10.1		Transition to Implementation Class	SW-LR-10.1	Class Contract source file	# Class Contract files					
10.2		Represent Inter-Class Visibility	SW-LR-10.2	Class Contract source file	# Class Contract files					
10.3		"Represent Class ""Body"" Structure"	SW-LR-10.3	Class Implementation source file	# Class Implementation files					
10.4		Compile Class	SW-LR-10.4	Compiled Class source file	# Classes compiled (success)	0.20				
10.5		Integrate Controller Class PDL	SW-LR-10.5	Controller Class source file	# Controller Classes identified/ designed	0.20				
10.6		Process PDL	SW-LR-10.6	PDL Reports	Report Summaries					
10.7		Implement_View Classes	SW-LR-10.7	_View Class source file	# _View Classes implemented	0.30				
10.8		Develop Database Schema	SW-LR-10.8	ERD	# ERDs	0.30				
11	***Method Design***		***SW-MPDL-11***							
11.1		Decide Representation Mechanism	SW-MPDL-11.1							
11.2		Develop Method PDL	SW-MPDL-11.2	Method PDL source file	# Methods PDLd	0.50				
11.3		Process PDL	SW-MPDL-11.3	PDL Reports	Report Summaries	0.50				
12	***Class Implementation/Class Test***		***SW-CICT-12***							
12.1		Implement Class Methods	SW-CICT-12-1	Method implemented	# Methods implemented (%)	0.50				
12.2		Determine Class Test Strategy	SW-CICT-12-2	Class Test Strategy	1 Class Test Strategy completed					
12.3		Develop Class Test Drivers	SW-CICT-12-3	<class>_ctd_#.ext source file	# Class Test Drivers & Test Cases	0.25				
12.4		Perform Class Test	SW-CICT-12-4	Result files	# tests run & % passed	0.25				
13	***Category Test***		***SW-CT-13***							
13.1		Develop Cateory Test Strategy	SW-CT-13.1	Categry Test Strategy	1 Category Test Stratgey completed					
13.2		Develop Category Test Drivers	SW-CT-13.2	<class>_ctd_#.ext source file	# Category Test Drivers & Test Cases	0.50				
13.3		Perform Intra-Catgory Test	SW-CT-13.3	Result files	# Intra-tests run & % passed	0.25				
13.4		Perform Inter-Category Test	SW-CT-13.4	Result files	# Inter-tests run & % passed	0.25				
14	***SWIT***		***SW-UCT-14***							
14.1		Develop SWIT Test Plan	SW-UT-14.1	SWIT Test Plan	1 SWIT Test Plan competed	0.25				
14.3		Perform SWIT Test	SW-UT-14.2	PTRs	"# PTRs, #Test Cases, #Use Cases tested (%passed)"	0.75				
15	***System Test***		***SYS-TST-15***							
15.1		Develop System Test Plan	SYS-TST-15.1	System Test Plan	1 System Test Plan completed	0.25				
15.2		Perform System Test	SYS-TST-15.2	PTRs	"# PTRs, #Test Cases, #Use Cases tested (%passed)"	0.75				
16	***Requirements Trace***		***SYS-RT-16***							
16.1		Generate Forward Requirements Trace	SYS-RT-16.1	FRT Reports		0.50				
16.2		Generate Reverse Requirements Trace	SYS-RT-16.2	RRT Reports		0.50				
17	***Maintenance***		***MAINT-17***							
17.1		Requirements Engineering	MAINT-17.1							
17.2		System OOA Static	MAINT-17.2							
17.3		System OOA Dynamic	MAINT-17.3							
17.4		Hardware/Software Split	MAINT-17.4							
17.5		Software OOA Static	MAINT-17.5							
17.6		Software OOA Dynamic	MAINT-17.6							
17.7		Software OOD Process Architecture	MAINT-17.7							
17.8		Software OOD Static	MAINT-17.8							
17.9		Software OOD Dynamic	MAINT-17.9							
17.10		Language Representation	MAINT-17.10							
17.11		Method PDL	MAINT-17.11							
17.12		Class Implementation/Class Test	MAINT-17.12							
17.13		Category Test	MAINT-17.13							
17.14		SWIT Test	MAINT-17.14							
17.15		System Test	MAINT-17.15							
17.16		Requirements Trace	MAINT-17.16							

David G. Mullens
4650 89th Avenue S.E.
Mercer Island, WA 98040

USE CASES COMBINED WITH BOOCH/OMT/UML: PROCESS AND PRODUCTS

Putnam P. Texel
Charles B. Williams

Prentice Hall PTR
Upper Saddle River, NJ 07458
http://www.prenhall.com

Library of Congress Cataloging-in-Publication Data

Texel, Putnam P.

Use cases combined with BOOCH/OMT/UML: process and products / Putnam Texel, Charles Williams.

p. cm.

Includes bibliographical references and index.

ISBN 0-13-727405-X (cloth : alk. paper)

1. Object-oriented methods (Computer science) 2. Computer software--Development. I. Williams, Charles. II. Title.

QA76.9.035T49 1997

005.1'17--dc21 97-61

CIP

Editorial/production supervision: *Patti Guerrieri*
Cover design director: *Jerry Votta*
Cover designer: *Design Source*
Manufacturing manager: *Alexis R. Heydt*
Acquisitions editor: *Paul W. Becker*
Editorial assistant: *Maureen Diana*
Marketing manager: *Dan Rush*

Published by Prentice Hall PTR
Prentice-Hall, Inc.
A Simon & Schuster Company
Upper Saddle River, NJ 07458

The publisher offers discounts on this book when ordered in bulk quantities. For more information, contact: Corporate Sales Department, Phone: 800-382-3419; Fax: 201-236-7141; E-mail: corpsales@prenhall.com; or write: Prentice Hall PTR, Corp. Sales Dept., One Lake Street, Upper Saddle River, NJ 07458.

Printed in the United States of America
10 9 8 7 6 5 4 3 2 1

ISBN 0-13-727405-X

Prentice-Hall International (UK) Limited, *London*
Prentice-Hall of Australia Pty. Limited, *Sydney*
Prentice-Hall Canada Inc., *Toronto*
Prentice-Hall Hispanoamericana, S.A., *Mexico*
Prentice-Hall of India Private Limited, *New Delhi*
Prentice-Hall of Japan, Inc., *Tokyo*
Simon & Schuster Asia Pte. Ltd., *Singapore*
Editora Prentice-Hall do Brasil, Ltda., *Rio de Janeiro*

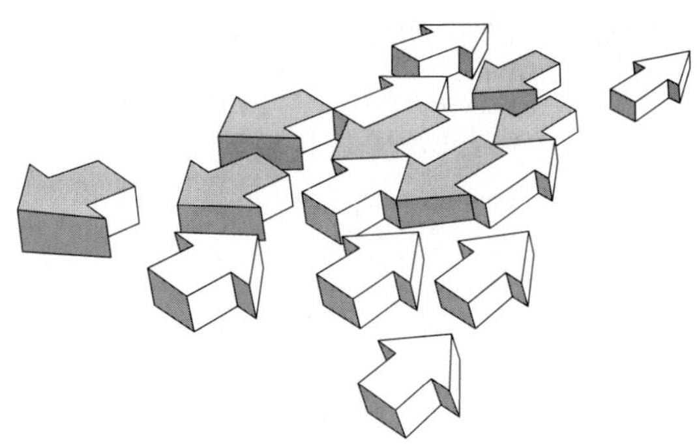

Dedication

To my son Ray—I love you heaps, always will.

Mom

To Arlene, Yale and Zachary,
Thank you for the time and understanding needed to complete this project.
I love you all.

Me

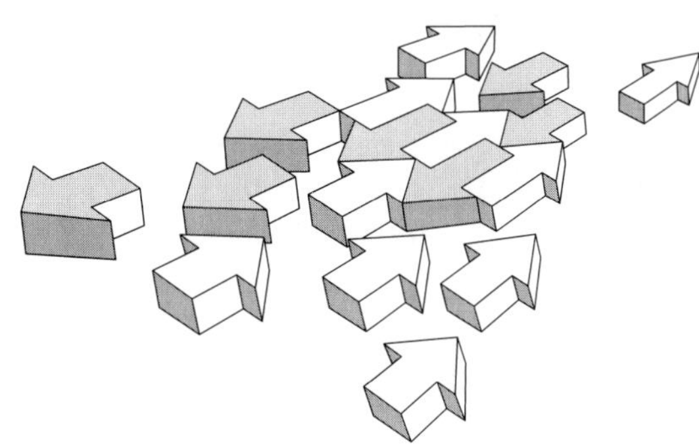

Contents

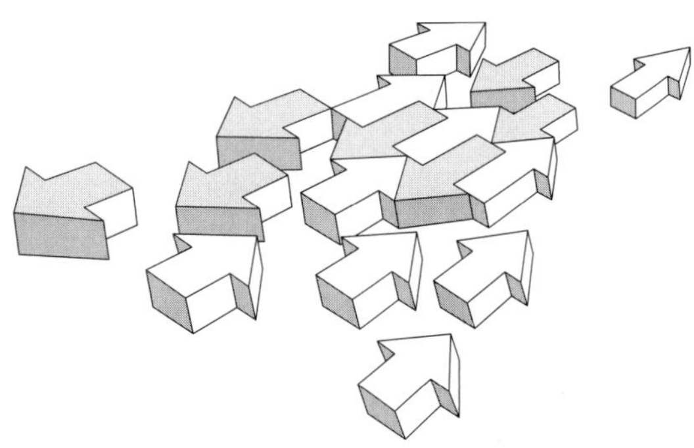

List of Figures

PHASE 6 SOFTWARE OOA—DYNAMIC VIEW

PHASE 7 SOFTWARE OOD—PROCESS VIEW

PHASE 8 SOFTWARE OOD—STATIC VIEW

PHASE 9 SOFTWARE OOD—DYNAMIC VIEW

PHASE 10 SOFTWARE OOD—LANGUAGE REPRESENTATION

PHASE 11 METHOD DESIGN

PHASE 12 CLASS IMPLEMENTATION/CLASS TEST

PHASE 13 CATEGORY TEST

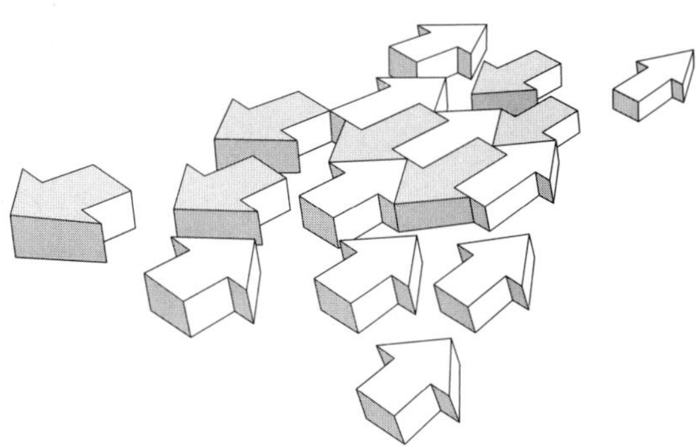

List of Tables

PHASE 15 SYSTEM INTEGRATION AND TEST (SIT)

PHASE 16 REQUIREMENTS TRACE

PHASE 17 MAINTENANCE PHASE OVERVIEW

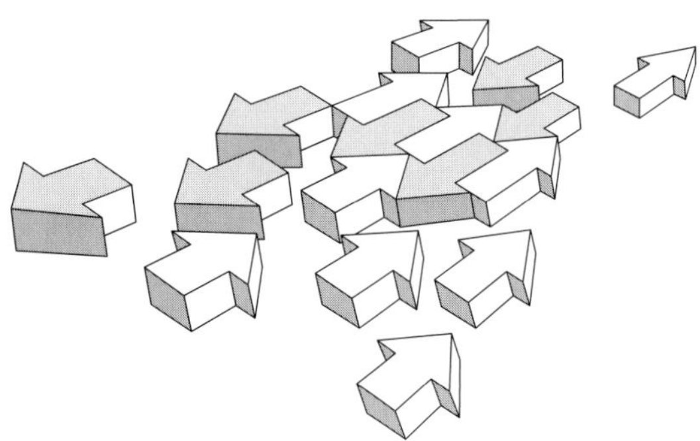

Preface

Purpose

The purpose of this text is to introduce the reader to a complete Object-Oriented (OO) system and software development process. The word "complete" is used because the process begins with Requirements Engineering and ends with Maintenance[TEX96]. Current methodologies, for example, Booch[BOO94] and Object Modeling Technique (OMT)[RUM91], are geared to and address the software development phases of analysis and design. The front-end activities of Requirements Engineering based on Use Cases and the back-end activities of Testing, Requirements Trace, and Maintenance have *not* yet been fully integrated. This text provides a *framework* that *encapsulates* existing OO software development methodologies, for example Booch, OMT, and Unified Modeling Language (UML)[1], within a complete OO systems development process.

The process presented herein is intended to be *evolutionary*, not *revolutionary*. The process does *not* require that you learn a new methodology, but rather addresses how to *extend* your current software development methodology. If you are now using Booch, OMT, or UML, there is no requirement for you to change; but rather, we present the opportunity to *augment* what you are currently doing and *extend* your OO process to phases of the software life cycle that precede and succeed software analysis and design.

Intended Audience

Use Cases Combined with Booch/OMT/UML: Process and Products was written to address the various needs of a Project Team either currently working on an OO project, or contemplating one. For both Project Management and Engineering staff, this

[1]This book is compatible with and presents UML Version 1.0, the latest version available at the time of this writing.

text provides a very detailed road map and answers the following two proverbial questions:

> **"Where Are We Going?"**
> Without the experience of a previous OO project, engineers do *not* realize what benefits an OO approach provide for future software development activities. Without the experience of a previous OO project, the adage, "Without knowing where you are going, any road will get you there," is applicable. However, incorrect decisions made early in an OO project can have major negative impact later on. This process provides such a road map. The benefits, of course, are that knowing what road you are taking leads to sounder early decisions. This text helps both managers and engineers answer the proverbial question, "*Where are we going?*".
>
> **"What Do I Do Next?"**
> Without the experience of a previous OO project, technical decisions are hard to make because, as previously stated, this road has *not* been previously traveled. The process presented herein provides a clear definition of what the software developer is to do next. This text helps managers and engineers answer the proverbial question, "*What do I do next?*".

It is important to realize that this book is *not* an OO tutorial. This book focuses on presenting a *process* and its resulting *products* to provide both a management and technical infrastructure to OO projects. We assume you have some knowledge of the OO software development community, and may even have tried to model. The more background knowledge you have, the easier this book will be to understand and apply. There is no intent on the part of the authors to define or introduce for the first time concepts like Use Case, Category, Subsystem, Class, Attribute, and Method. Definitions of these terms *are* provided herein to provide consistency within the book, but this particular book is *neither meant nor designed* to be a tutorial on OO technology. There are many books in the marketplace that provide that information.

Basis for the Process

The basis for the process presented herein is the Use Case, as introduced by Ivar Jacobson in his book *Object-Oriented Software Engineering: A Use Case Approach* [JAC93]. It is precisely Jacobson's introduction of Use Cases that provides the ability to address phases of the software life cycle *not* previously addressed in the marketplace. Requirements Engineering revolves around the identification and description of Use Cases, while Requirements Trace focuses on the cross-referencing of Use Cases to Booch/UML Categories (or OMT Subsystems), Classes, and their Methods. In addition to Requirements Engineering and Requirements Trace, the authors' OO project experience indicates that Use Cases provide the basis for:

- Booch/UML Categories, OMT Subsystems and therefore, software source code directory structure

- Project management infrastructure
- Work allocation
- Software integration and test
- System test
- Project management metrics capture
- Project technical metrics capture

The Process

The process consists of multiple life cycle Phases[TEX94][TEX96]. Each Phase is a major step in the system/software development life cycle for OO projects. The Phases, as identified in Figure P-1, support and are consistent with Booch's concept of a "macro process"[BOO96]. Additionally the Phases are consistent with Jacobson's phi-

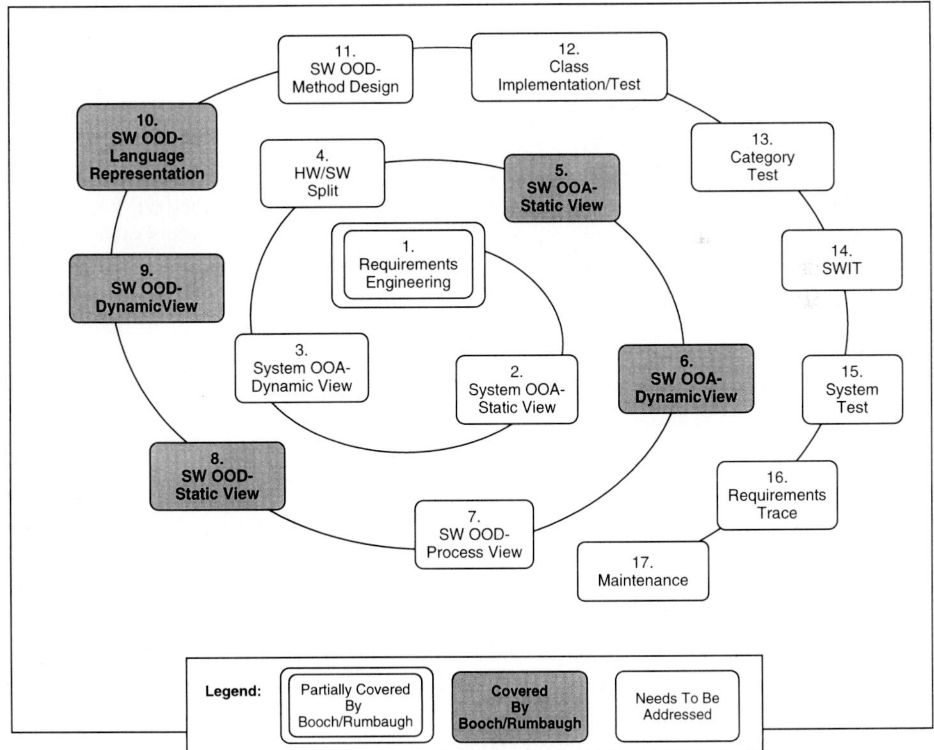

Figure P-1. Phases of the Process

losophy of Use Case engineering [JAC96]. Jacobson proposes a three-pronged approach as follows:

- Analyze the Use Cases
- Design the system to implement the Use Cases
- Test that the Use Cases have indeed been fulfilled.

We can map the Phases proposed in this book to this approach as follows:

- Phases 1–6: Analyze the Use Cases
- Phases 7–13: Design the system to implement the Use Cases
- Phases 14–16: Test that the Use Cases have indeed been fulfilled.

A project "spirals" through the Phases as shown in Figure P-1 with a well-defined, small, initial subset of Use Cases. By first following the entire process for a small subset of Use Cases and completing all Phases for these carefully chosen Use Cases, both management and engineering staff gain confidence. Confidence is gained in the process itself and in the ability to perform, because both groups understand what is expected and required. The spiral is then repeated for a second set of Use Cases, then a third set, and so on. This approach supports either the same individuals performing Object-Oriented Analysis (OOA), Object-Oriented Design (OOD), and Object-Oriented Programming (OOP), or the division of work where one group of analysts provides the OOA view, while another distinct group of designers produces the OOD view to the provided analysis. Regardless of who is actually performing OOA and OOD, more and more confidence is gained with each subset of Use Cases that is produced. This approach to the development of Use Cases is far more successful than the "big bang" approach where all Use Cases are analyzed at once. Addressing a small subset of Use Cases enables productivity to improve continually. As productivity improves, metrics become more stable, and confidence increases in meeting expected completion dates.

Finally, the process, in addition to being iterative, is incremental. The process is incremental because one Phase typically builds upon a previous Phase, thus work products are developed in a step-by-step, or incremental, fashion. For example, consider the development of a Class Diagram. Class Diagrams produced in OOA are restricted to Domain, Interface, and View Classes. Class Diagrams are then refined during OOD to include Abstract, Collection, Parameterized and Association Classes. This incremental approach to the development of OO work products helps developers because what is required has been *precisely* specified. This incremental approach aids managers because they now have a metric by which they can measure the progress of the project.

Case Study Approach

As opposed to fragmented examples, a single case study is utilized throughout this book to demonstrate the process and provide examples of the work products produced. In essence, the Case Study is the requirement for a software system to monitor occupied living quarters in a sealed environment. Each living quarter has three sensors that monitor air pressure, oxygen percent, and temperature in degrees Fahrenheit, respectively. The software must detect the current value of all three environmental conditions for each occupied living quarter and calculate the deviation of the current value from a nominal value stored in a database. Based on the percent deviation from the nominal value, a display is highlighted and/or an audible alarm is sounded. An operator has the capability to modify the nominal values in the database and to turn off the alarm.

We strongly recommended that you familiarize yourself with the Case Study Problem Statement. Although the Case Study Problem Statement initially appears to be relatively simple, it has been carefully chosen because the solution embodies and illustrates the following concepts:

- *Use Cases*
- *Categories*
- *Inheritance hierarchy*
- *Aggregation hierarchy*
- *Hardware interface*
- *Graphical User Interface (GUI)*
- *Database*
- *Multiple processes.*

The Case Study allows the reader to see these concepts implemented in an application that is *not* difficult to comprehend and remember. The reader does *not* drown in the application, thus losing the ability to understand and implement the proposed process.

OO model solutions for the Case Study in Booch, OMT, and UML notation are found in Appendix D on the enclosed CD-ROM, as are complete language-dependent solutions in Ada95, C++, Java, and SNAP[2].

Organization

This book is divided into parts. Part I, Introduction, provides an overview of the process, followed by the Case Study Problem Statement that is used throughout the book to illustrate the process and resulting products. The remaining parts represent a cohesive collection of Phases. The remaining parts of this book, and their respective Phases, are specified below:

Part II: Systems Engineering

1. Requirements Engineering
2. System OOA–Static View

[2]SNAP is an integrated OO development environment of Template Software, Inc.

3. System OOA–Dynamic View
4. Hardware/Software Split

Part III: Software OOA

5. Software OOA–Static View
6. Software OOA–Dynamic View

Part IV: Software OOD–Language-Independent

7. Software OOD–Process View
8. Software OOD–Static View
9. Software OOD–Dynamic View

Part V: Software OOD–Language-Dependent

10. Software OOD–Language Representation
11. Method Design

Part VI: Implementation

12. Class Implementation/Class Test

Part VII: Test

13. Category Test
14. Software Integration and Test (SWIT)
15. System Test
16. Requirements Trace

Part VIII: Post Delivery

17. Maintenance

Describing a Phase

As previously stated, Figure P-1 identifies the Phases of the process. It is important that we as authors explicitly state that the Phases of the process are ***iterative***, can be ***concurrent***, and may ***overlap***.

Figure P-2 depicts the legend for the graphical notation that is utilized to define *each* Phase. This notation can be easily transitioned into whatever process notation is currently utilized by an organization (e.g., IDEF to add controls and mechanisms). An Object-Oriented notation can also express the process and products, but we have found more success in transitioning technology using this more functional notation.

Note in Figure P-2 that an ellipse represents an item that is required to perform an Activity (a required resource, or input), a numbered rectangle reflects an Activity

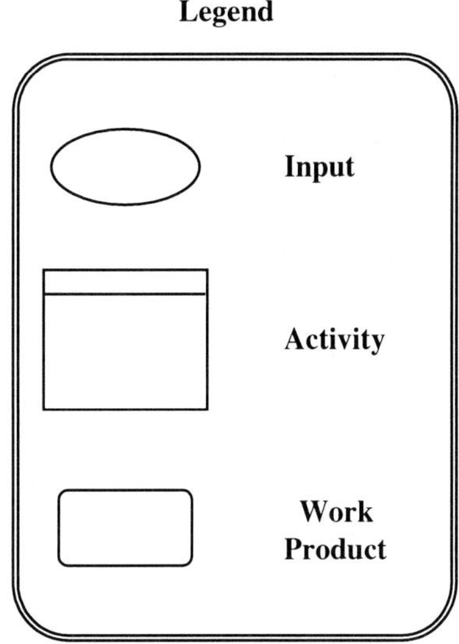

Figure P-2. Legend for Phase Description Diagram

(work to be performed), and a rounded rectangle represents a work product of an Activity (in some cases, a new work product, and in other cases, an update of an existing work product). How these work products are incorporated into actual deliverables is project-specific.

Use of the notation to represent a Phase is shown in Figure P-3. A Phase is composed of many Activities, each of which requires inputs and produces some work product(s). This particular representation of the sequence in which the Activities flow has proved to be extremely helpful on four projects. Although the Activities are numbered sequentially, they are ***iterative***. Again, some Activities are actually ***concurrent***, while others may ***overlap***. The sequential numbering scheme for Activities within a Phase is simply to get a project started, provide management with the ability to monitor project progress, and provide a vehicle to describe to engineers what technical Activity is required. Iteration *within* the Activities of a Phase is purposefully *not* graphically depicted to minimize the number of arrows on a diagram, but is understood to be ongoing. The same holds for iteration between Phases.

How do you read these diagrams? Figure P-3 shows that Phase 1, Requirements Engineering, consists of four Activities, numbered 1.1 through 1.4, respectively. A System Specification and any available OO products related to a generic object model of the problem domain are nice to have on hand when starting Activity 1.1, Identify External Interfaces. Activity 1.1 results in a product called a Context Diagram. Activity 1.2 extracts individual sentences that include the word "shall" from an initial basic set of documents associated with a project and enters these "shall" sentences into a Requirements Trace Matrix (RTM). An initial set of documents might include a

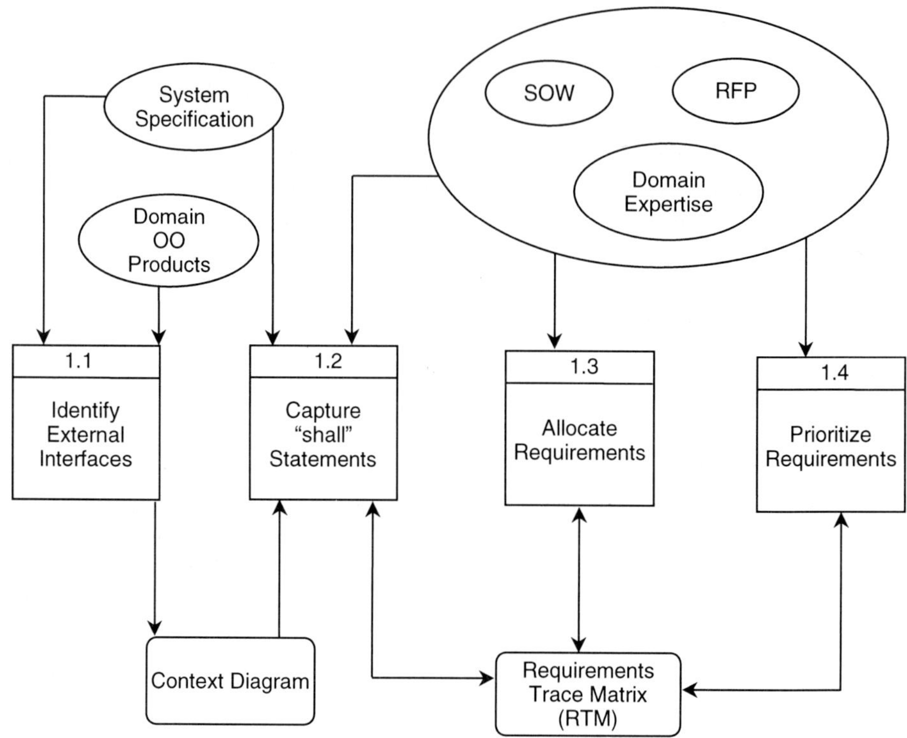

Figure P-3. Phase 1: Requirements Engineering Phase Diagram

System Specification, Statement Of Work (SOW), Request For Proposal (RFP), or an Operational Concept Document (OCD). If the initial documents are *not* written with "shalls," the documents can still be used to derive the requirements. If the Project Team does *not* have any such written documentation, discussions with individuals who have domain expertise must be conducted to formulate a set of "shall" sentences for the project.

The RTM is used as an input to Activity 1.3, where the individual "shall" statements (requirements) are initially allocated to either hardware, software, or a combination of both. These allocations are recorded in the RTM. Finally, Activity 1.4 focuses on prioritizing the requirements with respect to builds, releases, or both[3]. The intent here in the Preface is to show that this mechanism for defining and documenting a process is easy to read, easy to understand, and easy to modify. Large projects require simple solutions. In fact, very simple solutions have been utilized successfully on numerous projects, both large and small.

Following the last Activity of each Phase, three topics are introduced by icons. Each of the topics, and their corresponding icons, are specified below.

[3]Precise definitions of build and release are provided in Phase 1, Activity 1.4.

First, *Phase Transition Criteria* provide guidelines for *transitioning* to the next Phase. A Phase is *never complete;* therefore, to wait to start a new Phase until the previous Phase is completed makes no sense whatsoever.

The *Review Criteria* topic appears once, within the *Phase Transition Criteria*, and provides input for deciding if transitioning to the next Phase makes sense. The *Review Criteria* provide answers to questions like the following:

- "What constitutes a good Class?"
- "How do I know if I have a good inheritance hierarchy?"
- "How do I write a Class description?"
- "How do I review a Class description? What am I looking for?"
- "How do I know when I am done?"

and thus provides guidance for both developers and reviewers. The *Review Criteria* can be categorized as High (H), Medium (M), or Low (L), depending on the importance of the criteria for transitioning to the next Phase[4]. For example, transitioning to the next Phase should *not* take place when a work product under review fails a High criteria. However, transitioning to the next Phase can take place when a work product fails a Low criteria (as long as the action item is taken, and the action item is closed at the next review).

Finally, each Phase terminates with a *Tracking Progress* section. This topic summarizes, in an Excel spreadsheet, the Activities performed in the Phase and metrics for tracking the progress of the project. The *Tracking Progress* section provides metrics for *tracking progress*. Each Phase builds on the information provided in the preceding Phase, culminating in a project spreadsheet that can be imported into Microsoft Project® for the addition of staffing estimates and project milestone dates. The spreadsheet for the entire process is included on the enclosed CD-ROM in Appendix E. Technical metrics are addressed on the enclosed CD-ROM.

Describing an Activity

The Activities, as presented for each Phase, support and are consistent with Booch's concept of a "micro process"[BOO96]. *Each* Activity within a Phase is described using the same format, and contains the following topics:

- *Purpose*
- *Definition(s)*
- *Process*

[4]The review criteria have *not* been categorized in this book because each organization has different drummers to which the organization marches.

- *Example*
- *Pragmatic Project Issues*
- *Product(s).*

Each of the topics, and their corresponding icons, are specified below. When a specific topic is *not* applicable to an Activity, the topic is omitted.

The *Purpose* describes the reason behind an Activity, or why the Activity is to be performed. Knowing *why* an Activity is necessary helps engineers focus on the issues at hand, thus minimizing digression and endless discussion.

The *Definition(s)* identify and define a term being introduced for the first time. These definitions provide consistency within this book for terms that may have multiple definitions in the industry.[5]

The *Process,* a more *detailed road map*, identifies the specific step-by-step procedures (e.g., copy an existing diagram, add View Classes, add inter-process communication calls, and so on) required to complete an Activity. This format helps make the process "definable and repeatable," thus enabling an organization to acquire an acceptable level of maturity as measured by the Capability Maturity Model (CMM).

The *Example* shows the specific portion of the Case Study that was created during the Activity. The notation utilized will sometimes be Booch, sometimes OMT, and sometimes UML. Recall that complete models in Booch, OMT, and UML notation are included on the enclosed CD-ROM in Appendix D.

Pragmatic Project Issues focuses on specific questions that have been asked by developers on projects we have been supporting, and the responses we provided for the customers. Some pragmatic issues point out project decisions that need to be made, while other pragmatic issues provide suggestions as to how to avoid common pitfalls.

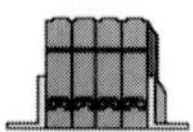

The *Product(s)* topic summarizes the anticipated outputs of the Activity. The *Product(s)* identifies "work products" produced, *not* project deliverables. How the "work products" are incorporated into project deliverables is project-specific. A commercial project could (and should) deliver the "work products" as a deliverable; however, military projects often need to accommodate specific standards governing the format and content of deliverables.

[5]An example of an "overloaded" term in the industry is *Object:* one methodology defines *Class* as a *set* of entities, while another uses the term *Object* to mean a *set* of entities. The methodology that defines Object as a set of entities uses the term Instance to represent a member of the set. The methodology that uses Class as a set of entities uses the term Object as a member of the set.

Cookbook Approach?

Some individuals might call this a ". . . cookbook approach to OO software development", and follow that statement with another statement, ". . . that OO *cannot* be done according to a cookbook!" We *agree* that it is impossible to develop software using a cookbook-like process. The process, Phases, Activities, and review criteria presented in this text are intended to put ***structure*** around projects. This proposed ***structure*** is necessary to ***manage***, as well as to ***implement***, an OO effort of any size. There is plenty of room for creativity within the process. Creativity is required to discover the Categories, Classes, Methods, implementation strategies, process architecture, and on and on. It is *intended* that projects will *revise* this process once a project is accomplishing its goals. *Not* all organizations work the same, *not* all projects within an organization work the same, and *not* all project managers manage the same. What is proposed herein is a process to gain an understanding of *what* must be *done* and *one way* to go about accomplishing it. Once that understanding is achieved, have a wonderful time revising and refining this process! Like any recipe, once confidence is gained in the resulting product, you can have fun experimenting with the ingredients!

Acknowledgments

Without hesitation, the first acknowledgments go to Grady Booch, Ivar Jacobson, and Jim Rumbaugh for their respective contributions to the OO community. Without their insight and foresight, this book would never have been conceived or written.

The next acknowledgment goes to all our customers, who continually support and provide opportunities to learn and grow and try. Our customers include, but are *not* limited to:

- GTE
- Harris Corporation
- NASA
- National & Provincial Building Society, Ltd.
- U. S. Army
- U. S. Air Force.

Each customer provided an opportunity to learn and contribute to a different piece of this process. Stated differently, our learning has been a little bit here, a little bit there, and now finally, the opportunity exists to put it all together in one text.

Thank you to the reviewers: Bob Auchter, Corrine Gregory, Tim Kaiser, and Tony Wood. Their comments were insightful, valuable, and helped improve the structure, content, and readability of this book. A very special thank you to Patty Southard for giving up a weekend to proof the entire manuscript, finding many last-minute inconsistencies, and providing some very helpful suggestions to improve the presentation.

Thank you to Ken Lusby for implementing the C++ GUI Classes and to Paul Smith for researching all the trademarks. Finally thank you to Barbara Ardary for providing McCabe's Class and OO metrics on the C++ code.

Within Prentice Hall, thanks go first to Paul Becker for realizing the value of this work, his support in coming to contract in a timely manner, and his support in its timely production. To Camie Goffi for her extensive, thorough, and accurate copy editing; to Patti Guerrieri for her impressive capabilities as a production manager.

To list all of the individuals who contributed to this effort is impossible, but some stand out for their contributions: Tony Wood at N&P for his incredible perception of the reader's point of view and, more importantly, his patience during a very rough time in my life; Carl Joeckel for his immediate, "Oh just call the process flow diagram a "Process Interaction Graph." (we decided, however, that PIG was *not* an appropriate acronym, so we changed it to Process Interaction Diagram with the acronym PID); Melissa D'Agostino for the original layout of the Use Case Worksheet; Lisa Heidelberg who, when I was designing the Requirements Trace, asked, "What if a Method changes," thus leading to the Reverse Requirements Trace; Dave Amrhein and John Widere for a discussion that led to the Process Architecture Diagram; and, Bob Auchter for reminding me to do the State Transition Diagrams for the Process and Processor Classes. These individuals, each in their own way, contributed to the technical content herein.

Most of all, my personal and very public thank you to four very special people: Ralph Crafts who taught me to believe in myself; Mark Ellinger for passing on to me the most valuable skills of my life; Lil White for her support and encouragement; and, to the best massage therapist in Palm Beach County, Vincent Torchia, for keeping my C-Spine under control. Although the process presented in this book has been under development and refinement for the past seven years and is based on experience on both real-time and MIS application efforts which encompassed over three and one half million lines of code written in Ada, C++, and SNAP, there would *not* be a process, or even this book, if it weren't for these four people.

Putnam P. Texel (ptexel@flinet.com)
12685 White Coral Drive
West Palm Beach, FL 33414

I would like to extend my personal thanks to several people: to my sons Yale and Zachary for sacrificing their evenings and weekends with Daddy so I could work on the book; to Randy Maroney for instantly realizing my talents and extracting me from a bad situation; to Mary Ann Stoops for being there when the stress of the book, work, and home needed to be vented. Lastly, I would like to extend a big public thank you to my co-author for putting up with me over the time it has taken to produce this book. When we started, she warned me that it was "going to be a lot of work." I now know how true that statement was!

Charles B. Williams (chuck.williams@template.com)
9210 Easton Court
Manassas, VA 20110

PART I

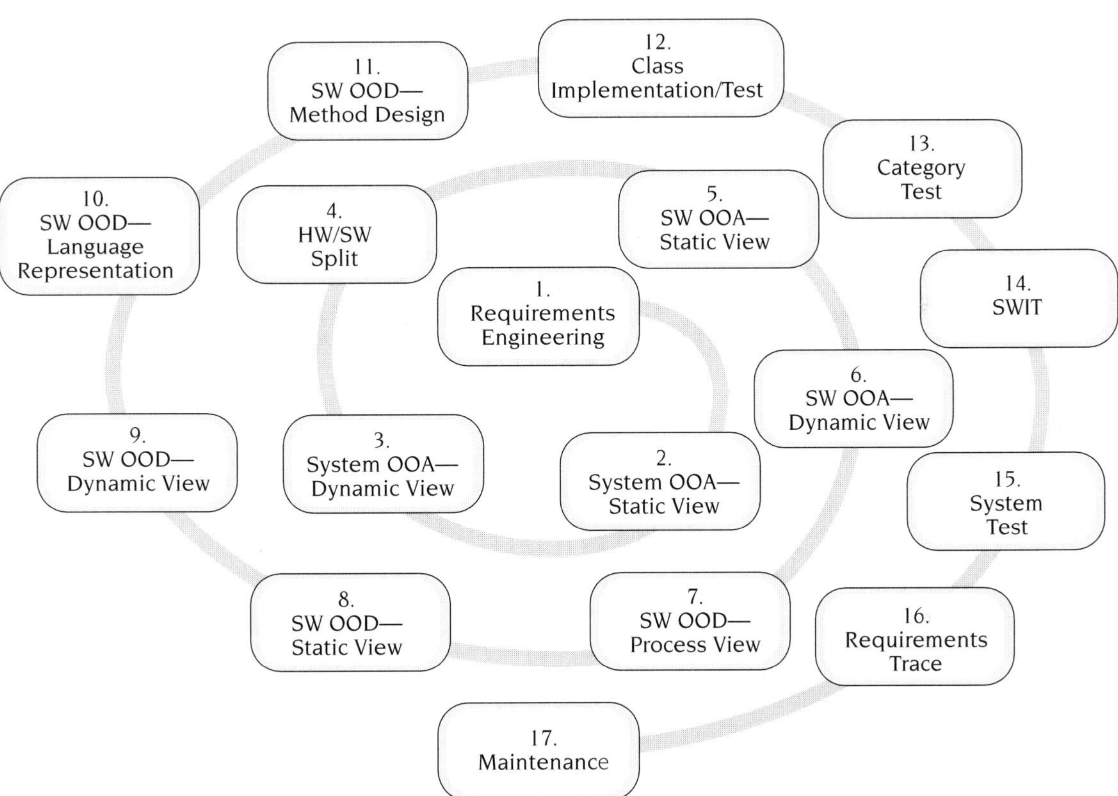
1. Requirements Engineering
2. System OOA—Static View
3. System OOA—Dynamic View
4. HW/SW Split
5. SW OOA—Static View
6. SW OOA—Dynamic View
7. SW OOD—Process View
8. SW OOD—Static View
9. SW OOD—Dynamic View
10. SW OOD—Language Representation
11. SW OOD—Method Design
12. Class Implementation/Test
13. Category Test
14. SWIT
15. System Test
16. Requirements Trace
17. Maintenance

Introduction

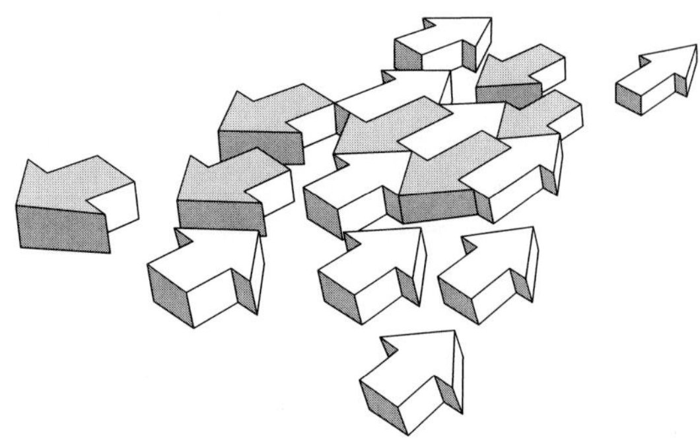

Process Overview

The purpose of this overview is to summarize the development philosophies that form the backbone of the process presented in this book. The philosophies of the process include

- Iterative development,
- Incremental development, and
- Development by levels of abstraction.

Details are intentionally left out of this overview. Rather, the detail is supplied within the description of each Phase. Lastly, recall that all terms are defined within the book.

The process presented in this book is simple. Figure O-1 repeats the spiral diagram from the Preface that identifies the 17 Phases of the process. The process iterates over all 17 Phases for a small subset of requirements, plus the process iterates within the Activities of a Phase for a specific set of requirements.

The process begins with the explicit representation of requirements as a table, called the Requirements Traceability Matrix (RTM), which maintains all the requirements for a system as individual entries. Phases 1 and 2 concentrate on the development of the RTM for a project. Table O-1[1] shows the beginning of a very simple hypothetical RTM for a software system that collects staff hours expended by project charge number. In the RTM, each software *functional* requirement is expressed in a format that clearly defines the actions performed by the software system. A functional requirement expressed in this way is called a Use Case. Use Cases are then assigned to a specific software build. The allocation of RTM entries to Use Cases is critical because in Phase 2, the Categories (a logical collection of Classes) for the project are extracted from the Use Cases.

Once the requirements are agreed-upon by the customer and the developer, static and dynamic views of the solution are produced in increments. The production of the static view is discussed next.

[1]Many more columns are included in the actual table that is developed throughout Phases 1 and 2.

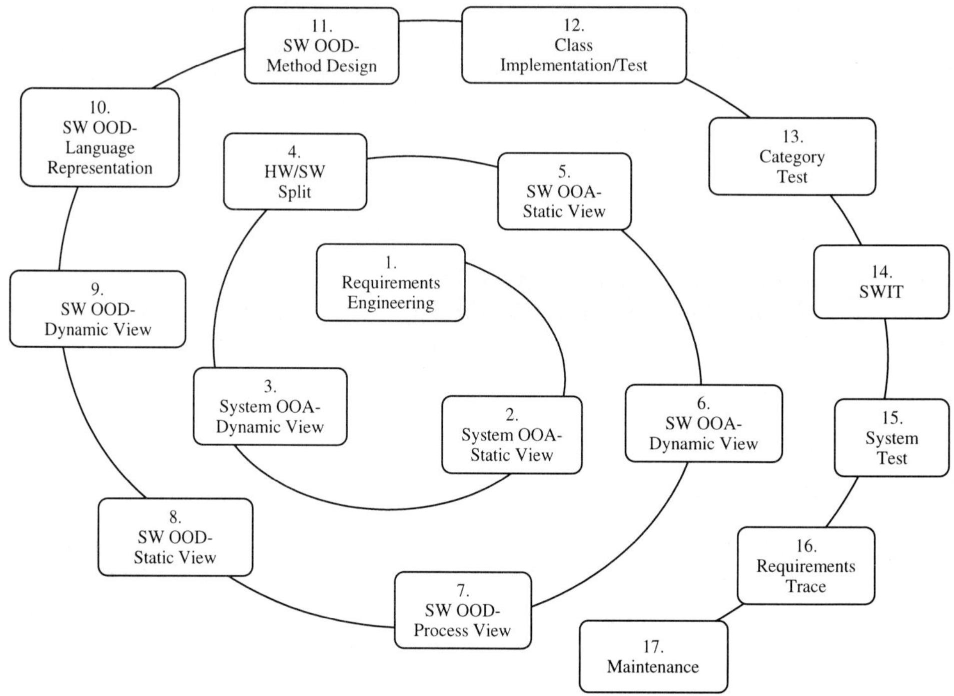

Figure O-1. Phases of the Process

Table O-1. Sample Requirements Traceability Matrix (RTM)

Entry #	Para #	XYZ System Requirements	Build #	Use Case Name
1	2.0	The staff hours data entry system shall permit a staff member to enter a staff member's name.	B1	UC1_Operator_Add_Name
2	2.0	The staff hours data entry system shall permit a staff member to enter the staff member's company affiliation number.	B1	UC2_Operator_Add_Affiliation_Number
3	2.0	The staff hours data entry system shall permit a staff member to view an entire week's entry.	B2	UC3_Operator_View_Data_By_Week
...	...	...	...	...
n	6.7	The staff hours data entry system shall allow a staff member to enter the hours in .25 hour increments by project number.	B1	UC*n*_Operator_Enter_Hours_Per_Project

Figure O-2 shows that the static view, represented by Class Diagrams, is started in Phase 2 when a diagram is produced that identifies the abstract associations between the identified Categories. The development of this diagram at the Category level

- Validates the Categories
- Identifies the responsibility for each Category
- Identifies the associations (hierarchy) among the Categories.

As Figure O-2 shows, during Phase 2, emphasis is placed on the associations between Domain and Interface Categories. Then in OOA (Phase 5), the static view is refined, developing one Class Diagram for each Category, that concentrates solely on

- Application Domain Classes,
- Interface[2] Classes, and
- View[3] Classes.

This diagram focuses on the *logical* view of the solution by limiting the focus to *what* Classes are required to satisfy the requirements. The Class Diagram is then refined again during OOD (Phase 8), when the following are identified and added to the Class Diagram:

- Abstract Classes
- Collection Classes
- Controller Classes
- Parameterized Classes
- Process Classes.

These kinds of Classes are defined within the text and examples are provided from the Case Study. In addition to the previously identified Classes, these Class stereotypes represent the *physical* Classes that are required to represent the solution. Finally, the associations that were established during OOA are refined in OOD to dependencies, an indication of what other Classes are required by a Class to fulfill its responsibility (i.e., specifying visibility requirements).

[2]Use of the term "Interface Class" here is *not* consistent with Jacobson's use of the term "Interface Class." Here, Interface Class means those Classes that require access to either hardware or other existing software systems.

[3]Use of the term "View Class" means a Class that provides a view of the data, for example, a GUI or a report. Use of the term "View Class" here is equivalent to Jacobson's use of the term "Interface Class."

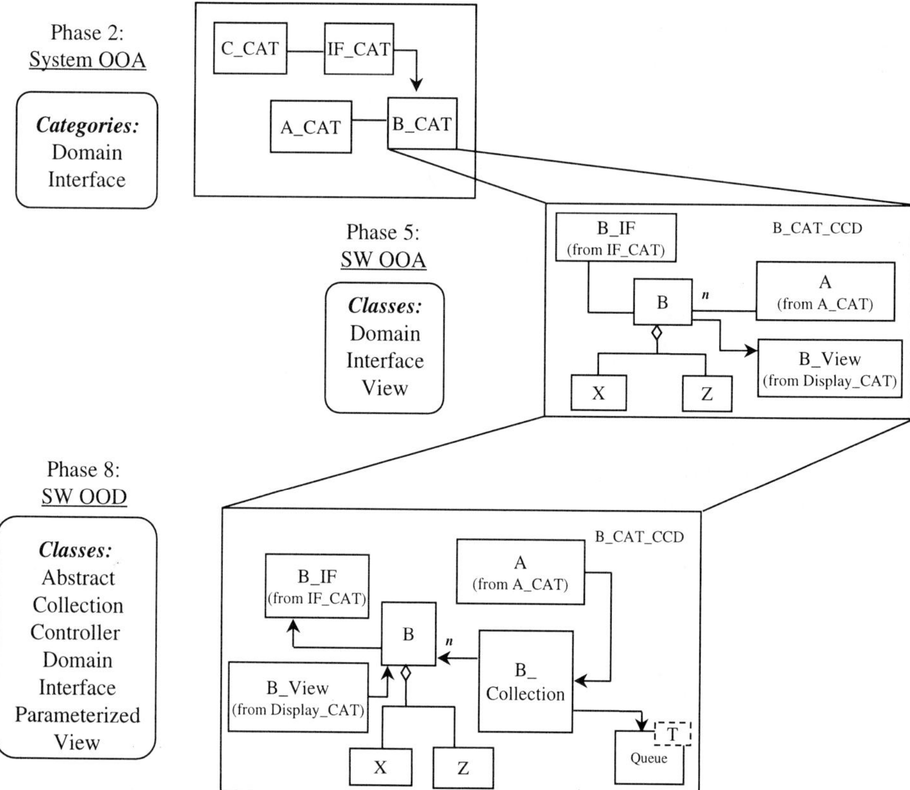

Figure O-2. Levels of Abstraction: Static View

Similarly, the dynamic view is developed in incremental steps. Figure O-3 depicts the process for developing Interaction Diagrams (IDs). As Figure O-3 shows, IDs are produced first at the Category level in Phase 3. By producing an Interaction Diagram at the Category level, called a Category Interaction Diagram (CID), the Categories and their respective responsibilities are again validated. Validation of Categories is extremely critical because Categories form the basis for

- Work allocation
- Directory structure
- Test
- Management metrics capture
- Technical metrics capture.

CIDs are refined during OOA (Phase 6), where the focus changes from Categories to the application Domain, View, and Interface Classes identified during OOA. Finally, in OOD (Phase 9), the IDs are refined once again, by adding

- Abstract Classes,
- Controller Classes,
- Process Classes,
- Inter-process communication calls,
- Exception propagation, and
- Collection Classes.

In summary, and as shown in Figures O-2 and O-3, both the static and dynamic views provided during OOA and OOD are well-defined in terms of *what* a developer does *when*, and *what* the *contents* of a specific work product are to be.

Figure O-4 highlights the testing philosophy proposed. In Phase 12, Class Test, the focus is on testing a single Class in isolation to ensure that it functions as expected. Once the Classes within a Category have been successfully tested, the set of Class connections within a Category is tested to ensure that a Category functions as expected (intra-Category testing). Next, a Category is further tested by evaluating the connections that the Classes in the Category have with Classes in foreign Categories,

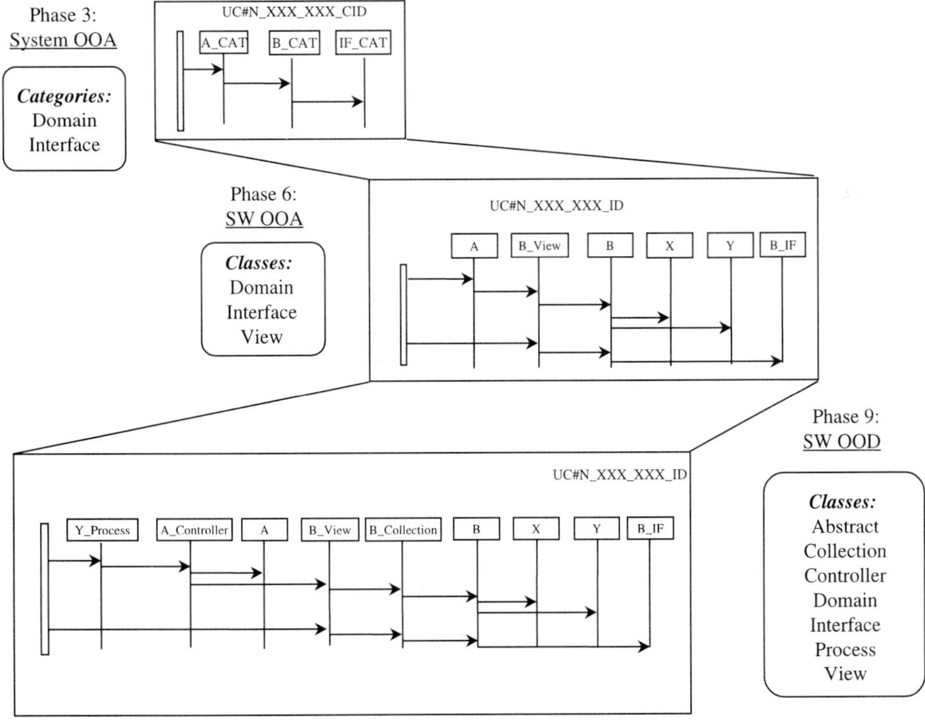

Figure O-3. Levels of Abstraction: Dynamic View

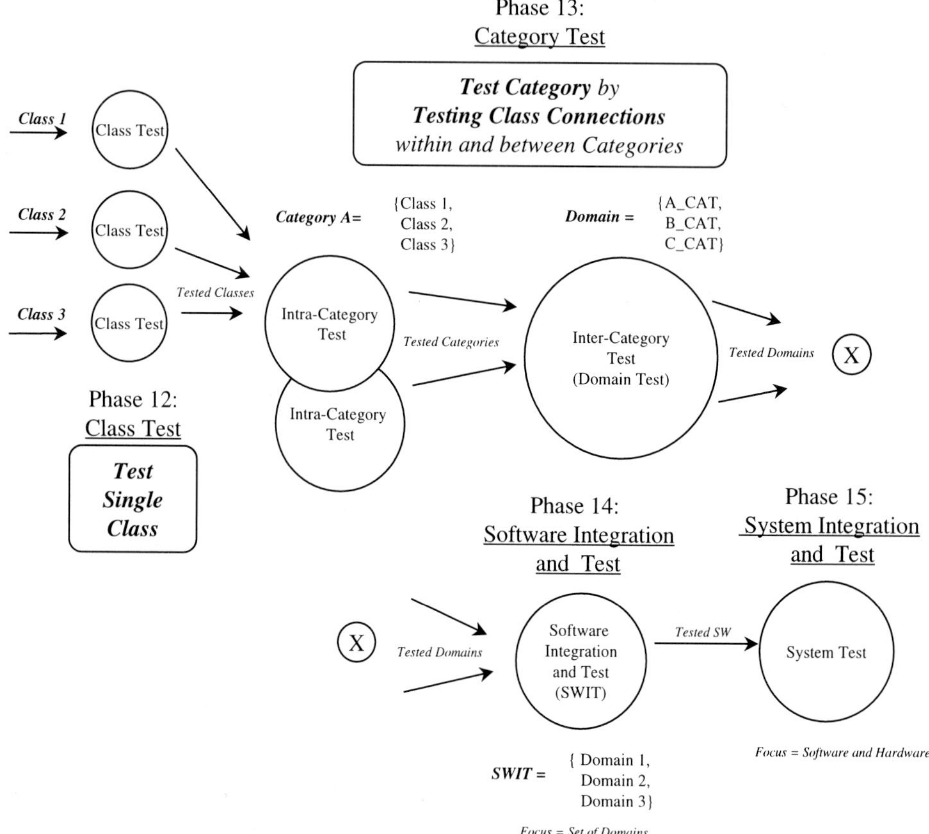

Figure O-4. Testing Philosophy

in the same Domain[4] (inter-Category testing). Stated differently, once a Category is tested internally, the set of Categories that comprise a Domain are tested to ensure that a Domain functions as expected. And finally, all Domains are integrated during Phase 14, Software Integration and Test. Testing terminates with Phase 15, System Test, and the delivery of the system. The process presents a recommendation for when stubs for Classes are appropriate and at what point in the testing process Class stubs are replaced by actual Classes for interfacing to

- Hardware
- Existing software systems
- The database.

[4]A Domain is a collection of Categories that represents a large functional portion of the system to be developed.

The process also provides a trace, or map, of Use Cases *to* the Categories, Classes, and Methods that are required to fulfill the Use Cases. This mapping is called a Forward Requirements Trace (FRT) because it starts with a Use Case and goes *forward* to the actual Categories, Classes, and Methods that are used in the implementation of the Use Case. Consequently, when a Use Case changes, the FRT identifies exactly which Categories, Classes, and Methods are impacted by the change. Additionally, a Reverse Requirements Trace (RRT) maps an actual source code Method *back to* its Class and Category, as well as maps the source code Method *back to* the set of Use Cases that utilize that Method in their implementation. Consequently, a change in a Method can be traced back to all the Use Cases affected by that change. All of this helps in regression testing and in Phase 17, Maintenance.

This overview is *not* complete without a small discussion of Phase 7, Process View. A process and processor are Classes, like any other Class. They have Attributes and Methods like any other Class, but more importantly, they root inheritance hierarchies that reflect the actual process and processor architecture of the intended system. Class Diagrams are used to reflect these hierarchies and the associations between processes and processors; they therefore represent the static view. The dynamic view of the process and processor Classes is reflected by 1) State Transition Diagrams (STDs) that reflect the behavior of a process or processor in a multiprocessor system, and 2) an Interaction Diagram (ID) that represents the interaction between the processes that comprise the system.

Lastly, Phase 17, Maintenance, is viewed as an iteration through the previous 16 Phases, based on either the detection of an error or the request for new or changed requirements.

The next section introduces the Case Study that will be developed using the process just described. Familiarization with the Case Study is imperative as all examples in the text are derived from it.

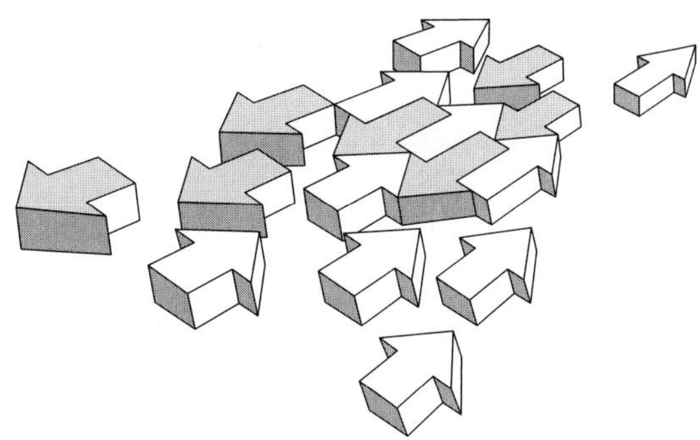

Case Study Problem Statement: Habitat Control Center (HCC)

HCC-1.0 INTRODUCTION

A Habitat Control Center (HCC) is to contain 48 living quarters and a software system, named Sealed Environment Monitor (SEM), which is to act as a monitor of all the living quarters for the habitat personnel in the HCC[1].

HCC-2.0 SEALED ENVIRONMENT MONITOR (SEM)

The SEM shall monitor all *occupied* living quarters. There shall be a total of 48 living quarters, each of which may, or may not, be occupied at any one time.

HCC-2.1 MONITORED DATA

For each occupied living quarter, the SEM shall obtain, once per minute, the following data:

- Current air pressure (pounds per square inch)
- Current temperature (degrees Fahrenheit)
- Current oxygen level (as a percentage).

This information shall be obtained from three sensors that are located inside each living quarter. There shall be one sensor per environmental condition.

[1]It is important to note that the authors do not have access to actual alarms and sensors, consequently the interfaces are emulated in the software.

HCC-2.2 ALARM CONDITIONS

For each of the items in Paragraph HCC-2.1, the SEM shall immediately react to the following situations as indicated:

- For a changed value that represents a deviation of >= 1% but <2% from the nominal values found in the database, the appropriate window in the panel shall be lit.
- For a changed value that represents a deviation of >= 2% but less than 3% from the nominal values found in the database, the appropriate window in the panel shall be lit and flash at a rate of two times per second.
- For a changed value that represents a deviation of >= 3% from the nominal values found in the database, the appropriate window in the panel shall be lit and flash at a rate of four times per second. Additionally, an audible alarm shall be sounded.

There shall be only one audible alarm.

HCC-3.0 ANNUNCIATOR PANEL

The annunciator panel is located in the control center of the sealed habitat. The panel of annunciators shall consist of 48 annunciators, arranged in six rows (A–F) of eight annunciators in each row (numbered 1–8, respectively). Additionally, each annunciator shall be mapped to a unique living quarter by the location in the annunciator panel. For example, annunciator C-5 corresponds to living quarter C-5. Figure HCC-1 depicts the envisioned panel display.

Each annunciator in the panel shall be composed of three parts: an air pressure warning window, an oxygen warning window, and a temperature warning window. Each window shall be identified by an appropriate legend. Figure HCC-2 depicts a typical annunciator display that is composed of three windows, one for each environmental condition.

HCC-4.0 NOMINAL VALUES

All nominal values shall be found in the database. There shall be an option for an Operator to redefine the values of the environmental conditions maintained in the database. The Operator shall be able to redefine all three environmental nominal values to be used for all living quarters and apply this change to SEM processing.

HCC-5.0 ALARMS

The audible alarm-sounding and window-flashing features shall be only turned ***on*** by the SEM. The SEM shall continue to turn on these warning indicators as long as the alarm condition continues to exist. The warning indicators shall only be turned ***off*** by the Operator.

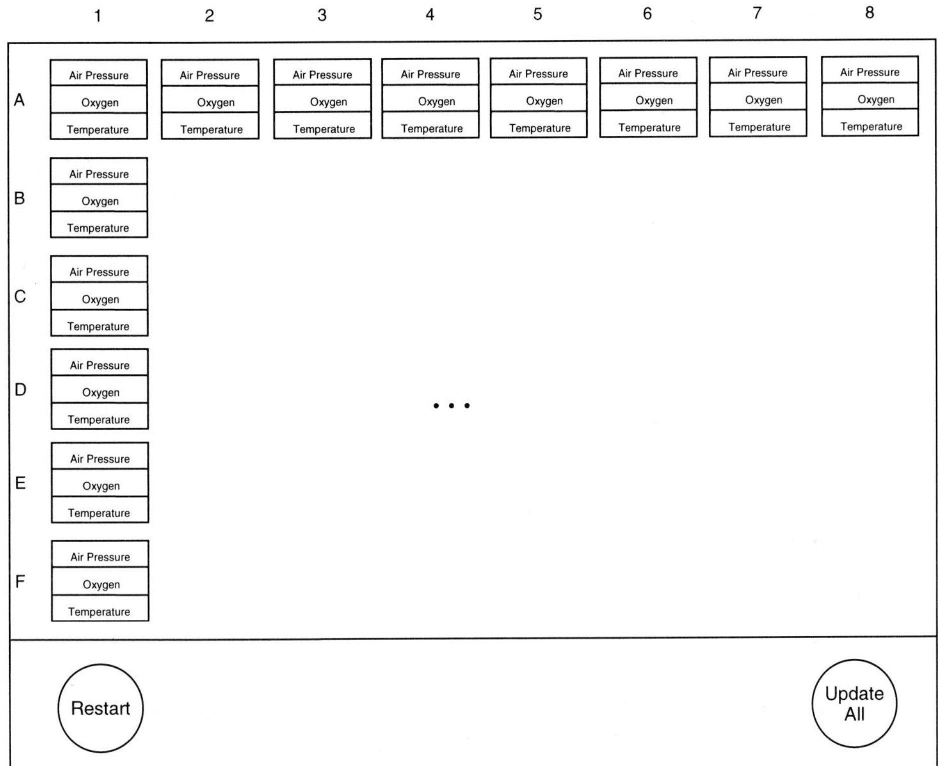

Figure HCC-1. Panel Display

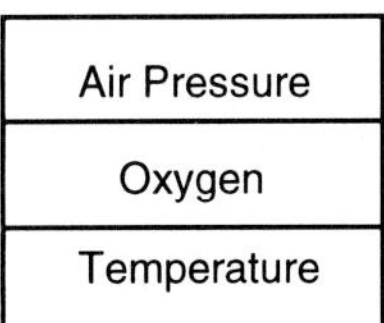

Figure HCC-2. Annunciator Display

PART II

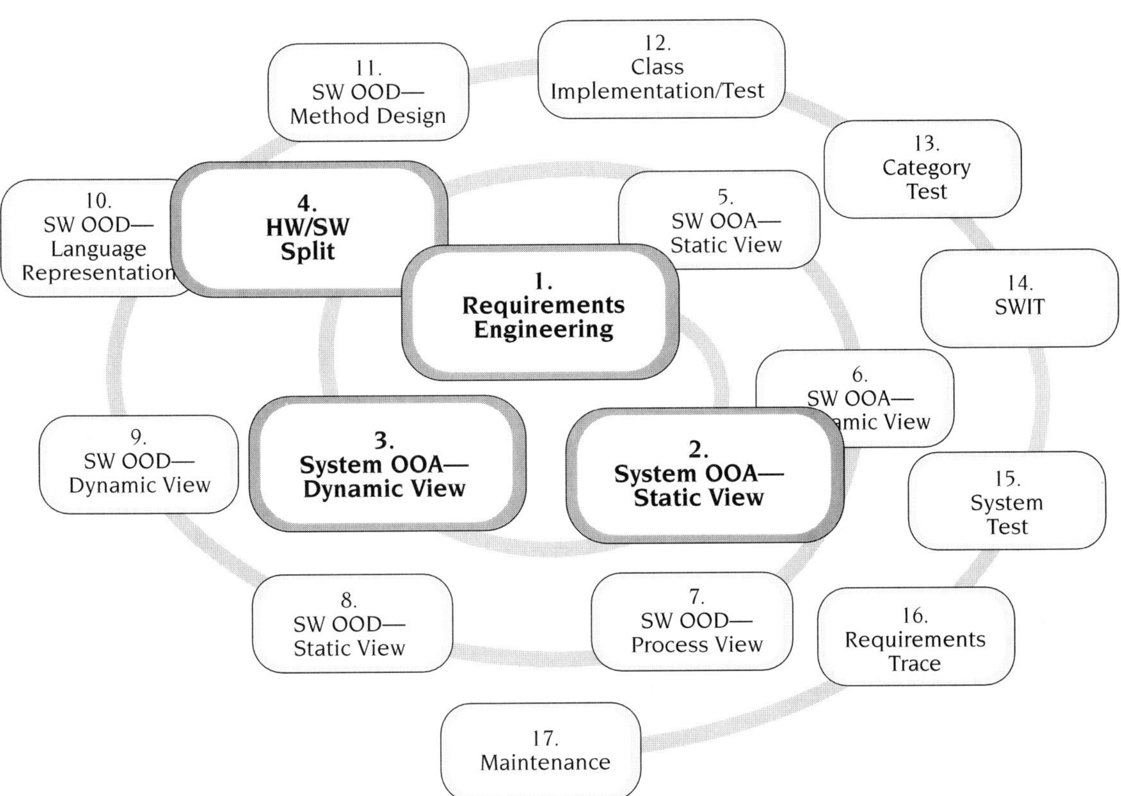

Systems Engineering

PHASE 1

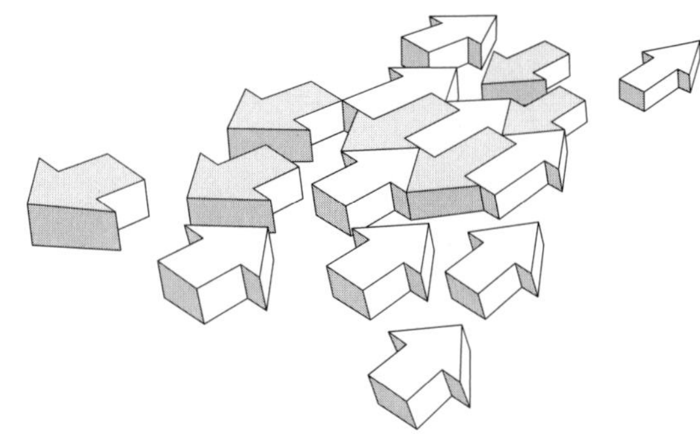

Requirements Engineering

PHASE OVERVIEW

The entire system[1] development process begins with Requirements Engineering, which can be loosely defined as the process of establishing a set of requirements, both hardware and software, for a system development effort. Figure 1-1 depicts the Activities for this Phase. As the figure shows, the goals of this Phase are to

- Identify the external interfaces for the system
- Identify, categorize, and prioritize the system requirements in a Requirements Trace Matrix (RTM).

This Phase first focuses on establishing the external interfaces for the system and representing that information in a traditional Context Diagram. Context Diagrams have been part of the industry for years, and there is no intent or attempt to recreate the wheel with instructional material in this book.

Next, the set of "shall" sentences is extracted from an agreed-upon set of documents and an initial Requirements Trace Matrix (RTM) is developed. Because some projects have multiple documents on hand, it may be necessary to first define the set of documents to be utilized for establishing a requirements baseline. Once specified, the documents are examined for sentences that include the word "shall". The sentences that include the word "shall" are the initial set of requirements with which we work, and they are entered into rows in the RTM. If documents do *not* exist, or if documents exist that are *not* written using the word "shall", requirements can still be discovered through discussions with domain experts and then they can be entered into the RTM.

Next, each requirement ("shall") in the RTM is *initially* categorized as to whether the requirement is to be satisfied by hardware, software, or both. This allocation is usually driven by cost factors. In some cases, it is less expensive to purchase required

[1]Use of the word "system" here implies both hardware and software components.

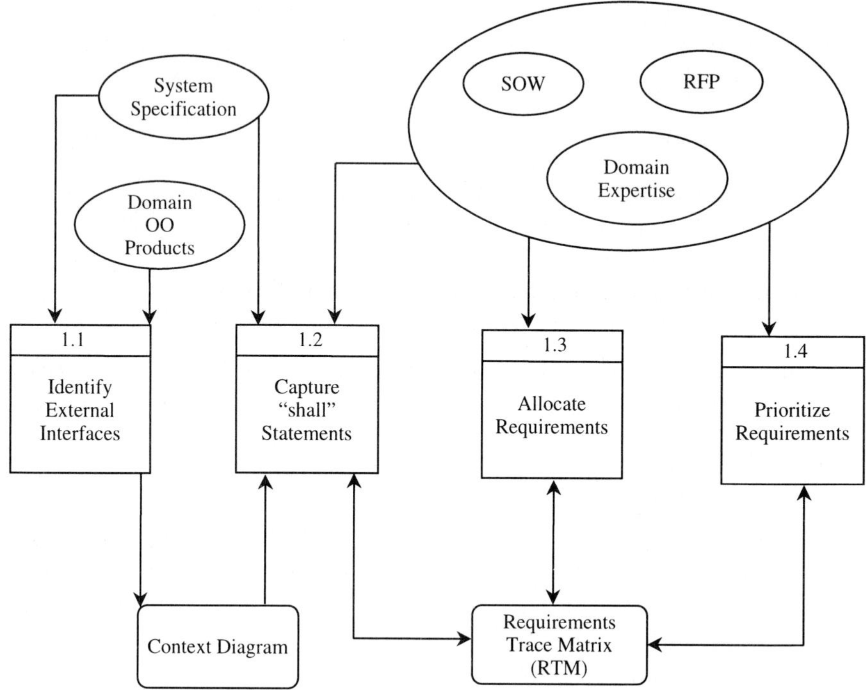

Figure 1-1. Requirements Engineering Phase Description Diagram

functionality in hardware than it is to develop equivalent functionality in software. Sometimes, no hardware alternative exists, in which case the functionality must be allocated entirely to software. Lastly, the requirements are prioritized for development.

1.1 IDENTIFY EXTERNAL INTERFACES

Purpose

> The purpose of this Activity is simply to identify and document the set of external interfaces for the system: hardware, software, and data store.

The benefits of producing a Context Diagram are well-documented in the industry and again, there is no intent here to reinvent the wheel. It is difficult to imagine developing a system without clear identification and definition of the external interfaces.

As for the OO benefit of this Activity, as will be shown in later Activities, identification of the external interfaces leads to the discovery of Interface Classes that are required for implementation[2].

Definition(s)

Context Diagram: A **Context Diagram** is a diagram consisting of one circle (or ellipse), which represents the system, that is typically placed in the **center** of the diagram; rectangles are used to represent entities, both hardware and software, that are external, yet required interfaces, to the system to be developed; and finally, a pair of double lines represents any data store that is required/produced.

Commercial Off-The-Shelf Software (COTS): **COTS** is software that is already written, or under development, that can be used to implement a portion of the required software functionality. The **COTS** copyright is typically owned by the organization that developed the software. Some examples of **COTS** products are Oracle, Microsoft Office, Netscape, and so on.

Customer-Furnished Software (CFS): CFS is software that is supplied by a customer, and that is to be incorporated into the software under development. **CFS** is a term that is commonly used in the commercial arena. The copyright to **CFS** is typically owned by the customer.

Data Store: A **data store** is used to represent persistent data that are accessed by the system.

External Interface: An **external interface** is an entity that is *not* currently part of the system being developed, yet provides resources that are required by or affected by the system currently under development.

Government-Furnished Software (GFS): **GFS** is software that is already written, or under development, that can be used to implement a portion of the required software functionality. The **GFS** copyright is typically owned by the Government and therefore is public domain software.

Persistent Data: **Persistent data** are data that remain after the termination of an application. There are various implementation mechanisms for **persistent data**, for example: a database, flat file, and so on.

Repository: Each CASE tool maintains its information in a database, the format and content of which are typically vendor-specific. This book utilizes the word "**repository**" to represent a CASE tool database for one specific project. Thus, if a CASE tool supports two projects named A and B, respectively, there are two **repositories**—one for Project A and one for Project B.

[2]As we shall see later, external interfaces become Interface Classes that are owned by either an Interface Category or a child Category of the Interface Category.

Process

Step 1: Examine Existing Documentation

Read existing documentation to discover the external interfaces. Look for operators, hardware devices, software systems, and persistent data. These four entities represent typical external interfaces.

When thinking of software systems with which the current system interfaces, look for COTS and GFS/CFS. Most large systems typically require the functionality of existing software. One project, for example, had a requirement to launch word processors, spreadsheets, and e-mail. Consequently, those COTS entities appeared on the Context Diagram as external interfaces. Another project had a requirement to interface to existing software that provided map images to the system under development. That GFS software system appeared on the Context Diagram.

Step 2: Produce the Context Diagram

Before using your OO CASE tool to produce the Context Diagram, investigate whether the CASE tool supports the development of a Context Diagram within the same repository that is to be used for developing the OO model. If the CASE tool has a mechanism to support the development of a Context Diagram in the same repository as the project, by all means use it. If a Context Diagram is *not* included in the OO CASE tool's capability, then using existing OO symbols to represent a Context Diagram will corrupt the integrity of the repository, and will introduce nodes in the repository that are *not* related to the OO model.[3] When a repository is corrupted, reports generated from the repository are confusing to read.

Step 3: Review with Domain Experts

Everything is *not* always written down! There is also a great deal of knowledge that resides in the domain experts' heads. Have the Context Diagram reviewed to ensure its correctness and to facilitate discussions that may lead to *significant* leaps in knowledge.

Example

Figure 1-2 shows the Context Diagram for the HCC. Note that it includes the following: the Operator interface with the system (to reset the software, update the database, and turn off the alarm); the alarm interface with the system (the alarm is sounded when the deviation goes above 3%); an interface to the sensor that is required to read the current value of an environmental condition; and, an interface to the database that is required to acquire/reset the current nominal value for an environmental condition.

[3]Either the Category or the Class symbol must be utilized to represent the external interfaces, resulting in these entities becoming nodes in the CASE tool repository. The "lines" connecting the external entities to the system symbol become association nodes in the repository, and are listed when all associations are listed. And finally, the system itself becomes either a Category in the repository if the Category symbol is utilized, or a Class in the repository if the Class symbol is utilized. In summary, utilizing an OO CASE tool to draw a Context Diagram can result in three different kinds of nodes being entered into the repository that have nothing whatsoever to do with the OO model!

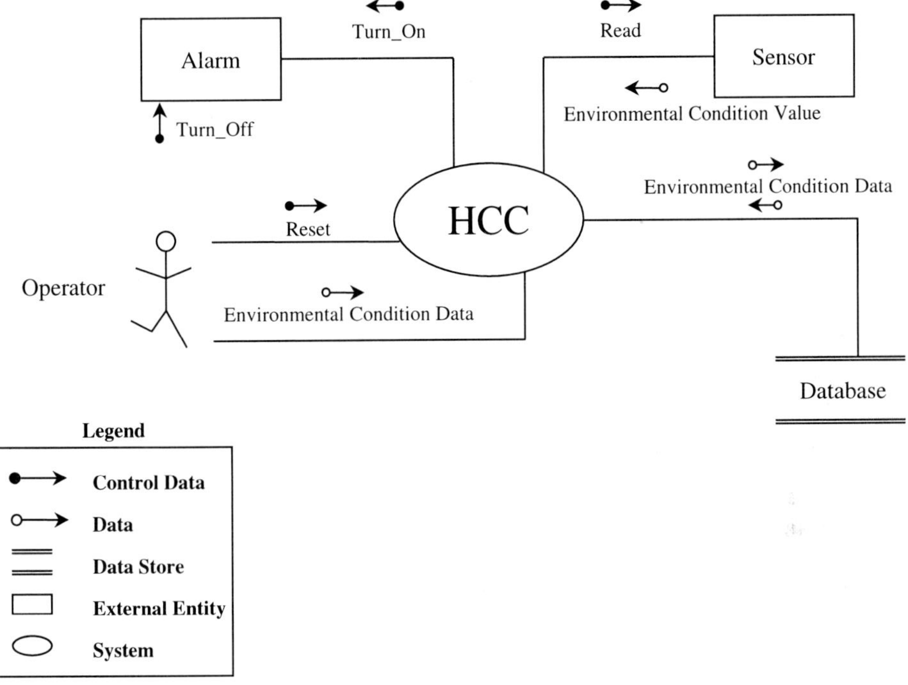

Figure 1-2. HCC Context Diagram

Pragmatic Project Issues

Think about External Systems in Terms of Classes

The entities that are external to the system are *not* eliminated from the system analysis and design efforts because of their relationship to the system. As previously stated, external entities imply the need for Interface Classes. More on this later.

1.2 CAPTURE "SHALL" STATEMENTS

Purpose

The purpose of this Activity is to produce an initial Requirements Trace Matrix (RTM) that contains the entire set of sentences from the System Specification, and any other agreed-upon documents, that include the word "shall". A sentence that includes the word "shall" represents a requirement that must be satisfied.

Many projects proceed without such a list of requirements and end up producing something other than what the customer originally wanted! Alternatively, without such a list, requirements "creep" occurs and more functionality is developed than originally conceived. Forcing the identification of *single shalls* during a project's early stages means that agreement can be reached, between developer and customer, as to exactly what the system is supposed to do—i.e., defining what the real requirements are. Requirements defined during this Activity become the cornerstone of all future software development activity, and more importantly, become the mechanism for tracing requirements (both statically and dynamically) through to the implemented and tested Use Cases, Categories, Classes, and Methods.

Definition(s)

"shall" statement: A single **"shall" statement** is a sentence that includes the word **"shall"**. A **"shall" statement** is extracted from the System Specification (and any other agreed-to documentation). A **"shall" statement** indicates a contractual requirement for the system to be developed.

Derived Requirement: A **derived requirement** is a specification of system functionality that is conceived as knowledge of the semantics of the "shall" sentences accumulates. A **derived requirement** does *not* represent a sentence that includes the word "shall". A **derived requirement** is a requirement that is deduced from other system knowledge, yet is *not* explicitly stated in the System Specification (or any other document).

Requirements Trace Matrix (RTM): An **RTM** is a matrix that initially contains the set of requirements for a system. The **RTM** is continually enhanced throughout Phases 1 and 2. The **RTM** is continually maintained throughout the lifetime of a project.

Rational Rose®: Rational Rose is a software CASE tool developed by the Rational Software Corporation that supports the Booch, OMT, and UML methods.

Software through Pictures (StP) OMT®: StP OMT is a CASE tool developed by Aonix that supports the OMT methodology.

Process

Step 1: Agree to a Starting Set of Documents

The first Step of this Activity is to identify the document, or set of documents, that form the baseline of a search for "shall" statements. Some projects have a myriad of documents, all of which are considered "Requirements Documents". For example, one project had two System Specification documents. Each System Specification was produced by a different organization: one by a contractor and one by the customer because the customer felt that the contractor's System Specification was neither accurate nor complete. Needless to say, the two documents were not always consistent!

Other projects have absolutely no documentation with which to begin, except the existing code, which is *not* usually documented. We will see what to do in this case in the next Step.

Step 2: Extract the "shall" Statements

Start at the beginning of the identified document(s) and search for the word "shall". Each sentence that includes the word "shall" forms an entry in a matrix called the Requirements Trace Matrix (RTM). If two sentences appear to mean the same thing, and both use the word "shall", do *not* do any analysis now, simply add both sentences as *unique entries* in the RTM. Analysis of these entries is performed in a later Activity.

If the selected set of documents is *not* written in terms of "shall" statements, simply extract from the documents the statements that imply requirements and add the word "shall" to the text. If there are *no* documents at all, hold discussions with domain experts and produce the initial set of "shalls" from these discussions. In these cases, be sure to obtain both customer and management buy-in to insure these "derived" shalls are within the scope of the current contract.

Step 3: Start the Requirements Trace Matrix (RTM)

Whether a "shall" sentence comes directly from a document, comes from adding the word "shall" to an existing sentence in a document, or comes from discussions with domain experts, each single "shall" sentence becomes a unique entry in the RTM, reproduced in the RTM exactly as it appears in the original document. A unique sequence number identifies each row in the RTM.

Example

Figure 1-3, Entries 1 through 22 inclusive, depicts the initial RTM for the HCC. Note that all sentences that include the word "shall" have been extracted from the HCC Problem Statement, and that each "shall" sentence occupies its own row in the RTM. Next, note the column headings, which are project-specific. The entries in the RTM will be analyzed and categorized in subsequent Phase 1 and Phase 2 Activities.

Now the project has a starting point. The importance and significance of the RTM *cannot be over emphasized.* This initial Activity leads to the establishment of Use Cases and Categories, which form the basis for the OO software development effort.

Pragmatic Project Issues

Use Scanner and Search Tool

If the document(s) in question can be scanned into the development environment and electronically searched for the word "shall", so much the better. Otherwise, the search must be done manually.

What About the Word "will"?

Many documents include sentences that utilize the word "will". These are not "shall" sentences, but "will" sentences. "Will" sentences typically indicate something that the customer would like to have, but they do *not* represent requirements. The Project Team can decide whether to include or exclude "will" sentences in the RTM. There are

Entry #	Para #*	HCC Requirements Traceability Matrix	Type
1	2.0	The SEM shall monitor all occupied living quarters.	
2	2.0	There shall be a total of 48 living quarters.	
3	2.1	Air Pressure, Temperature, and Oxygen % shall be obtained once per minute.	
4	2.1	There shall be three sensors in each living quarter.	
5	2.1	There shall be one sensor for each environmental condition.	
6	2.2	A current value representing a deviation >= 1% but <2% from the nominal value shall cause the window in the panel to be lit.	
7	2.2	A current value representing a deviation >= 2% but < 3% from the nominal value shall cause the window in the panel to be lit and flash two times per second.	
8	2.2	A current value representing a deviation >= 3% from the nominal value shall cause the window in the panel to be lit and flash four times per second and sound an audible alarm.	
9	2.2	There shall be one audible alarm.	
10	3.0	The panel shall accommodate 48 annunciators arranged in six rows.	
11	3.0	Each annunciator shall be mapped to a unique living quarter.	
12	3.0	Each annunciator shall accommodate three windows.	
13	3.0	Each window shall be identified with an appropriate legend.	
14	4.0	All nominal values shall be found in the database.	
15	4.0	The Operator shall be capable of redefining the nominal values in the database.	
16	4.0	The Operator shall be capable of redefining all three nominal values in the database to be used for all living quarters.	
17	4.0	The Operator shall be able to redefine the nominal value for a specific living quarter.	
18	5.0	Only the software shall turn on the audible alarm.	
19	5.0	Only the software shall flash a window.	
20	5.0	The software shall continue to turn on the warning indicators as long as the alarm condition exists.	
21	5.0	The Operator shall turn the audible alarm off.	
22	5.0	The Operator shall turn the window off.	
23	3.0	Each environmental condition will be represented by a different color.	
24	3.0	All windows for the same environmental condition will be the same color.	
25	—	Because the Operator can reset the nominal values in the DB, he/she needs to be able to reset the SEM to operate on those new values.	
26	—	The SEM does not need to monitor unoccupied living quarters, so the Operator can set living quarters to occupied/unoccupied to enable the SEM to operate more efficiently.	

*The paragraph number represents the paragraph number from the Case Study Problem Statement section with the prefix "HCC-" omitted.

Figure 1-3. Initial Habitat Control Center (HCC) RTM

two "will" sentences in the HCC Problem Statement, both appearing in Paragraph 3.0. For the SEM, the decision was made to include the "will" sentences in the RTM. The two sentences are as follows:

> Each environmental condition will be represented by a distinct color.
>
> All windows for the same environmental condition will be the same color.

These two "will" sentences appear as Entries 23 and 24 in the RTM, respectively. Note that the "will "sentences appear at the end of the RTM, grouped together. They could equally as well appear in the body of the RTM in proper chronological order. Grouping them together makes it easy to evaluate them for possible inclusion in the system. Keeping them in-line sequentially according to the order of their appearance in the original document makes the RTM a bit more tidy. This is a project-specific decision.

Electronically Maintain the RTM

The RTM needs to be electronically maintained by whatever tool is available, CASE or otherwise, including Microsoft Excel®, FileMaker Pro®, and so on. Choose the tool to support the RTM and use it from the start. It is important to choose a tool that supports "sorting" the matrix by columns because the information in the RTM, when completed, will get sorted many times in many ways for both the management and development teams.

Capture Derived Requirements—If Possible

As knowledge of an application is gained, it is possible to formulate derived requirements. Although this is not the focus of this Activity, derived requirements should *not* be ignored. Enter derived requirements into the RTM when conceived, so they will *not* be lost and can later be confirmed with the customer. Entries 25 and 26 in Figure 1-3 represent two derived requirements for the HCC that need to be approved by the customer for implementation in the SEM software. The fact that there is no paragraph reference indicates that these entries are potential derived requirements.

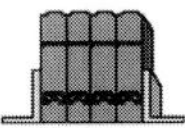

Product(s)

The result of this Activity is the *initial* Requirements Trace Matrix (RTM). The row entries represent the entire set of single "shalls" and "wills" extracted from the set of documents previously identified for examination. The RTM, *at this point in its development*, simply captures the initial set of requirements for the project.

There is one (1) RTM per project.

1.3 ALLOCATE REQUIREMENTS

Purpose

Without a stable set of requirements that are allocated to respective organizations for development, how can a system be developed?

> The purpose of allocating the requirements is to begin to define clearly what requirements are the responsibility of software and what requirements are the responsibility of hardware.

Definition(s)

Performance Requirement: A **performance requirement** is a statement that specifies either a timing or sizing restriction on either a hardware device or a functional subset of the software.

Software Constraint: A **software constraint** is a restriction potentially placed on the software implementation. For example, consider the fact that a living quarter has three sensors. The number three is a potential software ***constraint***, and can be implemented as an array upper bound, size of a bounded linked list, and so on. The same can be said for the number of halls, rooms, and therefore, the number of living quarters.

Process

Step 1: Categorize the RTM Entries

Categorize each entry in the RTM according to its "type". Each Project Team will, of course, define the valid "types" for its project, but at a minimum, the following are suggested:

DR => Derived Requirement

HW => Hardware requirement

NTH => Nice To Have

P => Performance requirement

SW => Software requirement

SWC => Software Constraint

D(#nn) => Duplicate of RTM entry #nn

Example

Figure 1-4 shows the RTM, which now reflects the results of completing the "type" column. Note that an entry may have more than one "type," for example, Entry 3, which has both a software and a performance categorization.

What is important from the system engineer's view is that all requirements are captured and categorized. What is important from the software developer's point of view is that the software requirements are established, because it is the software requirements that will be rewritten as Use Cases in the next Phase.

Entry #	Para #*	HCC Requirements Traceability Matrix	Type
1	2.0	The SEM shall monitor all occupied living quarters.	SW
2	2.0	There shall be a total of 48 living quarters.	HW, SWC
3	2.1	Air Pressure, Temperature, and Oxygen % shall be obtained once per minute.	SW, P
4	2.1	There shall be three sensors in each living quarter.	HW, SWC
5	2.1	There shall be one sensor for each environmental condition.	HW, SWC
6	2.2	A current value representing a deviation >= 1% but <2% from the nominal value shall cause the window in the panel to be lit.	SW
7	2.2	A current value representing a deviation >= 2% but < 3% from the nominal value shall cause the window in the panel to be lit and flash two times per second.	SW
8	2.2	A current value representing a deviation >= 3% from the nominal value shall cause the window in the panel to be lit and flash four times per second and sound an audible alarm.	SW
9	2.2	There shall be one audible alarm.	HW, SWC
10	3.0	The panel shall accommodate 48 annunciators arranged in six rows.	SW[4]
11	3.0	Each annunciator shall be mapped to a unique living quarter.	HW, SWC
12	3.0	Each annunciator shall accommodate three windows.	SW[5]
13	3.0	Each window shall be identified with an appropriate legend.	SW
14	4.0	All nominal values shall be found in the database.	SW
15	4.0	The Operator shall be capable of redefining the nominal values in the database.	SW
16	4.0	The Operator shall be capable of redefining all three nominal values in the database to be used for all living quarters.	SW
17	4.0	The Operator shall be able to redefine the nominal value for a specific living quarter.	SW
18	5.0	Only the software shall turn on the audible alarm.	SW
19	5.0	Only the software shall flash a window.	SW
20	5.0	The software shall continue to turn on the warning indicators as long as the alarm condition exists.	SW
21	5.0	The Operator shall turn the audible alarm off.	SW
22	5.0	The Operator shall turn the window off.	SW
23	3.0	Each environmental condition will be represented by a different color.	NTH
24	3.0	All windows for the same environmental condition will be the same color.	NTH
25	—	Because the Operator can reset the nominal values in the DB, he/she needs to be able to reset the SEM to operate on those new values.	SW, DR
26	—	The SEM does not need to monitor unoccupied living quarters, so the Operator can set living quarters to occupied/unoccupied to enable the SEM to operate more efficiently.	SW, DR

*The paragraph number represents the paragraph number from the Case Study Problem Statement section with the prefix "HCC-" omitted.

Figure 1-4. HCC RTM with "Type" Column Completed

[4]The allocation is to SW because the panel will be reflected on a monitor.

[5]The allocation is to SW because the annunciator will be reflected on a monitor.

Pragmatic Project Issues

Project Direction Required

For those entries in the RTM with a software constraint (SWC), a project decision is required to establish how the constraints are to be implemented in the software. Are the constraints to be hard coded? Are the constraints to be read in from a flat file or a database, thus permitting changes without recoding or recompiling? A decision is also required as to how the constraints are to be represented in the OO model. In other words, should the Class Diagram show ***3*** sensors or ***n*** sensors (* in UML)?

For this project the decision was made to show the constraints in the OO model. This means that the number '***3***' is to be placed on the OO diagrams, not *n* (or * in UML*)*. The implementation of these constraints is to be decided at a later time. The implementation options include, but are *not* limited to

- Named constants in the code
- A flat file containing the constraints, read upon system start-up
- Input from the Operator upon system start-up.

This choice is application-dependent. For this application, we chose the first option.

Maintain Consistent Staff

This effort takes time to complete, and it is suggested *not* to change the personnel assigned to this Activity.

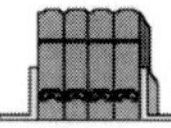

Product(s)

The product produced is the updated RTM with the "Type" column completed. Again, there is only one (1) RTM per project.

1.4 PRIORITIZE REQUIREMENTS

Purpose

> The purpose of prioritizing the requirements is to allocate the Use Cases to a reasonable development schedule.

Definition(s)

Build: A **build** is a specification of software functionality to be developed by a specific date. A **build** is part of a release, used for internal management purposes to track the development of a release to a customer. For inheritance hierarchies, the first **build** implements the root Class and one branch of an inheritance hierarchy down to a leaf Class. Subsequent **builds** add respective Subclass branches.

Release: A **release** is a distribution of software functionality to the customer. A **release** is made up of one or more builds. A **release** has a specific version number associated with it to help identify the specific set of functionality included in the delivered software.

Process

Step 1: Establish Definition of Build and Release

The two words, "build" and "release", are overloaded in the industry. Agree upon definitions for the two terms for the project. The definitions to be used in this book are provided above.

Step 2: Identify Releases

Partition the software functionality into multiple releases. Releases are typically easier to define when they focus on the Methods within a Class.

Step 3: Identify Builds/Releases

Partition each release into multiple builds. Builds are typically easier to define and implement when they focus on the selection of Classes, where, as previously stated, releases are typically easier to define when they focus on the Methods within a Class. Consequently, subsequent builds add Classes to existing software, whereas subsequent releases add functionality to existing Classes.

Example

Figure 1-5 shows a completed release/build schedule for the SEM software requirements and Figure 1-6 maps each specific software requirement in the RTM to a build.

Note that Builds 1 and 2 do *not* require the `Alarm`[6] Class. Note that Release 2 (Builds 3 and 4) adds functionality to the already incorporated `Living_Quarter` Class, specifically changing the state of the `Living_Quarter`. This recommended way to define builds and releases is just a guideline to get started and is *not* a hard and fast rule. Frankly, nothing in OO is a hard and fast rule!

Build 1 could have been restricted to just the air pressure sensor and the air pressure environmental condition, adding the oxygen sensor and oxygen environmental

Release #	Basic Functionality	Builds
1	Monitor all occupied living quarters (based on initial values) and display the panel and deviations. Omit all Operator interaction and the audible alarm.	B1, B2
2	Incorporate audible alarm functionality. Incorporate Operator interaction with the SEM software: changing the state of a living quarter and changing values in the database.	B3, B4

Figure 1-5. Release to Build Allocation

[6]Although an Alarm Class and a Living Quarter Class have not yet officially been identified, they need to be referenced here for clarity.

Entry #	Para #*	HCC Requirements Traceability Matrix	Type	Build
1	2.0	The SEM shall monitor all occupied living quarters.	SW	B1
2	2.0	There shall be a total of 48 living quarters.	HW, SWC	B1
3	2.1	Air Pressure, Temperature, and Oxygen % shall be obtained once per minute.	SW, P	B1
4	2.1	There shall be three sensors in each living quarter.	HW, SWC	B1
5	2.1	There shall be one sensor for each environmental condition.	HW, SWC	B1
6	2.2	A current value representing a deviation >= 1% but <2% from the nominal value shall cause the window in the panel to be lit.	SW	B2
7	2.2	A current value representing a deviation >= 2% but < 3% from the nominal value shall cause the window in the panel to be lit and flash two times per second.	SW	B2
8	2.2	A current value representing a deviation >= 3% from the nominal value shall cause the window in the panel to be lit and flash four times per second and sound an audible alarm.	SW	B2, B3
9	2.2	There shall be one audible alarm.	HW, SWC	B3
10	3.0	The panel shall accommodate 48 annunciators arranged in six rows.	SW	B1
11	3.0	Each annunciator shall be mapped to a unique living quarter.	HW, SWC	B1
12	3.0	Each annunciator shall accommodate three windows.	SW	B1
13	3.0	Each window shall be identified with an appropriate legend.	SW	B1
14	4.0	All nominal values shall be found in the database.	SW	B1
15	4.0	The Operator shall be capable of redefining the nominal values in the database.	SW	B4
16	4.0	The Operator shall be capable of redefining all three nominal values in the database to be used for all living quarters.	SW	B4
17	4.0	The Operator shall be able to redefine the nominal value for a specific living quarter.	SW	B4
18	5.0	Only the software shall turn on the audible alarm.	SW	B3
19	5.0	Only the software shall flash a window.	SW	B2
20	5.0	The software shall continue to turn on the warning indicators as long as the alarm condition exists.	SW	B2, B3
21	5.0	The Operator shall turn the audible alarm off.	SW	B3
22	5.0	The Operator shall turn the window off.	SW	B3
23	3.0	Each environmental condition will be represented by a different color.	NTH	
24	3.0	All windows for the same environmental condition will be the same color.	NTH	
25	—	Because the Operator can reset the nominal values in the DB, he/she needs to be able to reset the SEM to operate on those new values.	SW, DR	B4
26	—	The SEM does not need to monitor unoccupied living quarters so the Operator can set living quarters to occupied/unoccupied to enable the SEM to operate more efficiently.	SW, DR	B4

*The paragraph number represents the paragraph number from the Case Study Problem Statement section with the prefix "HCC-" omitted.

Figure 1-6. HCC RTM with Build/Requirement Allocation

condition in Build 2, and temperature in Build 3. Then, Build 4 could have added the panel display, which requires the `Panel`, `Annunciator`, and `Window` Classes. This could have constituted Release 1. This partitioning of functionality would more closely follow the recommendation provided earlier. However, this approach for the SEM, *not* a very complex system, would have resulted in too many builds. Again, as with any approach, engineering judgment is required.

Pragmatic Project Issues

Achieving Success

To achieve success, customer satisfaction, and management buy-in, keep the first release and its builds relatively simple. Keep the required functionality for the first few builds and release simple enough to enable the development staff to gain a full understanding of the process. Once success is achieved and progress has been demonstrated to both the customer and upper-level management, life is ever so much simpler!

Maintain Consistent Staff

Again, utilize the same individuals for this effort that performed the categorization of the requirements. Building a core set of individuals that have knowledge of the requirements, builds, and releases is necessary for any project.

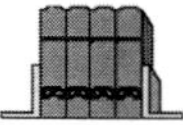

Product(s)

The product of this Activity is the updated RTM, showing the completion of the "Build" column. Note how the RTM is growing! And, we are *not* anywhere near finished yet!

Phase Transition Criteria

Time ***must*** be spent on this initial Phase. Without a fairly stable RTM, a project *cannot* move forward. Do *not* progress until at least the Build 1 requirements have been agreed-upon. By at least agreeing upon Build 1 requirements, once Phase 3 is complete, the software effort can begin. The review criteria shown in Table 1-1 may prove helpful in deciding whether or not to move on and start the next Phase.

Review Criteria

Table 1-1. RTM Review Criteria: Phase 1

#	RTM Review Criteria	Phase 1
1	Are the "shall" sentences from the agreed-upon set of documents included?	√
2	Is each "shall" a unique entry in the RTM?	√
3	Are any known derived requirements included, and marked "DR"?	√
4	Are the "will" sentences included, and marked "NTH"?	√
5	Are all entries categorized?	√
6	Are duplicates identified?	√
7	Is Build 1 identified?	√

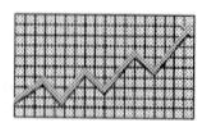

Tracking Progress

Table 1-2 indicates what has been accomplished in this Phase. Table 1-2 also includes suggested management metrics that can be collected and monitored to track the progress of a project. As previously stated in the Preface, this specific table is expanded in every Phase. By the end of this book, a complete project management spreadsheet, implemented in Microsoft Excel 7.0, will have been produced. This Excel spreadsheet is included on the enclosed CD-ROM in Appendix E and can be imported into Microsoft Project for the addition of staffing requirements and a milestone schedule.

The first column identifies the specific Phase and Activity by number. The second and third columns provide the name of the Phase and each Activity in the Phase, respectively. The fourth column provides suggested development staff charge-back numbers for internal tracking purposes. This information can be collected, analyzed, and used as input to future estimates. The fifth and sixth columns respectively define the final product(s) produced and the associated management metrics that can be utilized to monitor the progress of the effort, as well as to achieve an earned value approach to compensation. The final column assigns weights to the actual work products within a Phase (with *each* Phase providing a base of 100%). The weights are used as a vehicle for an earned value approach to compensation for work accomplished to date. For Phase 1, equal weight (50%) is applied to the development of the Context Diagram and the RTM. Weight assigned to the incremental development of the RTM is also equally divided. Of course, these actual weights are project-specific and are provided as food for thought. It is anticipated that an organization will modify these weights.

Table 1-2. Project Management Spreadsheet: Phase 1

HCC Project Management Spreadsheet						
Number	**Phase Name**	**Activity**	**Charge Number**	**Product**	**Progress Metric**	**% Weight**
1	**Requirements Engineering**		**RE-1**			
1.1		Identify External Interfaces	RE-1.1	Context Diagram	1 Context Diagram completed	0.50
1.2		Capture "shall" Statements	RE-1.2	RTM ("shall" Statements)	# "shall" sentences	0.16
1.3		Allocate Requirements	RE-1.3	RTM ("Type" Column)	# entries typed (%) #SW entries (%)	0.17
1.4		Prioritize Requirements	RE-1.4	RTM ("Build" Column)	# entries prioritized (%) #Use Cases/build(%)	0.17

PHASE 2

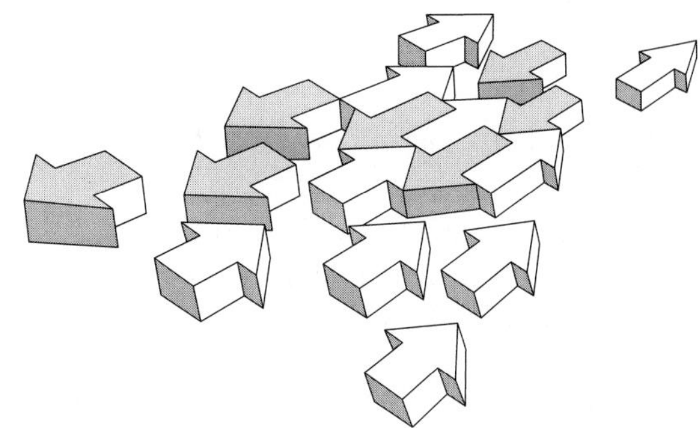

Systems OOA–Static View

PHASE OVERVIEW

Figure 2-1 depicts the Activities for this Phase. As the figure shows, the goals of this Phase are the:

- Transition of a software requirement to a Use Case
- Establishment of a Category List
- Development of Scenarios and draft GUIs for each Use Case
- Development of a System Category Diagram (SCD) that represents the Categories and their associations.

Phase 2 begins with reformatting the subset of *software* requirements identified in the RTM into Use Case format. Next, Scenarios are produced, along with draft GUI designs, to describe the envisioned operational concept, or sequence of actions, behind each Use Case. Next, by examining the Actors and Subjects extracted from the Use Cases, a list of Categories is developed. Each Use Case is then allocated to an appropriate software Category for development based on the Subject of the Use Case. The Phase ends with the completion of a Booch/UML Class Diagram (or OMT Object Diagram) that depicts the Categories, and their Associations at the very highest level of abstraction. If UML is the notation of choice, only dependencies can be drawn between Categories in a package diagram.

A project must choose whether to keep all or some of these products in separate, distinct repositories for maintenance by Systems Engineering, or whether to maintain *all* model products, systems, and software in one repository. It certainly makes sense to keep the RTM in a separate repository, thus enabling and facilitating early configuration management of the RTM. The System Category Diagram (SCD) however is a different story. Keeping the SCD in its own repository (thus creating a copy in a new repository for subsequent refinements made in the software OOA and OOD Phases) means that the SCD, which shows Associations among Categories, must be manually updated throughout the lifetime of the project. The alternative is to actually *refine* (modify) the

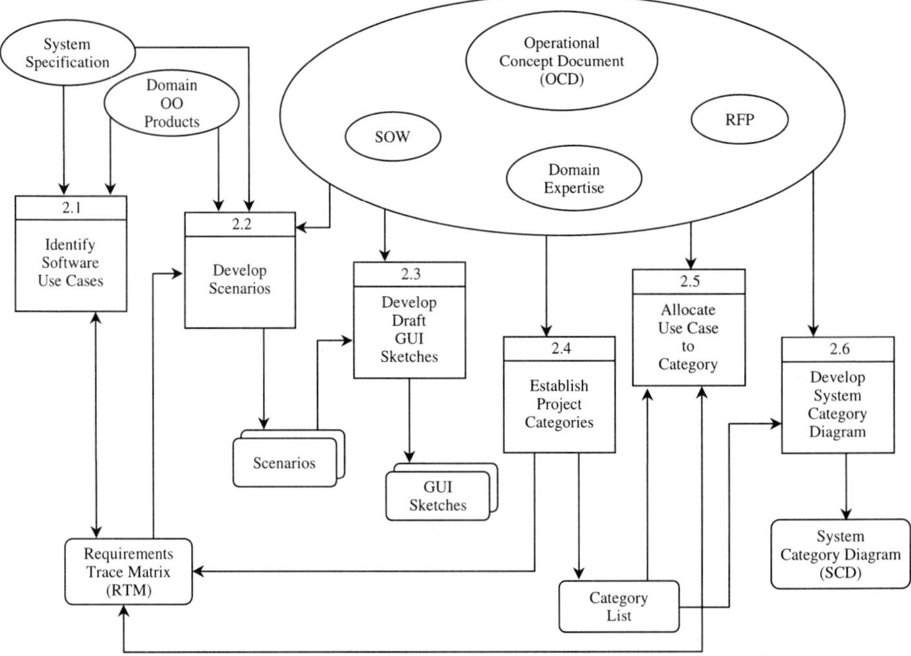

Figure 2-1. System OOA—Static View Phase Description Diagram

SCD to reflect changes discovered during OOA and OOD, thus losing the original system view. For the HCC Case Study, the decision was made to maintain the system view (RTM and SCD) in a *separate* repository and perform manual updates. Although this approach means extra work now, the benefits occur when having to incorporate new or changing requirements. On a real project, because of staffing considerations, typically one repository is maintained. Most projects simply do *not* have time to manually update previous views. But, this is a decision that is made for each specific project.

2.1 IDENTIFY SOFTWARE USE CASES

Purpose

The purpose of this Activity is to extract the software requirements from the RTM and reformat these requirements to aid in the discovery of potential Categories. The reformatting Activity transitions a "shall" sentence into Use Case format.

Definition(s)

Action: An **Action** represents a capability requested of the software. An **Action** is a specific subset of functionality that can be requested by an Actor. An **Action** is a statement of requested processing.

Actor: An **Actor** represents a stimulus to the software system. The stimulus can be external to the software system, or internally created by the software itself. An **Actor** requests a specific thread of control (functionality).

Qualifier: A **qualifier** is a mechanism for refining a Use Case Actor or Subject, and thus aids in the discovery of inheritance hierarchies. There are three kinds of qualifiers: Frequency Qualifier, Filter Qualifier, and Time Qualifier. When adding a qualifier to a Use Case in the RTM, place the qualifier in parentheses after the Use Case name. Consider the following:

Manager Views Activity Code (by life cycle phase) - Filter Qualifier

Manager Requests Activity Code Report (Monthly) - Frequency Qualifier

Manager Requests Hours (January) - Time Qualifier

The three kinds of qualifiers are discussed in more detail in the Pragmatic Project Issues section.

Software Requirement: A **software requirement** is a requirement that must be satisfied by the software. There are many kinds of requirements: hardware only, software functional, software performance, and so on. A Use Case is a re-statement of a *functional* **software requirement**. A software performance requirement is a constraint that is placed on one or more software functional requirements.

Role: A **Role** represents a set of responsibilities for an Actor of a software system. An Actor may play several **Roles**. Use of the word "**Role**" here is not to be confused with the use of the word "role" within OMT.

Subject: A **Subject** represents the item acted *upon* by an Action requested *of* the software. A **Subject** is a domain entity that has the responsibility of fulfilling the request for the functionality of a specific Use Case. A **Subject** satisfies the request for an Action, either entirely by itself, or in collaboration with other entities in the software system.

Use Case: A **Use Case** is a statement of functionality required of the software. A **Use Case** is written in a specific format. The specific format for a **Use Case** is

Actor Action Subject

where "Actor," "Action," and "Subject" are as defined above.

Process

Step 1: Establish Naming Conventions

Establish the naming conventions for Use Cases[1]. The convention adopted in this text is UC##_Use_Case_Name, with each word of the Use Case name 1) separated by one underscore, and 2) written with an initial capital letter. The double pound sign (##) is a placeholder for the sequence number of the Use Case, without zero filling. Another quite common convention is to name a Use Case UC##UseCaseName with no underscores at all, and with the first letter of each word capitalized.

Step 2: Agree upon Allowable Use Case Stimuli

Some developers believe that the only allowable Actors are external stimuli, indeed, *tangible* external stimuli; examples of these include an Operator, ATM Card, and so on. Other developers believe that a Use Case represents a specific use of the software, and that an Actor is *any* requester of software functionality. This latter group permits an entry such as "SW" (for software-requested functionality), "IN" (for functionality requested by an interrupt), or "COTS" (for functionality requested by COTS software), in the RTM ***and*** in the name of the Use Case. Constraining Actors to just Operators is quite inflexible with respect to requirements definition. Agree upon the Project Team's view of an Actor before performing Step 5.

Step 3: Agree on the Quantity of Use Cases

Some developers feel that six or seven Use Cases for a million-lines-of-code software system is quite sufficient. Other developers feel that 5000 Use Cases for a million-lines-of-code software system is more reasonable. Each position has a *major* impact on system development. Too few Use Cases do *not* enable Categories to be selected early in the project. Too many Use Cases make for very detailed requirements and a very thorough Requirements Trace. Experience has shown that too many Use Cases is more beneficial than too few.

Step 4: Determine Strategy for Use Cases on Inheritance Hierarchies

Suppose an entry in the RTM is worded like Entry 3 in the HCC RTM. Entry 3 states that

> Air Pressure, Temperature, and Oxygen % shall be obtained once per minute.[2]

Does this statement migrate to one Use Case,

> UC3_Timer_Triggers_Living_Quarter_Sensor

that covers all three Subclasses? If this is the decision, then there will be only one Interaction Diagram (or Sequence Diagram in UML) produced and the RTM can be an-

[1]When defining the naming conventions for Use Cases, consider the CASE tool utilized. For example, StP OMT does not permit a colon (:) in the name, therefore UC##:Use_Case_Name is not a possible naming convention. However an underscore is permited in a name, consequently UC##_Use_Case_Name was utilized.

[2]This statement means to obtain a sensor's current value once per minute, for each of the three kinds of sensors.

notated with the Use Case repeated for all three Subclasses to ensure that the Subclasses are explicitly captured. The entry in the RTM is then traceable to one Use Case. This is the approach adopted by the authors. Another approach is to migrate the single entry to three distinct Use Cases named UC3a, UC3b, and UC3c, respectively, one for each environmental condition or Subclass. Although more work, the more precise a Use Case, the easier it is to implement, test, and reuse. Lastly, with precise Use Cases, customer confidence is gained quite easily. Again this is a project-specific decision.

Step 5: Extract Software Requirements as Use Cases

Examine each entry in the RTM that has a categorization of SW. For each software functional requirement, restate the requirement in the format of a Use Case, specifically as Actor - Action - Subject.

Example

Figure 2-2 shows the RTM, which now reflects the result of identifying Use Cases for the *unique* software entries. Note the following:

Duplicate entries are so noted and do not need to be considered again.

An Actor is *not* always external to the software system; therefore, the convention of using the capital letters "SW" to indicate that the software is requesting the Action was adopted. Additionally a Use Case may be requested as the result of an interrupt, in which case "IN" indicates that an interrupt is the stimulus for a specific Use Case. Use the name of the COTS/CFS/GFS software system as the Actor when the system under-development is stimulated by either COTS/CFS/GFS.

Also realize that what has been initiated is the start of a Forward Requirements Trace (FRT). Each software entry in the RTM is now mapped to a Use Case to be implemented in software. As we shall see in later Phases, a Use Case is subsequently mapped to the software OO model entities, both logical (OO CASE tool repository) and physical (language-specific source code). More on the FRT later, in Phase 16.

Pragmatic Project Issues

Avoid Analysis Paralysis

The RTM is perhaps one of the *most important products* in an OO project. The RTM establishes the software functional threads to be implemented, represented as Use Cases, and as is soon to be shown, the project Categories. In the initial stages of a project, take your best guess and move on. The RTM is a living document and, properly configuration-managed, continues to be the backbone of the project. You want to be as "right" as possible initially, but wanting to be perfect holds up the forward motion of a project. Configuration management of the RTM permits change in a controlled fashion. Consider a project where the Project Team held quarterly system requirements reviews for over a year. That project was subsequently canceled because the customer perceived a lack of understanding of the domain by the team.

Entry #	Para #*	System Specification Text	Type	Build	Use Case Name
1	2.0	The SEM shall monitor all occupied living quarters.	HW, SW	B1	UC1_SW_Monitors_Living_Quarters
2	2.0	There shall be a total of 48 living quarters.	HW, SWC	B1	n/a
3	2.1	Air Pressure, Temperature, and Oxygen % shall be obtained once per minute.	SW, P	B1	UC3_Timer_Triggers_Living_Quarter_Sensor Timer_Triggers_LQ_Air_Pressure_Sensor Timer_Triggers_LQ_Temperature_Sensor Timer_Triggers_LQ_Oxygen_Sensor
4	2.1	There shall be three sensors in each living quarter.	HW, SWC	B1	n/a
5	2.1	There shall be one sensor for each environmental condition.	HW, SWC	B1	n/a
6	2.2	A current value representing a deviation >= 1% but <2% from the nominal value shall cause the window in the panel to be lit.	SW	B2	UC6_SW_Lights_Window
7	2.2	A current value representing a deviation >= 2% but < 3% from the nominal value shall cause the window in the panel to be lit and flash two times per second.	SW	B2	UC7_SW_Flashes_Window_2X
8	2.2	A current value representing a deviation >= 3% from the nominal value shall cause the window in the panel to be lit and flash four times per second and sound an audible alarm.	SW	B2, B3	UC8_SW_Flashes_Window_4X
9	2.2	There shall be one audible alarm.	HW, SWC	B3	n/a
10	3.0	The panel shall accommodate 48 annunciators arranged in six rows.	SW	B1	UC10_SW_Displays_Panel
11	3.0	Each annunciator shall be mapped to a unique living quarter.	HW	B1	n/a
12	3.0	Each annunciator shall accommodate 3 windows.	SW	B1	UC12_SW_Displays_Annunciator
13	3.0	Each window shall be identified with an appropriate legend.	SW	B1	UC13_SW_Displays_Window

14	4.0	All nominal values shall be found in the database.	SW	B1	n/a
15	4.0	The Operator shall be capable of redefining the nominal values in the database.	SW	B4	Duplicate(#16)
16	4.0	The Operator shall be capable of redefining all three nominal values in the database to be used for all living quarters	SW	B4	UC_16_Operator_Updates_Nominal_Values_In_DB
17	4.0	The Operator shall be able to redefine the nominal value for a specific living quarter.	SW	B4	UC17_Operator_Updates_Living_Quarter_Nominal_Value
18	5.0	Only the software shall turn on the audible alarm.	SW	B3	UC18_SW_Sounds_Alarm
19	5.0	Only the software shall flash a window.	SW	B2	Duplicate (#7 and #8)
20	5.0	The software shall continue to turn on the warning indicators as long as the alarm condition exists.	SW	B2, B3	Duplicate (#18 and #19)
21	5.0	The Operator shall turn the audible alarm off.	SW	B3	UC21_Operator_Turns_Off _Alarm
22	5.0	The Operator shall turn the window off.	SW	B3	UC22_Operator_Turns_Off_Window
23	3.0	Each environmental condition will be represented by a different color.	NTH		
24	3.0	All windows for the same environmental condition will be the same color.	NTH		
25	—	Because the Operator can reset the nominal values in the DB, he/she needs to be able to reset the SEM to operate on those new values.	SW, DR	B4	UC25_Operator_Resets_SEM
26	—	The SEM does not need to monitor unoccupied living quarters, so the Operator can set living quarters to occupied/unoccupied to enable the SEM to operate more efficiently.	SW, DR,	B4	UC26_Operator_Sets_Living_Quarter_State

Legend:
D => Duplicate, DR => Derived Requirement, HW => Hardware, NTH => Nice To Have, P => Performance, SW => Software, SWC => Software Constraint

*The paragraph number represents the paragraph number from the Case Study Problem Statement section with the prefix "HCC-" omitted.

Figure 2-2. HCC RTM with Use Cases Identified

Understand the Meaning of the Word "Subject"

The Subject is the entity whose data structure is accessed (read or written to) by the Action. Be careful when naming a Use Case. Examine Use Case 16. If the Use Case were written as UC16_Operator_Updates _Nominal_Values, the Subject would *not* be as obvious as UC16_Operator_Updates_Nominal_Values_In_DB. The DB is the Subject that is affected by the Use Case. The DB *contains* the nominal values. Make sure to include the word "DB" in the Use Case name. Again, what is important is to do the best you can and move on. Anomalies will be discovered and can be easily corrected during the lifetime of the RTM.

Guidelines for External Stimuli

Think of people (e.g., different kinds of Operators or users of the system), things (e.g., cards, hardware device, interrupts), and COTS/CFS/GFS software systems that are external forces of the software system.

When thinking of people, names of specific individuals may come to mind. That is fine as long as when the Use Case is written, the name of the person is changed to the Role that the person plays. To identify Roles, think of job categories, organizational titles, and/or project titles. Roles such as:

- Manager
- Team Leader
- Data Entry Clerk
- Tester
- Developer
- Administrator
- Network Manager
- Designer

are examples of potential Roles of a system user. Use these terms as the Actors in a Use Case; do *not* use the names of individuals.

Think of Reading and Writing Roles

The point is that different users of a software system (Actors) use the system to perform different sets of actions. A software developer uses a software environment differently from a software tester. A project manager may use a metrics capture software system to monitor staff hours, which is entirely different than the software engineers, who use the system to enter their weekly time-related data.

The Roles May Form an Inheritance Hierarchy

Roles become Classes, and possibly a Category exists centered around a root Class named Role. Be sure to think in terms of nouns, because nouns typically represent Classes.

Actions Are Verbs or Verb/Noun Pairs

Initially, state the Action to be performed in terms of a verb or verb/noun pair acting on a Subject (noun). Later, with more experience, more complete names like Timer_Triggers_ Living_Quarter_Sensor will become quite natural.

Think of Qualifiers for the Subject

Previously, three kinds of qualifiers for a Subject were introduced. As time progresses, more qualifiers will most probably arise in the industry. The three qualifiers currently identified are

- Time (how much time is covered by a Use Case)
- Filter (a specific subset of the Actor or Subject)
- Frequency (how often is a Use Case performed)

The time qualifier helps discover inheritance hierarchies based on periods of time. Consider, for example, monthly reports, daily reports, and so on. These two Classes form Subclasses of a parent `Report` Class.

The filter qualifier aids in the discovery of inheritance hierarchies. Consider, for example, an air pressure sensor, oxygen sensor, and temperature sensor. These Classes are Subclasses of the parent `Sensor` Class. Adjectives typically represent a filter qualifier. The frequency qualifier leads to the number of iterations for a specific functional capability.

Naming in General

Avoid using plural case; keep the Subject and Action singular. Write Operator instead of Operators and sensor instead of sensors. This convention simply provides consistency within a project, and after all, a Class is an abstraction of all its Instances.

Use Case or Method on a Class: VERY IMPORTANT!

Suppose there are 3000 entries in the RTM and 2875 of them are software functional requirements. If a project decides to produce one Interaction Diagram (UML Sequence Diagram) per Use Case, 2875 Interaction Diagrams need to be produced. The project schedule may positively *prohibit* this "clean" approach; but, there is an alternative that maintains the clean specification and trace of the requirements as captured in the RTM.

The alternative centers around the concept of *complex* and *simple* Use Cases. Basically, a *complex* Use Case requires many Classes in its implementation, while a *simple* Use Case requires only one, or maybe two, Classes. The idea is that for each *complex* Use Case, an Interaction Diagram is produced. For each *simple* Use Case, allocating the RTM entry to a Method on a Class, rather than to a Use Case, might be sufficient, as long as the Class Test strategy mandates dynamic testing for such Class Methods. But, it is clear that for simple Use Cases, an Interaction Diagram may *not* be necessary, and in fact, may be overkill.

Consider allocating Entries 18 and 21 to the Methods `Sound_Alarm()` and `Silence_Alarm()`, respectively of the `Alarm Class`. With this approach, the RTM requires two more columns, "Class" and "Method", as shown in Figure 2-3. For the purposes of the Case Study and its solution, we have chosen this alternative approach. Now there are only 13 Interaction Diagrams to complete, not 15—a 13% decrease.

How can we know that there is an `Alarm` Class and how can we know that it has the Methods `Sound_Alarm()` and `Silence_Alarm()`? Experience pays off here. Whether to allocate an RTM entry to a Use Case or a Method on a Class is, of course, a judgment call. Is there really an `Alarm` Class with these Methods? There most probably is an `Alarm` Class. As for the Method names, take your best guess and move on. If the decision is made to allocate an entry to a Method on a Class, be flexible, because it may change in the future. Again recall that the RTM needs to be a managed product.

Avoid the Word "Find"

The word "find" is overloaded. Confusion reigns in a project when the word "find" is used in any Use Case. The word "find" can mean all, or none, of the following:

- Extract a subset of values based on a filter criteria
- Extract from the database
- Locate a pattern (e.g., a search string).

The word "find" means none of these when 1) none of the above is applicable within the context of a Use Case, and 2) no other meaning can be deduced. Use of the word "find" basically highlights the fact that the Use Case has *not* been defined precisely enough to enable software developers to understand the intent of the Use Case. Instead of using the word "find", use the following for the above three situations:

- Filter qualifier
- Read
- Search.

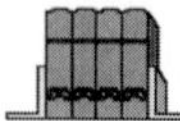

Product(s)

The product produced in this Activity is an updated RTM with the completion of the "Use Case," "Class," and "Method" columns.

2.2 DEVELOP SCENARIOS

Purpose

To develop the software, the software developers need much more information than a Use Case statement.

Entry #	Para #*	System Specification Text	Type	Build	Use Case Name	Class	Method
1	2.0	The SEM shall monitor all occupied living quarters.	SW	B1	UC1_SW_Monitors_Living_Quarters		
2	2.0	There shall be a total of 48 living quarters.	HW	B1	n/a		
3	2.1	Air Pressure, Temperature, and Oxygen % shall be obtained once per minute.	SW, P	B1	UC3_Timer_Triggers_Living_Quarter_Sensor Timer_Triggers_LQ_Air_Pressure_Sensor Timer_Triggers_LQ_Temperature_Sensor Timer_Triggers_LQ_Oxygen_Sensor		
4	2.1	There shall be three sensors in each living quarter.	HW	B1	n/a		
5	2.1	There shall be one sensor for each environmental condition.	HW	B1	n/a		
6	2.2	A current value representing a deviation >= 1% but <2% from the nominal value shall cause the window in the panel to be lit.	SW	B2	UC6_SW_Lights_Window		
7	2.2	A current value representing a deviation >= 2% but < 3% from the nominal value shall cause the window in the panel to be lit and flash two times per second.	SW	B2	UC7_SW_Flashes_Window_2X		
8	2.2	A current value representing a deviation >= 3% from the nominal value shall cause the window in the panel to be lit and flash four times per second and sound an audible alarm.	SW	B2, B3	UC8_SW_Flashes_Window_4X		
9	2.2	There shall be one audible alarm.	HW	B3	n/a		
10	3.0	The panel shall accommodate 48 annunciators arranged in six rows.	SW	B1	UC10_SW_Displays_Panel		
11	3.0	Each annunciator shall be mapped to a unique living quarter.	HW	B1	n/a		
12	3.0	Each annunciator shall accommodate three windows.	SW	B1	UC12_SW_Displays_Annunciator		
13	3.0	Each window shall be identified with an appropriate legend.	SW	B1	UC13_SW_Displays_Window		
14	4.0	All nominal values shall be found in the database.	SW	B1	n/a		

Figure 2-3. HCC RTM with "Class" and "Method" Columns Added

Entry #	Para #*	System Specification Text	Type	Build	Use Case Name	Class	Method
15	4.0	The Operator shall be capable of redefining the nominal values in the database.	SW	B4	Duplicate (#16)		
16	4.0	The Operator shall be capable of redefining all three nominal values in the database to be used for all living quarters.	SW	B4	UC_16_Operator_Updates_Nominal_Values_In_DB		
17	4.0	The Operator shall be able to redefine the nominal value for a specific living quarter.	SW	B4	UC17_Operator_Updates_Living_Quarter_Nominal_Value		
18	5.0	Only the software shall turn on the audible alarm.	SW	B3		Alarm	Sound
19	5.0	Only the software shall flash a window.	SW	B2	Duplicate (# 7 and #8)		
20	5.0	The software shall continue to turn on the warning indicators as long as the alarm condition exists.	SW	B2, B3	Duplicate (#18 and #19)		
21	5.0	The Operator shall turn the audible alarm off.	SW	B3		Alarm	Silence
22	5.0	The Operator shall turn the window off.	SW	B3	UC22_Operator_Turns_Off_Window		
23	3.0	Each environmental condition will be represented by a different color.	NTH				
24	3.0	All windows for the same environmental condition will be the same color.	NTH				
25	—	Because the Operator can reset the nominal values in the DB, he/she needs to be able to reset the SEM to operate on those new values.	SW, DR	B4	UC25_Operator_Resets_SEM		
26	—	The SEM does not need to monitor unoccupied living quarters, so the Operator can set living quarters to occupied/unoccupied to enable the SEM to operate more efficiently.	SW, DR,	B4	UC26_Operator_Sets_Living_Quarter_State		

*The paragraph number represents the paragraph number from the Case Study Problem Statement section, with the prefix "HCC-" omitted.

Figure 2-3. HCC RTM with "Class" and "Method" Columns Added (*continued*)

> The purpose of a Scenario is to provide the operational concept behind a Use Case.

Definition(s)

Scenario: A **Scenario** is a formatted description of the steps required for the completion of a Use Case. A **Scenario** consists of text that represents the concept of how an Operator interacts with the software to achieve the desired result. For a **Scenario** that does *not* have Operator interaction, the **Scenario** describes the sequence of software actions required to complete the specified functionality.

Process

Step 1: Agree upon the Format of a Scenario

Agree upon what information should be included in a Scenario. Identify a format that facilitates the specification of the required information to the software development staff and provides consistency for the project. Should the GUI be included? Should failure conditions be identified and error correction processing be specified? Should pre/post conditions be identified? A sample format is shown in Figure 2-4. All Scenarios for the SEM are written in this format.

Step 2: Complete the Draft Scenario for each Use Case

Only the Scenarios for the build in question need to be produced. Although UML permits multiple Scenarios per Use Case, experience has shown that this is perhaps *not* the best way to go. One Scenario per Use Case has worked much better. With multiple Scenarios per Use Case, common functionality in the system is difficult to detect. Common functionality is easier to detect from the RTM than from pages and pages of written documentation. Requirements Trace is easier, more precise, and more complete if there is one Scenario per Use Case. Finally, projects need precise requirements definition, otherwise how does a Project Team know what to implement? This is why the statement was made earlier that too many requirements (Use Cases) are better than too few.

Step 3: Review with Software Test and System Test Organizations

Review the Scenario with the Software, Software Integration and Test, and Systems Test organizations. The review is critical because

- Software needs to know what is to be implemented
- Software Integration and Test needs to know so a Software Integration and Test strategy can be determined
- System Test needs to know so that a System Test Plan can be developed.

The review at this stage *cannot* be expected to answer or even raise all questions. Carry on with what is known at this point. Remember, the process is iterative.

Use Case xx: Title

Overview:

< Text that provides a high-level description of the Use Case.>

Preconditions:

<List numerically the assumptions required before this Use Case can be executed.>

Scenario:

Action	Software Reaction
1. <Specify an Action>	1. <Describe the software reaction>
2. <Specify an Action>	2. <Describe the software reaction>

Scenario Notes:

<Indicate concurrency of Actions, any additional information, such as optional steps and branching and iteration steps. When indicating same, refer to specific sequence number.>

Post Conditions:

<List sequentially the conditions expected at the completion of the Scenario.>

Required GUI:

<List the names of the GUIs utilized in this Scenario.>

Exceptions:

<List sequentially any failure conditions that can affect the Scenario, and how the system should respond.>

Use Cases Utilized:

<List other Use Cases used.>

Timing Constraints:

<Specify any timing constraints for the Use Case or portion of the Use Case.>

Figure 2-4. Sample Scenario Format

Step 4: Review with Training Organizations

The organization associated with producing training materials for the users of the system needs to be involved at this stage as well. Early involvement enables the staff to start gaining the necessary knowledge to structure and write the user training materials.

Example

A draft Scenario is shown in Figure 2-5.[3] The Scenario is self-explanatory.

[3]Remember that the entire set of Scenarios for the SEM are on the enclosed CD-ROM in Appendix D.

Use Case 16: Operator_Updates_Nominal_Values_In_DB

Overview:

This Use Case enables the Operator to change the nominal values of all three environmental conditions in the database. These updated values are the nominal values against which the values detected by the sensors are compared to reflect percent deviation.

Preconditions:

1. There are no alarms currently active.
2. SEM_Desktop_View is displayed.
3. The database is accessible.

Scenario:

Action	Software Reaction
1. Operator clicks on the Update All button on the SEM_Desktop_View.	1. Update_All_View pop-up appears.
2. Disable the alarm.	2. Alarm disabled.
3. Enter Air Pressure value.	3. Air Pressure field is updated.
4. Enter Oxygen value.	4. Oxygen field is updated.
5. Enter Temperature value.	5. Temperature field is updated.
6. Operator clicks on the OK button.	6. The Update_All_View pop-up is destroyed, the DB is updated, and the Operator is returned to the SEM_Desktop_View.
7. Operator clicks on the Cancel button.	7. The Update_All_View is destroyed and monitoring continues. The database is not updated.
8. Enable alarm.	8. Alarm is enabled.

Scenario Notes:

Items 3, 4, and 5 may be done in any order. Additionally the Operator does not have to update all three values. This Use Case *permits* the modification of all three values, *but* the Operator may choose to update one, two, or all three. Steps 6 and 7 are mutually exclusive. Step 8 happens regardless of whether 6 or 7 was selected.

Post Conditions:

1. The nominal Air Pressure value is updated in the DB (if OK button was selected).
2. The nominal Oxygen value is updated in the DB(if OK button was selected).
3. The nominal Temperature value is updated in the DB(if OK button was selected).
4. The Operator is returned to the Desktop.
5. The alarm is enabled.

Exceptions:

1. The DB cannot be accessed.

Required GUI:

1. SEM_Desktop_View
2. Update_All_View pop-up

Use Cases Utilized:

None

Timing Constraints:

None

Figure 2-5. Example Scenario: Use Case 16

Pragmatic Project Issues

Avoid Implementation Issues

A Scenario represents an operational concept; consequently, a Scenario should be implementation-independent. Avoid any mention of files, pointers, and records.

Write White Papers

While writing Scenarios, Systems Engineering often discovers issues that need to be resolved for the entire project. Examples of such issues are:

- Configuration/versioning (How many versions of an entity, if any, should be maintained?)
- Database update (Should the validation of updated data in a GUI occur at *each* field completion, or at the end of *all* field completions?)

When issues like these are discovered, white papers need to be written that cover the decisions made. They need to be uniquely identified and maintained online for all developers to access. These white papers are then referenced in the Scenario, in the "Notes" section, so that their existence is made known to the project.

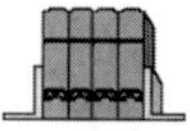

Product(s)

One Scenario is produced per Use Case.

2.3 DEVELOP DRAFT GUI SKETCHES

Purpose

> To provide a draft of the GUI for the system, as envisioned during the development of the Scenarios.

By initiating GUI activity now, requirements can be solidified with respect to Scenario content, user documentation can be drafted, and both the Software Integration and Test and System Test organizations can initiate their respective test plans.

Definition(s)

Graphical User Interface (GUI): **GUI** is the term used for the dialogs that comprise the interface between the software system and the user of the software system.

Process

The development of the GUI really occurs *in parallel with* the previous Activity. It is difficult to envision either this Activity or the previous Activity occurring independently of the other.

Step 1: Establish GUI Project Standards

To maintain consistency within a project, identify a set of allowable widgets for the project and follow good human factors engineering guidelines for the combination of widgets within a dialog.

Step 2: Develop Draft GUI

Using either pencil and paper, a drawing tool, or a GUI tool, draft the initial concept of the GUI(s) that support(s) each Scenario.

Step 3: Provide a Unique ID for Each GUI

Label each prototype GUI with a unique ID that can be referenced in the Scenario. Because a single GUI can potentially be utilized in multiple Use Cases, and because Categories have *not* yet been identified, neither the Use Case number nor the Category name should be used within the unique identifier. For the SEM, we have simply chosen to name the GUI with a unique name. This of course might be difficult to scale up for a large project, consequently, sequential numbers, letters, or a combination of both can be utilized.

Example

Figures 2-6 and 2-7 show two draft GUIs for Use Case 16: the envisioned desktop GUI (`SEM_Desktop_View`) that enables an Operator to monitor living quarters, and the `Update_All_View` pop-up that is displayed when an Operator selects the Update All button in the SEM_Desktop_View (Figure 2-6). The Update_All_View pop-up permits an Operator to change one, two, or all three of the environmental conditions. Figure 2-7 is also utilized if an Operator chooses to update just one environmental condition, with those fields representing the environmental conditions that *cannot* be modified grayed out.

Pragmatic Project Issues

Assign a GUI Architect

Decisions must be made with respect to the implementation of the GUI to provide a consistent look and feel for the project. For moderate to large projects, a GUI Architect is required, whose sole responsibility is to establish and monitor the GUI standards and resulting implementation of the GUI for the project.

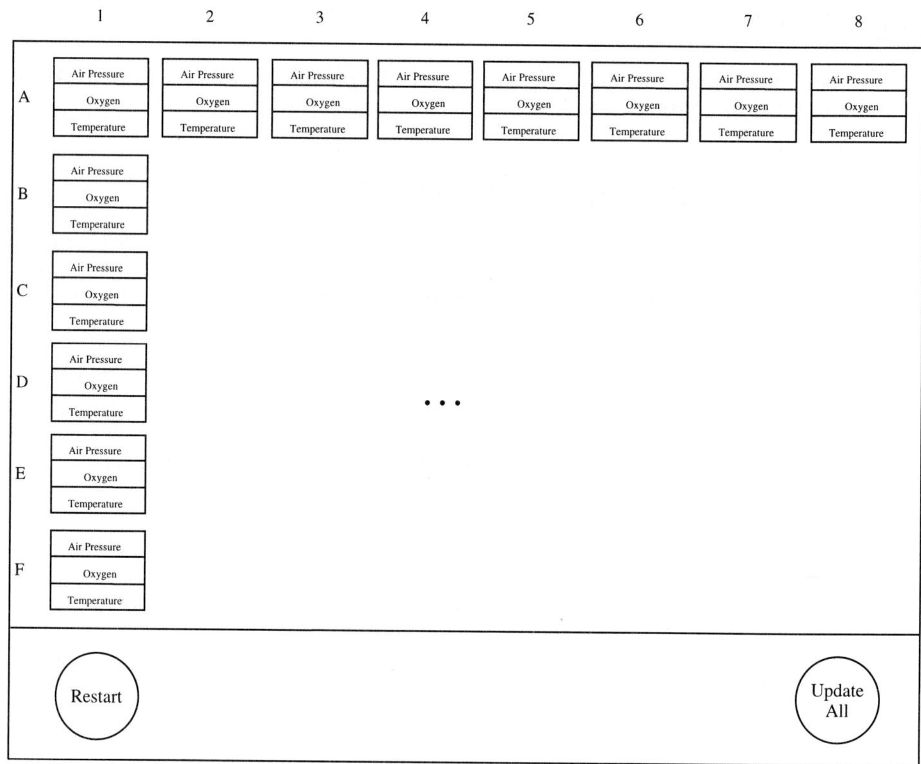

Figure 2-6. SEM Desktop Draft GUI

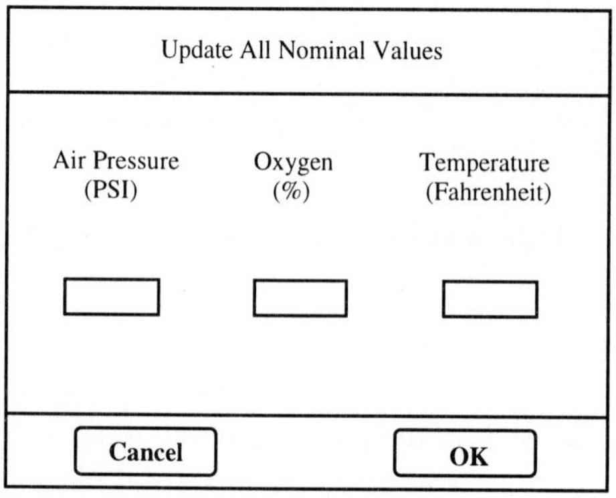

Update All Nominal Values

Air Pressure (PSI)
Oxygen (%)
Temperature (Fahrenheit)

Cancel
OK

Figure 2-7. Update All Draft GUI

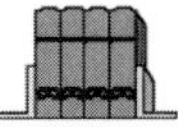

Product(s)

The product of this Activity is a set of draft GUIs, each with a unique identifier, that represents the initial set of GUIs for the system.

2.4 ESTABLISH PROJECT CATEGORIES

Purpose

> The purpose of this Activity is to develop an initial Category List. Categories provide the kernel for all future software development effort.

Quite simply, Categories form the foundation for the *entire project structure*, including, but *not* limited to the

- Software static architecture
- Use Case development effort
- Software source code directory structure
- Management metrics capture
- Technical metrics capture.

These claims will be substantiated as the process unfolds.

Definition(s)

Category: A **Category** is a collection of logically related Classes. Within this text, the definition of logically related Classes is a collection of Classes related through single inheritance, a collection of Classes related through aggregation (composition), or a collection of Classes based on meaningful context (for example, Interim_CAT, Reusable_CAT, UNIX_IF_CAT, and so on). A **Category** should *not* be based on functional capability unless it is a Process Category (see Phase 7) or an Interface Category, for example, UNIX_IF_CAT, and so on. A **Category** is one kind of package stereotype in UML.

UML Domain: A logical collection of Categories represents a functional area and is called a ***Domain*** in UML.

Process

Step 1: Develop a Candidate Category List

Extract the Actors and Subjects from the Use Cases and form a candidate list of Categories. The Actors and Subjects are the candidate Categories.

Step 2: Extract as a Category the Root of an Inheritance Hierarchy

Examine the list for inheritance hierarchies, a set of Classes based on similarities and dissimilarities. Ask yourself, "Is this <Candidate Category> a kind of <Another Candidate Category>?" For example, is Temperature Sensor a kind of Sensor? If yes, maintain the root Class name as the Category name, as the Subclasses will be Classes that are owned by the Category. Do *not* make a separate Category for each Subclass. Single inheritance across Categories is difficult, to say the least. As another example, Environmental Condition is a Category, while the Subclasses Air Pressure, Oxygen, and Temperature Environmental Conditions are Classes in the Environmental Condition Category. Looking for filter qualifiers helps here.

Step 3: Extract as a Category the Root of an Aggregation Hierarchy

Examine the list for aggregation hierarchies, a set of Classes based on a "whole/part" Association. Ask yourself "Is this <Candidate Category> made up of <Another Candidate Category>?" For example, is a Panel made up of Annunciator(s)? If yes, maintain the "whole" Class as the Category name because the "part" Class will be either a Class that is owned by the Category, *or a Category in its own right*. Whether the "part" Class becomes a Category in its own right is application-specific. The number of Classes in each Category should not exceed 20 or so. Let this upper limit, as well as sound engineering judgment, be the driving factor as to whether a "part" Class becomes a Category as well.

Step 4: Extract Remaining Categories

"To be or not to be, that is the question."[4] For example, should Operator be a Category? Should Alarm be a Category? Neither Operator nor Alarm represent the root Class of any hierarchy (inheritance or aggregation) for this application. But, they ***might*** as the system expands. The recommendation is to have more Categories rather than less. Making a Category now sets the project up for easier modification. Although there is no requirement to maintain any information now for an Operator, there may be at a later point in time. For example, there may be a need to record which Operator is on which shift, or there may be the requirement to restrict the Update All operation to only certain Operators. Setting up an Operator Category now makes life easier in the future.

Step 5: Establish Naming Conventions

This Case Study uses the convention of adding the suffix _CAT to the name of the Category. On another project which utilized StP OMT, the name of the Subsystem was suffixed with _SS. For the SEM, _CAT was utilized to be more in-line with UML.

Step 6: Establish Abbreviations for Categories

Establish either a two-letter or three-letter abbreviation for each Category. The abbreviation will be used later on, when directory structure and file naming conventions are

[4]From Shakespeare's *Hamlet*.

developed. Most projects name the source files beginning with the abbreviation of the Category that owns the Class. More on this later.

Step 7: Allocate Categories to Domains

Typically, most projects have a functional organization already in place. For example, for a tracking system, there might be functional areas named Network, Radar, Telemetry, and so on. These represent the Domains for the project. Typically, budget and functional responsibility for the Domains have already been allocated by project management. Now is the time to assign Categories to the appropriate Domain.

Step 8: Assign Subject Matter Expert (SME) to Each Domain

For the lifetime of a project, a SME needs to be assigned to each Domain. The SME has the responsibility of

- Answering on-call questions about the Domain
- Reviewing all products
- Attending all reviews
- Coordinating with the customer for clarification.

By assigning a SME to each Domain, the responsibility for domain knowledge is distributed between the Software Category Lead and Domain SME. Using this approach, the Category Lead is free to worry about software development, and the Domain SME can assume the responsibility of coordination with the customer with respect to requirements.

Example

The HCC draft Candidate Category List, containing the list of Actors and Subjects from the RTM, is shown in Figure 2-8. The entries follow the order of occurrence in the Use Cases, and do *not* conform to any naming conventions because the final list has *not* yet been produced.

HCC Candidate Category List	
Living_Quarter	Alarm
Sensor	Operator
Air_Pressure_Sensor	Timer
Oxygen_Sensor	Nominal_Values
Temperature_Sensor	Environmental Condition
Window	Air Pressure
Panel	Oxygen
Annunciator	Temperature
Database	Deviation

Figure 2-8. HCC Candidate Category List

The final Category List is shown in Figure 2-9(a). The figure also specifies a two-letter abbreviation[5] for each Category. The Category names follow the naming convention previously indicated and each Category has been initially allocated to the Domains identified for the HCC. Figure 2-9(a) also shows the SME assignment for each Category.

The three sensor Subclasses (air pressure, oxygen, and temperature) do *not* appear as final Categories because they will be Classes owned by the `Sensor_CAT`. The annunciator and window do *not* appear as final Categories in the HCC either. This application does *not* lend itself to architecture where annunciator and window are separate Categories. The annunciator and window are Classes owned by the `Panel_CAT`.

Experience has also shown that the following four Categories exist on any project. They can be added now, or later, in Phase 5. We have chosen to add them now.

- `IF_CAT`
- `Interim_CAT`
- `Process_CAT`
- `Reusable_CAT`.

`IF_CAT` owns Classes that are required to interface to existing external software or hardware (for example to existing COTS/CFS/GFS software, existing equipment, and so on). `IF_CAT` owns the Classes that represent interfaces to the external entities identified in the Context Diagram. In the SEM, `IF_CAT` will own an `Alarm_IF` Class and a `Sensor_IF` Class.

Throughout the lifetime of a project, `Interim_CAT` holds the entities (Classes) that are *not* immediately assignable to an existing Category. When the system is delivered, `Interim_CAT` should be empty.

HCC Category Name	Abbreviation	Domain	SME
`Alarm_CAT`	AL	Error Notification	Paul M.
`DB_CAT`	DB	Database	Peter H.
`Environmental_Condition_CAT`	EC	Monitor	Jack G.
`IF_CAT`	IF		
`Interim_CAT`	IM		
`Living_Quarter_CAT`	LQ	Monitor	Jack G.
`Operator_CAT`	OP	Monitor	Jack G.
`Panel_CAT`	PL	Error Notification, Monitor	Paul M./Jack G.
`Process_CAT`	PS		
`Sensor_CAT`	SR	Monitor	Jack G.
`Reusable_CAT`	RU		
`Timer_CAT`	TR	Monitor	Jack G.

Figure 2-9(a). HCC Final Category List and Initial Domain Allocation

[5]Recall that the abbreviation for the Category is used later in establishing directory structure for the source code and in establishing file naming conventions.

Reusable_CAT holds Classes representing existing entities (either hardware or software) that are to be reused.

Process_CAT holds the Process and Processor Classes, as well as process architecture static and dynamic diagrams (see Phase 7).

With respect to Domain allocation, the Domains Error Notification, Monitor, and Database are initially identified. Note in Figure 2-9(a) that the Panel_CAT is assigned to two Domains. When a Category can be allocated to more than one Domain, a decision needs to be made as to which Domain to assign the Category. In the case of Panel_CAT, the Panel_CAT can be assigned to either the Error Notification or Monitor Domain. The decision that was made for the Case Study assigns the Panel_CAT to the Monitor Domain, consequently Figure 2-9(b) represents the final Category List, as well as the final Domain and SME allocations for the Case Study.

Interim_CAT is *not* assigned to any Domain because Interim_CAT holds Classes that must be reallocated at some point in time. As you will soon see, the OO Project Team monitors and manages Interim_CAT.

Reusable_CAT is *not* assigned to any domain because Reusable_CAT owns Classes that are used in multiple Categories, and typically cross Domain boundaries.

IF_CAT is *not* assigned to any specific Domain or SME because IF_CAT also crosses many Domain boundaries. Typically, child Categories exist within IF_CAT and it is the child Categories that are assigned to a Domain and SME. For the SEM, IF_CAT could have two child Categories, Alarm_IF_CAT and Sensor_IF_CAT. In this case, Alarm_IF_CAT would be assigned to the Domain Error Notification, while Sensor_IF_CAT would be assigned to the Domain Monitor.

Pragmatic Project Issues

What about Subcontractors?

Subcontractors are typically assigned to a specific functional area. Ideally, if a Subcontractor can work with the prime contractor as a member of the development team, the subcontractor can work directly in the same Categories as the prime contrac-

HCC Category Name	Abbreviation	Domain	SME
Alarm_CAT	AL	Error Notification	Paul M.
DB_CAT	DB	Database	Peter H.
Environmental_Condition_CAT	EC	Monitor	Jack G.
IF_CAT	IF		
Interim_CAT	IM		
Living_Quarter_CAT	LQ	Monitor	Jack G.
Operator_CAT	OP	Monitor	Jack G.
Panel_CAT	PL	**Monitor**	**Jack G.**
Process_CAT	PS		
Sensor_CAT	SR	Monitor	Jack G.
Reusable_CAT	RU		
Timer_CAT	TR	Monitor	Jack G.

Figure 2-9(b). HCC Final Category List and Final Domain Allocation

tor. In this case, the technical integrity of the Categories is maintained. Although it may be difficult to achieve management understanding of the necessity for a subcontractor to have write access to the entire project repository to enable the subcontractor to work on the same diagrams that the prime contractor is developing, this is the preferred approach. The alternative is to have the subcontractor work in the *same repository* as the prime, but to work with *distinct Categories*, thus allowing the subcontractor write access to only the subcontractor's Categories. In this latter case, the integrity of the Category List is *not* protected if the subcontractor's functionality crosses Domains and/or Categories. How to incorporate subcontractors is a very project-specific decision.

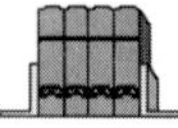

Product(s)

The product of this Activity is a Category List, with appropriate abbreviations identified for the Categories and their allocation to a project Domain. There is one Category List for a project.

2.5 ALLOCATE USE CASES TO CATEGORIES

Purpose

> The purpose of assigning Use Cases to Categories is to allocate the responsibility for Use Case development to a Category (and thus to a software Category Lead). This allocation makes it perfectly clear who is responsible for the development of a specific Use Case.

Process

Step 1: Assign Use Cases/Methods to Categories for Development

This is a difficult step, especially for those new to OO thought processes. Examine each Use Case for the build in question and make sure that the Subject is clear. Next, allocate the Use Case to one *and only one* of the Categories on the Category List based on the Subject of the Use Case. For example, assign Use Case 1: SW_Monitors_Living_Quarter to `Living_Quarter_CAT`. Assign Use Case 6: SW_Lights_Window to `Panel_CAT` because the `Window` Class will be owned by the `Panel_CAT` (because the `Panel` is made up of `Annunciators`, which are made up of `Windows`). Assign Use Case 16: Operator_Updates _Nominal_Values_In_DB to `DB_CAT`. If the Subject is *not* an exact match to the Category (and 50% may *not* be), imagine the inheritance hierarchy, or aggregation hierarchy, for the Categories and ask yourself, "Is the Subject of the Use Case to be allocated, a Subclass of one of the Categories on the Category List, or a "part" of one of the Categories on the Category List?" If the answer to the question is yes, then allocate the Use Case to the Superclass or "whole" Class Category, as appropriate. For those Use

Cases that are difficult to allocate, assign them to the `Interim_CAT` for now. But, be careful *not* to use the `Interim_CAT` as a "catchall".

Step 2: Update Category List

The process of assigning Use Cases to Categories may cause an iteration to the Category List. This iteration can result in additional Categories being identified, Categories being divided, or Categories being combined. Be open minded to changes in the Category List. Like everything else in OO, nothing is final and everything is subject to iteration!

Step3: Update the RTM

Update the RTM by completing the "Category" column for each Use Case. Remember that because the RTM is managed, decisions made now can be reversed later if necessary.

Example

Figure 2-10 depicts the updated RTM as a result of allocating Use Cases to Categories. Note that all the Use Cases allocated to the `Panel_CAT` include those that affect the panel, the annunciator, and the window. The "part" Class `Window` is the Subject of the Use Case in Entry 13, but `Window` will be owned by the `Panel_CAT` because the `Panel` is made up of `Annunciators`, and an `Annunciator` is made up of `Windows`.

The RTM will be expanded *again* in subsequent Phases. If you are getting the feeling that this matrix plays an important role in the project, you are correct!

Pragmatic Project Issues

Degree of Difficulty

This particular task is difficult to do if there is no prior OO experience upon which to draw. A small team of individuals needs to be assigned to this task. One member of the team needs to have strong domain knowledge and another needs to be an individual extremely strong in OO. Sometimes, it takes real insight to determine which Category a Use Case is to be assigned for development. Take your best guess and move on!

Software Organization Input

Software and Systems organizations need to work this effort together. Systems needs to be sure that the requirements are well-defined and understood. Software needs to watch the allocation of Use Cases to Categories.

Remember the Interim_CAT

Any Use Case that is difficult to assign can be assigned to `Interim_CAT`. Of course, the goal is to deliver the project with an `Interim_CAT` that is empty. As time marches on and domain knowledge increases, it will become clearer as to which Category these Use Cases should be allocated. At the appropriate point in time, the Use Cases can be reallocated to a more appropriate Category.

Entry #	Para #*	System Specification Text	Type	Build	Use Case Name	Class	Method	Category
1	2.0	The SEM shall monitor all occupied living quarters.	SW	B1	UC1_SW_Monitors_Living_Quarters			Living_Quarter_CAT
2	2.0	There shall be a total of 48 living quarters.	HW	B1	n/a			
3	2.1	Air Pressure, Temperature, and Oxygen % shall be obtained once per minute.	SW, P	B1	UC3_Timer_Triggers_Living_Quarter_Sensor Timer_Triggers_LQ_Air_Pressure_Sensor Timer_Triggers_LQ_Temperature_Sensor Timer_Triggers_LQ_Oxygen_Sensor			Living_Quarter_CAT
4	2.1	There shall be three sensors in each living quarter.	HW	B1	n/a			
5	2.1	There shall be one sensor for each environmental condition.	HW	B1	n/a			
6	2.2	A current value representing a deviation >= 1% but <2% from the nominal value shall cause the window in the panel to be lit.	SW	B2	UC6_SW_Lights_Window			Panel_CAT
7	2.2	A current value representing a deviation >= 2% but < 3% from the nominal value shall cause the window in the panel to be lit and flash two times per second.	SW	B2	UC7_SW_Flashes_Window_2X			Panel_CAT
8	2.2	A current value representing a deviation >= 3% from the nominal value shall cause the window in the panel to be lit and flash four times per second and sound an audible alarm.	SW	B2, B3	UC8_SW_Flashes_Window_4X			Panel_CAT
9	2.2	There shall be one audible alarm.	HW	B3	n/a			
10	3.0	The panel shall accommodate 48 annunciators arranged in six rows.	SW	B1	UC10_SW_Displays_Panel			Panel_CAT
11	3.0	Each annunciator shall be mapped to a unique living quarter.	HW	B1	n/a			
12	3.0	Each annunciator shall accommodate three windows.	SW	B1	UC12_SW_Displays_Annunciator			Panel_CAT
13	3.0	Each window shall be identified with an appropriate legend.	SW	B1	UC13_SW_Displays_Window			Panel_CAT

14	4.0	All nominal values shall be found in the database.	SW	B1	n/a			
15	4.0	The Operator shall be capable of redefining the nominal values in the database.	SW	B4	Duplicate (#16)			
16	4.0	The Operator shall be capable of redefining all three nominal values in the database to be used for all living quarters.	SW	B4	UC_16_Operator_Updates_Environmental_ Condition_Nominal_Values_In_DB			DB_CAT
17	4.0	The Operator shall be able to redefine the nominal value for a specific living quarter.	SW	B4	UC17_Operator_Updates_Living_Quarter_ Nominal_Value			DB_CAT
18	5.0	Only the software shall turn on the audible alarm.	SW	B3		Alarm	Sound	Alarm_CAT
19	5.0	Only the software shall flash a window.	SW	B2	Duplicate (# 7 and #8)			
20	5.0	The software shall continue to turn on the warning indicators as long as the alarm condition exists.	SW	B2, B3	Duplicate (#18 and #19)			
21	5.0	The Operator shall turn the audible alarm off.	SW	B3		Alarm	Silence	Alarm_CAT
22	5.0	The Operator shall turn the window off.	SW	B2	UC22_Operator_Turns_Off_Window			Panel_CAT
23	3.0	Each environmental condition will be represented in a different color.						
23	3.0	All windows for the same environmental condition will be the same color						
25	—	Because the Operator can reset the nominal values in the DB, he/she needs to be able to reset the SEM to operate on those new values.	SW, DR	B4	UC23_Operator_Resets_SEM			Process_CAT
26	—	The SEM does not need to monitor unoccupied living quarters, so the Operator can set living quarters to occupied/ unoccupied to enable the SEM to operate more efficiently.	SW, DR,	B4	UC24_Operator_Sets_Living_Quarter_State			Living_Quarter_CAT

*The paragraph number represents the paragraph number from the Case Study Problem Statement section, with the "HCC-" prefix omitted.

Figure 2-10. HCC RTM with Category Allocation Completed

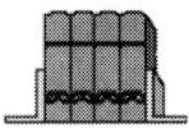

Product(s)

The product of this Activity is the RTM with the "Category" column completed.

2.6 DEVELOP SYSTEM CATEGORY DIAGRAM (SCD)

Purpose

> The purpose of developing a System Category Diagram (SCD) is to depict the high-level Associations that exist between the Categories, and thus validate the Categories.

The SCD serves many purposes. First, the diagram can be used to explain to the customer the overall view of the system, thus increasing the customer's confidence in the developer's domain knowledge. Second, the SCD helps to validate the Categories. And last of all, the SCD provides a base from which the impact of new or changing requirements can be analyzed.

Definition(s)

Aggregation Relationship: An **aggregation relationship** is an Association that is based on a "whole/part" Association between two Categories (or Classes) in question. The two kinds are explored in Phase 5.

Association: An **Association** is a semantic relationship that exists between two Categories or two Classes. There are three kinds of **Associations**:

- Aggregation relationship
- Inheritance relationship
- Association relationship.

Association Relationship: An **association relationship** is an Association that is based on a semantic relationship between two Categories (or Classes) and that is *not* inheritance and *not* aggregation. When graphically depicted, an **association relationship** requires a label that describes the relationship, as well as the definition of its multiplicity (how many instances participate).

Inheritance Relationship: An **inheritance relationship** is an Association between two Categories (or Classes) that is based on similarities/dissimilarities between two Categories (or Classes) in question.

Multiplicity: **Multiplicity** defines the number of Instances that participate in either an association relationship or aggregation relationship. **Multiplicity** is synonymous with cardinality.

System Category Diagram (SCD): An **SCD** is a Category-level diagram. An **SCD** for a project is a Class Diagram (either a Booch Class Diagram or OMT Object Diagram) that depicts all known Categories and all Associations between the Categories. In UML, the **SCD** is drawn between UML packages, and the SCD portrays a UML *dependency*, rather than an Association.

UML Dependency: A **UML dependency** between two entities, whether the two entities are Categories or Classes, indicates that one of the entities depends upon, or requires the resources of, the other entity. A **UML dependency** is depicted with a dashed line, with an arrow at one or both ends. The entity at the tail of the arrow depends upon the entity at the head of the arrow. A **UML dependency** between two entities means that the dependent entity requires visibility, or access, to the unit upon which it depends.

UML Package: A **UML package** is a collection of cohesive entities. There are different kinds of **UML packages**: a Category (a collection of Classes), a Subsystem (a collection of source code files), and so on. Each different kind of **UML package** is called a stereotype. A **UML package** has its own distinct symbol, a tabbed rectangle.

UML Stereotype: A **UML stereotype** identifies a kind of element in UML. The **stereotype** Category package indicates that Category is a kind of package, while the **stereotype** Exception Class indicates that Exception is a kind of Class. A **UML stereotype** has its own distinct symbol, the name of the **stereotype** enclosed in double angled brackets, as in <<Category>>[6].

Uses Relationship: A Booch **"uses" relationship** is identical to a UML Dependency, indicating required visibility from the source Class (requires resources) of the "uses" relationship to the target Class (supplies resources). The symbol utilized to represent a **"uses" relationship** is an unfilled circle attached to the source Class with a solid line to the target Class.

Process

Step 1: Define SCD Naming Conventions

Decide on a naming convention for the SCD. With distinct suffixes, diagram types[7] are easily located in a large repository, and scripts that search for diagram types are easily written. One suggestion is to name the System Category Diagram <SystemName>_SCD, and that is what has been done for the HCC Case Study. The SCD for the HCC is named HCC_SCD.

Step 2: Initiate the System Category Diagram

This, of course, is the easiest step. Utilize a CASE tool to provide a canvas for the development of the SCD. Make sure the diagram is named properly.

[6] The double angled brackets (<<>>) are appropriately called "guillemets" in UML.

[7] Actually, to be precise with respect to UML, diagram is another package stereotype because there are several kinds of diagrams: Class, Interaction, and so on.

Step 3: Place the Correct Symbol for a Class (or Category) on the Blank Canvas

For each Category, decide whether it appears on the SCD. For example, it is *not* necessary, or even advisable, to place `Interim_CAT` on the SCD. The same can be said for `Process_CAT`. More on this in the Pragmatic Project Issues section.

Step 4: Add Association Relationships

The SCD should represent the Associations between Categories: inheritance relationship, aggregation relationship, and association relationship. If UML is being utilized, only the dependencies between Categories can be depicted.

Step 5: Agree Whether Attributes/Methods Are to Be Identified

This issue centers around whether it is necessary, or even advisable, to discover the Attributes and Methods for a Category. Experience indicates that this is *not* advisable as the Attributes and Methods for a Category are eventually distributed to multiple Classes within the Category and the trace is lost from the original Category. Consequently, the suggestion is that the SCD in Booch or OMT notation *not* portray Attributes and Methods. In UML, this is *not* an issue as a Category is a stereotype of a package and a package does *not* have Attributes and Methods at the current time.

Example

Figure 2-11(a) shows the associations between the OMT Subsystems (Categories) on the HCC_SCD as represented in OMT. Figure 2-11(b) shows the same diagram in Booch notation, with rectangles to represent Categories, and Uses Relationships. Note that multiplicity is specified for association relationships and aggregation relationships, and that only primary Associations are shown. The last sentence may need some clarification. A primary Association is an Association that exists "directly" between two Categories (or Classes). An example of a primary Association is the Association between `Living_Quarter_CAT` and `Environmental_Condition_CAT`. The association that a `Living_Quarter_CAT` is described by three `Environmental_Condition_CAT`s exists, and is a direct association. The fact that the `Environmental_Condition_CAT` is detected by `Sensor_CAT` is also a direct, primary association. However, there is no need for an Association between the `Living_Quarter_CAT` and the `Sensor_CAT` that is labeled "values are read by" a `Sensor_CAT`. This is a transitive association, an association that exists *indirectly* between two Categories (`Living_Quarter_CAT` and `Sensor_CAT`) because of primary associations that exist between other Categories (specifically, `Living_Quarter_CAT` and `Environmental_Condition_CAT`, and `Environmental_Condition_CAT` and `Sensor_CAT`). Of course, there is a primary aggregation association, "owns" or "has", between the `Living_Quarter_CAT` and the `Sensor_CAT` because each living quarter has three sensors. This is a *different and necessary* Association than the one previously discussed and is therefore included on the SCD.

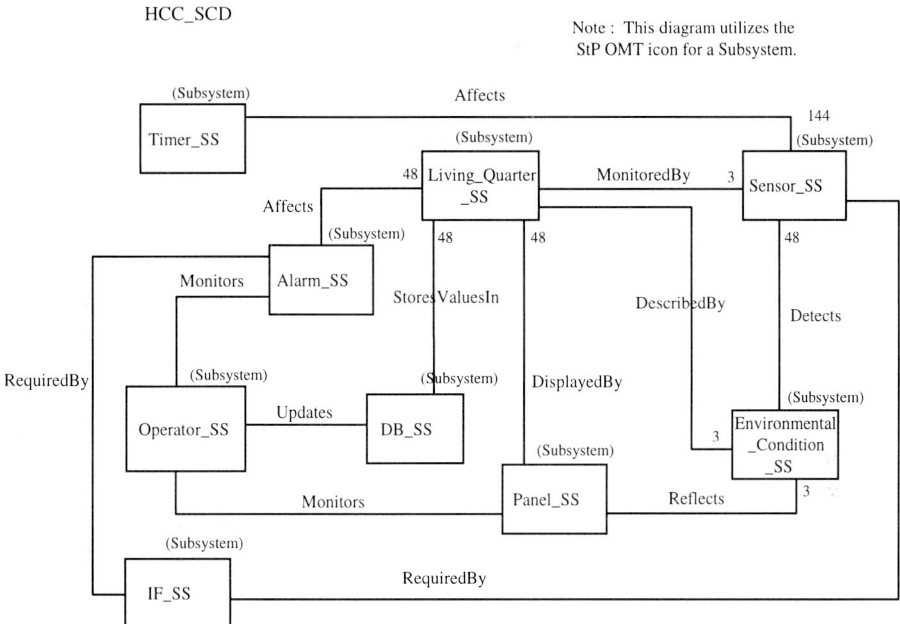

Figure 2-11(a). HCC SCD: OMT Notation

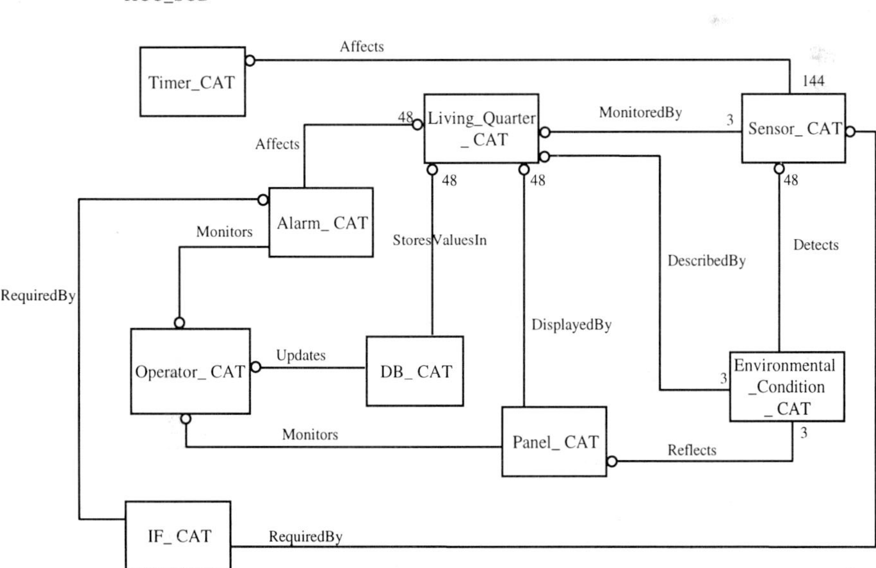

Figure 2-11(b). HCC SCD: Booch Notation

Figures 2-12 and 2-13 show how the SCD could be reflected in UML notation. In UML you must depict the *dependencies* between packages (one kind of package is a Category). Figure 2-12 shows the diagram *without* the stereotype indicated, while Figure 2-13 shows the diagram *with* the stereotype indicated. The symbol for a package in UML is a tabbed rectangle, and the indication of the particular package stereotype, here a Category, may or may not be depicted. UML requires that a *dependency* be drawn between packages, consequently, the lines are dashed, rather than solid. The arrowhead points to the unit upon which the package at the tail of the arrow depends. Stated differently, Figures 2-12 and 2-13 both indicate that `Living_Quarter_CAT` depends on `DB_CAT` and therefore in design, that *some* Class in `Living_Quarter_CAT` depends on, or needs visibility to, *some* Class in `DB_CAT`. These figures *additionally* indicate that `Living_Quarter_CAT` depends on `DB_CAT` for its resources rather than `DB_CAT` depending on `Living_Quarter_CAT` for any resources. Finally, note that the kind of dependency has been indicated on the dependency line—calls or references. There are no instantiated dependencies on this diagram. Note the difference between Figure 2-11(a) and 2-13 with respect to the `Timer_CAT`. More on this in the Pragmatic Project Issues section.

Pragmatic Project Issues

To Show or Not to Show All Categories

This issue centers around whether to show `IF_CAT`, `Interim_CAT`, `Process_CAT`, and `Reusable_CAT` on the SCD. `IF_CAT` is useful to show, but the other Categories do *not* provide any real useful information at the *system* level. `Interim_CAT`, `Process_CAT`, and `Reusable_CAT` are mainly Categories that support software *design and implementation*. `DB_CAT` is questionable. If `DB_CAT` appears as a direct requirement (as it does in the SEM), include it on the SCD. If `DB_CAT` is more of an implementation decision, omit it. Remember that the purpose of the SCD is to focus on the Associations between domain Categories to ensure a correct understanding of the application at its highest level of abstraction.

Check Your Tool

Some CASE tools do *not* support Associations between Categories. As a matter of fact, that is the situation with the Rational Rose version used for this book. In another CASE tool, the SCD is developed using the capability of the Data Flow Diagram tool! Definitely a kluge, but this approach allows the script writers to "pull" the diagram into a deliverable document because the Data Flow Diagram tool is just another capability within the CASE tool suite being used.

UML Issue

In UML, the Association between UML packages is one of "dependency". As previously stated in the definitions section, a UML dependency implies visibility requirements in the subsequent design. Do *not* stall the project by debating whether the `Timer_CAT` "pops" the `Living_Quarter_CAT` or the `Sensor_CAT`. This issue

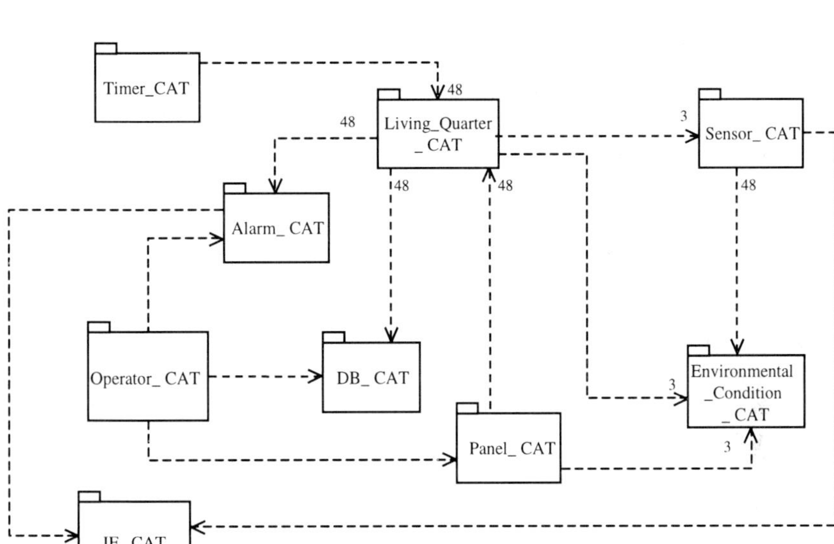

Figure 2-12. HCC SCD in UML: without Stereotype

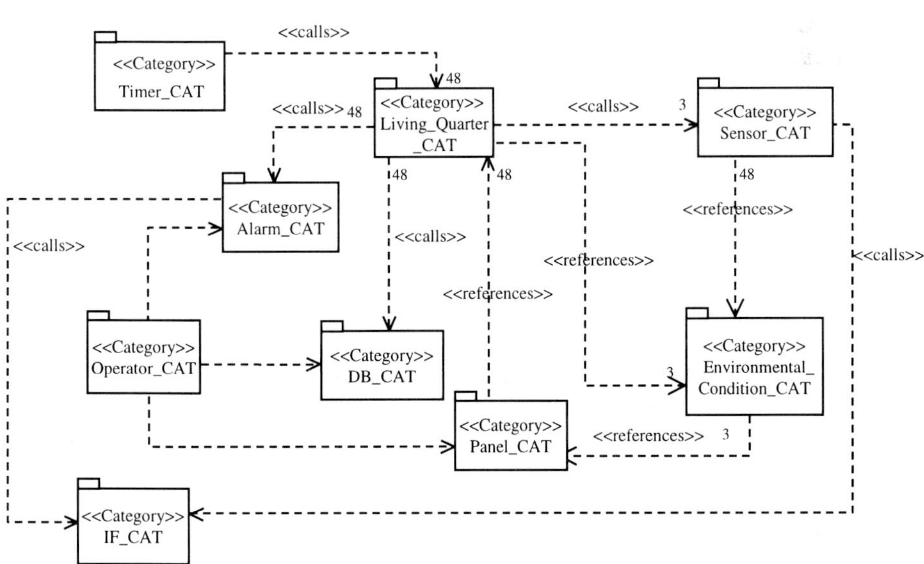

Figure 2-13. HCC SCD in UML: with Stereotype

is primarily a design issue and the SCD is about identifying and portraying *abstract* Associations between Categories! Make a best guess as to which way the dependency exists and move on. The best guess for the SEM, as shown in Figure 2-13, is that the timer will "pop" the living quarter because the living quarter owns its sensors. In other words, the timer accesses a sensor by navigating through the living quarter. As knowledge is gained, the correctness of the decision will be verified. The decision can be reversed later if it turns out to be incorrect.

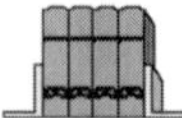

Product(s)

The product of this Activity is the SCD showing Categories and the primary Associations between Categories. There is one SCD per project.

Phase Transition Criteria

It is safe to transition to the next Phase for the build in question, when

- All Use Cases have been identified for the current build
- All Use Cases have been assigned to a Category for the build
- The SCD has been completed and agreed upon for the entire set of releases
- The RTM has been updated.

The review criteria, shown in Tables 2-1, 2-2, and 2-3 below, may help in deciding whether or not to transition to the next Phase. Table 2-1 represents a refinement to Table 1-1.

Review Criteria

Table 2-1. RTM Review Criteria: Phase 2

#	RTM Review Criteria	Phase 1	Phase 2
1	Are the "shall" sentences from the agreed-upon set of documents included?	√	
2	Is each "shall" a unique entry in the RTM?	√	
3	Are any known derived requirements included, and marked "DR"?	√	
4	Are the "will" sentences included, and marked "NTH"?	√	
5	Are all entries categorized?	√	
6	Are duplicates identified?	√	
7	Is Build 1 identified?	√	
8	Are duplicates identified?		√
9	Do all SW entries have a corresponding Use Case? Method on a Class?		√
10	Is the Actor identified as a domain entity or as SW?		√
11	Is the Subject correct? Is the Subject's data structure the one affected by the Use Case?		√
12	Is the word "find" never utilized in a Use Case name?		√
13	Is each SW Use Case allocated to a single Category?		√

Table 2-2. SCD Review Criteria

#	SCD Review Criteria
1	Are all Categories from the Category List included on the SCD, with the exception of `Interim_CAT`, `Process_CAT`, and `Reusable_CAT`?
2	Is multiplicity shown for aggregation and association relationships?
3	Are Associations between Categories valid?
4	Does the diagram name follow diagram naming conventions?
5	Do the Category names follow Category naming conventions?
6	Are crossing lines minimized?
7	Can all requirements be allocated to Categories on the SCD?

Table 2-3. Category Review Criteria

#	Category Review Criteria
1	Is the Category based on either an inheritance or aggregation hierarchy?
2	If the Category is *not* based on either an inheritance or aggregation hierarchy, are the envisioned Classes within the Category cohesive? In other words, are the Classes a collection of logically related Classes?
3	Is the Category envisioned to have approximately 15-20 Classes?
4	Does the Category name follow Category naming conventions? *Is the Category name a noun?* *Does the Category name have the correct suffix?*
5	Is the Category *not* functionally based (unless it is a Category that is being developed by a third party or unless it is to be allocated to COTS or GFS)?
6	Are there Use Cases that are allocated to the Category? If not, justify the Category.
7	Does the set of Categories consume the Use Cases?
8	Is the set of miscellaneous Categories, like `Interim_CAT`, `IF_CAT`, and so on agreed upon?
9	Have the Categories been allocated to a single domain?

Tracking Progress

Table 2-4 updates the previous project management spreadsheet and adds the Activities and products produced in this Phase. Within this Phase the

- Number of Use Cases identified as a percentage of total Use Cases for the build
- Number of Scenarios written as a percentage of total Scenarios required for the build
- Number of draft GUIs developed as a percentage of total draft GUIs anticipated for the build
- Number of Use Cases allocated to a Category as a percentage of Uses Cases per build

can be monitored. These data need to be collected on a Category-by-Category basis, summarized on a Domain-by-Domain basis, and if desired, further summarized for the project.

Table 2-4. Project Management Spreadsheet: Phase 2

HCC Project Management Spreadsheet						
Number	**Phase Name**	**Activity**	**Charge Number**	**Product**	**Progress Metric**	**% Weight**
1	**Requirements Engineering**		**RE-1**			
1.1		Identify External Interfaces	RE-1.1	Context Diagram	1 Context Diagram completed	0.50
1.2		Capture “shall” Statements	RE-1.2	RTM (“shall” Statements)	# “shall” sentences	0.16
1.3		Allocate Requirements	RE-1.3	RTM (“Type” Column)	# entries typed (%), #SW entries(%)	0.17
1.4		Prioritize Requirements	RE-1.4	RTM (“Build” Column)	# entries prioritized (%), #Use Cases/build(%)	0.17
2	**System OOA–Static View**		**SYS-OOAS-2**			
2.1		Identify Software Use Cases	SYS-OOAS-2.1	RTM (“Use Case” Column)	# Use Cases (%)	0.20
2.2		Develop Scenarios	SYS-OOAS-2.2	Scenario	# Scenarios (%)	0.20
2.3		Develop Draft GUIs	SYS-OOAS-2.3	Draft GUI	# GUI sketches	0.20
2.4		Establish Project Categories	SYS-OOAS-2.4	Category List	# Categories	0.20
2.5		Allocate Use Cases to Category	SYS-OOAS-2.5	RTM (“Category” Column)	# Use Cases allocated (%), # Use Cases/Category	0.10
2.6		Develop System Category Diagram	SYS-OOAS-2.6	1 SCD	1 SCD completed	0.10

Finally, note that equal weight has been assigned to the products produced in this Phase. Each product is equally important for the stability of the project because each product represents a different piece of the requirements definition.

From this point in the project onward, the total number of Use Cases per build (initially specified in Phase 1) can be continually monitored throughout the remaining Phases. A large increase or decrease in the number of Use Cases is cause for concern.

PHASE 3

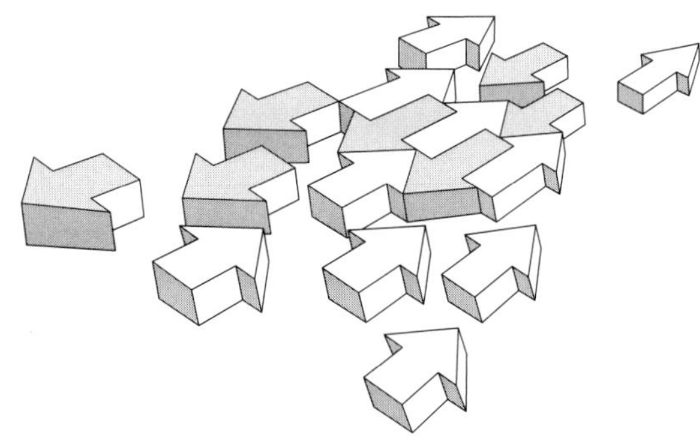

Systems OOA—Dynamic View

PHASE OVERVIEW

The previous Phase focused on the identification of the major components of the system, Categories, and the primary Associations (or dependencies, in UML) between them. Figure 3-1 summarizes the Activities of this Phase, which focuses on the dynamic view of the system, or the behavioral interactions *between Categories* necessary to implement a Use Case. Once the Categories are allocated to Category Managers and Category Leads, the dynamic view is provided by producing Interaction Diagrams (either UML Sequence Diagrams or Collaboration Diagrams) where instead of showing interactions between Classes, interactions *between Categories* are depicted. This Activity is *extremely* beneficial because it continues to validate the list of Categories *and* defines, at a *high level of abstraction*, the functional behavior of the system.

3.1 ALLOCATE CATEGORIES TO CATEGORY MANAGERS/LEADS

Purpose

> The purpose of this Activity is to assign responsibility for the development of a Category to one individual.

There *must* be an individual, a Category Manager, who is responsible and held accountable for the development of a Category, regardless of whether the Category is all hardware, all software, or both hardware and software. A Category Manager can be assigned multiple Categories, but each Category must be assigned to one Category Manager. Once a Category has been assigned to a Category Manager, he/she can then

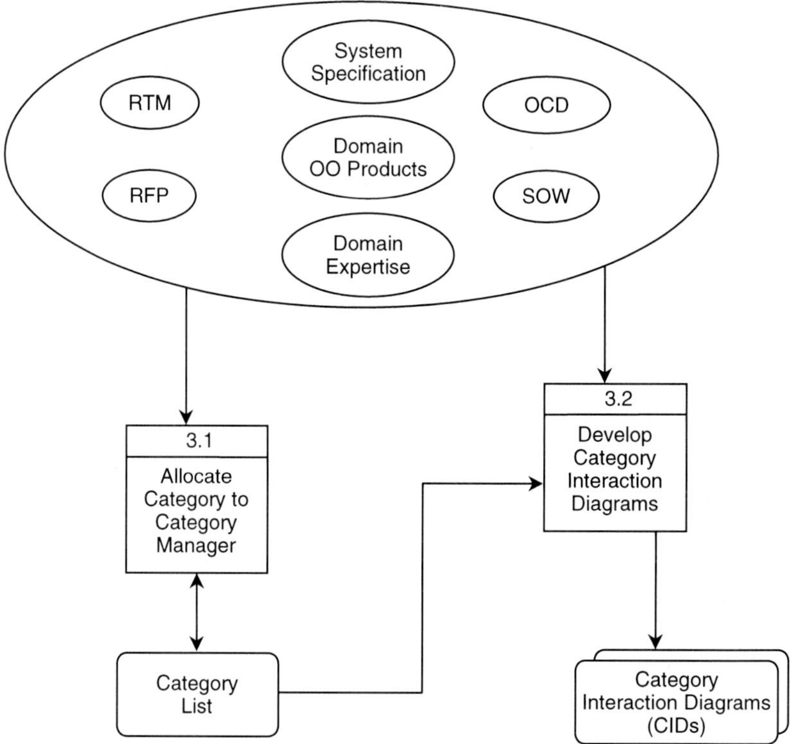

Figure 3-1. System OOA: Dynamic View Phase Description Diagram

assign the hardware portion of the Category and the software portion of the Category to Hardware and Software Category Leads, as required.

Definition(s)

Category Manager: A **Category Manager** is an individual who is assigned both administrative and technical responsibility for the development of one or more Categories.

Category Lead: A **Category Lead** is an individual who is responsible for either the hardware *or* software portion of one or more Categories.

Process

Step 1: Assign Category Manager

The position of Category Manager *cannot* be allocated to junior staff members. Consider only senior staff members, who have previous project management experience, and preferably an individual who has some OO experience.

Step 2: Assign Category Leads

These are excellent growth positions. Category Leads have minor administrative responsibility and full technical responsibility for a Category.

Step 3: Establish an OO Team

The Category Managers and Category Leads, or a subset of that collective group, need to form the core of an OO Team for the project. Simply stated, it helps if they can work together! Initially, the OO Team meets weekly to make decisions regarding the OO practices and standards for the project, for example naming conventions. Additional responsibilities of the OO Team include but are *not* limited to the following:

- Managing `Interim_CAT`
- Managing the repository.

As the project progresses, the OO Team transitions to meeting every other week.

Example

Table 3-1 shows a sample allocation for the HCC. Note that Harry Brown has responsibility for all the Categories that involve hardware because Harry has both hardware and software experience. Sue Smith is assigned the remaining Categories, except for the `Reusable_CAT` and `Interim_Cat`, as Kathryn has worked with these Categories on other projects and has experience interfacing with the corporation's reuse library. The importance of Harry, Sue, and Kathryn having previous management responsibility and OO experience *cannot be over-emphasized*. Harry and Sue can now assign Hardware/Software Category Leads, respectively.

The "N/As" in Table 3-1 indicate that there is no requirement for a Category Lead for that portion of the Category. The blank portions of the table indicate assignments that need to be made.

Table 3-1. HCC Category Development Responsibilities

Category Name	Category Manager	Hardware Lead	Software Lead	Use Case Assignment
Alarm_CAT	Harry Brown	Sam Smith		UC18, UC21
Database_CAT	Sue Smith	N/A		UC16, UC17
Environmental_CAT	"	N/A		
IF_CAT	Harry Brown/Sue Smith	N/A		
Interim_CAT	Kathryn Santini	Kathryn	Kathryn	
Living_Quarter_CAT	Sue Smith	N/A		UC1, UC23, UC24
Operator_CAT	"	N/A	N/A	
Panel_CAT	"	Sam Smith		UC6-UC8, UC10, UC12, UC13, UC22
Process_CAT	Michael Jones	N/A		
Reusable_CAT	Sue Smith	Kathryn	Kathryn	
Sensor_CAT	Harry Brown	Sam Jones		UC3
Timer_CAT	Michael Jones			

Pragmatic Project Issues

The Triangle

Figure 3-2 is an interesting and accurate figure[1]. Simply stated, it takes all three corners of the triangle to effectively transition technology and effect a change within an organization. If any of the three vertices are missing, the technology transfer, or change, *will not*, and *cannot*, take place. Notice that one vertex is management commitment. The individuals selected as Category Managers and Category Leads must be committed to making OO work within their organization and for this specific project. Without their commitment, it is extremely difficult, *if not impossible*, to have success. Higher-level management *must* provide support to the Category Managers and Leads as well.

The second vertex, Agent of Change, is an external agent that brings a fresh perspective, new enthusiasm, and solid OO experience to the effort. Most organizations get tired of listening to the same people over and over.

Finally, the third vertex indicates that an effort needs to be designated as the target for the learning process, either a small project or a pilot project.

3.2 DEVELOP CATEGORY INTERACTION DIAGRAMS (CIDS)

Purpose

> The purpose of this Activity is to identify how the Categories collaborate to implement a Use Case.

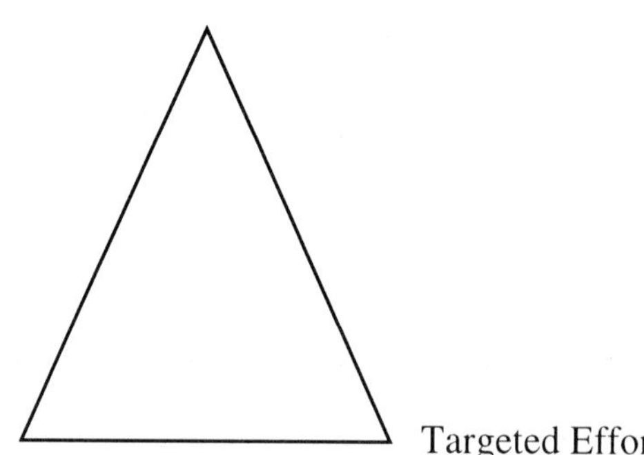

Figure 3-2. Three Requirements for Transitioning Technology

[1]This initial concept is attributed to IMA (Implementation Management Associates) and a course IMA provided in change management.

The development of a Category Interaction Diagram (CID) determines which Category has the *responsibility* for implementing a specific portion of functionality for a Use Case.

Definition(s)

Category Interaction Diagram (CID): A **CID** is a graphical representation of the interactions between Categories required to satisfy, or implement, a Use Case using the notation of the CASE tool. OMT provides Event Traces while Booch provides Interaction Diagrams and Object Scenario Diagrams**.** In UML 1.0 terminology, an Interaction Diagram is any diagram that depicts interaction at the Instance level, and can be either a Sequence Diagram or a Collaboration Diagram.

Program Design Language (PDL): **PDL** is a language used to represent design information. **PDL** is often called pseudo code because it resembles code and indicates, in its own syntax, the behavior of a specific functionality.

Supporting Interaction Diagram: A **Supporting Interaction Diagram** is an Interaction Diagram that represents common processing, utilized by many Use Cases, that itself is *not* a Use Case. Again a Supporting Interaction Diagram is drawn using the notation provided by the CASE tool.

UML Collaboration Diagram: A **UML Collaboration Diagram** is the new UML name for the Booch Object Scenario Diagram.

UML Interaction Diagram: A **UML Interaction Diagram** refers to both UML Sequence Diagrams and UML Collaboration Diagrams. Both kinds of diagrams represent general behavior, specifically interactions between Objects (Instances).

UML Sequence Diagram: A **UML Sequence Diagram** is the UML name for the Jacobson Interaction Diagram. Whereas a Jacobson Interaction Diagram portrayed collaboration between Classes, a **UML Sequence Diagram** shows the collaboration required between Objects (Instances). Additionally a UML Sequence Diagram provides new notational enhancements for representing creation/destruction of Instances, conditional flow of control and so on.

Process

Step 1: Establish Naming Conventions

For this book, all Category Interaction Diagrams (CIDs) that represent the implementation of a Use Case are named <UC##_Use_Case_Name>_CID, as in UC16_Operator_Updates _Nominal_Values_In_DB_CID. UML Sequence Diagrams are named <UC##_Use_Case_Name>_CSD, for Category Sequence Diagram (CSD), as in UC16_Operator_Update_Nominal_Values_In_DB_CSD.

Step 2: Agree upon a Representation Mechanism

Agree on whether

- OMT Event Traces
- Jacobson Interaction Diagrams
- Booch Object Scenario Diagrams
- UML Sequence Diagram
- UML Collaboration Diagrams

are to be produced. The contents of each diagram are semantically similar, if *not* identical in some cases. For the SEM, Jacobson Interaction Diagrams have been produced.

Step 3: Agree upon Diagram Contents

Agree on what the contents of each diagram should be. Consider including the following in addition to the title of the diagram and the actual diagram itself (whether Classes or Instances are depicted is *not* relevant to this step):

- Textual overview of the Use Case
- Exceptions
- GUI Classes.

For the HCC, the decision was made to keep it simple, as should be the basis for all decisions. The textual overview is *not* included as additional text on a diagram because an overview and a full description is included in the Scenario for each Use Case. Exceptions are *not* included because more detailed knowledge of the application is required and because the focus of a CID is Category interaction, *not* Class interaction. GUI Classes are *not* necessary to include at this level, as again the focus is on Category interaction, *not* Class interaction. GUI Classes are included in OOA and OOD refinements to these initial CIDs. Of course, these decisions can be *reversed* for your project. This step is to agree on exactly ***what*** the contents of the CIDs are to be.

Step 4: Number each Message

Each Message on a CID needs a sequence number, either as part of the Message or as a comment attached to the Message. Rational Rose supports automatic resequencing of Message numbers when a Message is inserted or deleted. If the CASE tool of choice does *not* support Message numbering, see if the Message numbers can be added as comments. Of course, renumbering is then a manual process.

Step 5: Comment each CID

All branching, looping, and exception handling (if included) needs to be described as a note on the diagram, otherwise the construct available for the specific diagram must be used. This information, in effect, represents a PDL for the Use Case.

Step 6: Agree to Notation for Use Cases Using/Referencing Other Use Cases

There should be at least one CID for each Use Case. However, there may be more than one Use Case involved in the representation of the implementation of one specific Use Case. For example, consider Use Case 1, which utilizes many other Use Cases, specifically 6, 7, and 8, among others. One suggested way to represent a Use Case referencing another Use Case on a CID is to 1) enter a Category (or Class) into the CASE tool repository with a unique and distinct name (so that it can be overlooked for certain reports [e.g., report on Classes owned by each Category]), and then 2) use the name of the Use Case as the name of the Message to this Category. Figure 3-3 shows how to do this. The unique Class named `$Use_Case` has been created. Using a dollar sign character ($) as the first character of the name makes it easy to generate reports on the repository that recognize this Class and either discard or include it depending on the nature of the report.[2] Note that the name of the Message to the `$Use_Case` Class is the same as the name of the Use Case being utilized in the solution.

Whatever notation is agreed-upon, make sure that the selected CASE tool supports the notation for naming the unique Class. When using a special character, make

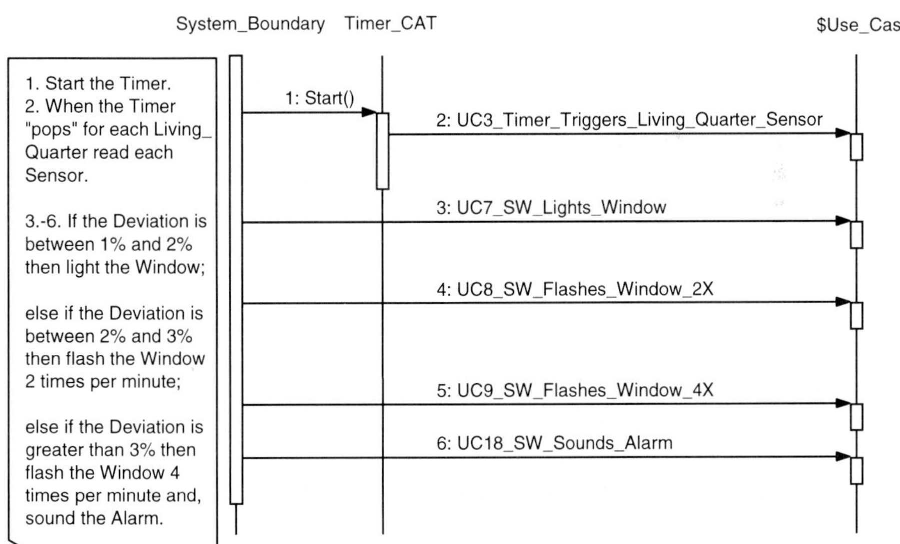

Figure 3-3. Sample CID: Referencing Other Use Cases: UCI

[2]Care should be taken when using any special character to ensure that the character chosen does *not* interfere with or impact the tool's capabilities.

sure that both the character selected and the position of the character in the name are supported by the CASE tool.

Example

Because of the existing diversity of notations to represent collaboration between Classes and/or Instances, we have chosen to represent all IDs using a simplified version of IDs.

Figure 3-3 serves a dual purpose because it represents an actual CID for Use Case 1, *and* it references other Use Cases. A second example is shown in Figure 3-4, the CID for Use Case 3: Timer_Triggers_Living_Quarter_Sensor. Both of these figures are drawn using Booch/Jacobson notation for Interaction Diagrams.

Figure 3-5 shows the same information that is contained in Figure 3-3, but Figure 3-5 utilizes UML notation for a Sequence Diagram. Note how UML displays timing information on a Sequence Diagram; a lower case letter identifies a Message, time required between 2 Messages is included between opening and closing curly braces ({}).

Note how alternate paths are depicted in UML, as well as the use of backward arrows to indicate return of control flow. In UML Sequence Diagrams, Messages are sent to Objects (Instances) rather than Classes. To reflect that an entity is an Instance, the name of the Instance is underlined. The Instance name may also be preceded by the Class name, followed by the scope resolution operator (::), as in

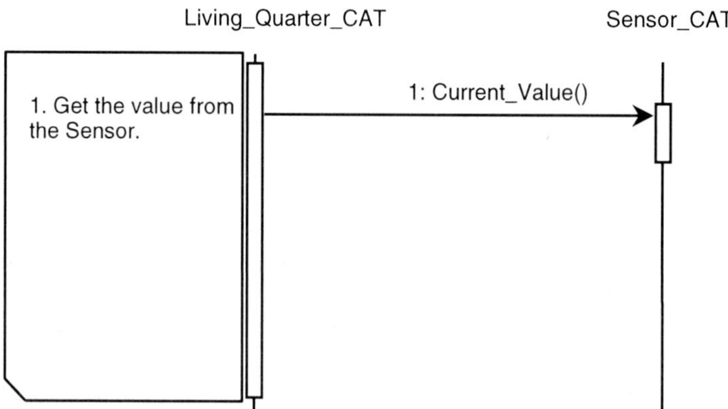

Figure 3-4. CID: UC3_Timer_Triggers_Living_Quarter_Sensor

UC1_SW_Monitors_Living_Quarters_CID

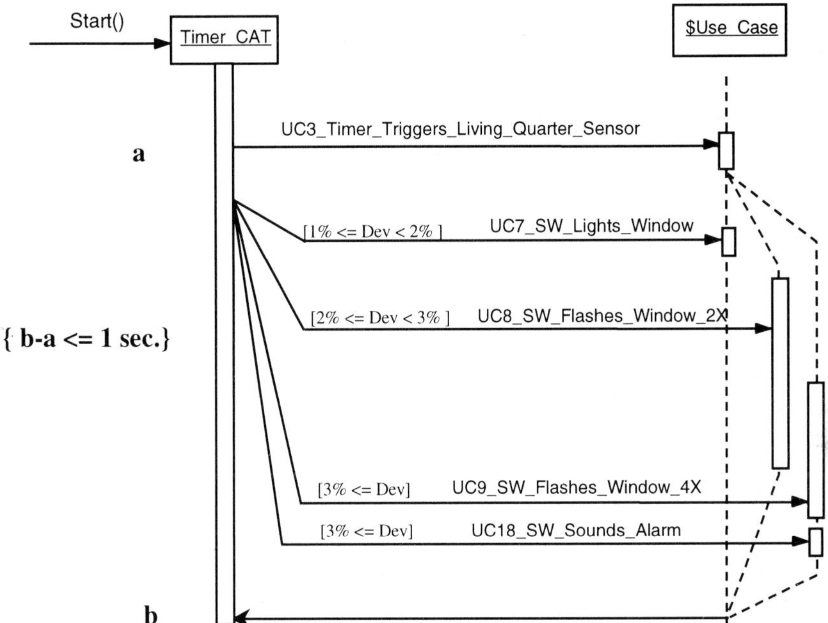

Figure 3-5. CID: UC1: UML Sequence Diagram Notation

ClassName::InstanceName. Because real-time systems can have numerous Instances, and *not* all Instances are persistent, one convention that can be adopted is to precede the name within the rectangle with the Class's name only when it is important to distinguish Instances. For a CID, just leave the name of the Category underlined, as has been done in Figure 3-5. Worrying about Instances is *not* important yet.

It is important to distinguish Instances when the software being developed resides in many geographical locations and the locations communicate, or when *not* all locations have the same software composition. To be more specific, consider software that tracks launched vehicles. If a Tracking Operator at Location A wants to send a message to the Supervising Operator at Location B, it is important to show Instances. Visually seeing the Instance `TrackingOperator::A` sending the Message `SendCodeBlue()` to the Instance `SupervisingOperator::B` is extremely helpful and important to show on a Sequence Diagram. But, *not* all situations require Instances to be identified. And in many situations, there are so many Instances that the diagram would become too cluttered. For the SEM, it is *not* important to show Instances on the CID. Interaction or collaboration at the Category level is sufficient to depict.

Pragmatic Project Issues

Stay away from Classes

Keep the CIDs at the level of Category-to-Category interactions. Refrain from adding Classes that may become evident as the CIDs are produced.

Look for Common Processing

Processing required by multiple Use Cases is very common. Consider adding to Use Cases 16, 17, 21, and 22 the capability of logging Operator actions to a flat file. Agree to a notation for representing common processing in its *own* Interaction Diagram so that it can be referenced from multiple CIDs. One suggestion is to name a CID that represents common processing according to the following guidelines:

- Do not use any Use Case number prefix
- Use all capital letters
- Use the _CID suffix.

Additionally, any Messages to this new supporting CID, from another CID, need to be sent to the `$Use_Case` Class. Figures 3-6 and 3-7 show this suggested notation as an Interaction Diagram, *not* in UML notation. Figure 3-6 represents the common processing of adding a message to a log. Note that the supporting CID remains at the Category

ADD_ENTRY_TO_LOG_CID

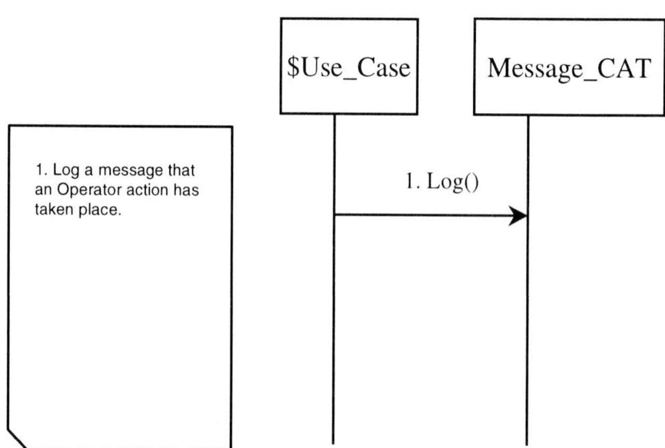

Figure 3-6. A Supporting CID

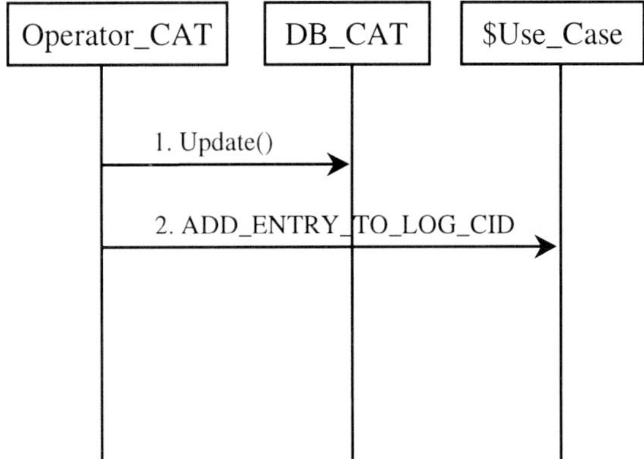

Figure 3-7. Referencing a Supporting CID

level as well. The details of first checking to see if a log file already exists, and if it does, then adding an entry, or creating the log file first and then adding an entry are flushed out during OOA and OOD. For the purposes of this book, any CID that does *not* map directly to a Use Case is called a *Supporting CID;* consequently, Figure 3-6 represents a Supporting CID. Figure 3-7 shows how in Message 2, the `$Use_Case` Class is used to receive the request for logging an Operator action. Note that the name of the Message is the exact name of the Supporting CID and appears in all capital letters. Using a visual clue, like all capital letters, makes the supporting CID easy to find in a repository of diagrams, *and* easy to see on any CID on which it is referenced.

Facilitating Software Integration and Test

One major benefit of the CIDs is that this early identification of Use Case dependency facilitates an early start to the development of Software Integration and Test Plans.

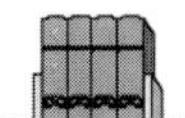

Product(s)

The result of this Activity is a set of CIDs and derived Supporting Interaction Diagrams for the current build. In actuality, a CID may be an Interaction Diagram á la Jacobson, an Object Scenario Diagram á la Booch, an Event Trace á la Rumbaugh, or a UML Interaction Diagram, which can be either a Sequence Diagram or a Collaboration Diagram.

Phase Transition Criteria

Transition to the next Phase when the CIDs have been produced and reviewed by both the Systems and Software organizations. The review criteria shown below in Table 3-2 might help to decide whether or not to transition to the next Phase.

Review Criteria

Table 3-2. CID Review Criteria

	CID Review Criteria
1	Is there at least one CID for each Use Case?
2	Are the naming conventions followed?
3	Are supporting CIDS named according to the naming conventions?
4	Is a Category that accepts a Message the Category that will have the responsibility for fulfilling the request?
5	Is there only one `$Use_Case` class that accepts all Messages that represent requests for other Use Cases or Supporting CID capability?
6	Does each Category appear only once on the CID?
7	Does the sequence of messages represent the operational concept as specified in the Scenario?
8	Are all exception conditions (if included) specified in the Scenario represented in the CID?
9	Are the exceptions (if included) propagated appropriately?
10	Is each Message numbered sequentially from top to bottom?
11	Is any branching, looping, and exception handling (if included) described in a note to the left of the diagram and do these notes refer to the Message number?

Tracking Progress

Table 3-3 updates Table 2-4 by adding the Activities and products of this Phase. Basically, this Phase concentrated on producing Interaction Diagrams (or UML Sequence Diagrams) for Use Cases at the Category level.

The minimum number of CIDs for a build is the same as the number of Use Cases for the build. A project can track the actual number of CIDs developed to date and compare that to the number of Use Cases required for the build. Recall however that CIDs may have Supporting CIDs. The Supporting CIDs should *not* be included in the comparison, but rather, should be monitored separately.

Table 3-3. Project Management Spreadsheet: Phase 3

HCC Project Management Spreadsheet						
Number	**Phase Name**	**Activity**	**Charge Number**	**Product**	**Progress Metric**	**% Weight**
1	**Requirements Engineering**		**RE-1**			
1.1		Identify External Interfaces	RE-1.1	Context Diagram	1 Context Diagram completed	0.50
1.2		Capture "shall" Statements	RE-1.2	RTM ("shall" Statements)	# "shall" sentences	0.16
1.3		Allocate Requirements	RE-1.3	RTM ("Type" Column)	# entries typed (%) #SW entries(%)	0.17
1.4		Prioritize Requirements	RE-1.4	RTM ("Build" Column)	# entries prioritized (%) #Use Cases/build(%)	0.17
2	**System OOA–Static View**		**SYS-OOAS-2**			
2.1		Identify Software Use Cases	SYS-OOAS-2.1	RTM ("Use Case" Column)	# Use Cases (%)	0.20
2.2		Develop Scenarios	SYS-OOAS-2.2	Scenario	# Scenarios (%)	0.20
2.3		Develop Draft GUIs	SYS-OOAS-2.3	Draft GUI	# GUI sketches	0.20
2.4		Establish Project Categories	SYS-OOAS-2.4	Category List	# Categories	0.20
2.5		Allocate Use Cases to Category	SYS-OOAS-2.5	RTM ("Category" Column)	# Use Cases allocated (%), # Use Cases/Category	0.10
2.6		Develop System Category Diagram	SYS-OOAS-2.6	1 SCD	1 SCD completed	0.10
3	**System OOA–Dynamic View**		**SYS-OOAD-3**			
3.1		Allocate Category to Category Manager	SYS-OOAD-3.1		# Categories allocated	
3.2		Develop Category Interaction Diagrams	SYS-OOAD-3.2	CID	#CIDs (%)	1.00

PHASE 4

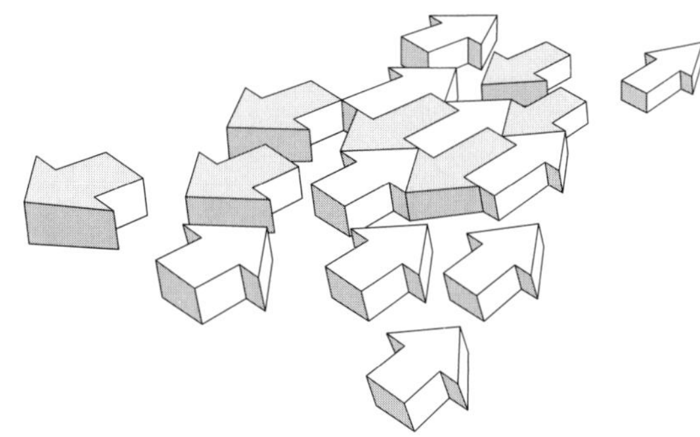

Hardware/Software Split

PHASE OVERVIEW

Up until now, the focus has been on establishing a set of requirements, allocating the requirements to a build, identifying Categories, and allocating Use Cases (representing re-statements of software functional requirements) to specific Categories for development. Static and dynamic views of the system were developed that represented the Categories and their Associations (in an SCD) and the interaction of the Categories to implement a Use Case (in CIDs). The basic architecture of the system under development has been established. This Phase, represented by Figure 4-1, focuses on the allocation of Category capability to hardware, software, or both.

4.1 PARTITION CATEGORIES

Purpose

> The purpose of this Activity is to identify what Categories are hardware, software, or a combination of both.

Remember that although a Category may be totally implemented in hardware, a software interface Class may need to be identified during software OOA.

Definition(s)

Category Class Diagram (CCD): A **CCD** is a diagram for a Category that represents the Classes owned by the Category and their Associations to other Classes in the Category, as well as their Associations to Classes from foreign Categories. A **CCD** is drawn as a Booch Class Diagram, an OMT Object Diagram, or a UML Class Diagram.

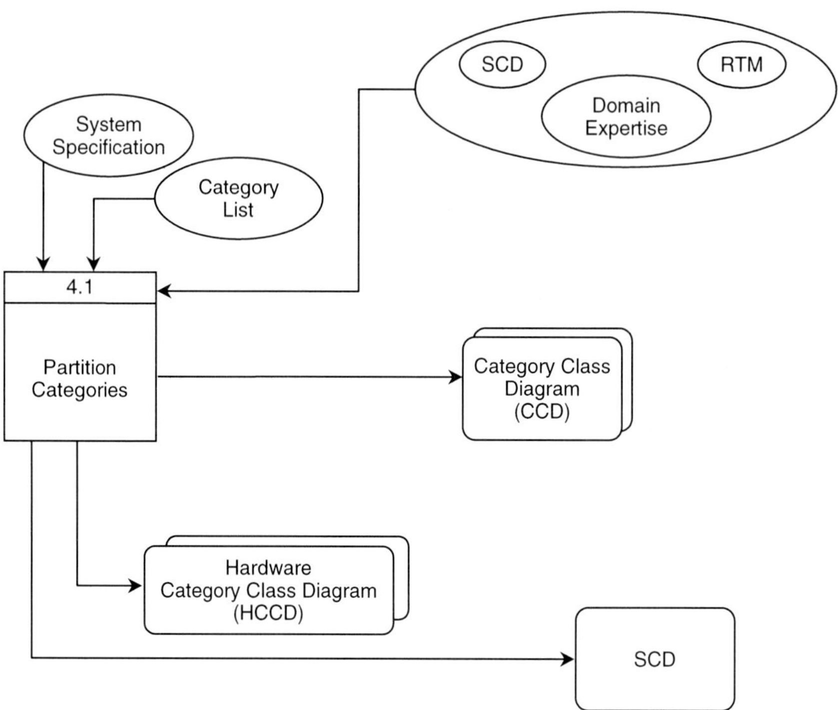

Figure 4-1. Hardware/Software Split Phase Description Diagram

Hardware Category Class Diagram (HCCD): An **HCCD** is a diagram for a Category that represents the hardware Classes owned by the Category and their Associations to other Classes in its Category, as well as to Classes in foreign Categories. An **HCCD** is drawn as a Booch Class Diagram, an OMT Object Diagram, or a UML Class Diagram.

UML Aggregation: In UML, there are two terms: **aggregation** and composition. **Aggregation** is indicated by an *unfilled* diamond and specifies that the "whole" Class maintains a *reference* to its "part" Class(es), thus the "whole" Class may *not* have created the "part" Class(es). In C++, this means that the "whole" Class maintains either a reference (&) or a pointer (*) to its "part" Class(es). Additionally, the lifetime of the whole Class is not dependent upon the lifetime of the part Class.

UML Composition: In UML, there are two terms: **composition** and aggregation. **Composition** is indicated by a *filled* diamond and specifies that the "whole" Class *is responsible* for creating its "part" Class(es). In C++, this means that when an Instance of a "whole" Class is declared (or dynamically allocated) the constructors for the "part" Class(es) are called, the "part" Classes are constructed, and then the constructor of the "whole" Class is executed.

Process

Step 1: Establish Naming Conventions

Because each Category is partitioned into its hardware and software components, naming conventions must be agreed-upon for Classes that consist of all hardware, all software, and Classes that represent a combination of both hardware and software. Naming conventions must also be agreed-upon for diagrams that might represent hardware-only Categories, depicting their Classes and their Associations.

The convention adopted in this book is as follows: hardware-only Classes are suffixed with an asterisk (*), Classes that are a combination of hardware and software are suffixed with a pound, or sharp, sign (#), and Classes that are all software are *not* suffixed with any special symbol. Of course, this is only a suggestion—the final choice is up to a Project Team to decide.

The following conventions are also used: For a Class Diagram that reflects a software-only Category, or a Category that is a combination of hardware and software, the diagram is named <CategoryName>_CAT_CCD. For a Class Diagram that reflects a hardware-only Category, the diagram is named <Category Name>_CAT_HCCD.

Step 2: Specify a Category as Hardware, Software, or Both

For each Category, ask the following question: "Is the capability of Category X to be totally implemented in hardware, software, or a combination of both?" The rationale for this decision is typically based on hardware availability and cost. Usually, it is less expensive to purchase a commercial hardware item than it is to build the equivalent capability in software. `Process_CAT` does *not* need to be considered here because `Process_CAT` is for software processes only. With respect to `Interim_CAT` and `Reusable_CAT`, the Project Team can decide whether these two Categories are strictly for software Classes, hardware Classes, or both. For example, `Interim_CAT` could have two child Categories: `SW_Interim_CAT` and `HW_Interim_CAT`.

If the answer to the question posed in the previous paragraph is hardware, then 1) initiate an HCCD for Category X (X_CAT) named X_CAT_HCCD, and 2) add a Class named X* to the X_CAT_HCCD. The asterisk (*) suffixing the Class name follows the naming conventions specified in Step 1 and indicates that the Class is a hardware Class.

If the answer to the question posed above is software, then 1) initiate a CCD for Category X (X_CAT) named X_CAT_CCD, and 2) add a Class named X to the X_CAT_CCD. Note that the name of the Class on the X_CAT_CCD does *not* have any special symbol or naming convention. This permits a seamless transition for the software developers.

If the answer to the question posed above is both, then 1) initiate a CCD for Category X (X_CAT) named X_CAT_CCD and 2) add a Class named X# to the X_CAT_CCD that has an aggregation relationship (is made up of) with two Classes: X*, representing the hardware portion of the Class, and X, representing the software portion of the Class. The pound sign (#) suffixing the name of the Class follows the naming conventions specified in Step 1 and indicates that the Class is made up of both hardware and software. The asterisk (*) suffixing the "part" Class name indicates that the "part" Class is a hardware Class. Again, note that the simple name of the Class, X, carries down to the software developers. Figure 4-2 shows a decision tree that summarizes the above decision process.

Example

Figure 4-3(a) shows the CCD for the `Alarm` Category in OMT notation. Note the name of the diagram is Alarm_SS_CCD. The Class at the root of the hierarchy is named `Alarm#`, indicating that it is made up of both hardware and software. The aggregation hierarchy rooted at `Alarm#` is made up of two "part" Classes, `Alarm*`, representing the hardware part of the Class, and `Alarm`, representing the software part of the Class. Now the Attributes and Methods for the hardware and software portions can be allocated to the appropriate part of the `Alarm#` Class. Figure 4-3(b) shows the same information in Booch notation.

Figure 4-3(c) shows the `Alarm_CAT` CCD in UML notation. Note that the symbol has transitioned from the tabbed folder for a package (Category stereotype) in the SCD to a symbol for a Class (rectangle). Also note that the form of aggregation chosen is UML composition, rather than UML aggregation.

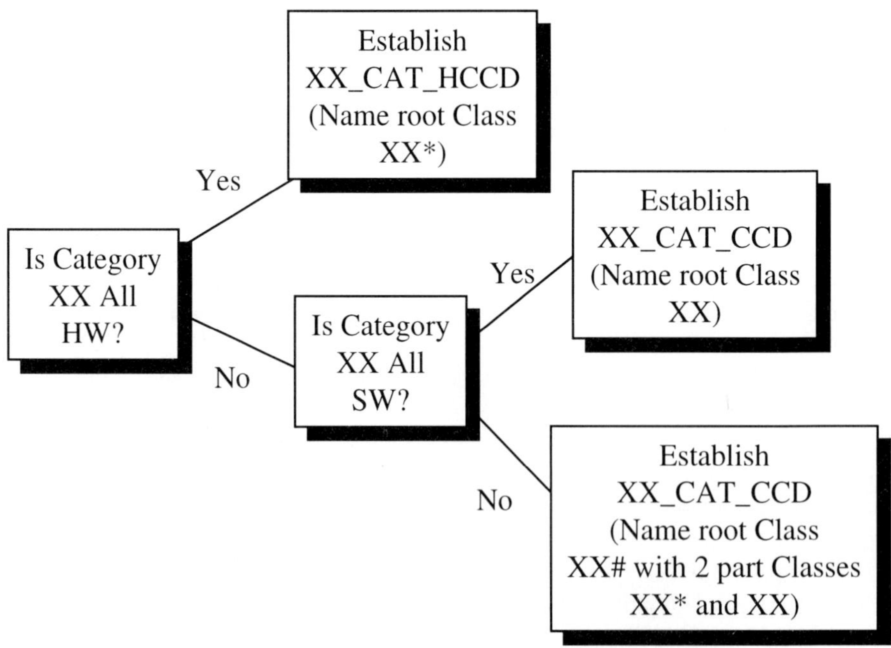

Figure 4-2. HW/SW Split Decision Tree

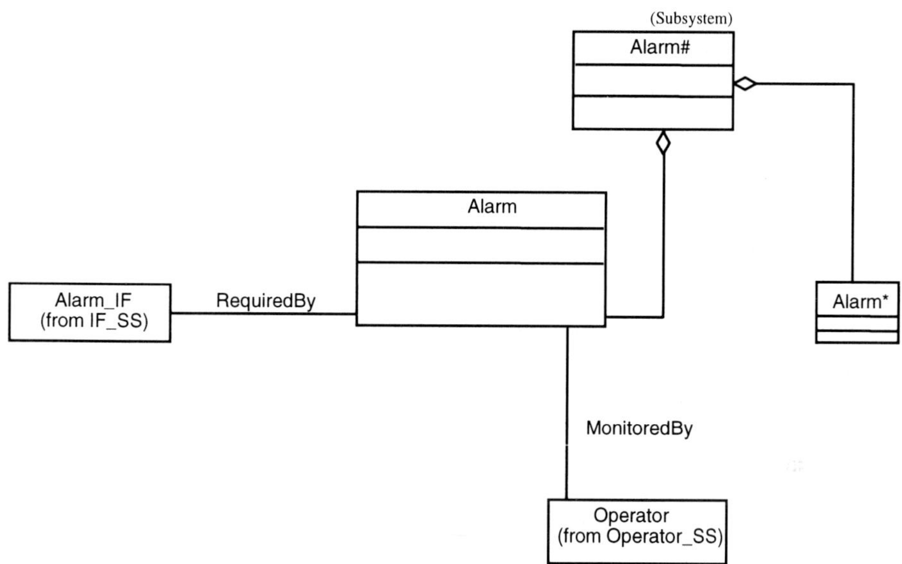

Figure 4-3(a). Alarm_SS_CCD : OMT Notation

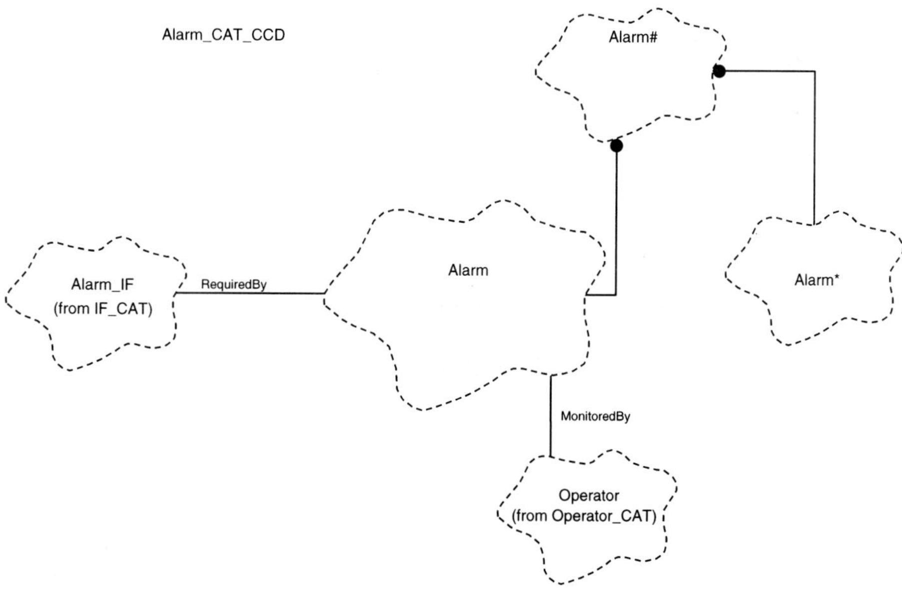

Figure 4-3(b). Alarm_CAT_CCD : Booch Notation

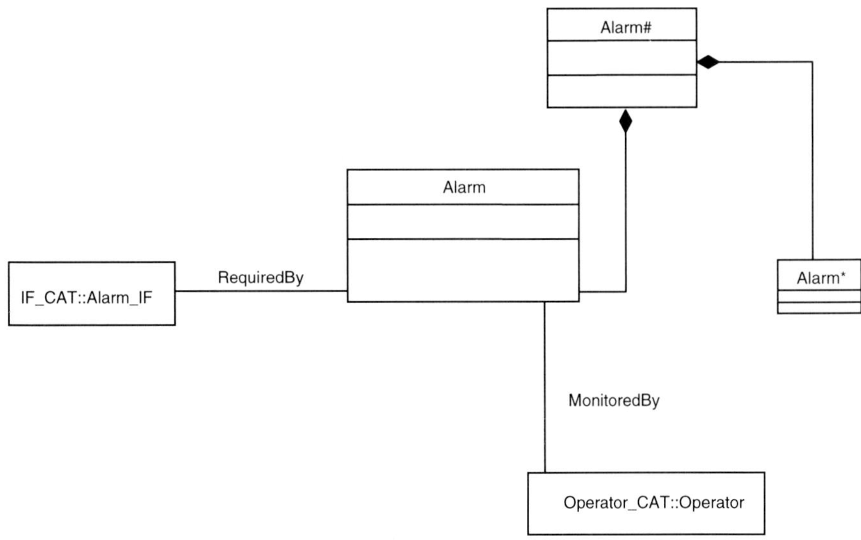

Figure 4-3(c). Alarm_CAT_CCD : UML Notation

Figure 4-4(a) shows the Environmental_Condition_SS_CCD in OMT notation. The fact that the `Environmental_Condition` Class is *not* suffixed by either an asterisk (*) or pound sign (#) indicates that the OMT Subsystem (equivalent to Booch Category) and Class are made up entirely of software. Figure 4-4(b) shows the same CCD in Booch notation, while Figure 4-4(c) represents UML notation. Inheritance in UML is in-

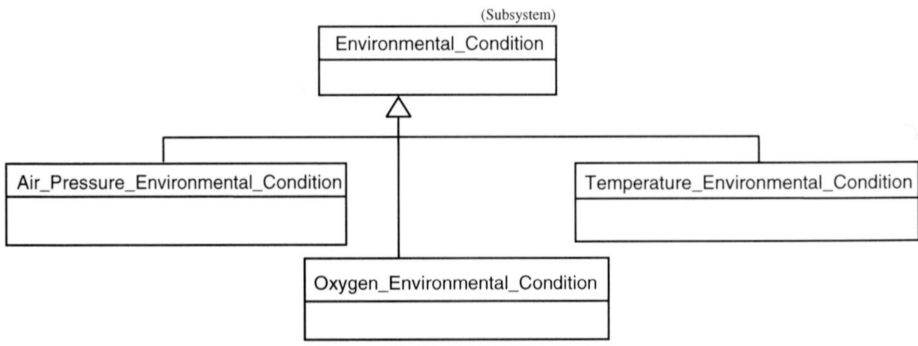

Figure 4-4(a). Environmental_Condition_SS_CCD : OMT Notation

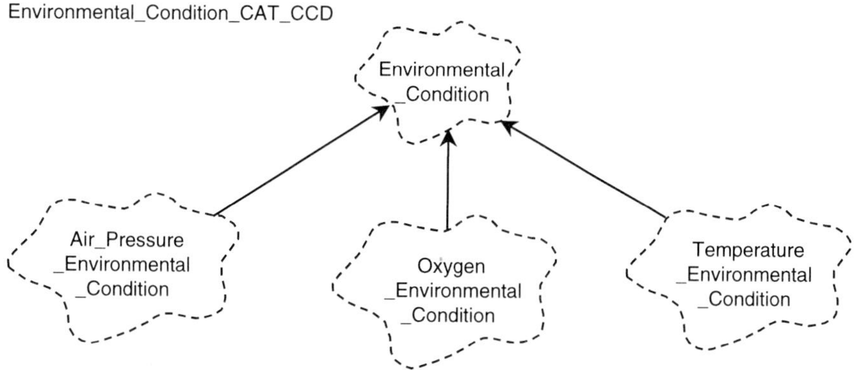

Figure 4-4(b). Environmental_Condition_CAT_CCD : Booch Notation

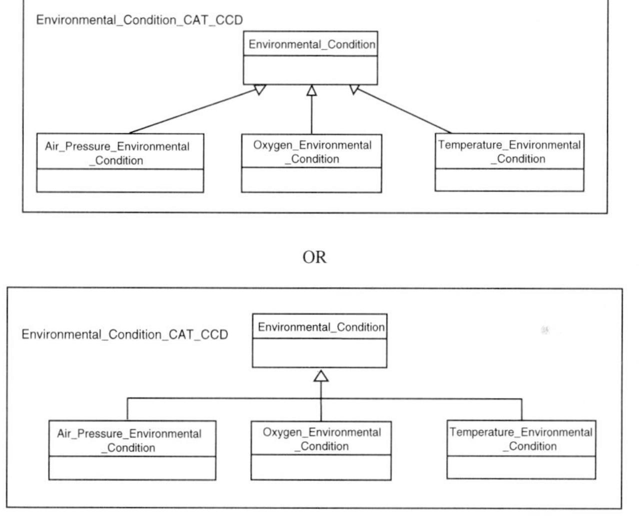

Figure 4-4(c). Environmental_Condition_CAT_CCD : UML Notation

dicated by arrows with unfilled arrowheads drawn *from* the Subclass *to* the Superclass. Figure 4-4(c) also depicts two UML alternatives for representing inheritance.

The HCC does not have any Classes that are 100% hardware.

Pragmatic Project Issues

Hardware Responsibility

The hardware Category Lead responsible for a Category decides whether the hardware portion of a Category needs to have its own HCCD, or whether the Attributes and Methods for the hardware Classes can be incorporated into an all-purpose CCD. The point is that there is no reason why the hardware portions of a system cannot be modeled, just as the software portions are modeled, and maintained in the same repository that maintains the software Classes.

Pre-empting Phase 5

The first Activity of the next Phase, Phase 5, *again* addresses establishing a set of CCDs, one for each software Category. Although examples of CCDs are shown in this Activity, refer to the next Activity for more detailed information on CCDs.

Alternative Notations

There are other possible notations for representing the hardware/software partitioning of a Category. For example, `System_Alarm` can be the name of the aggregation "whole" Class, `Alarm_Hardware` can be the name of the hardware "part" Class, and `Alarm` can be the name of the software "part" Class. The point is to choose one notation that can be supported by the CASE tool of choice.

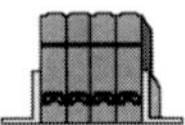

Product(s)

The result of this Activity is a subset of initial CCDs (and optionally, HCCDs) established for the Categories of the project.

Phase Transition Criteria

Transition to the next Phase when the initial CCDs have been produced, reviewed, and agreed-upon by both the Systems and Software organizations.

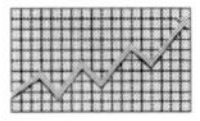

Tracking Progress

Table 4-1 once again augments the previous project management spreadsheet by adding the Activities and products of this Phase. Note that 100% of the weight is allocated to the identification of the type of Category, rather than being allocated to the actual representation of the decision in CCDs and HCCDs. These particular diagrams can be initiated in the next Phase without any consequence to the project. What *is* important is to agree upon the actual allocation of a Category to hardware components, software components, or a combination of both.

Table 4-1. Project Management Spreadsheet: Phase 4

HCC Project Management Spreadsheet						
Number	**Phase Name**	**Activity**	**Charge Number**	**Product**	**Progress Metric**	**% Weight**
1	**Requirements Engineering**		**RE-1**			
1.1		Identify External Interfaces	RE-1.1	Context Diagram	1 Context Diagram completed	0.50
1.2		Capture “shall” Statements	RE-1.2	RTM (“shall” Statements)	# “shall” sentences	0.16
1.3		Allocate Requirements	RE-1.3	RTM (“Type” Column)	# entries typed (%) # SW entries(%)	0.17
1.4		Prioritize Requirements	RE-1.4	RTM (“Build” Column)	# entries prioritized (%) # Use Cases/build(%)	0.17
2	**System OOA–Static View**		**SYS-OOAS-2**			
2.1		Identify Software Use Cases	SYS-OOAS-2.1	RTM (“Use Case” Column)	# Use Cases	0.20
2.2		Develop Scenarios	SYS-OOAS-2.2	Scenario	# Scenarios (%)	0.20
2.3		Develop Draft GUIs	SYS-OOAS-2.3	Draft GUI	# GUI sketches	0.20
2.4		Establish Project Categories	SYS-OOAS-2.4	Category List	# Categories	0.20
2.5		Allocate Use Cases to Category	SYS-OOAS-2.5	RTM (“Category” Column)	# Use Cases allocated (%), # Use Cases/Category	0.10
2.6		Develop System Category Diagram	SYS-OOAS-2.6	1 SCD	1 SCD completed	0.10
3	**System OOA–Dynamic View**		**SYS-OOAD-3**			
3.1		Allocate Category to Category Manager	SYS-OOAD-3.1		# Categories allocated	
3.2		Develop CIDs	SYS-OOAD-3.2	CID	#CIDs (%)	1.00
4	**HW/SW Split**		**HWSW-4**			
4.1		Partition Categories	HWSW-4.1	CCD HCCD	# CCDs initiated # HCCDs initiated	1.00

PART III

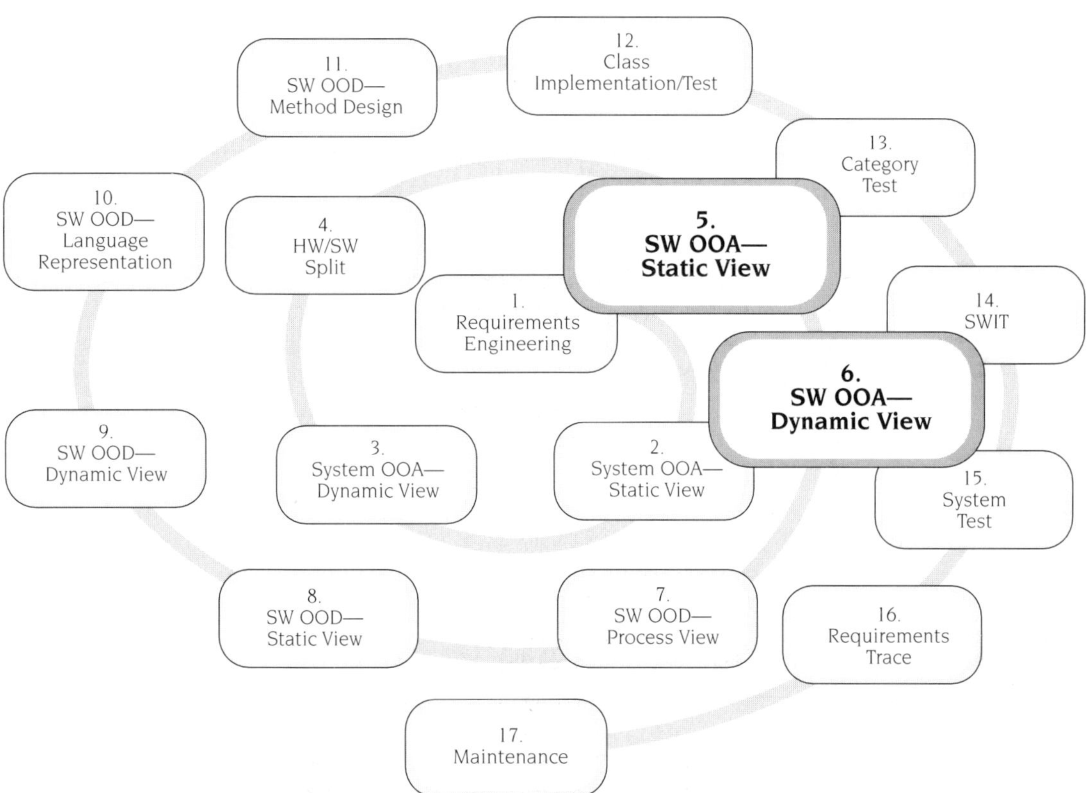

Software Object-Oriented Analysis

PHASE 5

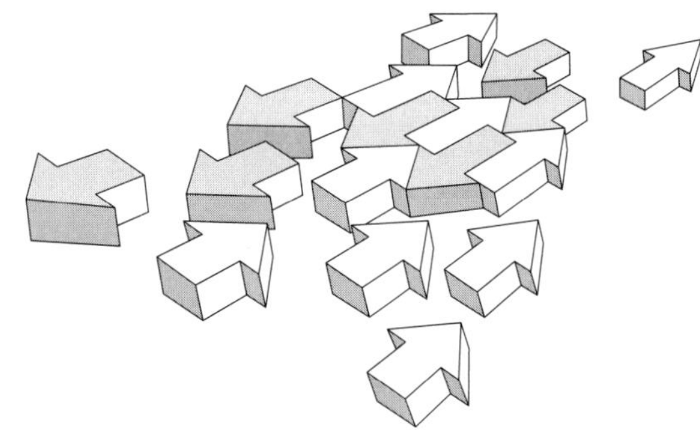

Software OOA–Static View

PHASE OVERVIEW

Figure 5-1 identifies the Activities to be performed in this Phase. For each Category, the following are produced:

- One Category Class Diagram (CCD)
- Multiple Class-Centric Class Diagrams (CCCDs) (at most, one for each Class in a Category)
- Class Specifications (CSs) (one for each Class).

The CCDs, representing a refinement of the SCD, are created using either Booch or UML Class Diagrams or OMT Object Diagrams. A CS is created using either the Booch or UML Class Specification capability, or the OMT Class Table, plus any additional OMT annotations that have been defined for the project.

In summary, this Phase focuses on the most stable part of the software system—its basic atomic elements, Classes. Thus, this Phase results in the specification of the non-behavioral software system requirements.[1] Although all Phases are critical to the success of any OO software development effort, this Phase, and the next, form the cornerstone for the resulting code. Time spent in this Phase and the next reduces the amount of design and coding errors, and therefore, the time required for testing.

5.1 INITIATE CATEGORY CLASS DIAGRAM (CCD)

Purpose

> The purpose of this Activity is simply to produce a "canvas" for a Category Class Diagram (CCD) for any Category whose CCD was not initiated during the previous Phase (Phase 4).

[1]The next Phase, Software OOA–Dynamic View, focuses on the dynamic behavior of the software by investigating the internal behavior of a Class (State Transition Diagram) and the collaborative behavior required of Classes to implement a Use Case (Interaction Diagram or UML Sequence Diagram).

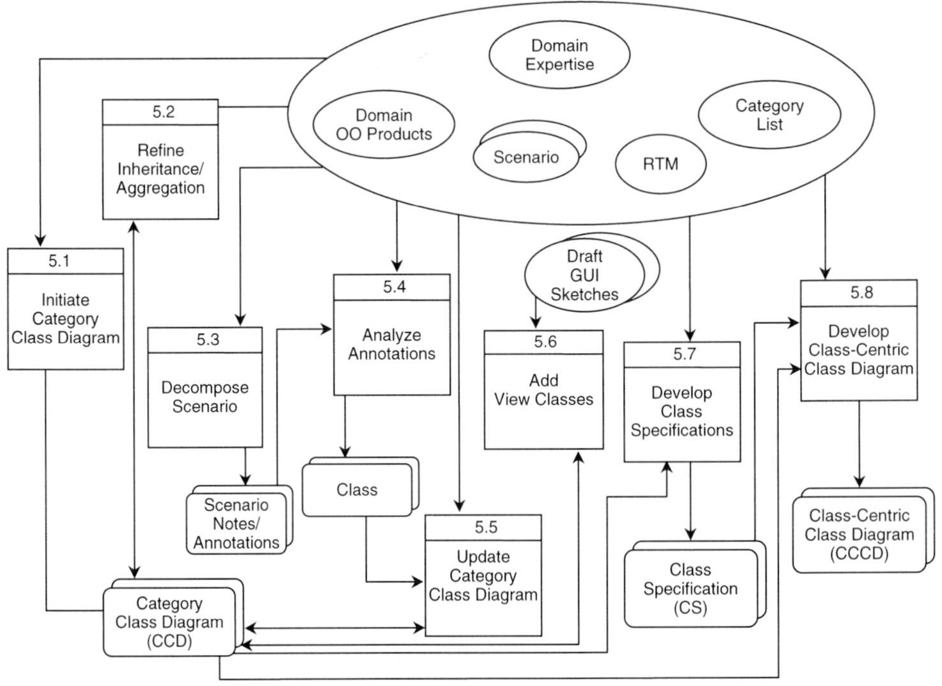

Figure 5-1. Software OOA - Static View Phase Description Diagram

Definition(s)

Category Class Diagram (CCD): A **CCD** for *one* Category is a Class Diagram that depicts all Classes owned by the Category, all Classes required by the Classes in the Category that are owned by other Categories (imported Classes), and all Associations between these Classes. There is one CCD per Category. Recall that a CCD is created as a Booch or UML Class Diagram or an OMT Object Diagram.

Child Category: A **child Category** is a Category that is *owned* by another Category —the parent Category—and represents a logical collection of Classes of the parent Category, or equivalently, a subset of the parent Category.

Parent Category: A **parent Category** represents a Category that, because of its size, is decomposed into a logical collection of child Categories.

Process

Step 1: Establish Naming Conventions

Give the CCD diagram the name of the Category, suffixed with _CCD, as in <<Category_Name>>_CCD. Note that by naming the diagram <<Category_Name>>_CCD, the entire repository is easily browsed for the CCDs. For OMT, the suffix suggested is _SS. Establish naming conventions for CCDs for child Categories.

Step 2: Initiate the CCD

Recall that a CCD may have been established in the preceding Phase. Using the CASE tool selected for the project, establish a CCD for each Category *not* previously created during Phase 4. Remember that this Activity does nothing more than establish the canvas upon which developers can produce CCDs.

Step 3: Add the Root Class

For those Categories that are represented by an inheritance or aggregation hierarchy, place the Class that represents the root of the hierarchy, on the CCD. Name the root Class the same as the name of the Category, but omit the _CCD (or_SS, if using OMT) suffix. For example, place an `Environmental_Condition` Class on the Environmental_Condition_CAT_CCD. Place a `Panel` Class on the Panel_CAT_CCD.

For those Categories that are *not* rooted by such a hierarchy, place a Class with the same name as the Category on the diagram. For example, place an `Alarm` Class on the Alarm_CAT_CCD, and a `Living_Quarter` Class on the Living_Quarter_CCD. Although neither the `Alarm` nor the `Living_Quarter` are represented by either an inheritance or aggregation hierarchy, both the `Alarm_CAT` and `Living_Quarter_CAT` will have a Class that is named the same as the Category. Typically, *most* Categories own a Class that is named the same as the Category. Exceptions do exist; for example, `Interim_CAT`, `Reusable_Cat`, and so on.

Step 4: Establish Diagram Traversal[2] Capability

Within the selected CASE tool, traversal capability between the SCD and a CCD needs to be provided. Rational Rose provides this capability automatically, while the traversal capability must be manually created within OMT. Traversal capability provides a developer/reviewer with the capability to "click" on a Category icon on the system-level SCD and automatically traverse to, and display, the Category CCD for either update or review purposes.

Step 5: Establish Diagram Ownership

Establish ownership of the diagram in the CASE tool to the appropriate Category. Doing so now will facilitate the generation of project deliverables by Category. In OMT, this is accomplished using an OMT annotation. In Rose, this is accomplished automatically because any new diagram must be created within a Category, thus automatically establishing ownership.

[2]The word "navigation" could have been used rather than the word "traversal", but then, navigation would have become confused with the word navigation as used in UML. Here, traversal (navigation) means the ability to move directly from one diagram in the repository to another diagram in the repository. In UML, navigation means the existence of an Attribute in a Class that allows two Classes to communicate.

Example

The initial CCD for the `Environmental_Condition_CAT` is shown in Figure 5-2. Note that the diagram is named properly, and a single Class, `Environmental_Condition`, has been added to the diagram. The Environmental_Condition_CAT_CCD will be completed during Activities 5.2, 5.5, and 5.6, and continually updated until the code is delivered to the customer.

Pragmatic Project Issues

Acquire a CASE Tool Administrator

At this point, it is wise to consider creating, and filling, a position known as the CASE Tool Administrator. This person can create the traversal capabilities, thus freeing the development staff from this task. Future responsibilities for the CASE Tool Administrator[3] are identified in the text as the OO process unfolds. In summary however, it is difficult to conceive of a moderate to large project without a CASE Tool Administrator.

Reduce Clutter

By creating the CCD canvas now for each Category, clutter within the repository is reduced. With many developers creating diagrams, it is inevitable that additional diagrams will populate the repository. Because of time constraints, typically it is extremely difficult for developers to find time to clean up the repository. Creating empty, or skeleton, diagrams now helps to maintain consistency within the repository.

Identification of New Categories

In any project, it is also inevitable that new Categories will be identified as the project progresses. This is *not* an issue at all, or worded differently, it is a non-issue. Just set up the Categories *now* for those Categories that have been identified. As new Categories

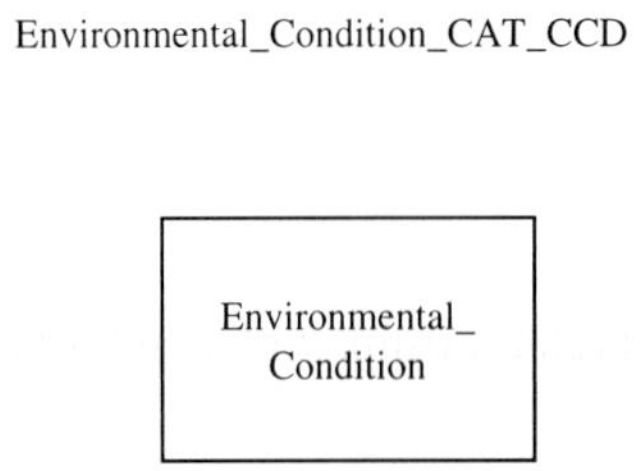

Figure 5-2. Initial Environmental_Condition_CAT CCD

[3]A CASE Tool Administrator can also be made responsible for the integrity of the repository by producing inconsistency reports (more on this later), monitoring interfaces between the Categories, and having write permission to the entire repository to update interfaces between Categories.

are discovered, or as it is determined that a Category is *not* really needed, simply inform the CASE Tool Administrator to create (or delete) the specified Category.

Manage the Categories

Provide a mechanism to manage the creation/deletion of Categories for the project. Typically, the OO Team has the responsibility of approving/disapproving all Categories other than child Categories of a previously identified Category. Approving or *not* approving *child* Categories belongs at the parent Category Manager level, *not* the OO Team level.

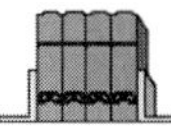

Product(s)

The result of this Activity is the initial set of Category CCDs, one for each Category in the software model, with traversal capability established from the system-level SCD to each CCD in the repository. These initial CCDs should represent the hardware/software split as previously established in Phase 4.

5.2 REFINE INHERITANCE/AGGREGATION HIERARCHIES

Purpose

> The purpose of this Activity is to focus on developing and representing the inheritance hierarchy and/or aggregation hierarchy for each Category in a CCD. Additionally, this Activity continues to justify and validate the Category List.

This Activity does *not* result in completed CCDs. At this point, it is important to justify and validate the envisioned inheritance and aggregation hierarchies for the project. The CCDs are continually evolved throughout this entire Phase, and are further refined in Phase 8.

Definition(s)

Aggregation Hierarchy: An **aggregation hierarchy** is a set of Classes related through an aggregation relationship, with one root Class. All remaining Classes in the hierarchy are parts of, either directly or indirectly, and help comprise, the root Class.

Aggregation Relationship: An **aggregation relationship** is an Association between Classes that focuses on one Class being "made up of" another Class. An **aggregation relationship** is an Association that exists between "whole" Classes and "part" Classes. In UML there are two kinds of **aggregation relationships**: aggregation and composition.

Association: An **Association** represents a relationship between two Classes that is one of the following:

- Aggregation relationship
- Inheritance relationship
- Association relationship.

Association Relationship: An **association relationship** defines the nature of the coupling between two Classes that are *not* coupled through inheritance or aggregation. An **association relationship** between two Classes is named, identifies how many Instances of each Class participate (multiplicity), and specifies whether or not it is permissible for Instances of a Class not to participate in the relationship at all (conditionality).

Attribute: An **Attribute** is a single characteristic of a Class that needs to be remembered by the software. An **Attribute** can either be transient or persistent. A **transient Attribute** is an Attribute of a Class whose value is *not* maintained after the application terminates. A **persistent Attribute** is an Attribute of a Class whose value *is* retained after the application terminates.

Class: A **Class** is a static abstraction of a set of real world entities that have the same characteristics (Attributes) and exhibit the same behavior (Methods).[4]

Inheritance Hierarchy: An **inheritance hierarchy** is set of Classes related through inheritance relationships, with one root Class. All remaining Classes in the hierarchy are descended, either directly or indirectly, from the root Class.

Inheritance Relationship: An **inheritance relationship** is an Association between Classes that focuses on similarities and dissimilarities between the Classes with respect to the Classes' Attributes and Methods. An **inheritance relationship** is an Association that exists between a Superclass and its Subclasses.

Instance: An **Instance** is a single, unique, real world entity that belongs to a Class. The term Object is used synonymously with **Instance** in this text.

Method: A **Method** is a single functional capability of a Class that can be performed on an Instance of the Class.

Subclass: A **Subclass** is a Class that is derived from another Class, its Superclass or base Class. A **Subclass** inherits all the Attributes and Methods of its parent Superclass.

Superclass: A **Superclass** is a Class from which other Classes, named Subclasses, are derived. A Superclass provides Attributes and Methods that are in common to all its Subclasses.

[4]This definition is a combination of Shlaer/Mellor's and Meyer's. Shlaer/Mellor initiated the concept of an abstraction of a set of entities, while Meyer made the distinction between static and dynamic [SHL88], [MEY88A].

UML Aggregation: Aggregation is an aggregation relationship where the "whole" Class does *not* have to create its "part" Classes, but rather, refers to the "part" Classes by reference or pointer. An Instance of a "part" Class has been potentially created by another Class and the "whole" Class requires access to the Instance to complete its aggregation. **Aggregation** permits parts to be easily replaced. **Aggregation** indicates a weaker coupling between the "whole" and its "part" Classes than is indicated with composition. The graphical representation of **aggregation** is an unfilled diamond (◊).

UML Composition: Composition is an aggregation relationship where the "whole" Class is responsible for creating its "part" Classes directly. With composition the lifetime of an Instance of a "whole" Class is dependent on the lifetime of its "part" Class. If an Instance of a "part" Class "dies", so does the Instance of the "whole" Class (unless the multiplicity permitted '0' Instances to participate). **Composition** indicates a tighter coupling between the "whole" and "part" Classes than is indicted with aggregation by reference. The graphical representation of **composition** is a filled diamond (♦).

Process

Step 1: Identify Kind of Hierarchy

For each Category, examine the name of the Category and ask the following questions:

- Are there different **"kinds"** or **"types"** of <<Category_Name>>?
- Is the <<Category_Name>> **"made up of"** other, distinct Classes?

Answering "Yes" to the first question identifies a potential inheritance hierarchy, while answering "Yes" to the second question identifies a potential aggregation hierarchy. Simply asking these two questions starts the process of developing a CCD.

Step 2: Validate Hierarchy

To justify that a Class is a potential root of an inheritance hierarchy, identify the Attributes and Methods of the root Class. If these Attributes and Methods are applicable to the different "kinds" or "types" of the Class, an inheritance hierarchy probably exists. The "types" or "kinds" of the root Class define possible Subclasses. Repeat this process on each Subclass until as much of the hierarchy as possible has been uncovered. *No amount of discussion can validate an inheritance hierarchy!* Only the identification of Attributes and Methods for the root Class and its Subclasses can justify the hierarchy. As a final check, validate that the Superclass *may be* a Subclass and that the Subclass *is a* Superclass. For example, a sensor *may be* a Temperature_Sensor (or an Air_Pressure_Sensor or an Oxygen_Sensor), while a Temperature_Sensor *is a* sensor.

To justify that a Class is a potential root of an aggregation hierarchy, identify that the Association that exists between the "whole" Class and the "part" Classes is "*made up of*". If, for this domain, deletion of a "part" Class requires deletion of the "whole"

Class, the Association is indeed aggregation (specifically composition). However, if deletion of a "part" Class does *not* require deletion of the "whole" Class (because the "whole" Class has a lifetime of its own, with Methods that are applicable to it whether or not it contains the "part" Class), the Association between the two Classes could either be aggregation, or merely an Association Relationship, whose multiplicity and conditionality need identification.[5]

Step 3: Populate the CCD

Using the selected CASE tool, populate the CCD with the Classes identified that belong to the hierarchy, using the appropriate notation for multiplicity and conditionality provided by the CASE tool.

Step 4: Add Categories

Phase 4 identified the following Categories that appear in any software system. They are repeated here for convenience. If CCDs were *not* previously established for these Categories, add these CCDs to the repository now so that they are in place for subsequent activities.

`IF_CAT`[6,7]	To hold Interface Classes, which are Classes that are utilized to interface to external software systems or to hardware devices.
`Interim_CAT`	To serve as a TBD Category, owning Classes that have yet to be allocated to a Category[8].
`Process_CAT`	To hold the Process/Processor Classes[9] and their associated Controller[10] and top-level GUI Classes.
`Reusable_CAT`	To hold low-level, non-domain-specific Classes [e.g., Name, DTG[11]] utilized by more than one Category and that have potential utilization in other applications.

[5]Stated differently, a "whole" Class may be made up of 0 or more of its "part" Classes. Thus, deletion of a "part" Class requires processing to determine whether or not the "whole" Class must also be deleted. In this case, simply make a decision as to whether to represent the association relationship as an aggregation relationship or an association relationship. The specific case usually indicates which is more appropriate.

[6]For example, on one project, there were four child IF_CAT Categories established: 1) GFS_API_IF_CAT to hold Interface Classes to GFS application software that was utilized to perform some functionality of the project software; 2) COTS_API_IF_CAT to hold Interface Classes to COTS application software that was incorporated into the project's software; 3) COTS_USER_IF_CAT to hold Classes that would launch COTS applications (word processor, spreadsheet, and so on); and 4) External_Net_IF_CAT to hold Classes that would interface to external networks.

[7]Assign management responsibility for IF_CAT now. Implementation of _IF Classes is dispersed over several Categories.

[8]There are times when it is difficult to decide which Category should own a Class: perhaps the Class is applicable to more than one Category, or perhaps budget constraints inhibit the assignment.

[9]These Classes are addressed in Phase 7.

[10]Controller Classes are discussed in Phases 9 and 10.

[11]DTG means Date Time Group.

Step 5: Setup Traversal Capability for New Categories

Remember to set up the CASE tool traversal capability for any newly created CCDs.

Example

Figures 5-3(a), 5-3(b), and 5-3(c) show the CCD for the `Environmental_Condition_CAT` in Booch, OMT, and UML notations, respectively. Note that all diagrams are named properly and contain a Class that is named the same as the Category and is the root of an inheritance hierarchy. Within the hierarchy, the known Subclasses are identified, specifically the `Air_Pressure_Environmental_Condition`, `Oxygen_Environmental_Condition`, and `Temperature_Environmental_Condition`. This inheritance hierarchy is initially validated because of the requirement for conversion routines within each Subclass to convert from the raw data detected by a sensor to the appropriate unit of measure for the Subclass, and vice versa.

For the `Sensor_CAT`, the inheritance hierarchy is validated initially by the identification of the Attributes `Sensor.State` and `Sensor.Address` that are applicable to all `Sensor` Subclasses, and the Methods `Current_State()` and `Current_Value()` that are also applicable to all `Sensor` Subclasses.

Figure 5-4(a), in Booch notation, shows the result of examining the `Panel_CAT`'s `Panel` Class and the identification of the `Panel` Class' aggregation hierarchy. Note the diagram is named properly, contains a Class that is named the same as the Category, specifically `Panel`, and represents the root of an aggregation

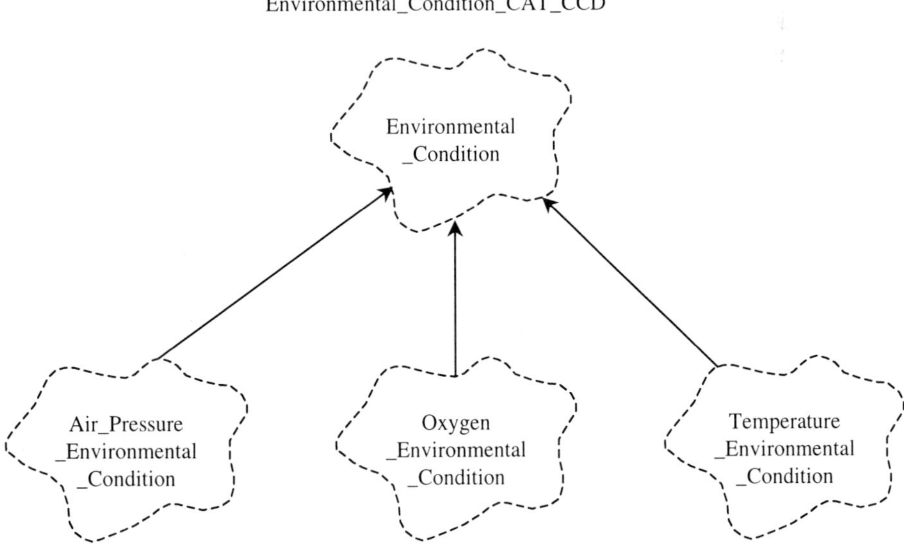

Figure 5-3(a). Environmental_Condition_CAT CCD : Booch Notation

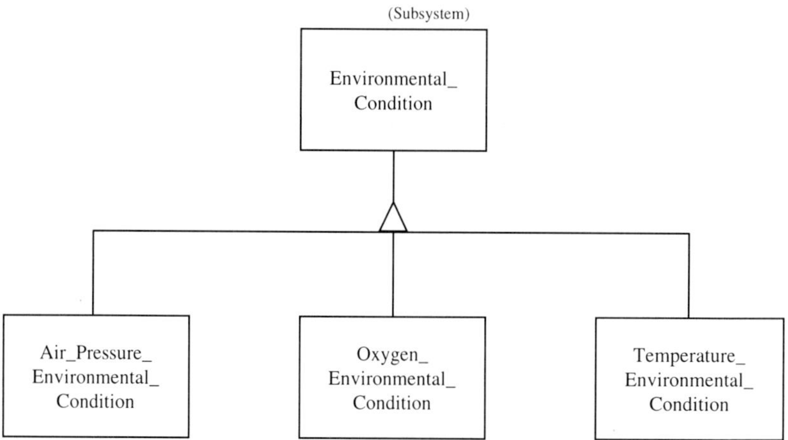

Figure 5-3(b). Environmental_Condition_CAT CCD : OMT Notation

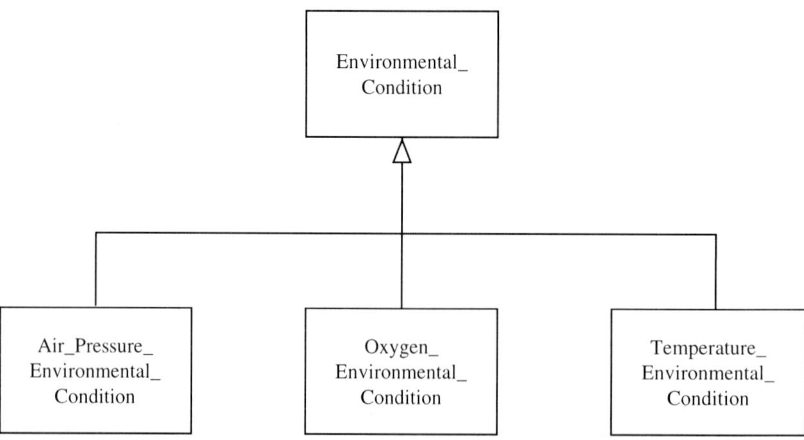

Figure 5-3(c). Environmental_Condition_CAT CCD : UML Notation

hierarchy. The aggregation hierarchy has been initially justified because if a `Window` is deleted, there is no `Annunciator`. If an `Annunciator` is deleted, there is no `Panel`. The `Panel` Class is truly "composed of" or "made up of" the `Annunciator` Class, and the `Annunciator` Class is truly "composed of" or "made up of" the `Window` Class. This is a much stronger binding of the Classes than that of a simple association relationship. Figure 5-4(b) shows the `Panel_CAT` CCD in OMT notation, while Figure 5-4(c) shows the `Panel_CAT` CCD in UML notation. Note the use of composition in Figure 5-4(c). Composition was used rather than aggregation because the `Panel` should create its own `Annunciators` and be responsible for them. The same is true for the `Annunciator` and `Window` Classes.

Recall the previous discussion that addressed whether or not to place the number of parts on the diagram? Some developers take this as direction to "hard code" the values into the code, thus providing an inflexible solution. What if the number of rooms changes? What if the number of environmental conditions to be monitored changes (perhaps there will be a requirement at some point to monitor humidity)? Project direction at the outset of a project, as well as project schedule input, is required to resolve this kind of issue. Note that in both Figures 5-4(a) and 5-4(b), the currently

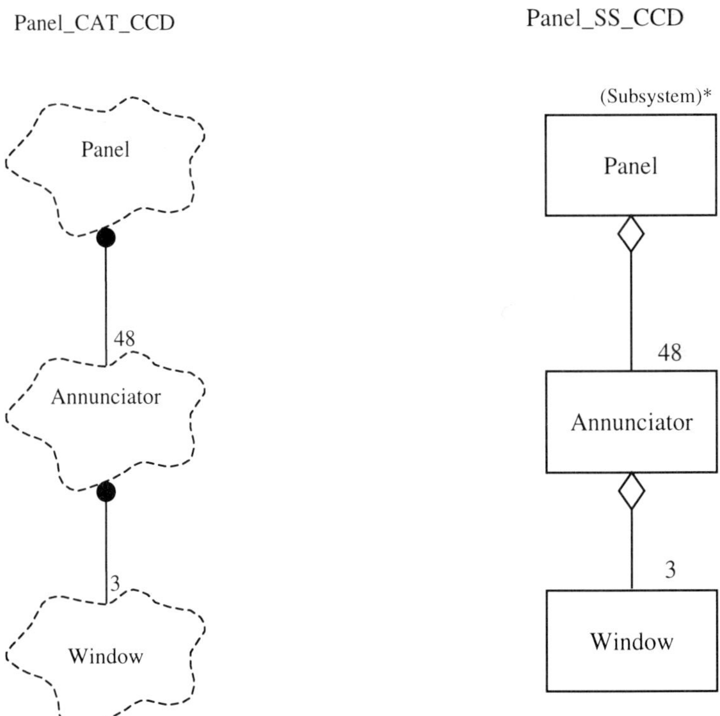

Figure 5-4(a). Panel_CAT CCD : Booch Notation

* StP OMT requires the Subsystem icon to support diagram traversal.

Figure 5-4(b). Panel_CAT CCD : OMT Notation

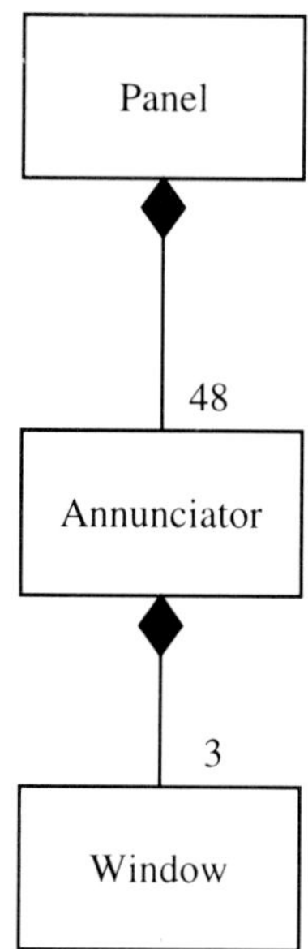

Figure 5-4(c). Panel_CAT CCD : UML Notation

known multiplicity of the parts is identified on the CCD following the decision made earlier to place the specific software constraints on the OO model.

Pragmatic Project Issues

Stay Focused on Hierarchy

At this point, try and stay focused on validating and identifying the inheritance and aggregation hierarchies. The temptation is to start adding Classes, outside of the hierarchy, with which the Classes of the hierarchy have association relationships; but, stay focused on just validating and identifying the hierarchy. These hierarchies form the basis for Category validation, management of the software effort, work allocation, Use Case development allocation, metrics collection, documentation, requirements trace, and so on. Categories are the cornerstone of OO development. Make sure they are identified as correctly as possible now.

Decide Superclass Relationships Modifications

A decision needs to be made by the Project Team as to whether to maintain the Associations between Superclasses on the SCD. As analysis progresses, many Associations initially discovered to exist at the Superclass level on the SCD are refined and exist at the Subclass level. Either the initial Associations need to be deleted on the SCD (because they have been refined to Subclass Associations) or they need to remain on the SCD (in addition to the Subclass Associations). How this decision affects the way Associations are collected for the Class Specification is CASE tool- and project-dependent.

Multiple Inheritance

The Project Team must also make a decision concerning the use of multiple inheritance. For a first or even second project, it is recommended to focus on single inheritance and ignore multiple inheritance. As time goes by and strength is developed in OO software development in general, incorporate multiple inheritance into the technical representation of the system. To represent multiple inheritance in a model that is utilizing only single inheritance, select which is the most significant inheritance for the application and turn the least important inheritance into an Attribute for the root Class, which is then inherited by all Subclasses.

Establish Naming Conventions for Inheritance

Establish naming conventions for an inheritance hierarchy. One suggestion is to add a suffix to the name of the Subclass, which is an underscore, followed by the name of the Superclass. For example, note that the temperature Subclass of the `Environmental_Condition` Class is named `Temperature_Environmental_Condition`. There are certainly other acceptable naming conventions; the point is to choose one and follow it.

Aggregation Relationship vs. Association Relationship

In Booch or OMT, because an aggregation relationship and an association relationship have the same implication for basic code constructs (Class visibility and the relationship coded as an Attribute) do *not* get bogged down in whether to model something as an aggregation relationship or an association relationship. The significant impact in the resulting code comes from deciding which Class creates the Instances, thus the impact is felt when defining and identifying the representation of Attributes and Methods. For UML composition, the "whole" Class should be responsible for creating and deleting its "part" Classes. For UML aggregation or ordinary association relationship, typically some other Class has already created the Instance and Classes that reference that Instance use a pointer, or reference.

A guideline follows: When a decision *cannot* be made between aggregation relationship and association relationship, simply choose the association relationship to capture the fact that there is a relationship between the two Classes. Later, when developing the Interaction Diagrams (UML Sequence Diagrams), it will become apparent if the relationship is aggregation. If it is determined that the original relationship is indeed an aggregation relationship, the model can be changed. Once again, the real implication in the design, and the major decision that needs to be made, is which Class creates, and therefore deletes, the Instance that is the Attribute of the Class in question.

Add/Delete Categories

This is the time to validate the Categories. This is also the time to delete a Category if it does *not* appear to be correct or necessary. Perhaps the Category turned out to be a single Class that could be assigned to another Category. Perhaps the Category was originally thought to be required, but upon further research, appears to be unnecessary. Remember, a ***Category does not have to be an inheritance or aggregation hierarchy.*** Consider, for example, `Alarm_CAT` and `Living_Quarter_CAT`. Neither the `Alarm` nor the `Living_Quarter` Class form the foundation for an inheritance or aggregation hierarchy at this point in time, yet are valid Categories.

Establish Inheritance Depth

The Project Team needs to agree on the maximum acceptable inheritance depth for the software. For example, one level of Subclasses is *not* sufficient to reflect the problem domain, and 15 levels of Subclasses is far too deep.

Class with Category Name

There is always a Class with the same name as a Category, that is based on an inheritance or aggregation hierarchy. For example, in the `Sensor_CAT`, there is a Class named `Sensor` and in the `Panel_CAT`, there is a Class named `Panel`.

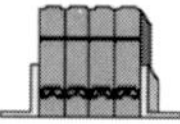

Product(s)

The result of this activity is a *set* of refined CCDs for the software model, with initial inheritance and aggregation hierarchies developed.

For any new Categories discovered or *not* previously initiated (e.g., `Interim_CAT` and `Reusable_CAT`), CCDs are now initiated with traversal capability established in the CASE tool. Additionally, all Categories have been assigned to Category Leads who are responsible for their development.

5.3 DECOMPOSE SCENARIO

Purpose

> The purpose of this Activity is to gain as complete an understanding of the Use Case Scenario as possible within the time constraints imposed by the project schedule. The goal is to understand exactly what the implementation must do to support the Use Case.
>
> Another purpose of this Activity is to identify the Attributes and Methods appropriate for a Class.

Definition(s)

Annotation[12]**:** An **annotation** is simply a set of notes, compiled by the developer, that records his/her understanding of the Scenario resulting from further research on the Scenario and/or discussions with domain experts/Systems Engineering. In other words, an **annotation** is a clarification of a Scenario.

Process

Step 1: Read and Discuss

The process is to 1) read the Scenario for the Use Case, 2) read any other existing material that addresses the Scenario, and 3) hold discussions with domain experts and Systems Engineering about the Scenario.

Step 2: Take Copious Notes

Take copious notes and document the findings, either in the CASE tool, if possible and reasonable[13], or simply in a text file. These annotations will be analyzed in the next Activity because typically the notes reflect a functional view of the satisfaction of a Use Case.

Step 3: Identify Attributes and Methods

To support an OO approach to software development, new Classes, Attributes, and Methods need to be extracted from the Scenarios and annotations.

Example

The following example represents information gathered as a result of discussions with Systems Engineering, with respect to Use Case 16: Operator_Updates_Nominal_Values_In_DB. The Scenario for this Use Case, that was developed in Phase 2, is repeated in Figure 5-5 for convenience.

When the software developer began working with this Scenario, the developer realized the need to return to Systems Engineering and ask three questions. The questions, and their answers, form the basis for an annotation for Use Case 16. Figure 5-6 shows how this annotation could be recorded.

Pragmatic Project Issues

Acquire Domain Expertise

At this point in the development of Object-Oriented methodologies, it seems as if the benefits of a domain expert are still *not* widely accepted. Simply stated, it is the

[12] Not to be confused with an *StP OMT annotation*, a named "note" attached to a "node" in the OMT repository.

[13] An *StP OMT annotation* can be used to capture Scenario annotations.

Use Case 16: Operator_Updates_Nominal_Values_In_DB

Overview:

This Use Case enables the Operator to change the nominal values of all three environmental conditions in the database. These updated values are the nominal values against which the values detected by the sensors are compared to reflect percent deviation.

Preconditions:

1. There are no alarms currently active.
2. SEM_Desktop_View is displayed.
3. The database is accessible.

Scenario:

Action	Software Reaction
1. Operator clicks on the Update All button on the SEM_Desktop_View.	1. Update_All_View pop-up appears.
2. Disable the alarm.	2. Alarm disabled.
3. Enter Air Pressure value.	3. Air Pressure field is updated.
4. Enter Oxygen value.	4. Oxygen field is updated.
5. Enter Temperature value.	5. Temperature field is updated.
6. Operator clicks on the OK button.	6. The Update_All_View pop-up is destroyed, the DB is updated, and the Operator is returned to the SEM_Desktop_View.
7. Operator clicks on the Cancel button.	7. The Update_All_View is destroyed and monitoring continues. The database is not updated.
8. Enable alarm.	8. Alarm is enabled.

Scenario Notes:

Items 3, 4, and 5 may be done in any order. Additionally the Operator does not have to update all three values. This Use Case *permits* the modification of all three values, *but* the Operator may choose to update one, two, or all three. Steps 6 and 7 are mutually exclusive. Step 8 happens regardless of whether 6 or 7 was selected.

Post Conditions:

1. The nominal Air Pressure value is updated in the DB (if OK button was selected).
2. The nominal Oxygen value is updated in the DB (if OK button was selected).
3. The nominal Temperature value is updated in the DB (if OK button was selected).
4. The Operator is returned to the Desktop.
5. The alarm is enabled.

Exceptions:

1. The DB cannot be accessed.

Required GUI:

1. SEM_Desktop_View
2. Update_All_View pop-up

Use Cases Utilized:

None

Timing Constraints:

None

Figure 5-5. Sample Scenario: Use Case 16

Annotation:

Use Case 16: Operator_Updates_Nominal_Values_In_DB

Q1: If Update_All is chosen in Step 1 of the Scenario, must all three conditions be updated?
A1: No, the Operator could update one , two, or all three of the Environmental_Conditions.
Q2: Can the Operator override a previously submitted value?
A2: Yes, because the value is not recorded until the Operator selects OK.
Q3: What happens if an alarm occurs while the Operator is updating the nominal values?
A3: All alarms must be disabled at the start of the update and then enabled after the Operator selects OK.

Figure 5-6. Sample Annotation: Use Case 16

domain expert who should have the knowledge of how the current system works, what future enhancements are desired, and the operational concepts conceived for the new system. More projects bog down due to unnecessary discussion by individuals who simply do *not* have the knowledge, but love to talk. Frankly, Project Teams just don't have time for this. The right people are the key to the success of this Activity.

Acquire Consensus on Scenario

Typically, it is difficult to reach consensus on exactly how the software should produce its desired effect. While clarifying a Scenario, it is possible to get multiple interpretations of a step in the Scenario. It is important that this Activity be managed and assumptions documented for future reviews. Annotations serve this purpose.

Develop Common Implementation Approaches: White Papers

The development of annotations drive the necessity for common approaches to the implementation of the software. For example, common approaches may need to be identified to manage versioning of data within the software, to handle event logging, and so on. These issues, if they don't surface during systems OOA, typically surface now. The Systems Engineering organization continues to assist the software developers by producing white papers that explain common strategic approaches to implementation issues. These white papers, as previously stated, can be referenced by the Scenario, in the "Notes" section.

Annotation Requirements

Not all Scenarios require an annotation. Use judgment to determine which Scenarios require further clarification and which do not.

Annotation Added to Scenarios

It is a project-specific decision as to whether annotations should be added to Scenarios; perhaps they can be referenced in the "Notes" section.

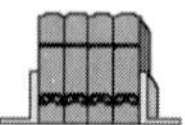

Product(s)

The result of this Activity is a *set* of notes, called *annotations,* for the Scenarios that support a Use Case. Not all Scenarios require annotations.

5.4 ANALYZE ANNOTATIONS

Purpose

> The purpose of this Activity is to discover new Classes, Attributes, and Methods by examining Scenarios and their annotations for nouns, verbs, adjectives, and so on.

Process

Step 1: Extract Classes

This process consists of reading each Scenario annotation and examining the annotation for nouns, adjectives, and verbs. This is the original Booch concept of OO design and is fully documented in his many texts.

Example

Figure 5-7 represents the result of analyzing the annotation previously shown in Figure 5-6. No new Classes were identified, but the Attribute `Alarm.State` was identified as were the Methods `Enable()` and `Disable()` for the `Alarm` Class.

Pragmatic Project Issues

Extract Low-Level Data Items

Look for low-level data items like date, time, name, readiness[14], health[15], and so on. For now, add these Classes to the `Reusable_CAT`. But, be forewarned that a

New/Existing Classes	New Attributes	New Methods
Alarm	Alarm.State (enabled, disabled)	Enable() Disable()

Figure 5-7. Sample Annotation Analysis: Use Case 16.

[14]Readiness here refers to the concept of readiness in the U. S. Army.

[15]Health here refers to the "go" or "no go" status of equipment.

heated discussion may follow. A developer, caught by a time crunch, may argue the following:

> *Developer:* "We do not have time to implement these as distinct Classes! This is just an example of Class proliferation! This is just a language type in a common types Class in C++ or a package of common types in Ada95."
>
> For example, in C++, the following Class can be developed:

```
class Common_Types // C++ Class
{
        // operational readiness
        enum Readiness {C1, C2, C3, C4};
        // go, no go status of equipment
        enum Health {go, nogo, maintenance};
};
```

> while the same Class looks like the following in Ada95:

```
package Common_Types is -- Ada95 package
        --operational readiness
        type Readiness_Type is (C1, C2, C3, C4);
        --go, no go status of equipment
        type Health_Type is (Go, No_Go, Maintenance);
end Common_Types;
```

> *OO Mentor:* "By starting *now* to identify the low-level data items (Classes) , the Project Team can begin to build a library of reusable components at the lowest level, and thus provide Classes, ready for implementation by junior staff, that will be ready to provide services (either by C++s `#include` or Ada's `with`) when needed. By identifying the simple Classes now, we enable both a bottom-up and a top-down approach to the implementation of Classes. Finally, if there really is a time constraint during implementation, by examining the Classes in `Reusable_CAT`, it becomes clear what types need to be developed in a common types C++ Class or Ada package, as well as a vehicle to communicate that information to the developers."

Look for Adjectives

Often, an adjective indicates the possibility of an inheritance tree. For example, consider the two words "temperature sensor". "Temperature" is an adjective modifying the noun "sensor". Consequently, "sensor" needs to be investigated as a potential inheritance tree. As it turns out, `Sensor` certainly is a Class that roots an inheritance hierarchy, with three Subclasses: `Air_Pressure_Sensor`, `Oxygen_Sensor`, and `Temperature_Sensor`.

Is the Noun an Attribute or a Class?

Should a noun be represented as a Class or an Attribute? The answer is *both*. The noun in question becomes a Class, **and** is an Attribute of any Class with which it has an association relationship. For example, consider the `Hall` Class. A `Living_Quarter` is identified by a `Hall` letter and `Room` number. Is `Hall` a Class or an Attribute? The answer, of course, is both. Create a Class `Hall` that is owned by the `Living_Quarter_CAT`. The `Living_Quarter` Class then has an Attribute, `Living_Quarter.HallId` that represents the association relationship that `Living_Quarter` has with a `Hall`. The same is true for `Room` and `Living_Quarter.RoomId`. `Room` is a Class, and the `Living_Quarter` Class has an Attribute, `Living_Quarter.RoomID`, that represents the association relationship that `Living_Quarter` Class has with `Room`.

Is the Word a Noun or a Verb?

Consider the context of a word to determine whether the word under examination is being used as a noun or verb. For example, if the word "record" appears in a sentence, is the word a noun, as in information or data record, or is the word being used as a verb, meaning to *record* something. Another example is the word "log". Does "log", considered as a noun, refer to an actual file of messages, or does "log" represent the verb, to *log* an entry into a file.

Double-Check Method Allocation

Again, following the Booch philosophy, verbs become Methods. Be extremely careful to associate a Method with the Class that owns the data structure that will be affected by the Method. For example, consider setting a new temperature value for all living quarters in the database. This Method belongs to the `Database` Class, not the `Temperature_Environmental_Condition` Class. The `Temperature_Environmental_Condition` Class does *constraint checking* on a value to ensure that it is between the specified bounds, and then converts it to a raw value to be sent to the `Database` Class `Write()` Method.

Establish Method Names for the Project

Set up a list of Method names that can be used consistently throughout a project. Consistent naming will facilitate an understanding of the software by developers, reviewers, and customers alike. For example, use the name `Create()`[16] to create an Instance of a Class, and `Delete()` for actually deleting an Instance from the application. `Use Add()` to add an Instance to a collection or group, and use `Remove()` to remove an Instance from a collection or group, but *not* to delete it from the application. Thus, the difference between `Delete()` and `Remove()` becomes clear. Use `Write()` to store in the database, and use `Read()` to retrieve from the database.

The Word "Status"

The word "status" is another example of an overloaded term in the industry. The word "status" can mean the

[16]Sequence Diagrams in UML now provide the ability to represent the creation and deletion of Instances. Therefore whether a Method is required that is named Create() is project-specific.

- Success/failure of an operation (the status code returned)
- Availability of equipment ("go" or "no go" status)
- Availability of parts of a dysfunctional piece of equipment (parts status)
- Values of the Attributes, some or all, of an Instance of a Class (Instance status).

Each of these has a distinct meaning and requires its own carefully named Method. Suggestions are as follows: either exceptions or an enumeration type named `Op_Status` for the first item listed above, a Method named `Health()` for the second item, a Method named `Detailed_Health()` for the third item, and appropriately named query Method(s) for the last item.

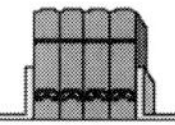

Product(s)

The result of this Activity is a *set* of Classes, Attributes, and Methods extracted from the annotations. The Classes are added to the CCD in Activity 5.5, and then documented in Class Specifications (CSs) in Activity 5.7.

5.5 UPDATE CCD

Purpose

> The purpose of this Activity is to augment the existing CCD with the Classes discovered in the previous Activity.

Process

Step 1: Assign Ownership of New Classes

Remember that all Classes discovered may *not* belong to the Category in which they were discovered. Consequently, it is important to assign ownership to them by allocating them to the correct Category. If in doubt, remember the `Interim_CAT`. Its purpose is to "own" Classes whose ownership is initially difficult to determine. Recall the OO Team? As previously stated one responsibility for the OO Team is to manage the `Interim_CAT`.

Step 2: Add New Classes to the CCD

Examine whether a new Class is, or is not, a member of a hierarchy that already exists. Remember, a CCD is *not* limited to just a hierarchy. Classes in the Category that are related, and therefore belong to the Category, also belong on the CCD. For example, the `Deviation` Class is a Class that is owned by `Living_Quarter_CAT` and appears on the Living_Quarter_CAT_CCD; yet, it is *not* part of any inheritance or aggregation hierarchy.

Step 3: Add the Associations Appropriate for the New Class

New Associations can be discovered in one of two ways: First, examine the Attributes discovered to see if new Associations need to be added to the CCD. An Attribute is the mechanism by which an Instance of a Class maintains its link to another Class Instance. Second, look for sentences that mention two or more Classes for a potentially new Association, and consequently new Attributes.

Step 4: Add Attributes and Methods

Add the Attributes and Methods for the Classes that are owned by the Category, optimally with access rights if known. For overloaded Methods, add them *all*. Add parameters that distinguish the overloaded Methods from each other. The `Database` Class has the overloaded Methods `Read()` and `Read(bool)`. The `Read()` Method reads an environmental condition value from the database, while the `Read(bool)` Method returns whether a living quarter is occupied or not. Distinguishing overloaded Methods in this manner creates unique entries in a repository and therefore contributes to more complete and consistent reports on the repository.

Example

Figure 5-8(a) shows the CCD for the `Panel_CAT` in Booch notation while figure 5-8(b) shows the CCD for the `Panel_CAT` in UML notation. Note that the CCD shows the `Panel` Class' aggregation hierarchy as originally conceived, as well as the Associations that these Classes have with other Classes in the model. The GUI Classes are *not* included yet because GUI Classes are added in a later Activity in this Phase.

Pragmatic Project Issues

Size of the CCD

The CCD can get quite large (particularly if the number of Categories is small), and because of the large number of Classes, it may become difficult to read. Consider printing to a plotter to facilitate the ease of use of the CCD by developers and reviewers. Alternatively, consider decomposing the Category into smaller Categories; in other words, decompose the CCD into a set of integrated child CCDs.

Display the CCD

After printing out the CCD, no matter what size paper is utilized, display the CCD outside your office so others can see it as they go by. A successful project is one where the teams are proud of the CCD, display it, and discuss it. The real benefit comes from the fact that the CCD is available for discussions with engineering staff from other

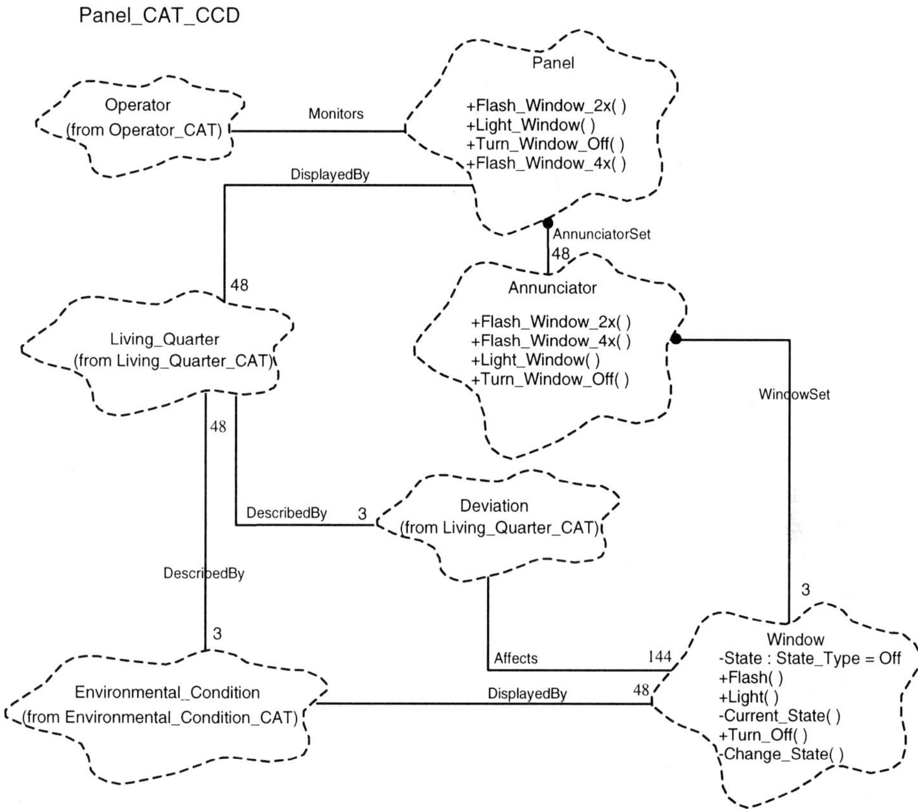

Figure 5-8(a). Panel_CAT CCD : New Classes/Associations Added : Booch Notation

Categories! Displaying the CCD fosters communication across the Categories, which of course is necessary to secure the interfaces.

Remember Interim_CAT

Sometimes it is difficult to assign ownership of a Class. Remember the `Interim_CAT`? Allocate the Classes whose ownership is difficult to determine, or is unknown, to the `Interim_CAT`. Eventually, all Classes owned by the `Interim_CAT` will be allocated to other Categories. Upon delivery of the final code, the `Interim_CAT` should be empty.

Search Interim_CAT

Again, don't forget the `Interim_CAT`. Search the `Interim_CAT` for any Classes that may belong to your Category. Perhaps now, with more knowledge of the domain, it is possible to reassign ownership of some Classes from the `Interim_CAT` to your Category.

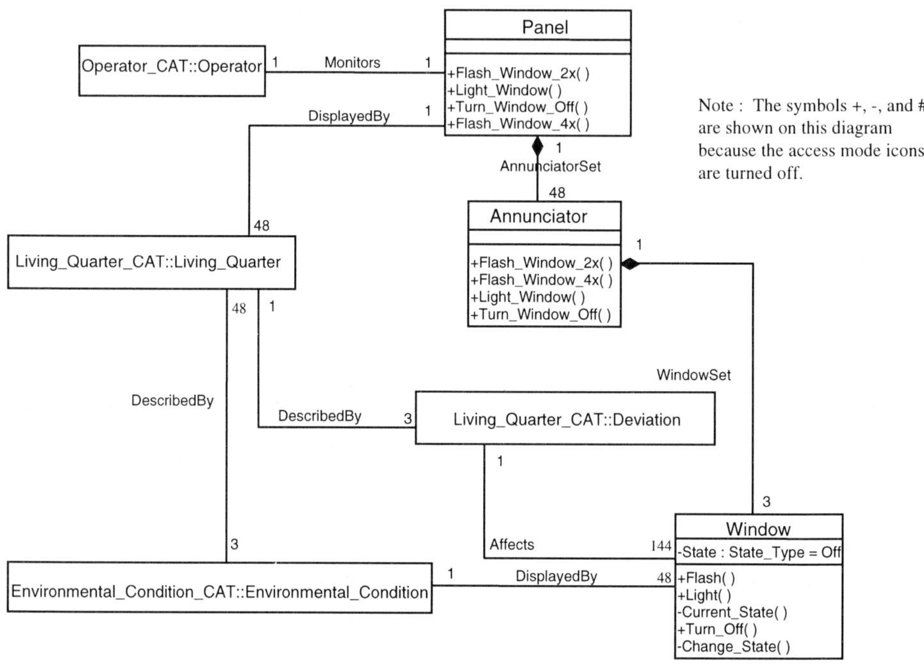

Figure 5-8(b). Panel_CAT CCD : New Classes/Associations Added : UML Notation

Identify External Interfaces

Establish which Classes in your Category interface with external software systems or hardware. Examine the Context Diagram, produced in Phase 1, Requirements Engineering, to identify whether any of the Classes in a Category need to interface with the external interfaces identified on the SCD. Establish those Interface Classes (_IF) that are necessary, add them to the appropriate CCD, and finally, assign ownership of those _IF Classes to the `IF_CAT`. Depending upon the application and the kinds of interfaces that exist, the `IF_CAT` may need to be decomposed into a few child _IF Categories. Consider where an external software system, say ZZ, is used in multiple ways, thus requiring multiple interfaces to ZZ. Then, provide a child Category, ZZ_IF_CAT, to hold the Classes that model the distinct interfaces to the ZZ system.

Establish Interface Control Board

At this point, it is wise to establish an Interface Control Board (ICB) that can begin to manage all interfaces *between* Categories. Interfaces between Classes *within* a Category are under the control of the Category Lead, while interfaces between Classes in *different* Categories are managed by the ICB. An ICB needs to be chaired by the Software Lead, and the Category Software Leads need to be ICB members.

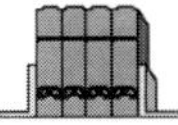

Product(s)

The result of this Activity is an *updated* CCD that depicts all Classes owned by the Category, and those Classes from foreign Categories with which a Category Class has an Association. The diagrams do *not* show Attributes and Methods, unless desired for everyday work purposes. Each customer is different with respect to what should be included on the CCDs.

For the SEM, we decided to show the Attributes and Methods on a CCD only for those Classes that are owned by the Category.

5.6 ADD VIEW CLASSES TO THE CCD

Purpose

The purpose of this Activity is to add the GUI Classes to the OO model.

Note that there is no intention in this text to specify everything that a GUI Architect needs to consider when building a user interface. This Activity simply presents various options for modeling GUI Classes.

Definition(s)

Domain Class: A **Domain Class** is a Class which defines a real world entity extracted from the problem space.

View Class: A **View Class** is a Class which defines how information in a Domain Class is displayed by the system. A **View Class** may provide controls to interact with the system.

Process

Step 1: Examine the Scenarios

Start with the Scenarios. Each Scenario identifies the initial set of GUIs required. Name the Classes with `_View` as a suffix. Undoubtedly, new `_View` Classes will be discovered, so simply coordinate with the Scenario writer to ensure that these new `_View` Classes will be documented in the Scenarios.

Step 2: Initiate the View_CAT

There are several different ways to handle the modeling of View Classes. For the HCC Case Study, the following approach was used. For alternative approaches, see the Pragmatic Project Issues section in this Activity.

Step 2.1 Add View_CAT to the Category List

Update the Category List to include a View_CAT.

Step 2.2 Create View_CAT CCD

Create a new View_CAT_CCD. The View_CAT_CCD is initially populated with the following Class:

`View` – Superclass of an inheritance hierarchy

Figure 5-9 shows the starting point for the View_CAT_CCD, with just the root `View` Class.

Step 2.3 Update the SCD

Because the `View_CAT` is *not* a child Category of any other Category, the SCD is updated to reflect the new Category, and association relationships with the `Operator_CAT` and `Panel_CAT` need to be diagrammed as well. Lastly establish traversal capability to `View_CAT` from the SCD.

Step 2.4 Reallocate Use Cases in the RTM

Do any Use Cases need to be reallocated to the `View_CAT`? The answer is project-specific. For the SEM, the decision made was *not* to reallocate any Use Cases to the `View_CAT`. The developers within a specific Category develop the GUI associated with the Category. Stated differently, for the SEM there are not any developers whose only assignment is to develop the GUI.

Step 3: Add the Required View Classes to the Appropriate CCDs

There are two parts to this step: adding `_View` Classes, and their Associations, to the `View_CAT`, and adding `_View` Classes to the appropriate domain CCD(s).

Step 3.1 Add _View Classes To The View_CAT

In the first part, `_View` Classes are added as Subclasses of the `View` Class on the View_CAT_CCD. Adding the `_View` Classes to the View_CAT_CCD avoids inheritance across Categories (which is messy to manage and implement) and provides a single Category, `View_CAT`, that owns all the displays in the system. Having a single `View_CAT` does *not* prohibit a management/development structure that supports developers currently assigned to a domain Category from implementing the `_View` Classes that are applicable to their Category. Similarly, it does *not* prohibit one (or

View

Figure 5-9. View_CAT CCD

more) special GUI developer(s) from developing all the GUIs. To summarize, the actual development staff assigned to implement the various `_View` Classes in the `View_CAT` is flexible; therefore, this is a project-specific decision.

Figure 5-10(a), in Booch notation, shows four `_View` Classes added to the View_CAT_CCD. Figures 5-10(b) and 5-10(c) represent the same information in OMT and UML notation respectively. To keep the diagrams uncluttered for this book, only the Association of the `Panel_View` Class to the `Panel` Class is depicted.

Step 3.2 Add _View Classes to the Category CCD

In the second part of this step, add the View Classes to the View Class' domain CCD (e.g., add the `Panel_View` Class to the Panel_CAT_CCD, as shown in Figures 5-11(a) and 5-11(b)).

Step 4: Add Association Relationships

Add an association relationship from the `_View` Class to the appropriate domain Class (e.g., from the `Panel_View` Class to the `Panel` Class), also shown in Figures 5-11(a) and 5-11(b)[17].

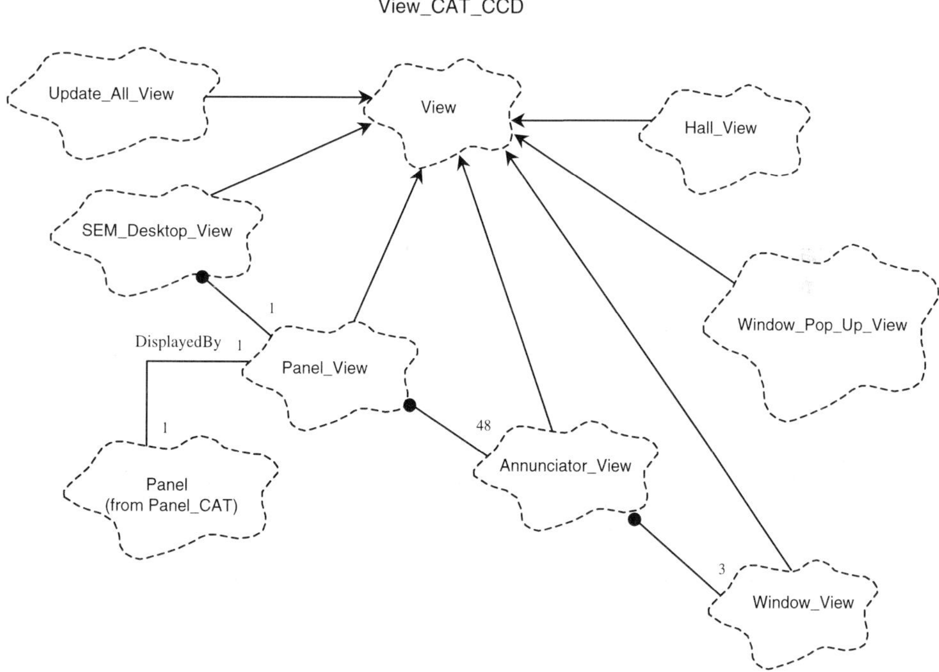

Figure 5-10(a). View_CAT CCD : Panel_View Class Added : Booch Notation

[17]Dependencies are deferred until the OOD portion of the book.

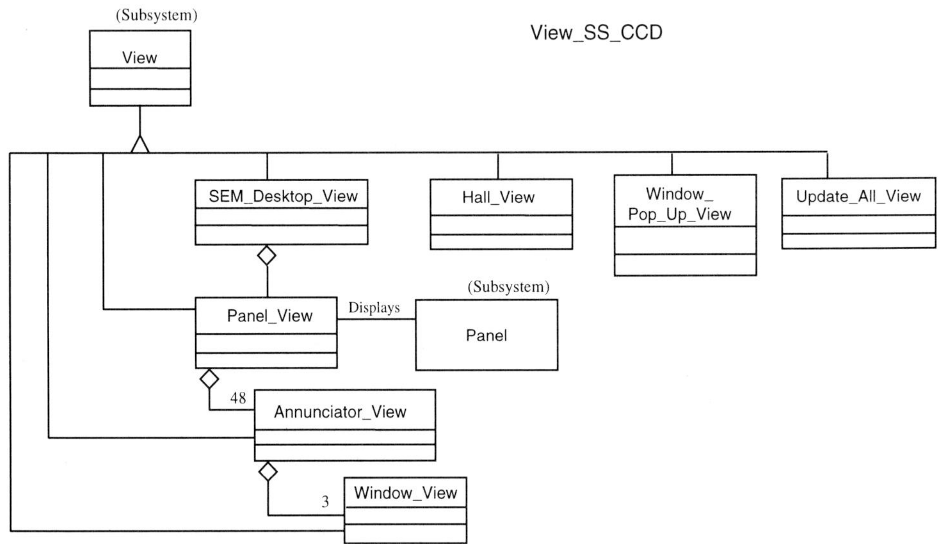

Figure 5-10(b). View_CAT CCD : Panel_View Class Added : OMT Notation

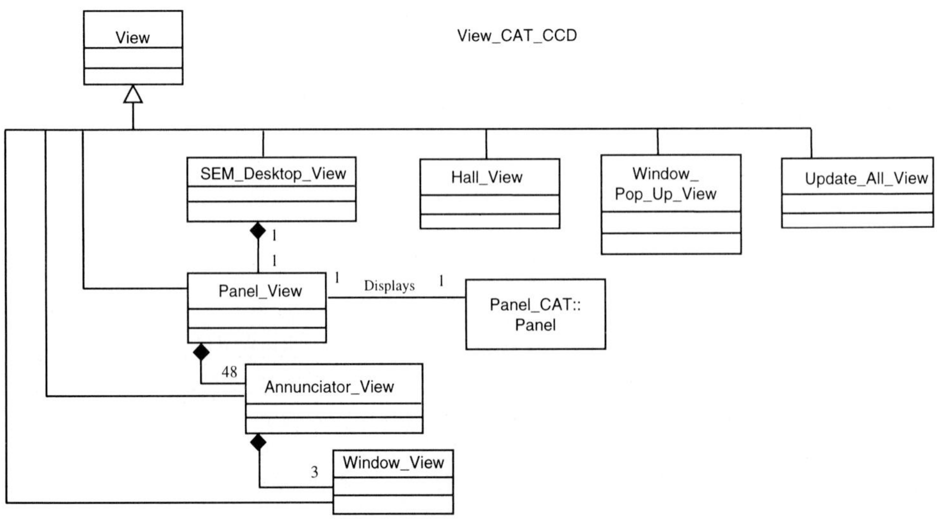

Figure 5-10(c). View_CAT CCD : Panel_View Class Added : UML Notation

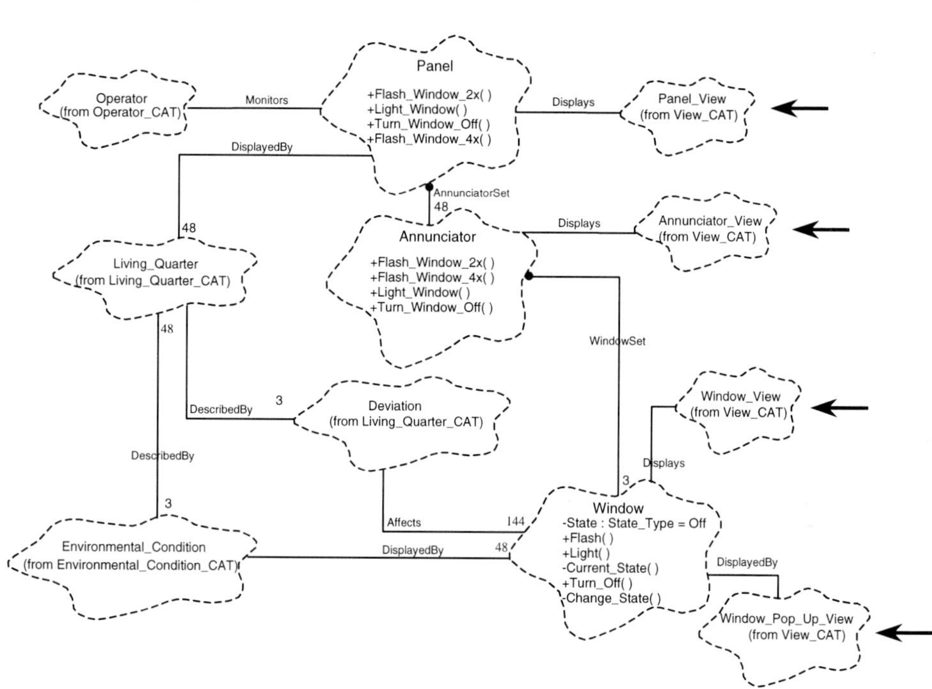

Figure 5-11(a). Panel_CAT_CCD: Panel_View Class Added : Booch Notation

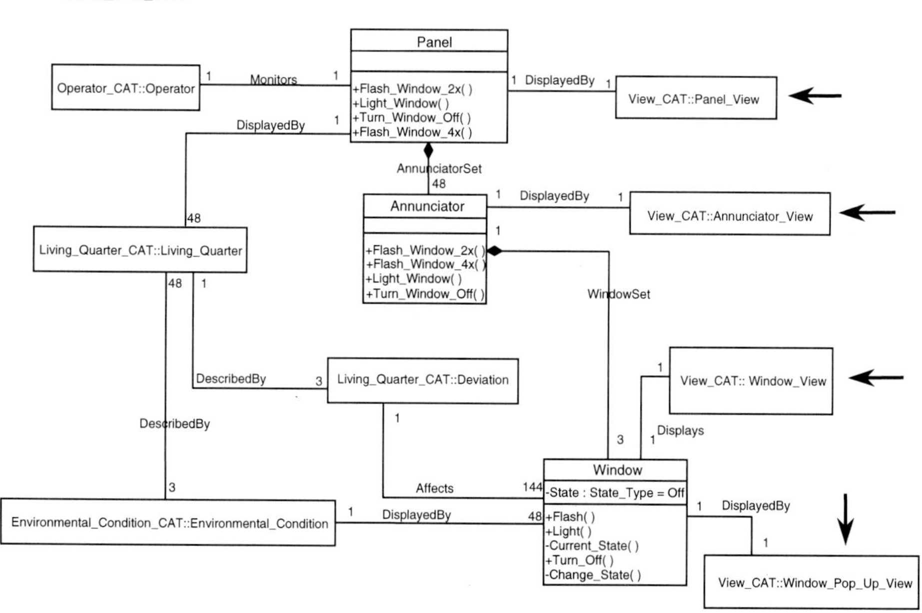

Figure 5-11(b). Panel_CAT_CCD : Panel_View Class Added : UML Notation

Example

Because the discussion of the GUI modeling technique was lengthy, we included the examples in that discussion. The example for the Case Study is therefore already represented by Figures 5-10 and 5-11, respectively. Note in Figure 5-11 that the other appropriate `_View` Subclasses for the `Panel_CAT` have also been added to the CCD.

Pragmatic Project Issues

View Class Modeling Options

As previously stated, there are many ways to model the displays required by a system. Three modeling options follow:

Option 1

The first option is the same as that exemplified in the Case Study, which is shown in Figures 5-10 and 5-11. Each display is described in terms of a `_View` Class that is related to one or more Domain Classes (whose data the `_View` Class displays). Each `_View` Class becomes a Subclass in the `View` Class inheritance hierarchy, and has an association relationship to its appropriate Domain Class(es). This modeling strategy applies regardless of the GUI implementation environment used for the project.

Option 2

The second way to model displays is a refinement of the first option, with refinement defined as going to the next level of detail. The `View` Class, in addition to its inheritance hierarchy, also has an aggregation hierarchy[18], with the `View` made up of `Widgets`. The `Widget` Class is the root Class of another inheritance hierarchy of different types of widgets, for example `List_Widget` (which is also a Superclass with a Subclass `Scrollable_List_Widget`), `Button_Widget`, `Text_Widget`, and so on. The actual `Widget` Subclasses, determined by the project's GUI implementation mechanism, are added to the `View_CAT`. Now, each data item that is displayed can be associated with the exact `Widget` Subclass that is used to display it. The Subclasses in the `Widget` hierarchy can be owned and modeled in the `View_CAT`, or they can belong to a new Category, `Widget_CAT`. Regardless, all appropriate Associations are then drawn to the appropriate Domain Classes as required. Figure 5-12 shows the `View_CAT` with the `Widget` hierarchy added.

Figure 5-13 shows how specific Domain Classes can be associated with the specific widgets that will be used to display the Class data. This figure shows a sample message Category, where messages recording Operator actions are logged. In the Message_CAT_CCD, note the association relationship from the `Scrollable_List_Widget` to the `Message_Collection` Class.

[18]It is most certainly permissible and natural for a Class to be the root of both an inheritance hierarchy and an aggregation hierarchy at the same time.

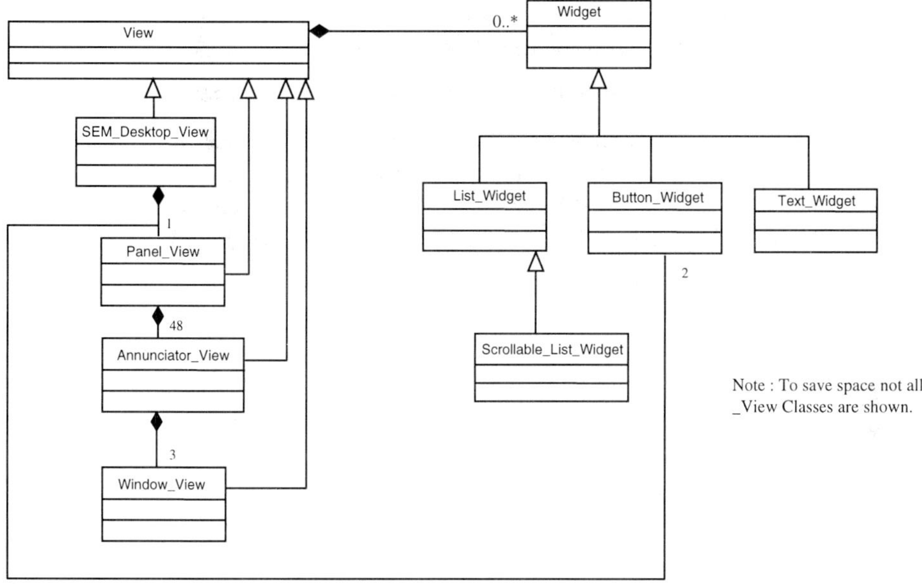

Figure 5-12. View_CAT_CCD : Widget Hierarchy Added : UML Notation

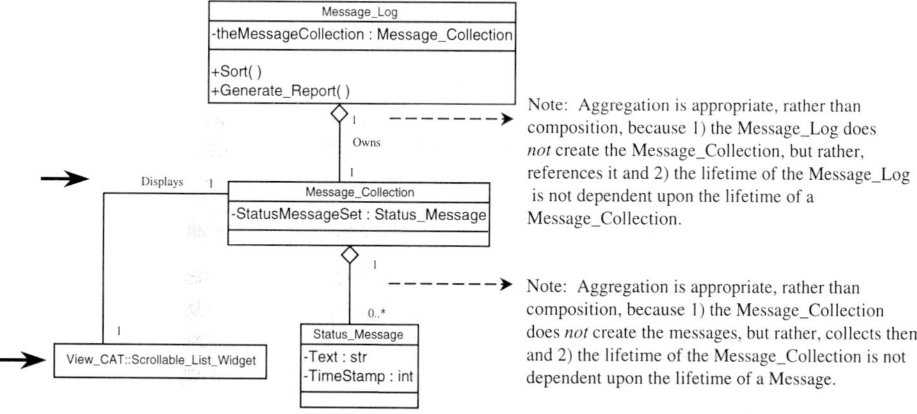

Figure 5-13. Scrollable_List_Widget Association Added to Message_CAT_CCD : UML Notation

Option 3

The third way to model the GUI Classes is *not* to have any `View_CAT` at all, and simply to place all the `_View` Classes with their appropriate Domain Classes in the Domain Class Category. This particular approach is very useful if the GUI implementation is generated from a GUI builder tool, with no inheritance hierarchy whatsoever. An example of this might be when the GUI tools generate straight C code (not C++). In this case, the `Panel_View` Class would be owned by the `Panel_CAT`. Figure 5-14 reflects the change from Figure 5-11 and shows that the `Panel_View` Class is no longer a Class imported from the `View_CAT`, but rather a Class that is now owned by the `Panel_CAT`. Similarly, the `Message_Log` Class can now have a `Message_Log_View`, with an association to the `Message_Log` Class. No other View Classes or Associations need to be identified.

What about View Classes that Cross Categories?

This is *not* an issue. The View Class is simply owned by the `View_CAT` and then appears on each CCD that has a Domain Class that is accessed by the View Class. If the third option above is chosen and a `View_CAT` does *not* exist, simply determine an "owner" Category for the View Class and proceed as previously stated.

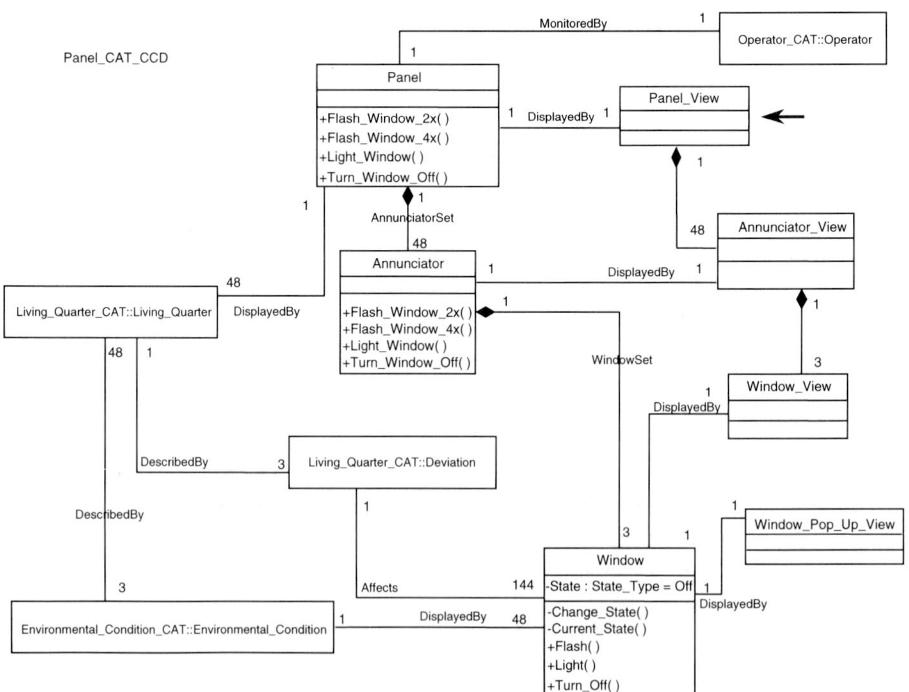

Figure 5-14. Panel_View Class Owned by Panel_CAT : UML Notation

Who's Responsible?

Each project should have a GUI Architect who has overall responsibility to maintain the displays and ensure a consistent look and feel. No matter which method is used to model the displays, the Project Team must decide who is responsible for the implementation of each display.

Multiple Views

Remember that a single Domain Class may require multiple `_View` Classes, each of which should be created as a distinct `_View` Class. Of course, good naming conventions are needed.

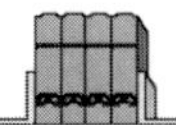

Product(s)

The result of this Activity is a set of completed[19] CCDs.

5.7 COMPLETE CLASS SPECIFICATIONS (CSS)

Purpose

> Classes and their descriptions, as well as Attributes, Methods, Associations, and their descriptions, are now documented.
>
> A second purpose of this Activity is to identify as much information as possible to assist in sizing the database.

Definition(s)

Class Specification (CS): A **CS** is a description of a Class that includes, at a minimum, a textual description of the Class, the list of Class Attributes and Methods, a description of each Class Attribute and Method, and so on. The specific contents of a **CS** are project-specific. The specific implementation of a **CS** in a CASE tool is vendor-dependent. For example, StP OMT keeps some information in a Class Table, while the rest is kept as annotations to a Class. Rose captures this information in a window, and produces a pre-formatted document including the information for each Class. To summarize, the contents of a **CS** are project-specific because of the dependency upon time available and the CASE tool being utilized. In the author's opinion, some CASE tools go overboard on the data to be entered to describe a Class.

[19]Use of the word "completed" here means "completed at this point in time". It does NOT imply that there isn't any more work to be done. Actually, the CCDs are not "completed" until the code is delivered.

Class Specification Document (CSD): A **CSD** is a project deliverable that contains CSs at a minimum, organized by Category. A **CSD** might also include CCDs and STDs.

Process

In general, CSs are Class-based, therefore this Activity focuses on 1) documenting the knowledge gained about each Class, and 2) identifying the database information required to design and implement the database. Therefore, for each Class in a Category, the process consists of the steps outlined below.

Step 1: Agree on the Domain Class Templates

The information documented for each Class, specifying which fields of information are to be provided by the developers, must be agreed-upon and maintained in the CASE tool repository. As has been previously stated, each CASE tool is distinct with respect to how this information is associated with a Class. Provide *specific guidance* as to what information is required to ensure that all documents generated from the repository are consistent.

The following templates, at a minimum, must be agreed-upon. For each template, a suggested minimum set of information is also specified.

- Class Template
  Textual description, parent Category, constraints, persistence, Superclass, Subclasses, "whole" Class, "part" Classes, database partition[20]*, number of Instances, indication as to whether it is a GUI Class (_VIEW), Controller Class (_Controller), Interface Class (_IF), or Domain Class*
- Attribute Template
  Textual description, range of values, persistence, rules of derivation, expected number of associations, Unit of measure
- Method Template
  Textual description, parameter list , mode of each parameter, algorithm overview or citation
- Association Relationship Template
  Textual description, multiplicity description , conditionality description (twice, if conditionality is biconditional).

Project schedule, tool capability, in-house tool enhancement capability, and in-house script generation capability all play roles in determining exactly which fields of the templates can be *successfully* accommodated on a project.

Step 2: Complete the Agreed-Upon Domain Template for each Class

For the current build, document each Class according to the agreed-upon templates.

[20]If applicable.

Step 3: Estimate DB Requirements

Now is the time to estimate how many Instances of the Class there may be, and for the Attributes that represent Associations to other Classes, how many Instances of the Associations there may be. This information is very helpful to initially size the database.

Step 4: Do It!

Take the time to produce the CSs.

Step 5: Write Class Specifications for Classes in the View_CAT

Don't forget the Classes in the `View_CAT`. Identify the Attributes and Methods required by each View Class in the `View_CAT`. For example, some Attributes for the `View` Class could be

- Screen location
- Foreground color
- Background color
- Modal dialog
- Active.

Of course, these Attributes are then inherited from the `View` Class by all of its Subclasses. Some Methods for the `View` Class could be

- Clear()
- Update()
- Manage() (bring the display to the terminal)
- Unmanage() (remove the display from the terminal)
- Resize()
- Move().

Project schedule will determine how far a project goes in documenting the View Classes of a system.

Example

Figure 5-15 represents the CS for the `Temperature_Environmental_Condition` Class—including its Attributes, Methods, and association relationships. Although the OO model does *not* identify an Attribute, it seems wise to include a simple Attribute anyway and update the CCD. This decision turns out to be correct as will be shown in Phase 12, when the Class is implemented.

Temperature_Environmental_Condition

Category: : Environmental_Condition_CAT
Persistent/Transient : Transient
Description : Indicates the degree of intensity of heat (or cold) in a Living_Quarter
Constraints: : Maintained in the DB as raw float value, but constrained to be >= 50.0 and <= 95.0 degrees Fahrenheit
Superclass(es) : Environmental_Condition
Subclass(es) : N/A
Aggregate(s) : N/A
Part(s): : N/A
Expected Instances : 0

Attributes:

theTempValue
Persistent/Transient : Transient
Description : An actual value in degrees Fahrenheit
Domain Of Values : Degrees Fahrenheit 50° <= X <= 95°, in gradations of a tenth (.1) of a degree
Rules: : N/A

Methods:

The_Percent()
Description : Calculates the deviation between two Temperature_Environmental_Condition Instances
Input(s) : Two Instances: a base value and a current value in Fahrenheit units
Output : Floating point value as a percent
Algorithm : [|DB_Value - Actual_Value|[21]/DB_Value]*100.0

Convert_To_Raw()
Description : Converts a value in degrees Fahrenheit to a float
Input(s) : One Fahrenheit value
Output : Float equivalent
Algorithm : Type-casting

Convert_To_Unit()
Description : Converts a raw value in float to a degrees Fahrenheit value
Input(s) : One raw value
Output : Fahrenheit equivalent
Algorithm : Checks to ensure input is within range.

Relationships:

Temperature_Environmental_Condition (Detected_By) Temperature_Sensor
A Temperature_Sensor detects zero or more Temperature_Environmental_Conditons, while a Temperature_Environmental_Condition can be detected by zero or more Temperature_Sensors.

Condition: Temperature_Sensor: If a Living_Quarter is not occupied, the Temperature_Sensor in that Living_Quarter will not detect any Temperature_Environmental_Conditions.

Condition: Temperature_Enviromental_Condition: It is possible that a specific temperature will never be detected.

Figure 5-15. Temperature_Environmental_Condition CS

[21]The use of the two bars (||) represents absolute value.

Pragmatic Project Issues

Find the Right Compromise

The Project Team must agree upon what information should be provided in the templates. A balance must be achieved between the capability provided by the CASE tool and what can reasonably be accomplished by the developers.

Including the CCD in a Class Specification Document (CSD)

Typically, the CSD, in addition to the CSs, includes the CCD for each Category. If the CCDs are physically large and appear on plotter paper, use a large envelope to hold the diagrams. This package can be bound with the document. Alternatively, provide guidelines for decomposing a CCD into one main CCD with multiple supporting CCDs, where each piece can be represented electronically (e.g., each diagram must fit onto either letter-sized or ledger-sized paper)[22]. One such guideline is to decompose a CCD that represents an inheritance hierarchy into supporting CCDs based on the Subclasses at the first level of inheritance. Stated differently, let each first-level Subclass on a Category CCD initiate a new child Category, and therefore a new CCD.

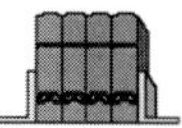

Product(s)

The result of this Activity is a set of CSs that can later be grouped into a contractual deliverable, a CSD, organized by Category.

5.8 DEVELOP CLASS-CENTRIC CLASS DIAGRAM (CCCD)

Purpose

> The purpose of this Activity is to provide a precise diagrammatic view of a single Class. Specifically, the view provided is that of the Class, and all Associations that Class has with any other Classes in the model.

Definition(s)

Class-Centric Class Diagram(CCCD): A **CCCD** for a Class within a Category is a kind of Class Diagram that represents, for *one* Class, all Classes and Associations in which the Class participates. These diagrams, of course, are optional. Remember that **CCCD**s are created as Booch/UML Class Diagrams or OMT Object Diagrams.

[22]In our previous experiences, one customer required plotter paper, while another customer required ledger-sized paper.

Process

Step 1: Agree upon Naming Convention

The Project Team must agree on the naming convention for the CCCDs. One suggestion is to use the name of the Category, followed by the Class name, followed by the suffix _CCCD. For example the CCCD for the `Panel` Class in the `Panel_CAT` would be Panel_CAT_Panel_CCCD, while the CCCD for the `Annunciator` Class would be Panel_CAT_Annunciator_CCCD. Another possibility is the abbreviated name of the Category, followed by an underscore, followed by the Class name, followed by _CCCD, as in PL_Window_CCD, where PL is the agreed-upon abbreviation for the `Panel_CAT`.

Step 2: Develop the CCCD

Basically, this is a mechanical activity that simply provides a different view of the information previously provided in various CCDs. For the Class in question, generate a new diagram, add the Class in question, and then add all Classes and Associations from the set of CCDs onto the CCCD. In Rose, this is easily accomplished with the following steps[23]:

1. Create a new Class Diagram and name it appropriately (e.g., <<Class_Name>>_CCCD).
2. Select "Query -> Add Classes".
3. Select and add the Class that is the subject of the CCCD.
4. Select the Class on the CCCD and select "Query -> Expand Class".
5. In the pop-up, select "Expand to n levels" and set n = 1.
6. Select "Tools -> Layout Diagram".

With this capability in Rose, consistency checking between the CCD and CCCD is automatic. With StP OMT, the CCCD must be created manually, and any consistency check is therefore manual as well.

Example

Figures 5-16(a) and 5-16(b) represent the CCCD for the `Window` Class owned by the `Panel_CAT` in Booch and UML notation respectively. Note that the focus is on the `Window` Class and all its Associations.

Pragmatic Project Issues

A CCCD for Every Class?

The Project Team must agree on what Classes require a CCCD. Not every Class does. Consider doing a CCCD for a Class if the Class interfaces with at least one Class from another Category. Of course, this entire Activity could be tailored out by a project.

[23]Of course, these exact steps could change with future versions of the tool.

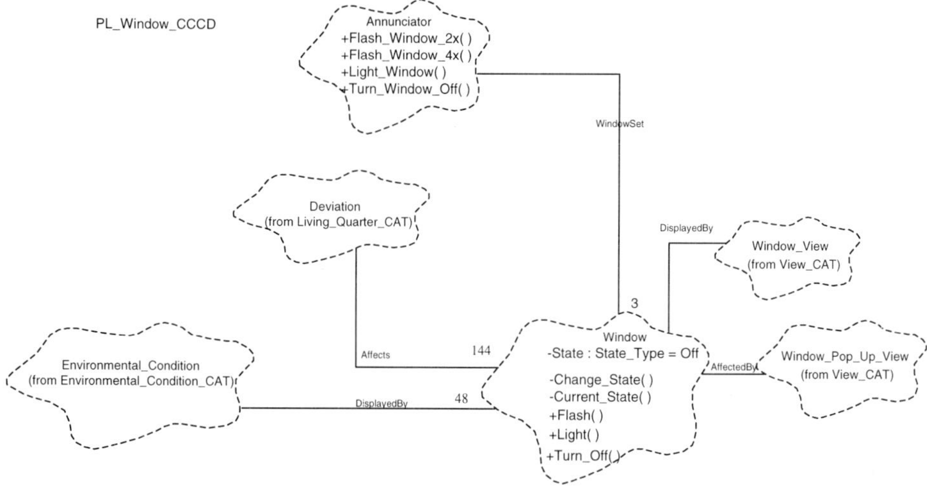

Figure 5-16(a). Window CCCD : Booch Notation

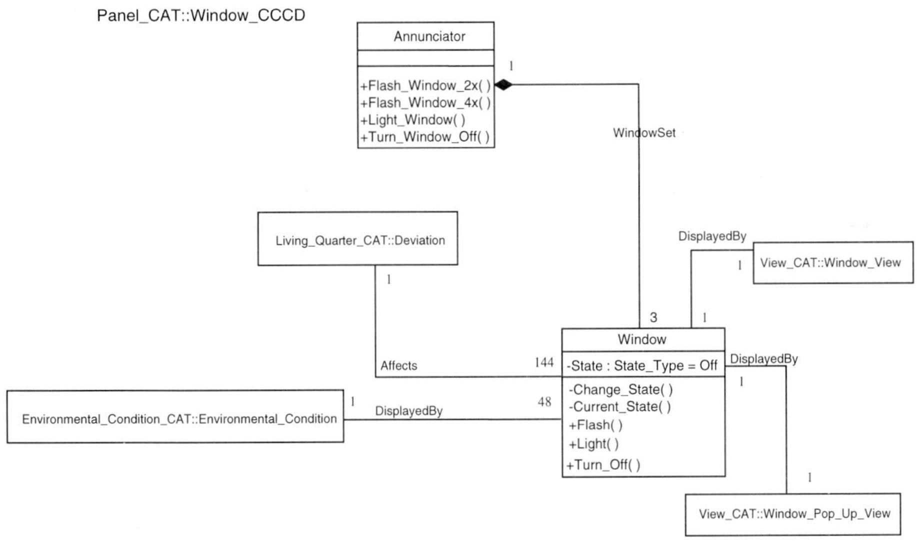

Figure 5-16(b). Window CCCD : UML Notation

Include in Project Deliverable?

A decision must be made whether to include the CCCD in a project deliverable that collects the CSs by Category. A CCCD is particularly helpful when trying to understand a single Class. A reviewer can have the CCD, CS, and CCCD for the Class at his/her fingertips, making the reviewer's job ever so much easier.

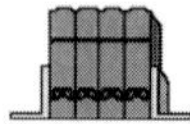

Product(s)

The result of this Activity is a *set* of CCCDs for a Category, at most one for each Class owned by the Category.

Phase Transition Criteria

The CCDs, CCCDs, and CSs will *not* be "*completed*" for a set of Use Cases until the code is actually delivered. Keep in mind that the CCDs and CSs are continually updated in subsequent Phases. However, it is certainly possible, and often necessary, to move on to the next Phase. But, how do we know when to move on? The criteria for transitioning on to the dynamic view of OOA, or developing Interaction Diagrams, are listed below:

- All known sources of resource material have been examined.
- The Systems Engineering organization and/or domain experts can provide no new information.
- Required annotations are completed/analyzed.
- All known requirements have been consumed.
- No more Classes have been discovered.
- No new Associations have been discovered.
- All known Classes are assigned to a Category.
- The CCDs, CCCDs, and CSD have had a successful review.
- All action items have been closed.[24]
- Previous work products have been updated.

The review criteria, shown in Tables 5-1 through 5-6, might also help to decide whether it is possible to move on to the next Phase or whether more time needs to be spent in this Phase to produce a more robust and complete product.

[24]It is also possible to transition to the next Phase with open action items, as long as their closure is managed properly.

[25]Rose maintains an association relationship in its repository as drawn from the source Class to the target Class. Consequently, when extracting the information for deliverable documents, it is relatively easy in Rose. StP OMT requires that a directional arrow be added to an association to extract the association from the repository in a fashion that is readable in deliverable documentation.

Review Criteria

Table 5-1. CCD Review Criteria

#	Category Class Diagram Review Criteria	OOA
1	Are all Categories represented by a CCD?	√
2	Does every CCD in the repository represent a legitimate Category?	√
3	Has the naming convention been followed, e.g., <<Category_Name>>_CCD?	√
4	Has navigation capability between diagrams been established?	√
5	Are the Categories consistent with the Category List?	√
6	Has the initial Class been added to the CCD?	√
7	Are the CCDs consistent with the hardware/software split?	√
8	*Have all inheritance hierarchies been validated?*	√
	Are all Subclass names suffixed with an underscore followed by the Superclass name?	√
	Is the answer to the following question "True"? A Superclass *may be* a Subclass, while a Subclass *is* a Superclass.	√
	Do Attributes in Subclasses have a different domain of values or units of measure?	√
	Do the Subclasses have additional Attributes?	√
	Do the Subclasses have additional Methods or override an inherited Method?	√
	Do the Subclasses represent different "kinds" or "types" of the Superclass?	√
	Do the Subclasses inherit all Attributes and Methods from the Superclass?	√
9	*Have all aggregation hierarchies been validated?*	√
	Methods on the "whole" Class are generally distinct from Methods on the "part" Class. There are exceptions, for example, a "whole" Class may need to configure all of its parts as part of configuring itself.	√
	Multiplicity for the "part" Classes is identified.	√
	Does the "part" Class exist to support the "whole" Class? This does not mean that a "part" Class cannot have an association with other Classes. It means that within the hierarchy being validated, does the "part" Class exist to support the "whole" Class? If the "whole" Class can exist without the "part" Class, re-examine the model and investigate the possibility of just a 1:M association relationship.	√
10	Have all Classes been reviewed? (See Table 5-2.)	√
11	Have Class Attributes been reviewed? (See Table 5-3.)	√
12	Have Class Methods been reviewed? (See Table 5-4.)	√
13	Does the CCD consist solely of horizontal and vertical lines? Diagonal lines are to be minimized.	√
14	*Have association relationships been reviewed?*	√
	Is every association relationship labeled?	√
	Are multiplicity and conditionality identified for all association relationships?	√
	Are association relationship labels placed to facilitate reading from top to bottom on a vertical line, and from left to right on a horizontal line? Are the associations labeled to support the CASE tool?[25]	√
	Does each association relationship follow association naming conventions: no underscores and each word Capitalized except the first?	√
15	No Process or Controller Classes?	√
16	*Are all _View Classes identified in the Scenarios accounted for?*	√
	Do all Classes that require a _View Class have an association relationship on the CCD with their _View Class?	√
	If appropriate, have the GUI Classes from a GUI library been added to the View_CAT_CCD?	√
17	Are the _IF Classes consistent with the Context Diagram?	√

Table 5-2. Class Review Criteria

#	Class Review Criteria
1	Does the Class follow naming conventions? • Name is singular, not plural • Name uses initial capital letter for all words, with an underscore separating words • Suffixed by _IF for an Interface Class • Suffixed by _View for a GUI Class • Suffixed by _Controller for a Controller Class.
2	The Class is *not* an implementation Class (unless mandated by a requirement), for example, "`File`" is not a good name for a Class unless a requirement specifically states that some kind of data is either found or stored in a file.
3	Does the Class represent an entity, not a functional capability (unless the Class is an _IF or _Controller Class)?
4	Is the Class cohesive (represents a single entity)?
5	Is the Class loosely coupled (depends upon a minimum number of other Classes)?
6	Does the Class represent one of the following? • *Tangible entity*[26] • *Specification entity* • *Incident entity* • *Interaction entity* • *Role entity* • *Interface (_IF)* • *COTS (SW or HW)* • *Controller (OOD only)* • *Collection Class (OOD only)* • *Subclass* • *Superclass* • *"Whole" Class* • *"Part" Class* • *Low-level data item* • *Parameterized Class (OOD only)* • *View Class* • *Abstract Class (OOD only).*

Table 5-3. Attribute Review Criteria

#	Attribute Review Criteria
1	Does the Attribute represent a single characteristic of the Class?
2	Is the Attribute independent (not derivable)[27]?
3	Can the domain of the Attribute be represented as either a language predefined type or another Class?
4	Is the Attribute named appropriately?
5	Is the Attribute one of the following kinds of Attributes?[28] • *Descriptive* (helps define) • *Referential* (an association) • *Naming* (a label) • *Kind* (to reflect inheritance) • *State.*
6	Is each Attribute named with an initial capital letter for each word, with underscores separating words?
7	Is the existence of the Attribute justified by the existence of at least one Method that accesses that Attribute?

[26]These first five entries are attributable to Shlaer/Mellor [SHL88].

[27]This rule is difficult to follow and needs to be relaxed on any project.

[28]The first three kinds of Attributes were identified by Shlaer/Mellor [SHL88].

Table 5-4. Method Review Criteria

#	Method Review Criteria
1	Does the Method access an Attribute of the Class? If not, justify its existence.
2	Follow naming conventions? • *Methods that perform "setting" or calculation activities should be named as a verb or verb/noun pair (e.g., Set_Temperature()).* • *Methods that return the value of an Attribute should be named the value returned (e.g., Current_Temperature()).* • *Methods that test a condition should be named for the condition (e.g., End_Of_File()).*
3	Is the Method performing a single capability (functionally cohesive)?
4	Are the Methods named from the following list of project-wide Method names? • *Create (create an Instance)* • *Delete (delete an Instance)* • *Add (to a group or collection)* • *Remove (from a group or collection)* • *Print (produce hard copy)* • *Display (produce screen display)* • *Update (modify an Instance)* • *Update_X (modify Attribute X of an Instance)* • *Read (retrieve from the database)* • *Write (store into the database)* • *Archive (store to a remote device)* • *Calculate_X (determine the value for X)* • *Log (log an event into a collection of events)* • *Change_State (updates the State Attribute)* • *Current_State (queries the State Attribute)* • *Status (returns the values of the set of Attributes that represent the requested information)* • *Calibrate (equipment)* • *Configure (HW or SW).*

Table 5-5. CS Review Criteria

#	Class Specification Review Criteria	OOA
1	*Have all Class descriptions been reviewed?*	√
	Is each Class description brief, clear, concise, and correct?	√
	Has the Class template been followed?	√
	References to other Classes refer to the model name of the referenced Class, and the name and case is identical to the Class name in the models?	√
	If a word is a Category, any reference to that word refers to the Category. Stated differently, any word that is identical to a Category name should *not* be used in any manner other than to represent the Category.	√
	If a word is a Class, any reference to that word refers to the Class. Stated differently, any word that is identical to a Class should *not* be used in any manner other than to represent the Class.	√
	Attributes support the Methods, and Methods access the Attributes.	√
	Do not use implementation terms, for example, "database record" in either the name of the Class or the description of the Class. For example, do not name the Sensor Class Sensor_Record or Sensor_Pointer.	√
	Is the Class description scoped to the application?	√
2	*Have the Attributes been reviewed (Table 5-3)?*	√
	Is each description short, clear, concise, and correct?	√
	Is the Attribute named appropriately?	√
	Can the domain of the Attribute be represented by a language type or by another Class?	√
	Do not precede the name of the Attribute in the actual Attribute description by the name of the Class, e.g., do not write Alarm.State, just write State. Of course, when making references to an Attribute of *another* Class, the name of the Attribute must be preceded by the name of the Class.	√
	Has the Attribute template been followed?	√
3	*Have all Methods been reviewed (Table 5-4)?*	√
	Does the description specify the intended processing of the Method?	√
	Does the description identify all required interfaces to externals where required?	√
	Does the description identify the Attributes (by their model name) affected by the Method?	√
	Are Attributes affected by the Method written in initial upper-case notation?	√
	Are locally required Methods identified in the description?	√
	If the Method is a well-known algorithm, is a reference cited where the algorithm is specified?	√
	Are internal support Methods referenced?	√
	Has the Method template been followed?	√
4	*Have all association relationships been reviewed?*	√
	Is the association relationship named correctly—without being control-specified?	√
	Has the association template been followed?	√
	Is the association description consistent with the association as represented on the CCD?	√
	Has multiplicity been described?	√
	Has conditionality been described?	√
5	*Have the View Classes been reviewed?*	√
	Do the `_View` Classes have the appropriate Attributes?	√
	Do the `_View` Classes have the appropriate Methods and redefined Methods?	√
	Do the `_View` Classes inherit from a predefined GUI Class (if appropriate)?	√

Table 5-6. CCCD Review Criteria

#	Class-Centric Class Diagram Review Criteria
1	Is the Class of focus in the center of the diagram?
2	Is the CCCD consistent with the CCD? • *Associations the same?* • *Multiplicity and conditionality the same?* • *Association label the same?* • *Classes the same?*
3	Are diagonal lines minimized?
4	Is the diagram named appropriately, with the agreed-upon prefix and the_CCCD suffix?

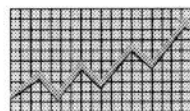

Tracking Progress

Another vehicle can be initiated in this Phase to help the developers from this point on. A report generated on the repository, that provides a representation of the Categories and Classes owned by the Category, can be very beneficial to a Project Team. Category Managers and Category Leads can watch the growth (or decline) of Classes for the project. Figure 5-17 shows a sample report that can be generated from the repository. The report shows the current status of the Classes in the project. Generating this report on a biweekly basis can help keep Classes from proliferating in the repository due to misconceptions and misspellings, as well as help identify Classes that are owned by Categories with which a developer needs to interface.

Figure 5-17 currently shows the "static" diagrams upon which a Class appears. This information is extremely helpful if changes need to be made. After the next Phase, another column can be added that lists the "dynamic" diagrams upon which the Class appears. The column for child Categories is *not* needed for the Case Study, but is definitely needed on large projects where a Category may have several child Categories.

This report will be generated again at the end of OOD Static View in Phase 8, and the difference between OOA and OOD will be striking.

Table 5-7 shows the project management spreadsheet updates made for this Phase. The portion of the spreadsheet that represents Part I (Phases 1-4, inclusive) is *not* repeated, but recall that the entire spreadsheet is included in Appendix E on the enclosed CD-ROM. Note that the total number of CCDs required is the same as the number of Categories, including child Categories. Consequently, the actual number of CCDs completed can be compared, as a percentage, to the total number of CCDs required to monitor progress.

The number of CSs produced can begin to be tracked here, and monitored throughout the rest of the project. In addition to the above, along with the continued

Class Listing By Category

Category	Child Category	Class	Static Diagram
Alarm_CAT			**SCD**
		Alarm	Alarm_CAT_CCD, IF_CAT_CCD, Operator_CAT_CCD, Living_Quarter_CAT_CCD
DB_CAT			**SCD**
		Database	DB_CAT_CCD, Living_Quarter_CAT_CCD, Operator_CAT_CCD
Environmental_Condition_CAT			**SCD**
		Environmental_Condition	Environmental_Condition_CAT_CCD, Panel_CAT_CCD
		Air_Pressure_Environmental_Condition	Environmental_Condition_CAT_CCD, Sensor_CAT_CCD
		Oxygen_Environmental_Condition	Environmental_Condition_CAT_CCD, Sensor_CAT_CCD
		Temperature_Environmental_Condition	Environmental_Condition_CAT_CCD, Sensor_CAT_CCD
IF_CAT			**SCD**
		Alarm_IF	IF_CAT_CCD, Alarm_CAT_CCD
		Sensor_IF	IF_CAT_CCD, Sensor_CAT_CCD
Interim_CAT			
Living_Quarter_CAT			**SCD**
		Deviation	Living_Quarter_CAT_CCD, Alarm_CAT_CCD, Panel_CAT_CCD
		Hall	Living_Quarter_CAT_CCD
		Living_Quarter	Living_Quarter_CAT_CCD, Environmental_Condition_CAT_CCD, DB_CAT_CCD, Panel_CAT_CCD, Sensor_CAT_CCD, Timer_CAT_CCD
		Room	Living_Quarter_CAT_CCD
Operator_CAT			**SCD**
		Operator	Operator_CAT_CCD, Alarm_CAT_CCD, Panel_CAT_CCD, Operator_CAT_CCD, View_CAT_CCD

Panel_CAT		SCD
	Annunciator	Panel_CAT_CCD, Living_Quarter_CAT_CCD
	Panel	Panel_CAT_CCD,
	Window	Panel_CAT_CCD, Environmental_Condition_CAT_CCD, Living_Quarter_CAT_CCD
Process_CAT		
Reusable_CAT		
Sensor_CAT		**SCD**
	Air_Pressure_Sensor	Sensor_CAT_CCD, Living_Quarter_CAT_CCD, Environmental_Condition_CAT_CCD
	Oxygen_Sensor	Sensor_CAT_CCD, Living_Quarter_CAT_CCD, Environmental_Condition_CAT_CCD
	Sensor	Sensor_CAT_CCD, IF_CAT_CCD, Living_Quarter_CAT_CCD
	Temperature_Sensor	Sensor_CAT_CCD, Living_Quarter_CAT_CCD, Environmental_Condition_CAT_CCD
Timer_CAT		**SCD**
	Timer	Timer_CAT_CCD, Living_Quarter_CAT_CCD
View_CAT		**SCD**
	Annunciator_View	View_CAT_CCD, Panel_CAT_CCD
	Hall_View	View_CAT_CCD, Living_Quarter_CAT_CCD, Operator_CAT_CCD
	Panel_View	View_CAT_CCD, Panel_CAT_CCD, Operator_CAT_CCD
	SEM_Desktop_View	View_CAT_CCD, Operator_CAT_CCD
	Update_All_View	Panel_CAT_CCD, Living_Quarter_CAT_CCD, Operator_CAT_CCD
	Window_View	View_CAT_CCD, Panel_CAT_CCD, Operator_CAT_CCD
	Window_Pop_Up_View	View_CAT_CCD, Operator_CAT_CCD, Panel_CAT_CCD

Figure 5-17. Project Classes Reported by Category

Table 5-7. Project Management Spreadsheet: Phase 5

HCC Project Management Spreadsheet						
Number	**Phase Name**	**Activity**	**Charge Number**	**Product**	**Progress Metric**	**% Weight**
5	**Software OOA–Static View**		**SW-OOAS-5**			
5.1		Initiate CCD	SW-OOAS-5.1	CCD	# initiated CCDs	
5.2		Refine Inheritance/Aggregation Hierarchies	SW-OOAS-5.2	CCD (Updated)		
5.3		Decompose Scenario	SW-OOAS-5.3	Annotation	# Annotations	
5.4		Analyze Annotation	SW-OOAS-5.4		# Annotation analyzed	
5.5		Update CCD	SW-OOAS-5.5	CCD (Updated)		
5.6		Add View Classes	SW-OOAS-5.6	CCD (Updated)	# CCDs	0.50
5.7		Develop CSs	SW-OOAS-5.7	CS	# CSs completed	0.45
5.8		Develop CCCDs	SW-OOAS-5.8	CCCD	# CCCDs	0.05

monitoring of the number of Use Cases per build, the Project Team can also begin to monitor the

- Number of Classes per Category
- Average number of Methods per Class
- Average number of Attributes per Class.

Again, these data should be collected on a Category-by-Category basis, summarized on a Domain-by-Domain basis, and, if desired, summarized on a project-wide basis. These data need to be collected periodically so that radical changes in data can be detected early, thus permitting corrective action to take place in a timely manner.

PHASE 6

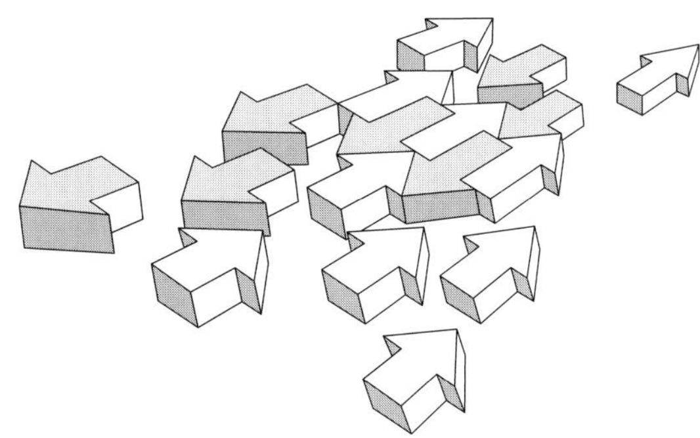

Software OOA–Dynamic View

PHASE OVERVIEW

The previous Phase focused on the most stable part of the software system, its basic atomic elements, or Classes. Now it is time to focus on the dynamic behaviors of a system, specifically the

- Individual internal behavior of a Class, and
- Collaborative behavior of Classes

that are required to satisfy requirements. As Figure 6-1 shows, the individual behavior of a Class is represented by a State Transition Diagram (STD), while the collaborative behavior of Classes is represented by Interaction Diagrams (IDs). Table 6-1 compares the *focus* of both the static and dynamic views, while Table 6-2 compares the *products* produced. The tables do *not* attempt to compare, or make analogies about, the entities listed. Stated differently, do *not* try and make any analogy between Category and State just because they are on the same line. Quite simply, the "STATIC" view focuses on Categories, Classes, Attributes, Methods, and Associations, while the "DYNAMIC" view focuses on different entities, specifically states, state transitions, and Use Cases.

This Phase describes the *process/products* for developing/documenting the behavioral requirements, both intra-Class and inter-Class, of a software system.

6.1 DEVELOP STATE TRANSITION DIAGRAM (STD)

A State Transition Diagram (STD) is a graphical representation of the life cycle of the Instances of a Class. STDs focus on the life cycle phases of a Class, whose values represent the domain of values for an Attribute of a Class, typically named `State`.

Determining the existence of a State Attribute and its set of legal values is the very first step in producing the OOA dynamic view. A State Attribute represents the center of the dynamic behavior of a Class, and therefore is the basis for an STD.

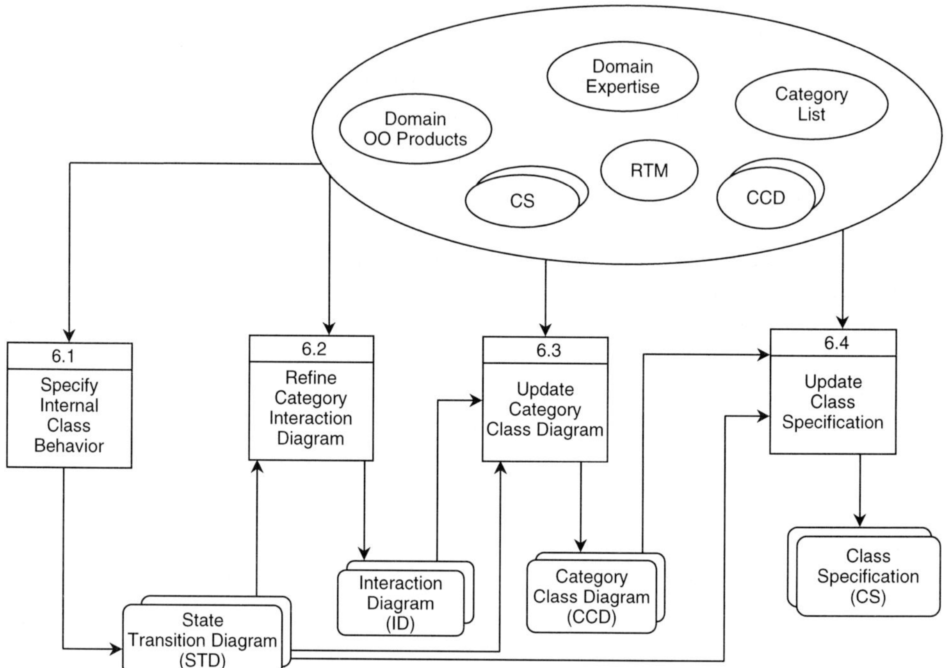

Figure 6-1. Software OOA - Dynamic View Phase Description Diagram

Table 6-1. Comparing Static/Dynamic Atomic Components

Static	Dynamic
Category	State
Class	State Transition
Attribute	Use Case
Method	
Association	

Table 6-2. Comparing Static/Dynamic Atomic Products

Static	Dynamic
Graphic	**Graphic**
Category Class Diagram (CCD)	State Transition Diagram (STD)
Class-Centric Class Diagram (CCCD)	Interaction Diagram (ID)
Textual	**Textual**
Class Specification (CS)	State Attribute

Purpose

The purpose of identifying a State Attribute is to determine whether or not an STD is warranted. *Not* all Classes warrant an STD.

Definition(s)

State Attribute: A **State Attribute** is an Attribute for a Class, named `State`, whose set of values represents the phases of the life cycle of the Class. Phases of a life cycle represent "snapshots" of a Class as it progresses through its lifetime. Each phase of a Class' life cycle becomes one value of the **State Attribute** of a Class.

State Transition Diagram (STD): An **STD** is a diagram that represents the internal behavior of a Class. An **STD** depicts the life cycle phases of a Class and the events that cause an Instance to transition from one state to another.

Process

Step 1: Establish Naming Conventions for STDs

Name the STDs <Class_Name>_STD, as in Alarm_STD. Other naming conventions are possible; the point is to choose one.

Step 2: Develop the STD

Because this Step involves many substeps, a separate figure, Figure 6-2, explicitly shows one thought process that can be used to develop an STD. The thought process is described next in more detail.

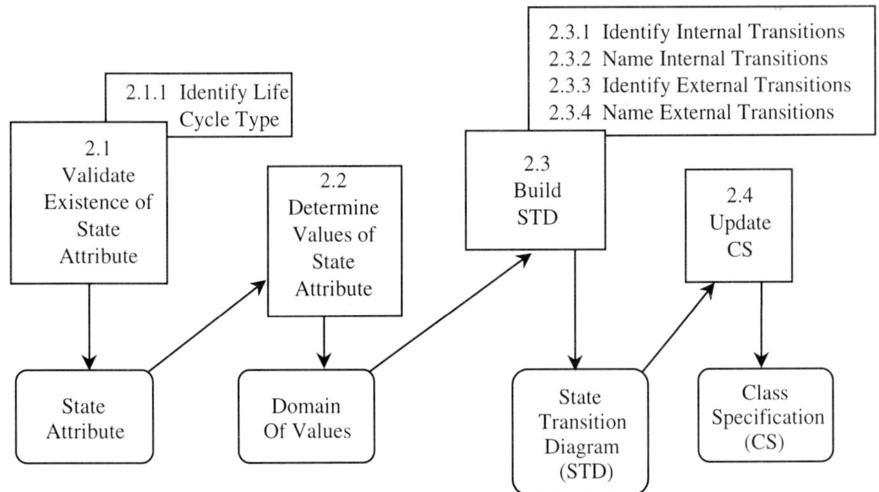

Figure 6-2. Activity 6.1, Step 2, Sub-Activities

Step 2.1 - Validate Existence of State Attribute

Determine whether or not a Class has a State Attribute. *Not* all Classes have a State Attribute. Any Class whose processing differs depending upon the state of the Class requires a State Attribute, and therefore, an STD needs to be produced. Classes that do *not* have a State Attribute, and therefore do *not* require an STD, are Classes that have very simple dynamic behavior.

Consider the Class `Temperature_Environmental_Condition`. `Temperature_Environmental_Condition` simply provides a range of values for one Attribute and simple Methods, for example `ConvertToRaw()`, `ConvertToUnit()`, `The_Percent()`, and so on. There are no *significant* behavioral requirements for this Class. Consequently, there is no requirement for an STD for the `Temperature_Environmental_Condition` Class.

Next, consider the `Window` Class. A window can only transition to a more severe alarm condition, a window *cannot* degrade gracefully by transitioning from flashing four times a second to flashing two times a second. However, a window can always transition *up* a level of severity. If a window is currently in the Flash_2X state, the window *can* transition to the Flash_4X state. Consequently, the behavior of a window differs depending upon the current value of the `Window.State` Attribute. Developing an STD for the `Window` Class forces a complete understanding and representation of when a window can change state and when it *cannot*. The implementation of Methods that act on a `Window` need to query the current value of `Window.State` before permitting further processing of the Method. To summarize, the existence of a State Attribute for the `Window` Class, and therefore an STD, has been justified.

Step 2.1.1 Identify Life Cycle Type

To help determine whether a Class has a State Attribute, first see if it has a recognizable life cycle. There appear to be three different kinds of life cycles:

1) Birth/Death

2) Cyclic

3) Hybrid (e.g., a Cyclic cycle embedded in a Birth/Death cycle).

Each of these is discussed below.

Birth/Death Life Cycle: To see if a Class has a birth/death life cycle, examine the Class to see if it goes through specific transitions and then dies. For example, a Class named `Person` might have the following life cycle:

newborn, infant, toddler, child, teenager, young adult, adult, elderly, deceased

The fully-qualified name of the State Attribute for `Person` that describes its life cycle is `Person.State`. The domain of values for `Person.State` are as listed above. These values represent the phases of the life cycle of the Class.

Cyclic Life Cycle: When a Class is represented by a cyclic life cycle, the final phase transitions to another phase of the life cycle, typically the first phase (but not always); thus, an Instance of the Class never "dies." Consider the `Alarm` class in the Case Study. An Instance of `Alarm` transitions from Enabled to Disabled and back to Enabled, and so on.

Hybrid Life Cycle: A Class can have a cyclic "sub-cycle" embedded in a birth/death life cycle, or even within a cyclic life cycle. For example, consider the `Alarm` Class just discussed. The `Alarm` Class has an Attribute `Alarm.Audible` with values (True, False) embedded in the `Alarm.State` cycle (Enabled, Disabled).

Finally, consider the UNIX® program, `xbiff`[1]. This program is an example of when a cyclic cycle is embedded within a birth/death cycle. An `xbiff` window is created when `xbiff` is started and immediately transitions to the No Mail phase or New Mail phase, depending if the mailbox has any new mail. The `xbiff` window then transitions back and forth between the No Mail phase and the New Mail phase as new mail arrives and is read by the user. The `xbiff` window is destroyed when `xbiff` is terminated.

Step 2.2 - Determine Values of State Attribute

Values of a State Attribute represent the phases of the life cycle of a Class. Obtaining the phases and therefore, the values of the State Attribute, is perhaps the most difficult part of producing the dynamic model. There is no "cookbook" approach to identifying the values of a State Attribute. Experience leads to a more timely identification of the existence of a State Attribute, as well as to the identification of its values. The first attempt is very rarely the correct representation. The previous sub-activity of identifying whether a Class has a birth/death, cyclic or hybrid life cycle, and staying focused on the application being modeled, will help.

The domain of values for the `Alarm.State` Attribute are

`Alarm.State` (Enabled, Disabled)

The values for the `Window.State` Attribute are

`Window.State` (Off, Lit, Flash_2X, Flash_4X)

Step 2.3 - Build the STD

The next sub-activity is to build the STDs for those Classes for which a State Attribute has been identified. As an aid to building STDs, follow the steps below:

[1]The `xbiff` program is a program that displays a mailbox in a window under X-windows. When new mail arrives, the `xbiff` window changes color and the flag on the mailbox is raised.

Step 2.3.1 Identify Internal Transitions

Examine all possible permutations[2] of pairs of phases within the Class to determine if a transition between two phases is possible. If a transition between the phases is possible, an internal transition exists between the two phases. An internal transition therefore represents the fact that a transition is possible between two phases within a Class.

When analyzing a Class and the possible transitions between two phases of a Class, be sure to treat the two possible transitions between the two phases as two distinct transitions. Just because a Class can transition from phase A to phase B does not mean that the Class can, or will, transition from phase B to phase A. Furthermore, if a Class can transition from phase B to phase A, that transition should be viewed as an activity independent from the activity of transitioning from phase A to phase B[RUM91].

Below are sample questions a developer might ask to illustrate the above concept.

> Can a window transition from Off to Flash_2x? (Yes)
>
> Can a window transition from Flash_2x to Flash_4x? (Yes)
>
> Can a window transition from Flash_4x to Flash_2x? (No)

The use of a State Transition Table (STT) is helpful, particularly when the number of states is large or confusing (see Table 6-3). To build an STT, name the rows and columns of the table with the phases (values) of the State Attribute. Then, simply place a "Y" for Yes or an "N" for No in each cell if a transition *from* the phase named in the row *to* the phase named in the column is possible. Use an STT to help organize your thinking.

Step 2.3.2 Name Internal Transitions

To name the transitions, choose either a verb/noun pair or a conditional clause. If choosing a verb/noun pair, use the name of the Class for the noun, and for the verb, modify the phase value to reflect the action on the Class. For example, when

Table 6-3. STT for Window Class

	Off	Lit	Flash_2x	Flash_4x
Off	—	Y	Y	Y
Lit	Y	—	Y	Y
Flash_2x	Y	N	—	Y
Flash_4x	Y	N	N	—

[2]The word "permutation" is used in the mathematical sense, as opposed to the word "combination".

choosing the name of the transition to the Off state, take the state value, Off, and turn it into a verb acting on the Class, for example, Turn_Off_Alarm()[3]. Taking this approach leads to Methods that may *not* have been previously identified.

When dealing with conditions, the Class name typically appears first, as in Deviation>=3%, and so on. Remember that these transitions represent required processing for a Class, and therefore help identify Methods for the Class.

Step 2.3.3 Identify External Stimuli

An external stimulus is a stimulus initiated from outside a Class, that, when received by a Class in a specific state, causes the Class to perform some processing, followed by a transition to another state, or possibly, retention in the same state.

To identify external stimuli, examine the Class in each state and ask the following question:

> What external stimuli can affect the Class in this state?

Begin by examining the Use Case list, because each Use Case represents a potential external stimulus to a Class. First, identify the Class whose responsibility it is to satisfy the Use Case. Then, ask yourself in which state(s) can the Class accept the Use Case?

Step 2.3.4 Name External Stimuli

External stimuli, other than Use Cases, are named in the same manner as internal transitions, except the name of the Class that is the source of the external stimuli, followed by a semi-colon (;), is prepended to the transition name. For example, if the `Window` Class sends a stimulus named Disable_Alarm to the `Alarm` Class, the name of the transition is `Window:Disable_Alarm`. This naming convention allows you to look at a Class STD and immediately separate the internal transitions from the external stimuli. Additionally, the name of the external transition indicates precisely which Class is the source of the event causing the transition, thus clearly indicating with which other Classes the Class in question interfaces.

In UML, the notation is the name of the event on one line (e.g., Start Flashing), followed on a separate line by the fully qualified name of the Message (preceded by a ^), as in `^Alarm.Sound_Alarm()`.

Example

Figure 6-3(a) depicts the STD for the `Window` Class in Booch notation, while Figure 6-3(b) represents the same STD in UML notation. Figure 6-4(a) depicts the STD for the `Alarm` Class in Booch notation, while 6-4(b) represents the same STD in UML notation.

[3]The Method `Turn_Off_Alarm()` was changed to `Silence_Alarm()` in the solution, to be more compatible with `Sound_Alarm()`.

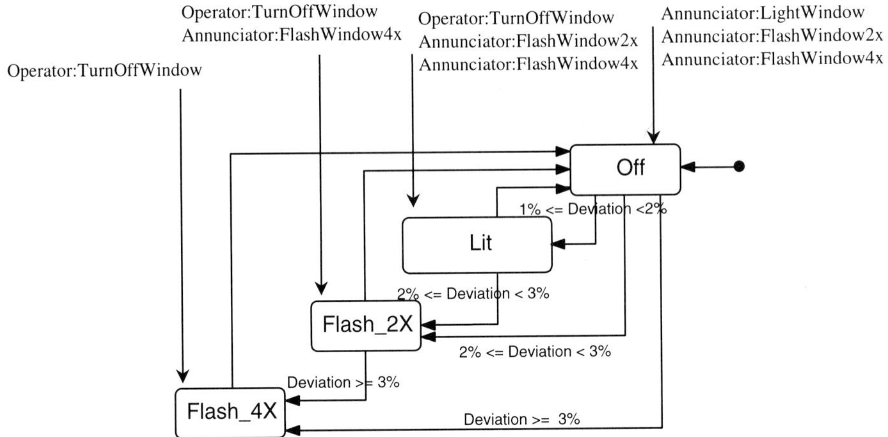

Figure 6-3(a). Window Class STD : Booch Notation

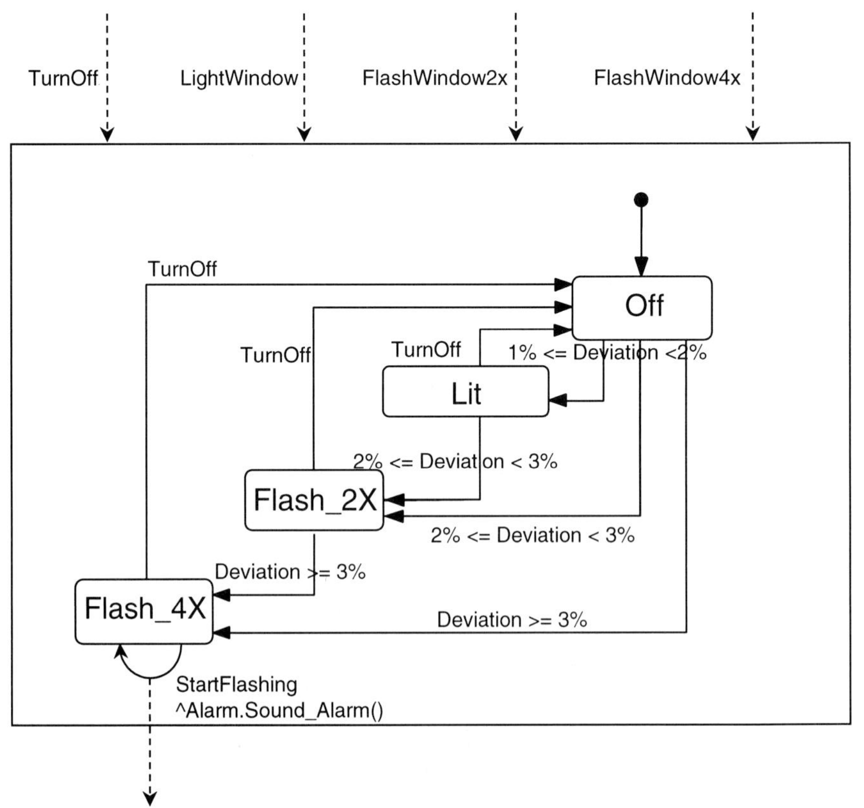

Figure 6-3(b). Window Class STD : UML Notation

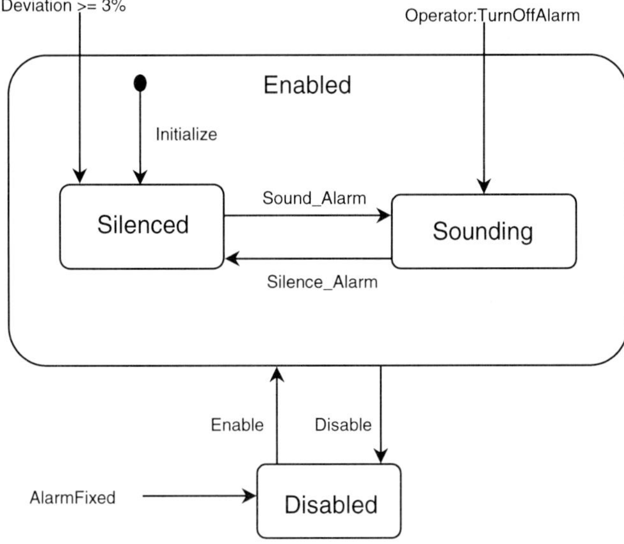

Figure 6-4(a). Alarm Class STD : Booch Notation

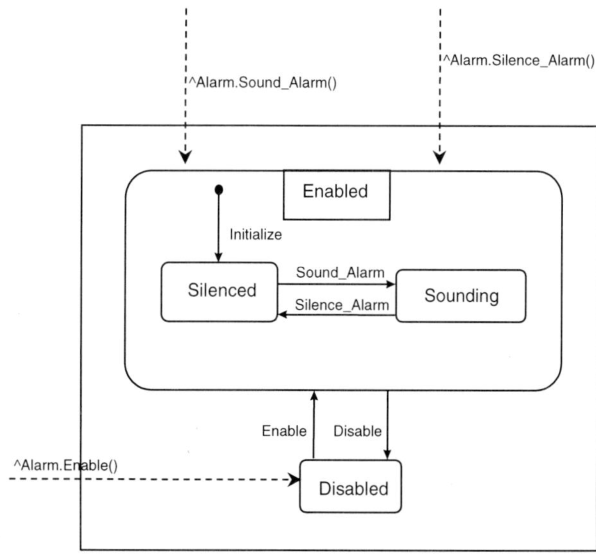

Figure 6-4(b). Alarm Class STD : UML Notation

Pragmatic Project Issues

Do Not Consider Creation/Deletion of Instances

It is easier to model and present the resulting STDs when an STD assumes the existence of an Instance of a Class. Consequently, the recommendation is *not* to include states associated with the creation/deletion of Objects/Instances.

Pay Attention to Inheritance Hierarchies

If the State Attribute is identified for a Superclass, all the Subclasses inherit that State Attribute and only one STD needs to be produced for the entire hierarchy. If however the Subclasses have their own distinct behavior, and therefore distinct State Attributes, an STD needs to be provided for each of the Subclasses, and potentially another STD needs to be produced for the Superclass.

Pay Attention to Aggregation Hierarchies

Typically the State Attribute of a "whole" Class is different than the STD for its "part" Classes. This makes sense, of course, because a "part" Class is a Class in its own right.

Stay Domain-Specific

Focus on identifying the State Attribute for *this specific application.* Don't get confused or sidetracked by thinking of other application domains. In one application, a `Person.State` Attribute might have the values Active and Retired. In another application domain, the `Person.State` Attribute might have a different set of values. Consider, for example, a license registration system. The values for the `Person.State` Attribute might be as follows: No_Points, Less_Than_6_Points, Twelve_Points_or_ More, etc.

This clearly shows how a State Attribute for a Class can have a different domain of values from application to application. A State Attribute for one application might *not* be needed, might need to be redefined for another application, or might lead to an inheritance tree, based on different State Attributes to permit the reuse of the Class in different applications.

Remembering the requirements will help focus the identification of the domain of values of a State Attribute within a *specific application domain.*

Birth/Death STD

Birth/Death STDs always have an initial and a terminal state.

Put Something on Paper

When starting to build an STD, it is important to take an initial educated guess as to the values for the State Attribute, and to begin to model the behavior. The model will be refined as the work progresses. Procrastination, hesitation, and fear of making a mistake do *not* allow a project to move forward.

Structure the Thinking

Use additional tables, like STTs, if necessary, to structure your thought process.

Examine the Use Cases

Use Cases identify external stimuli. Be sure to include these external stimuli on the STDs.

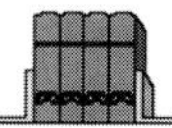

Product(s)

The end result of this Activity is a collection of STDs produced for those Classes whose internal behavior warrants a State Attribute. There will *not* be an STD for every Class.

6.2 REFINE CATEGORY INTERACTION DIAGRAM (CID)

The reason for producing the *system*-level Category Interaction Diagrams (CIDs), during Phase 3, System OOA, was to help validate the identified Categories, validate the intended purpose of each Category, and ensure that each Use Case was satisfied, at the highest level of abstraction. Now it is time to refine the CIDs and provide the level of detail necessary for implementation. The refined CIDs are renamed Interaction Diagrams (IDs).

Purpose

> The purpose of refining the CIDs and developing a software-level ID is to show at a finer (more precise) level of detail all the Classes and Methods within each Class that are required to implement a Use Case.

Definition(s)

Interaction Diagram (ID): An **ID** is a diagram, using the graphical notation previously introduced in Phase 3, System OOA, when the CIDs were produced, that represents the *refinement* of a CID or supporting CID. An **ID** portrays the functionality of a thread of control (Use Case) at the software level, in a manner that identifies which Classes, and which Methods of each Class, are required to satisfy a Use Case.

Process

Step 1: Decide Whether to Refine the CID or to Copy the CID

Because this Activity refines the CIDs, decide at this point whether to maintain the system view as separate diagrams and *copy them* over for refinement during OOA. If copied over, the diagrams must be renamed with an _ID suffix to clearly show that they are distinct from the CIDs. The alternative is to actually modify the CID, thus maintaining only one set of behavioral diagrams. This choice loses the system view.

The decision made for the SEM software was to produce a second set of diagrams, specifically a set of IDs. These IDs are refined one more time, in Phase 9, OOD Dynamic View, when the physical view of the solution is developed.

Step 2: Decide What to Include on an Interaction Diagram

This issue centers around exactly which kinds of messages to include on an ID *in this Activity*, and which messages to *exclude in this Activity and defer to OOD* (specifically, Phase 9). The issue arises because there are so many different kinds of Classes and Messages in an OO software system. Consider the following questions:

- *Should calls to the database be included?*
- *Should a Database Class be included?*
- *Should exceptions[4] propagation be included?*
- *Should Controller Classes be included?*
- *Should GUI Classes(_View Classes) be included?*
- *Should Process Classes be included?*
- *Should callbacks be included?*
- *Should IPC Messages be explicitly annotated as such?*
- *Should _IF Classes be included?*

In reality, answers to these questions center around the concept of a logical view of the satisfaction of the Use Case, and a physical (or implementation) view of the satisfaction of a Use Case. Consistency throughout a project is achieved by providing guidance to the Development Team with respect to the questions posed above. The following represents one possible set of answers that strives to focus this activity on *"what"* the software must do (logical view), as opposed to *"how"* the software will satisfy the Use Case (physical view). Stated differently, the proposed set of answers focuses this activity on the logical view, and helps to defer design and implementation issues. The benefit, of course, is the achievement of an understanding of a requirement *before* its implementation.

- *Should calls to the database be included?*

  Optional. The magnitude of the number of calls adds nothing to the overall understanding of the Use Case. Furthermore, the number of Messages to the database, if shown, can yield a terribly messy and cluttered diagram which is difficult to read. Yet most projects prefer to include these Messages because working with a data-

[4]An exception is defined as a situation where the Method cannot complete its intended processing. Exceptions are limited to real failure conditions, not status reporting. Status reporting should be handled by one or more Attributes and Methods.

base is familiar. If excluded from this Activity, database calls need to be included in Phase 9 when the IDs are refined once again in OOD.

- *Should a Database Class be included?*

  Optional. If the Messages to the database are included, then, of course, the Database Class needs to be included.

- *Should exception propagation be included?*

  Optional. Adding exception propagation to IDs is optional during this Phase. If the failure of a Method to perform its required processing is known, by all means include known exception propagation as a backward arrow[5]. The appearance of the arrowhead indicates where the exception should be handled. However, all exception propagation must be identified during OOD, and need to be added to the IDs, when the diagrams are again refined (Phase 9).

- *Should Controller Classes be included?*

  No. Whether or not to include Controller Classes is very controversial. Justifying either position is quite easy. Frankly, we have had more success by deferring the addition of Controller Classes because Controller Classes are strictly a design construct. Again, the recommendation is that developers defer adding Controller Classes until Phase 9.

- *Should GUI Classes be included?*

  Absolutely, positively, yes. Here is where the real GUI requirements are refined. Identifying the types of GUIs now aids in the development of GUIs that have a common look and feel across the project.

- *Should Process Classes be included?*

  No. Process Classes are identified in Phase 7 and are added to IDs in Phase 9.

- *Should callbacks be included?*

  No. Callbacks are at too low a level of implementation detail, and the recommendation is that callbacks be added to IDs in Phase 9.

- *Should Inter-Process Communication (IPC) Messages be explicitly annotated?*

  No. Again, Process Classes are not identified until Phase 7, OOD Process Architecture; therefore, IPCs are added to IDs in OOD (Phase 9).

- *Should _IF Classes be included?*

  Absolutely!

[5]Another option here is that a separate symbol (hashed arrow) be used to indicate an exception. Jacobson takes this approach, while neither Booch nor Rumbaugh do. Using OMT, a project can require that all Messages be indicated by forward arrows, requiring proper placement of the Classes to support forward arrows for all Messages. With forward arrows restricted to Messages, backward arrows can be used to represent exceptions.

Step 3: Idenitfy Supporting IDs

Each project needs a project standard for decomposing IDs, just as CIDs were decomposed in Phase 3, Systems OOA–Dynamic View. Recall from Phase 3 that many Use Cases may have, as part of their thread, some common processing, for example, event logging. Event logging first requires a query as to whether the log has been established. If the log has *not* been established, it must be created. Once created, the log *entry* must be created. Finally, the log entry must be added to the log. Figure 3-6 indicated how common processing was represented at the CID level.

Common processing is also possible and, in fact, is quite probable at the ID level. To represent a supporting ID, write the name of the diagram in upper-case and add a suffix of _ID to the name. This convention identifies the diagram as a supporting ID. To reference a supporting ID, add the $Use Case Class to the ID and name the Message to the $Use Case Class the same as the name of the supporting ID, using all capital letters.

Step 4: Update the Diagram

Now, update the ID by adding the new Classes and Messages that are appropriate for the Use Case in question, and taking into account the decisions made in Step 2.

Example

Figure 6-5 represents the CID for Use Case 16: Operator_Updates_Nominal_Values_In_DB. Recall that this diagram was produced during Phase 3, System OOA–Dynamic View. The CID indicates that the Operator selects the Update All button, the `Alarm` is disabled, then Use Case 17 is invoked (which enables the Operator to update the nominal values for the three `Environmental_Conditions`). After the `Environmental_Conditions` are updated, the `Alarm` is enabled. At the system level, this CID validated the Categories and made the delegation of responsibility of the Categories quite clear.

Figure 6-6 shows how the ID has changed from the initial system-level CID. Note the new Classes that have been added, and their Methods. These Classes were identified

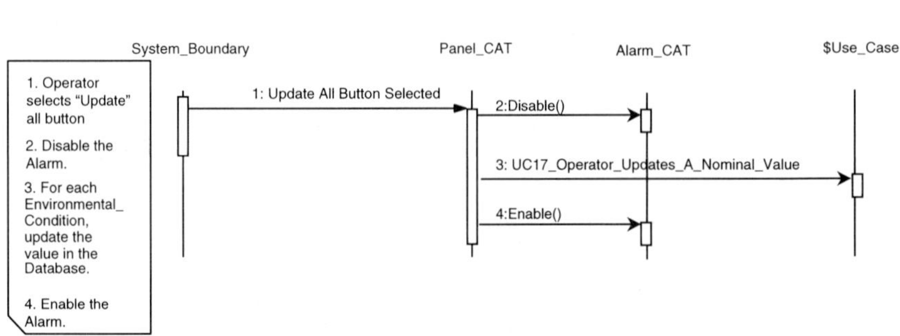

Figure 6-5. CID for UC16_Operator_Update_Nominal_Values_In_DB

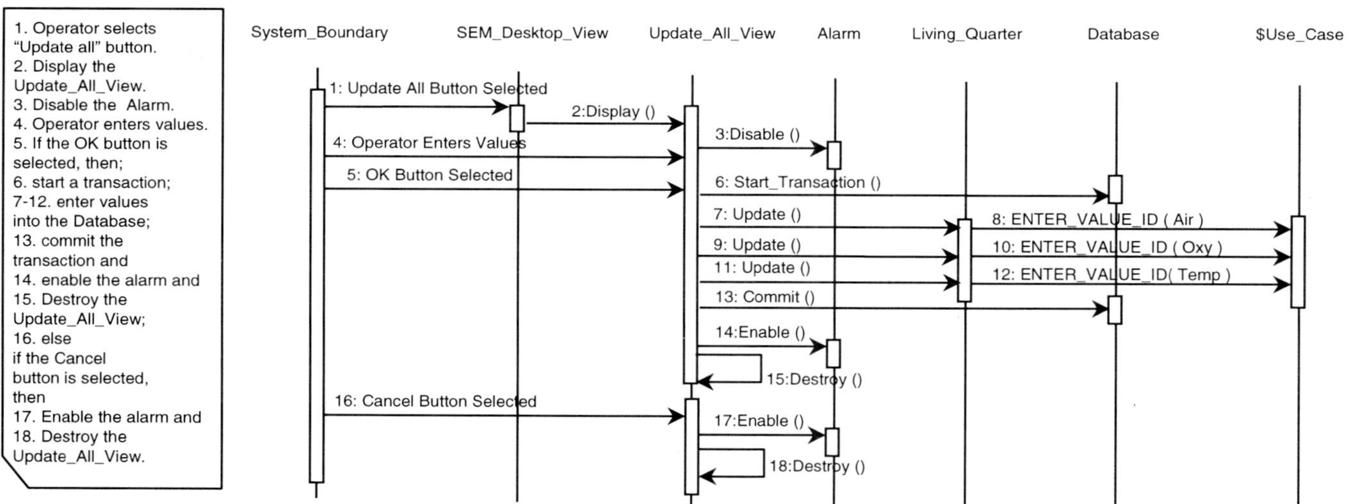

UC16_Operator_Updates_Nominal_Values_In_DB_ID
1. Operator selects "Update all" button.
2. Display the Update_All_View.
3. Disable the Alarm.
4. Operator enters values.
5. If the OK button is selected, then;
6. start a transaction;
7-12. enter values into the Database;
13. commit the transaction and
14. enable the alarm and
15. Destroy the Update_All_View;
16. else if the Cancel button is selected, then
17. Enable the alarm and
18. Destroy the Update_All_View.
System_Boundary
SEM_Desktop_View
Update_All_View
Alarm
Living_Quarter
Database
$Use_Case
1: Update All Button Selected
2:Display ()
3:Disable ()
4: Operator Enters Values
5: OK Button Selected
6: Start_Transaction ()
7: Update ()
8: ENTER_VALUE_ID (Air)
9: Update ()
10: ENTER_VALUE_ID (Oxy)
11: Update ()
12: ENTER_VALUE_ID(Temp)
13: Commit ()
14:Enable ()
15:Destroy ()
16: Cancel Button Selected
17:Enable ()
18:Destroy ()

*NOTE: The parent Database Class is shown on this ID, but at the time the IDs are drawn it may not be known what database implementation (e.g., which Subclass) will be used. In the solution, the SNAP implementation uses the MSAccess_Database Class, while the C++ implementation uses the Flat_File_Database Class.

Figure 6-6. Interaction Diagram : UC16_Operator_Updates_Nominal_Values_In_DB

during the previous Phase, when the CCDs were expanded. Just as a quick comparison, the CID identifies that two Categories and four Messages are required to represent the Use Case, while the software OOA–level ID identifies five Classes and 18 Messages are required, and the Supporting ID ENTER_VALUE_ID (Figure 6-7) represents three additional Classes (one for each Subclass of the `Environmental_Condition` Class) and three additional Messages that are required.

Note in Figure 6-6 that the reference to Use Case 17 has disappeared. Upon further analysis, it became apparent that Use Case 17 could no longer be embedded within Use Case 16 as there was too much common processing, for example, enabling and disabling the alarm.

Pragmatic Project Issues

Handling Creation/Deletion of Instances

UML 1.0 now includes the capability to portray the creation and deletion of Instances in a Sequence Diagram. The icon for the Instance (□) is drawn at the same level with the arrow whose Message creates the Instance. For the destruction of Instances, a large upper-case X indicates that the Instance is destroyed. A hashed line is used as the stem for the Instance icon to represent *existing* Instances. This notation was previously shown in Figure 3-5.

Naming Creation/Deletion Messages

If not using UML, the issue focuses on whether to name a Message (and therefore a Method) `Create()`. The resolution of the issue depends on the CASE tool being utilized and the implementation language of choice. If, on an ID, a Message is sent to a Class, and the Message is named `Create()`, this may cause (*automatically* within the CASE tool[6]) a Method named `Create()` to be added to the Class. In a C++ implementation, duplicate Methods will be provided in the C++ generated code: a `Create()` function, *as well as* a constructor function. In C++, constructors are *not* named `Create()`, but rather they are given the name of the Class. Consequently, the developer must do some manual clean-up before implementing the code automatically generated by the tool. In Ada83, a Method named `Create()` must be automatically generated. And, in Ada95, the Method name, in the generated code, will depend upon whether the Class is a Subclass of the Ada95 `Controlled_Type` Class.

With respect to a C++ implementation, one Project Team decided to name the message `Create()`, ignoring the fact that the tool provided constructors. The Project Team felt that too much information was lost by *not* including the Message `Create()` on the ID. Additionally, by utilizing a `Create()` Message, and indicating the parameters, it became clear how many overloaded constructors were required. The function prototypes for constructors that were automatically generated by the CASE tool, as well as those provided for the overloaded `Create()` capability, were manually updated to reflect the intent of the ID.

[6]Rose automatically populates the CS for a Class with the Method.

ENTER_VALUE_ID

*Note: This supporting ID occurs once for each Environmental_Condition Subclass (<sub>).

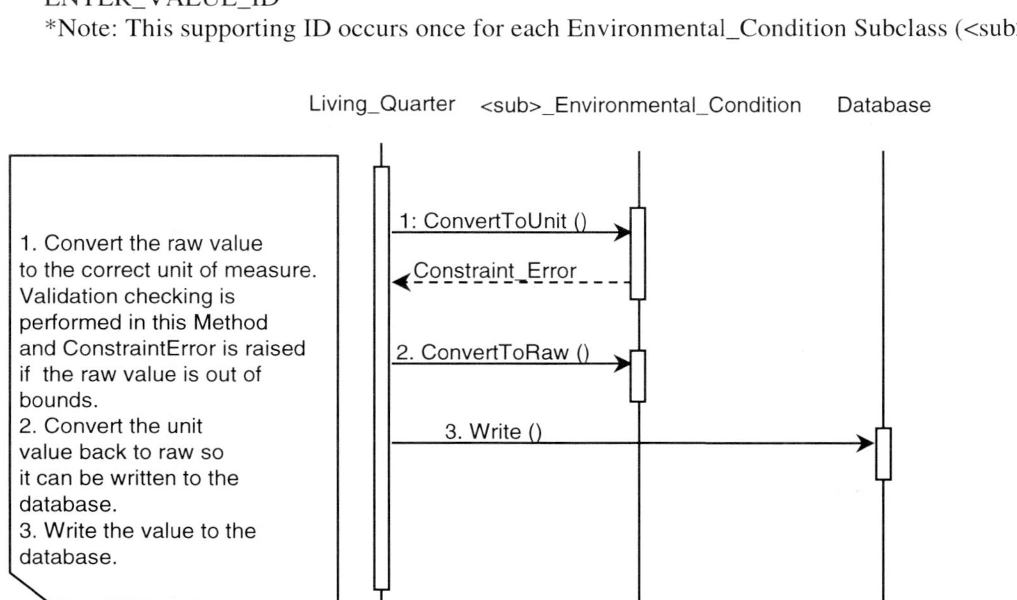

Living_Quarter
<sub>_Environmental_Condition
Database
1: ConvertToUnit ()
Constraint_Error
2. ConvertToRaw ()
3. Write ()
1. Convert the raw value to the correct unit of measure. Validation checking is performed in this Method and ConstraintError is raised if the raw value is out of bounds.
2. Convert the unit value back to raw so it can be written to the database.
3. Write the value to the database.

*NOTE: The parent Database Class is shown on this ID, but at the time the IDs are drawn it may not be known what database implementation (e.g., which Subclass) will be used. In the solution, the SNAP implementation uses the MSAccess_Database Class, while the C++ implementation uses the Flat_File_Database Class.

Figure 6-7. A Supporting ID—ENTER_VALUE_ID

The Word "Find"

The word "find" is typically overloaded on a large project. The word "find" can mean

- Implement a Use Case action
- Return an Attribute Value
- Use a filter based on some selection criteria.

A Project Team would be wise to prohibit use of the word "find" in a Use Case. Typically, use of the word "find" in a Use Case, for example, Operator_Find_Panel_Values, means that the Use Case has *not* been stated precisely enough. The Use Case should be written more explicitly, for example, Display_All_Environmental_Conditions.

"Find"ing a value in the database is really a requirement of an individual Method, and the name `Read()` is far more appropriate and in keeping with the Method naming conventions presented earlier.

A Method returning an Attribute value, according to the Method naming conventions discussed in Phase 3 should be named the same as the name of the Attribute. Therefore, a Message to return the temperature of a `Living_Quarter` should be named `Temp_Value()`, or `Temperature()`, *not* `Find_Temperature()`.

Following these conventions turns the confusing ID, as shown in Figure 6-8 into the more precise, and much more understandable, ID shown in Figure 6-9.

Instance Existence

Remember to check for the existence of an Instance before processing the Instance. If the Instance does *not* exist, include an exception, a situation where the Method *cannot* perform its intended processing.

Challenge the Use Case

Just because a Use Case has been defined does *not* mean that the Use Case is cast in concrete. A Use Case that reads as follows:

Operator_Updates_the_Database

is *not* precise enough. Does the Use Case imply that the Operator updates all three `Environmental_Conditions`, or just the `Environmental_Conditions` for a single `Living_Quarter`, or both (in which case, there is another Use Case). When it is *not* clear exactly what a Use Case describes, *challenge* the Use Case to obtain a more precise definition.

Creation/Deletion Again

When sending `Create()/Delete()` messages, utilize and analyze the CCD, specifically the multiplicity and conditionality that is specified there. If Class A has a one-to-one (1:1) and unconditional association with Class B, then deletion of an Instance of Class B *requires* deletion of the referenced Instance of Class A. If Class A has a one to many (1:M) association with Class B, then deletion of an Instance of Class B requires deletion of the referenced Instance of Class A *only if* the Class A Instance is *not* associated with any other Class B Instances. This is also true when the relationship between Class A and Class B is aggregation.

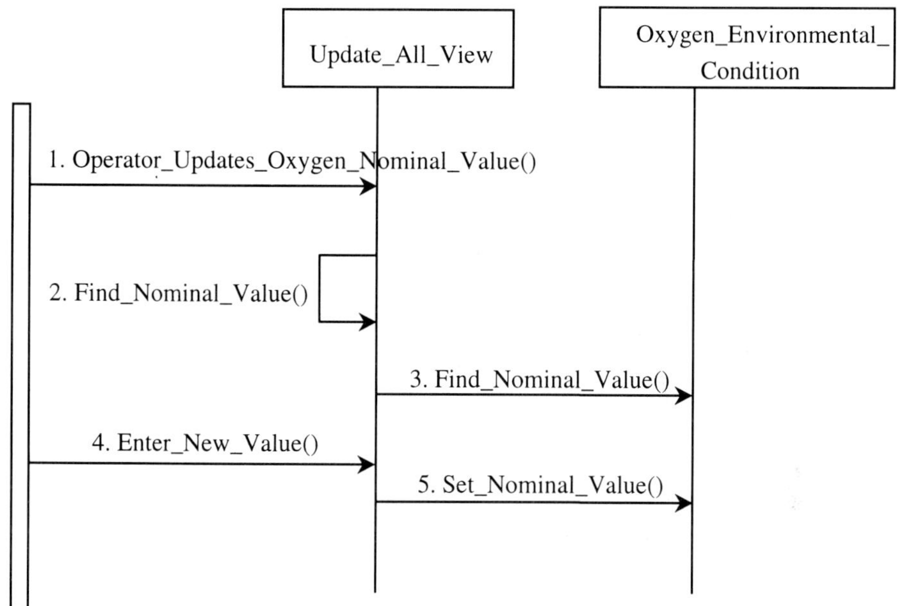

Figure 6-8. The Word "find" : A Confusing ID

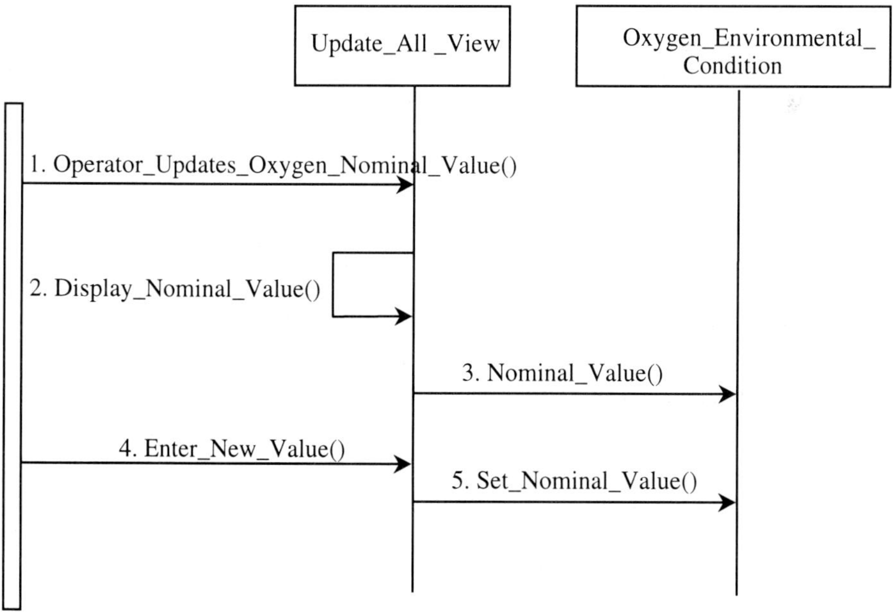

Figure 6-9. The Word "find" : A Precise ID

Class-Level Interaction Diagrams or Instance-Level Interaction Diagrams–IMPORTANT!!

The Project Team must choose whether to develop IDs where the entities that receive Messages are Classes, or, whether to be more precise, and develop IDs where the entities that receive Messages are Instances. This is a project-specific decision, and depends upon the CASE tool and application being developed. A large million-lines-of-code effort, that is distributed across multiple geographic locations, surely needs to develop *some* IDs at the Instance level. Doing so enables tracking of functionality from one Operator to the next, from one geographical location to the next, and so on. For a small or even moderately-sized application that is self contained, Instance-level diagrams really add nothing, so Class-level diagrams are sufficient.

With UML, both Sequence Diagrams and Collaboration Diagrams are drawn using Instances, rather than Classes.

Plotter Required

Interaction Diagrams can become quite large. Once again, a plotter may be required to print the diagram because, quite simply, an ID on a substantial project will not fit on an 8 1/2" × 11" piece of paper. Most of the CASE tools do *not* currently support a plotter, therefore it becomes a requirement for an organization's CASE Tool Support Team to develop the required software interface.

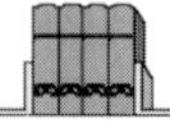

Product(s)

The result of refining all system-level CIDs is a numerically greater set of software IDs. However, each system-level CID still maps to at *least* one software-level ID.

6.3 UPDATE CATEGORY CLASS DIAGRAM (CCD)

Once IDs are developed, a greater degree of understanding of the behavioral aspect of the system is gained. As a result of developing IDs, more Classes and/or Associations may be discovered. These new Classes and Associations need to be placed on the CCD to keep the diagram up-to-date and current.

Purpose

> The purpose of updating the CCDs is to keep them current and to reflect the new information discovered while developing the STDs and IDs.

Process

The process of updating the CCD is very simple. Make sure to do the following:

- Add any newly discovered Classes to the CCD, and
- Add new Associations to the CCD, with associated multiplicity.

Example

No new Classes or Methods were discovered for the SEM in this Activity.

Pragmatic Project Issues

Maintenance: A Necessary Evil!

Updating pre-existing material is *not* the most favorite part of any software development effort. Again, a very frequent review schedule helps to ensure that the updates take place.

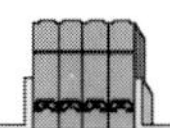

Product(s)

The products of this Activity are IDs that represent both a refinement of the CIDs and represent a more detailed view of the solution. It really doesn't matter whether the IDs are drawn using Object Scenario Diagrams, Sequence Diagrams, Collaboration Diagrams, or Jacobson Interaction Diagrams. The products of this Activity are updated CCDs that reflect newly discovered Classes and Associations as a result of producing the IDs.

6.4 UPDATE CLASS SPECIFICATION (CS)

Purpose

> The purpose of updating the CS is to keep the Class description current and to reflect the information gleaned from developing STDs and IDs.

Once STDs and IDs are complete, a greater degree of understanding of the behavioral aspects of each Class is gained. As a result, the CS for each Class needs to be updated.

Process

The process of updating a CS is very simple. Simply

- Add any newly discovered Class information to the description of the Class
- Add a State Attribute to the Class
- Add the description of the State Attribute according to the Attribute template
- Add the phases of the life cycle to the domain of values for the State Attribute
- Add Methods named `Current_State()` and `Change_State()`, and add their descriptions to those Classes that have a State Attribute
- Add newly discovered Methods and Attributes.

Example

Adding the Attribute named `Alarm.State` to the Class description for the `Alarm` Class, according to the Attribute template, adds the following entry to the CS:

State

Persistent/Transient	: Transient
Description	: The life cycle phases of the Alarm Class
Domain Of Values	: (Enabled, Disabled)
Rules	: Initialized to Enabled; only disabled when the Operator requests to update the environmental condition values in the database. Enabled upon database update completion.

Adding the Methods named `Current_State()` and `Change_State()` cause the following to be added to the Method portion of the `Alarm` CS:

Change_State()

Description	: Modifies the current value of the State Attribute
Inputs	: Instance of Alarm, new value of `AlarmState`
Outputs	: N/A
Algorithm	: Toggles between Enabled and Disabled

Current_State()

Description	: Returns the current value of the `AlarmState`
Inputs	: Instance of Alarm
Outputs	: Value of state (Enabled, Disabled)
Algorithm	: N/A

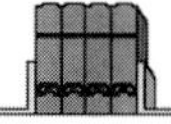

Product(s)

The products of this Activity are updated CSs. The updates reflect any newly discovered Classes, Attributes and Methods and their descriptions discovered as a result of producing IDs.

Phase Transition Criteria

Move on to the next Phase when

- All Use Cases for the current build have been modeled in CIDs and IDs
- Scenarios have been represented accurately
- STDs for appropriate Classes have been developed
- Static products (CCDs, CSs) have been updated
- No new Classes, Attributes, and Methods seem appropriate.

The review criteria shown in Tables 6-4 and 6-5 might also help make the decision to transition to the next Phase:

Review Criteria

Table 6-4. STD Review Criteria

#	State Transition Diagram Review Criteria
1	Name each transition.
2	External stimuli names should be prefixed by the name of the source Class of the stimuli followed by a period (.) (or preceded by a (^) in UML).
3	Diagonal and intersecting lines should be minimized.
4	Validate that each potential path through the STD is valid.
5	The phases on the STD are consistent with the values of the State Attribute in the CS.
6	Validate that a transition is owned by only one Class and is not duplicated by another Class.
7	Validate that the lack of a transition between two states is valid.
8	If an external transition stimulates a Class in more than one state, validate the correctness of the stimulus (or lack of stimulus) for that transition for all indicated states of the Class.
9	Keep the same transitions with the same name within a Class.
11	Birth/Death STDs have an initial and a terminal state.

Table 6-5. ID Review Criteria

#	Interaction Diagram Review Criteria	OOA
1	Each Message is a Method of the Class and appears as part of the Class description.	√
2	Branching and iteration appear either as comments or by using provided syntax (e.g., UML).	√
3	Are diagram naming conventions followed? An ID is named either i) <<UC#_Use Case Name>>_ID ii) all capitals for a supporting ID, suffixed by _ID.	√
4	Each Message is numbered, even "Messages" to supporting IDs.	√
5	Instances are identified (optional).	√
6	Is a Message sent to the correct Class? Does the Method have access to the right data to complete its processing?	√
7	Does the Method need access to additional Classes to perform the Message?	√
8	Do Message names follow Method naming conventions?	√
9	Do the notes reflect the correct Message Numbers?	√
10	Are DB messages included (optional at OOA, required at OOD)?	√
11	There are no Process Classes at OOA (required at OOD).	√
12	There are no Controller Classes at OOA (required at OOD).	√
13	Exceptions represent failure, not status.	√
14	Exception propagation is reasonable.	√
15	Do comments exist that annotate collections of Messages? These comments, in essence, represent PDL for a Use Case, not PDL for an individual Method.	√
16	There is only one incoming Message per Class Method; however, multiple outgoing Messages per Class Method are permitted.	√
17	Classes on the ID appear in the CCD.	√
18	The word "find" is not utilized.	√
19	Create()/Delete() Messages are validated against the CCD for multiplicity/conditionality consistency.	√
20	For Classes with a State Attribute, messages for Current_State() and Change_State() exist.	√
21	Are known View Classes included?	√
22	Do View Classes send Messages to domain Classes, and not vice versa?	√
23	Does the View Class have a "Populate()" Message if it autofills data?	√

Tracking Progress

Figure 6-10 shows how the Class Listing by Categories (initiated in the previous Phase) is augmented to reflect the STDs and IDs produced during this Phase. Examining the inconsistencies in Class names helps to precisely and unambiguously identify which Classes interface with which other Classes. The report also identifies when an ID assumes the existence of a Class and the Class has *not* yet been identified by the Category that would own the Class! The figure represents *only* those Classes on the ID for Use Case 16. The entire table has *not* been completed, just enough to illustrate the concept. This report needs to be generated every two weeks. This report will *not* appear again in this book.

Another report can be initiated, if desired, that enables the identification of inconsistencies between Methods in a CS and Messages on IDs. Methods are listed that appear in a CS yet *never* appear on an ID. Messages are listed that appear on an ID that do *not* have a corresponding entry in a CS.

These reports are invaluable to a project. They serve to maintain consistency of information in the CASE tool repository.

Table 6-6 depicts the project management spreadsheet that we have been building for Part II. The number of IDs required is the same as the number of Use Cases. Consequently, progress can be monitored by tracking how many IDs have been produced (and reviewed), as compared to the number required. A suggestion is to monitor the number of supporting IDs separately.

In addition, the ongoing monitoring by project, Domain, and Category of

- Use Cases to build
- Number of Classes per Category
- Average number of Methods and Attributes per Class
- Number of CSs completed

provide valid indicators of the status of the Categories, the Domains, and therefore the project.

Table 6-6. Project Management Spreadsheet: Phase 6

HCC Project Management Spreadsheet						
Number	**Phase Name**	**Activity**	**Charge Number**	**Product**	**Progress Metric**	**% Weight**
5	**Software OOA–Static View**		**SW-OOAS-5**			
5.1		Initiate CCD	SW-OOAS-5.1	CCD	# initiated CCDs	
5.2		Refine Inheritance/Aggregation Hierarchies	SW-OOAS-5.2	CCD (Updated)		
5.3		Decompose Scenario	SW-OOAS-5.3	Annotation	# Annotations	
5.4		Analyze Annotation	SW-OOAS-5.4		# Annotation analyzed	
5.5		Update CCD	SW-OOAS-5.5	CCD (Updated)		
5.6		Add View Classes	SW-OOAS-5.6	CCD (Updated)	# CCDs	0.50
5.7		Develop CSs	SW-OOAS-5.7	CS	# CSs completed	0.45
5.8		Develop CCCDs	SW-OOAS-5.8	CCCD	# CCCDs	0.05
6	**Software OOA–Dynamic View**		**SW-OOAD-6**			
6.1		Specify Internal Class Behavior	SW-OOAD-6.1	STD	# STDs	0.10
6.2		Refine CID	SW-OOAD-6.2	ID	# IDs	0.60
6.3		Update CCD	SW-OOAD-6.3	CCD (Updated)	# CCDs updated	0.15
6.4		Update CSs	SW-OOAD-6.4	CS (Updated)	# CSs	0.15

Class Listing by Category

Category	Child Category	Class	Static Diagram	Dynamic Diagram
Alarm_CAT			**SCD**	
		Alarm	Alarm_CAT_CCD, IF_CAT_CCD, Operator_CAT_CCD, Living_Quarter_CAT_CCD	Alarm_STD, UC 16_ID
DB_CAT			**SCD**	
		Database	DB_CAT_CCD, Living_Quarter_CAT_CCD, Operator_CAT_CCD	UC 16_ID
Environmental_Condition_CAT			**SCD**	
		Environmental_Condition	Environmental_Condition_CAT_CCD, Panel_CAT_CCD	UC 16_ID
		Air_Pressure_Environmental_Condition	Environmental_Condition_CAT_CCD, Sensor_CAT_CCD	UC 16_ID
		Oxygen_Environmental_Condition	Environmental_Condition_CAT_CCD, Sensor_CAT_CCD	UC 16_ID
		Temperature_Environmental_Condition	Environmental_Condition_CAT_CCD, Sensor_CAT_CCD	UC 16_ID
IF_CAT			**SCD**	
		Alarm_IF	IF_CAT_CCD, Alarm_CAT_CCD	
		Sensor_IF	IF_CAT_CCD, Sensor_CAT_CCD	
Interim_CAT				
Living_Quarter_CAT			**SCD**	
		Deviation	Living_Quarter_CAT_CCD, Alarm_CAT_CCD, Panel_CAT_CCD	
		Hall	Living_Quarter_CAT_CCD	
		Living_Quarter	Living_Quarter_CAT_CCD, Environmental_Condition_CAT_CCD, DB_CAT_CCD, Panel_CAT_CCD, Sensor_CAT_CCD, Timer_CAT_CCD	
		Room	Living_Quarter_CAT_CCD	

Category	Class	SCD	
Operator_CAT		**SCD**	
	Operator	Operator_CAT_CCD, Alarm_CAT_CCD, Panel_CAT_CCD, Operator_CAT_CCD, View_CAT_CCD	
Panel_CAT		**SCD**	
	Annunciator	Panel_CAT_CCD, Living_Quarter_CAT_CCD	
	Panel	Panel_CAT_CCD	
	Window	Panel_CAT_CCD, Environmental_Condition_CAT_CCD, Living_Quarter_CAT_CCD	Window_STD
Process_CAT			
Reusable_CAT			
Sensor_CAT		**SCD**	
	Air_Pressure__Sensor	Sensor_CAT_CCD, Living_Quarter_CAT_CCD, Environmental_Condition_CAT_CCD	
	Oxygen_Sensor	Sensor_CAT_CCD, Living_Quarter_CAT_CCD, Environmental_Condition_CAT_CCD	
	Sensor	Sensor_CAT_CCD, IF_CAT_CCD, Living_Quarter_CAT_CCD	
	Temperature_Sensor	Sensor_CAT_CCD, Living_Quarter_CAT_CCD, Environmental_Condition_CAT_CCD	
Timer_CAT		**SCD**	
	Timer	Timer_CAT_CCD, Living_Quarter_CAT_CCD	

Figure 6-10. Project Classes Reported by Category—Augmented Version

Class Listing by Category				
Category	**Child Category**	**Class**	**Static Diagram**	**Dynamic Diagram**
View_CAT			**SCD**	
		Annunciator_View	View_CAT_CCD, Panel_CAT_CCD	
		Hall_View	View_CAT_CCD, Living_Quarter_CAT_CCD, Operator_CAT_CCD	
		Panel_View	View_CAT_CCD, Panel_CAT_CCD, Operator_CAT_CCD	
		SEM_Desktop_View	View_CAT_CCD, Operator_CAT_CCD	UC 16_ID
		Update_All_View	Panel_CAT_CCD, Living_Quarter_CAT_CCD, Operator_CAT_CCD	UC 16_ID
		Window_View	View_CAT_CCD Operator_CAT_CCD Panel_CAT_CCD	
		Window_Pop_Up_View	View_CAT_CCD Operator_CAT_CCD Panel_CAT_CCD	

Figure 6-10. Project Classes Reported by Category—Augmented Version (*continued*)

PART IV

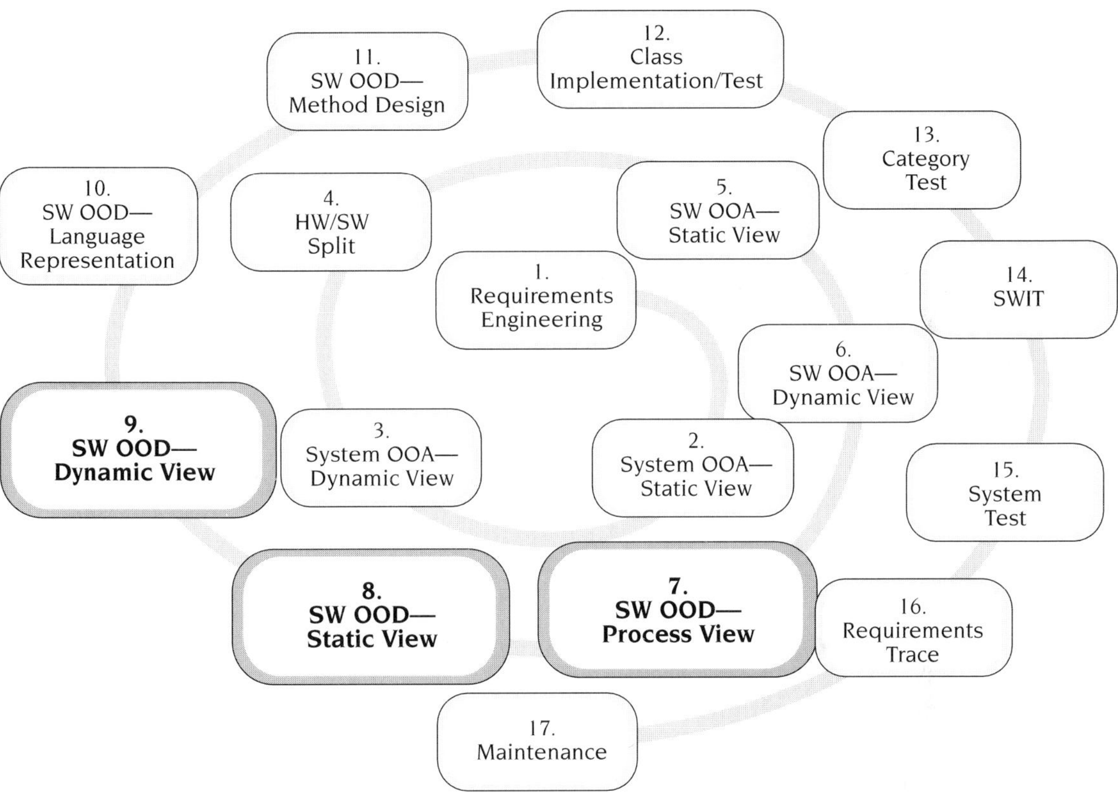

Software Object-Oriented Design—Language-Independent

PHASE 7

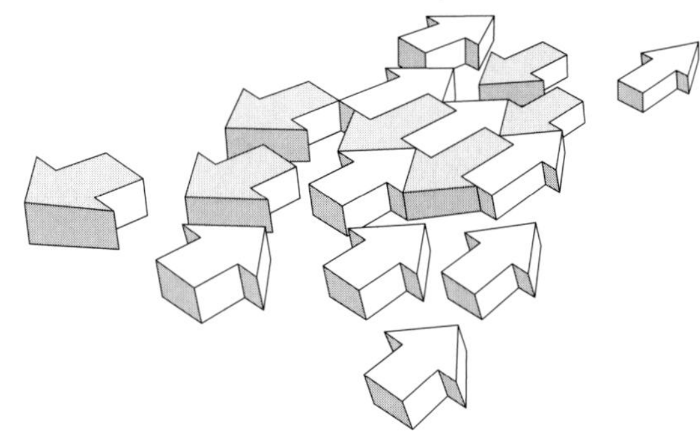

Software OOD–Process View

PHASE OVERVIEW

Now it is time to look at process architecture, or more specifically, which processes are required and how these processes are allocated to processors. The process/products for developing/documenting the process architecture are identified in Figure 7-1. Figure 7-1 indicates that two distinct products are produced during this Phase to represent the static process architecture: 1) a Process Architecture Diagram (PAD) that identifies system processes and what processor(s) they are allocated to, and 2) Process-to-Class Allocation Diagrams (PCAD) that depict the allocation of Classes to a process. One PAD[1] is produced per software system, while one PCAD is produced for each process.

Next, IDs are utilized to represent the collaboration of processes, or the dynamic view of the process architecture.

Finally, CSs are developed for the newly discovered `Process` and `Processor` Classes identified during this Phase. You might ask what are the Attributes and Methods for these Classes? Activity 7.8 will answer these questions for you.

Instead of developing the process architecture at this point, a Project Team may elect to continue with the static and dynamic views of the system at the OOD level by continuing to refine the CCDs and the IDs (Phases 8 and 9, respectively). This approach can help a developer move from a logical view of the solution, to a more physical, or implementation, view. However, most Project Teams do *not* feel comfortable iterating the CCDs and IDs. Typically, the response is that, "We have modeled enough. What is the process architecture?"

However, early knowledge of the process architecture yields a different understanding of the system and, depending on the implementation of Inter-Process Communications (IPCs), may actually yield more conventions for developing both the static and dynamic views at OOD time. For example, if UNAS[2] is utilized as the IPC

[1]Although one PAD is the goal, on some systems it is impossible to depict the information in one diagram in a readable fashion. For instance, on one project there were over forty processes (way too many—poor design) and the PAD became quite cluttered; consequently, we resorted to multiple PADs.

[2]UNAS™ stands for Universal Network Architecture System, software developed by TRW. UNAS represents one possible IPC implementation. UNAS is a vendor proprietary IPC vehicle.

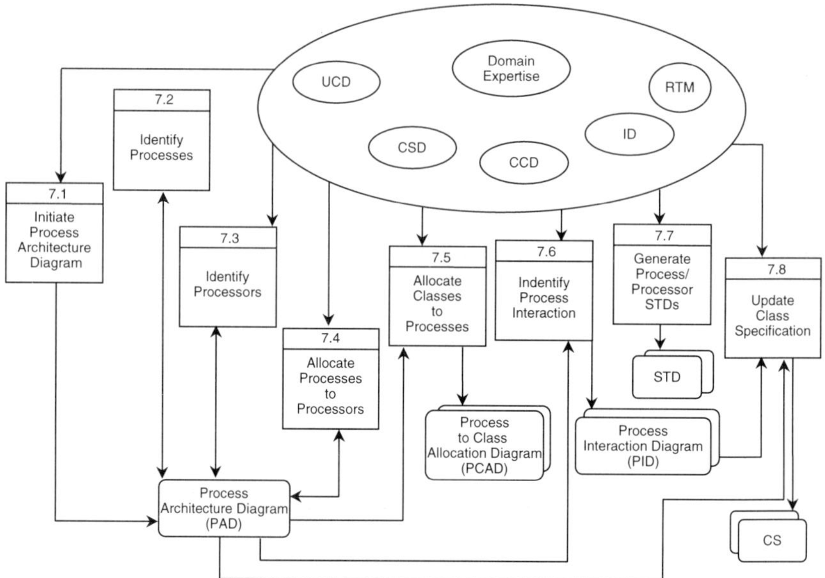

Figure 7-1. Software OOD - Process Architecture Phase Description Diagram

implementation mechanism, domain IPC message Classes need to be identified as Classes on the CCD and their creation and transmission need to be included on the IDs. However, if Distributed Computing Environment (DCE)[3] is utilized, IPC message Classes do *not* need to be identified because an IPC call is made to look exactly like a Remote Procedure Call (RPC). Regardless, a decision needs to be made as to whether RPCs are included (notationally) on IDs. More on this subject in Phase 9.

7.1 INITIATE THE PROCESS ARCHITECTURE DIAGRAM (PAD)

Purpose

> The purpose of creating a PAD is to emphasize that this diagram, the PAD, is a **distinct** diagram from those diagrams that have been previously created. Although the PAD is a Class Diagram, the PAD does *not* reflect domain Classes per se, but rather depicts distinct types of Classes (specifically `Processor` and `Process` Classes) and only one association relationship (`IsAllocatedTo`).

[3]DCE stands for Distributed Computing Environment. DCE represents another possible implementation mechanism. DCE is actually a standard for IPC that different vendors can implement.

Definition(s)

Process Architecture Diagram (PAD): A **PAD** is a Class Diagram that depicts the identified `Processor` and `Process` Classes in the software system, and the `Process` to `Processor` allocation.

Process

Step 1: Establish Naming Convention

Name the PAD <System_Name>_PAD.

Step 2: Initiate the Diagram

Using the CASE tool for the project, establish a new Category named `Process_CAT` if it was not previously introduced as a Category.

Step 3: Establish Diagram Ownership

Insure that the `Process_CAT` is the owner of the PAD. Recall that ownership of Classes and diagrams is essential to produce documents from the OO model repository by Category.

The PAD is now ready for Activity 7.2.

Example

Figure 7-2 shows the PAD that was initiated for the SEM. The diagram is now ready for the addition of the `Process` and `Processor` Classes that are identified in the following Activities.

Pragmatic Project Issues

Analyze the Processes

We have found it easier to model with just one PAD, but sometimes a system dictates that there be more than one PAD. When creating multiple PADs, engineering judgment must be utilized as to how best to decompose the PAD, or whether the PAD is necessary at all in light of the fact that a matrix can be utilized to depict the information. A significant benefit of the PAD is that by representing `Processes` and `Processors` as Classes, they get documented in CSs (see Activity 7.8). This information is *not* typically documented and now a vehicle exists to document the static process architecture in a manner consistent with the rest of the project.

Instance Diagrams

For "composable"[4] systems, the PAD at the Class level is *not* sufficient because the PAD is a Class Diagram. For "composable" systems, "Instance" PADs can indicate the specific configuration of processes for a system.

[4]A "composable" system is a system that resides at many sites in different configurations. Not all sites have the same process configuration.

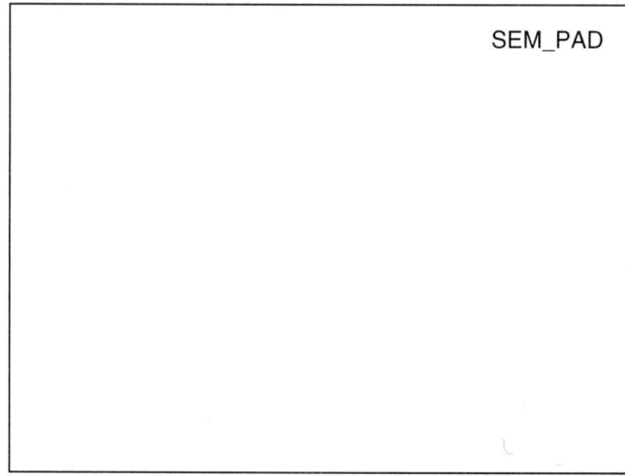

Figure 7-2. Developing The PAD - Step 1 : Initiating the Diagram

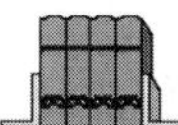

Product(s)

The product of this Activity is an empty Class (or Object) Diagram, named <System_Name>_ PAD. The PAD is completed within this Phase, specifically within Activities 7.2 through 7.4, inclusive.

7.2 IDENTIFY PROCESSES

Purpose

> The purpose of identifying processes is to specify the executable elements of the software system.

Definitions(s)

Process: A **process** is an executable entity that comprises Classes (and their Methods). A process executes on a processor.

Transient Process: A **transient process** is a process that is temporally active. In other words, a transient process is activated for a short period of time to perform specific functionality, and then it is deactivated when its processing has completed.

Persistent Process: A **persistent process** is a process that is active for the lifetime of an application.

Process

Step 1: Add Initial Process Classes to the PAD

A new Category, `Process_CAT`, was added to the model in the previous Activity. Now, add the following three Classes to the <System_Name>_ PAD: the Superclass `Process`; the two Subclasses `Transient_Process` and `Persistent_Process`.

Step 2: Identify Domain Processes

Identifying application-specific processes is dependent upon the degree of experience of the software engineer. But, the following list of typical processes [SHU92] might help provide guidelines for the identification of processes:

- Functionally Cohesive Process[5]
  - Database Interface Process
  - Computationally-Intensive
- Hardware Driver Process[6]
  - I/O Driver for Antenna, Sensor, Printer
- Time-Critical Process[7]
  - Data Capture
  - Data Display
- Periodic Process[8]
  - Sampling (readings)
  - Status Gathering (equipment, readings)
  - Displaying (data)

Step 3: Categorize Processes as Transient or Persistent

For each process identified, categorize the process as either persistent or transient.

Step 4: Add Application Process Classes to PAD

Once the application processes are identified, the next step is to add these identified processes to the PAD as Subclasses of either the `Transient_Process` or the `Persistent_Process`. The software system application processes inherit from either `Transient_Process` or `Persistent_Process` as appropriate.

[5]A functionally cohesive process is a process that performs multiple functional capabilities, all relating to the same overall function. For example, consider a database interface process which performs add, delete, and query capabilities, all relating to the database.

[6]A hardware driver process is a process that interfaces to an external hardware device.

[7]A time-critical process is a process that must be completed in a specific amount of time.

[8]A periodic process is a process that executes periodically and within a specific amount of time. Some periodic processes also require a certain percentage of spare time within the time allowed.

Example

Figure 7-3 depicts the updated PAD, utilizing UML notation. The Subclasses of the `Process` Class are themselves Superclasses that will further extend the `Process` Class' inheritance hierarchy.

The three distinct application processes that have been identified for the SEM are:

1. Display process (handles all displays)
2. Monitor process (monitors environmental conditions)
3. Database process (interface with the DB).

The first and third processes are examples of functionally cohesive processes, while the second process, the monitor process, is an example of a periodic process.

Next, these processes need to be categorized as to whether the process is a transient process (invoked only for a specific purpose and then terminated) or a persistent process (a process that is active for the lifetime of the application). For the SEM, we have determined that all three processes are persistent processes: the database process is persistent because the monitoring process queries the database for the current nominal value of an environmental condition for a living quarter; and, the monitor and display processes must always be available, because the software is constantly monitoring and displaying the status of the living quarters. Figure 7-4 depicts the results of this analysis.

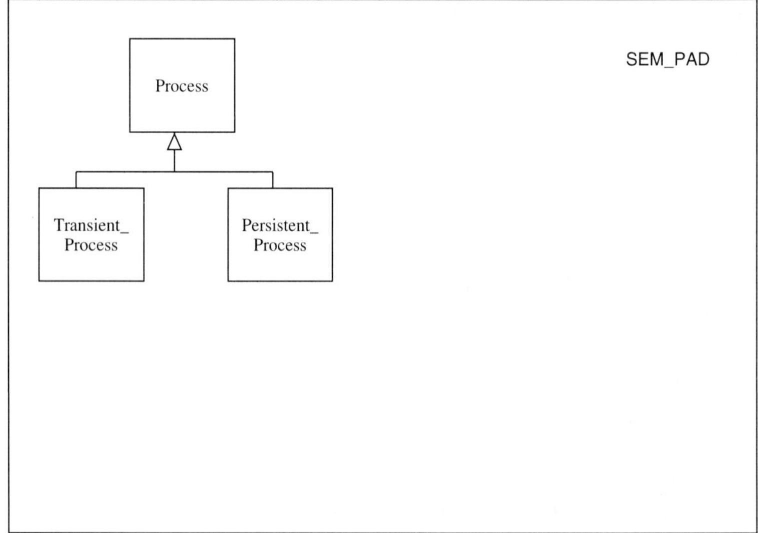

Figure 7-3. Developing The PAD - Step 2 : Adding Process Inheritance Hierarchy : UML Notation

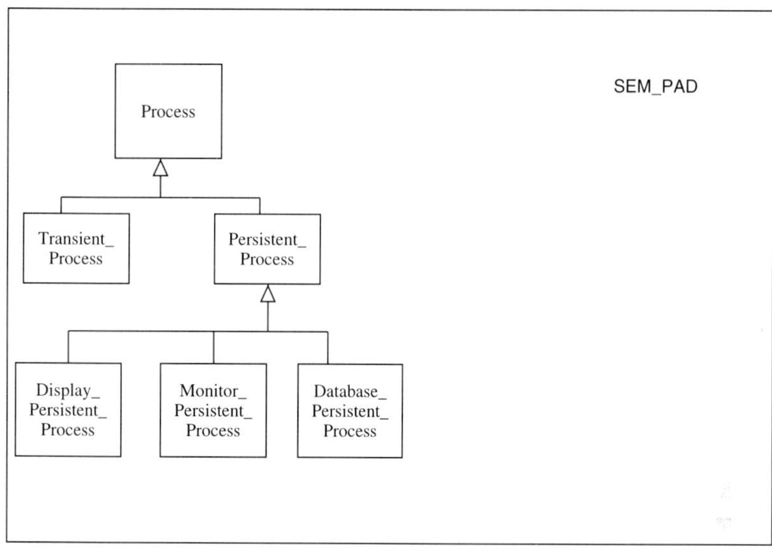

Figure 7-4. Developing The PAD - Step 3 : Adding Application Process Subclasses : UML Notation

The SEM does *not* have an example of a transient process. But, consider if the Operator had to log onto the SEM to use the SEM software. If this were the case, there would need to be a `Login_Transient_Process` that would activate when the SEM was invoked, validate the `Operator`, and then spawn the appropriate `Persistent_Process` Subclasses. In this case, Figure 7-4 would look like Figure 7-5.

Pragmatic Project Issues

Adding External Processes

You may want to consider adding processes to the PAD that are part of foreign software systems to which your system interfaces. In this situation, you have external and internal software processes, as well as transient and persistent processes. Either multiple inheritance must be used, or the model must be modified, by removing the `Transient_Process` and `Persistent_Process` Subclasses and adding an Attribute to the `Process` Class, named `Process.Persistence` (with values Persistent and Transient), that is inherited by all `Process` Subclasses. Then, `Internal_Process` and `External_Process` become Subclasses of the `Process` Class. Alternatively, make an Attribute, `Process.Internal` (with values Internal and External), and keep the `Transient_Process` and `Persistent_Process` as Subclasses of `Process`. The choice is yours.

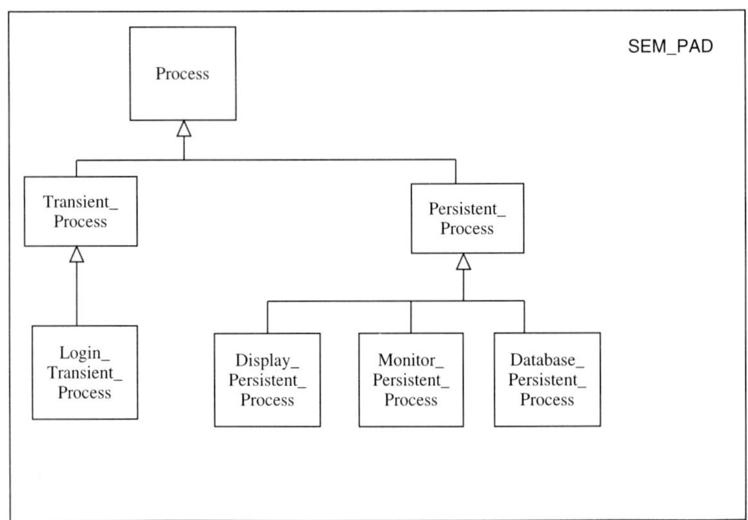

Figure 7-5. SEM PAD Depicting Login_Transient_Process : UML Notation

Do Not Confuse Processes with Categories

One project equated a process and a Category, building a Category along process lines. This approach yielded Classes that were shared across Category boundaries and violated the concept of a Category "owning" a Class. A Category is a collection of Classes for modeling and development purposes. A process is a collection of Classes that represents an executable entity. A process can cross Category boundaries, and in fact, most often does.

Analyze the Processes

As previously stated, too many processes will make for a very cluttered PAD. Too many processes may be the result of a poor design, so re-evaluate the design before proceeding; but, multiple PADs may need to be developed instead of one PAD. In this case, use engineering judgment, as well as good naming conventions, when decomposing the PAD.

Deciding between Transient and Persistent Processes

Sometimes the decision as to whether a process should be transient or persistent is *not* clear. Arguments for either case make sense and are sound. In this situation, make a decision and move on. The decision can be reversed later. Too many projects falter due to lack of a decision. It is better to make a bad decision, and correct it later, than *not* to make a decision at all.

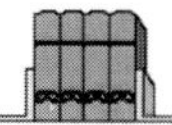

Product(s)

The product of this Activity is the partially completed PAD. All that the PAD indicates at the end of this Activity is the `Process` Class inheritance hierarchy. Processors are addressed in the next Activity.

7.3 IDENTIFY PROCESSORS

Once the `Process` Class hierarchy has been identified, the next step is to identify the physical processors that are required to support the software. Multiple processes may be executed by the same processor, while a process may execute on more than one processor.

Purpose

> To identify the physical processors required to run the processes of a system.

Definition(s)

Processor: A **processor** is a physical hardware device that can execute processes.

Process

Step 1: Add Processor Class

Add a `Processor` Class to the PAD. The `Processor` Class is the root Class of a `Processor` inheritance hierarchy. `Processor` Subclasses are the kinds of processors selected for the system.

Step 2: Add System Processor Aggregation Class

Next, add a UML composition (or Booch/OMT aggregation) Class for the system (e.g., `SEM_Processor_Collection`) to the PAD. This collection Class is to be composed of each identified processor selected for the system. The processors are identified in the next Step.

Step 3: Identify Processor Subclasses

Identify the kinds and number of application processors that are required to support the software system. These processors are Subclasses of the `Processor` Class.

Although the focus of this Activity is the identification of processors, remember to consider the number of concurrent processes that may be required for each processor. Consider how many process Instances will need to be connected simultaneously to other processes. Consider the kind of processing that each process will be performing. Processes that will be performing user interface operations may be best suited for PC-based processors, while server processes that will be handling complex transactions may be best suited for workstation-based processors. The kinds of processors selected may need to be re-examined after the processes are allocated to the processors (see Activity 7.4).

Step 4: Add Hierarchy Associations to the PAD

Add the inheritance relationship between the application `Processor` Subclasses and the `Processor` Superclass. Then, add a composition, or aggregation, relationship from the `SEM_Processor_Collection` Class to the domain `Processor` Subclasses, indicating the number of each kind of processor required in the aggregation.

Example

Figure 7-6 shows the updated PAD for the SEM. The SEM has two kinds of processors, a PC/Pentium and a Sun SPARC5. These processors were selected to support the three previously identified processes. The PC/Pentium processor was selected to support the `Display_Persistent_Process` because this process will *not* be performing any computationally intensive tasks. The SPARC5 processor was selected for the `Monitor_Persistent_Process` and `Database_Persistent_Process` because it is capable of supporting both processes. Note that both processors inherit from the `Processor` Class. Finally, note that the `SEM_Processor_`

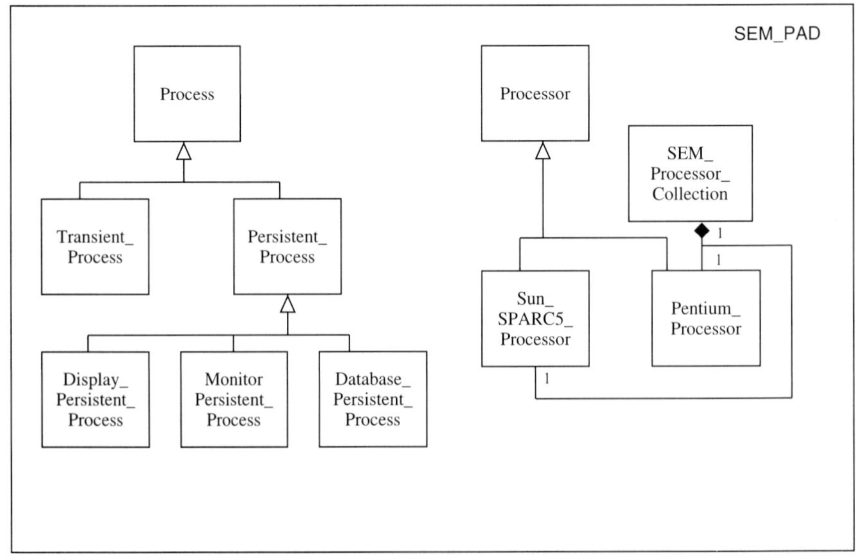

Figure 7-6. Developing the PAD - Step 4 : Adding Processor Hierarchy : UML Notation

`Collection` Class specifies that the SEM requires only one Pentium processor and one Sun SPARC5. The processes are allocated to the processors in the next Activity.

Pragmatic Project Issues

Consider the Processes

Remember to consider the functionality for which each process is responsible when identifying processors. GUI processes may be best suited to PC-class machines, while more complex application processes may be best suited to workstations.

Consider the Pending Allocation of Processes to Processors

The allocation of `Process` Subclasses to `Processor` Subclasses can affect the kinds of processors selected. If multiple processes are to be allocated to the same processor, a larger capacity processor type should be considered. Although these allocations are *not* made until the next Activity, they can, and will, influence the selection of the processors.

Consider Communication between Processors

Processor communication requirements may require even more processing capability. For example, PCs running Windows 3.1 cannot handle multiple simultaneous connections to other processors, while PCs running Windows 95 or Windows NT can.

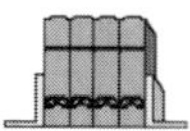

Product(s)

The product of this Activity is an updated PAD with the `Process` and `Processor` Class hierarchies depicted.

7.4 ALLOCATE PROCESSES TO PROCESSORS

Purpose

> To allocate the processes identified in Activity 7.2 to the processors identified in Activity 7.3.

Process

Step 1: Add Associations to the PAD

In this Activity, the PAD is updated by adding "IsAllocatedTo" association relationships between the `Process` Subclasses and `Processor` Subclasses. These association relationships identify which processes are allocated to which processors. [SHU92] also provides guidelines for this Step.

Example

Figure 7-7 shows the PAD with three "IsAllocatedTo" association relationships added. The diagram shows that the Display_Persistent_Process is allocated to the Pentium_Processor, while both the Monitor_Persistent_Process and Database_Persistent_Process are allocated to the Sun_SPARC5_Processor.

Pragmatic Project Issues

Too Many Processes per Processor

Make sure that the number of processes allocated to each processor does *not* exceed the operational capability of the processor.

Enough Processors?

Make sure that there are enough processors to account for all the Instances of each process. For example, if the SEM was expanded to 500+ living quarters, multiple Monitor_Persistent_Process Instances would be needed, which might also require additional Sun_SPARC5_Processor Instances.

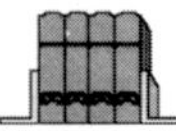

Product(s)

The product of this Activity is a completed PAD.

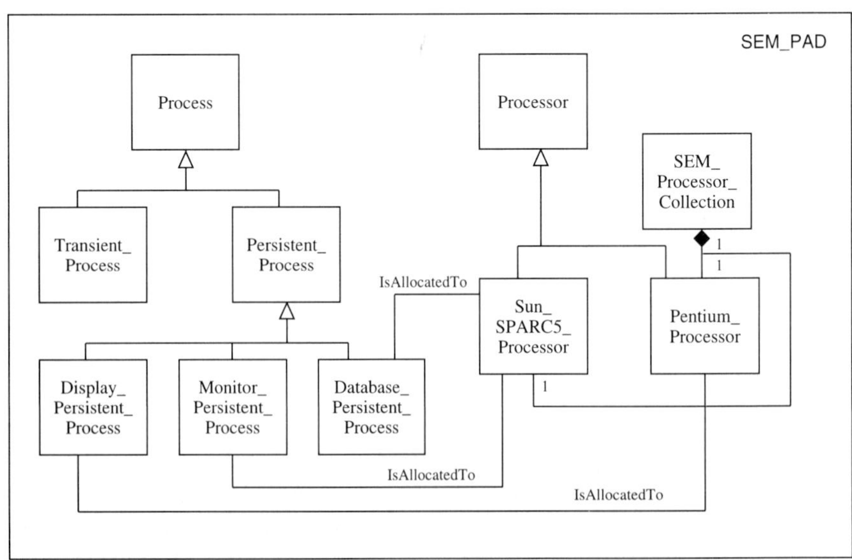

Figure 7-7. Developing the PAD - Step 5 : Adding "Is Allocated To" Association Relationship : UML Notation

7.5 ALLOCATE CLASSES TO PROCESSES

Now that the `Process/Processor` identification and categorization is conceived and documented in the PAD, this Activity focuses on allocating Classes to the processes previously specified in the PAD.

Purpose

> To allocate each identified Class to one or more specified process(es) for the purpose of building executables and identifying Classes that are "shared" by multiple processes.

Definition(s)

Processor-to-Class Allocation Diagram (PCAD): A **PCAD** is a Booch/UML Class Diagram or OMT Object Diagram that for each identified process, depicts the set of Classes required by the process. One PCAD is produced for each process.

Shared Class: A **shared Class** is a Class that has Instances that are required by more than one process, regardless of whether the processes are on the same or different processors. When an Instance of a Class is required by more than one process, a strategy must be devised to keep the Instances of the Class synchronized. Shared memory is one approach, where the Instances are maintained in shared memory and all processes access the Instance through shared memory. If the processes require non-intersecting portions of the Class in question, the Class can perhaps be decomposed into two Classes, with each process utilizing the appropriate partition of the Class. For example, if only one of multiple processes needs to access the Instance information in the *database*, the Class can be broken into two Classes providing direct access to the database Methods in the process that requires those services, thus avoiding database activity being linked into all processes. Another alternative is message passing to keep the Instances synchronized. Each Project Team makes its own decision here.

Process

Step 1: Create Initial PCADs

For each `Process` Subclass that is a leaf in the `Process` Class inheritance hierarchy, create a new, distinct PCAD, named <Process_Name>_PCAD. Place the `Process` Subclass that is the subject of the PCAD at the top center of the diagram. Review the CCD, CSs, and for each Domain Class, _View Class, and _IF Class, determine if that Class needs to be allocated to the specified `Process` Subclass. If a

Class is to be allocated to a process, add that Class to the appropriate PCAD and create a UML composition or Booch/OMT aggregation between the `Process` Subclass and domain Class in question.

Step 2: Insure PCAD Ownership

Again, make sure that the PCADs are owned by the `Process_CAT` Category.

Step 3: Consider Alternative Representation

If there are a large number of Classes, a matrix can be created for allocating Classes to processes. Create an N × M matrix, where N = the number of Classes and M = the number of processes. Place an 'X' in each column to show that the Class in the row has been allocated to the process in the indicated column. This is a less than desirable documentation strategy however, because it is a table, in a separate database, and thus is more difficult to include in project documentation. Again, by utilizing Booch/UML Class Diagrams or OMT Object Diagrams, all diagrams are accessible for inclusion in automatically generated project documentation.

Example

Figures 7-8 through 7-10, are the three PCADs for the SEM in UML notation. With PCADs, it is not necessary to represent multiplicity because only one Class is required to build the process. As previously stated, an alternative representation mechanism is,

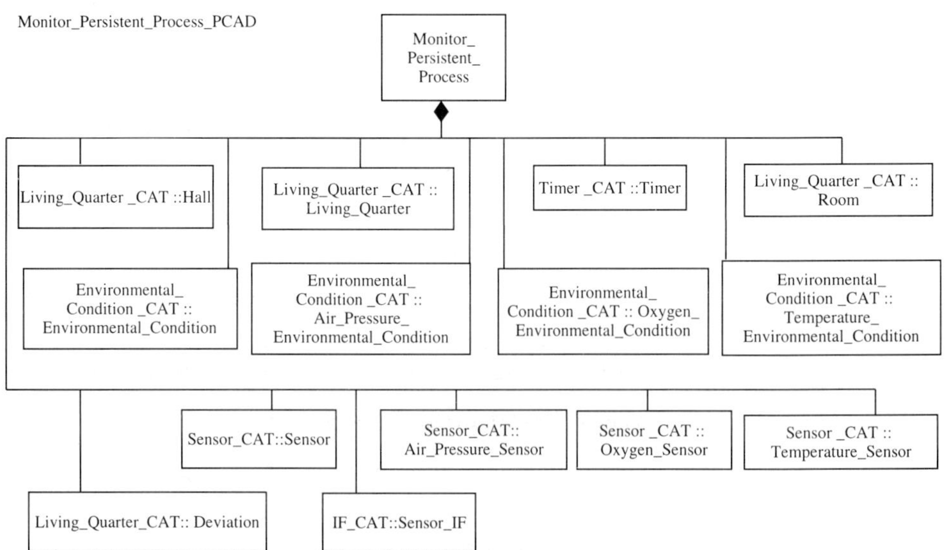

Figure 7-8. PCAD : Monitor_Persistent_Process : UML Notation

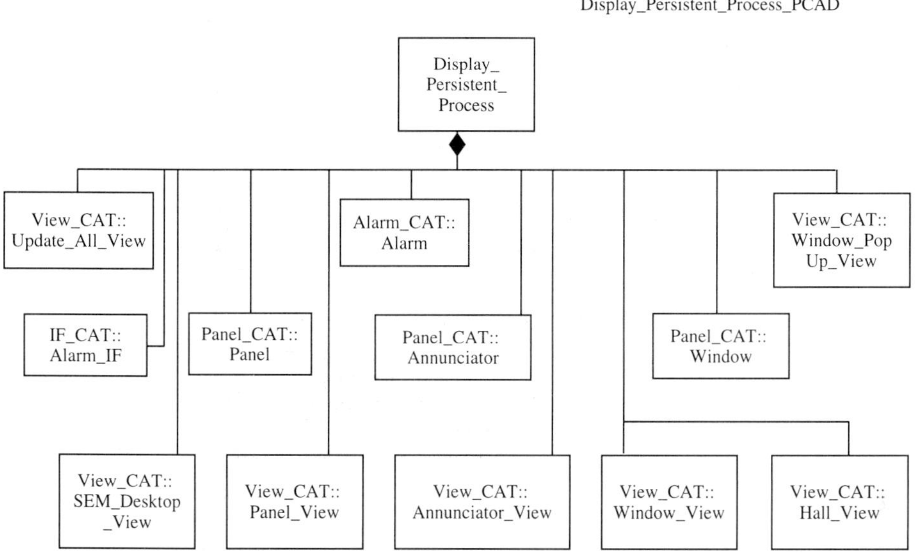

Figure 7-9. PCAD : Display_Persistent_Process : UML Notation

Database_Persistent_Process_PCAD

Database_ Persistent_ Process

DB_CAT::Database

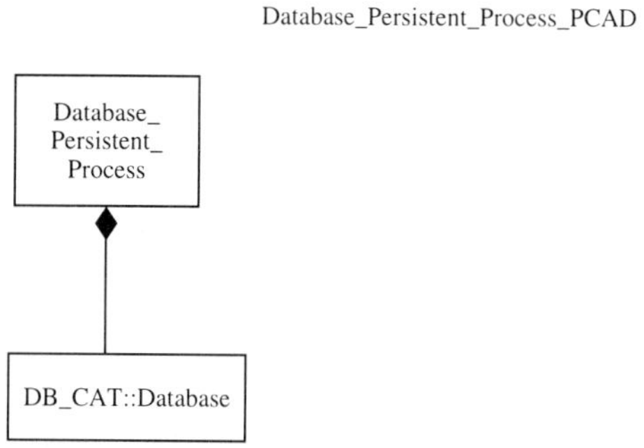

Figure 7-10. PCAD : Database_Persistent_Process : UML Notation

of course, a matrix. Table 7-1 shows the Process-to-Class Allocation Matrix for the SEM software.

The PCADs are the preferred vehicle to represent the information because the information is then maintained in the OO model repository, thus extractable from the repository for documentation purposes just as any other Class information is extractable.

The table and three figures show that for the SEM, there are *not* any Classes that need to be shared.

Table 7-1. Process-to-Class Allocation Matrix

	Display_Persistent_ Process	Monitor_Persistent_ Process	Database_Persistent_ Process
Air_Pressure_Environmental_ Condition		X	
Air_Pressure_Sensor		X	
Alarm	X[9]		
Alarm_IF	X		
Annunciator	X		
Annunciator_View	X		
DB			X
Deviation		X	
Environmental_Condition		X	
Hall		X	
Hall_View	X		
Living_Quarter		X	
Operator[10]			
Oxygen_Environmental_ Condition		X	
Oxygen_Sensor		X	
Panel	X		
Panel_View	X		
Room		X	
Sensor		X	
Sensor_IF		X	
Temperature_Environmental_ Condition		X	
Temperature_Sensor		X	
Timer		X	
Update_All_View	X		
Window	X		
Window_Pop_Up	X		
Window_View	X		
SEM_Desktop_View	X		

Pragmatic Project Issues

Consider Composition Hierarchy

If a Composite (or Aggregation) Class has been allocated to a process, then allocate all of its Parts to the same process. If the "part" Class is a member of another hierarchy that is used by another process, then of course this Class will appear on multiple

[9]Although it seems that the `Alarm` Class belongs to the `Monitor_Persistent_Process`, having `Alarm` in `Display_Persistent_Process` made life easier!

[10]Note the Operator Class does not require implementation.

PCADs, and thus is shared across the processes. If the shared Class participates in a composition relationship, no further analysis is necessary. Only if Instances of a shared Class are truly shared is there a requirement for further analysis.

Consider Splitting a Class

As previously introduced, if a Class is shared, meaning it is allocated to more than one process, and communication between processes needs to be minimized, consider splitting the Class into two (or more) Classes, if applicable, and allocate the new Classes appropriately. Otherwise, consider using shared memory for the Class, or some other alternative strategy.

Consider Inter-process Communication (IPC) Strategy

Another benefit of identifying shared Classes in this Activity is that *implementation issues* may cause a shared Class to be allocated to more than one process. For example, when implementing in SNAP, a Class that sends an RPC needs to be in *both* the sending process and the receiving process; but, when using DCE, the Class only needs to be in the sending process (with appropriate *compatible* code in the receiving process).

What Depth to Go to on a PCAD?

If Process A requires Class B, and Class B requires Class C, and Class C requires Class D, how many Classes get portrayed on a PCAD? To what level of detail should the PCAD go? Should the PCAD for process A just show Class B? Or, should the PCAD represent *all* Classes that are required for the process, meaning the PCAD would show all Classes: B, C, and D? The recommendation for large projects is to just show the Classes at the first level, meaning to just show Class B. The PCAD gets much too cluttered if all Classes are shown, and the purpose of the PCAD is *not* to create a make (`.mak`) file. But this of course is a project specific decision.

Product(s)

The product of this Activity is a collection of PCADs. The PCADs are used to update the CSs, which are the focus of the last Activity of this Phase, Activity 7.8, Update Class Specifications.

7.6 DEVELOP PROCESS INTERACTION DIAGRAM (PID)

Purpose

> The previous Activities in this Phase focused on the static view of the process architecture. The purpose of this Activity is to define the interaction between processes, or to develop a dynamic view of the process architecture.

How do the identified processes interact? Do they communicate directly with another process? Do they communicate through the database? Does any process spawn another process? The purpose of developing a Process Interaction Diagram (PID) is to explicitly indicate the process communication mechanisms envisioned for the system.

Definition(s)

Process Interaction Diagram (PID): A **PID** is a diagram that is drawn just like an ID (Jacobson Interaction Diagram, Booch Object Scenario Diagram, OMT Event Trace Diagram, or UML Sequence Diagram), and which shows how the processes interact.

Process

Step 1: Establish Naming Conventions

In the project CASE tool, develop one PID. Name the diagram as follows:

<System_Name>_PID, as in SEM_PID.

Step 2: Develop an Interaction Diagram

The only Classes permitted on a PID are process Classes from the `Process` inheritance hierarchy and the Database Class[11]. Some View Classes may be appropriate, particularly if a selection on a View Class invokes a transient process. On a PID, backward arrows *are* permitted to avoid replicating Process Classes on the PID.

Step 3: Establish Diagram Ownership

Make sure that the PID is owned by the `Process_CAT` Category.

Example

The PID for the SEM is shown in Figure 7-11.

Pragmatic Project Issues

The Process Subclasses `Initialize()` *Method*

In establishing IPCs, decisions must be made, based on the IPC mechanism selected, as to which processes are server processes (i.e., they open a connection) and which are client processes (i.e., they connect to an open connection). Once these connections are established, the process at one end of the connection sends RPCs to the process at the other end of the connection. For example, in the SEM, the processes communi-

[11]Controller Classes are also beneficial to show on a PID, but they have not yet been identified. The PID can be updated when the Controller Classes are identified (Phase 10), if a Project Team so chooses.

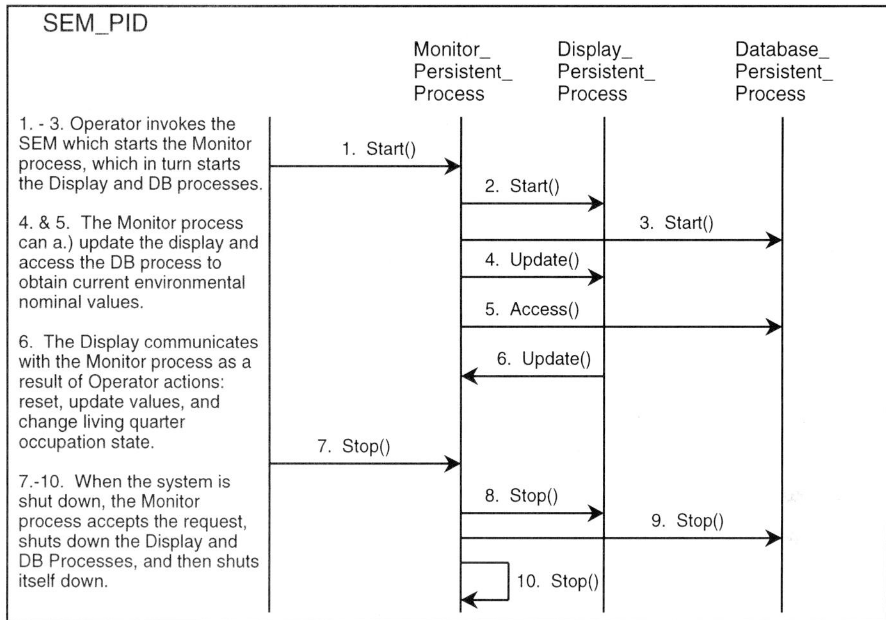

Figure 7-11. SEM PID

cate via RPCs. This means that certain processes open connections to send and receive RPC calls and others connect to the open connections. In the SEM, the `Monitor_Persistent_Process` opens a single connection for both the `Database_Persistent_Process` and `Display_Persistent_Process`. This Client/Server relationship can be reflected on the PAD. Figure 7-12 reflects the updated PAD.

Decomposing a PID

If there are too many processes, the PID can get quite large. Either print the PID on a plotter or decompose the PID into multiple smaller PIDs, which are then related by some higher-level PID (use the same philosophy as presented in Phase 3 for Supporting CIDs, and in Phase 6 for Supporting IDs).

Instance Diagrams

For "composable" systems, the PID as a Class Diagram may not be sufficient. IDs at the Instance level can better specify the process-to-process interaction for a specific configuration of the system.

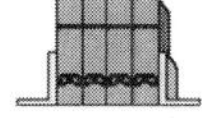

Product(s)

The product of this Activity is at least one PID that is owned by the `Process_CAT`.

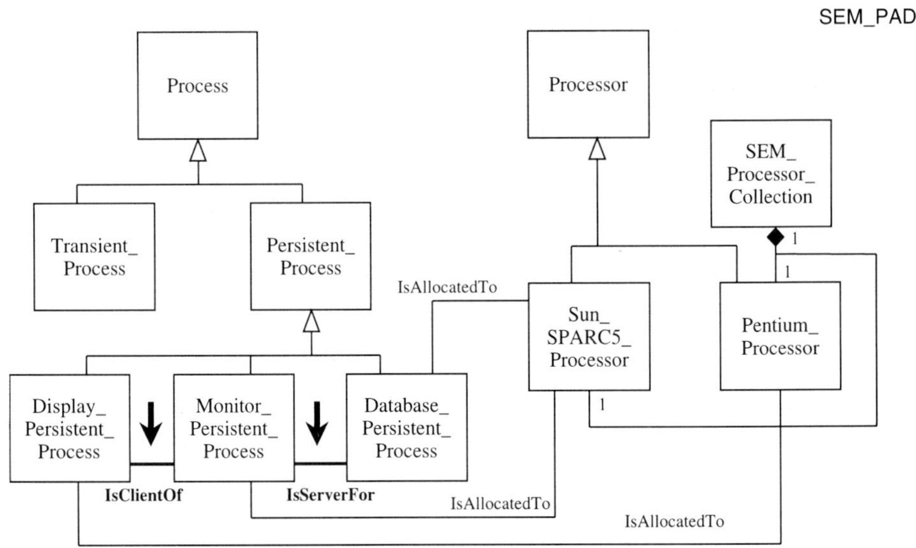

Figure 7-12. Updated PAD : UML Notation

7.7 DEVELOP STATE TRANSITION DIAGRAMS (STDs)

Purpose

The purpose of this Activity is to specify the internal behavior of processors in a fail/recovery mode, and to capture the internal behavior of processes, when applicable.

Process

Step 1: Determine Necessity for Processor STD

When viewing a processor as a Class, the `Processor` Class may or may *not* require an STD. For the SEM, an STD is *not* necessary because the `Processor` Class has a very simple behavior in the SEM, namely to keep processing! If the processor fails, the SEM does *not* have a backup processor to support automatic fail and recovery. However, in a two-server configuration, one server is the primary and the other server is the backup. In this case, the server Class has a State Attribute, `Server.State`, with two values: initialize and operational. When in the initialize state, a server determines whether it is to be the primary or backup server and then transitions to the operational state and the appropriate sub-state; primary or backup. Transitioning between primary and backup occurs when the heartbeat that the primary sends to the backup is lost and the backup must become the primary. In this situation an STD can be used to depict the behavior.

Step 2: Determine Necessity for Process STD

When viewing a process as a Class, the `Process` Class may or may *not* require an STD. This of course depends upon the complexity of the process. When an STD is appropriate, consider values for the `Process.State` Attribute as follows: running, ready, blocked, and terminated [BOO87A].

Step 3: Determine STD Appropriateness to Inheritance Hierarchy

There are times when the STD that represents the internal behavior of a Superclass is appropriate to all the Subclasses, and there are times when the STD for a Superclass is *not* appropriate to its Subclasses. Examine the `Processor` and `Process` Classes' inheritance hierarchies and create distinct STDs for Subclasses when appropriate.

Example

Figure 7-13(a) shows the STD for the `Processor` Class in the Client/Server configuration discussed above, in Booch notation. Although this is a very simplistic example, the concept of developing STDs for the `Processor` and `Process` Classes can be quite helpful in documenting their behavior in a fashion that is consistent with the rest of the project. Figure 7-13(b) represents the same STD in UML notation.

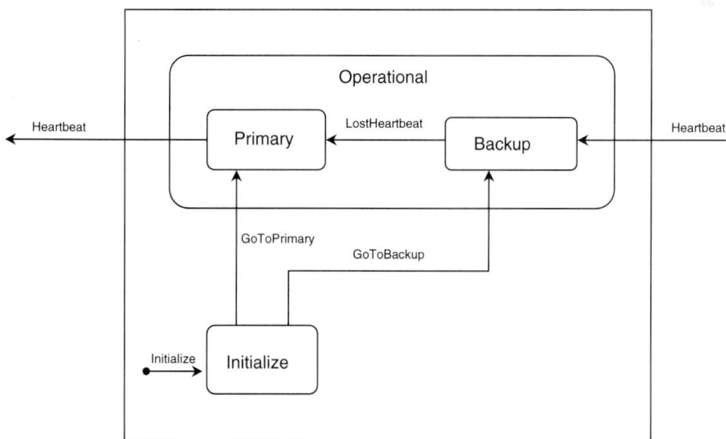

Figure 7-13(a). Sample Processor Class STD : Booch Notation

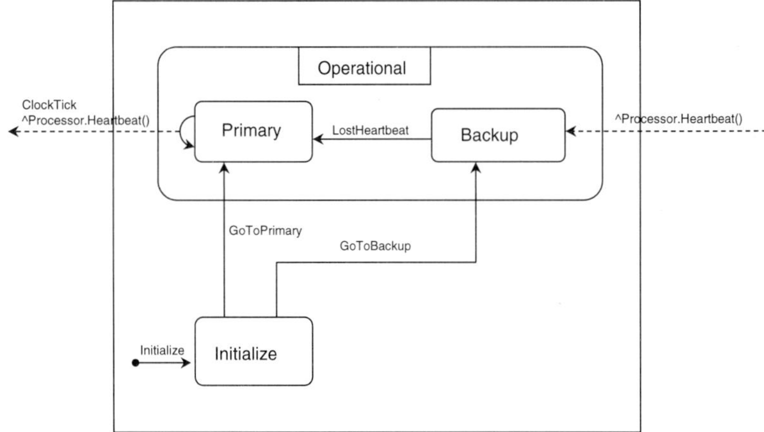

Figure 7-13(b). Sample Processor Class STD : UML Notation

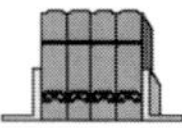

Product(s)

The product of this Activity is a set of STDs for the `Process_CAT` Classes that have interesting behavior.

7.8 UPDATE CLASS SPECIFICATIONS(CSs)

Purpose

> The previous Activities in this Phase identified new `Process` and `Processor` Class hierarchies, including the `Process` and `Processor` Subclasses that belong to those hierarchies.
>
> The purpose of this Activity is to capture and document, in CSs, the Attributes and Methods of all `Process` and `Processor` Classes in those hierarchies.

Although we tend to think of Instances of processes as functional (because a process provides for a specific functionality), the Instances *really belong* to a `Process` Class. To justify the previous statement, consider the following Attributes for a `Process` Superclass: `Process.Name`, `Process.Id`, `Process.Execution_Time`, `Process.Class_Collection`, `Process.Size`, and so on. `Process` Class Methods might include `Start()`, `Stop()`, `Pause()`, `Resume()`, `Time()`,

Initialize(), and so on. Attributes appropriate for the Processor Class are Processor.Speed, Processor.RAM, Processor.Kind, Processor.State, and so on. Sample Methods for the Processor Class are Current_State(), Boot(), Shutdown(), and so on. Obviously, the specific Attributes and Methods documented in the CSs for a specific project are those that reflect the customer's and project's requirements.

Process

Step 1: Add Class Specifications

The PAD introduces new Classes to the model which need to be documented in a CS. In the project CASE tool, complete the CSs for the Classes that have been introduced in this Phase, specifically:

- Process
- Transient_Process
- Persistent_Process
- Application Subclasses of Transient_Process
- Application Subclasses of Persistent_Process
- Processor
- Application Subclasses of Processor
- <<SystemName>>_Processor_Collection[12]

The PCAD is simply a *new* Class Diagram that represents the allocation of *previously identified* Classes to a process. No *new* Classes are introduced on the PCADs, consequently, *no new CSs* are required for those Classes.

Step 2: Add Association Descriptions

Finally, the Associations on the PAD and PCADs need to be documented, with rationale provided for the specific process/processor allocation.

Example

Figure 7-14 shows the CS for the Process Class. Projects will vary with respect to how much detail is provided, and of course, the choice of CASE tool drives the specific format. Recall that Transient_Process and Persistent_Process are Subclasses of the Process Class that were previously identified, and therefore, they are described in their own CSs. Recall that these Subclasses will inherit all the Attributes and Methods of the Process Class.

[12]For the SEM, the Class is named SEM_Processor_Collection.

Process

Category	: Process_CAT
Persistent/Transient	: N/A
Description	: A Process is an executable entity. Processes execute on processors. Processes are the vehicle by which the program achieves its desired effect. There are two kinds of processes: Transient_Process and Persistent_Process.[13]
Constraints:	: N/A
Superclass(es):	: N/A
Subclass(es):	: Persistent_Process, Transient_Process
Aggregate(s):	: N/A
Part(s):	: N/A
Number of Instances	: 0 (It is an Abstract Class.)

Attributes:

Class_Collection

Persistent/Transient	: Transient
Description	: A list of Classes allocated to the process
Domain of Values	: List (Alphabetically ordered)
Rules:	: N/A

File_Name

Persistent/Transient	: Transient
Description	: The full path name representing the .exe file
Domain of Values	: String
Rules:	: N/A

Last_Execution_Time

Persistent/Transient	: Transient
Description	: The last recorded time of execution
Domain of Values	: HH:MM:SS in 24-hour time
Rules:	: N/A

Maximum_Execution_Time

Persistent/Transient	: Persistent
Description	: The required maximum execution time, in milliseconds
Domain of Values	: Natural number
Rules:	: N/A

Name

Persistent/Transient	: Persistent
Description	: The name of the process

Figure 7-14. Process CS

[13]Actually there are more kinds, specifically bootable or non-bootable, bootable and transient, bootable and persistent, and so on. The specific hierarchy tree chosen for a project will depend on the decision-maker and time allotted to documenting the process architecture. We have found that simply using `Transient_Process` and `Persistent_Process` has been sufficient.

Domain of Values	: The domain of values, restricted to between one and eight **alphabetic** characters, inclusive
Rules:	: N/A
Process_ID	
Persistent/Transient	: Transient
Description	: The identification assigned to the process by the operating system at run-time
Domain of Values	: Dependent on the hardware upon which the process executes
Rules:	: N/A
State	
Persistent/Transient	: Persistent
Description	: The current status of a process
Domain of Values	: (Running, Ready, Blocked, Terminated)
Rules:	: N/A
Methods:	
Initialize()	
Description	: Set-up for the process, must be defined by each Subclass
Input(s)	:
Output	:
Algorithm	:
Resume()	
Description	: Resumes a previously suspended process
Input(s)	: N/A
Output	: A status indicator
Algorithm	: Sets Process.State to ready; manages the time interruption
Start():	
Description	: Starts a Process
Input(s)	: A Process_ID
Output	: A status indicator
Algorithm	: Sets Process.State to running; starts a clock and sets Process.Last_Execution_Time
Stop()	
Description	: Stops the execution of a process
Input(s)	: A Process_ID
Output	: A status indicator
Algorithm	: Sets Process.State to terminated; terminates the clock count
Suspend():	
Description	: Suspends a process for the indicated time in milliseconds
Input(s)	: Time in milliseconds
Output	: A status indicator
Algorithm	: Frees the CPU; sets Process.State to blocked; manages the time interruption

Figure 7-14. Process CS (*continued*)

Pragmatic Project Issues

The Process Class Initialize() Method

Each `Process` Class needs to have an `Initialize()` Method that is called as a part of the normal startup routine for the Class. The `Initialize()` Method functions as the main setup routine for the `Process` Class, executing anything that needs to be executed for the `Process` Class to be ready to execute. This includes, but is *not limited to,*

- Displaying the main GUI of the process,
- Connecting to the database (if required), and
- Establishing IPCs.

Consider the Schedule

Some Project Teams simply do *not* have time to properly document the process architecture. The counter-argument is that typically this information must be documented somewhere before the code is delivered. Why not as CSs, with the rest of the Class documentation?

Hardware Not Selected

If the hardware has *not* been selected, then obviously this information will need to be reverse-engineered at the time the decisions are made.

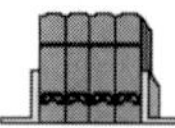

Product(s)

The product of this Activity is a set of new CSs for the `Process_CAT` Classes.

Phase Transition Criteria

This Phase can proceed concurrently with Phases 8 and 9, and most likely will. But, when all processes have been allocated to acceptable processors and all Classes have been allocated to processes, this Phase is considered completed. This Phase will be reviewed throughout the development process to verify that the specified processors are capable of meeting the timing and performance requirements of the system. This Phase involves the Systems Engineering organization; therefore, Systems Engineering needs to be included if any processor changes are required later in the development process. Using the review criteria in Table 7-2 will help determine whether transitioning to the next Phase is feasible.

Review Criteria

Table 7-2. PAD Review Criteria

#	Process Architecture Diagram Review Criteria
1	Has the PAD(s) been created?
2	Is the PAD named properly?
3	Has diagram ownership to the Process_CAT been established?
4	Is the process hierarchy depicted?
5	Do the domain processes inherit from Transient_Process and Persistent_Process?
6	Does the categorization of the domain processes make sense?
7	Is the number of processes reasonable?
8	Is each domain process: • Functionally cohesive • A hardware driver • Time-critical • Periodic
9	Ensure that all processes have been allocated to at least one processor.
10	Ensure that each processor can support the processes that have been allocated to it.
11	Ensure that there are enough processors to support the number of Instances of each process.

Tracking Progress

Table 7-3 shows the project management spreadsheet initiated for Part III. What is important here is that initial versions of the PAD, PCADs, and the PID(s) are produced. These diagrams form the basis for future iterations. Of course, the number of Classes in the `Process` Class' inheritance hierarchy, plus the number of Classes in the Processor inheritance hierarchy, plus one (for the processor Aggregation Class), determine how many CSs need to be written.

Ongoing monitoring of the previous metrics (e.g., Number of Classes per Category) will also reflect the additional `Process` and `Processor` Hierarchy Classes and their respective CSs.

Table 7-3. Project Management Spreadsheet: Phase 7

HCC Project Management Spreadsheet						
Number	**Phase Name**	**Activity**	**Charge Number**	**Product**	**Progress Metric**	**% Weight**
7	**Software OOD Process View**		**SW-OOD-PA-7**			
7.1		Initiate PAD	SW-OOD-PA-7.1	PAD	1 PAD completed	0.25
7.2		Identify Processes	SW-OOD-PA-7.2			
7.3		Identify Processors	SW-OOD-PA-7.3			
7.4		Allocate Processes to Processors	SW-OOD-PA-7.4			
7.5		Allocate Classes to Processes	SW-OOD-PA-7.5	PCADs	# PCADs (%)	0.30
7.6		Identify Process Interaction	SW-OOD-PA-7.6	PID	1 PID completed	0.25
7.7		Generate Process/Processor STD	SW-OOD-PA-7.7	STD	#STDs	0.10
7.8		Update Class Specifications	SW-OOD-PA-7.8	CSs	#CSs	0.10

PHASE 8

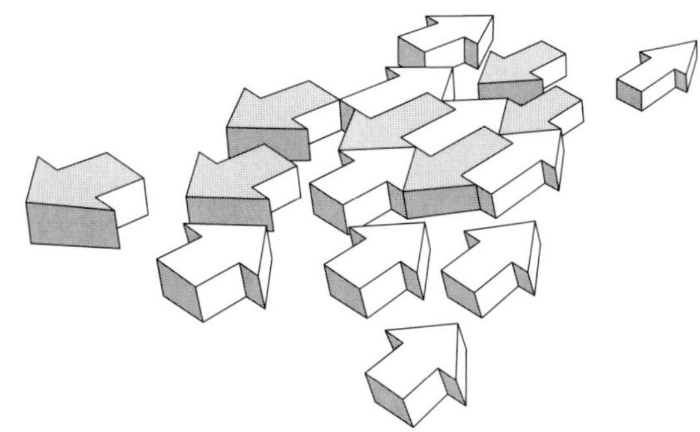

Software OOD–Static View

PHASE OVERVIEW

The purpose of this Phase is to migrate the static logical view produced in Phase 5 into a physical, or implementation view. Figure 8-1 identifies the Activities to be performed in this Phase. Basically the Phase consists of updating the

- Category Class Diagrams (CCDs), and
- Class Specifications (CSs).

This Phase does *not* introduce any new work products, but rather *refines previous* work products by adding more detail.

Refinements to the OOA CCDs performed during this Phase include: the addition of Parameterized Classes, Collection Classes, and the identification of Abstract Classes. Refinements to the OOA CSs consist of the specification of access rights for Attributes and Methods, the discovery of what exceptions each Class needs to raise/throw, and the identification of which Methods in a Class raise/throw the exception.

What is implicitly being said, *not* explicitly until now, is that Booch Module Diagrams (UML Component Diagrams) are *not* produced. Experience has shown that Booch Module Diagrams (UML Component Diagrams) simply reflect another view of the updated CCD and do *not* provide any new semantic information.

8.1 UPDATE CATEGORY CLASS DIAGRAM (CCD)

Purpose

> The purpose of this Activity is to provide more detail in the CCD; specifically, to identify new Classes and association relationships, as well as to identify visibility requirements for Classes and Class resources.

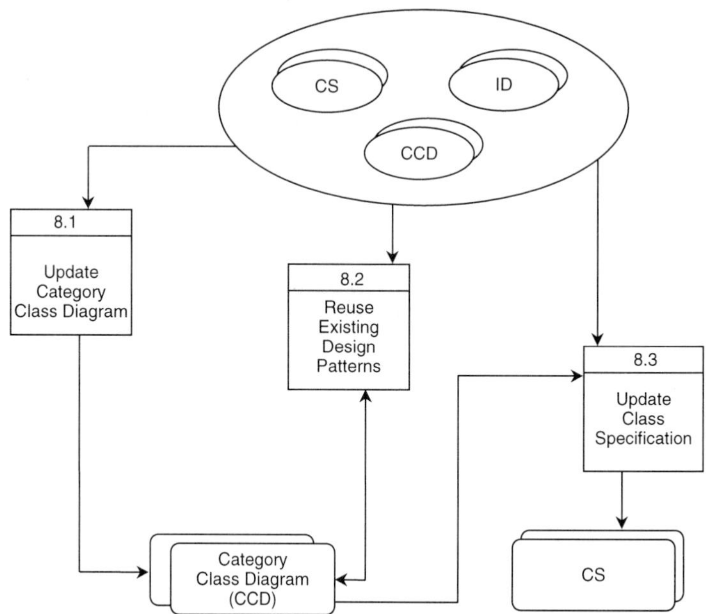

Figure 8-1. Software OOD - Static View Phase Description Diagram

The Steps for this Activity are identified in Figure 8-2. Because this Activity has many Steps and is rather lengthy, the Definition, Process, Example, and Pragmatic Project Issues subsections are included for each Step, rather than just once for the Activity.

Process

Step 1: Specify Inter-Class Visibility

Association Relationships, as modeled up to now, do *not* imply any direction. That means that there is no explicit identification as to which Class in the Association Relationship *provides* the services and which Class *uses* the services. Changing Association Relationships into Booch Uses Relationships (UML Dependencies) implies control, or direction. Changing Association Relationships into Booch Uses Relationships (UML Dependencies) identifies which Class is the client (requires resources) and which Class is the supplier (supplies resources).

Definition(s)

Client Class: A **Client Class** is a Class which is the owner of a Booch Uses Relationship (UML Dependency). A **Client Class** contains a reference to its Supplier Class in the form of an Attribute.

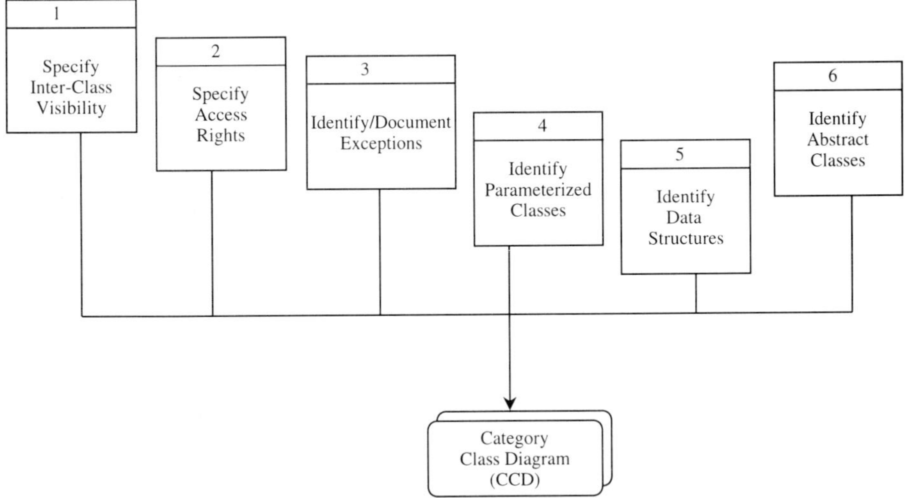

Figure 8-2. The Six Steps of Activity 8.1

Supplier Class: A **Supplier Class** is a Class that is the target of a Booch uses relationship (UML Dependency). A **Supplier Class** is a Class that provides services to a Client Class.[1]

Uses Relationship: A **uses relationship** shows that the Client Class *depends* on the Supplier Class to provide services, and implies that the Client Class needs visibility to the Supplier Class in the implementation language. Recall that this is the same definition as provided earlier for a UML Dependency.

Process

Step 1.1 Migrate Association Relationship to Uses Relationship (UML Dependency)

For example, consider the association relationship "Affects" between the `Timer` and `Living_Quarter` Classes. As currently modeled, there is no indication whether the `Timer` *interrupts* the `Living_Quarter`, or whether the `Living_Quarter` *polls* the `Timer`. If the `Timer` *interrupts* the `Living_Quarter`, the `Timer` has control, and the Association Relationship between the `Timer` and `Living_Quarter` should become a Uses Relationship *from* the `Timer` *to* the `Living_Quarter`. Stated differently, the `Timer` is the client and the `Living_Quarter` is the supplier. On the other hand, if the `Living_Quarter` *polls* the `Timer`, the `Living_Quarter` has control, and the Association Relationship should become a Uses Relationship *from* the `Living_Quarter` *to* the `Timer`. In this case, the

[1]A Supplier Class is `with`'ed (in Ada) or `#include`'d (in C++) by the corresponding Client Class.

`Living_Quarter` is the client and the `Timer` is the supplier. This identification of control is vital, because as will be shown in Phase 10, the direction of an Association Relationship transitions directly to language visibility constructs[2].

Revisit each CCD. Examine *each* Association Relationship and determine which Class is the Supplier Class and which Class is the Client Class. If the CASE tool being used supports the *changing* of relationship types, *change* Association Relationships into Booch Uses Relationships (UML Dependency). If the CASE tool does *not* support changing relationship types, delete the Association Relationships and draw Booch Uses Relationships (UML dependency) *from* the Clients *to* the Suppliers.

Step 1.2: Pay Special Attention to One-to-One and Many-to-Many Association Relationships

A one-to-many Association Relationship is easy to transition. The Class with the one cardinality will be the client and the Class with the many cardinality will be the supplier. For one-to-one and many-to-many associations, *each* Class in the Association Relationship *may* need to be *both* supplier and client. Note that if the implementation language does *not* support circular references between Classes, an OMT Link Association Class (UML Association Class) needs to be created to handle bi-directional Uses Relationships.

Figure 8-3(a) shows a many-to-many Association Relationship between two Classes and Figure 8-3(b) shows how this many-to-many Association Relationship changes when a UML Association Class is introduced. In Figure 8-3(a), the

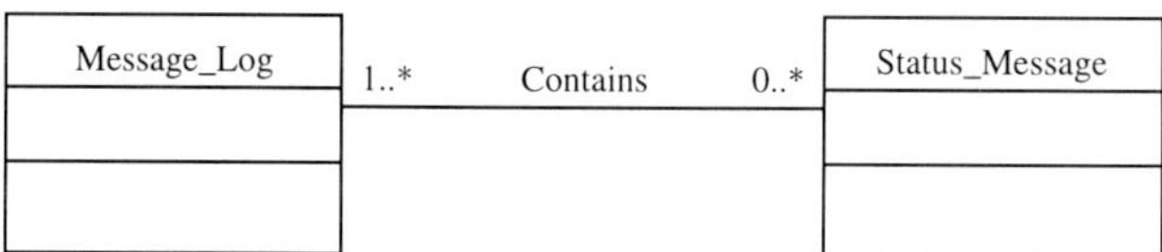

Figure 8-3(a). Many-to-Many Association : UML Notation

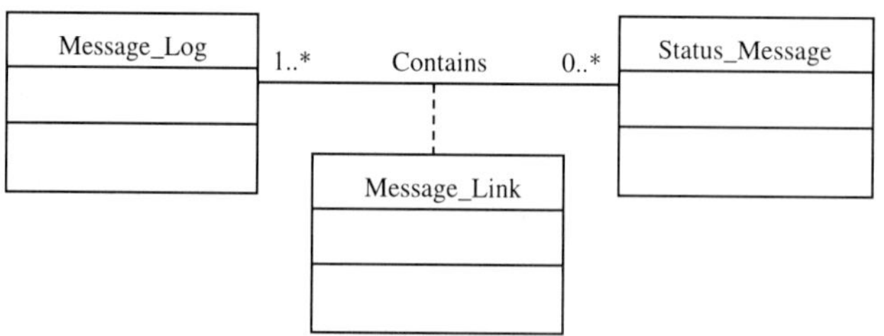

Figure 8-3(b). Many-to-Many Association with UML Association Class : UML Notation

[2]A Client Class `with`'s (in Ada) or `#include`'s (in C++) the corresponding Supplier Class.

Association Relationship between Message_Log and Status_Message represents the hypothetical situation where an Operator may sort a Message_Log and store the results in another Message_Log that holds the sorted set of Status_Messages. In this hypothetical case, a Status_Message is contained in many Message_Logs and a Message_Log possibly contains many Status_Messages. Now, see in Figure 8-3(b) how this many-to-many association changes with the addition of the Message_Link Class. Finally, the Message_Link Class has a Uses Relationship (UML Dependency) to both the Message_Log and Status_Message Classes, as shown in Figure 8-4.

Step 1.3: Name Uses Relationships

Make sure each Uses Relationship is labeled with a meaningful name because, in some CASE tools, that name is used for the Attribute in the Client Class that references the Supplier Class. For example, the Living_Quarter Class uses the Hall Class. The Uses Relationship is labeled HallId, which becomes the name of the Attribute in the Living_Quarter Class that contains the reference to the Instance of the Hall Class. If the CASE tool directly supports this Activity, fine. If not, the Project Team needs to define conventions to provide for this capability; in other words, good conventions identified here can result in more consistent code.

Step 1.4: Assign/Validate Cardinality

Assign cardinality to the target end (Supplier Class) of the Uses Relationship. Make sure the cardinality is correct as specified by the analysis models. The cardinality will help define the implementation type of the Attribute.

Step 1.5: Do Not Transition Inheritance Hierarchies

Do *not* transition an inheritance hierarchy to a Uses Relationship because this may inhibit automatic code generation by the selected CASE tool. Additionally you do not want to lose the visual specification of inheritance.

With respect to Client/Supplier relationships in an inheritance hierarchy: a Subclass is always a client to its parent, and a Superclass is always a supplier to its Subclasses.

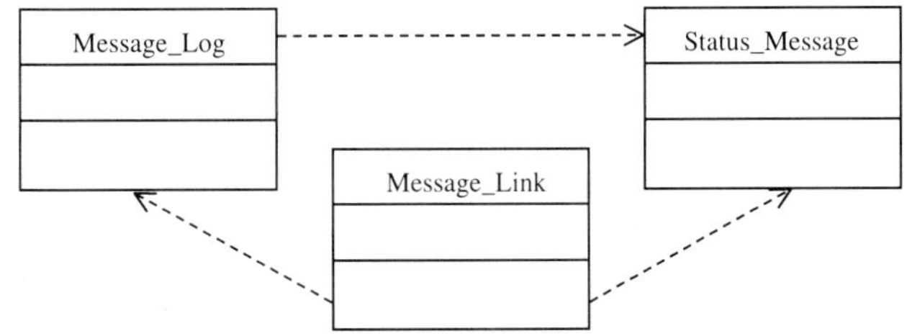

Figure 8-4. Transitioning a Many-to-Many Association : UML Notation

Step 1.6: Transition Aggregation Hierarchies

A "part" Class in an aggregation hierarchy is the Supplier Class to its "whole" Class, consequently, transition composition, or aggregation, such that the "whole" Class has a Uses Relationship to its "part" Class. Alternatively, because it is so clear that a "whole" Class depends on its "part" Class, a Project Team may decide *not* to change the aggregation symbol. When making the decision, consider the CASE tool being utilized and whether or not code is automatically generated from an aggregation symbol.

At the time of this writing, there is a great deal of discussion in the industry about whether a "part" Class can also be a client of its "whole" Class. One position is that a "whole" Class is responsible for managing its "part" Classes, and therefore, any requests for services on a part must *first* go through the "whole" Class. First, the requested part is extracted from the "whole" Class (through a get operation) and the "whole" Class (or a Controller Class) then sends the part to the appropriate "part" Class for the specific service. This mechanism permits the "whole" Class to always have knowledge of services performed on its parts. An alternate position is that a "part" Class can be called directly, particularly when the "whole" Class really doesn't need knowledge of its parts. The authors prefer the first position, as it is hard to imagine when a "whole" Class won't require knowledge of its parts; otherwise, why would it have "part" Classes in the first place?

Example

Figure 8-5 shows the Living_Quarter_CAT_CCD updated to reflect the changing of Association Relationships to Uses Relationships. In the figure, note that each Uses Relationship has its cardinality specified.

Figure 8-6 shows *part* of the CS for the `Living_Quarter` Class as a result of the decision that the `Living_Quarter` Class is the Client Class and the `Hall` Class is the Supplier Class. The `Living_Quarter` Class now has an Attribute that identifies the Instance of the `Hall` Class referenced by a `Living_Quarter` Instance. The same discussion can be repeated for the `Room` Class. Note also that the Association Relationships are described.

Pragmatic Project Issues

To Add or Not to Add an OMT Link Association Class/UML Association Class

Recall that either a one-to-one or many-to-many association is an indication that each Class may need to be both a client and supplier to the other Class in the association, which in turn can result in a Uses Relationship in each direction. Some languages, C++ for example, permit circular references, in which case the OMT Link Association Class/UML Association Class is *not* needed when moving to implementation. (So, why model it?) Other languages, such as Ada, do *not* support circular referencing, so this type of Class is needed in the model. A good policy is to *always* model a Link Association Class/UML Association Class for the sake of clarity. Just because a language permits circular references does *not* mean that the capability must be utilized!

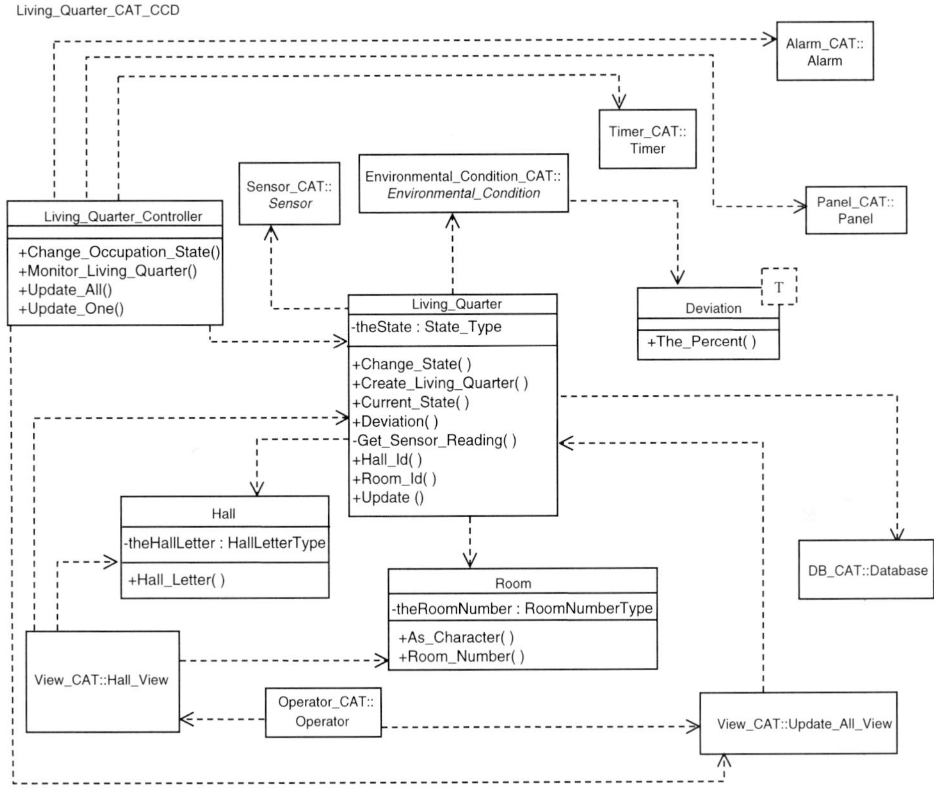

Figure 8-5. Living_Quarter_CAT_CCD : UML Notation

Step 2: Specify Access Rights

Now, establish the visibility of each of the Class resources: first establish the visibility for each Attribute and then establish the visibility of each Method. Focusing on the Attributes first helps to both identify new Methods, as well as to establish the required visibility for an individual Method.

Definition(s)

Private[3]: A **private** access right *prohibits* access by external Classes to a Class' Attributes and/or Methods that are designated as **private**. A **private** access right permits access by Subclasses that inherit privately from the Class in question. The graphical symbol to represent private access is a minus sign (–).

[3]This definition is consistent and compatible with the UML v1.0 [RAT97] definition.

Living Quarter

Category:	: Living_Quarter_CAT
Persistent/Transient	: Persistent
Description	: Maintains data with respect to Living Quarter
Constraints:	: There are 48 Living Quarters
Superclass(es)	: None
Subclass(es)	: N/A
Aggregate(s)	: None
Part(s):	: N/A
Expected Instances	: 48

Attributes:

HallId

Persistent/Transient	: Persistent
Description	: The hall identifier for the living quarter
Domain of Values	: A through E, inclusive
Rules:	: No more than eight rooms per hall

RoomId

Persistent/Transient	: Persistent
Description	: The room identifier for the living quarter
Domain of Values	: 1 through 8, inclusive
Rules:	: No more than eight rooms per hall

. . .

Methods:

Deviation ()

Description	: Obtains current value, obtains nominal value, and returns the deviation between the two values as a %
Input(s)	: aLivingQuarter, aBaseValue, and aCurrentValue
Output	: Float (representing a %)
Algorithm	: Two retrieves followed by a send to ThePercent()

. . .

Relationships:

Living Quarter (IdentifiedBy) Hall

Description	: Each living quarter is identified by a hall letter and a hall letter is associated with eight living quarters

Living Quarter (IdentifiedBy) Room

Description	: Each living quarter is identified by a room number and a room number is associated with six living quarters

. . .

Figure 8-6. Living Quarter CS

Protected[4]: A **protected** access right *permits* access by Subclasses to their Superclasses' Attributes and Methods that have been designated as **protected**. A **protected** access right *prohibits* access by *non*-Subclasses to a Class' Attributes and/or Methods. The graphical symbol to represent protected access is a pound sign (#).

[4]This definition is consistent and compatible with the UML v1.0 [RAT97] definition.

Public[5]**:** A **public** access right allows *all* Client Classes visibility to a Class' Attributes and/or Methods that are designated as **public**. The graphical symbol to represent public access is the plus sign (+).

Process

Step 2.1: Establish Attribute Visibility

Review *each* CS for the current build's Classes. For *each* Attribute in *each* Class, ask the following question:

> Does any other Class need access to this Attribute?

If the answer to the above question is "Yes," and all of the Classes requiring access are Subclasses of the Class in question, make the Attribute a protected Attribute and do not worry about Get and Set Methods for the Attribute of the Subclasses because each Subclass (and each Subclass of that Subclass) will have direct access to the Attribute. However, if the answer to the question posed above is "No" and there are Classes that are *not* Subclasses that require access, make the Attribute private and then ask yourself the next question:

> What type of access is needed, Get, Set, or both?

Step 2.2: Identify New Methods

Based on the answer to the above question, ensure that the appropriate Get[6] and Set Methods already exist, then make sure these Methods are public Methods; otherwise, add the new Get and Set Methods as public Methods.

Figure 8-7 shows a decision tree that summarizes Steps 2.1 and 2.2.

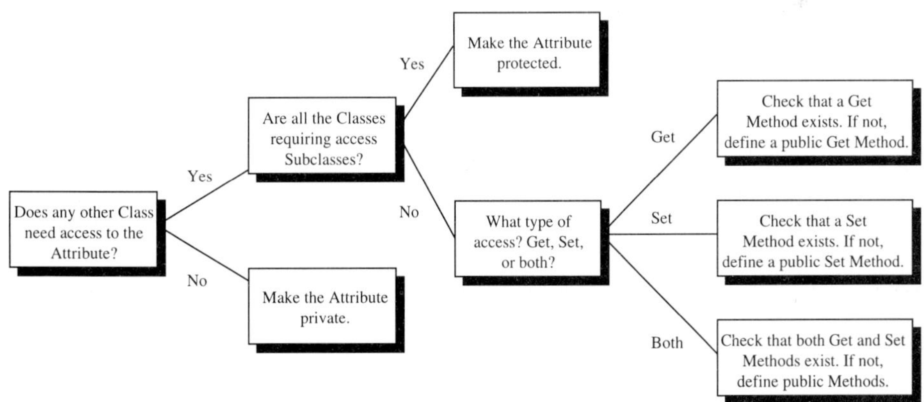

Figure 8-7. Decision Tree for Determining Attribute Access Rights

[5]This definition is consistent and compatible with the UML v1.0 [RAT97] definition.

[6]Recall that Get Methods are named for the Attribute being retrieved and Set Methods are named Set_<Attribute_Name>.

Step 2.3: Establish Method Visibility

Review each CS. For *each* Method in *each* Class, ask the following question:

Do any other Classes need to call the Method in question?

If the answer to this question is "Yes," and all of the Classes that need to call the Method are Subclasses of the Class which owns the Method, make the Method a protected Method because the Subclasses will then acquire direct access to the Method. If the answer to the question posed above is "Yes" and all of the Classes that need to call the Method are *not* Subclasses of the Class which owns the Method, make the Method public. If the answer to the question posed above is "No," make the Method private. Figure 8-8 shows a decision tree that summarizes this decision-making process.

Example

Figure 8-9 shows the updated CS for the `Living_Quarter` Class. Note that a new field, Visibility, has been added for each Attribute and Method. When specified, this visibility assignment is portrayed on the CCDs *when* the Attributes and Methods are displayed for each Class.

Pragmatic Project Issues

Visibility

It is considered good OO practice *not* to have any public Attributes, that is, all Attributes should be private or protected, and public Methods should be used to set and query Attributes within a Class. There may be several implementation reasons to make an exception to this rule. For example, in cases of time-critical performance, it may be faster to directly access a public Attribute in another Class than it is to make a function call. If language-supplied mechanisms for optimization (e.g., pragma Inline

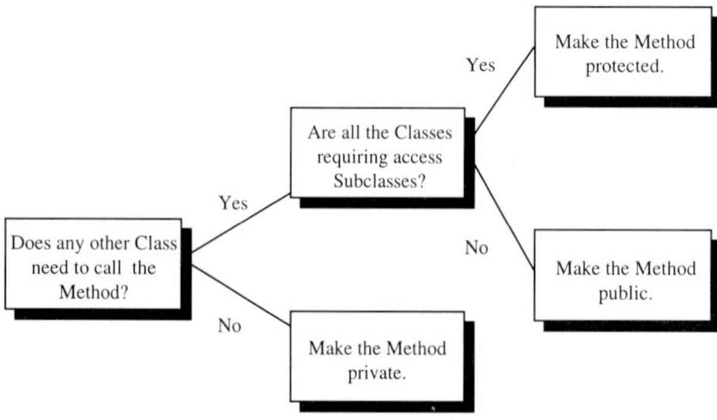

Figure 8-8. Decision Tree for Determining Method Access Rights

Living Quarter

Category:	: Living_Quarter_CAT
Persistent/Transient	: Persistent
Description	: Maintains data with respect to living quarter
Constraints:	: There are 48 Living Quarters
Superclass(es)	: None
Subclass(es)	: N/A
Aggregate(s)	: None
Part(s):	: N/A
Expected Instances	: 48

Attributes:

HallId

Persistent/Transient	: Persistent
Description	: The hall identifier for the living quarter
Domain of Values	: A through E, inclusive
Rules:	: No more than eight rooms per hall
Visibility	***: private***

RoomId

Persistent/Transient	: Persistent
Description	: The room identifier for the living quarter
Domain Of Values	: 1 through 8, inclusive
Rules:	: No more than eight rooms per hall
Visibility	***: private***

. . .

Methods:

Deviation ()

Description	: Obtains current value, obtains nominal value, and returns the deviation between the two values as a %
Input(s)	: aLivingQuarter, aBaseValue and aCurrentValue
Output	: Float (representing a %)
Algorithm	: Two retrieves followed by a send to ThePercent()
Visibility	***: public***

. . .

Relationships:

Living Quarter (IdentifiedBy) Hall	
Description	: Each living quarter is identified by a hall letter and a hall letter is associated with eight living quarters
Living Quarter (IdentifiedBy) Room	
Description	: Each living quarter is identified by a room number and a room number is associated with six living quarters

. . .

Figure 8-9. Living Quarter CS

in Ada, and inline functions in C++) do *not* provide the timing required and additional optimization techniques fail, try making the Attribute in question a public Attribute, noting the reason for making the Attribute public in the CS.

Private vs. Protected

In most OO programming languages, private Attributes and Methods are *not* visible to their Subclasses[7]. Attributes and Methods in Superclasses should only be private if the Superclass is *not* an Abstract Class (see Activity 8.6), and the Attribute/Method in question is only required by Instances of the Superclass.

Step 3: Identify/Document Exceptions

The purpose of this Step is to identify the exceptions for a Class and the Methods that raise/throw them. Identifying exceptions is *not* easy.

Definition(s)

Exception: An **exception** is an error condition that occurs during run-time, and that without associated corrective processing, results in system failure.

Process

A general rule of thumb for finding exceptions is to look for conditions under which a Method will ***fail***, that is, look for conditions when the Method ***cannot execute to completion*** without crashing the system. An example of an exception is an attempt to divide by zero. Examine the Method `The_Percent()` in the `Temperature_Environmental_Condition` Class[8]. Note that if the input value for the base parameter is zero, the Method will fail due to an attempt to divide by zero. If this condition is *not* detected, the program will crash. Consequently, an exception, `DivideByZero`, needs to be thrown by the `The_Percent()` Method in the Class. On the other hand, if the `Temperature_Environmental_Condition.theTempValue` *cannot* be read from the database, this is *not* an exception *if* the design of the system is such that the system can use a last known value. If there is no last known value, this condition would be an exception.

Step 3.1: Identify Exceptions

Examine the Scenarios. Look for the "Exceptions:" section in each Scenario. For each of the conditions, identify an exception in the Class whose Method might encounter the error condition in question. Examine each Method currently identified for a Class. Ask yourself "Under what condition(s) will this Method fail?"

[7]As previously stated, private inheritance can be used to gain access in a Subclass to private Attributes and Methods. This is *not* recommended as it breaks the principle of information hiding.

[8]The CS for the `Temperature_Environmental_Condition` Class was initiated in Phase 5.

Step 3.2: Associate Exceptions with Methods

For each of the above identified exceptions, determine which Method(s) raises/throws each exception.

Step 3.3: Document the Exception

Be sure to document, in the CS, the fact that a Class defines an exception, as well as which Method(s) raises/throws the exception.

Example

Figure 8-10 shows the Scenario for UC1_SW_Monitors_Living_Quarters. Note the exception condition that the deviation, that is identified in the Scenario, *cannot* be computed.

Name the exception `CantCompute`, to be owned by the `Living_Quarter` Class. Next, determine which Method(s) causes the exception to occur. It is clear that the `Deviation()` Method raises/throws this exception, because it is this Method that needs to return the calculation to a client. Figure 8-11 shows the updated CS for the `Living_Quarter` Class. Note that two new sections have been added to the CS: 1) a general "Exceptions" field preceding the Attributes Section, and 2) an "Exceptions Raised" field in the Method section for a Method.

Pragmatic Project Issues

All OO Languages Do Not Support Exceptions

Exceptions are *not* supported in all OO languages[9]. If the implementation language being used does *not* support exceptions and an "`if...then...else`" construct is used instead to perform the required error detection and handling, still perform this Activity as the identification of the exceptions helps the implementer determine what Methods require the "`if...then...else`" construct!

A Very Fine Line

When does a condition justify the definition of an exception? If a condition can occur that causes a Method to fail, define an exception for that condition. If a condition can occur that is an expected part of processing (i.e., a user enters an invalid password when logging into a system), this is *not* an exception and the condition should be dealt with using normal decision logic (e.g., `if...then...else`, or case/switch). Consequently, an exception, `CantDegrade` for the `Window` Class, was ***not*** introduced because the code can work around this situation by ignoring the request to degrade and continuing to flash at the same rate until either 1) the condition is corrected, or 2) the Operator turns off the window.

[9]SNAP does not currently support exceptions.

Use Case 1: SW_Monitors_Living_Quarters

Overview:

This Use Case allows an operator to monitor ***all*** occupied living quarters by viewing the main display.

Preconditions:

1. The database is accessible.
2. The SEM software is properly linked and the executable exists.
3. The SEM_Desktop_View is displayed.

Scenario:

Action	Software Reaction
1. Initialize/Start timer	1. Timer initialized (set time interval)
2. Pop timer	2. Timer triggers loop of monitoring living quarters
3. For each living quarter, check occupation state	3. Return living quarter occupational status
4. If occupied, for one environmental condition acquire nominal value from DB	4. Nominal value for living quarter for one environmental condition
5. If occupied, acquire sensor reading for the environmental condition for the living quarter	5. Current value obtained (UC3)
6. Calculate deviation	6. Deviation calculated as a percent
7. Update display and sound alarm, if required	7. Display updated
8. Operator selects Update_All button	8. UC16
9. Operator selects Restart button	9. UC25
10. Operator changes occupation state of a living quarter	10. UC26
11. Operator turns off window (and alarm, if deviation was >= 3%)	11. UC22 (and if appropriate, UC21)

Scenario Notes:

Steps 3–7 are repeated for each living quarter. Steps 4 and 5 are repeated for each environmental condition.
Step 2 automatically repeats until there is Operator intervention
Steps 8–12 represent action upon Operator intervention.

Post Conditions:

1. The SEM_Desktop_View is displayed reflecting current conditions for each living quarter.
2. The timer is (re)set.

Required GUI:

1. The main display (SEM_Desktop_View)

Use Cases Utilized:

Uses UC 3, 7, 8, 9, and 18. Also uses UC 21, 22, 25, and 26.

Exceptions:

1. The database is not accessible.
2. The deviation cannot be calculated.

Timing Constraints:

Must be performed within one minute.

Figure 8-10. Scenario for UC1

Living Quarter

Category:	: Living_Quarter_CAT
Persistent/Transient	: Persistent
Description	: Maintains data with respect to living quarter
Constraints:	: There are 48 living quarters
Superclass(es)	: None
Subclass(es)	: N/A
Aggregate(s)	: None
Part(s):	: N/A
Expected Instances	: 48
Exceptions	***: CantCompute***

Attributes:

HallId

Persistent/Transient	: Persistent
Description	: The hall identifier for the living quarter
Domain of Values	: A through E, inclusive
Rules:	: No more than eight rooms per hall
Visibility	: private

RoomId

Persistent/Transient	: Persistent
Description	: The room identifier for the living quarter
Domain of Values	: 1 through 8, inclusive
Rules:	: No more than eight rooms per hall
Visibility	: private

. . .

Methods:

Deviation ()

Description	: Obtains current value, obtains nominal value, and returns the deviation between the two values as a %
Input(s)	: aLivingQuarter, aBaseValue, and aCurrentValue
Output	: Float (representing a %)
Algorithm	: Two retrieves followed by a send to ThePercent()
Visibility	: Public
Exceptions Raised	***: CantCompute***

. . .

Relationships:

Living Quarter (IdentifiedBy) Hall

Description	: Each living quarter is identified by a hall letter, and a hall letter is associated with eight living quarters

Living Quarter (IdentifiedBy) Room

Description	: Each living quarter is identified by a room number, and a room number is associated with six living quarters

. . .

Figure 8-11. Living Quarter CS

Watch out for Status Codes

Sometimes status codes are generated as a result of making a system call. These status codes should *not* be passed around the system because it is difficult to remember what a status code means. Bury the system call in a more abstract user interface and raise/throw exceptions.

Step 4: Identify Domain Parameterized Classes

The purpose of this Activity is to determine which *Domain* Classes are Parameterized Classes and which Classes are Instances of a Parameterized Class. This Step does *not* concern itself with data structure Parameterized Classes. That Step is a subsequent Step.

Definition(s)

Parameterized Class: A **Parameterized Class** is a Class that is used as the base Class description for a new Class. **Parameterized Classes** are implemented as templates in C++, or as generics in Ada95.

Process

Step 4.1: Examine Domain Classes

Examine the Domain Classes in the model. Look both for Domain Classes that have similar specifications and for Domain Classes that have Attributes or Methods that are duplicated in other Classes. These Domain Classes are candidates to become Parameterized Classes. Use the CASE tool, if possible, to represent Parameterized Classes.

Step 4.2: Add Relationships

If the selected CASE tool provides a notation for instantiation, draw instantiations *from* the Classes that require a Parameterized Class *to* the Parameterized Class. If the selected CASE tool does *not* support a notation for this kind of relationship, simply choose an appropriate naming convention for Parameterized Classes and draw a Uses Relationship *from* the Class that requires a Parameterized Class *to* the Parameterized Class. If using UML, draw a dependency to the Parameterized Class and label the dependency <<instantiates>>.

Step 4.3: Develop Class Specifications for Parameterized Classes

Because a Parameterized Class is a Class, the Parameterized Class requires a CS.

Example

Recall the `Temperature_Environmental_Condition` CS from Phase 5. This CS defines a public Method named `The_Percent()`. The `Environmental_`

`Condition` Class family has two other Subclasses that require this capability as well. This suggests that the `Deviation` Class is really a Parameterized Class. Figure 8-12(a) shows the Environmental_Condition_CAT_CCD in Booch notation. Note that the `Deviation` Class is a Parameterized Class and note the corresponding Uses Relationship from the `Environmental_Condition` Subclasses to the `Deviation` Parameterized Class. Figure 8-12(b) shows this in UML notation.

Pragmatic Project Issues

Designing for Reuse

Parameterized Classes are one way that a project can take advantage of reuse; either by using existing Parameterized Classes or by establishing new Parameterized Classes. The problem in establishing new Parameterized Classes is that designing

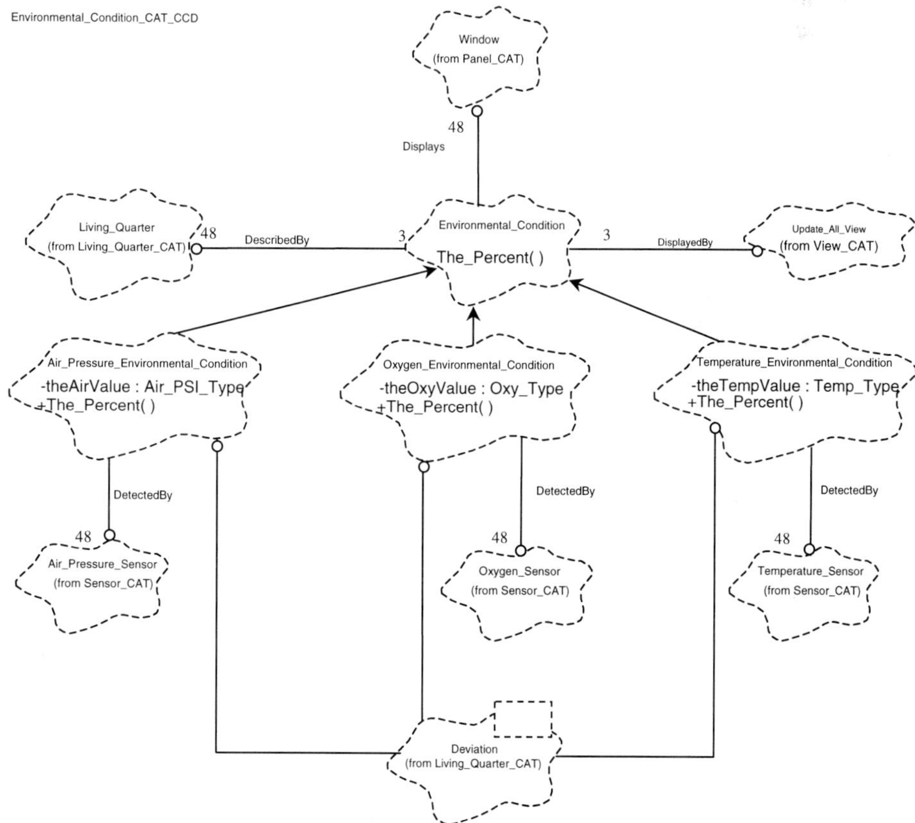

Figure 8-12(a). Environmental_Condition_CAT_CCD Deviation Parameterized Class : Booch Notation

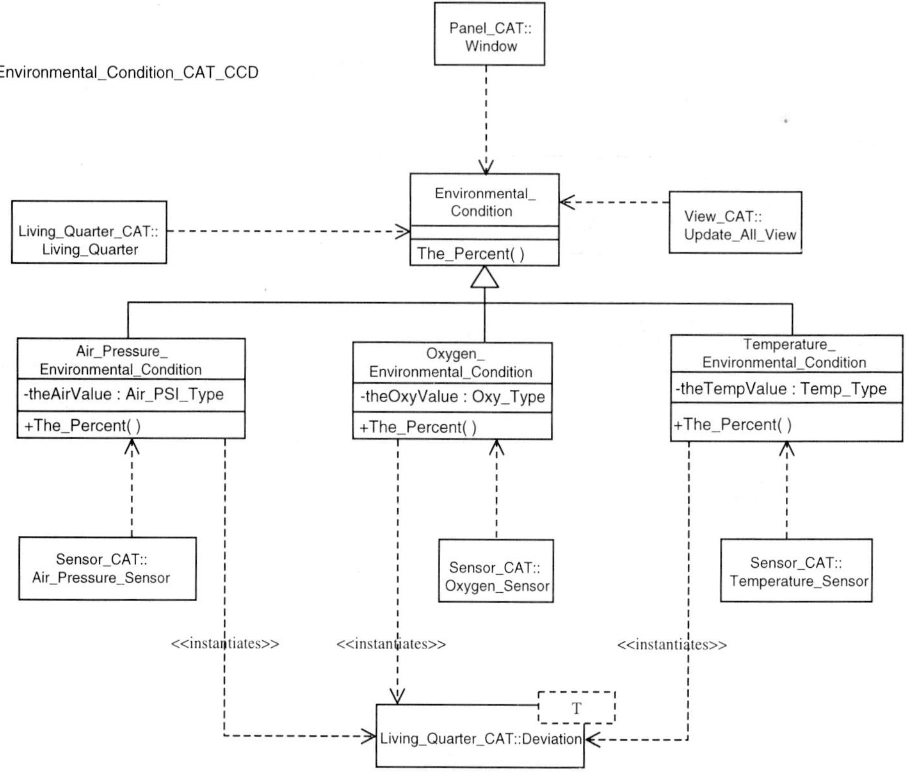

Figure 8-12(b). Environmental_Condition_CAT_CCD with Deviation Parameterized Class : UML Notation

Domain Parameterized Classes for reuse takes time and, on most projects, time is money. A larger issue here is that there are too many definitions of reuse!

Not Invented Here (NIH)

Most projects have a very strong notion of "not invented here" (NIH). This NIH syndrome causes projects to define their own Parameterized Classes rather than looking for reusable Classes in a reuse library.

Technology Is Lagging

In addition to the issues stated above, browser technology for reuse libraries is far behind the rest of the OO industry. Often, it is less expensive for a project to define its own Classes rather than browse libraries of reusable Classes in search of required functionality.

Step 5: Identify Data Structures

This Step examines how one-to-many and many-to-many Uses Relationships are implemented. Uses Relationships with one-to-many or many-to-many cardinality require the Client Class to reference many Instances of the Supplier Class. These references need to be maintained in some type of standard data structure (e.g., a linked list, stack, or queue). The purpose of this step, therefore, is to identify the data structures used for the implementation of a Class.

Process

Step 5.1: Review Class Specifications

Review the CSs and CCDs. Look for Classes that contain Uses Relationships (i.e., an Attribute) with one-to-many or many-to-many cardinality, and determine how that relationship needs to be implemented. The implementation is typically one of the following:

- Unordered list
- Indexed list
- Linked list (singly, doubly)
- Queue (FIFO, priority)
- Stack.

For a more complete taxonomy of data structures, see Booch's taxonomy [BOO91].

Step 5.2: Add Data Structure Parameterized Classes to the Reusable_CAT

Add any required data structure Parameterized Classes to the `Reusable_CAT` so the `Reusable_CAT` maintains ownership of the Parameterized Class. Note that adding these Parameterized Classes to the `Reusable_CAT` implies the creation of CSs for those Parameterized Classes.

Step 5.3: Add Data Structure Classes to CCDs

Add the required domain data structures as Collection Classes on the domain CCDs as needed. The convention we have adopted is that all Collection Classes end with the word "Collection", for example, `Message_Collection`. This convention is independent of the implementation mechanism used for the data structure.

Step 5.4: Add Relationships

First, add a Uses Relationship from the Domain Class needing the collection data structure to the collection data structure. Next, add a dependency (or a Uses Relationship) between the Collection Class and the Parameterized Class.

Example

Suppose an additional requirement was added to the SEM to log a message whenever an Operator interacts with the system. These messages are to be logged to a file. Figure 8-13 shows the hypothetical Message_CAT_CCD at the end of OOA. Note the one-to-many association relationship from the `Message_Log` Class to the `Operator_Action_Message` Class. A `Message_Log` contains many `Operator_Action_Messages`. How should this one-to-many Association Relationship be refined in OOD? Once a decision is made to use a "queue" to hold all of the messages, the modelling of the decision is easy. Figure 8-14 shows a `Queue` Parameterized Class added to the Reusable_CAT_CCD, and Figure 8-15 shows the `Queue` Class added to the Message_CAT_CCD. Lastly, note the dependency from the `Message_Collection` Class to the `Queue` Class.

Pragmatic Project Issues

Consider the Implementation Language

There are many different ways to implement data structures. Take into account the most effective way the implementation language can be used to handle data structure definitions.

Step 6: Identify Abstract Classes

The purpose of this Activity is to determine which Superclasses are Abstract Classes and which Classes are Concrete Classes. The recognition that a Class is an Abstract Class aids in the transition to a language-dependent solution.

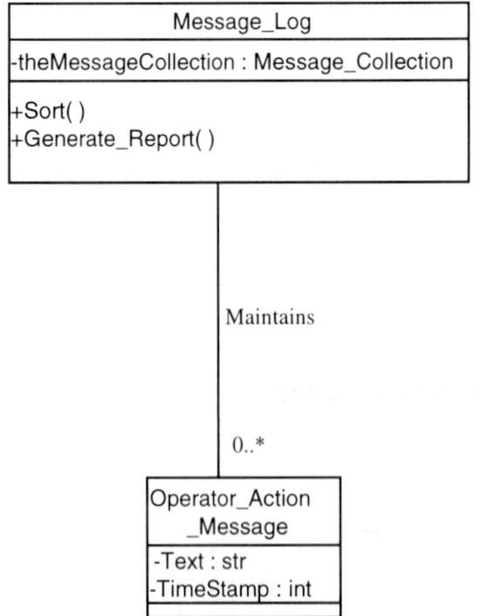

Figure 8-13. Message_CAT_CCD : UML Notation

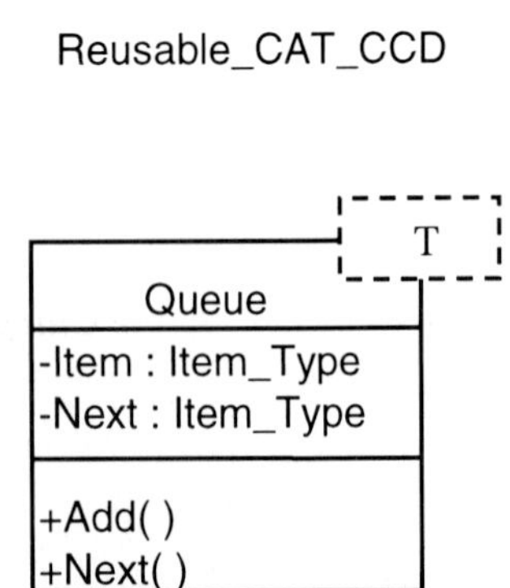

Figure 8-14. Reusable_CAT_CCD : UML Notation

Message_CAT_CCD

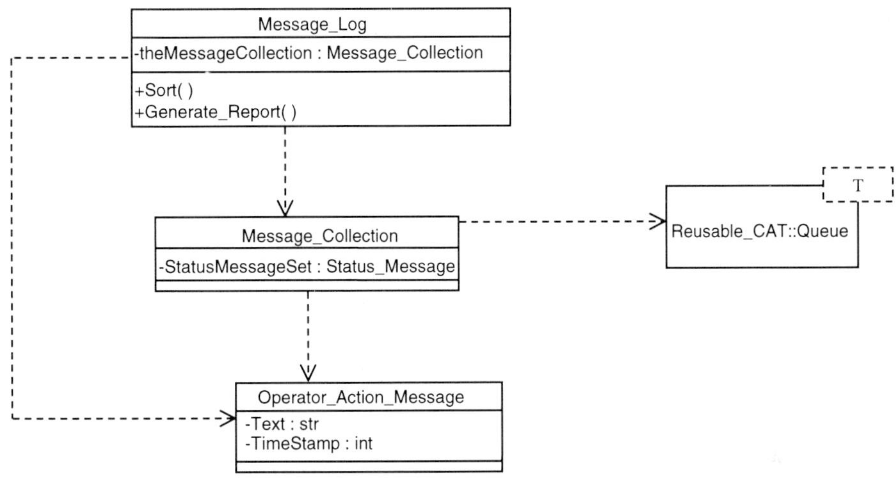

Figure 8-15. Message_CAT_CCD with Queue Parameterized Class : UML Notation

Definition(s)

Abstract Class: An **Abstract Class** is a Superclass in an inheritance hierarchy that does *not* have any Instances (Objects).

Concrete Class: A **Concrete Class** is a Class that has Instances.

Process

Step 6.1: Examine each Inheritance Hierarchy

Look at each Superclass and determine if the Superclass will ever have Instances. Ask, "Is there an Instance of this Class in the domain?" Or, "Do all the Instances belong to a Subclass?". Note that a Superclass is *not* always just the root of an inheritance hierarchy tree. Subclasses of the root Class may themselves be Abstract Classes, consequently, examine each Class in each branch of the tree until a Concrete Class is found in the branch.

Step 6.2: Update Category Class Diagram (CCD)

On the CCD, mark a Class as an Abstract Class; the selected CASE tool should have a way to mark a Class as such. For example, the symbol in Rational Rose for an Abstract Class is an "A" in an inverted triangle (▽), and the symbol appears *inside* the Class. The UML notation for an Abstract Class is to italicize both the name of the Class (as in `Sensor`), as well as the abstract Method[10] names. If using UML, the stereotype

[10] An abstract Method is a Method that must be overridden.

<<Abstract>> can be added to the diagram, if desired, to indicate that this Class is an Abstract stereotype of the package Class.

If the selected CASE tool does *not* have a way to mark an Abstract Class, consider using a special symbol as part of the Class name (e.g., !Class_Name, Class_Name!, etc.) to annotate Abstract Classes.

Step 6.3: Update Class Specification (CS)

For the SEM, note that there is no requirement for an entry in the CS for Abstract Classes because the "Expected Instances" field of the CS will be zero.

Example

Figure 8-16(a) shows the updated Sensor_CAT_CCD with the `Sensor` Class marked as "Abstract" in Booch notation. Figure 8-16(b) reflects the same information in UML notation (note the italics).

Figure 8-17 shows the `Sensor` CS. Because `Sensor` is an Abstract Class, the Expected Instances field of the CS is zero. The `Sensor` Class is simply acting as a placeholder for information (Attributes and Methods) that is common to all `Sensor` Subclasses. However, there *are* Instances of `Air_Pressure_Sensor`, `Oxygen_Sensor`, and `Temperature_Sensor`; consequently, these Classes are *not*

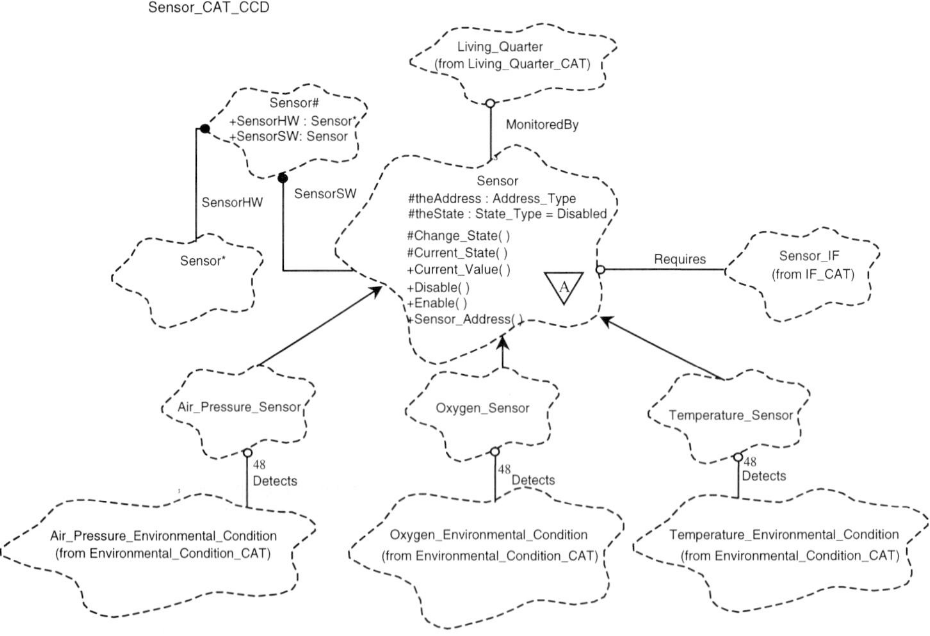

Figure 8-16(a). Sensor_CAT_CCD Depicting Abstract Class : Booch Notation

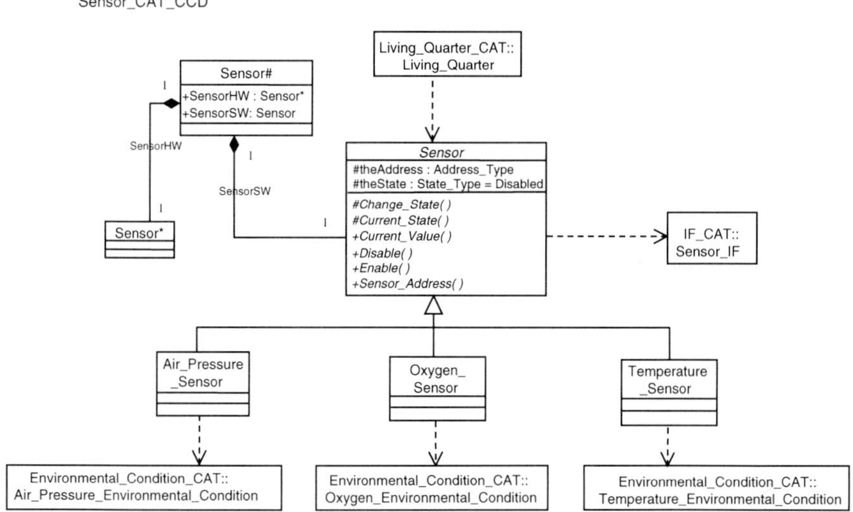

Figure 8-16(b). Sensor_CAT_CCD Depicting Abstract Class : UML Notation

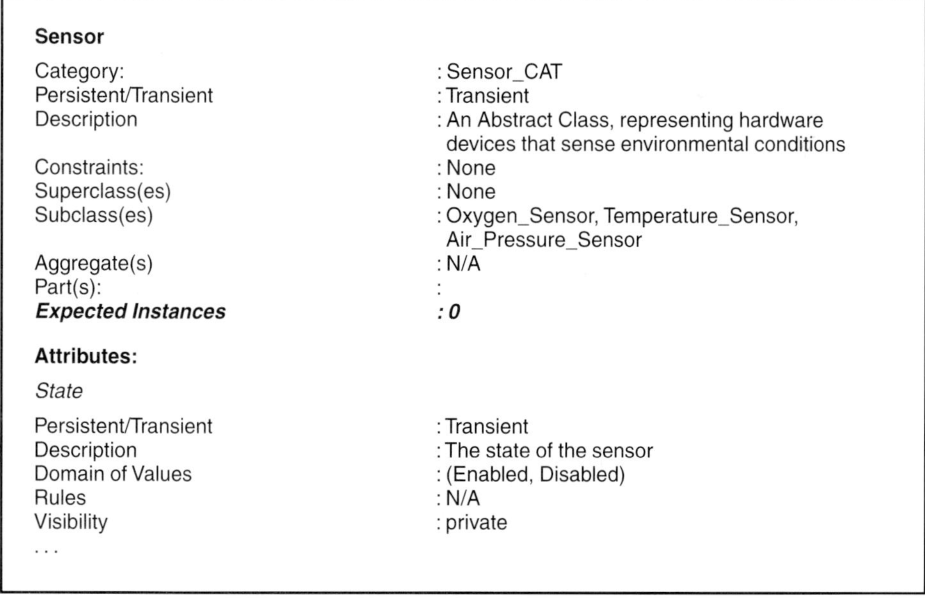

Sensor

Category:	: Sensor_CAT
Persistent/Transient	: Transient
Description	: An Abstract Class, representing hardware devices that sense environmental conditions
Constraints:	: None
Superclass(es)	: None
Subclass(es)	: Oxygen_Sensor, Temperature_Sensor, Air_Pressure_Sensor
Aggregate(s)	: N/A
Part(s):	:
Expected Instances	***: 0***

Attributes:

State

Persistent/Transient	: Transient
Description	: The state of the sensor
Domain of Values	: (Enabled, Disabled)
Rules	: N/A
Visibility	: private

. . .

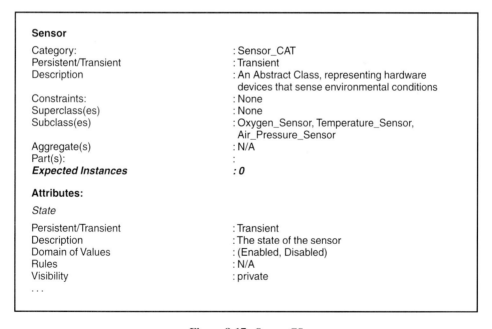

Figure 8-17. Sensor CS

Methods:

Change_State ()

Description	: Toggles the current state of the sensor
Input(s)	: Sensor
Output	: None
Algorithm	: Toggle
Visibility	: private
Exceptions Raised	: Device_Unresponsive

Current_State ()

Description	: Returns the current state of the sensor
Input(s)	: Sensor
Output	: (Enabled, Disabled)
Algorithm	: N/A
Visibility	: private
Exceptions Raised	: Device_Unresponsive

Enable ()

Description	: Enables the sensor
Input(s)	: Sensor
Output	: None
Algorithm	: N/A
Visibility	: public
Exceptions Raised	: Device_Unresponsive

Disable ()

Description	: Disables the sensor
Input(s)	: Sensor
Output	: None
Algorithm	: N/A
Visibility	: public
Exceptions Raised	: Device_Unresponsive

Current_Value ()

Description	: Returns the current value of the sensor
Input(s)	: Sensor
Output	: Float
Algorithm	: N/A
Visibility	: public
Exceptions Raised	: Device_Unresponsive

Relationships:

None.

Figure 8-17. Sensor CS (*continued*)

Abstract Classes, they are Concrete Classes. The same discussion is true for the Environmental_Condition family as well. The `Environmental_Condition` Class is an Abstract Class, while its Subclasses are Concrete Classes.

Step 7: Analyze _View Classes

Many times, Attributes and/or Methods that are originally perceived to belong to a Domain Class will become part of the _View Class for that Domain Class. For example, during OOA, the Methods `Light()`, `Flash_2X()`, and `Flash_4X()` were identified for the `Window` Class. In actuality, upon further analysis during OOD, the Methods were found *not* to be appropriate to the `Window` Class at all, but rather to belong to the `Window_View` Class.

8.2 REUSE EXISTING DESIGN PATTERNS

Purpose

> The purpose of this Activity is to reuse design patterns that have already been identified in the industry.

Process

The work done by Gamma [GAM95] identifies and documents design patterns into three Categories:

- Creational patterns
- Structural patterns
- Behavioral patterns.

These patterns are classic patterns, and the Project Team needs to include an individual or individuals who are extremely familiar with these patterns. The recognition and inclusion of these patterns in CCDs during OOD can save an enormous amount of time and provide consistency for a project that anticipates changes in the implementation model.

Example

The `Database` Class is an excellent example of a Class that can be designed according to the Abstract Factory design pattern [GAM95]. The Abstract Factory design pattern provides an inheritance hierarchy where the hierarchy represents a family of products and the Subclasses represent abstractions of the different kinds of products. Consider Figure 8-18. The `Database` Class now roots an inheritance hierarchy of

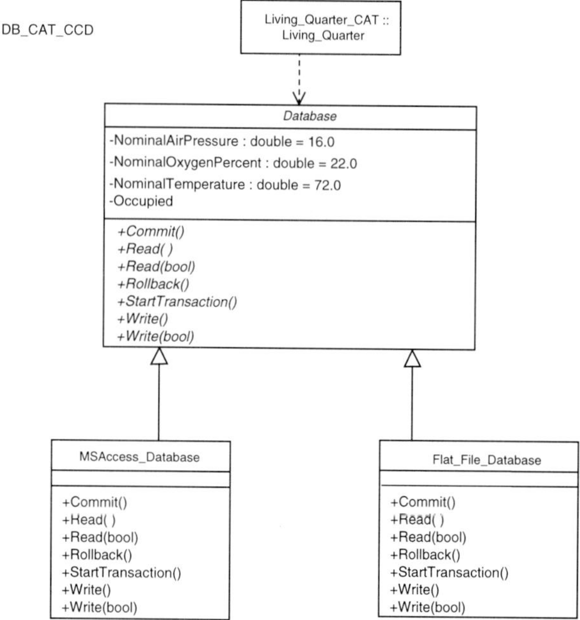

Figure 8-18. DB_CAT_CCD Depicting Abstract Factory Design Pattern : UML Notation

two Subclasses, `MSAccess_Database` and `Flat_File_Database`. The SNAP solution utilizes the `MSAccess_Database` Subclass to interface to Microsoft Access, and the C++ solution utilizes the `Flat_File_Database` Subclass to maintain the data in a flat file. However, both solutions have the same look and feel, specifically the Methods that are inherited from the `Database` Class; the Methods are simply implemented differently for each Subclass.

Product(s)

The products of this Activity are updated CCDs.

8.3 UPDATE CLASS SPECIFICATION (CS)

Purpose

> The purpose of this Activity is to update the definitions of the Classes to reflect the new information, thus keeping the CCD and the CS synchronized.

Process

The CSs were actually already updated during Activity 8.1.

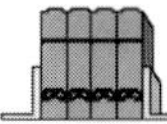

Product(s)

The products of this Activity are updated CSs.

Phase Transition Criteria

This Phase is ready to transition to the next Phase when all Association Relationships have been converted to Uses Relationships (dependencies); Attributes and Methods have access rights defined; Parameterized Classes have been identified; Collection, Concrete, and Abstract Classes have been identified; and finally, the CCDs and CSs have been updated. Remember that none of the decisions made in this Phase are irreversible. Phase 12, Implementation, may cause some of the choices made here to be revisited. The following can help in deciding whether or not to transition to the next Phase.

Review Criteria

The review criteria shown below in Tables 8-1 and 8-2, update the tables introduced in OOA. These tables now include criteria for Uses Relationships, Parameterized Classes, Abstract Classes, Collection Classes, and visibility requirements.

Tracking Progress

Table 8-3 depicts the Activities of this Phase added to the project management spreadsheet. Of course, the number of CCDs and CSs to be updated can be monitored as a percentage of the actual number of CCDs and CSs identified after Phase 5 (OOA). These numbers will change as a result of new diagrams (if multiple CCDs are produced for a Category due to page limitations) and/or new Classes (Parameterized, Controller, Collection, and so on) that require CSs.

Table 8-1. CCD Review Criteria

#	Category Class Diagram Review Criteria	OOA	OOD
1	Are all Categories represented by a CCD?	√	√
2	Does every CCD in the repository represent a legitimate Category?	√	√
3	Has the naming convention been followed, e.g., <<Category_Name>>_CCD?	√	√
4	Has navigation capability between diagrams been established?	√	√
5	Are the Categories consistent with the Category List?	√	√
6	Has the initial Class been added to the CCD?	√	√
7	Are the CCDs consistent with the hardware/software split?	√	√
8	*Have all inheritance hierarchies been validated?*	√	√
	Are all Subclass names suffixed with an underscore followed by the Superclass name?	√	√
	Is the answer to the following question "True"? A Superclass *may be* a Subclass, while a Subclass *is* a Superclass.	√	√
	Do Attributes in Subclasses have a different domain of values or units of measure?	√	√
	Do the Subclasses have additional Attributes?	√	√
	Do the Subclasses have additional Methods or override inherited Method?	√	√
	Do the Subclasses represent different "kinds" or "types" of the Superclass?	√	√
	Do the Subclasses inherit all Attributes and Methods from the Superclass?	√	√
9	*Have all aggregation hierarchies been validated?*	√	√
	Methods on the "whole" Class are generally distinct from Methods on the "part" Class. There are exceptions, for example, a "whole" Class may need to configure all of its parts as part of configuring itself.	√	√
	Multiplicity for the "part" Classes is identified.	√	√
	Does the "part" Class exist to support the "whole" Class? This does not mean that a "part" Class cannot have an association with other Classes. It means that within the hierarchy being validated, does the "part" Class exist to support the "whole" Class? If the "whole" Class can exist without the "part" Class, re-examine the model and investigate the possibility of just a 1:M association relationship.	√	√
10	Have all Classes been reviewed? (See Table 5-2.)	√	√
11	Have Class Attributes been reviewed? (See Table 5-3.)	√	√
12	Have Class Methods been reviewed? (See Table 5-4.)	√	√
13	Does the CCD consist solely of horizontal and vertical lines? Diagonal lines are to be minimized.	√	√

14	*Have association relationships been reviewed?*	√	√
	Is every association relationship labeled?	√	√
	Are multiplicity and conditionality identified for all association relationships?	√	√
	Are association relationship labels placed to facilitate reading from top to bottom on a vertical line, and from left to right on a horizontal line? Are the associations labeled to support the CASE tool?	√	√
	Does each association relationship follow association naming conventions: no underscores, and each word capitalized except the first?	√	√
15	*No Process or Controller Classes?*	√	√
16	*Are all View Classes accounted for?*	√	√
	Do all Classes that require a View Class have an association relationship on the CCD with their View Classes?	√	√
	If appropriate, have the GUI Classes from a GUI library been added to the View_CAT_CCD?	√	√
17	*Have uses relationships been reviewed?*		√
	Have all association relationships been converted into uses relationships, as well as inheritance and aggregation hierarchies (optional)?		√
	Do uses relationships exist in both directions for many-to-many associations, or has a Link Association Class been created with uses relationships to the appropriate Classes?		√
	Are all uses relationships named correctly?		√
	Each uses relationship has the correct multiplicity (cardinality)?		√
	All relationships now expressed as uses relationships?		√
18	*Have Parameterized Classes been reviewed?*		√
	Have the data structure Parameterized Classes been added to the Reusable_CAT?		√
	Have the domain Collection Classes been added to the appropriate domain Category?		√
	Have uses relationships been added from the Collection Class to the Domain Class?		√
	Has a uses relationship been added from Collection Classes to the data structure Parameterized Class in the Reusable_CAT?		√
19	*Does the CCD reflect Abstract Classes?*		√
	Has each Abstract Class been so noted in the appropriate CCDs?		√
20	*Has visibility been reviewed?*		√
	Does each Attribute in each Class have a visibility specification?		√
	Does each Attribute in each Class have the correct visibility?		√
	Does each Method in each Class have a visibility specification?		√
	Does each Method in each Class have the correct visibility?		√

Table 8-2. CS Review Criteria

#	Class Specification Review Criteria	OOA	OOD
1	*Are all Class descriptions reviewed?*	√	√
	Is the Class description brief, clear, concise, and correct?	√	√
	Has the Class template been followed?	√	√
	References to other Classes refer to the model name of the referenced Class, and the name and case is identical to the Class name in the models?	√	√
	If a word is a Category, then any reference to that word refers to the Category. Stated differently, any word that is identical to a Category name should *not* be used in any manner other than to represent the Category.	√	√
	If a word is a Class, then any reference to that word refers to the Class. Stated differently, any word that is identical to a Class should *not* be used in any manner other than to represent the Class.	√	√
	Attributes support the Methods, and the Methods access the Attributes.	√	√
	Do not use implementation terms, for example, "database record", in either the name of the Class or in the description of the Class. For example, do not name the Sensor Class Sensor_Record or Sensor_Pointer.	√	√
	Is the Class description scoped to the application?	√	√
2	*Have the Attributes been reviewed (Table 5-3)?*	√	√
	Is the description short, clear, concise, and correct?	√	√
	Is the Attribute named appropriately?	√	√
	Can the domain of the Attribute be represented by a language type or by another Class?	√	√
	Do not precede the name of the Attribute in the actual Attribute description by the name of the Class, e.g., do not write Alarm.State, just write State. Of course, in references to an Attribute of another Class, the name of the Attribute must be preceded by the name of the Class.	√	√
	Has the Attribute template been followed?	√	√
3	*Have all Methods been reviewed (Table 5-4)?*	√	√
	Does the description specify the intended processing of the Method?	√	√
	Does the description identify all required interfaces to externals where required?	√	√
	Does the description identify the Attributes (by their model name) affected by the Method?	√	√
	Are Attributes affected by the Method written in initial upper-case notation?	√	√

	Are locally required Methods identified in the description?	√	√
	If the Method is a well-known algorithm, is a reference cited where the algorithm is specified?	√	√
	Are internal support Methods referenced?	√	√
	Has the Method template been followed?	√	√
4	*Have all association relationships been reviewed?*	√	√
	Is the association relationship named correctly - without control specified?	√	√
	Has the association template been followed?	√	√
	Is the association description consistent with the association as represented on the CCD?	√	√
	Has multiplicity been described?	√	√
	Has conditionality been described?	√	√
5	*Have the View Classes been reviewed?*	√	√
	Do the `_View` Classes have the appropriate Attributes?	√	√
	Do the `_View` Classes have the appropriate Methods and redefined Methods?	√	√
	Do the `_View` Classes inherit from a predefined GUI Class (if appropriate)?	√	√
6	*Have the inheritance hierarchies been examined for Abstract Classes?*		√
	Has the Class Specification for an Abstract Class been updated, specifically the "Expected Instances" field?		√
7	*Have exceptions been reviewed?*		√
	Are all exceptions specified in the Scenarios represented?		√
	Is the list of exceptions in the "Exception" field?		√
	Have the Method sections been updated with the exceptions raised/thrown?		√
	Is each exception for a Class raised by at least one Method?		√
8	*Has visibility been reviewed?*		√
	Does each Attribute in each Class have a visibility specification?		√
	Does each Attribute in each Class have the correct visibility?		√
	Does each Method in each Class have a visibility specification?		√
	Does each Method in each Class have the correct visibility?		√

Table 8-3. Project Management Spreadsheet: Phase 8

HCC Project Management Spreadsheet						
Number	**Phase Name**	**Activity**	**Charge Number**	**Product**	**Progress Metric**	**% Weight**
7	**Software OOD—Process View**		**SW-OOD-PA-7**			
7.1		Initiate PAD	SW-OOD-PA-7.1	PAD	1 PAD completed	0.25
7.2		Identify Processes	SW-OOD-PA-7.2			
7.3		Identify Processors	SW-OOD-PA-7.3			
7.4		Allocate Processes to Processors	SW-OOD-PA-7.4			
7.5		Allocate Classes to Processes	SW-OOD-PA-7.5	PCADs	# PCADs	0.30
7.6		Identify Process Interaction	SW-OOD-PA-7.6	PID	1 PID completed	0.25
7.7		Generate Process/Processor STD	SW-OOD-PA-7.7	STD	#STDs	0.10
7.8		Update CS	SW-OOD-PA-7.8	CS	#CSs	0.10
8	**Software OOD—Static View**		**SW-OODS-8**			
8.1		Update CCD	SW-OODS-8.1	CCD (Updated)	#CCDs	
8.2		Reuse Existing Design Patterns	SW-OODS-8.2	CCD (Updated)	#CCDs	0.50
8.3		Update CSs	SW-OODS-8.3	CS (Updated)	#CSs	0.50

PHASE 9

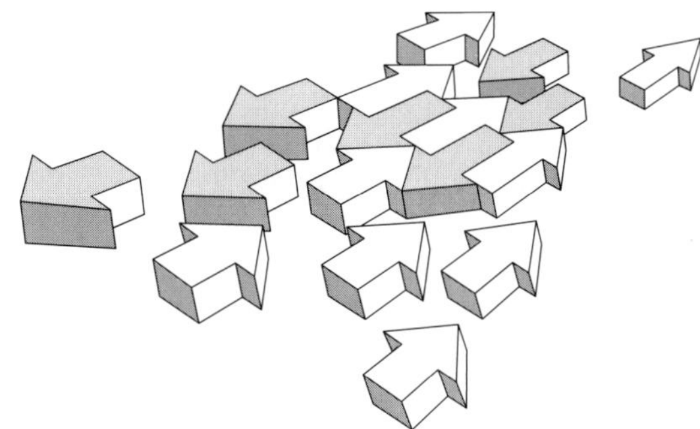

Software OOD–Dynamic View

PHASE OVERVIEW

Now that the static design is complete, the dynamic design of the system can be developed. The Interaction Diagrams (IDs) produced during OOA (Phase 6) are updated to include all newly discovered Classes; specifically Process, Controller, and Collection Classes. And finally, IPC and exception propagation are added to the IDs. The Activities for this Phase are shown in Figure 9-1.

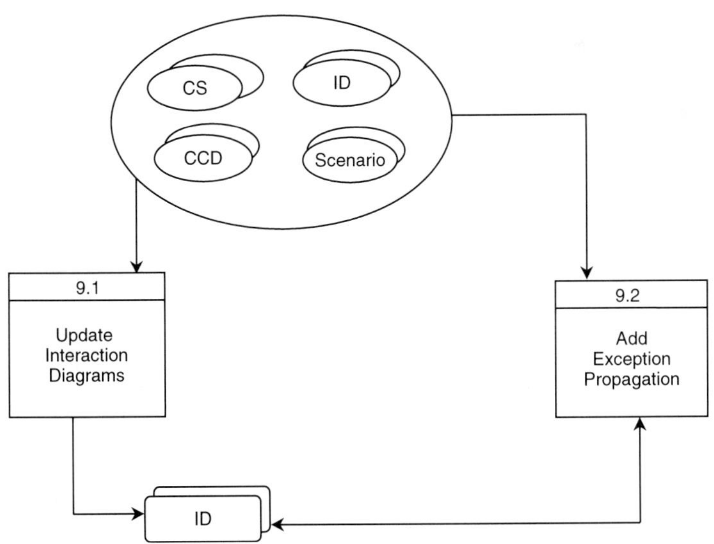

Figure 9-1. Software OOD - Dynamic View Phase Description Diagram

9.1 UPDATE CLASSES/MESSAGES ON INTERACTION DIAGRAMS (IDs)

Purpose

> The purpose of this Activity is to refine the OOA IDs by adding Classes discovered in the previous Phase (Phase 8), as well as the appropriate Messages to these Classes.

Again, this is a refinement Activity, specifically the refinement of the collaborative behavior of the Classes. Most Project Teams, specifically the developers, *cannot* complete an entire ID in one step. During OOA (Phase 6), the CIDs (developed in Phase 3), which depict required interaction *between Categories*, were refined to reflect the *Classes* within Categories required to satisfy a Use Case. During OOA, emphasis was placed on the logical view; consequently, only Domain, _IF, and _View Classes and their respective Messages were added to the CIDs and the CIDs were renamed Interaction Diagrams (IDs). The purpose of this *next* refinement is to add those remaining Classes that participate in the physical implementation of the logical view (Process, Controller, and Collection Classes), as well as the Messages that are sent to these Classes.

Definition(s)

Controller Class: A **Controller Class** is a Class that is responsible for defining the necessary collaboration between Domain and View Classes to achieve a specific functionality. Basically, a **Controller Class** is an example of a Facade Design Pattern [GAM95]. (See Step 3 of this Activity for more detail on Controller Classes.)

Facade: A **Facade** design pattern is a mechanism that supplies an interface to a collection of interfaces. A **Facade** design pattern is a paradigm where one Class filters requests for services from a collection of Classes, routing a request to the correct Class.

Process

Step 1: Add Process Classes

For each ID, add the appropriate Classes from the `Process` Class hierarchy[1], ensuring that all Classes allocated to a process appear to the right of the process on the diagram. If a shared Class exists on the ID, the Class will appear more than once on the

[1]Refer to the Process Architecture Diagram (PAD) and Process-to-Class Allocation Diagrams (PCADs) created in Phase 7, Software OOD—Process View.

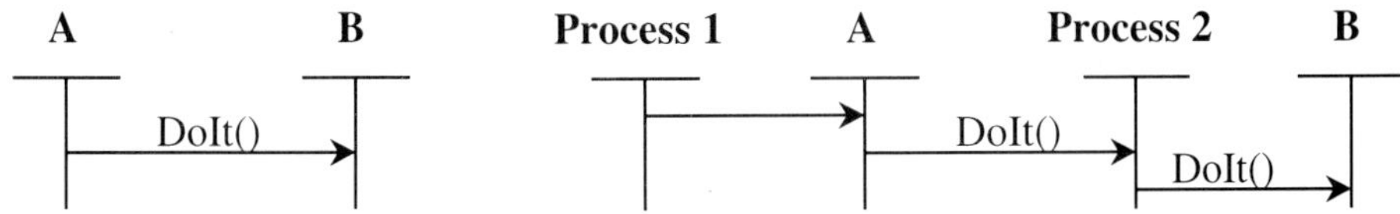

Figure 9-2(a). "Before" Adding Process Class

Figure 9-2(b). "After" Adding Process Class

ID, to the right of *each* process that requires the Class. This step may result in significantly reworking and laying out the ID. This effort is worthwhile, because during maintenance, knowing which process is involved helps significantly! Figure 9-2(a) and 9-2(b) represent *before and after* views of adding a Process Class. Note that in Figure 9-2(a), which reflects the logical, or OOA view, Class A sends a message, DoIt(), to Class B. When refined in this Activity, Class A, which is used in Process 1, now sends the DoIt() Message to Process 2, which contains Class B. Then, the Process 2 Class sends the DoIt() Message to Class B. This will be modified one more time when Controller Classes are added to the ID in Step 3.

In summary, the original Message between two Classes transitions into two Messages. The first Message starts at the source Class of the original Message and terminates on the process that owns the target Class of the original Message. The second Message starts on the Process Class that owns the target Class of the original Message and terminates on the target Class of the original Message.

Step 2: Add _View Classes

Although _View Classes are added during OOA, typically *not* all _View Classes are identified during OOA. Consequently, this Step really focuses on getting the *newly discovered* _View Classes added to the IDs.

Add the _View Classes to the ID to accept any display/input Messages that currently exist to the Domain Class on the ID. To do this, change the target of the display. Input Messages from the Domain Class should now terminate on the Domain Class' _View Class. Finally, add the Operator Class to depict how an Operator interacts with the _View Class. Figures 9-3(a) and 9-3(b) represent *before and after* views of adding a _View Class. Note in Figure 9-3(a), which represents the OOA view, Class A sends a message, Update_B(), to Class B. During this Activity, this is refined by adding the Operator and B_View Classes to the ID; and, assuming that Class A causes the B_View Class to be displayed, A sends a Display() Message to the B_View Class, which causes the B_View Class to be displayed and thus enables the Operator to interact with the system to update Class B by setting the X, Y, and Z Attributes of Class B. Finally, Class B is updated when the Operator Selects_OK(). In this example, the issue of validating the Operator's input has *not* been addressed. On a real project validation, of course, needs to take place, and a Project Team must decide whether each Attribute is validated on input, or whether all three Attributes are validated at the completion of the Operator input, specifically, when the Operator selects the OK button.

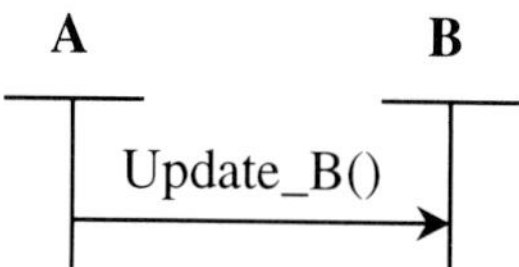

Figure 9-3(a). "Before" Adding View Class

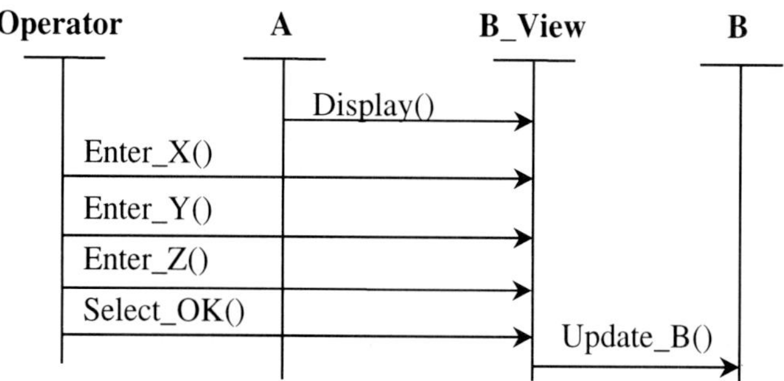

Figure 9-3(b). "After" Adding View Class

Step 3: Add Controller Classes

Examine the Categories to determine if a Category requires one or more Controller Classes. In general, *at least one* Controller Class is needed by a Category if the Category has any Use Cases allocated to it. A Category's Controller Class then has a Method for each Use Case allocated to the Controller Class' Category. In actuality, there may be *more than one* Controller Class per Category because processes cut across Categories[2]. Stated differently, a process, because it manages a certain set of functionality for Category A, would have a Controller Class to manage only the functionality required of Category A. Another process, that manages a *different* part of functionality for the same Category A, would then require a *different* Controller Class for Category A. Consequently, Category A may require two Controller Classes.

If an ID is for a software action (i.e., the ID name starts with "SW_"), add the Controller Class to the right of the system boundary. Otherwise, add the Controller Class to the right of the _View Class that appears to the right of the system boundary, because it is the _View Class that will interact with the Controller Class. Figures 9-4(a) and 9-4(b) represent *before and after* views of adding a Controller Class. Note that Figure 9-4(a) is a repeat of Figure 9-2(b), and that in 9-4(b), the Process 2 Class now sends the Message DoIt() to the Controller Class. Recall that the Controller Class may require services from other Supplier Classes, as well as services from Class B. The

[2]Recall the previous discussion in which it was indicated that processes and Categories do not equate.

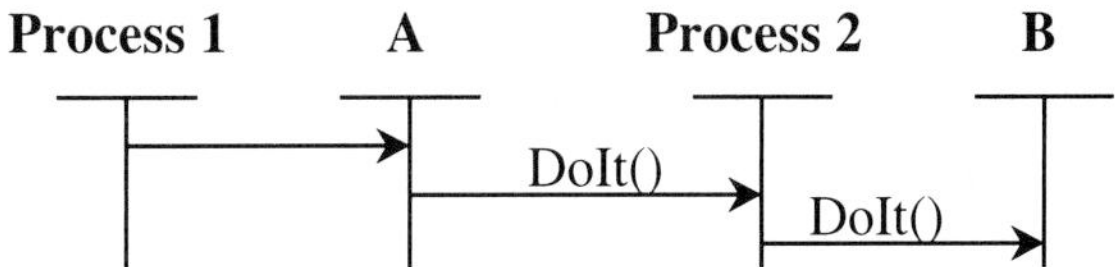

Figure 9-4(a). "Before" Adding Controller Class

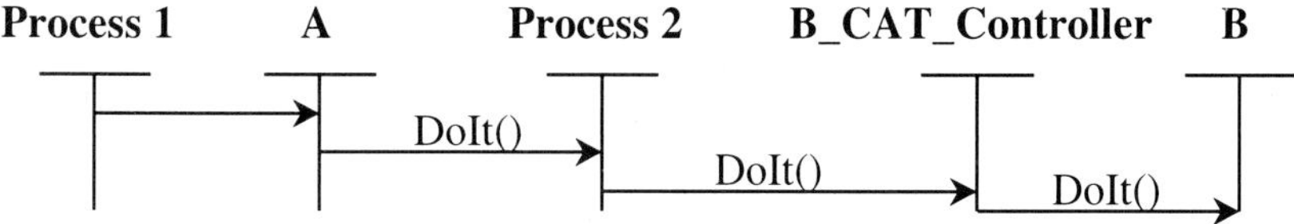

Figure 9-4(b). "After" Adding Controller Class

Controller Class is smart enough to finish the request for DoIt(); among other Messages that the Controller Class sends (e.g., to the database, perhaps, or to other Domain Classes), the Controller Class sends one Message to Class B to a Method named DoIt(), where DoIt() in Class B performs the *domain*-specific processing of the request.

Step 4: Add Collection Classes

Finally, add the newly discovered Collection Classes to the ID, as well as their respective Messages. Figures 9-5(a) and 9-5(b) depict the *before and after* views for this Step. In Figure 9-5(a), produced during OOA, Class A has Collection_Of_B as an Attribute and a corresponding Method, Collection_Of_B(), to obtain the actual collection from an Instance of A, which in turn requests a single B from the B Class.

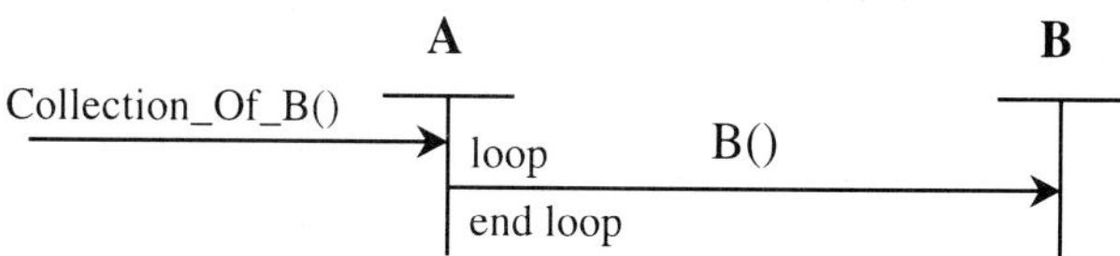

Figure 9-5(a). "Before" Adding Collection Class

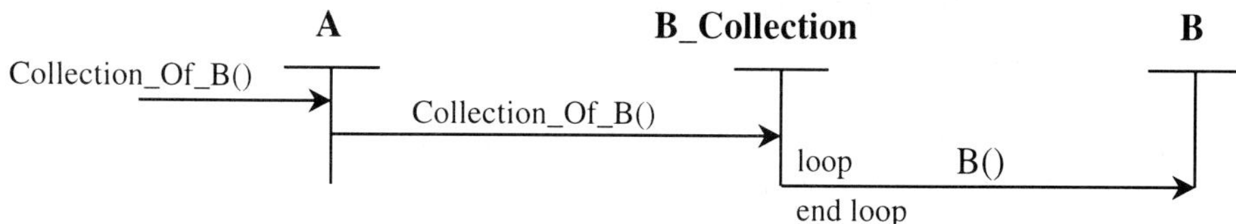

Figure 9-5(b). "After" Adding Collection Class

In 9-5(b), note the addition of the B_Collection Class, which is still an Attribute of A, and the Collection Class, which is now an aggregation of B's. Note that the Message that originally went to a Collection member Class in OOA now is sent to the Collection Class, which may, or may *not*, send a Message to the Collection Member Class.

Step 5: Establish Naming Conventions for IPCs

On an ID, suffix the Messages that communicate between processes with _RPC or _IPC. For the SEM, the decision was made to suffix the name of inter-process messages with _RPC. Figures 9-6(a) and 9-6(b) show *before and after* views for this Step.

Example

Figure 9-7 repeats the Category Interaction Diagram (CID) developed in System OOA (Phase 3) for UC16_Operator_Updates_Nominal_Values_In_DB. Figure 9-8 shows the result of refining the original CID, during OOA (Phase 6). Figure 9-9(a) shows the updated ID. Three `Process` Subclasses have been added (specifically `Monitor_Persistent_Process`, `Display_Persistent_Process`, and `DB_Persistent_Process`) as well as the `SEM_Desktop_View` and `Update_All_View` Classes. The Supporting ID is shown in Figure 9-9(b).

Also note that at this point in the production of the solution, the allocation of Use Cases 16 and 17 has changed. Originally, these Use Cases were allocated to the `DB_CAT`. But, as a result of our analysis and design efforts, it is more appropriate to assign them to the `Living_Quarter_CAT`, and have the `Living_Quarter_CAT` store the appropriate values in the database by calling the `Database Write()` Method. Consequently, the RTM is updated, the two Uses Cases are reassigned to the `Living_Quarter_CAT`, and the project proceeds.

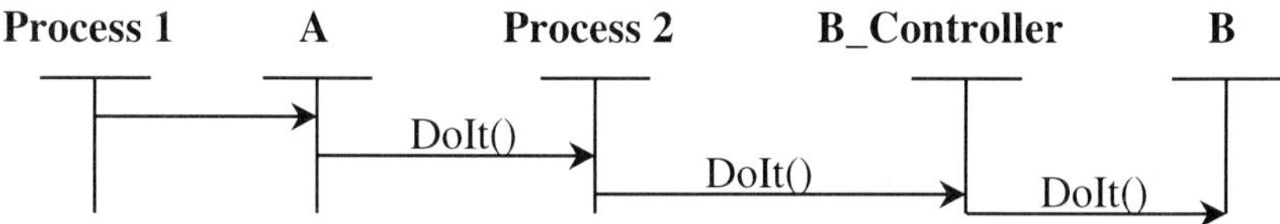

Figure 9-6(a). "Before" Indicating RPC

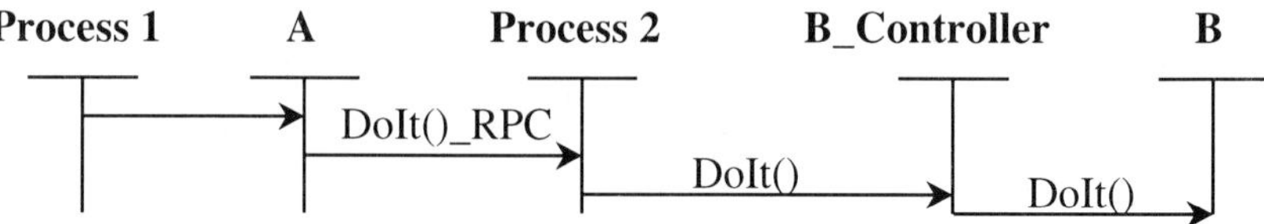

Figure 9-6(b). "After" Indicating RPC

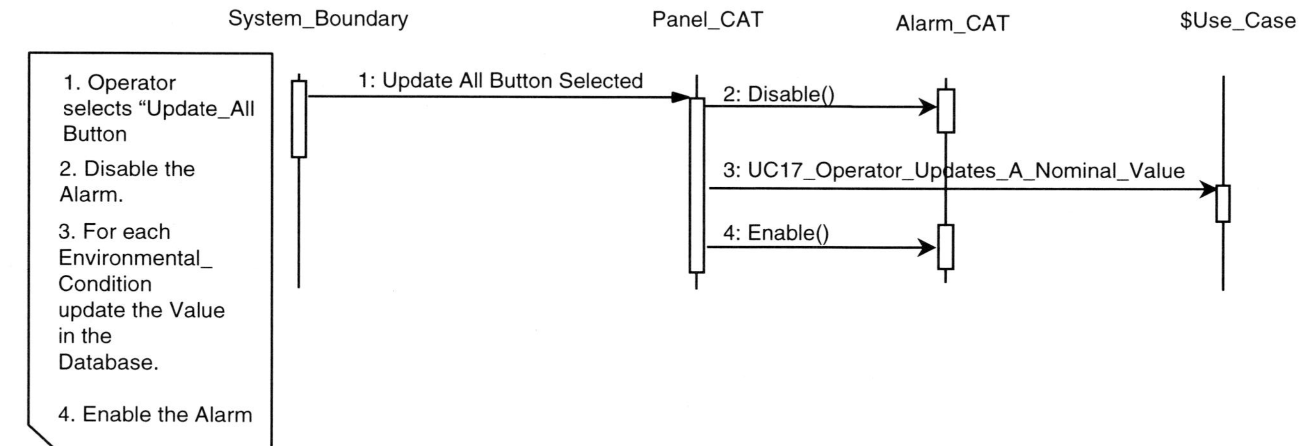

Figure 9-7. UC16’s CID

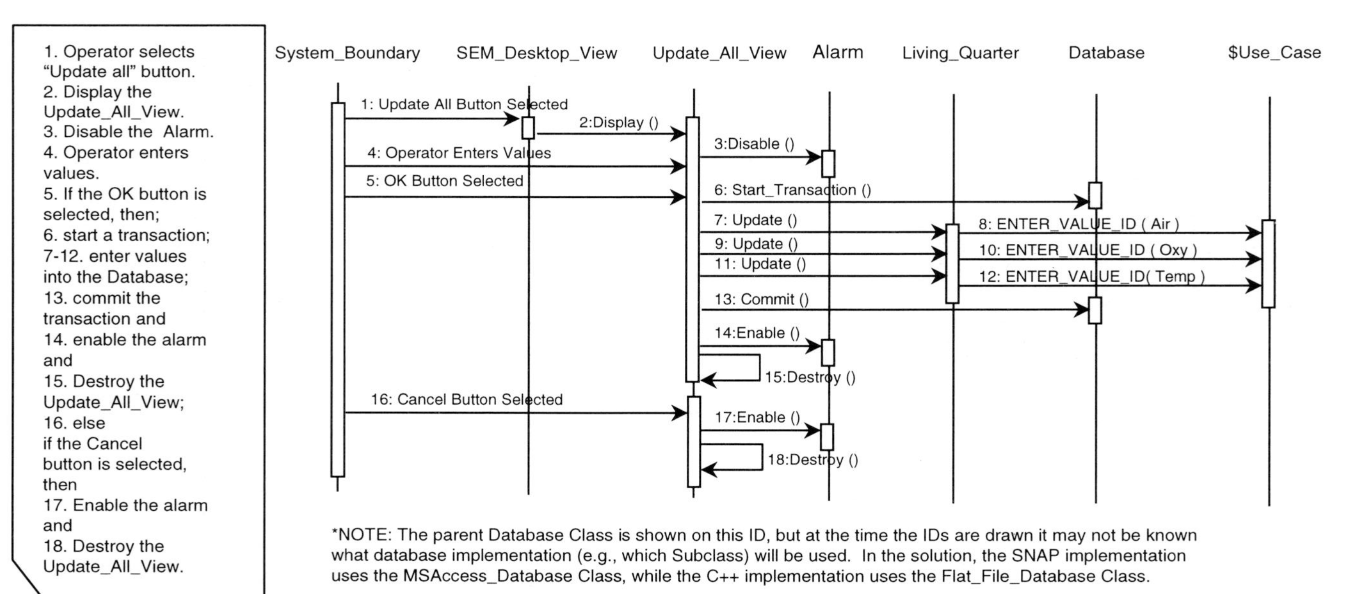
UC16_Operator_Updates_Nominal_Values_In_DB_ID
1. Operator selects "Update all" button.
2. Display the Update_All_View.
3. Disable the Alarm.
4. Operator enters values.
5. If the OK button is selected, then;
6. start a transaction;
7-12. enter values into the Database;
13. commit the transaction and
14. enable the alarm and
15. Destroy the Update_All_View;
16. else if the Cancel button is selected, then
17. Enable the alarm and
18. Destroy the Update_All_View.
System_Boundary
SEM_Desktop_View
Update_All_View
Alarm
Living_Quarter
Database
$Use_Case
1: Update All Button Selected
2:Display ()
3:Disable ()
4: Operator Enters Values
5: OK Button Selected
6: Start_Transaction ()
7: Update ()
8: ENTER_VALUE_ID (Air)
9: Update ()
10: ENTER_VALUE_ID (Oxy)
11: Update ()
12: ENTER_VALUE_ID(Temp)
13: Commit ()
14:Enable ()
15:Destroy ()
16: Cancel Button Selected
17:Enable ()
18:Destroy ()
*NOTE: The parent Database Class is shown on this ID, but at the time the IDs are drawn it may not be known what database implementation (e.g., which Subclass) will be used. In the solution, the SNAP implementation uses the MSAccess_Database Class, while the C++ implementation uses the Flat_File_Database Class.

Figure 9-8. UC16's ID after OOA

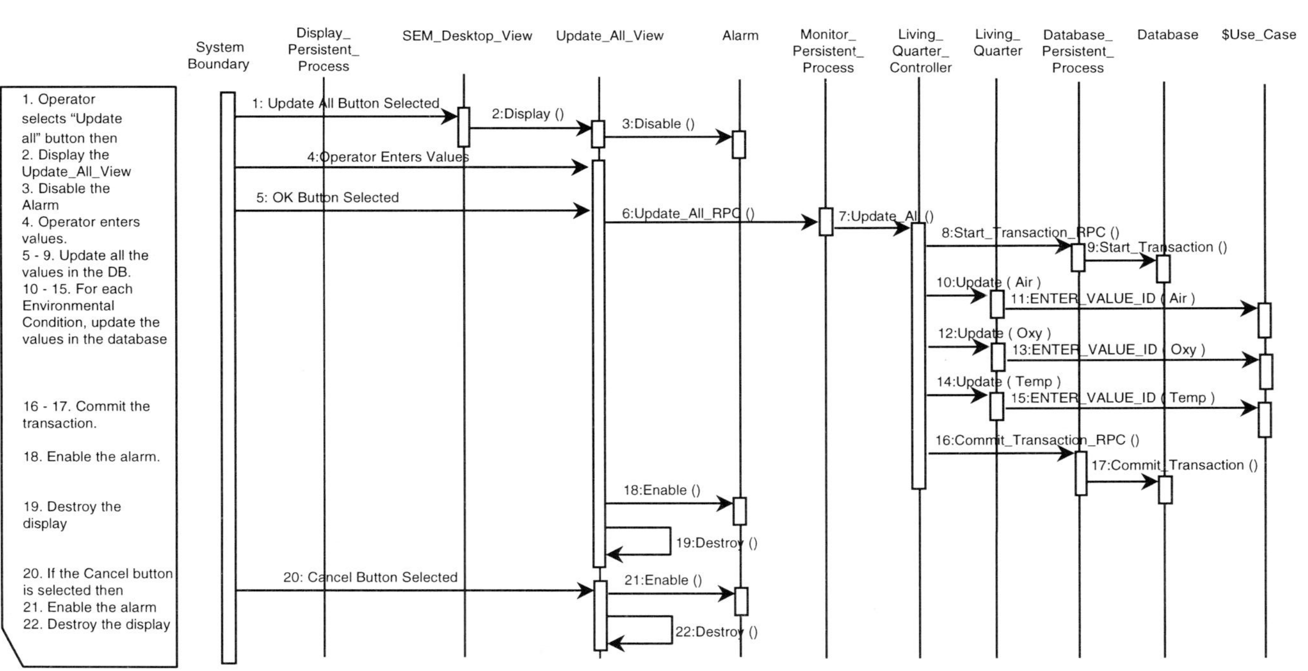
UC16_Operator_Updates_Nominal_Values_In_DB_ID
System Boundary
Display_ Persistent_ Process
SEM_Desktop_View
Update_All_View
Alarm
Monitor_ Persistent_ Process
Living_ Quarter_ Controller
Living_ Quarter
Database_ Persistent_ Process
Database
$Use_Case
1. Operator selects "Update all" button then
2. Display the Update_All_View
3. Disable the Alarm
4. Operator enters values.
5 - 9. Update all the values in the DB.
10 - 15. For each Environmental Condition, update the values in the database
16 - 17. Commit the transaction.
18. Enable the alarm.
19. Destroy the display
20. If the Cancel button is selected then
21. Enable the alarm
22. Destroy the display
1: Update All Button Selected
2:Display ()
3:Disable ()
4:Operator Enters Values
5: OK Button Selected
6:Update_All_RPC ()
7:Update_All ()
8:Start_Transaction_RPC ()
9:Start_Transaction ()
10:Update (Air)
11:ENTER_VALUE_ID (Air)
12:Update (Oxy)
13:ENTER_VALUE_ID (Oxy)
14:Update (Temp)
15:ENTER_VALUE_ID (Temp)
16:Commit_Transaction_RPC ()
17:Commit_Transaction ()
18:Enable ()
19:Destroy ()
20: Cancel Button Selected
21:Enable ()
22:Destroy ()

*NOTE: The parent Database Class is shown on this ID, but at the time the IDs are drawn it may not be known what database implementation (e.g., which Subclass) will be used. In the solution, the SNAP implementation uses the MSAccess_Database Class, while the C++ implementation uses the Flat_File_Database Class.

Figure 9-9(a). UC16's ID after Adding Process and Controller Classes

ENTER_VALUE_ID
*Note: This supporting ID occurs once for each Environmental_Condition Subclass (<sub>).

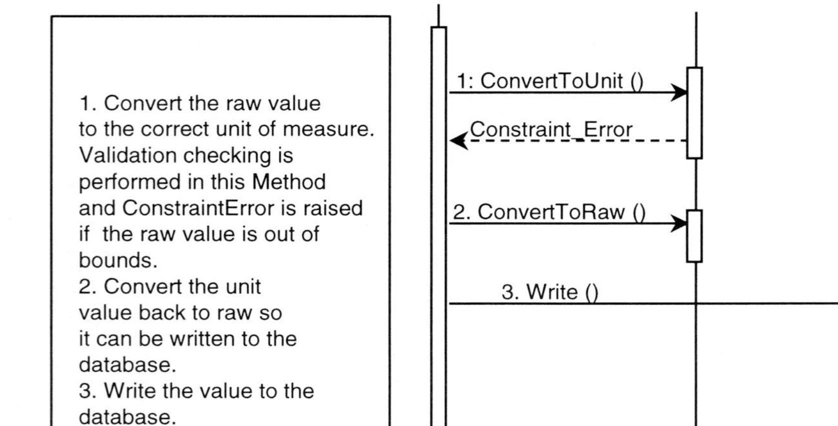
Living_Quarter
<sub>_Environmental_Condition
Database
1. Convert the raw value to the correct unit of measure. Validation checking is performed in this Method and ConstraintError is raised if the raw value is out of bounds.
2. Convert the unit value back to raw so it can be written to the database.
3. Write the value to the database.
1: ConvertToUnit ()
Constraint_Error
2. ConvertToRaw ()
3. Write ()

*NOTE: The parent Database Class is shown on this ID, but at the time the IDs are drawn it may not be known what database implementation (e.g., which Subclass) will be used. In the solution, the SNAP implementation uses the MSAccess_Database Class, while the C++ implementation uses the Flat_File_Database Class.

Figure 9-9(b). Supporting ID : ENTER_VALUE_ID

There is only one Controller Class required for the SEM software—Living_Quarter_Controller Class. The Living_Quarter_Controller Class has four Methods

- Monitor_Living_Quarters() - UC1
- Change_Occupation_State() - UC24
- Update_All() - UC16
- Update_One() - UC17

that represent the referenced Use Case. The Method Monitor_Living_Quarters() is responsible for looping through the living quarter Instances and, for each living quarter, requesting the deviation. Based on the deviation, the controller requests the appropriate Method from the Panel and/or Alarm Class. Keeping the Living_Quarter Class *independent* of the Panel and Alarm Classes, and building that functionality into the Controller Class, makes the Living_Quarter more reusable in other applications. Note in Figure 9-9(a) the addition of the Living_Quarter_Controller Class and its receipt of the update request from the Monitor_Persistent_Process and how this Controller Class controls the functionality of Use Case 16.

A Controller Class for the Panel Category, Panel_Controller, was deemed *not* necessary because the Panel Class can perform the capability just as well. Another designer might well put a Panel_Controller Class in the design and that would *not* be wrong. Within Object-Oriented technology, there are many different degrees of "right"!

A Controller Class for the Environmental_Condition_CAT was considered to handle Use Cases 16 and 17 (updating the values of the environmental conditions in the database). Having an Environmental_Condition_Controller Class would require that the Environmental_Condition Class have knowledge of the Living_Quarter Class. Stated differently, having an Environmental_Condition_Controller Class would require a bi-directional association relationship between the Living_Quarter Class and Environmental_Condition Class. For the SEM, this was considered unnecessary; consequently, the two Use Cases are handled by the Living_Quarter_Controller Class.

Currently there are *not* any Collection Classes in the SEM; therefore, an example of Step 4 is *not* included. Refer to Phase 17 to see an example of a Collection Class being added, during maintenance, to an ID for the SEM.

Pragmatic Project Issues

Whether or Not to Add Process Classes

In this Case Study, Process Classes were added to all the IDs, regardless of the fact that some IDs were contained entirely by a single process, and therefore the Use Case (as shown by its ID) did *not* require any IPC. The addition of Process Classes on an ID provides support during the Maintenance Phase because the ID will indicate exactly which Process is involved in any required changes/updates to the requirements.

Whether or Not to Add Parameterized Classes

It does *not* make much sense to add Parameterized Classes to the IDs as their instantiations are usually programming language declarations, not Messages.

Add Controller Classes to the CCD?

Adding a Controller Class to a CCD does *not* seem to yield any positive benefits. Rather, adding a Controller Class to a CCD seems to yield negative benefits, supporting a functional development of the CCD. Consider adding Controller Classes to the PAD instead, to indicate which Controller Classes are required by which processes.

A Lot of Work!

Completing the IDs is a lot of work, but the rewards reaped as a result are great. Most customers have difficulty understanding Class (or Object) Diagrams and do *not* fully appreciate the necessity for CSs. Most Customers are concerned with understanding that *their required functionality* is included in the OO model. Consequently, we have achieved greater success by presenting precise and clear IDs to a Customer, rather than Class Diagrams. IDs are easy to learn to read, are easy to present, and represent the system functionality as currently conceived by the developers. Time spent here pays significant dividends with respect to customer confidence and with respect to specifying implementation requirements for the development staff.

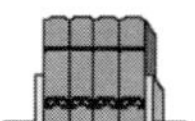

Product(s)

The products of this Activity are updated IDs.

9.2 ADD EXCEPTION PROPAGATION

Purpose

> The purpose of this Activity is to identify corrective action that will execute under predefined failure conditions.

Definition(s)

Exception: An **exception** is an error condition that occurs at run-time and that causes the software system to crash.

Exception Handler: An **exception handler** is a piece of code, or processing, that executes and provides corrective action when an exception occurs.

Propagation: **Propagation** is the re-raising of an exception to the next level, where "level" is defined by the programming language. The next "level" can be a block, calling routine, and so on.

Process

Step 1: Examine Scenarios

Extract the exceptions identified in the Scenarios and build a table that allocates exceptions first to Categories, and then to the appropriate Class within the Category that raises the exception. Table 9-1 shows a typical table that facilitates exception management *within* a Category. With modifications, the table can be used to facilitate exception management *between* Categories.

Step 2: Update ID

If a Class that raises an exception appears on an ID, determine first if the Message being sent to the Class is the Message that could cause the specific exception to occur. If it is the Message that causes the exception to occur, determine if the Class can handle the exception locally, whether the Class needs to propagate the exception to the calling Class, or both. Figure 9-10 shows a decision tree that represents this concept.

We tend to draw a distinct exception symbol to each of the Classes that are involved in the propagation chain rather than one symbol from the Class that first throws the exception to the last Class in the propagation chain. If the CASE tool does *not* support a distinct symbol for an exception, consider restricting ordinary Messages to be forward arrows, and then backward arrows can be used to represent exception propagation.

Repeat this process for each Class on the ID until the propagation chain is completed, meaning that the exception is *not* propagated any further.

Example

Figure 9-11 now shows the ID for Use Case 16, with exception propagation included.

Table 9-1. Exception Identification Table

Exception Name	Use Case/Scenario	Category	Class
Database_Down	1	DB_CAT	Database
Device_Unresponsive	16	Sensor_CAT	Air_Pressure_Sensor, Oxygen_Sensor, Temperature_Sensor
etc.			

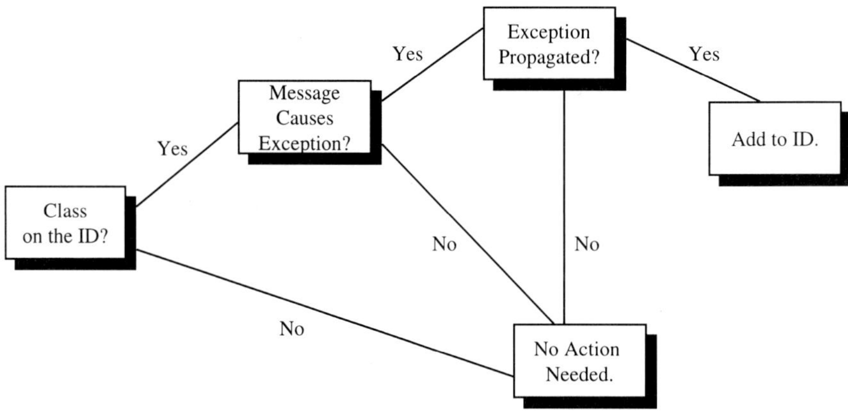

Figure 9-10. Decision Tree for Exception Handling

Pragmatic Project Issues

How Far to Show the Exception Propagation Trail

Should exception propagation be just shown to the first Class in a chain of propagation, or should it be shown as propagated to every Class until the propagation chain terminates? Sometimes the propagation chain crosses IDs. Should that be represented? These answers depend upon the time allowed for completion of the IDs and the support provided by the selected CASE tool. The ideal, of course, is to show the entire propagation chain until the exception is no longer propagated, for the two reasons previously cited: customer confidence and implementation direction to the development staff.

Can Exceptions Propagate to Another Process?

Should exception propagation be *limited* to *within* a process? Stated differently, should exceptions be allowed to propagate between processes? The answer depends upon the project's implementation of IPC; therefore, the answer is project-dependent.

What If the Implementation Language Doesn't Support Exceptions?

Hopefully this is *not* the case, but if it is, then of course implement exceptions using an `if..then..else` construct.

What to do with Status Codes?

As previously stated, many system calls return status codes. When these calls need to be made, bury the system call in a Method for the Class, and define an enumeration type for normal return values and exceptions for failure conditions.

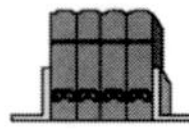

Product(s)

The products of this Activity are updated IDs.

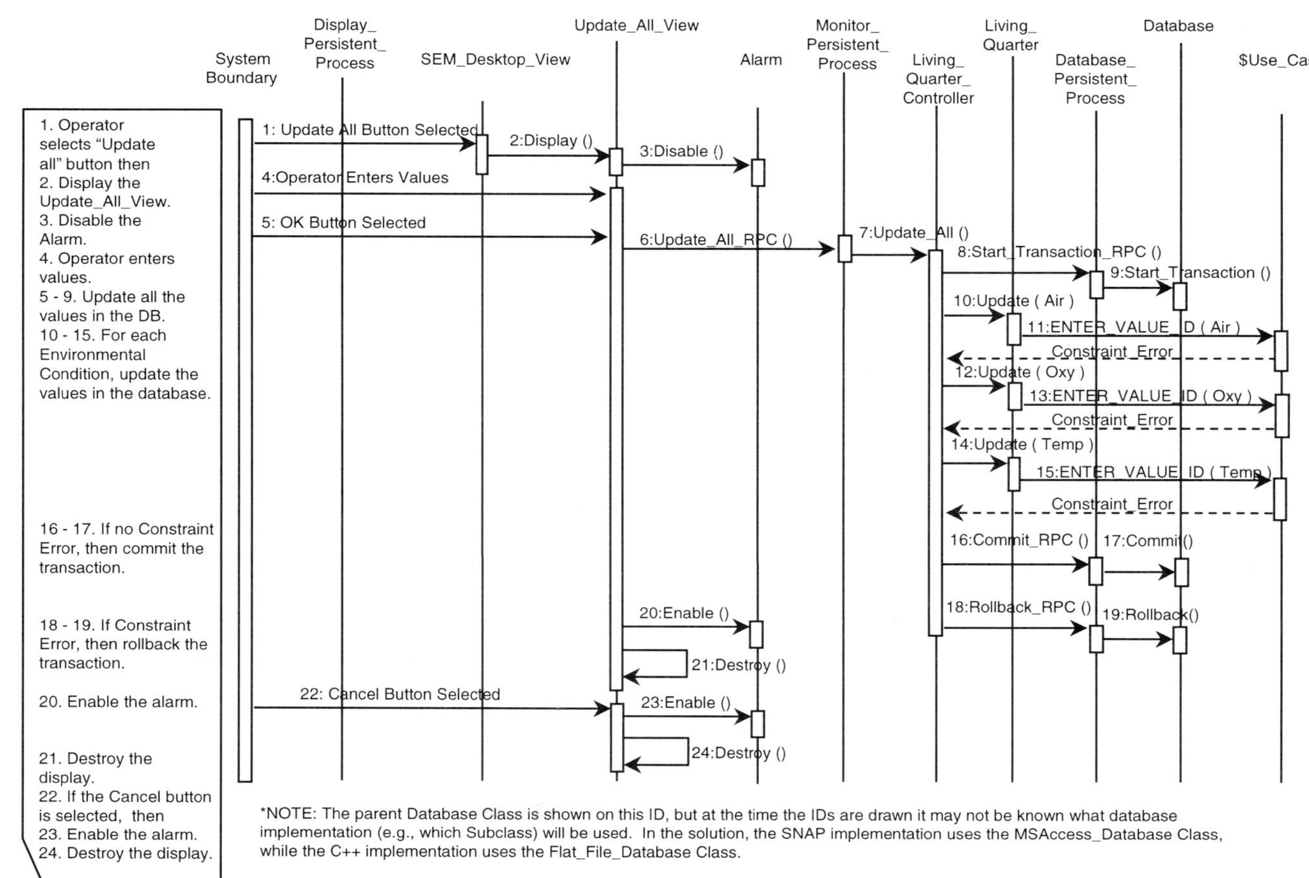

UC16_Operator_Updates_Nominal_Values_In_DB_ID
System Boundary
Display_ Persistent_ Process
SEM_Desktop_View
Update_All_View
Alarm
Monitor_ Persistent_ Process
Living_ Quarter_ Controller
Living_ Quarter
Database_ Persistent_ Process
Database
$Use_Case
1. Operator selects "Update all" button then
2. Display the Update_All_View.
3. Disable the Alarm.
4. Operator enters values.
5 - 9. Update all the values in the DB.
10 - 15. For each Environmental Condition, update the values in the database.
16 - 17. If no Constraint Error, then commit the transaction.
18 - 19. If Constraint Error, then rollback the transaction.
20. Enable the alarm.
21. Destroy the display.
22. If the Cancel button is selected, then
23. Enable the alarm.
24. Destroy the display.
1: Update All Button Selected
2:Display ()
3:Disable ()
4:Operator Enters Values
5: OK Button Selected
6:Update_All_RPC ()
7:Update_All ()
8:Start_Transaction_RPC ()
9:Start_Transaction ()
10:Update (Air)
11:ENTER_VALUE_ID (Air)
Constraint_Error
12:Update (Oxy)
13:ENTER_VALUE_ID (Oxy)
Constraint_Error
14:Update (Temp)
15:ENTER_VALUE_ID (Temp)
Constraint_Error
16:Commit_RPC ()
17:Commit()
18:Rollback_RPC ()
19:Rollback()
20:Enable ()
21:Destroy ()
22: Cancel Button Selected
23:Enable ()
24:Destroy ()
*NOTE: The parent Database Class is shown on this ID, but at the time the IDs are drawn it may not be known what database implementation (e.g., which Subclass) will be used. In the solution, the SNAP implementation uses the MSAccess_Database Class, while the C++ implementation uses the Flat_File_Database Class.

Figure 9-11. UC16's ID with Exception Handling

Phase Transition Criteria

Transition to the next Phase when the IDs are complete and ready to transition to a language representation of the design. The review criteria shown in Table 9-2 can be used to aid in the transition decision process.

Review Criteria

Table 9-2. ID Review Criteria after OOD

#	Interaction Diagram Review Criteria	OOA	OOD
1	Each Message represents a Method of a Class and appears as part of the Class description.	√	√
2	Branching and iteration appear as comments.	√	√
3	Are diagram naming conventions followed? An ID is named either i.) <<UC#_Use Case Name>>_ID ii.) all upper-case letters for a supporting ID, suffixed by _ID	√	√
4	Each Message is numbered, even "Messages" to supporting IDs.	√	√
5	Instances are identified (optional).	√	√
6	Is a Message sent to the correct Class? Does the Method have access to the right data to complete its processing?	√	√
7	Does the Method need access to additional Classes to perform the Message?	√	√
8	Do Message names follow Method naming conventions?	√	√
9	Do the notes reflect the correct Message numbers?	√	√
10	Are DB Messages included (optional at OOA,required at OOD)?	√	√
11	No Process Classes at OOA (required at OOD).	√	√
12	No Controller Classes at OOA (required at OOD).	√	√
13	Exceptions represent failure, not status.	√	√
14	Exception propagation is reasonable.	√	√
15	Do comments exist that annotate collections of Messages. These comments, in essence, represent PDL for a Use Case, not PDL for an individual Method.	√	√
16	There is only one incoming Message per Class Method, however, multiple outgoing Messages per Class Method are permitted.	√	√
17	Classes on the ID appear in the CCD.	√	√
18	The word "find" is not utilized.	√	√
19	Create()/Delete() Messages are validated against the CCD for multiplicity/conditionality consistency.	√	√
20	For Classes with a State Attribute, Messages for Current_State() and Change_State() are issued.	√	√
21	Are known View Classes included?	√	√
22	Do View Classes send Messages to Domain Classes, and not vice versa?	√	√
23	Does a View Class have a "populate()" Message if it autofills data?	√	√
24	Are Process Classes included?		√
25	Are the Process Classes consistent with the PAD?		√
26	Are the Classes to the right of a Process Class consistent with the PCAD for the process?		√
27	If a Class is shared by multiple processes, does the Class appear to the right of each process?		√
28	If a Class is shared by multiple processes, is the Message to the Class the right Message for the process?		√
29	Do exceptions represent failure?		√
30	Does the exception propagation depicted reflect the Scenario?		√
31	Does the Controller Class support decoupling of Domain Classes?		√

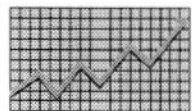

Tracking Progress

Table 9-3 once again shows an update to the project management spreadsheet. For this Phase, the number of IDs updated, compared to the actual number of IDs that were produced during OOD (Phase 6), can be monitored as a percentage.

Finally, any new Classes, Methods, and Attributes identified are reflected in the ongoing monitoring of the number of Classes per Category, as well as the average number of Methods and Attributes per Class.

Table 9-3. Project Management Spreadsheet: Phase 9

HCC Project Management Spreadsheet						
Number	**Phase Name**	**Activity**	**Charge Number**	**Product**	**Progress Metric**	**% Weight**
7	**Software OOD—Process View**		**SW-OOD-PA-7**			
7.1		Initiate PAD	SW-OOD-PA-7.1	PAD	1 PAD completed	0.25
7.2		Identify Processes	SW-OOD-PA-7.2			
7.3		Identify Processors	SW-OOD-PA-7.3			
7.4		Allocate Processes to Processors	SW-OOD-PA-7.4			
7.5		Allocate Classes to Processes	SW-OOD-PA-7.5	PCADs	# PCADs	0.30
7.6		Identify Process Interaction	SW-OOD-PA-7.6	PID	1 PID completed	0.25
7.7		Generate Process/Processor STD	SW-OOD-PA-7.7	STD	#STDs	0.10
7.8		Update CSs	SW-OOD-PA-7.8	CS	#CSs	0.10
8	**Software OOD—Static View**			**SW-OODS-8**		
8.1		Update Category Class Diagram	SW-OODS-8.1	CCD (Updated)		
8.2		Reuse Existing Design Patterns	SW-OODS-8.2	CCD (Updated)	#CCDs	0.50
8.3		Update Class Specifications	SW-OODS-8.3	CS (Updated)	#CSs	0.50
9	**Software OOD—Dynamic View**		**SW-OODD-9**			
9.1		Update Classes/Messages on ID	SW-OODD-9.1	IDs (Updated)	# IDs	
9.2		Add Exception Propagation	SW-OODD-9.2	IDs (Updated)	# IDs	1.00

PART V

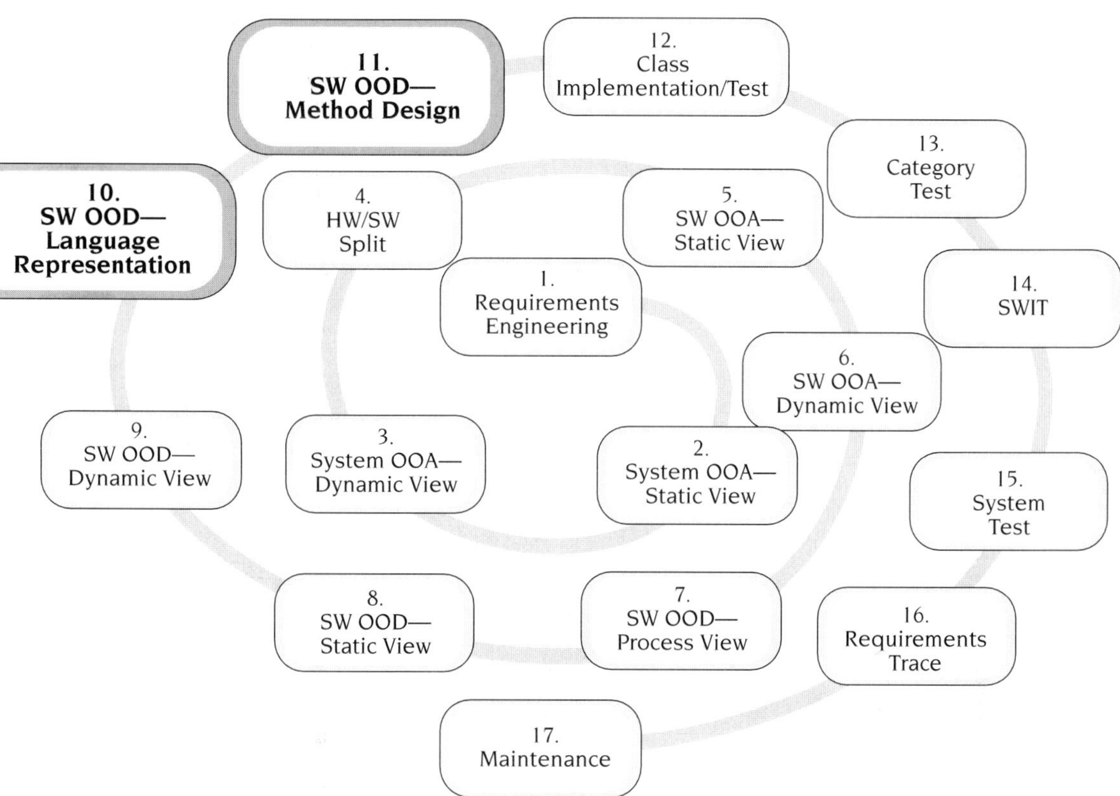

Software Object-Oriented Design—Language-Dependent

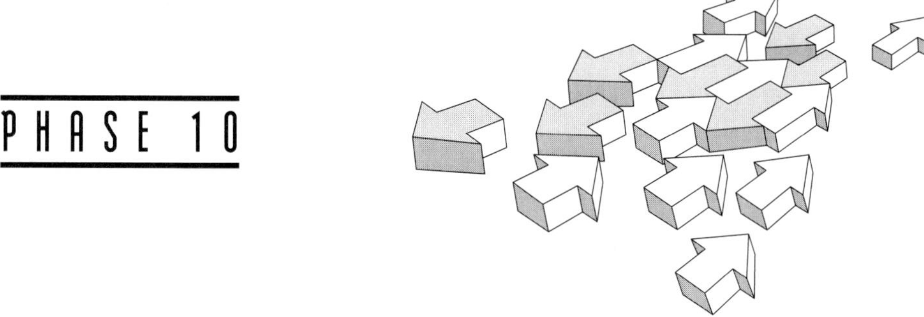

PHASE 10

Software OOD—Language Representation

PHASE OVERVIEW

Now that the *language-independent* design is complete, it is time to move to a *language-dependent* representation of the solution. As Figure 10-1 shows, Phase 10 focuses on producing a *language-dependent, compilable* representation of the static Class architecture. In this Phase, the Classes that have been discovered are transi-

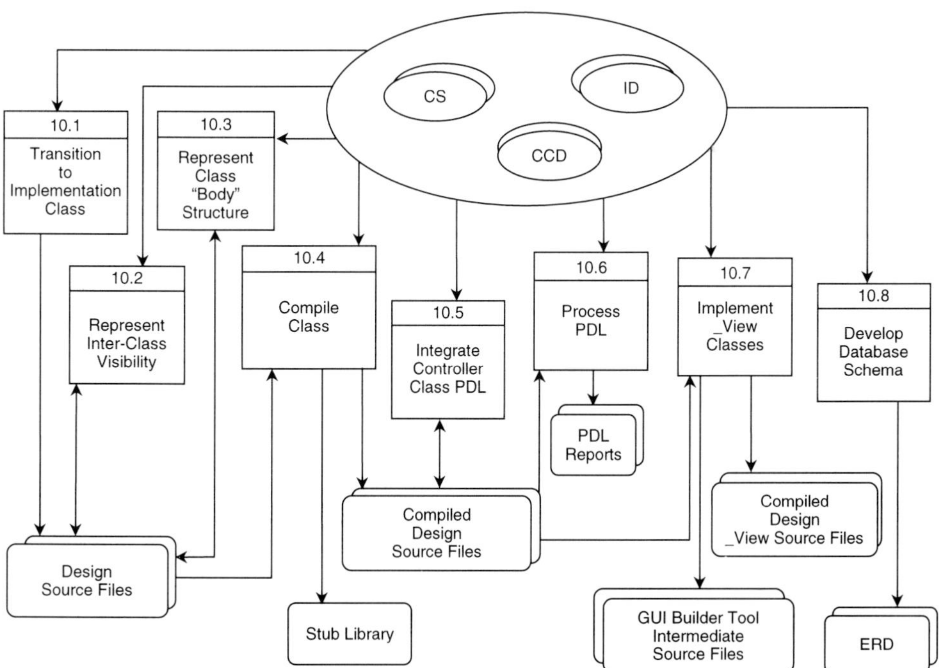

Figure 10-1. Software OOD - Language Representation Phase Description Diagram

tioned to the appropriate language construct, *without* implementing the Methods. Language representations of the structure of a Class are developed and *compiled* to ensure that visibility requirements are satisfied. If a project has selected to let the language serve as a Program Design Language (PDL) as well, the appropriate PDL processor can be utilized to generate both technical and managerial reports that support the entire development process.

At this time, in *parallel* Activities, the `_View` Classes are implemented and integrated with the compiled Class skeletons, and the initial database schema is developed. By implementing the front-end (`_View` Classes) and back-end (database) pieces of the solution, they can be integrated with the compilable design and thus, they can be ready for subsequent Class implementation.

Of course, it goes without saying that a project's file naming conventions, language design guidelines, and coding standards impact the resulting language representation.

Examples for this section are provided in four languages, in the following order: C++, Ada95, Java, and SNAP. Complete language solutions for the SEM in all four languages are provided in Appendix D on the enclosed CD.

10.1 TRANSITION TO IMPLEMENTATION CLASS

Purpose

> The purpose of this Activity is to develop a language-dependent representation of a Class contract.

Definition(s)

Ada95 Package: A **package** is an Ada95 construct that is utilized to represent a Class. A package has two parts: a package specification (specifies the contract, or interface, to clients) and a package body (provides the implementation of the Class).

.cpp File: A **.cpp file** is a file that typically contains the C++ implementation of the Class Methods, with the exception of those functions coded in-line in the C++ header file. A **.cpp file** is *not* part of the interface, or contract, of a Class.

C++ Class: A **C++ Class** is a C++ language construct that is utilized to represent a Class. A **C++ Class** is represented by both a header file that provides the contract or interface to the clients and a `.cpp` file that provides the set of all function definitions appropriate to the Class.

C++ Header File: A **C++ header file** is a file that specifies the interface of a C++ Class to its clients. The contract that a Class makes with its clients is represented in the **C++ header file**.

Class Contract: A **Class contract** is the interface of a Class to its clients. A **Class contract** represents the resources of a Class that are accessible by the clients of a Class.

Java Package: A **Java package** is a Java construct that provides a mechanism to group-related Classes and interfaces.

Package Body: A **package body** is an Ada95 construct that is utilized to represent the implementation of a Class. A **package body** is *not* part of the interface to the Class' clients.

Package Specification: A **package specification** is an Ada95 language construct that is utilized to represent the interface of a Class. A **package specification** represents the interface, or contract, that the Class makes with its potential clients.

SNAP Class Definition File: A **SNAP Class Definition File** (`.cd` file) is a file that typically contains the SNAP interface and implementation of a Class.

Process

Step 1: Determine Implementation Mechanism for Software Constraints

When the RTM was initially developed (Phase 1), a code was assigned to each entry in the RTM that indicated the entry's type, e.g., software, hardware, performance requirement, and so on. One of the codes used was SWC, meaning a software constraint; a specification of a certain limit on the software. At that time it was stated that later, during implementation, a decision would need to be made about how those constraints would be implemented. Options for implementation include hard coded bounds on arrays or lists, named constants, constraint access through a flat file or database, or perhaps, Operator action to enter the initial values for these constraints.

Now is the time to make the decision about how to implement the constraints, as some of them may need to be included in the Class contract. For the SEM, the decision was made to use named constants in the code.

Step 2: Establish the Source Code Directory Structure

Define the directory structure to follow the Category structure. In other words on the development platform, establish an `/src` directory with one subdirectory for each Category. Name the subdirectory the two- or three-letter Category acronym established earlier (see Figure 2-9(b)). For the SEM, subdirectories were established as follows:

`/src/PL`,

`/src/LQ`,

and so on.

For *each* of these subdirectories, establish two more subdirectories, `/code` and `/test`, for example, `/src/PL/code` and `/src/PL/test`. The `/code` subdirectory is used for maintaining the source code files for a specific Category, while the `/test` subdirectory is used for maintaining all the test drivers and test results for a specific Category.

Step 3: Develop the Class Structure for the Class Contract

For a Class, develop just the skeleton of the Class. The word "skeleton" has a different meaning depending upon the implementation language. Both C++ and Ada95 separate their Class contract and implementation into distinct files. For C++, use of the word "skeleton" implies the basic structure of the C++ header file. For Ada95, use of the word "skeleton" means the basic structure of the Ada95 package declaration. Java and SNAP do *not* have distinct language constructs for the Class contract and Class implementation. For Java and SNAP, the contract and implementation of a Class reside in the same basic enclosing language construct and in the same file. Consequently, the word "skeleton," when applied to those languages, implies the Class structure without the implementation of any Methods.

Of course, follow the file naming conventions and coding standards established for the project. Most file naming conventions require that each file name begin with the two- (or three-) letter abbreviation for the Category that owns the Class.

The Class from the SEM that has been selected to illustrate this Activity is the Temperature_Environmental_Condition Class. For reference, Figure 10-2 shows the CCD, at the end of OOD, for the `Environmental_Condition_CAT` that owns the `Temperature_Environmental_Condition` Class.

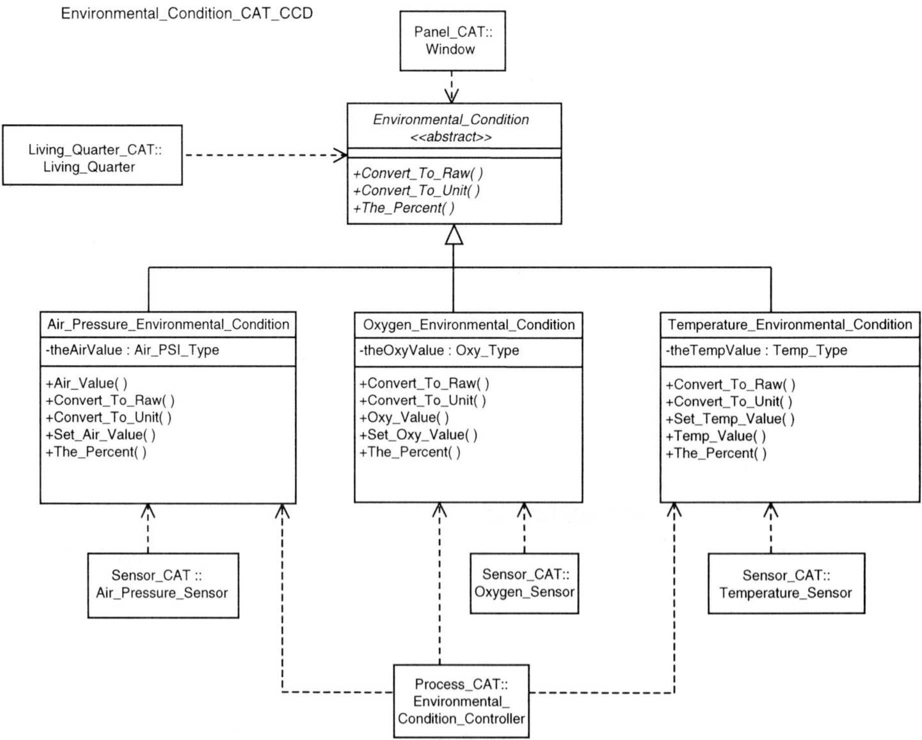

Figure 10-2. Environmental_Condition_CAT_CCD : UML Notation

Example

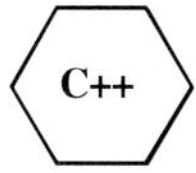


```
/* =================================================================
// Copyright P. P. Texel & C. B. Williams 1996
//
// FILENAME: ec_tempenv.h
//
// AUTHOR: P. Texel
//
// DESCRIPTION: Subclass of Class EnvironmentalCondition
//
// DATE CREATED: 3 July 1996
//
=================================================================*/
#ifndef _TEMPENVIRON_H
#define _TEMPENVIRON_H

#include "ec_environ.h"

class TemperatureEnvironmentalCondition
          : public EnvironmentalCondition
{
public:

protected:

private:
};
#endif
```

Note that the C++ header file “skeleton” includes the following:

- Variable definition to prohibit multiple `#includes`
- `#includes` (Classes required) - optional
- Inheritance, where applicable
- Establishment of public, protected, and private partitions of the Class.

```
--=================================================================
-- Copyright P. P. Texel & C. B. Williams 1996
--
-- FILENAME: ec_temp_ec_s.ada
--
-- AUTHOR: P. Texel
--
-- DESCRIPTION:    Subclass of Class Environmental Condition
--
-- DATE CREATED: 3 July 1996
--
--=================================================================
with Environmental_Condition;
package Temperature_Environmental_Condition is
   -- renaming declarations
   package EC renames Environmental_Condition;

   -- Abstract Data Type
   type Temperature_Environmental_Condition_Type is new
      EC.Environmental_Condition_Type with private;

private
   type Temperature_Environmental_Condition_Type
      is new EC.Environmental_Condition_Type with
      record
         null;
      end record;
end Temperature_Environmental_Condition;
```

Note that the Ada95 package specification "skeleton" includes the following:

- `withs` (Classes required) - optional
- Renames for `with`ed packages - optional
- Type for the Class[1]
- Inheritance, where applicable
- Establishment of private partition of the Class.

[1]A type for a Class is *not* necessary to provide in C++ because a Class in C++ represents a user-defined type. The Ada95 package construct represents a collection construct and thus a type is required in Ada95 to represent the actual Abstract Data Type for the Class.

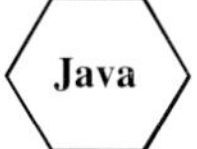

```
/* ==============================================================
// Copyright P. P. Texel & C. B. Williams 1996
//
// FILENAME: TemperatureEnvironmentalCondition.java
//
// AUTHOR: C. Williams
//
// DESCRIPTION: Subclass of EnvironmentalCondition
//
// DATE CREATED: 21 September 1996
//
//==============================================================*/
package EnvironmentalCondition;

import EnvironmentalCondition;

/*
 *
 * TemperatureEnvironmentalCondition
 *
 */
public class TemperatureEnvironmentalCondition
   extends EnvironmentalCondition
{

}
```

For Java, simply provide the following:

- owning package
- `import` (Classes required) - optional
- Inheritance (`extends`), where applicable
- Declaration as to whether the Class is `final`, `abstract`, or `public`[2]
- Opening/closing curly braces ({ }).

Private, protected, and public partitions are *not* established in Java. *Each* Class member, whether the member is an Attribute or a Method, has its access rights declared on a member-by-member basis.

[2]The modifier "final" when applied to a Class prohibits Subclasses from being defined. The modifier "abstract" prohibits Instances of the Class from being declared. The modifier "public" indicates that the Class is accessible outside the package within which the Class is defined.

SNAP

```
//=================================================================
// Copyright P. P. Texel & C. B. Williams 1996
//
// FILENAME: ec_tempenv.cd
//
// AUTHOR: C. Williams
//
// DESCRIPTION:Subclass of Class
//             EnvironmentalCondition
//
// DATE CREATED: 16 September 1996
//
//=================================================================
class
TemperatureEnvironmentalCondition
extends EnvironmentalCondition
{
}  // class TemperatureEnvironmentalCondition
```

For SNAP, simply provide the following:

- Inheritance (extends), where applicable

Note that in SNAP, there is no keyword for establishing visibility to required Supplier Classes. SNAP has a two-pass compiler which resolves references without requiring a keyword. Like Java, private, protected, and public partitions are *not* established. *Each* Class member, whether the member is an Attribute or a Method, has its access rights declared on a member-by-member basis.

Step 4: Transition Attributes

Using the CS, transition each Attribute to either a C++ , Java, or SNAP data member, or an Ada95 record component.[3] Be sure to follow the CS with respect to specifying the access rights to each Attribute.

The `Temperature_Environmental_Condition` Class did *not* have to have an Attribute in the model. A client of this Class can have two "raw" values, send them both to the `ConvertToUnit()` Method, which validates that each value lies within the specified bounds, and then pass the two raw values to `ThePercent()` Method. Earlier we chose to include an Attribute, even though the model did *not* require one. This latter approach requires a constructor that initializes the Attribute from a raw value, which then allows the Method `ThePercent()` to operate on Instances

[3]For this example, transition each Attribute as stated. However, on real projects, the actual type that represents the Class may be a pointer and may point to another type that contains the record components.

of the `TemperatureEnvironmentalCondition` Class. This clearly is an implementation issue. In the following C++ design, the Class provides the one Attribute, `theTempValue`, and the access right for `theTempValue` is specified as private.

C++

```
/* ===============================================================
// Copyright P. P. Texel & C. B. Williams 1996
//
// FILENAME: ec_tempenv.h
//
// AUTHOR: P. Texel
//
// DESCRIPTION: Subclass of Class
//              EnvironmentalCondition
//
// DATE CREATED: 3 July 1996
//
===============================================================*/

#ifndef _TEMPENVIRON_H
#define _TEMPENVIRON_H

#include "ec_environ.h"

class TemperatureEnvironmentalCondition: public
EnvironmentalCondition
{
public:

protected:

private:
   double theTempValue;
};
#endif
```

Note that the C++ header file now includes `theTempValue` Attribute as a data member in the private partition.

When specifying a data member declaration in C++, use the following as a guideline: if the data member is the result of an Association Relationship, consider making the data member a pointer to the Class, as in ***`double* theTempValue;`*** because the Instance of ***`double`*** can potentially be shared with other Classes. If, however, the data member is wholly owned by the Class in question (as in aggregation), consider either a reference to the Instance as in ***`double & theTempValue;`*** or simply ***`double theTempValue;`***, depending upon the actual size of the Instance and whether UML aggregation or composition was indicated on the CCD.

Ada95

```
--=================================================================
-- Copyright P. P. Texel & C. B. Williams 1996
--
-- FILENAME: ec_temp_ec_s.ada
--
-- AUTHOR: P. Texel
--
-- DESCRIPTION: Subclass of Class Environmental Condition
--
-- DATE CREATED: 3 July 1996
--
--=================================================================
with Environmental_Condition;
package Temperature_Environmental_Condition is
   -- renaming declarations
   package EC renames Environmental_Condition;
   -- types required for Attributes if Attribute is not
   -- another Class
   Minimum_Temperature: constant:= +50.0;
   Maximum_Temperature: constant:= +95.0;
   type Temperature_Type is digits 4 range
               Minimum_Temperature..Maximum_Temperature;
   -- Abstract Data Type, inherits from
   -- Environmental_Condition_Type
   type Temperature_Environmental_Condition_Type is new
      EC.Environmental_Condition_Type with private;
private
   type Temperature_Environmental_Condition_Type is new
      EC.Environmental_Condition_Type with record
         theTempValue: Temperature_Type;
      end record;
end Temperature_Environmental_Condition;
```

Note that the Ada95 package specification adds the following:

- `theTempValue` Attribute as a component of the record `Temperature_Environmental_Condition`
- Any additional types/constants required to satisfy any Attribute type declarations (here, `Temperature_Type` and the two named number declarations).

Java

```
/* ================================================================
// Copyright P. P. Texel & C. B. Williams 1996
//
// FILENAME: TemperatureEnvironmentalCondition.java
//
// AUTHOR: C. Williams
//
// DESCRIPTION: Subclass of EnvironmentalCondition
//
// DATE CREATED: 21 September 1996
//
//================================================================*/
package EnvironmentalCondition;

import EnvironmentalCondition;

/*
 *
 * TemperatureEnvironmentalCondition
 *
 */
public class TemperatureEnvironmentalCondition
             extends EnvironmentalCondition
{

      private double theTempValue;
}
```

There are no pointers in Java, consequently, the above declaration illustrates the typical manner in which a data member is declared.

SNAP

```
// ================================================================
// Copyright P. P. Texel & C. B. Williams 1996
//
// FILENAME: ec_tempenv.cd
//
// AUTHOR: C. Williams
//
// DESCRIPTION: Subclass of Class
```

```
//                EnvironmentalCondition
//
// DATE CREATED: 16 September 1996
//
//=====================================================================

class
TemperatureEnvironmentalCondition
extends EnvironmentalCondition
{

    static final double     MinimumTemperature = 50.0;
    static final double     MaximumTemperature = 95.0;

    double theTempValue
        [constraint: ConstraintOnlyVerifyTemp()];

    public truth
    ConstraintOnlyVerifyTemp()
    {
    return false; // Just to compile
    }
}       // class TemperatureEnvironmentalCondition
```

Note the addition of the two named constants for the maximum and minimum temperatures as well as the Attribute itself, `theTempValue`. These three declarations are private by default.[4] Finally, to enforce that the values for `theTempValue` are bounded, a constraint clause, with its associated Method, `ConstraintOnlyVerifyTemp()` has been added.

Step 5: Add Public Methods

Next, add the Methods to the Class. Again, pay attention to the CS with respect to specified access rights to the Methods. Stay focused on only the Methods that are in the CS, and of course, any Methods that may be required as a result of the implementation language (e.g., the copy constructor and overloaded assignment for C++). Finally, the names, types, and passing mechanism for all formal parameters must be identified.

[4]There is no reserved word "private" in SNAP. Any declaration not *explicitly* declared as public or protected is private.

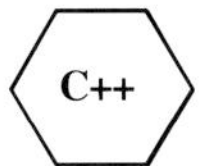

For C++, this step entails the addition of C++ function prototypes to the header file with access rights as specified in the CS.

```
/* =================================================================
// Copyright P. P. Texel & C. B. Williams 1996
//
// FILENAME: ec_tempenv.h
//
// AUTHOR: P. Texel
//
// DESCRIPTION: Subclass of Class EnvironmentalCondition
//
// DATE CREATED: 3 July 1996
//
=================================================================*/

#ifndef _TEMPENVIRON_H
#define _TEMPENVIRON_H

#include "ec_environ.h"

class TemperatureEnvironmentalCondition:
      public EnvironmentalCondition
{
public:
   // constructors & destructors
   TemperatureEnvironmentalCondition(); // default ctor
   // construct from raw value to acquire Instance
   TemperatureEnvironmentalCondition(double aTemp);
   TemperatureEnvironmentalCondition & // copy ctor
      (const TemperatureEnvironmentalCondition & aTemp);
   ~TemperatureEnvironmentalCondition(); // dtor
   // overloaded operators
   TemperatureEnvironmentalCondition &
      operator=(TemperatureEnviromentalCondition aTemp);

   // Attribute Queries
   double CurrentTemperature(); // returns temperature

   // Attribute Sets
   void SetTemperature(double aValue); // sets temperature

   // Domain Methods
      // determines percent deviation between two Instances
```

```
      double ThePercent
      (TemperatureEnvironmentalCondition & theBase);
   // conversion routines
   double ConvertToRaw ();
   void ConvertToUnit (double aRawValue);
protected:
private:
   double theTempValue;
};
#endif
```

Note that the C++ header file now includes the following:

- Constructors and a destructor
- An overloaded =
- A function prototype for each application-specific Method
- The parameter list for each Method
- The passing mechanism for each parameter
- The passing mechanism for each return specification

For Ada95, this step entails the addition of function, procedure, or task declarations to the package specification according to the access rights as specified in the CS.

```
--================================================================
-- Copyright P. P. Texel & C. B. Williams 1996
--
-- FILENAME: ec_temp_ec_s.ada
--
-- AUTHOR: P. Texel
--
-- DESCRIPTION: Subclass of Class Environmental Condition
--
-- DATE CREATED: 3 July 1996
--
--================================================================
with Environmental_Condition;
package Temperature_Environmental_Condition is
   -- renaming declarations
   package EC renames Environmental_Condition;
```

```
    -- types required for Attributes if not a Class
    Minimum_Temperature: constant:= +50.0;
    Maximum_Temperature: constant:= +95.0;
    type Temperature_Type is digits 4 range
                Minimum_Temperature..Maximum_Temperature;

    -- Abstract Data Type
    type Temperature_Environmental_Condition_Type is new
          EC.Environmental_Condition_Type with private;

    -- Attribute Queries
    function Temp_Value
       (aTEC: Temperature_Environmental_Condition_Type)
       return Temperature_Type;
    -- Attribute Sets
    procedure Set_TEC
       (aTEC: in out Temperature_Environmental_Condition_Type;
       aTempValue: in Temperature_Type);
    -- Domain Methods
    -- calculates the percent deviation between current and base
    function The_Percent
    (Current, Base: Temperature_Environmental_Condition_Type)
       return Float;
    -- conversion routines
    function ConvertToRaw
       (aTEC: Temperature_Environmental_Condition_Type)
       return Temperature_Type;
    function ConvertToUnit (aTempValue: Temperature_Type)
       return Temperature_Environmental_Condition_Type;
private
    type Temperature_Environmental_Condition_Type
          is new EC.Environmental_Condition_Type with
          record
             theTempValue: Temperature_Type;
          end record;
end Temperature_Environmental_Condition;
```

Note that the Ada95 package specification requires the following:

- For each Method, a decision must be made as to whether the Method is to be implemented as a procedure, function, or task
- For each parameter, the mode (`in`, `in out`, `out`) must be selected
- For each function, the return type must be specified
- For each task, the task entries, and their parameters, must be declared.

For Java, this step involves adding the *structure* of the function definitions for Class Methods. Here, use of the word "structure" means the *function contract,* or signature, and the required opening and closing curly braces. A return statement is required for those functions that return a value, e.g., an Instance of another Class or a predefined type.

```
/* ===============================================================
// Copyright P. P. Texel & C. B. Williams 1996
//
// FILENAME: TemperatureEnvironmentalCondition.java
//
// AUTHOR: C. Williams
//
// DESCRIPTION: Subclass of
//              EnvironmentalCondition
//
// DATE CREATED: 21 Sep 1996
//
//=============================================================*/
package EnvironmentalCondition;

import EnvironmentalCondition;

/*
 *
 * TemperatureEnvironmentalCondition
 *
 */
public class TemperatureEnvironmentalCondition
               extends EnvironmentalCondition
{

      private double theTempValue;

      public TemperatureEnvironmentalCondition ()
      {
      }

      public TemperatureEnvironmentalCondition
         (double aTempValue)
      {
      }
```

```
        public SetTemperature (double aTempValue)
        {
        }

        public double GetTemperature()
        {
            return 0.0;
        }

        public double ThePercent
            (TemperatureEnvironmentalCondition Base)
        {
            return 0.0;
        }

        public double ConvertToRaw ()
        {
            return 0.0;
        }

        public TemperatureEnvironmentalCondition
            ConvertToUnit (double aRawValue)
        {
        }
}
```

Note that Java, like C++, permits compilation without Method implementation. For this Activity, the following are required for Java:

- Each Method included as a function with an opening and closing curly brace ({ }), as a minimum
- For each function, the return type, if any, must be specified
- For each function that returns a value, a return statement that returns a dummy value of the return type
- Specification of member visibility on a member-by-member basis.

SNAP

```
// ==============================================================
// Copyright P. P. Texel & C. B. Williams 1996
//
// FILENAME: ec_tempenv.cd
//
// AUTHOR: C. Williams
```

```
//
// DESCRIPTION: Subclass of Class EnvironmentalCondition
//
// DATE CREATED: 16 September 1996
//
// ==============================================================
class
TemperatureEnvironmentalCondition
extends EnvironmentalCondition
{

   static final double     MinimumTemperature = 50.0;
   static final double     MaximumTemperature = 95.0;

   double    theTempValue
      [constraint: ConstraintOnlyVerifyTemp()];

   public truth
   ConstraintOnlyVerifyTemp()
   {
      return false;
   }

   // Constructor
   public static TemperatureEnvironmentalCondition
   New( in double aTempValue )
   {

      TemperatureEnvironmentalCondition Temp;
      return Temp;
   }

      {spec:"A constructor function to create new",
      "instances of, TemperatureEnvironmentalCondition."
      "This function has been created for ease of use",
      "but is not necessary."}
   // Attribute Queries
   public double
   CurrentTemperature()
   {
      return theTempValue;
   }

   // Attribute Sets
   public void
   SetTemperature ( in double aTempValue)
   {
```

```
    }

    // Domain Methods
    public double
    ThePercent ( in TemperatureEnvironmentalCondition
                theBase)
    {
       double Deviation;
       return Deviation;
    }
    {spec:"determines percent deviation between two",
          "values"}

// Note that ConvertToRaw and ConvertToUnit have not been
// implemented as their functionality has been replaced by the
// constraint clause on the theTempValue attribute definition.

}  // class TemperatureEnvironmentalCondition
```

The SNAP representation of a Class contract now includes:

- Parameter name, type, and passing mechanism (`in`, `inout`, `out`)
- Specification of return type
- Specification of member visibility on a member-by-member basis
- Specification of a constraint Method for each identified constraint clause

Step 6: Add Exceptions

Finally, add the exceptions identified in the Scenarios and summarized in the Exception Identification Table produced in the previous Phase. Associate each exception with the Method that throws the exception as a comment. Either comment the Method that raises the exception or comment the exception with the list of Methods that raise the exception.

C++

```
/* ==============================================================
// Copyright P. P. Texel & C. B. Williams 1996
//
// FILENAME: ec_tempenv.h
//
// AUTHOR: P. Texel
//
```

```
// DESCRIPTION: Subclass of Class EnvironmentalCondition
//
// DATE CREATED: 3 July 1996
//
==============================================================*/

#ifndef _TEMPENVIRON_H
#define _TEMPENVIRON_H

#include "ec_environ.h"

class TemperatureEnvironmentalCondition:
      public EnvironmentalCondition
{
public:

   // constructors & destructors
   TemperatureEnvironmentalCondition(); // default ctor
   TemperatureEnvironmentalCondition(double aTemp);

   TemperatureEnvironmentalCondition & // copy ctor
      (const TemperatureEnvironmentalCondition & aTemp);
   ~TemperatureEnvironmentalCondition(); // dtor
   // overloaded operators
   TemperatureEnvironmentalCondition &
      operator=(TemperatureEnviromentalCondition aTemp);

   // Attribute Queries
   Temperature CurrentTemperature(); // returns temp

   // Attribute Sets
   void SetTemperature(double aValue); // sets temp

   // Domain Methods
      // determines percent deviation between two values
      // throws "DivideByZero" exception if theBase == 0.0
   double ThePercent
      (TemperatureEnvironmentalCondition & theBase);
      // conversion routines
   double ConvertToRaw ();
   // throws "ConstraintError" if aRawValue is out of bounds
   void ConvertToUnit (double aRawValue);
protected:

private:
   Temperature theTempValue;
};
#endif
```

Note that in C++ the implementation of exceptions may be vendor/environment-specific because at this time, the C++ standard is *not* finalized. For this book, Borland C++ V4.5 was utilized, as well as Microsoft Visual C++™.

```
-- ==============================================================
-- Copyright P. P. Texel & C. B. Williams 1996
--
-- FILENAME: ec_temp_ec_s.ada
--
-- AUTHOR: P. Texel
--
-- DESCRIPTION: Subclass of Class Environmental Condition
--
-- DATE CREATED: 3 July 1996
--
-- ==============================================================

with Environmental_Condition;
package Temperature_Environmental_Condition is

   -- renaming declarations
   package EC renames Environmental_Condition;

   -- types required for Attributes if not a Class
   Minimum_Temperature: constant:= +50.0;
   Maximum_Temperature: constant:= +95.0;
   type Temperature_Type is digits 4 range
      Minimum_Temperature..Maximum_Temperature;

   -- Abstract Data Type
   type Temperature_Environmental_Condition_Type is new
      EC.Environmental_Condition_Type with private;

   -- Attribute Queries
   function Temp_Value
      (aTEC: Temperature_Environmental_Condition_Type)
      return Temperature_Type;
   -- Attribute Sets
   procedure Set_TEC
      (aTEC: in out Temperature_Environmental_Condition_Type;
      aTempValue: in Temperature_Type);
   -- Domain Methods
      -- calculates the percent deviation between current
      -- and base
```

```
   function The_Percent
      (Current, Base: Temperature_Environmental_Condition_Type)
      return Float;
   -- conversion routines
   function Convert_To_Raw
         (aTEC: Temperature_Environmental_Condition_Type)
         return Temperature_Type;
      -- raises Constraint_Error
   function Convert_To_Unit (aTempValue: Temperature_Type)
      return Temperature_Environmental_Condition_Type;

   Divide_by_Zero: exception; -- raised by The_Percent

private
   type Temperature_Environmental_Condition_Type
      is new EC.Environmental_Condition_Type with
      record
         theTempValue: Temperature_Type;
      end record;
end Temperature_Environmental_Condition;
```

Java

```
/* ================================================================
// Copyright P. P. Texel & C. B. Williams 1996
//
// FILENAME: TemperatureEnvironmentalCondition.java
//
// AUTHOR: C. Williams
//
// DESCRIPTION: Subclass of
// EnvironmentalCondition
//
// DATE CREATED: 21 Sep 1996
//
// ==============================================================*/
package EnvironmentalCondition;

import EnvironmentalCondition;
// Import the ConstraintError Class
// from the package SemExceptions
// import SemExceptions.ConstraintError;
/*
 *
```

```
 * TemperatureEnvironmentalCondition
 *
 */
public class TemperatureEnvironmentalCondition
extends EnvironmentalCondition
{
      private double theTempValue;

      public TemperatureEnvironmentalCondition ()
      {
      }
      public TemperatureEnvironmentalCondition
            (double aTempValue)
      {
         theTempValue = aTempValue;
      }
      public double ThePercent
         (TemperatureEnvironmentalCondition Base)
      {
         return 0.0;
      }

      public double ConvertToRaw ()
      {
            return 0.0;
      }
      public TemperatureEnvironmentalCondition
         ConvertToUnit (double aRawValue)
            throws ConstraintError    // must declare
                                      // in function declaration
   }
}
```

SNAP

SNAP does *not* support the concept of exceptions; consequently, the SNAP example does *not* change. SNAP provides a construct called an exit handler, that is used to control processing when an abnormal termination condition occurs.

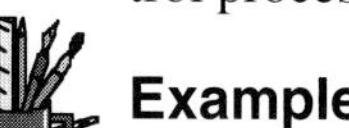

Example

The `Temperature_Environmental_Condition` Class was systematically developed in the above steps to show one way that a Class contract could be developed. Even though the `Temperature_Environmental_Condition` Class is a very *simple* Class, note that there is a *significant* amount of code in the Class contract.

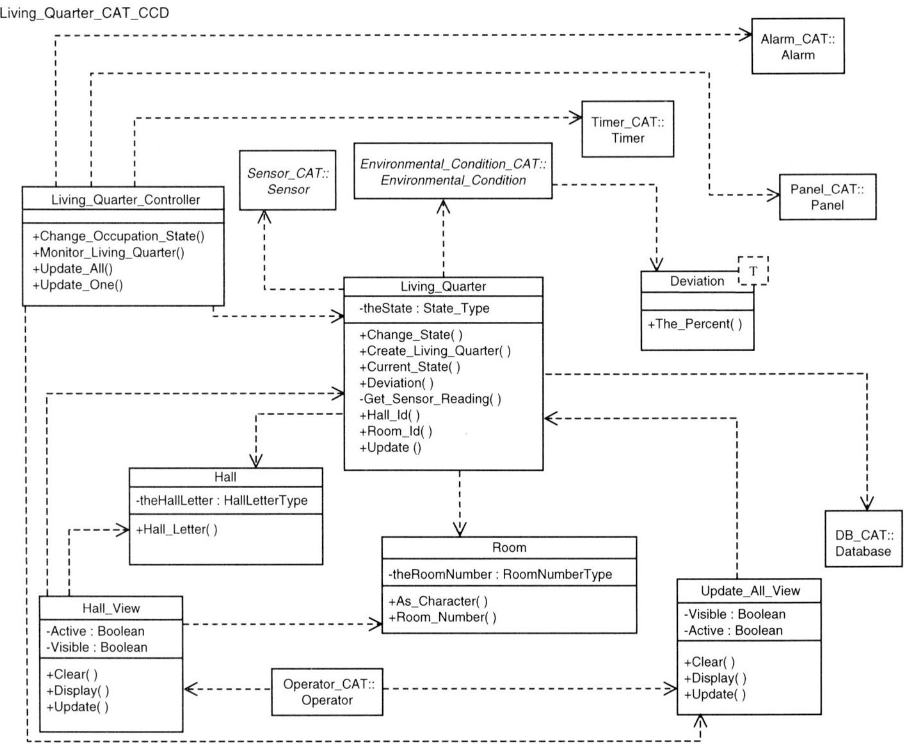

Figure 10-3. Living_Quarter_CAT_CCD : UML Notation

For this example, a more interesting Class, the `Living_Quarter` Class, is presented. For reference, Figure 10-3 depicts the Living_Quarter_CAT_CCD at the end of OOD.

C++

```
/* ==============================================================
// Copyright P. P. Texel & C. B. Williams 1996
//
// FILENAME: lq_lq.h
//
// AUTHOR: P. Texel
//
// DESCRIPTION: Concrete Class for Living Quarter
//
```

```
// DATE CREATED: 14 September 1996
//
============================================================*/
#ifndef _LQ_H
#define _LQ_H

#include "lq_hall.h"
#include "lq_room.h"
// SENSOR_CAT
#include "sr_sensor.h"
// ENVIRONEMNTAL_CONDITION_CAT
#include "ec_environ.h"

//
// this is a Concrete Class - instances can be declared
//
class LivingQuarter
{
public:
      // types for Attributes
      enum State {Occupied, Unoccupied};

      // constructors and destructors
      LivingQuarter();    // default constructor
      LivingQuarter(char aHallLetter, int aRoomNumber);
      LivingQuarter(const LivingQuarter & aLQ); // copy ctor

      ~LivingQuarter(); // destructor

      // overloaded operators
      LivingQuarter & operator=(LivingQuarter & aLQ);

      // Attribute Queries
      char Hall_Id(); // returns Hall Letter
      int Room_Id();  // returns Room Number
      State CurrentState(); // returns occupational
                            // status of a LQ

// Attribute Sets
void ChangeState(State newState);  // toggles
                                   // occupational status

// domain Methods
// throws "CantCompute" exception
double Deviation (EnvironmentalCondition::Kind aKind);

// Update Methods to update environmental condition
// is not included yet
```

```
private:
   Hall * HallId;  // pointer to Hall as Hall is shared
   Room * RoomId;  // pointer to Room as Room is shared
   Sensor * SensorSet[3];
   State theState; // occupational status

//local routine
double GetSensorReading // obtain sensor reading
      (EnvironmentalCondition::Kind aKind);
};
#endif
```

Ada95

```
--================================================================
-- Copyright P. P. Texel & C. B. Williams 1996
--
-- FILENAME: lq_lq_s.ada
--
-- AUTHOR: P. Texel
--
-- DESCRIPTION: The Living Quarter Class
--
-- DATE CREATED: 8 July 1996
--
--================================================================
with Hall, Room;
with Sensor;
with Air_Pressure_Sensor, Oxygen_Sensor, Temperature_Sensor;
with Environmental_Condition;
with Air_Pressure_Environmental_Condition,
   Oxygen_Environmental_Condition,
   Temperature_Environmental_Condition;

package Living_Quarter is
   -- renaming declarations
   package HL renames Hall;
   package RM renames Room;

   package EC renames Environmental_Condition;
   package APEC renames
      Air_Pressure_Environmental_Condition;
   package OEC renames Oxygen_Environmental_Condition;
   package TEC renames Temperature_Environmental_Condition;
```

```
   package SR renames Sensor;
   package AS renames Air_Pressure_Sensor;
   package OS renames Oxygen_Sensor;
   package TS renames Temperature_Sensor;

   -- types required for Attributes if not a Class
   type State_Type is (Occupied, Unoccupied);
      -- State Attribute values

   -- Abstract Data Type
      -- type for the Class
   type Living_Quarter_Type is private;
   procedure Create_Living_Quarter
            (aLvgQtr: in out Living_Quarter_Type;
             aHallId: in HL.Hall_Letter_Type;
             aRoomId: in RM.Room_Number_Type);

   procedure Living_Quarter_Ids (
                   aLvgQtr: in Living_Quarter_Type;
                   aHallId: out HL.Hall_Letter_Type;
                   aRoomId: out RM.Room_Number_Type);

   procedure Change_State
                (aLvgQtr: in out Living_Quarter_Type;
                      To: in State_Type);

   function Current_State (aLvgQtr: Living_Quarter_Type)
         return State_Type;
   function Deviation
         (aLvgQtr: Living_Quarter_Type;
          aSensor: EC.Environmental_Condition_Kind_Type)
      return Float;
   -- Update Methods to update the living quarter nominal
   -- value is not yet included
   Cant_Compute: exception; -- raised by Deviation

private
   -- set up array of pointers
   type Set_Of_Sensors_Type is array
         (EC.Environmental_Condition_Kind_Type) of
            SR.Sensor_Ptr_Type;
   -- pointer types for the Hall and Room attributes
   type Hall_Ptr_Type is access HL.Hall_Type;
   type Room_Ptr_Type is access RM.Room_Type;
```

```
    type Living_Quarter_Type[5] is
    record
       Hall_Id: Hall_Ptr_Type; -- pointer as association
       Room_Id: Room_Ptr_Type; -- pointer as association
       Sensor_Set: Set_Of_Sensors_Type -- owned by the
                                       -- Class
                   := (new AS.Air_Pressure_Sensor_Type,
                       new OS.Oxygen_Sensor_Type,
                       new TS.Temperature_Sensor_Type);
          -- default state for a LQ is unoccupied
          -- Operator must explicitly set a LQ to occupied
       State: State_Type:= Unoccupied; -- could be pointer
    end record;

end Living_Quarter;
```

In the full declaration of the Living_Quarter_Type, in the private part of the package specification, both the Hall_Id and Room_ID Attributes are declared as pointers, to be consistent with the recommendation that when an Instance is shared, a pointer is used to reference the Instance. However, in this Case Study, it really seems like overkill and frankly, if the Hall_Id and Room_ID Attributes were implemented as "owned" by the Living_Quarter_Type, as in

```
package Living_Quarter is
    -- as above
private
    type Living_Quarter_Type is
    record
       Hall_Id: HL.Hall_Type; -- no longer a pointer
       Room_Id: RM.Room_Type; -- no longer a pointer
       Sensor_Set: Set_Of_Sensors_Type
                   := (new AS.Air_Pressure_Sensor_Type,
                       new OS.Oxygen_Sensor_Type,
                       new TS.Temperature_Sensor_Type);
          -- default state for a LQ is unoccupied
          -- Operator must explicitly set a LQ to occupied
       State: State_Type:= Unoccupied; -- could be pointer
    end record;
end Living_Quarter;
```

this would *not* be a problem as the amount of space required is trivial. Remember, there are very few hard and fast rules. Guidelines can be provided for developers, but engineering judgment *must prevail.*

[5]The fully declared type can also be declared as a pointer to an incomplete type that is fully declared as a record type in the package body. This reduces recompilation required upon change.

Java

```
/* ===============================================================
// Copyright P. P. Texel & C. B. Williams 1996
//
// FILENAME: LivingQuarter.java
//
// AUTHOR: C. Williams
//
// DESCRIPTION: Implements a Class for a LivingQuarter
//
// DATE CREATED: 21 Sep 1996
//
// ============================================================*/
package LivingQuarter;

import Sensor.*; // the * means import all Classes in
                 // Sensor package
import EnvironmentalCondition.*;
import SemAddress.*;
import Database.FileDatabase; // import FileDatabase
                              // Class from Database package
import Sem; // the main applet is not in a package

/*
 *
 * LivingQuarter
 *
 */
public class LivingQuarter
{
   private Hall HallId;
   private Room RoomId;
   private boolean Occupied; // boolean predefined type
   private AirPressureSensor AirPressureSensorId;
   private OxygenSensor OxygenSensorId;
   private TemperatureSensor TemperatureSensorId;

   public LivingQuarter ()  // function declaration,
                            // no implementation
   {
   }

   public LivingQuarter (char aHallLetter, int aRoomNumber)
   {
   }
```

```
   public boolean CurrentState ()
   {
      return Occupied;
   }
   public char Hall_Id()
   {
      return HallId.HallLetter ();
   }

   public int Room_Id()
   {
      return RoomId.RoomNumber ();
   }

   public void ChangeState (boolean aState)
   {
   }

   // Update Method not yet included

   public double Deviation (int aKind)
   {
      double Answer = 0.0;   // dummy return value
      return Answer;
   }
}
```

SNAP

As with JAVA, a SNAP Class is contained in one file.

```
// ================================================================
// Copyright P. P. Texel & C. B. Williams 1996/1997
//
// FILENAME: lq_lq.cd
//
// AUTHOR: C. B. Williams
//
// DESCRIPTION: the Living Quarter Class
//
// DATE CREATED: 20 September 1996
//
// ================================================================
class
LivingQuarter
{
```

```
typedef public sgl {   // sgl is SNAP enum type
   Occupied,
   Unoccupied
} StateTP;   // StateTP is the sgl type name

StateTP  theState
   [default: Unoccupied];

set < Sensor > Sensors // no limit specified because
                       // truly a set, not an array
   [default: unknown];

Hall  theHall
   [default: unknown];

Room  theRoom
   [default: unknown];
public void
ChangeState  ( in StateTP  aState)
{
   theState = aState;
}

public static LivingQuarter
CreateLivingQuarter (in Hall aHall,
   in Room aRoom)
{

   LivingQuarter theLivingQuarter;
   return theLivingQuarter;
}
public StateTP
CurrentState()
{
return theState;
}
public double
Deviation( in EnvironmentalCondition
   anEnvironmentalCondition )
{

   double  Answer[ default: unknown];
   return Answer;
}

double
GetSensorReading( in Sensor  aSensor)
{
```

```
        return aSensor.CurrentValue();
    }

    public str
    HallId()
    {
        return theHall.HallLetter();
    }

    public str
    RoomId()
    {
        return theRoom.RoomNumber();
    }

}   // class LivingQuarter
```

Pragmatic Project Issues

Whether or Not to Automatically Generate Code

In two projects the automatic code generation capability of the selected CASE tool was *not* utilized by the developers because of the following:

- Poor naming conventions in the generated code
- Bi-directional implementation of all Association Relationships
- Automatic, inappropriate choices for data member types
- Lack of reverse engineering; thus, the only way to incorporate changes that occured in the OO model into the code was manual.

These projects simply generated the initial language-dependent representation of the Classes manually, and the developers were very satisfied.

Whether or Not to "`#include`", "`with`", or "`import`" Required Classes Now

It certainly makes sense to write the appropriate clauses that import required Classes now, rather than wait until the next Activity. It really doesn't matter whether it is done now or in the next Step. The above examples provide the required visibility in *this* Step, and are referenced in the discussion of the next Activity.

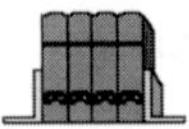

Product(s)

The products produced as a result of this Activity are contracts (no implementations) for a Class, represented in the project implementation language, with or without the clauses specifying required visibility. Although the clauses are required for compilation, compilation occurs during a subsequent Activity.

10.2 REPRESENT INTER-CLASS VISIBILITY

Purpose

> The purpose of this Activity is to add the required visibility to a Class contract, using the appropriate language construct; in other words, to provide access to the Class' Supplier Classes.

Process

Step 1: Inheritance Hierarchies

A Subclass in an inheritance hierarchy requires visibility to its Superclass. Visibility is achieved with an "`#include`" in C++ , with a "`with`" in Ada95, and with an "`import`" in Java. Consequently, a Subclass will `#include`, `with`, or `import` its Superclass. That is why the `Temperature_Environmental_Condition` Class `#included` its Superclass, `Environmental_Condition`, in C++, `with`ed it in Ada95, and `import`ed it in Java. Recall that SNAP does *not* require such a construct for specifying visibility requirements to Supplier Classes.

Step 2: Aggregation Hierarchies

A "whole" Class in an aggregation hierarchy requires visibility to its "part" Class. Thus, a "whole" Class must `#include`, `with`, or `import` its "part" Class. Note in the solution that the `Panel` Class `#includes` its "part" Class, `Annunciator`, in C++[6], `with`s it in Ada95, and `import`s it in Java.

Step 3: Uses Relationships

A Client Class' required visibility to its Supplier Classes is specified in the OO model as Booch "uses" relationships or UML Dependencies. Hence, a Client Class must `#include`, `with`, or `import` its Supplier Class. Note in Figure 10-3 that the `Living_Quarter` Class has a dependency on both the `Hall` and `Room` Classes and are `#included` in C++, `with`ed in Ada95, and `import`ed in Java.

Step 4: Validate the Visibility Requirement (C++ and Ada95 Only)

Make sure that the visibility is specified at the Class contract level when required, and deferred to the implementation level when appropriate. Stated differently, in Ada95 language terms, make sure that any "`with`"ing specified at the package specification level is necessary. "With"ing of a Class is necessary when the Class in question 1) has

[6]Depending upon the C++ design, a forward reference can be used at the .h level, followed by a #include at the .cpp level.

an Attribute of the `withed` Class, or 2) utilizes a Class as a parameter in a Method. Otherwise, defer the visibility to the implementation, or package body, level. In C++ terms, `#include` at the `.h` file level when the Class in question 1) has an Attribute of the `#included` Class, or 2) utilizes a Class as a parameter in a Method. Otherwise, defer the `#include` to the implementation, or `.cpp` file. Because Java and SNAP Classes are implemented in one construct, this particular Step is *not* applicable to Java and SNAP implementations.

Example

The previous examples specified the required visibility. The `Temperature_Environmental_Condition` Class required visibility to its Superclass, `Environmental_Condition`, and therefore `#includes` the file `ec_environ.h` in C++, `withs` the package `Environmental_Condition` in Ada95, and imports the `EnvironmentalCondition` Class in Java.

Pragmatic Project Issues

Defer, Defer, Defer!

Only provide visibility to those Classes that are required, *where* those Classes are required. If the inclusion can be deferred to a lower level (e.g., the Class implementation, or even to the Ada subunit level) then do so. Note that the `Database` Class is *not* included in the `.h` file for the `LivingQuarter` Class. Access to the `Database` Class is required as part of the implementation of the `LivingQuarter` Class `Update()` Methods, consequently the `Database` Class will be `#included` to the `.cpp` file.

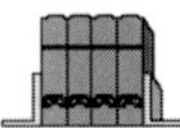

Product(s)

The products of this Activity are compilable Class contracts, represented in the selected implementation language.

10.3 DEVELOP CLASS "BODY" STRUCTURE

Purpose

> The purpose of this Activity is to create a Class implementation shell, or "body" structure, for a Class to complete the language representation of a Class.

Providing a Class "body" structure facilitates both compilation and early integration of multiple Classes. Once successfully compiled, appropriate Classes initiate a *stub library* that is then utilized by all developers for code integration across Categories.

Definition(s)

"Body": A **"body"** is the implementation of a Class contract. A **"body"** is represented as a compilable Ada95 package body or a `.cpp` file in C++. The concept of a "body" is not applicable to Java or SNAP.

"Body" Structure: A **"body" structure** is the overall structure of the implementation of the Methods of a Class, without the implementation of the Methods. A **"body" structure** does *not* contain the implementation of the algorithms. In Ada95, the **"body" structure** is developed using Ada95 stubs in the package body, while in C++ and Java, a **"body" structure** is developed by including the opening and closing curly braces ({ }) and a single return statement when required (when the function returns a value).

Stub Library: A **stub library** is a library of *Classes*, their *contracts* (interface specification) and "body" *structure*. The Classes in a **stub library** are those Classes that interface to any foreign Category, thus permitting developers to compile Classes within their Category that require access to Classes in foreign Categories, without relying on foreign Categories' development schedules.

Process

Step 1: Create the "Body" File

This step is applicable to C++ and Ada95 implementations only. Create a file to contain the "body" of the Class. For each Method, provide a stub in Ada95, or a function definition in C++, where for those functions that return a value, the function definition provides only a single return statement. In developing the structure of the Class implementation, pay attention to the following:

- `#include` or `with`, at the implementation level when appropriate
- Add new local declarations where applicable

  types, constants, Methods
- Identify package initialization, where applicable (Ada95 only).

Example

Here is the "body" structure for the `Temperature_Environmental_Condition` Class, in both C++ and Ada95, respectively:

C++

```
/* ==============================================================
// Copyright P. P. Texel & C. B. Williams 1996
//
// FILENAME: ec_tempenv.cpp
//
// AUTHOR: P. Texel
//
// DESCRIPTION: Implementation of the
// TemperatureEnvironmentalCondition Subclass of Class
// EnvironmentalCondition
//
// DATE CREATED: 3 July 1996
//
==============================================================*/
#include "ec_tempenv.h"

// constructors & destructors
TemperatureEnvironmentalCondition::
TemperatureEnvironmentalCondition()
{
}

TemperatureEnvironmentalCondition::
   TemperatureEnvironmentalCondition (double aTemp)
{
}

TemperatureEnvironmentalCondition &
TemperatureEnvironmentalCondition::
   TemperatureEnvironmentalCondition
   (const TemperatureEnvironmentalCondition & aTemp)
{
}

TemperatureEnvironmentalCondition::
   ~TemperatureEnvironmentalCondition()
{
}

// overloaded operators
TemperatureEnvironmentalCondition &
```

```
TemperatureEnvironmentalCondition::
   operator=(TemperatureEnvironmentalCondition aTemp)
{
   TemperatureEnvironmentalCondition DummyValue;
   return DummyValue; // dummy return statement
}

// Attribute Queries
Temperature TemperatureEnvironmentalCondition::
CurrentTemperature()
{
   Temperature DummyValue;
   return DummyValue; // dummy return statement
}

// Attribute Sets
void TemperatureEnvironmentalCondition::SetTemperature()
{
}

// Domain Methods

   // determines percent deviation between two values
   // throws "DivideByZero" exception if theBase == 0.0
double TemperatureEnvironmentalCondition::
ThePercent (TemperatureEnvironmentalCondition & theBase)
{
   return 0.0; // dummy return statement
}

   // conversion routines
double TemperatureEnvironmentalCondition::ConvertToRaw()
{
   return 0.0; // dummy return statement
}

   // throws "ConstraintError" if aRawValue
   // is out of bounds
void
TemperatureEnvironmentalCondition:: ConvertToUnit
   (double aRawValue)
{
}
```

Note that for those functions that do *not* return a value, only the opening and closing braces (e.g., { })are required for compilation. For those functions that *do* return a value, a dummy return statement is required for successful compilation.

Ada95

```
-- ==============================================================
-- Copyright P. P. Texel & C. B. Williams 1996
--
-- FILENAME: ec_tempenv_b.ada
--
-- AUTHOR: P. Texel
--
-- DESCRIPTION: Subclass of Class Environmental Condition
--
-- DATE CREATED: 3 July 1996
--
-- ==============================================================
package body Temperature_Environmental_Condition is

   -- Attribute Queries
   function Temp_Value
      (aTEC: Temperature_Environmental_Condition_Type)
       return Temperature_Type is separate;
   -- Attribute Sets
   procedure Set_TEC
      (aTEC: in out
       Temperature_Environmental_Condition_Type;
       aTempValue: in Temperature_Type)is separate;

   -- Domain Methods
      -- calculates the percent deviation between
      -- current and base
   function The_Percent
      (Current, Base: Temperature_Environmental_Condition_Type)
       return Float is separate;
      -- conversion routines
   function Convert_To_Raw
         (aTEC: Temperature_Environmental_Condition_Type)
          return Temperature_Type is separate;
      -- raises Constraint_Error
   function Convert_To_Unit (aTempValue: Temperature_Type)
          return Temperature_Environmental_Condition_Type
          is separate;

end Temperature_Environmental_Condition;
```

Note that the example has five stubs, one for each Method, which is quite straightforward for simple Classes like `Temperature_Environmental_Condition`. Importing (`withing`) the `Deviation` Class is *not* necessary because the implementation of `The_Percent()`, in its subunit, requires the instantiation of the `Deviation` Parameterized Class. Consequently, `withing` the `Deviation` Class has been deferred to the subunit level.

Other Classes, such as the `Alarm` Class, are *not* so simple. The "body" structure for the `Alarm` Class requires much more design than the Class contract because all an `Alarm` Class *needs* to provide to its clients is the ability to sound the alarm. For example, the Methods `Current_State()` and `Change_State()` do *not* appear in the package specification because they are *not* required by any clients; however, they *are* required by the implementation of the `Sound_Alarm()` and `Silence_Alarm()` Methods. Consequently, these two Methods appear as local Methods in the package body. The C++ equivalent is to provide these function definitions in the private portion of the `.h` file, or in the same `.cpp` file containing the Class "body"structure (scoped to the Class).

The package specification for the `Alarm` Class is very simple because the only interface required by its clients is the Method that sounds the alarm. In Ada, the `Sound_Alarm()` Method is an interrupt entry that can be designed into the package body.

Ada95

```
-- ============================================================
-- Copyright P. P. Texel & C. B. Williams 1995/1996
--
-- FILENAME: al_alarm_s.ada
--
-- DATE CREATED: 15 May 1996
--
-- AUTHOR: P. Texel
--
-- DESCRIPTION: Manages the interface to an Alarm
--
-- USE CASES SATISFIED: None - but RTM Entry #18, 21
--
-- ============================================================
package Alarm is
   procedure Sound_Alarm;
end Alarm;
```

The remainder of the Alarm Class' capability can be designed into the "body" structure of the Alarm Class, as follows:

```
-- ================================================================
-- Copyright P. P. Texel & C. B. Williams 1995/1996
--
-- FILENAME: al_alarm_b.ada
--
-- DATE CREATED: 15 May 1996
--
-- AUTHOR: P. Texel
--
-- DESCRIPTION: implements the package and provides an
-- interrupt handler for turning off the alarm
-- USE CASES SATISFIED: None - but RTM Entry #18, 21
-- ================================================================
package body Alarm is
   -- type for the state attribute
   type State_Type is (Silenced, Sounding);

      -- type for the Alarm with only one Attribute
      -- with default intitial value of Silenced
   type Alarm_Type is
   record
      State: State_Type:= Silenced;
   end record;

   -- the actual alarm Instance, automatically
   -- initialized to Silenced
   TheAlarm: Alarm_Type;

   task Alarm_Task is
      entry Sound_Alarm;
      entry Silence_Alarm;
      -- for Interrupt use at #56A#; -- platform dependent
   end Alarm_Task;

   procedure Change_State (To: in State_Type) is separate;

   function Current_State return State_Type is separate;

   -- calls the task entry Alarm_Task.Sound_Alarm;
   procedure Sound_Alarm is separate;

   task body Alarm_Task is separate;

end Alarm;
```

Pragmatic Program Issues

Can't Get Them All!

It is really impossible to envision *all* the required overloaded operators for a Class, although most of the domain's Methods can be identified from the IDs.

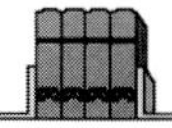

Product(s)

The products of this Activity are compilable "body" structures. At this point, C++ and Ada95 Classes are ready to compile (both the Class contract and structure of the implementation of the Class). Java and SNAP Classes were ready to compile following Activity 10.2.

10.4 COMPILE CLASS

Purpose

> The purpose of this Activity is to successfully compile each Class, to ensure that the static architecture is viable, to ensure that each Client Class has the required visibility to its suppliers, and to ensure that each Supplier Class provides the needed resources to its clients.

There is also an implicit purpose of this Activity, which is to ensure a correct syntactic and semantic language representation of the design.

Process

Step 1: Create a Stub Library Directory Structure

Create a new directory, with appropriate subdirectories for each Category, to act as a stub library.

Step 2: Compile Class

Compile the Classes. Use the Class stubs in the stub library for those Classes, inter-Category[7], with which the current Class requires an interface. Obviously, correct all compilation errors and applicable warnings before proceeding to Step 3.

[7]Of course this approach is equally applicable to intra-Category Class connections (visibility requirements).

Step 3: Update Stub Library

If the Class in question is a Class required by a Class in another Category, update the stub library for the current Class' Category.

Example

It is *not* necessary to provide an example of a clean compilation message. The goal is, of course, successful compilation of all Classes within a Category, using the stub library to permit compilation across Categories (or even within a Category, when necessary).

Pragmatic Program Issues

Commit to a Stub Library

The commitment to a stub library is one of manpower. But the benefits far outweigh the negatives. The initiation of a stub library *now*, provides the mechanism for interface management between Categories and within a Category. Without managing the interfaces, a project is doomed to chaos.

Interface Management

The stub library leads to a table, as shown in Table 10-1, that can evolve to provide a mechanism to manage the interfaces between Categories. The rows represent clients, while the columns represent suppliers. An upper-case letter, e.g., 'A', represents a Category, and a lower-case letter, e.g., 'a', represents a Class within the Category. Table 10-1 is read as follows: Category A, Class a1 requires an interface with Category B, Class b1; Category A, Class a2 requires an interface with Category B, Classes b1 and b2, and to Category C, Class c1. A table like this can be used to track interfaces at the Category and Class levels. The table can then be further refined to capture interface requirements at the Method level, or new tables can be generated that provide this next level of detail for tracking interfaces.

When dates required for Method completion are added to a table like this, a management schedule can be developed that begins to precisely nail down when Classes

Table 10-1. Interface Management Table

	A	a1	a2	**B**	b1	b2	**C**	c1
A								
a1					√			
a2					√	√		√
B								
b1								
b2								
C								
c1								

are expected to be completed. Of course, this then progresses to when a Use Case can be expected to be completed.

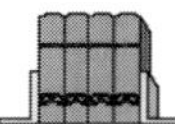

Product(s)

The products of this Activity are successfully compiled *design* source files that represent Class contracts and a Class "body" structure.

10.5 INTEGRATE CONTROLLER CLASS PDL

Purpose

> The purpose of this Activity is to successfully compile and integrate Category Controller Classes into the static architecture.

Definition(s)

UML Activity Diagram (AD): A **UML AD** is a diagram that depicts the execution steps to be performed by a Method[8]. A **UML AD** depicts the steps that a Method executes to perform its intended processing. The diagram considers the steps that a Method executes through as states of the state machine represented by the Method. The notation for a **UML AD** provides for concurrency, branching, and multiple Instances.

Process

Step 1: Select Mechanism for Representing Intended Controller Class Processing

Basically there are three choices of representation for the intended processing of the Methods of a Controller Class: AD, Sequence Diagram[9], or PDL.

If either an AD or Sequence Diagram is chosen to represent the intended execution of a Controller Class Method, that information resides in the CASE tool repository. If a PDL is produced, that information resides in the source code files. In any case, scripts can generate summary report information from either of these three work products, although the level of detail will differ. From the CASE tool repository, Class and Method utilization can be extracted, while from the PDL, variable set/used reports can be generated in addition to Method usage. If a PDL is utilized, depending upon the level of detail of the PDL, specific Instances and Methods can be indicated, (see Step 2 below).

[8]UML 1.0 indicates that an Activity Diagram is also applicable to a Use Case.

[9]A Sequence Diagram (or Collaboration) does provide constructs for representing control flow, therefore it too could be used to represent the intended processing of a Method in a Controller Class.

For the SEM, PDL was selected to represent the intended processing of a Controller Class. For a complete picture, a UML AD is also provided as Figure 10-4.

Step 2: Select Project PDL

PDLs range from a syntactically rigorous PDL to a very free-form PDL. Examples for the `Living_Quarter_Controller::Change_Occupational_State()` Method follow. However, first recall from the previous Phase that the Controller Class has a Method that is named the same as the Use Case *and* is named the same (or close to the same) as the Method in the `Living_Quarter` Class. The Method in the `Living_Quarter` Class manages the Attributes of the `Living_Quarter` Class, while the Method in the `Living_Quarter_Controller` Class coordinates the `Living_Quarter` Domain Class and requests services from other Classes as required.

In the following PDL[10], the symbol occurring as the first character *after* a language-dependent comment indicator, has the indicated meaning:

- % dictionary definition
- | design information.

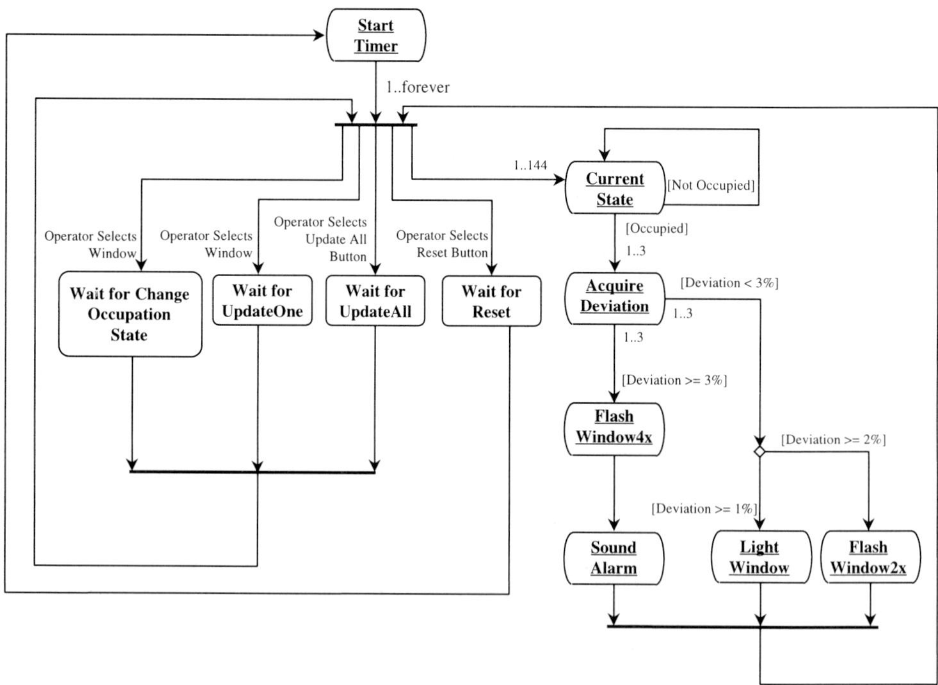

Figure 10-4. LivingQuarterController::MonitorLivingQuarters_AD

[10]This PDL is based on the AISLE® and CISLE™ family of tools. Surf to URL http://www.cyberg8t.com/ssd for more information.

Dictionary definitions are collected in reports that indicate, for all declared items,

- The declaration
- What unit owns the declaration
- The definition associated with the declaration
- The file and line number associated with the declaration

while the design information is utilized for pretty printing and set/used reports.

Following the contract and "body" structure below, the intended processing for the `Change_State()` Method of the `Living_Quarter_Controller` Class is first represented by a very rigorous PDL, and then by a very free-form PDL. The language utilized below is Ada, consequently the PDL is contained in an Ada subunit.

```
-- ================================================================
-- Copyright P. P. Texel & C. B. Williams 1995/1996
-- FILENAME: lq_controller_s.ada
-- DATE CREATED: 15 May 1996
-- AUTHOR: P. Texel
-- DESCRIPTION: manages all request for services for
-- Living_Quarter
-- USE CASES SATISFIED: UC#26
-- ================================================================
with Living_Quarter;
package Living_Quarter_Controller is --% Controller Class

   package LQ renames Living_Quarter;
   procedure Change_Occupation_State -- % controller
                                     -- Method (UC#26)
      (aLvgQtr: in out LQ.Living_Quarter_Type; --% the lg
       To: in LQ.State_Type); --% new state of lq
end Living_Quarter_Controller;

-- ================================================================
-- Copyright P. P. Texel & C. B. Williams 1995/1996
-- FILENAME: lq_controller_b.ada
-- DATE CREATED: 15 May 1996
-- AUTHOR: P. Texel
-- DESCRIPTION: implements the capability of changing the
--              occupational status of a Living Quarter
-- USE CASES SATISFIED: UC# 26
-- ================================================================
with Flat_File_Database; -- to update the database
with Hall, Room; -- to get the ids to update the database
package body Living_Quarter_Controller is
```

```
      procedure Change_Occupation_State
                  (aLvgQtr: in out LQ.Living_Quarter_Type;
                        To: in LQ.State_Type) is separate;
end Living_Quarter_Controller;
```

In the following PDL, each PDL statement is an actual call to a Method in a Class, but encapsulated in a comment. The call is written in expanded name notation using the abbreviation for the package that owns the Method. The call can be written either with or without parameters—that is a Project Team decision. Having a PDL this syntactically tight enables a PDL processor to indicate which Methods are referenced in the design and which are *not*, thus providing consistency reports.

```
-- ============================================================
-- Copyright P. P. Texel & C. B. Williams 1995/1996
-- FILENAME: lq_controller_chocc_b.ada
-- DATE CREATED: 15 May 1996
-- AUTHOR: P. Texel
-- DESCRIPTION: implements the changing of occupational
--  status of a living quarter
-- USE CASES SATISFIED: UC24
-- ============================================================
separate (Living_Quarter_Controller)
procedure Change_Occupation_State
                  (aLvgQtr: in out Living_Quarter_Type;
                        To: in State_Type) is
begin -- Change_Occupation_State
   --| LQ.Change_State()
   --| DB.Write()
   null; -- to permit compilation
end Change_Occupation_State;
```

Various choices exist for the definition of a syntactically rigid PDL. For example, do local declarations (e.g., for the local hall and room variables) get declared at this time or should they first appear during the coding effort? Should parameters get included in the call? And so on, and so on, and so on! The point is that if a rigid PDL is chosen for a project, time is required both to train the staff and to review the PDL to enable the accompanying PDL processor to extract the appropriate information and produce meaningful reports.

Here is an example of the same subunit, `Change_Occupation_State()`, with a very free-form PDL. Note that each PDL statement is a comment, and the comment is just free-form English. You can't get much simpler than this! At a minimum, a Project Team should consider a free-form PDL for complex Class Methods and Controller Class Methods.

```
--===========================================================
-- Copyright P. P. Texel & C. B. Williams 1995/1996
-- FILENAME: lq_controller_chocc_b.ada
-- DATE CREATED: 15 May 1996
-- AUTHOR: P. Texel
-- DESCRIPTION: implements the changing of occupational
-- status of a living quarter
-- USE CASES SATISFIED: UC24
--===========================================================
separate (Living_Quarter_Controller)
procedure Change_Occupation_State
                      (aLvgQtr: in out Living_Quarter_Type;
                           To: in State_Type) is
begin -- Change_Occupation_State
   -- just a pass through to LQ Method to change
   -- the state attribute
   -- update the database
   null; -- to permit compilation
end Change_Occupation_State;
```

Step 3: Decide on an Interface to the Database

Updating the database can be accomplished by a Domain Class or a Controller Class. If the access to values stored in the database is through the `Living_Quarter` Domain Class, the `Living_Quarter` Domain Class has a Method called `Current_State()` that is called by a Client Class, and the implementation of the Method `Current_State()` embeds the SQL calls to the database. Alternatively, a Controller Class could access the database directly when it reads/writes data. This approach requires the Controller Class to have knowledge of the database structure.

In the first alternative, accessing the database through a Domain class, the decision about the database selection is "hidden" in the implementation of the `Change_State()` and `Current_State()` Methods and the application code is *not* dependent upon this decision. If the database is changed, only the implementation of the appropriate Domain Class Methods need changing; the application code simply needs to be recompiled, linked, and regression tested. On the other hand, if a client requires access to the Domain Class, the client gets all the database code that comes along with the Class.

With the second alternative, all the database access is confined to a Controller Class, thus if the database changes, all the Controllers Classes require changing. This has a significant impact on the amount of regression testing to be performed. The benefit is that all the database code does *not* come along with the Domain Class.

Third, a domain Class can provide two interfaces to external Categories, one for clients that require database access and one for those clients that do not. The two distinct interfaces are provided by building an inheritance hierarchy for the Domain Class.

Finally, a distinct Database Class can be introduced to provide an interface to the database, thus hiding the implementation of the database from Domain Controller Classes. This approach, the approach chosen by the authors, decouples Domain and Controller Classes from knowledge of the structure of the database. Changes to the database implementation now require only recompilation and relinking of the Domain and Controller Classes. Recoding is not required, (except for the Database Class) because all code dependent upon the actual database is buried in the implementation of the Database Class.

The point is that the choice is yours; make an informed decision.

Example

The differences between two PDLs was illustrated above using a very simple Method, `Change_Occupation_State()`, in the `Living_Quarter_Controller` Class, assuming the Controller Class updated the database using a Database Class. Now, consider the PDL for the `Montior_Living_Quarters()` Method that manages Use Case UC1, Operator_Monitors_Living_Quarters .

First, the Method `Monitor_Living_Quarters()` is added to the `Living_Quarter_Controller` package specification, and an associated stub is added to the package body.

Ada95

```
-- ================================================================
-- Copyright P. P. Texel & C. B. Williams 1995/1996
-- FILENAME: lq_controller_s.ada
-- DATE CREATED: 15 May 1996
-- AUTHOR: P. Texel
-- DESCRIPTION: manages all request for services for
       Living_Quarter
-- USE CASES SATISFIED: UC#1, 26
-- ================================================================
with Living_Quarter;
package Living_Quarter_Controller is
   --% package that manages lqs

      package LG renames Living_Quarter;

      procedure Change_Occupation_State
          --% controller Method for lq
          (aLvgQtr: in out LQ.Living_Quarter_Type; --% the lg
           To: in LQ.State_Type)--% new state of lq
          );
```

```
    procedure Monitor_Living_Quarters;--% Controller Method
end Living_Quarter_Controller;
-- ================================================================
-- Copyright P. P. Texel & C. B. Williams 1995/1996
-- FILENAME: lq_controller_b.ada
-- DATE CREATED: 15 May 1996
-- AUTHOR: P. Texel
-- DESCRIPTION: implements the capability of changing the
--              occupational status of a Living Quarter
-- USE CASES SATISFIED: UC#1, 26
-- ================================================================
with Database; -- to update the database
with Hall, Room; -- to get the ids to update the database
package body Living_Quarter_Controller is
      procedure Change_Occupation_State
         (aLvgQtr: in out Living_Quarter_Type;
          To: in State_Type) is separate;
     -- the stub
     procedure Monitor_Living_Quarters is separate;
end Living_Quarter_Controller;
```

Here is the subunit for `Monitor_Living_Quarters()`, using a free-form PDL.

```
-- ================================================================
-- Copyright P. P. Texel & C. B. Williams 1995/1996
-- FILENAME: lq_controller_monlq_b.ada
-- DATE CREATED: 15 May 1996
-- AUTHOR: P. Texel
-- DESCRIPTION: implements the monitoring
-- of all living quarters
-- USE CASES SATISFIED: UC1
-- ================================================================
separate (Living_Quarter_Controller)
procedure Monitor_Living_Quarters is
begin -- Monitor_Living_Quarters
          -- start the timer[11]
          -- for each living quarter
          -- loop
          -- if living quarter occupied
          -- then
          -- for each Sensor
```

[11]Interrupt-driven design is very language-dependent. Although the ID for UC1 indicates that the Living_Quarter_Controller pops the timer, it might be that the timer is polled.

```
          -- loop
          -- acquire deviation
          -- set appropriate warning (Use Case #6,7,8,18)
          -- end loop
          -- end if
          -- end loop
          null; -- to permit compilation
end Monitor_Living_Quarters;
```

This PDL clearly shows that all this functionality is neither *wanted, nor required* in the Living_Quarter Domain Class. The Living_Quarter Domain Class would *not* be as reusable in other applications for the HCC if it was coupled to handling the interrupt requests for resetting the SEM software and sounding the alarm! It is best to put all that functionality in a Controller Class, with no requirement in this particular Case Study for a corresponding Monitor_Living_Quarters() Method in the Living_Quarter Domain Class.

Here is the same subunit with the algorithm represented in a rigorous PDL.

```
-- ================================================================
-- Copyright P. P. Texel & C. B. Williams 1995/1996
-- FILENAME: lq_controller_monlq_b.ada
-- DATE CREATED: 15 May 1996
-- AUTHOR: P. Texel
-- DESCRIPTION: implements the monitoring
-- of all living quarters
-- USE CASES SATISFIED: UC1
-- ================================================================

separate (Living_Quarter_Controller)
procedure Monitor_Living_Quarters is
begin -- Monitor_Living_Quarters
          -- Timer.Start()
          -- for aHall in HL.Hall_Type
          -- loop
          -- for aRoom in RM.Room_Type
          -- loop
          -- if LQ.Current_State = Occupied
          -- then
          --     for anEC in EC.Kind_Type
          --     loop
          --         if LQ.Deviation()>=.03
          --         then
          --             PL.FlashWindow_4X()
          --             AL.SoundAlarm()
          --         elsif LQ.Deviation >=.02
```

```
        --          then
        --              PL.FlashWindow_2X()
        --          elsif LQ.Deviation() >=.01
        --          then
        --              PL.LightWindow()
        --          end if
        --      end loop
        -- end if
        -- end loop
        null; -- to permit compilation
end Monitor_Living_Quarters;
```

An Activity Diagram (AD) can be produced for Controller Class Methods, instead of, or in addition to, developing a PDL. The steps for producing an AD are:

Step 1: Label the Diagram
Label the diagram as follows: <ClassName>>::MethodName_AD. More specifically, name the diagram with the name of the Class, followed by the scope resolution operator, followed by the Method name, and finally ending with the suffix _AD, as in Living_Quarter_Controller::MonitorLivingQuarters_AD.

Step 2: Establish Ownership
As always, establish ownership of the AD to the Category that owns the Class. The `Process_CAT`[12] should own the Living_Quarter_Controller::Monitor LivingQuarters_AD. Recall that ownership of diagrams makes deliverable documents easier to produce.

Step 3: Determine Initial/Termination Points for the Method
Because ADs have a symbol to represent where the algorithm begins (an arrow with a filled circle at the tail of the arrow, identical to the arrow that represents the initial state of a STD), and a termination symbol (two concentric circles with the inner circle filled) to represent where the algorithm terminates, it is helpful to establish these first.

Step 4: Develop the Diagram

Figure 10-4, previously shown, depicts the AD for the `LivingQuarter Controller::MonitorLivingQuarters()` Method.

Pragmatic Program Issues

GUIs Get Too Smart

Most projects have *not* yet fully grasped the concept of a Controller Class, and have difficulty understanding the benefit of providing a Controller Class for each Category

[12]Recall that Controller Classes are included on the Process_CAT_CCD.

to which Use Cases are assigned. On most projects, the GUI Classes are acting as Controller Classes because once the callback occurs, it is easy to include all the other required functionality in the callback. Pretty smart GUI!! As more changes are incorporated, the GUI gets more complex and incorporates more and more of the functionality that should be in the Controller Classes.

A Lot of Choices

There are lot of choices to be made in this Activity. For a large project, the simpler the better. And, once a decision is made, try *not* to reverse it when the impact affects 200+ programmers!

Getting It Done!

There is one major factor that impacts this decision—the project schedule.

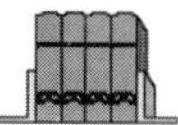

Product(s)

The products of this Activity are either compiled Controller Classes with the Methods described in a language-compilable PDL or ADs.

10.6 PROCESS PDL

Purpose

> The purpose of this Activity is to run reports that provide management and technical information on design source files that are based on the PDL chosen.

Process

Step 1: Select PDL Reports

PDL reports range from those that strictly provide management information (for example, how many Methods have been tested) to technical reports (for example, a data dictionary report listing the declared entities in a software system). Some PDL processors are customizable, permitting the Project Team to augment the standard set of reports. Make a decision as to which reports need to be generated.

Step 2: Decide How Often to Run the PDL Reports

Should the reports be run every week? Every two weeks? Every day? A suggestion is to run the reports in conjunction with the compilation schedule.

Example

The following is just an example of the kinds of reports that can be generated. Table 10-2 represents, in essence, a data dictionary for the project, listing all declared entities that have definitions in the PDL. In this case, the report is generated alphabetically by declared entity, and represents what would be produced from the following PDL. Although the table is simplified and represents items from one Class, consider the benefit of this table when dealing with a million lines of code! The following represents the PDL for the `Temperature_Environmental_Condition` package specification, with line numbers, because line numbers appear on PDL reports.

Ada95

```
(1)-- ==========================================================
(2)-- Copyright P. P. Texel & C. B. Williams 1996
(3)--
(4)-- FILENAME: ec_temp_ec_s.ada
(5)--
(6)-- AUTHOR: P. Texel
(7)--
(8)-- DESCRIPTION: Subclass of Abstract Class Environmental Condition
(9)--
(10)-- DATE CREATED: 3 July 1996
(11)--
(12)-- ==========================================================
(13)
(14)with Environmental_Condition;
(15)package Temperature_Environmental_Condition is -- % TEC Class
(16)
(17) -- renaming declarations
(18) package EC renames Environmental_Condition;
(19)
(20) -- types required for Attributes if not a Class
(21) Minimum_Temperature:constant:= +50.0; --% lowest acceptable temperature
(22) Maximum_Temperature:constant:= +95.0; --% highest acceptable temperature
(23) type Temperature_Type is digits 4 range --% type for temperature
(24)    Minimum_Temperature..Maximum_Temperature;
(25)
(26) -- Abstract Data Type
(27) type Temperature_Environmental_Condition_Type is new --% type for the TEC Class
(28)    EC.Environmental_Condition_Type with private;
                                        . . .
(48)private
(49) type Temperature_Environmental_Condition_Type
(50)            is new EC.Environmental_Condition_Type with
(51)            record
(52)                theTempValue: Temperature_Type; --% tempValue Attribute
(53)            end record;
(54) end Temperature_Environmental_Condition;
```

Table 10-2. Sample PDL Report: Data Dictionary

Declared Entity	Definition	Kind	Unit Owning Declaration	File Name	Line #
Maximum_Temperature	highest acceptable temperature	named number	Temperature_Environmental_Condition	ec_temp_ec_s.ada	22
Minimum_Temperature	lowest acceptable temperature	named number	Temperature_Environmental_Condition	ec_temp_ec_s.ada	21
Temperature_Environmental_Condition	TEC Class	package	Temperature_Environmental_Condition	ec_temp_ec_s.ada	15
Temperature_Environmental_Condition_Type	type for the TEC Class	private	Temperature_Environmental_Condition	ec_temp_ec_s.ada	27,49
Temperature_Type	type for temperature	floating point	Temperature_Environmental_Condition	ec_temp_ec_s.ada	23,52
theTempValue	tempValue Attribute	variable	Temperature_Environmental_Condition	ec_temp_ec_s.ada	52
. . .	. . .				

Pragmatic Program Issues

Is this Really Necessary?

With the advent of OO technology, is PDL really appropriate, or even necessary? Each Project Team must make this very project-specific decision. At this level of design, the benefits of PDL for Controller Class Methods are many, but perhaps, as we shall see, the requirements for PDL to describe the anticipated algorithm for a Class Method is *not* necessary because Methods in a well-designed Class should be quite simple!

Product(s)

The products of this Activity are management and technical reports that are generated by a PDL processor. The exact reports are vendor- and project-specific.

10.7 IMPLEMENT _VIEW CLASSES

Purpose

> The purpose of this Activity is to implement the _View Classes.

Process

Each project must complete (actually write) this section for itself as it is highly dependent upon the GUI builder chosen for the project. But, implementing the GUI Classes now provides a mechanism for integrating each GUI with its respective Domain and/or Controller Classes.

This book by intent does *not* explain how to design and develop the GUI interface for an OO project.

10.8 DEVELOP DATABASE SCHEMA

Purpose

> The purpose of this Activity is to design the database to ensure its readiness for the implementation of the Domain Classes.

Process

Step 1: Decide between RDBMS and OODBMS

Each Project Team must make this decision for itself. If an OODBMS is chosen, the database schema is *not* typically necessary to complete because Instances of Classes are stored with the database interface calls (e.g., store, retrieve) provided by the database vendor and sometimes coded within the Class itself. If an RDBMS is chosen, great care must be taken as to how to design the database. One table for each Class is a bit cumbersome. However, one table for an entire inheritance hierarchy, or a portion of a hierarchy, makes sense.

As with the previous GUI Activity, this book by intent does *not* describe how to develop an RDBMS to accommodate an OO model.

Step 2: Decide on a Database Class

A hierarchy of Database Connection Classes can be initiated, if so desired. The Class at the root of the inheritance hierarchy, named `Database`, with an Attribute like `Database.Connected` and Methods like `Connect()` and `Disconnect()`, can be provided for a project with Subclasses for Oracle®, Versant™, and so on. A carefully designed Database Class enables a database change with minimal effect on application code.

Phase Transition Criteria

Transition to the next Phase when, for the current build, the

- Design source files have been compiled
- Design sources files have been reviewed
- Previous work products have been updated

and the review criteria shown in Tables 10-3 and 10-4 below have been met.

Review Criteria

Table 10-3. Class Design Source File Review Criteria

#	Class Design Source File Review Criteria	OOD
1	Is there a Class contract and Class "body" structure for each Class required? (C++ and Ada95 only)	√
2	Do the source files follow file naming conventions?	√
3	Are the source files in the correct subdirectory?	√
4	Are project design guidelines followed, with waivers for deviations from the guidelines?	√
5	Are language coding standards followed?	√
6	Are access rights to Attributes and Methods consistent with the CS?	√
7	Are Attributes/Methods consistent with the CS?	√
8	Does PDL reflect PDL syntax?	√

Table 10-4. Additional Phase Transition Review Criteria

#	Miscellaneous Phase 10 Transition Criteria	
1	Have PDL reports been generated/examined (optional)?	√
2	Are the _View Classes implemented?	√
3	Have the _Controller Class' PDL been reviewed?	√
4	Has the database architecture been decided?	√
5	Has the stub library been initiated?	√

Tracking Progress

Table 10-5 once again shows an update to the project management spreadsheet. For this Phase, the number of source files established, compared to the actual number of Classes, can be monitored as a percentage. To be even more precise, the number of Class contracts can be monitored separately from the number of Class implementation files if desired. Again, if the numbers are monitored by Category, by Domain, and by project, it is relatively easy to identify problem areas.

Note that equal weight is applied to the development of the GUI and database, while the remaining 40% is divided equally among the Class design source files and Controller Class files.

It goes without saying that if an ODBMS is used and ERDs are not produced, then the 30% needs to be redistributed within this Phase to other Activities.

Table 10-5. Project Management Spreadsheet: Phase 10

HCC Project Management Spreadsheet						
Number	**Phase Name**	**Activity**	**Charge Number**	**Product**	**Progress Metric**	**% Weight**
10	**Language-Dependent Representation**		**SW-LR-10**			
10.1		Transition to Implementation Class	SW-LR-10.1	Class Contract source file	# Class contract files	
10.2		Represent Inter-Class Visibility	SW-LR-10.2	Class Contract source file	# Class contract files	
10.3		Represent Class "Body" Structure	SW-LR-10.3	Class Implementation source file	# Class implementation files	
10.4		Compile Class	SW-LR-10.4	Compiled Class source file	# Classes compiled (success)	0.20
10.5		Integrate Controller Class PDL	SW-LR-10.5	Controller Class source file	# Controller Classes identified/designed	0.20
10.6		Process PDL	SW-LR-10.6	PDL Reports	Report summaries	
10.7		Implement _View Classes	SW-LR-10.7	_View Class source file	# _View Classes implemented	0.30
10.8		Develop Database Schema	SW-LR-10.8	ERD	# ERDs	0.30

PHASE 11

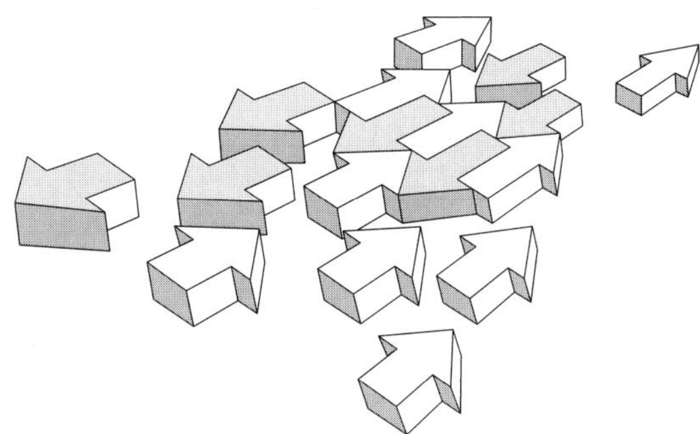

Method Design

PHASE OVERVIEW

Up to now, the language-dependent focus has been on establishing a static software architecture that is compilable. This Phase continues that focus by now identifying the algorithmic structure for applicable Methods of a Class. *Not all* Methods require further decomposition because with OO, most Class Methods are relatively simple and straightforward. For those Methods that are rather complex, some effort with respect to designing the Method is appropriate. As previously stated in Activity 10-5, the following options exist for the representation of a Method's algorithm:

- UML ADs (See Section 11.2)
- A PDL (See Sections 11.3 and 11.4)
- Interaction Diagrams (ID)

Consequently, this Phase, represented by Figure 11-1, focuses on establishing the design intent of complex Class Methods. As just stated, the representation for the algorithmic intent can be ADs, a PDL (and the processing of PDL reports), or IDs. Because IDs have been already presented, this option is not given any further consideration in this Phase.

In essence, this Phase prepares the Project Team for implementation, yielding a trivial implementation (hopefully). With emphasis on analysis and design, the actual coding, or implementation, should be relatively easy because at this point we should know what it is that we are coding! It is always difficult to code when it is not known what it is that is supposed to be produced!

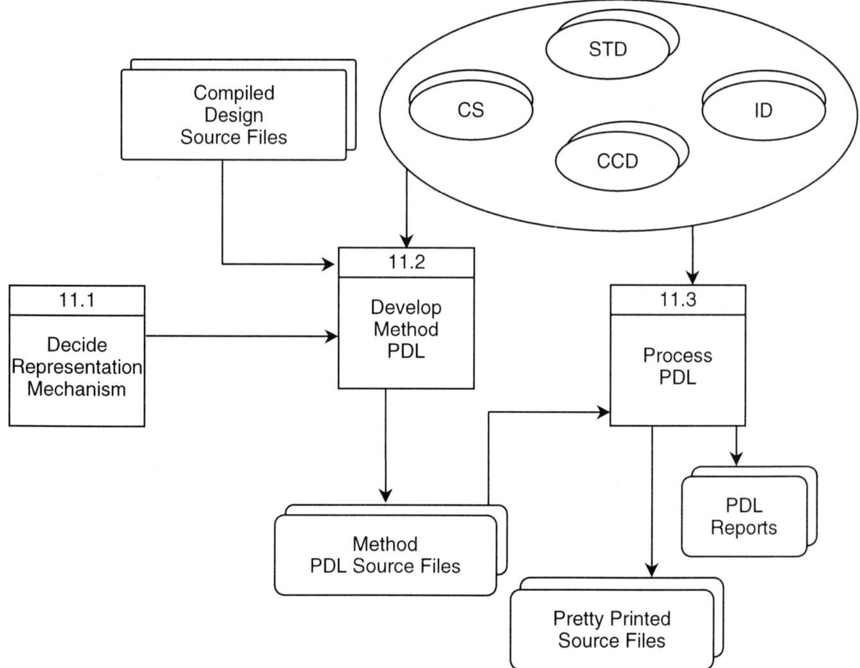

Figure 11-1. OOD-Method Design Phase Description Diagram

11.1 DECIDE ON REPRESENTATION MECHANISM

Purpose

> The purpose of this Activity is to decide what representation mechanism is to be used to represent the intended processing of complex Methods.

Process

Step 1: Make the Decision

As just stated, three representation mechanisms can be utilized to represent the intended processing for a complex method: an AD, ID, or a PDL.

For the SEM, the decision was made to use a PDL. An AD is also included to once again illustrate the differences.

11.2 DEVELOP METHOD PDL

Purpose

> The purpose of this Activity is to specify the algorithm for a Method in a pseudo language, or PDL, that can then be reviewed by an individual other than the developer who generated the PDL.

Process

Step 1: Determine Which Method Types Require PDL

There are several types of Methods that a Class can provide, for example:

- Constructor (Method that creates Instances)
- Destructor (Method that destroys Instances)
- Copy Method (Method that copies the contents of one Instance to another Instance)
- Conversion Method (Method that converts a value from one unit of measure to another unit of measure)
- Attribute set (Method that sets the values of one or more Attributes)
- Attribute get (Method that returns the values of one or more Attributes)
- I/O Methods (Methods that provide/receive data to/from a device)
- Overloaded operator (Method that redefines an arithmetic operator)
- Domain-specific (Method that is specific to the application).

Decide for which of the above a PDL is required. As a minimum, one suggestion is to require that a PDL be provided for the copy, overloaded operators, and the domain-specific Methods, as well as any Method that throws an exception. Remember, this recommendation can be modified for each project!

Finally, a PDL should be required for any Method that is deemed critical, either space- or time-critical, to the success of the system.

Step 2: Produce the PDL

Produce the PDL, according to the standards developed in the previous Phase.

Example

The following shows the PDL for the `Deviation()` Method in the `Living_Quarter` Class. According to the guidelines in Step 1, it is only necessary to complete the PDL for the `Deviation()` Method in the `Living_Quarter` Class because it is a domain-specific Method. The C++ example uses a free-form PDL, while the Ada95 example uses a more rigorous PDL. The use of a PDL to describe algorithmic intent is far more prevalent in the Ada community than in the C++ community (and therefore, probably the Java community as well).

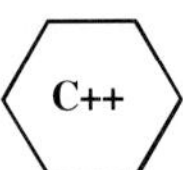

Recall the Class header for the `Living_Quarter` Class from the preceding Phase, repeated here for convenience. Following the Class header file is the `.cpp` file, with the PDL for the `Deviation()` Method added.

```
/* ==============================================================
// Copyright P. P. Texel & C. B. Williams 1996
//
// FILENAME: lq_lq.h
//
// AUTHOR: P. Texel
//
// DESCRIPTION: Concrete Class for Living Quarter
//
// DATE CREATED: 14 September 1996
//
==============================================================*/
#ifndef _LQ_H
#define _LQ_H

#include "lq_hall.h"
#include "lq_room.h"
//SENSOR_CAT
#include "sr_sensor.h"
// ENVIRONMENTAL_CONDITION_CAT
#include "ec_environ.h"

//
// this is a Concrete Class - instances can be declared
//
class LivingQuarter
{
public:

    // types for Attributes
    enum State {Occupied, Unoccupied};

    // constructors and destructors
```

```
    LivingQuarter();                  // default constructor
    LivingQuarter(char aHallLetter, int aRoomNumber);
    LivingQuarter // copy constructor
       (const LivingQuarter & aLQ)
    ~LivingQuarter(); // destructor

    // overloaded operators
    LivingQuarter & operator=(LivingQuarter & aLQ);

    // Attribute Queries
    char Hall_Id(); // returns Hall Letter
    int Room_Id();  // returns Room Number
    // returns occupational status of a LQ
    State CurrentState();
    // Attribute Sets
    // toggles occupational status
    void ChangeState(State newState);
    // domain Methods
    // throws "Cant Compute" exception
    double Deviation (EnvironmentalCondition::Kind aKind);
private:
    Hall * HallId; // pointer to Hall as Hall is shared
    Room * RoomId; // pointer to Room as Room is shared
    Sensor SensorSet[3]; // array of pointers to a Sensor
    State theState; // occupational status

    double GetSensorReading // obtain sensor reading
       (EnvironmentalCondition::Kind aKind);
};
#endif
```

In the previous Phase, it was shown that the requirements to compile the `.cpp` file were either empty braces (if the function did not return a value) or a dummy return statement (if the function returned a value). Below is the `lq_lq.cpp` file repeated, but with a PDL for the `Deviation()` Method now added. Note that the dummy return statement must still be included to permit compilation.

```
/* ========================================================
// Copyright P. P. Texel & C. B. Williams 1996
//
// FILENAME: lq_lq.cpp
//
// AUTHOR: P. Texel
//
// DESCRIPTION: Implements Living Quarter Class
```

```
//
// DATE CREATED: 14 September 1996
//
===========================================================*/

#include "lq_lq.h"
// other includes as required

// constructors & destructors
             ...

// overloaded operators
             ...

// Attribute Queries
             ...

// Attribute Sets
             ...

// Domain Methods
// throws "Cant Read" exception
double Deviation (EnvironmentalCondition::Kind aKind)
{
   // SWITCH statement based on kind of environmental
   // condition
   // case for each kind
   // get the current value for the lq & environmental
   // condition
   // get the nominal value from the database
   // convert them both to unit of measure
   // try EC.ThePercent()
   // catch "DivideByZero"
   //     throw "Cant Compute"
   // return the result
   //
      return 0.0; // dummy return statement
}
```

Ada95

Below is the Ada95 package specification for the `Living_Quarter` Class from the preceding Phase, repeated for convenience, with PDL constructs (indicated by --% or --|) added.

```
--===========================================================
-- Copyright P. P. Texel & C. B. Williams 1996
--
-- FILENAME: lq_lq_s.ada
--
-- AUTHOR: P. Texel
--
-- DESCRIPTION: The Living Quarter Class
--
-- DATE CREATED: 8 July 1996
--
--===========================================================

with Hall, Room;
with Sensor;
with Air_Pressure_Sensor, Oxygen_Sensor, Temperature_Sensor;
with Environmental_Condition;
with Air_Pressure_Environmental_Condition,
Oxygen_Environmental_Condition,
   Temperature_Environmental_Condition;

package Living_Quarter is --% class for lq

   -- renaming declarations
   package HL renames Hall;
   package RM renames Room;
   package EC renames Environmental_Condition;
   package APEC renames
      Air_Pressure_Environmental_Condition;
   package OEC renames Oxygen_Environmental_Condition;
   package TEC renames
      Temperature_Environmental_Condition;

   package SR renames Sensor;
   package AS renames Air_Pressure_Sensor;
   package OS renames Oxygen_Sensor;
   package TS renames Temperature_Sensor;

-- types required for Attributes if not a Class
type State_Type is (Occupied,Unoccupied);
      --% LQ State Attribute values

-- Abstract Data Type
type Living_Quarter_Type is private;
      --% ADT for the LQ Class
```

```
   procedure Create_Living_Quarter --% creates Instance of lq
      (aLvgQtr: in out Living_Quarter_Type; --% specific lq
       aHallId: in HL.Hall_Letter_Type; --% specific Hall letter
       aRoomId: in RM.Room_Number_Type --% specific Room #
      );

   procedure Living_Quarter_Ids (
       aLvgQtr: in Living_Quarter_Type; --% specific lq
       aHallId: out HL.Hall_Letter_Type; --% specific Hall letter
       aRoomId: out RM.Room_Number_Type --% specific Room #
      );

   procedure Change_State
         (aLvgQtr: in out Living_Quarter_Type; --% specific lq
          To: in State_Type --% the new State
      );

   function Current_State(aLvgQtr: Living_Quarter_Type
                                             --% specific lq)

     return State_Type;

   function Deviation
      (aLvgQtr: Living_Quarter_Type; --% specific lq
      aSensor: EC.Environmental_Condition_Kind_Type --% specific ec
      )
      return Float;

   Cant_Compute: exception; --% raised by Deviation Method

private

   -- set up array of pointers
   type Set_Of_Sensors_Type is array --% 3 sensors for lq
      (EC.Environmental_Condition_Kind_Type) of
         SR.Sensor_Ptr_Type;

   -- pointer types for the Hall and Room attributes
   type Hall_Ptr_Type is access HL.Hall_Type; --% ptr to Hall
   type Room_Ptr_Type is access RM.Room_Type; --% ptr to Room

type Living_Quarter_Type is --%ADT for lq
 record
      Hall_Id: Hall_Ptr_Type; --% lq Hall Attribute
      Room_Id: Room_Ptr_Type; --% lq Room Attribute
      Sensor_Set: Set_Of_Sensors_Type --% lq 3 sensors Attribute
         := (new AS.Air_Pressure_Sensor_Type,
              new OS.Oxygen_Sensor_Type,
```

```
            new TS.Temperature_Sensor_Type);
         -- default state for a LQ is unoccupied
         -- Operator must explicitly set a LQ to occupied
      State: State_Type:= Unoccupied; --% lq State Attribute

   end record;

end Living_Quarter;
```

Recall that the package "body" structure consists of stubs for the Class Methods, plus the declaration of any local data and/or initialization that may have been anticipated. For the `Living_Quarter` Class the local Method `Get_Sensor_Reading()` has been identified.

```
--================================================================
-- Copyright P. P. Texel & C. B. Williams 1996
--
-- FILENAME: lq_lq_b.ada
--
-- AUTHOR: P. Texel
--
-- DESCRIPTION: Implements the LQ specification
--
-- DATE CREATED: 10 July 1996
--
--================================================================

with Database; -- needed to access the Database
package body Living Quarter is --% class for lq
   package DB renames Database;

   -- Not sure what the parameters are yet so just a
   -- placeholder for now
   procedure Get_Sensor_Reading is separate; --% returns one ec

   procedure Create_Living_Quarter --% creates Instance of lq
      (aLvgQtr: in out Living_Quarter_Type; --% specific lq
       aHallId: in HL.Hall_Letter_Type; --% specific Hall letter
       aRoomId: in RM.Room_Number_Type --% specific Room #
      ) is separate ;

   procedure Living_Quarter_Ids
      --% returns Hall Letter & Room #
      (aLvgQtr: in Living_Quarter_Type; --% specific lq
       aHallId: out HL.Hall_Letter_Type; --% specific Hall Letter
       aRoomId: out RM.Room_Number_Type --% specific Room #
      ) is separate;
```

```
   procedure Change_State --% toggle lq occupational state
      (aLvgQtr: in out Living_Quarter_Type; --% specific lq
       To:      in State_Type  --% the new State
      ) is separate;

   function Current_State --% returns lq occupational status
      (aLvgQtr: Living_Quarter_Type --% specific lq
      ) return State_Type is separate;

   function Deviation --% calculates dev for 1 lq & 1 ec
      (aLvgQtr: Living_Quarter_Type; --% specific lq
       aSensor: EC.Environmental_Condition_Kind_Type
         --% specific ec
      ) return Float is separate;

end Living_Quarter;
```

In Ada95, the PDL for the Method `Deviation()` is provided in a subunit, a separately compilable entity that contains the implementation of a Method that has been stubbed out in another compilation unit (specifically here, the package body). What follows is the PDL for the subunit `Deviation()`:

```
--=================================================================
-- Copyright P. P. Texel & C. B. Williams 1996
--
-- FILENAME: lq_deviation_f.ada
--
-- AUTHOR: P. Texel
--
-- DESCRIPTION: calculates the deviation for 1 lq and 1 ec
--
-- DATE CREATED: 10 July 1996
--
--=================================================================
separate (Living_Quarter)
function Deviation --%calculates dev for 1 lq and 1 ec
      (aLvgQtr: Living_Quarter_Type; --% specific lq
      aSensor: EC.Environmental_Condition_Kind_Type
         --% specific ec)
      ) return Float is

   Answer: Float:=0.0; --% temp to hold The_Percent

begin -- Deviation
   --| case aSensor is -- for all 3 kinds
   --| Get_Sensor_Reading()
   --| DB.Read() database for the lq and ec kind
   --| Convert_To_Unit() -- appropriate Subclass
```

```
    --| Answer:= The_Percent() for the ec on the two values
    --| return Answer
    --| exception
    --|    when Divide_By_Zero =>
    --|          raise CantCompute
    return Answer;
end Deviation;
```

Note the local data declaration for `Answer`, and the references to `Answer` in the PDL design construct (indicated by the --|), as well as in the actual "code" return statement. The fact that there is a declared entity `Answer` is captured by the PDL processor, as are the references to `Answer` in both the PDL and code. Thus, `Answer` will appear in the generated reports.

Note that the references to called Methods in the PDL utilize the exact name of the called Method. These references can also be detected by the PDL processor and included in PDL reports.

Figure 11-2 depicts the UML AD for the `Deviation()` Method in the `Living_Quarter` Class. As indicated by the figure, the algorithm can begin by either obtaining the current value from the sensor or by reading the nominal value from the database. They can execute concurrently; however, both must have completed, and both must have synchronized at the synchronization point indicated by the darker horizontal bar, before the percent difference between the two values is completed.

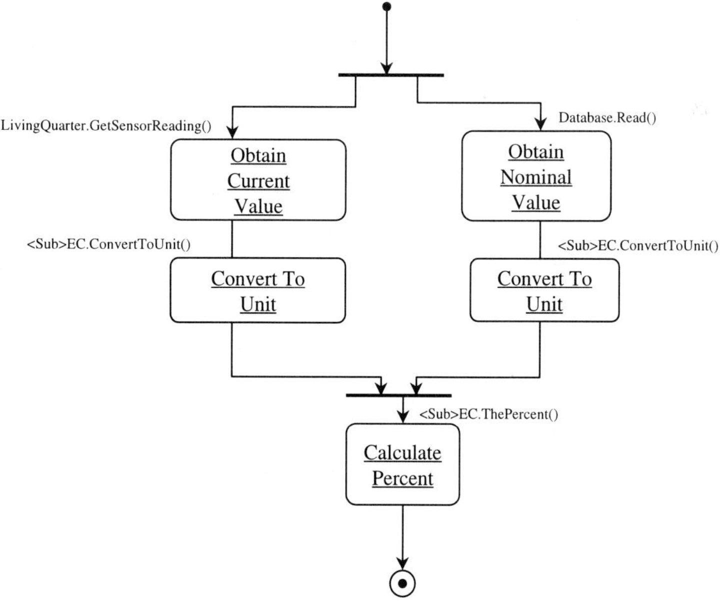

Figure 11-2. LivingQuarter::Deviation_AD

Pragmatic Project Issues

Getting It Done!

There is one major factor that impedes the completion of this Activity—making decisions. For example, "Should the local declaration for the variable `Answer` be required in the PDL? Is it necessary? If it is included, are definitions (`--%`) required for these local variables?" And, "Are definitions required for parameters?" Decisions on issues like these seem to be driven by egos lately, rather than by whether the project schedule and workload allocation can accommodate the Activities! Hours are wasted discussing these issues, when a clear-cut decision is all that is needed, plus the commitment of the development staff to abide by whatever decision is made.

Getting It Reviewed

If possible, someone other than the author of the PDL should review the PDL. Preferably, the reviewer is someone who needs the services of the Method, and actually calls the Method in his/her code.

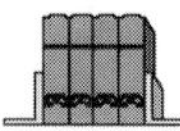

Product(s)

The result of this Activity depends upon the implementation language selected. For Ada95, the product is a set of subunits representing the PDL for those Methods for which the PDL is required. For C++, Java, and SNAP, the products produced as a result of this Activity are updated source files.

11.3 PROCESS PDL

Purpose

> The purpose of this Activity is to process the PDL to produce pretty printed source files and PDL reports that provide information on design source files.

Process

Step 1: Determine which Reports to Generate

Simply examine the standard set of reports provided and define any customizable reports (e.g., exception declaration/propagation). We have found the following kinds of reports to be helpful on many projects:

- Set/used reports
- Data dictionary reports
- Invocation reports
- Classes coded reports
- Classes tested reports
- Exception declaration/propagation reports
- Synchronization reports (for Ada tasking).

Step 2: Determine Frequency of Report Generation

Determine how frequently the reports are to be generated and by whom. Typically, a Category Lead generates the PDL reports, to analyze the status of his/her Category, thus collecting statistics that can then be provided to Category Managers. These statistics can then be summarized and provided to the Software Management organization, and so on up the management chain.

Step 3: Generate the Reports

Simply run the reports and analyze the data. Of course, analysis of the data indicates the kind of corrective action that needs to be taken. Data entities declared but *not* used can be deleted from the code. As another example, Methods *not* tested, as compared to Methods tested, yields management information with respect to work to be completed.

Example

Below is one example of a report that can be generated, a Declared/Referenced Report. This report indicates where a declared entity is referenced in the design and code. Basically, this report is an extension of the *Data Dictionary Report* introduced earlier. Note that by running the PDL processor now, on the *design* source files, the "Design Reference" column is completed. After the next Phase, Class Implementation/Class Test, the report can be generated again, on the *implementation* source files. When the PDL processor is run against the *implementation* source files, the "Code Line #" column is completed. Thus, the report can help identify entities declared, but *not* referenced, either in the design or the code. (It is also true that some compilers issue warnings for just such situations. Typically however, the PDL processor provides much more capability.) Table 11-1 depicts a sample Declared/Referenced Report.

The table shows that `theTempValue` is declared in the package specification, and referenced in both the package body (in the stub) and in the subunit for `Set_Temp()`, both in the design and code.

Similar reports can be generated to trace exception handling, task interaction (for Ada95), and so on. These additional reports are so valuable. It is difficult to imagine a

Table 11-1. A Sample Declared/Referenced PDL Report

Declared/Referenced Report: SEM					
Declared Entity	**File Name**	**Line #**	**File Reference**	**Design Line #**	**Code Line #**
Maximum_Temperature	ec_tempec_s.ada	9			
Minimum_Temperature	ec_tempec_s.ada	8			
Temperature_Environmental_Condition	ec_tempec_s.ada	1			
Temperature_Environmental_Condition_Type	ec_tempec_s.ada	14, 49			
Temperature_Type	ec_tempec_s.ada	9			
theTempValue	ec_tempec_s.ada	52	ec_temp_ec_b.ada	15	
			ec_settemp_p.ada	15, 24	35

large project succeeding (other than through sheer grit and determination) without the support of a PDL and PDL processors.

Finally, remember that these tables can be generated for an entire project, an entire directory (Category), or for just one Class.

Pragmatic Project Issues

Understanding the Value of the Reports

Everyone wants to code! The reports are just paper - right?

The biggest hurdle to overcome is the idea that development staff simply do *not* have the time to produce, and therefore do *not* use, the information provided in these kinds of reports. Examination of these kinds of data can yield technical improvement in the quality and quantity of the code, as well as valuable management information for discovering what *is* going right and what *is not* going right on a project, both at the Domain and Category levels.

Software Directory Structure

Lastly, further impediments to the use of a PDL are: 1) the fact that the current CASE tools do not really support a Category concept, and 2) unless the source code directory structure mimics the Category structure, the reports do not generate information organized around Category boundaries and therefore provide too much information at one time.

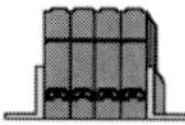

Product(s)

The products produced as a result of this Activity are the PDL processor reports that have been previously defined.

Phase Transition Criteria

Transition to the next Phase when the initial PDL has been produced and reviewed, and the agreed-upon reports have been generated and initially examined. Table 11-2 might help you to decide whether or not to make a phase transition.

Review Criteria

Table 11-2. PDL Review Criteria

#	PDL Review Criteria	OOD
1	Is there a Class contract and Class "body" structure for each Class required and subunits, as required?	√
2	Does a PDL exist for agreed-upon Methods?	√
3	Has the PDL been reviewed by someone other than the author?	√
4	Does the PDL follow the PDL standards established for the project?	√
5	Are the PDL reports available?	√
6	Have the PDL reports been analyzed?	√
7	Have the developers responded to the analysis?	√

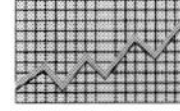

Tracking Progress

Table 11-3 shows the updated project management spreadsheet. For this Phase, the number of Methods that have an associated PDL, compared to the actual number of Methods, can be monitored as a percentage.

Table 11-3. Project Management Spreadsheet: Phase 11

HCC Project Management Spreadsheet						
Number	**Phase Name**	**Activity**	**Charge Number**	**Product**	**Progress Metric**	**% Weight**
10	**Language-Dependent Representation**		**SW-LR-10**			
10.1		Transition to Implementation Class	SW-LR-10.1	Class Contract source file	# Class contract files	
10.2		Represent Inter-Class Visibility	SW-LR-10.2	Class Contract source file	# Class contract files	
10.3		Represent Class "Body" Structure	SW-LR-10.3	Class Implementation source file	# Class implementation files	
10.4		Compile Class	SW-LR-10.4	Compiled Class source file	# Classes compiled (success)	0.20
10.5		Integrate Controller Class PDL	SW-LR-10.5	Controller Class source file	# Controller Classes identified/designed	0.20
10.6		Process PDL	SW-LR-10.6	PDL Reports	report summaries	
10.7		Implement _View Classes	SW-LR-10.7	_View Class source file	# _View Classes implemented	0.30
10.8		Develop Database Schema	SW-LR-10.8	ERD	# ERDs	0.30
11	**Method Design**		**SW-MPDL-11**			
11.1		Decide Representation Mechanism	SW-MPDL-11.1			
11.2		Develop Method PDL	SW-MPDL-11.2	Method PDL source file	# Methods PDL'd	0.50
11.3		Process PDL	SW-MPDL-11.3	PDL Reports	Report summaries	0.50

PART VI

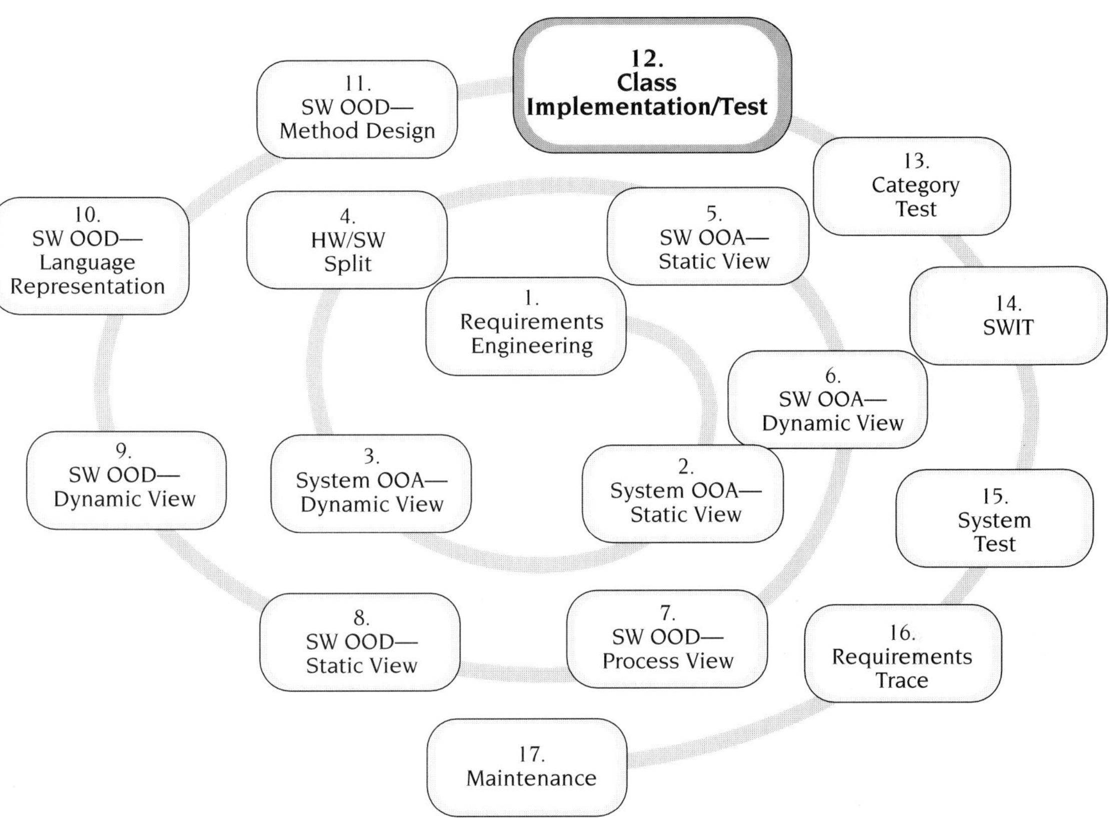

12.
Class
Implementation/Test
11.
SW OOD—
Method Design
13.
Category
Test
10.
SW OOD—
Language
Representation
4.
HW/SW
Split
5.
SW OOA—
Static View
14.
SWIT
1.
Requirements
Engineering
6.
SW OOA—
Dynamic View
9.
SW OOD—
Dynamic View
3.
System OOA—
Dynamic View
2.
System OOA—
Static View
15.
System
Test
8.
SW OOD—
Static View
7.
SW OOD—
Process View
16.
Requirements
Trace
17.
Maintenance

Implementation

PHASE 12

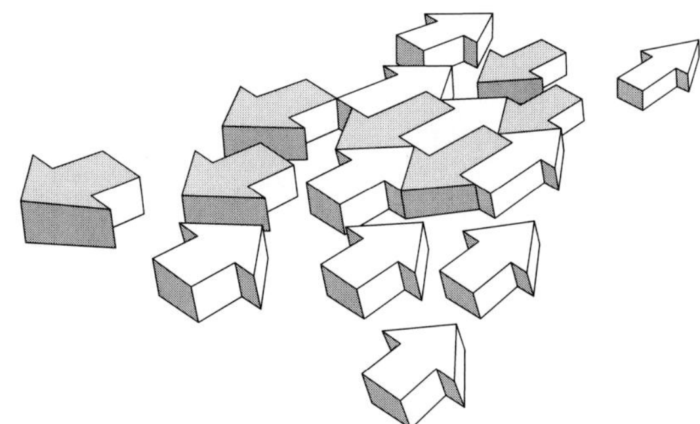

Class Implementation/Class Test

PHASE OVERVIEW

This Phase, represented by Figure 12-1, focuses on the

- Development of the actual code that implements the Methods,
- Agreement on a Class test strategy, and
- Testing of the Classes required for the current build.

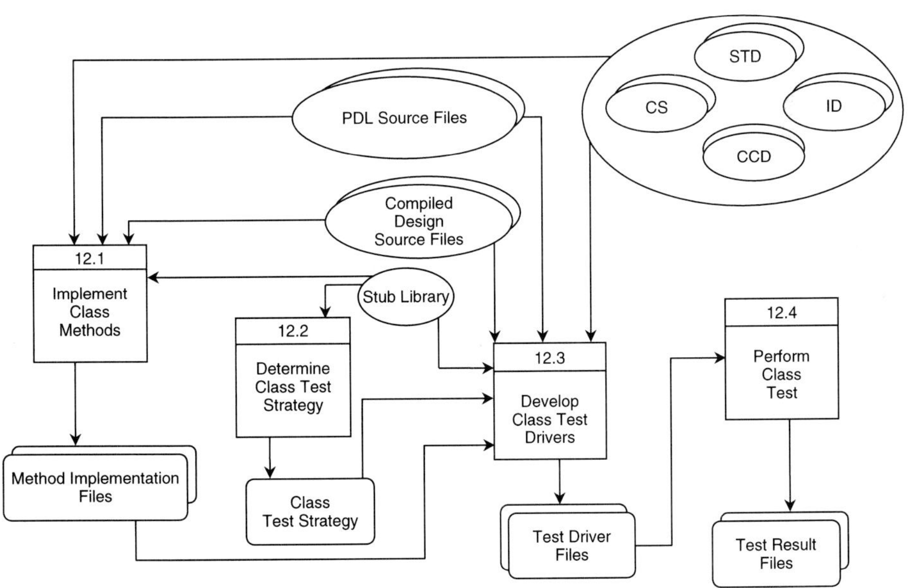

Figure 12-1. Class Implementation/Class Test Phase Description Diagram

The goal of this Phase is to ensure that a Class provides its contractual services as specified in the Class contract. This book emphasizes a robust Class Test strategy because

- Classes can become components in a corporate reuse library
- Classes are the cornerstone of all OO software development processes
- Collaboration of Classes satisfy a Use Case.

Inevitably, when projects fall behind, the testing portion of this Phase is perceived as an expendable activity, and untested code is pushed ahead to integration. The long hours, heated discussions, and finger-pointing that occur during integration are some of the primary reasons that software engineers spend many evening hours and weekends at the office during integration! A stronger emphasis on this Phase's testing activities helps reduce the number of conflicts.

Only sample code for C++ Classes and for testing C++ Classes is shown. There really is nothing to be gained in this book by showing the code/test driver/results files in Ada95, Java, or SNAP.

12.1 IMPLEMENT CLASS METHODS

Purpose

The purpose of this Activity is to produce the executable code for a Class.

Process

Step 1: Understand the PDL

Make sure the algorithmic intent is clear and well-defined. If the intent is *not* clear, clarify the intent *before* coding the Class Methods.

Step 2: Produce the Code

Produce the code. There really is *not* much more to say! Be sure to adhere to the coding standards specified for the project. Be sure to maintain the code in the appropriate directory as established in Phase 10.

Step 3: Produce PDL Reports

If necessary, produce PDL reports to help debug the code. A PDL processor can identify where an entity is declared, referenced in the design, and referenced in the code. This information can be very helpful to improve the quality of the code.

Step 4: Obtain Class Implementation Metrics

The next Activity deals with establishing a Class Test strategy. Part of the Class Test strategy is to decide which Methods require dynamic testing (actual execution of test drivers and capturing the results) and which Methods can be tested statically (for example, by inspection). As will be seen in the next Activity, one basis for making the decision as to which type of testing to use is to utilize McCabe's Cyclomatic Complexity Measure (CCM). If this measure is utilized, you must run the appropriate tool that provides the CCM for the Methods that are required for the current build. If a specified "cap" is exceeded by a specific Method, the Method needs to be redesigned.

Step 5: Update the Model

As a result of implementing the `Window_View` Class, it was discovered that the `Window_View` needed to know which annunciator it was a part of to allow the `Window_Popup_View` to obtain the address of the living quarter that needed to have its nominal value updated. This required visibility could *not* have been known at the time the View Classes were modeled, because at that time, it was *not* known exactly how the View Classes would be implemented. Because it is important to keep the source code and OO model synchronized, update the model by adding the appropriate Attribute/Methods to the `Window_View` Class. Updating the model with changes such as this may *seem* to be time-consuming to some, but it will pay *large dividends* during Phase 17, Maintenance.

Example

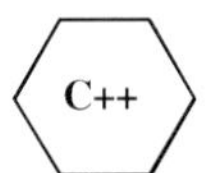

Figure 12-2 shows the implementation of the `LivingQuarter::Deviation()` Method. Note that the PDL for the `Deviation()` Method is maintained within the implementation of the Method in the `.cpp` file. When code is updated, it is easier to update the PDL, because the PDL is maintained in the same file that contains the code.

```
/* ==========================================================
// Copyright P. P. Texel & C. B. Williams 1996
//
// FILENAME: lq_lq.cpp
//
// AUTHOR: P. Texel
//
// DESCRIPTION: Implements Living Quarter Class
//
// DATE CREATED: 14 September 1996
//
==========================================================*/
#include "lq_lq.h"
// DATABASE_CAT
```

Figure 12-2. Implementation of LivingQuarter::Deviation() Method

```
#include "db_ffdatabase.h"
// SENSOR_CAT
#include "sr_address.h"
#include "sr_airsens.h"
#include "sr_oxysens.h"
#include "sr_tempsens.h"
// ENVIRONMENTAL_CONDITION_CAT
#include "ec_airenv.h"
#include "ec_oxyenv.h"
#include "ec_tempenv.h"

// constructors & destructors
...

// overloaded operators
...

// Attribute Queries
...

// Attribute Sets
...

// Domain Methods
   // throws "Cant Compute" exception
double Deviation (EnvironmentalCondition::Kind aKind)
{
   // SWITCH based on kind of ec
   // get the current value for the lq & environmental condition
   // get the nominal value from the database
   // convert to unit of measure
   // try EC.ThePercent()
   // catch "DivideByZero" {
   // throw "Cant Compute" }
   // return the result
   //
      double NominalValue;   // for nominal value from database
      double CurrentReading; // current Sensor reading
      double Answer;         // the deviation
      FlatFileDatabase dbInstance;  // instance of database
      Address lqAddress;     // address of the lq in question
   dbInstance.StartTransaction(FlatFileDatabase::toRead);
   switch (aKind)
      {
      case EnvironmentalCondition::AirPressure:
```

Figure 12-2. Implementation of LivingQuarter::Deviation() Method (*continued*)

```
        {
        AirEnvironmentalCondition EC1;
        AirEnvironmentalCondition EC2;
        // obtain the current reading
        try
        {
        CurrentReading = SensorSet[0]->CurrentValue();
        }
        catch (char * str) // catch DeviceUnresponsive
        {
           throw "Cannot Compute";
        }
        // obtain nominal value from database
        // get address
        lqAddress = SensorSet[0]->SensorAddress();
        // get nominal
        NominalValue = dbInstance.Read(lqAddress);
        // convert both raw values to units
        try
        {
           EC1.ConvertToUnit(CurrentReading);
           EC2.ConvertToUnit(NominalValue);
        }
           catch (char * str) // catch ConstraintError
        {
           throw "Cannot Compute";
        }
        // get percent difference
        Answer = EC1.ThePercent(EC2);
        break;
        }
  case EnvironmentalCondition::Oxygen:
        {
              // coded similarly
        }
  case EnvironmentalCondition::Temperature:
        {
              // coded similarly
        }
  }
  return Answer;
}
```

Figure 12-2. Implementation of LivingQuarter::Deviation() Method (*continued*)

Pragmatic Project Issues

Train Development Staff

This is one issue that has always been a puzzlement. Why do we ask Ada95 software engineers to code in C++ without any training? Why do we ask C++ software engineers to program in Ada95 without any training? And, why do we expect that the schedule will not slip?

Disseminate Information

This is another issue that has always been a puzzlement. Why do we find one software engineer spending four hours on understanding a particular aspect of the code (for example, how to launch a specific word processor from a C++ function), when it has already been solved by two other engineers, *each* of whom *also* spent four hours researching and understanding the same issue. Why do we not share knowledge?

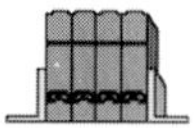

Product(s)

The result of this Activity is a set of source files for the current build that have *not* yet been tested.

12.2 DETERMINE CLASS TEST STRATEGY

Figure 12-3 introduces the overall strategy for Class, Category, and SWIT testing, covered in this Phase through Phase 15, inclusive. These Phases *structure* the testing process for an OO project. As was previously stated for the GUI and database issues, there are a wealth of texts in the marketplace that deal with testing, and there is no explicit intent here to reinvent the wheel. Each organization must build its own testing process with respect to

- Static testing
- Dynamic testing
- Coverage analysis

and so on.

In Figure 12-3, note that this Phase concentrates on testing a single Class, in isolation of other Classes. Classes that have been successfully tested are then migrated to Category Test. Category Test, covered in Phase 13, tests that the Classes owned by a Category collaborate properly to provide the subset of functionality provided by the Category. Successfully tested Categories within a Domain are then tested together to ensure that the collection of Categories for a specific Domain (e.g., radar, telemetry, network monitoring, and so on) collaborate together to satisfy the required functionality. Software Integration and Test (SWIT), covered in Phase 14, consists of integrating

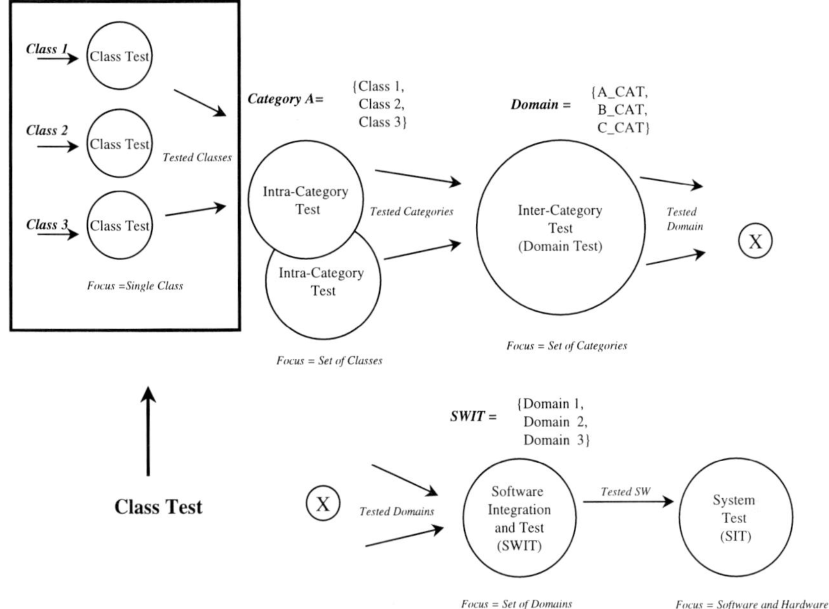

Figure 12-3. Overall Testing Philosophy : Class Test Focus

successfully tested Domains that comprise the system. SWIT then hands off the successfully tested software system to the System Test organization for system testing. System testing is covered in Phase 15.

This abstract view of the testing process is important to have in mind when defining and performing the Class Test. Finally, it must be stated that the Use Case provides the framework for the Category, SWIT, and System Test activities.

Purpose

> The purpose of this Activity is to develop a strategy for testing a Class in isolation of other Classes.

Definition(s)

Black Box Testing: Black box testing is the process of testing the contract that the entity under test has made with its clients. A test, or set of tests, that focus on **black box testing,** are designed to ensure that the specification of the contract, given specific inputs, produces the required outputs without attention to the actual control paths in the code.

Class Test: Class Test represents the process of testing a Class *in isolation of* other Classes in the software system.

Class Test Case: A **Class test case** describes, minimally, 1) what is being tested, 2) the required inputs, and 3) the expected results of a *single* test, along with the code that executes the single test.

Class Test Driver: A **Class test driver** is an executable piece of software that comprises one or more tests (called Class test cases) for an entity under test.

Class Test Results: **Class test results** record the results of executing a Class test driver.

Self-Documenting Test: A **self-documenting test** is a test case that is coded in such a way that when executed, can determine whether the test passed or failed, and outputs either a "PASS" or "FAIL" string to the results file. A **self-documenting test** therefore knows inputs and expected results, and compares actual results against expected results to determine whether a test passes or fails.

Test By Inspection: **Test by inspection** is a testing technique that relies on visual examination of an entity under test according to predefined criteria.

White Box Testing: White box testing is the process of testing the internal workings, or structure, of an entity under test. A test, or set of tests, that focus on **white box testing**, are designed to ensure that all paths, or a critical set of paths, are exercised during the test.

Process

Step 1: Determine Degree of Emphasis for Class Test

Typically, one group of developers supports a strong, robust Class test strategy, while a second group of developers typically sees little use for this entire Activity. Without deciding the degree of emphasis to be placed on Class Test, a strategy is impossible to develop.

Step 2: Agree upon Focus of Class Test

If the development staff can agree that the focus of Class Test is to force errors, *not* just to ensure that the code works well with one set of valid input, life will be ever so much easier!

Step 3: Agree upon Directory Structure for Class Test Files

Recall that an `/src` directory with subdirectories for each Category has already been established (Language Representation: Phase 10). Recall that each Category subdirectory has two subdirectories, `src/<<category>>/code` and `src/<<category>>/test`. The `test` subdirectory now needs two more subdirectories, `src/<<category>>/test/drivers` and `src/<<category>>/test/re-`

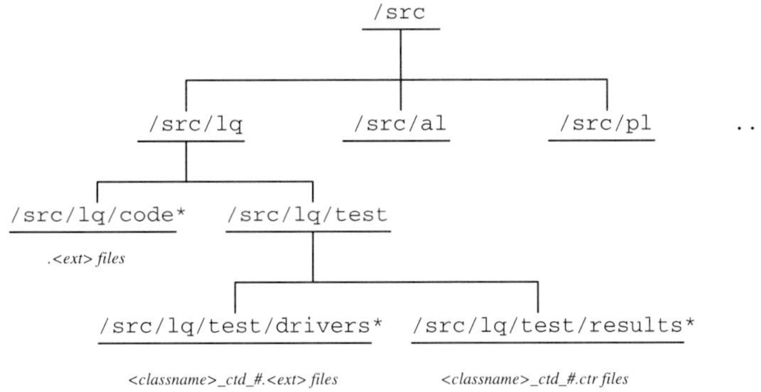

* These subdirectories can be further decomposed by Class.

Figure 12-4. Directory Structure

`sults`, to hold the Class test drivers and Class test results, respectively. Figure 12-4 shows this proposed directory structure in a C++ environment.

Step 4: Agree upon Naming Conventions for Class Test Drivers and Class Test Results

The naming conventions for the test files obviously depend on the language and implementation environment being utilized. One suggestion is to name a Class test driver `<<class name>>_ctd_#.<<ext>>` where `<<ext>>` represents the file extension for the chosen implementation language. The pound sign (#) reflects the test driver number because a Class has multiple test drivers with which it is associated, with each driver testing a different aspect of the Class. The corresponding results files can be named with the same name, with a different extension. For example, Class test results files in C++ would be named `lq_ctd_1.ctr` and `lq_ctd_2.ctr`, respectively. The `lq_ctd_1.cpp` and `lq_ctd_2.cpp` files would be placed in the `LQ/test/drivers` subdirectory, and the `lq_ctd_1.ctr` and `lq_ctd_2.ctr` results files would be placed in the `LQ/test/results` subdirectory. Refer to Figure 12-4, if needed, for a graphical representation of this information.

Step 5: Agree upon a Class Test Driver Template

Each Class test driver file should include, as a minimum, the

- Name of the file
- Name of the Class under test
- Name of the owning Category

- Date created
- Author

followed by one or more Class test cases, each contained in a block.

Step 6: Agree upon a Class Test Case Template

Minimally, each test case within a Class test driver should include the

- Inputs
- Expected results
- Purpose

and executable code, contained in a block.

Step 7: Agree upon Contents of Class Test Results Files

If tests must be self-documenting, the `.ctr` files would contain the

- Name of the test driver producing the results
- Date/time of the test's execution
- Indication of pass or fail for each test case within the driver
- Specification of execution time for those tests that have a performance requirement
- For those Methods that are tested by inspection, an entry in the results file that specifies the Method name and the fact that the Method passed by inspection.

Step 8: Determine if Class Test Drivers Can Contain Multiple Test Cases

Typically, it makes sense to permit a test driver to contain multiple test cases, as long as each test case within the driver is *independent* of all previous test cases. Test case results would *not* be reliable for a test case that relied on output from a previous test, if the previous test failed, yet provided results that were still usable by the test case in question. The test case could have passed with bad data, passed with good data, failed with bad data, or failed with good data.

Step 9: Determine Under What Conditions, if Any, Test by Inspection Is Permitted

Again, consensus is necessary to go forward and establish a test strategy. To require every Method in every Class to have a test case is one extreme, and to permit all Methods in a Class to be tested by inspection is the other extreme. Somewhere in between is the happy medium that must be struck. Here is where CASE tools can help. Consider a tool that provides McCabe's Cyclomatic Complexity Measure (CCM)[1] on the Methods in a Class. Consider specifying the test technique to be used for a Method

[1]Surf to http://www.mccabe.com for information on McCabe's tool.

Table 12-1. CCM Related to Test Technique

McCabe's CCM	Test Technique
CCM <= min	Test By Inspection
min < CCM <= max	Black Box Test
max < CCM <= cap	White Box Test[2]
cap < CCM	Redesign Required

in a Class based on CCM values, as shown in Table 12-1. This strategy requires that minimum, maximum, and cap values for McCabe's CCM be established for a project. Once established, the bounds are then used to establish the kind of testing technique to be utilized on a Class Method.[3]

A Class test results file can contain the text indicating that a specific Method passed by inspection.

Step 10: Agree upon Strategy for Testing Restricted Access Methods

How are private Methods to be tested? Are the private Methods to be moved to the public section for testing, and then returned to the private part for development? Hopefully not! Code should *never* be modified for testing purposes. What must be determined is *how* to test private Methods. Do private Methods get tested as a result of successful testing of the public Method that calls the private Method? Should tools like Cantata® and AdaTest[4] be utilized? These tools provide a philosophy for Class testing that incorporates a strategy for testing private Methods. Should the C++ "friend" capability be used? There are many options; again, the point is to make a decision, document it, and follow it.

Step 11: Agree upon Order of Method Testing

One suggestion is to test the Methods in a Class in the following order:

- Constructors/Destructor
- Attribute Set/Queries
- Overloaded Operators
- I/O Methods
- Domain Methods.

[2]White box testing can optionally be preceded by a structured walkthrough (which is considered part of a review process and is *not* addressed in this book).

[3]The McCabe Class Metrics and Object-Oriented Metrics for the SEM C++ solution are included in the C++ subdirectory in Appendix D on the enclosed CD-ROM.

[4]AdaTest provides Class test support for Ada code and Cantata provides Class test support for C++ code. This particularly robust set of tools was developed in the UK by IPL, Ltd. Surf to http://www.iplbath.com/p4.htm for more information.

Using this order results in Instances that first can be created and deleted. Next, you must test that the appropriate Attribute values can be assigned and manipulated, that Instances can be manipulated with overloaded operators, are receptive to I/O operations, and finally, that the domain-specific algorithms are functioning properly.

Step 12: Agree upon Kinds of Inputs

There is a great deal of material written on testing already in the marketplace. As with GUI and database issues, a detailed discussion of testing inputs is outside the scope of this book. Each Project Team must have an agreed-upon approach to specifying the inputs to be used in the test. For example, literature abounds with information indicating that when testing a Method, consider as inputs for testing the Method

- Boundary value
- Value out of range
- Value within range.

This kind of detail is beyond the scope of this book, but *not* beyond the scope of a project.

Step 13: What about Methods that Reflect RTM Entries?

Recall that during System OOA, certain RTM entries might be allocated to Methods on a Class to reduce the number of Use Cases, and hence IDs that need to be developed. Should the testing strategy for these Methods, for example `SoundAlarm()` and `SilenceAlarm()`, follow the strategy previously introduced? Should an alternate strategy be provided for these Methods?

One suggestion is to require test drivers to be developed and executed for those Methods to which an entry in the RTM has been allocated. The reason for this position is that without some sort of behavioral testing, how can the requirement be proven to be satisfied during System Test and eventually to the customer?

Step 14: What About _View Classes?

_View Classes do *not* lend themselves to the testing issues discussed above. To test _View Classes, the display itself can be visually tested by inspection, but callbacks need to be tested with a driver, or the actual GUI, to ensure that the correct Method is invoked upon callback.

Step 15: Agree upon/Develop a Timer Class

Some Class test cases need to have the elapsed time of execution recorded. This is true for Class Test, Category Test, and SWIT. Agree upon the unit of measure for capturing time. Is the unit of measure to be seconds, hundredths of seconds, milliseconds, and so on? Agree upon the `Timer` Class to be used by all developers. By providing a *`Timer`* Class with the Methods *`Start()`*, *`Stop()`*, and *`ElapsedTime()`*, all developers can execute timing tests in a similar fashion, with the same unit of measure.

Step 16: Investigate Current Activity on OO Testing

Testing OO systems is still a relatively new area. John McGregor at Clemson University provides a generic test harness in C++ which provides pure virtual functions that must be overridden in developers' derived Classes.[5]

Example

Below is a sample template for a Class test driver and a sample template for Class test cases within a Class test driver. Remember, modify these templates as required! Figure 12-5 shows a sample template for each individual Class test case, while Figure 12-6 shows a sample template for a Class test driver. Both Figures 12-5 and 12-6 represent samples for a C++ implementation. In Figure 12-6, note that **filename** and **filename.ctr** represent placeholders for an actual Instance of `fstream` and the corresponding operating system file with the extension `.ctr`, respectively. Note that each unique Class test case executes in a block, thus causing all declarations for each distinct test case to go out of scope when the test case completes. Also, note in Figure 12-6 that the I/O that is common to all results files is included in the template, thus ensuring that all results files have the same content in the same format.

C++

```
//==============================================================
// TEST CASE n
//
// INPUTS: << list required inputs by variable name >>
// EXPECTED RESULTS: << list expected results by variable name>>
// PURPOSE: << text to describe purpose of test case >>
// USES: << list other resources required>>
{
      //BLOCK FOR TEST CASE n:
      << code for test case n >>
      //END BLOCK FOR TEST CASE n:
}
//==============================================================
```

Figure 12-5. Sample C++ Class Test Case Template

[5]Surf to http://www.cs.clemson.edu:80/~johnmc/new/pact/node7.html#figgentestharness for the C++ Class header.

```
/*================================================================
//================================================================
// Copyright P. P. Texel & C. B. Williams 1996
//
// FILENAME: << Name of Class Test Driver File>>
//
// AUTHOR: << Name of author>>
//
// CLASS UNDER TEST: <<Class Name followed by Class file names>>
//
// OWNING CATEGORY: <<Name of owning Category>>
//
// DESCRIPTION: <<Words that describe the series of test cases
// within this Class Test Driver>>
//
// DATE CREATED: <<Date created >>
//
// TEST ENVIRONMENT: << Description of hardware and software
// environment used>>
// ===============================================================
// ==============================================================*/

// RESOURCES REQUIRED BY ALL TEST CASES
// #includes <<list all required Classes>>
void
main()
{
// global data
// establishing results file

      fstream filename; // C++ results file name is filename

      // open file as "filename.ctr"
      filename.open("filename.ctr", ios::out);
      if (!filename)
      {
         cout << "Error opening filename.ctr << "\n";
      }
      //position filepointer at the beginning of the file
      filename.seekp (0L, ios::beg);
      // write title to file
      filename << "========================================="
               << "\n";
      filename << "Results for filename " << "\n" ;
      // write date of execution to file
      struct date theDate;
```

Figure 12-6. Sample C++ Class Test Driver Template

```
        getdate(& theDate); // fills theDate with current date
        filename << "lq_1_ctd.cpp executed on: " << "\n" << "\n";
        filename << "month:" << (int)theDate.da_mon << "\n";
        filename << "day:" << (int)theDate.da_day << "\n";
        filename << "year:" << theDate.da_year << "\n" << "\n" ;
        // write the time of execution to file
        struct time theTime;
        gettime(& theTime); // fills theTime with current time
        filename << "lq_1_ctd.cpp executed at: " << "\n" << "\n";
        filename << "hour:" << (int)theTime.ti_hour << "\n";
        filename << "minutes:" << (int)theTime.ti_min << "\n";
        filename << "seconds:" << (int)theTime.ti_sec << "\n";

        filename << "=========================================="
                 << "\n";
        filename << "\n";
//=================================================================
// TEST CASE 1
//
// INPUTS: << list required inputs by variable name>>
// EXPECTED RESULTS: << list expected results by variable name>>
// PURPOSE: << text to describe purpose of test case >>
// USES: << list other resources required>>
{
    //BLOCK FOR TEST CASE 1:
        << code for test case 1>>
    //END BLOCK FOR TEST CASE 1:
}
//=================================================================
// TEST CASE 2
//
// INPUTS: << list required inputs by variable name>>
// EXPECTED RESULTS: << list expected results by variable name>>
// PURPOSE: << text to describe purpose of test case >>
// USES: << list other resources required>>
{
    //BLOCK FOR TEST CASE 2:
        << code for Test Case 2>>
    //END BLOCK FOR TEST CASE 2:
}
//===========================================================

// global clean up for all test cases
filename.close();                                   // close the file
}
```

Figure 12-6. Sample C++ Class Test Driver Template (*continued*)

Pragmatic Project Issues

Class Test CASE Tool

Class Test CASE tools exist in the marketplace.[6] If a Project Team has committed to using a specific tool, the template and content of the Class test case and Class test driver templates are influenced by the CASE tool.

How to Do I/O

Because there are many ways to do I/O in most languages, each Project Team must decide whether the I/O provided in the template *must* be used or whether a different I/O capability *may* be used. Remember that consistency goes a long way toward customer satisfaction!

An Alternate Approach

Rather than the template previously provided which must be copied into each developers test driver, consider a `ResultsFile` Class like the one shown in Figure 12-7, that provides resources like those in the template, but in a more Object-Oriented fashion. Note that all Instances must be created with an appropriate filename.

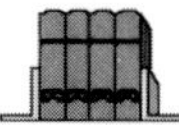

Product(s)

The products of this Activity are as follows:

- A Class test strategy
- A Class test driver template
- A Class test case template.

12.3 DEVELOP CLASS TEST DRIVERS

Purpose

> The purpose of this Activity is to develop the Class test drivers to be used to test a Class following the agreed-upon Class test strategy.

[6]As previously stated, AdaTest provides Class test support for Ada code and Cantata provides Class test support for C++ code. Both tools support the same strategy for testing a Class in the two languages. Another set of testing tools is provided by the previously mentioned AISLE and CISLE family of tools. This family of tools provides PDL and testing support for both Ada and C++, respectively.

```
/* ============================================================
//=============================================================
// Copyright P. P. Texel & C. B. Williams 1997
//
// FILENAME : results.h
//
// AUTHOR : Putnam Texel
//
// DESCRIPTION : Common aspects of a test results file
//              where the results are placed in a flat file
//
// DATE CREATED : 1 February 1997
//
// TEST ENVIRONMENT :  Borland C++ V4.5 and Micron P150
//=============================================================
//=========================================================== */
// RESOURCES REQUIRED BY ALL TEST CASES

#ifndef _RESULTS_H
#define _RESULTS_H

#include <iostream.h>
#include <fstream.h>
#include <dos.h>

class ResultsFile
{
public:
      //open results file with indicated name
      // prints title to the file
      // prints date and time of execution to the file
      ResultsFile(char * theName);  // ctor
      // closes the file
      ~ResultsFile();  // dtor

      // closes the results file
      void CloseResultsFile();

      void PrintPassed(int TestCaseNumber);
      void PrintFailed(int TestCaseNumber);
      void PrintLineOfText (char * theText);

private:

      fstream theResultsFile;  // file for results

};

#endif
```

Figure 12-7. ResultsFile Class

Process

Step 1: Determine which Methods Require Test Drivers

To determine which Methods *require* test drivers, run whatever tool is compatible with the strategy previously identified in Table 12-1. For the SEM, McCabe's CCM is used to determine which Methods require a dynamic test. Consequently, McCabe's Battlemap™ tool is run on the code in question to determine the CCM for the Methods of the Classes to be tested for the current build.

Step 2: Structure the Test Drivers for a Class

After determining which Methods must be tested with test drivers, determine how many test drivers are required for a Class and what the test cases in each driver are to be. A sample structuring might be as follows:

- `lq_ctd_1.cpp` => test cases to test `Deviation()` Method on Air Pressure
- `lq_ctd_2.cpp` => test cases to test `Deviation()` Method on Oxygen
- `lq_ctd_3.cpp` => test cases to test `Deviation()` Method on Temperature

and so on. Providing some initial thought to the structuring of test drivers and test cases can reap benefits when actually developing the cases. For example, the drivers `lq_ctd_2.cpp` and `lq_ctd_3.cpp` are so similar to `lq_ctd_1.cpp` that copying, pasting, and editing the test cases from `lq_ctd_1.cpp` produces many test cases in a short amount of time. Additionally, the same test case strategy can be used to test similar Classes. This is particularly valuable for test cases for Classes that belong to an inheritance hierarchy. For example, the goal would be to test the `Air_Pressure_Sensor` Class and then utilize the same strategy to test the `Oxygen_Sensor` and `Temperature_Sensor` Classes. C++ templates are invaluable here. See the Pragmatic Project Issues topic.

Step 3: Develop Class Test Drivers

Develop the actual test drivers, specifically producing the `.cpp` files (in C++) that are to be used to test Classes.

Example

Figure 12-8(a) shows one Class test driver, coded in C++. As previously stated, providing the code for the other three languages does *not* provide any significant benefit.

The test driver in Figure 12-8(a) contains multiple test cases that test the `Deviation()` Method in the `Living Quarter` Class. Other Methods in the `LivingQuarter` Class exhibit a CCM < minimum, therefore, those Methods do *not* require any test drivers.

The `LivingQuarter` Class was tested in isolation of other Classes by using Class stubs from the stub library. By changing the values returned in the Class stub, different run-time situations can be simulated. For example, in the first test case, represented by lq_ctd_1.cpp, a value of 0.0 was returned from the Class stub of the appropriate Sensor Subclass to represent the CurrentValue of the AirPressureSensor. A value of 20.0 was returned from the Class stub of the FlatFileDatabase Class to represent the NominalValue for the air pressure. The Class stub for the FlatFileDatabase Class is shown in Figure 12-8(b).

Next, in Phase 13, the LivingQuarter Class will be tested again, but it will use the *actual* Classes within the Living_Quarter_CAT with which it collaborates. This is called an intra-Category test. Any Classes with which the Living_Quarter Class collaborates that are owned by *other* Categories are again stubbed out, meaning that a Class from the stub library is used instead of the actual Class. Next, in inter-Category testing, or Domain testing, the LivingQuarter Class will be tested in conjunction with all other *actual* Classes from external Categories, still *within* a specific Domain. In inter-Category testing the *actual* Classes from Sensor_CAT, Database_CAT, and so on are used, *not* Class stubs from the stub library. Finally, all the Domains are integrated in SWIT.

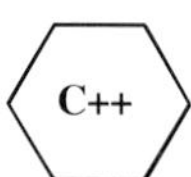

Figure 12-8(a) shows the Class test driver for the Living_Quarter Class that concentrates on testing the Deviation() Method for air pressure only. Additional test drivers contain test cases that focus on testing the Deviation() Methods for the oxygen and temperature environmental conditions.

In the C++ example that follows, note that the **filename** placeholder appearing in the template has been replaced with the actual Instance name for the Instance of fstream, and the corresponding operating system file name, **filename.ctr**, has been replaced with the name of the actual filename, lq_ctd_1.ctr. The goal of the test is to force the exception CantCompute to be raised by the Deviation() Method and indeed, with a value of 0.0 for the current value and 20.0 for the nominal value, the exception ConstraintError should be raised by the appropriate Environmental_Condition Subclass. Therefore, CantCompute should be raised by the Deviation() Method.

Figure 12-8(b) shows both the header file (.h) and implementation (.cpp) file for one of the Class stubs used in testing the LivingQuarter Class, specifically the FlatFileDatabase Class stub. Note that the header represents the interface as specified in the OO model. The implementation, on the other hand, is just a shell, providing the opportunity for a tester to provide any desired value for the value to be returned by the database.

```
/* ================================================================
//================================================================
// Copyright P. P. Texel & C. B. Williams 1996
//
// FILENAME: lq_ctd_1.cpp
```

Figure 12-8(a). LivingQuarter Class C++ Class Test Driver

```
//
// AUTHOR: Putnam Texel
//
// CLASS UNDER TEST: LivingQuarter (lq_lq.h & lq_lq.cpp)
//
// OWNING CATEGORY: Living_Quarter_CAT
//
// DESCRIPTION: All test cases in this file test the
// Deviation() Method for AirPressure only
//
// DATE CREATED: 1 October 1996
//
// TEST ENVIRONMENT: Borland C++ V4.5 and Micron P150
//==============================================================
============================================================= */
// RESOURCES REQUIRED BY ALL TEST CASES
// #includes
#include <iostream.h>
#include <fstream.h>
#include <dos.h>
#include <string.h>
// ENVIRONMENTAL_CONDITION_CAT
#include "ec_environ.h"
// LIVING_QUARTER_CAT
#include "lq_lq.h"

void
main()
{

// global for all test cases

   fstream lq_ctd_1; // file for results
            // open file
      lq_ctd_1.open("lq_ctd_1.ctr", ios::out);
      if (!lq_ctd_1)
      {
            cout << "Error opening lq_ctd_1.ctr" << "\n";
      }
      //position filepointer at the beginning of the file
      lq_ctd_1.seekp (0L, ios::beg);
      // write title to file
      lq_ctd_1  << "======================================"
                << "\n";
```

Figure 12-8(a). LivingQuarter Class C++ Class Test Driver (*continued*)

```
        lq_ctd_1  << "Results for lq_ctd_1.cpp test driver"
                  << "\n" ;

        // write date of execution to file
        struct date theDate;
        getdate(& theDate); // fills theDate with current date
        lq_ctd_1 << "lq_1_ctd.cpp executed on: " << "\n" << "\n" ;
        lq_ctd_1 << "month:" << (int)theDate.da_mon << "\n";
        lq_ctd_1 << "day:" << (int)theDate.da_day << "\n";
        lq_ctd_1 << "year:" << theDate.da_year << "\n" << "\n" ;

        // write the time of execution to file
        struct time theTime;
        gettime(& theTime); // fills theDate with current date
        lq_ctd_1  << "lq_1_ctd.cpp executed at: " << "\n" << "\n" ;
        lq_ctd_1  << "hour:" << (int)theTime.ti_hour << "\n";
        lq_ctd_1  << "minutes:" << (int)theTime.ti_min << "\n";
        lq_ctd_1  << "seconds:" << (int)theTime.ti_sec << "\n";
        lq_ctd_1  << "======================================"
                  << "\n";
        lq_ctd_1  << "\n";
//=============================================================
// TEST CASE 1
//
// INPUTS:   HallId = A, RoomId = 2,
//        CurrentValue = 0.0
//        NominalValue = 20.0
// EXPECTED RESULTS: expect exception "Cannot Compute" to be
   thrown
// PURPOSE: to force Cannot Compute exception to be thrown
// USES:
// EnvironmentalCondition Class
{
   //BLOCK FOR TEST CASE 1:

   LivingQuarter myLivingQuarter('A', 2);    // aLQ
   double theDeviation;                       // the result
   // for AirPressure only
   EnvironmentalCondition::Kind theKind =
                  EnvironmentalCondition::AirPressure;
   try
   {
   // get deviation
   theDeviation = myLivingQuarter.Deviation(theKind);
```

Figure 12-8(a). LivingQuarter Class C++ Class Test Driver (*continued*)

```
    // want to get the exception
    lq_ctd_1 << "TEST CASE 1 FAILED" ;
    }
    catch (char * str)
    {
       cout << "Error: " << str << "\n";
       // got the exception
       lq_ctd_1 << "TEST CASE 1 PASSED" ;
    }
    //END BLOCK FOR TEST CASE 1:
}
//===========================================================
// TEST CASE 2
{
         << This could test that when a value of 0.0 is
            returned from the database that the Deviation
            Method throws CantCompute as well >>
}
 //==========================================================
// TEST CASE 3

{
         << and so on >>
}
//===========================================================
//===========================================================

// global clean up for all test cases
      lq_ctd_1.close();                    // close the file
}
```

Figure 12-8(a). LivingQuarter Class C++ Class Test Driver (*continued*)

```
/* ============================================================
//Copyright P. P. Texel & C. B. Williams 1996
//
//FILENAME: db_ffdatabase.h
//
//AUTHOR: P. Texel
//
//DESCRIPTION: Database Class for maintaining nominal
//values for the Living Quarters as well as
//their occupational status.
```

Figure 12-8(b). FlatFileDatabase Class Stub

```
//
//DATE CREATED: 19 September 1996
//
==============================================================*/
#ifndef _FFDATABASE_H
#define _FFDATABASE_H

#include "db_database.h" // the Superclass
// SENSOR_CAT
#include "sr_address.h"

tyedef int bool; // bool not supported in Borland® C++ V4.5

class FlatFileDatabase: public Database
{
public:
      FlatFileDatabase();
      ~FlatFileDatabase();
      // commits the Operator entry
      void Commit(); // writes to and closes the file
      void Rollback(); // closes the file
      void StartTransaction(); // opens the file
      // the following four Methods throw "DatabaseDown"
      double Read(Address anAddress); // return a value
      bool ReadLQStatus(Address anAddress); // return T/F
      // change a value
      void Write(Address anAddress, double aValue);
      // change occupational status
      void WriteLQStatus (Address anAddress, bool aValue);
};
#endif
/* ==============================================================
// Copyright P. P. Texel & C. B. Williams 1996
//
// FILENAME db_ffdatabase.cpp
//
// AUTHOR: P. Texel
//
// DESCRIPTION: Current nominal values
// Implementation as Flat File - "semdata.dat"
//
// DATE CREATED: 19 September 1996
//
==============================================================*/
```

Figure 12-8(b). FlatFileDatabase Class Stub (*continued*)

```
#include "db_ffdatabase.h"
...
double FlatFileDatabase::Read(Address anAddress)
{
   return 20.0;
}

bool FlatFileDatabase::ReadLQStatus(Address anAddress)
{
   return 1;
}
...
```

Figure 12-8(b). FlatFileDatabase Class Stub (*continued*)

Pragmatic Project Issues

Review Class Test Cases

Review the set of Class test cases in each Class test driver to ensure proper coverage. Alternatively, if a CASE tool has been provided for the project that can detect test coverage, utilize that tool in conjunction with the next Activity.

Waiver Policy

Many times on projects, there is a perceived "justification" for allowing a Method that has a CCM greater than the cap specified in Table 12-1. Perhaps a subcontractor has developed code on a prior project that is being incorporated into the project. The point is that it is important to set in place a mechanism that provides for a waiver on a case-by-case basis.

Testing Subclasses in an Inheritance Hierarchy

Consider establishing C++ template Classes (Ada95 generics) to support the testing of the Subclasses in an Inheritance hierarchy. Figure 12-9 shows a C++ template class to test the SubClasses of the `EnvironmentalCondition` hierarchy. As currently designed, only the `ConvertToUnit()` Method in each Subclass is tested. More test cases need to be included for complete coverage. Finally, note the information from Table 12-5 is now included in the function definitions.

```
//
// This represents a test template for the
// environmental condition hierarchy
// and will only test the ConvertToUnit() Method.
//
```

Figure 12-9. C++ Test Template Class

```
// More Testn() Methods need to be added for a
// complete test of a Subclass of the heirarchy
//
#ifndef _TESTTEMPLATE_H
#define _TESTTEMPLATE_H

#include "results.h"   // access to the results file

template <class T>
class ECInheritanceTestTemplate
{
public:
      ECInheritanceTestTemplate();
      ~ECInheritanceTestTemplate();

      // testing ConvertToUnit()Method
      // value out of range
      void Test1
         (double  aValue, T aTInstance, ResultsFile & theFile);
      // value within range
      void Test2
         (double aValue, T aTInstance, ResultsFile & theFile);
      // value on boundary
      void Test3
         (double aValue, T aTInstance, ResultsFile & theFile);
} ;

template <class T>
ECInheritanceTestTemplate<T>::ECInheritanceTestTemplate()
{
}

template <class T>
ECInheritanceTestTemplate<T>::~ECInheritanceTestTemplate()
{
}

template <class T>
void ECInheritanceTestTemplate<T>::Test1
      (double aValue, T aTInstance, ResultsFile & theFile)
{
 // INPUTS:  raw value out of range for the Subclass
 //
 // EXPECTED RESULTS:  expect exception "ConstraintError"
 //                    to be thrown by the Subclass
```

Figure 12-9. C++ Test Template Class (*continued*)

```
 // PURPOSE: to catch ConstraintError and pass the test
 // USES:
 //    each Subclass of EnvironmentalCondition

    try
    {
           aTInstance.ConvertToUnit(aValue);
           theFile.PrintFailed(1); // want to catch exception
    }
    catch (char * str)
    {
           theFile.PrintPassed(1); // want to catch exception
    }
}

template <class T>
void ECInheritanceTestTemplate<T>::Test2
       (double aValue, T aTInstance, ResultsFile & theFile)
{
// INPUTS:  raw value within range for the Subclass
//
// EXPECTED RESULTS:  do not expect exception "ConstraintError"
//                        to be thrown by the Subclass
// PURPOSE: to ensure correct value is converted
// USES:
//    each Subclass of EnvironmentalCondition
    try
    {
           double Answer;
           aTInstance.ConvertToUnit(aValue);
           Answer = aTInstance.ConvertToRaw();
           if (Answer == aValue)
           {
              theFile.PrintPassed(2);
           }
           else
           {
              theFile.PrintFailed(2);
           }
    }
    catch (char * str)
    {
           theFile.PrintFailed(2);
    }
}
```

Figure 12-9. C++ Test Template Class (*continued*)

```
template <class T>
void ECInheritanceTestTemplate<T>::Test3
   (double aValue, T aTInstance, ResultsFile & theFile)
{
 // INPUTS:  raw value at boundary of range for the Subclass
 //
 // EXPECTED RESULTS: expect value to be converted
 // PURPOSE: to test boundary value is converted properly
 // USES:
 //    each Subclass of EnvironmentalCondition
       try
       {
              aTInstance.ConvertToUnit(aValue);
              theFile.PrintPassed(3);
       }
       catch (char * str)
       {
              theFile.PrintPassed(3);
       }
}

#endif
```

Figure 12-9. C++ Test Template Class (*continued*)

Figure 12-10 shows the test driver that utilizes this template Class. The driver also uses the `ResultsFile` Class to initiate and close a file named "xxx_1_ctd.ctr" to hold the test results. Next, three instantiations, one for each Subclass, are declared. Finally, each instantiation is used, and each test case in the instantiated Class is executed.

```
#include "results.h"   // to set up results file
#include "testt.h" // to use the ec test template

#include "airenv.h"// to test the subclasses
#include "oxyenv.h"
#include "tempenv.h"

void main()
{
   // open test results file
   ResultsFile myResultsFile("xxx_1_ctd.ctr");

   // the instantiations of test cases
   //  for the three Subclasses
   ECInheritanceTestTemplate<AirEnvironmentalCondition>
```

Figure 12-10. Test Driver Using C++ Template Class

```
    APTestCases;
ECInheritanceTestTemplate<OxyEnvironmentalCondition>
    OxyTestCases;
ECInheritanceTestTemplate<TempEnvironmentalCondition>
    TempTestCases;

// using the instantiation for the
// AirEnvironmentalCondition Class
AirEnvironmentalCondition myAirEC;
myResultsFile.PrintLineOfText
  ("AirPressure Subclass test results");
// out of range
    APTestCases.Test1(3.0, myAirEC, myResultsFile);
// within range
    APTestCases.Test2(19.0, myAirEC, myResultsFile);
// on range
    APTestCases.Test3(15.0, myAirEC, myResultsFile);

// using the instantiation for the
// OxyEnvironmentalCondition Class
OxyEnvironmentalCondition myOxyEC;
myResultsFile.PrintLineOfText
  ("Oxygen Subclass test results");
// out of range
OxyTestCases.Test1(-3.0, myOxyEC, myResultsFile);
// within range
OxyTestCases.Test2(19.0, myOxyEC, myResultsFile);
// on range
OxyTestCases.Test3(105.0, myOxyEC, myResultsFile);
// using the instantiation for the
// TempEnvironmentalCondition Class

TempEnvironmentalCondition myTempEC;
myResultsFile.PrintLineOfText
  ("Temperature Subclass test results");
//out of range
TempTestCases.Test1(-3.0, myTempEC, myResultsFile);
//within range
TempTestCases.Test2(72.0, myTempEC, myResultsFile);
// on range
TempTestCases.Test3(105.0, myTempEC, myResultsFile);

// close the results file
myResultsFile.CloseResultsFile();
}
```

Figure 12-10. Test Driver Using C++ Template Class (*continued*)

Product(s)

The products of this Activity are a set of Class Test Drivers, or `<<classname>>_ctd_#.cpp` files in C++, for each Class under test.

12.4 PERFORM CLASS TEST

Purpose

> The purpose of this Activity is to execute the Class Test Drivers to test the Classes required for the current build.

Process

Step 1: Execute the Tests

On a Class-by-Class basis, execute the Class test drivers. For each Class test case that fails, resolve the issue.

Step 2: Rerun PDL Processor

To aid in the debugging process, rerun the PDL processor to obtain an updated Declared/Referenced PDL Report (Table 11-1). Perhaps there are variables referenced in the design that do *not* appear in the code, and vice versa.

Example

Figure 12-11 shows the contents of the `lq_ctd_1.ctr` file that was produced as a result of executing the test driver `lq_ctd_1.cpp`. Note that Test Case 1 *passed*,

```
================================================================
Results for lq_ctd_1.cpp test driver
lq_1_ctd.cpp executed on:

month:10
day:4
year:1996

lq_1_ctd.cpp executed at:

hour:12
minutes:11
seconds:18
================================================================

TEST CASE 1 PASSED
```

Figure 12-11. LivingQuarter Class .ctr Class Test Results File

meaning the exception `CantCompute` was caught in the driver and therefore was thrown by the `Deviation()` Method.

Each `.ctr` file produced has the same initial heading that indicates the test driver executed and the date and time of execution. For each test case in the test driver, each `.ctr` file specifies whether the test case passed or failed, passed by inspection, and/or the elapsed execution time, if any, for the test case. This approach to providing test results makes it easier to see exactly which test cases failed, and in which test driver the test case is contained.

Figure 12-12 shows the contents of the "xxx_1_ctd.ctr" results file produced by executing the driver previously shown in Figure 12-10.

Pragmatic Project Issues

Review Results File

Someone other than the original developer needs to review the results file to ensure that all tests have passed. This can be easily accomplished if the test cases/test results are included in a code review.

```
==============================================================
Results for xxx_1_ctd.ctr test driver
xxx_1_ctd.ctr created on :

month :2
day :3
year  :1997

xxx_1_ctd.ctr created at :

hour     :9
minutes  :4
seconds  :46
==============================================================

AirPressure Subclass test results
TEST CASE 1 PASSED
TEST CASE 2 PASSED
TEST CASE 3 PASSED

Oxygen Subclass test results
TEST CASE 1 PASSED
TEST CASE 2 PASSED
TEST CASE 3 PASSED

Temperature Subclass test results
TEST CASE 1 PASSED
TEST CASE 2 PASSED
TEST CASE 3 PASSED
```

Figure 12-12. Results file xxx_1_ctd.ctr

Product(s)

The products of this Activity are a set of Class test results, or `.ctr` files, for each Class under test. There is one `.ctr` file for each Class test driver.

Phase Transition Criteria

Transition to the next Phase when the Classes required for the current build have been tested, the Class code and Class test results have been reviewed, and prior work products (CCDs, CSs, and so on) have been updated. Table 12-2 summarizes the criteria for transitioning to the next Phase.

Review Criteria

Table 12-2. Class Test Review Criteria

#	Class Test Review Criteria	Class Test
1	Is there a Class Test Strategy that provides direction for each of the Issues identified in Activity 12.2?	√
2	Is there a Timer Class coded and tested for the developers?	√
3	Has the test directory structure been established?	√
4	Is there a Class Test Driver Template? Have the developers been notified?	√
5	Is there a Class Test Case Template? Have the developers been notified?	√
6	Have the Classes required for the build been coded and tested?	√
7	Have the Class Test Drivers/Test Cases/Results been reviewed?	√

Tracking Progress

Table 12-3 shows the project management spreadsheet updated for this Phase. At a low level of detail, the number of Methods/Classes implemented can be monitored as a percentage based on the number of Methods per Class in the Model. Additionally, the number of test cases and test drivers per Class, per Category, per Domain, and per project can be monitored.

At a higher level of abstraction, the number of Classes implemented can be monitored as a percentage based on the number of Classes in the OO model. The number of Classes tested can then be monitored as a percentage based on the number of Classes implemented.

Finally, the number of test cases passed as a percentage of the total number of test cases can be monitored.

Table 12-3. Project Management Spreadsheet: Phase 12

HCC Project Management Spreadsheet						
Number	**Phase Name**	**Activity**	**Charge Number**	**Product**	**Progress Metric**	**% Weight**
12	**Class Implementation/Class Test**		**SW-CICT-12**			
12.1		Implement Class Methods	SW-CICT-12-1	Method implemented	# Methods implemented (%)	0.50
12.2		Determine Class Test Strategy	SW-CICT-12-2	Class Test Strategy	1 Class test strategy completed	
12.3		Develop Class Test Drivers	SW-CICT-12-3	<class>_ctd_#.ext source files	# Class test drivers and test cases (%)	0.25
12.4		Perform Class Test	SW-CICT-12-4	Result files	# tests run and % passed	0.25

PART VII

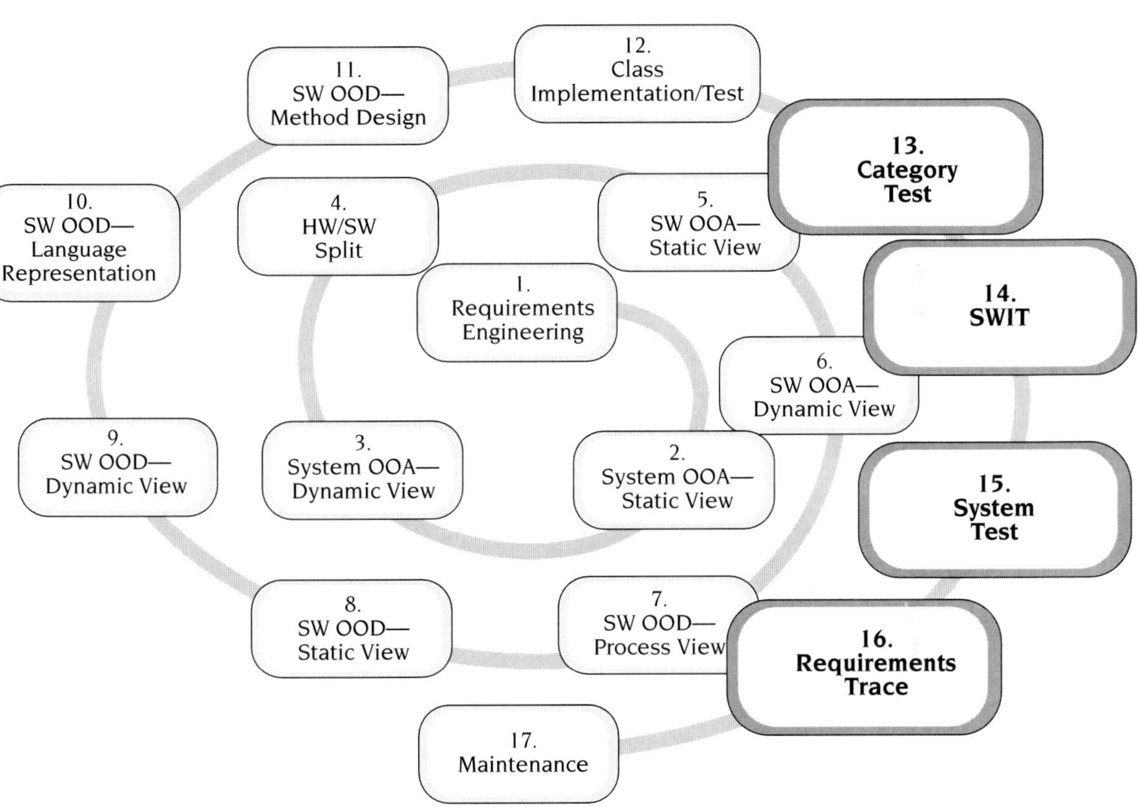

Test

PHASE 13

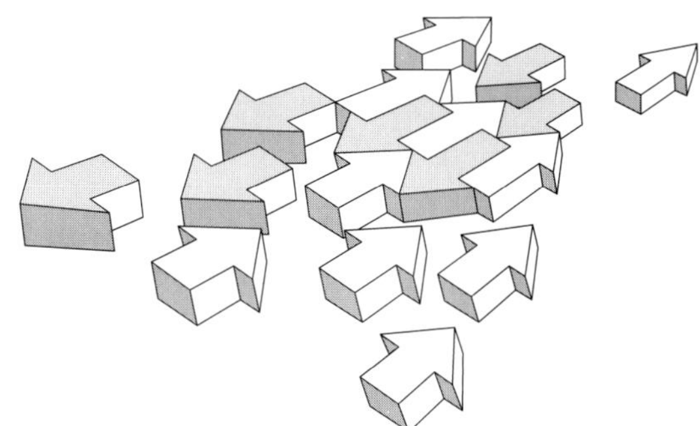

Category Test

PHASE OVERVIEW

This Phase, represented by Figure 13-1, focuses on the development of a Category test strategy, and finally, the testing of each Category that contributes to the current build. The goal of this Phase is to ensure that the Categories within a *Domain*, viewed as a collection of *successfully tested* Classes, provide their services with respect to Use Case requirements for the *Domain*. The goal of this Phase is to ensure that the Class connections *within* a Category, and the Class connections *between* Categories, all within the *same Domain*, collaborate to provide the intended functionality.

Figure 13-2 repeats the overall strategy for Class, Category, and SWIT testing, previously introduced in Phase 12 (Figure 12-2). Note that this Phase concentrates on testing a *single* Category, *first* in isolation of other Categories, and *then* in conjunction with other Categories *within* a specific functional area, or *Domain*. Finally, *all* Domains are migrated to SWIT. SWIT is covered next, in Phase 14.

As in Phase 12, only sample code for testing C++ Classes is shown.

13.1 DEVELOP CATEGORY TEST STRATEGY

Purpose

The purpose of this Activity is to develop and agree upon the strategy for testing a Category. The strategy must cover both *intra*-Category and *inter*-Category testing.

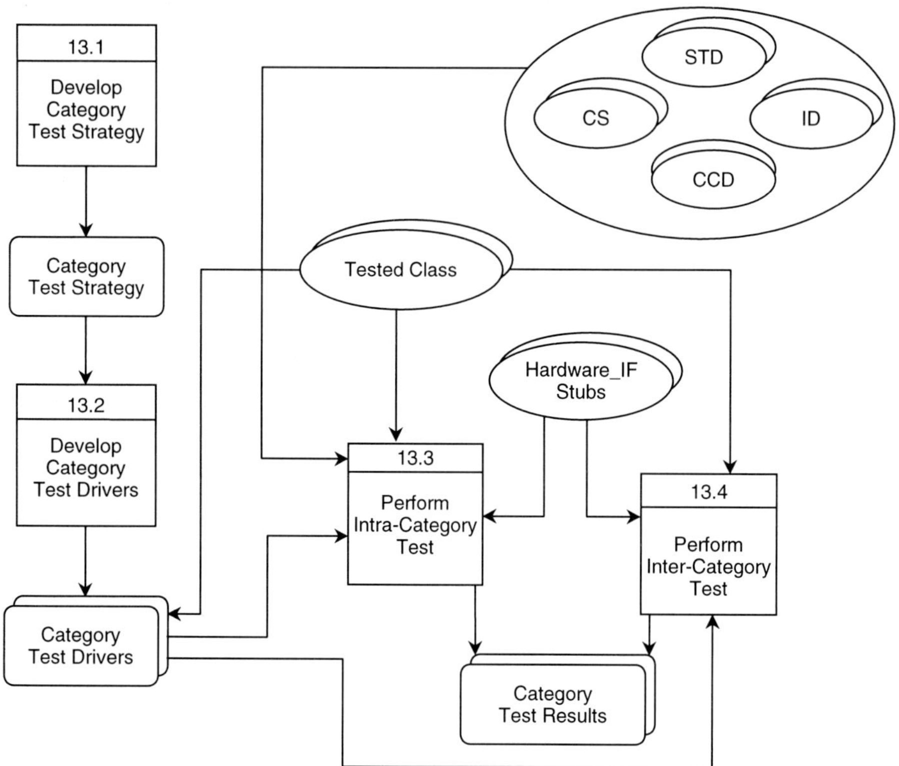

Figure 13-1. Category Test Phase Description Diagram

Definition(s)

Inter-Category Test: Inter-Category test is the process of testing the connections between successfully tested Classes in *different* Categories.

Intra-Category Test: Intra-Category test is the process of testing the connections between successfully tested Classes within the *same* Category.

Category Test Case: A **Category test case** is a description (minimally, in terms of 1) what is being tested, 2) required inputs, and 3) expected results) of a *single* test, along with the resulting code that executes the test.

Category Test Driver: A **Category test driver** is an executable piece of software that comprises one or more tests (called test cases) for the set of connections under test.

Category Test Results: **Category test results** record the results of executing a Category test driver.

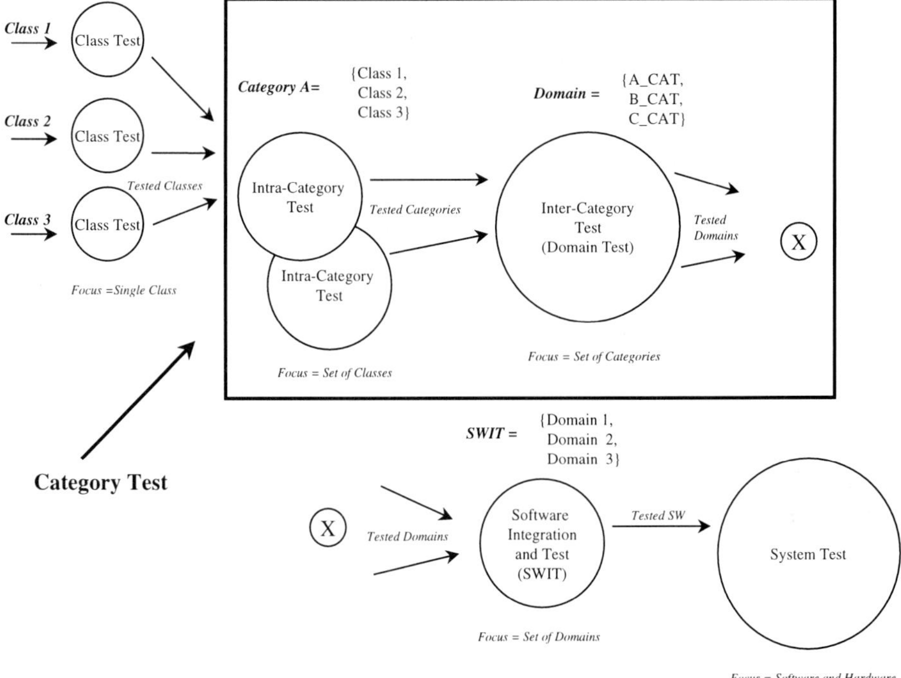

Figure 13-2. Overall Testing Philosophy : Category Test Focus

Leaf Class: A **leaf Class** is a Class that is the lowest-level Class in an inheritance or aggregation hierarchy. Within an aggregation hierarchy, a **leaf Class** does *not* have any "part" Classes. Within an inheritance hierarchy, a **leaf Class** does *not* have any Subclasses.

Process

Step 1: Identify the Intra-Category Connections to Be Tested

From the OOD CCDs, and the information contained in the IDs, identify exactly what Classes in the Category in question interface with each other.

Step 1.1: Develop an Intra-Category Connection Matrix

List the Classes *within* the Category that have connections with other Classes *within* the Category as the rows and columns of a matrix, respectively. An example for the `Living_Quarter_CAT` is shown in Table 13-1.

This table clearly shows that within the `Living_Quarter_CAT`, the `LivingQuarter` Class requires a connection to the `Hall` and `Room` Classes.

Table 13-1. Living_Quarter_CAT Intra-Category Connection Matrix

Living_Quarter_CAT Intra-Category Connection Matrix				
	Deviation	**Hall**	**LivingQuarter**	**Room**
Deviation				
Hall				
LivingQuarter		√		√
Room				

Within *this* Category, there are no other Class connections to be tested. The Hall and Room Classes support the Living_Quarter Class and do *not* require a connection to any other Classes in this or any other Category. The Deviation Class is *required by* the Environmental_Condition Subclasses and those connections are tested when testing the Environmental_Condition_CAT.

Step 1.2: Develop an Inter-Category Class Connection Matrix

List the Classes within the Category being tested that have connections with Classes from *foreign* Categories as the rows of the matrix. List, by Category, the Classes from foreign Categories with which the Category in question has connections as the columns of the matrix. Table 13-2 depicts the inter-Category connections for the Living_Quarter_CAT. Table 13-2 shows that the Living_Quarter_CAT interfaces with the Sensor_CAT, the Environmental_Condition_CAT, and the DB_CAT. The matrix also indicates precisely to which Classes (from the three Categories listed in the previous statement) the Classes in the Living_Quarter_CAT require an interface.

Note that because the Deviation Class is *not* listed, it does *not* have any requirement to interface with any Class from outside the Living_Quarter_CAT. Recall that it is the Environmental_Condition Subclasses that utilize the Deviation Class to provide the percent deviation. Consequently, the connection between the Deviation Class and three subclasses of Environmental-Condition will appear in the inter-Category Connection Matrix for Environmental_Condition_CAT. A Category Connection Matrix is developed from the Category point of view, in other words, from the point of view of what Class in a Category requires services from other Categories. A Category Connection Matrix shows a *uni-directional* dependency only, and is developed by and for the developers to aid in the structure and identification of the Category test cases to be developed.

Step 2: Develop Intra/Inter Category Test Case Template

The template for a Category test case that tests an intra-Category connection represents a simple refinement to the Class test case template. Specifically, add one more field to the Class test case template, "*CONNECTION TESTED,*" to identify the Class connection within/between the Category that is being tested. Figure 13-5 shows the

Table 13-2. Living_Quarter_CAT Inter-Category Connection Matrix

	Living_Quarter_CAT Inter-Category Connection Matrix											
	Sensor_ CAT	Sensor	AirP_ Sensor	Oxy_ Sensor	Temp_ Sensor	Environmental_ Condition_CAT	EC	Air_ EC	Oxy_ EC	Temp_ EC	DB_ CAT	DB
LivingQuarter	—	√	√	√	√	—	√	√	√	√	—	√

modified Class test case template, which yields a Category test case template. This template can be used for both intra- and inter-Category test cases.

Step 3: Develop Category Test Driver Template

The template for a Category test driver that tests either an intra- or inter-Category connection represents a simple refinement to the template of the Class test driver. Specifically, add one more field to the Class test driver template, named "*CATEGORY,*" to identify whether Class connections within or between the Category are being tested. If testing between Categories, list the foreign Categories in the test cases. Additionally, the test results file will contain an additional line that indicates that this Category test driver is either an INTRA-CATEGORY or INTER-CATEGORY driver. Figure 13-6 shows the modified Class test driver template, which yields a Category test driver template. This template can be used for both intra- and inter-Category test drivers. Simply add one line of code that prints to the file either INTRA- or INTER-CATEGORY TEST. If the driver represents INTER-CATEGORY testing, the names of the contributing Categories can also be added to the results file.

Although this template differs from the template for a Class test driver, the file naming conventions adopted for Class test drivers and results files do *not* need to be altered at the Category level. Category test drivers can be named <classname>_ctd_#.cpp and Category test results can be maintained in <classname>_ctd_#.ctr files. To avoid confusion, perhaps the Category test drivers and Category test results can be placed in a different directory. Alternatively, utilize different naming conventions for Category test drivers and Category test results.

Step 4: Agree upon a Directory Structure for Class Test Files

Based on the decision made in Step 3 to retain the same naming conventions for the drivers and results files, you could break the `<<category>>/test` subdirectory into three distinct subdirectories: `<<category>>/test/classtest`, `<<category>>/test/intracat`, and `<<category>>/test/intercat`, and you could maintain the drivers and results files in their respective subdirectories.

Step 5: Testing Inheritance Hierarchies

An inheritance hierarchy needs to be tested "from the top down." Use of the phrase "from the top down" means test the Class at the root of the hierarchy first, then test the first-level Subclasses, then test the second-level Subclasses, and so on. In other words, the phrase "from the top down" means test the Classes at the top of the inheritance hierarchy *down to* the leaf Classes in the hierarchy. This approach permits Subclass testing with knowledge that the Superclass has been tested.

When the root Class is an Abstract Class, however, test the first Concrete Subclass in a branch. This means that if a Subclass is also an Abstract Class, keep moving down a level until the first Concrete Class is reached. Test from that first Concrete Class down to the bottom leaves of the hierarchy, or until another Abstract Class is reached

Inheritance Hierarchy:
In the inheritance hierarchy rooted by the Abstract Class A, the connection between the Concrete Subclass B and B's Subclass D is tested first. Then, the connection from Subclass B to its Superclass A is tested. Testing progress "down" the hierarchy, starting with the first Concrete Class, then goes up the hierarchy, starting from the same Concrete Class.

Aggregation Hierarchy:
Class X is made up of Classes Y and Z. Class Z is made up of Classes ZZ1 and ZZ2. Assuming Classes ZZ1 and ZZ2 have passed Class Test, then the connections between Classes ZZ1 and ZZ2 with the whole Class Z are tested, in any order, before the connection between Class Z and its whole Class X is tested. Testing progresses up the hierarchy.

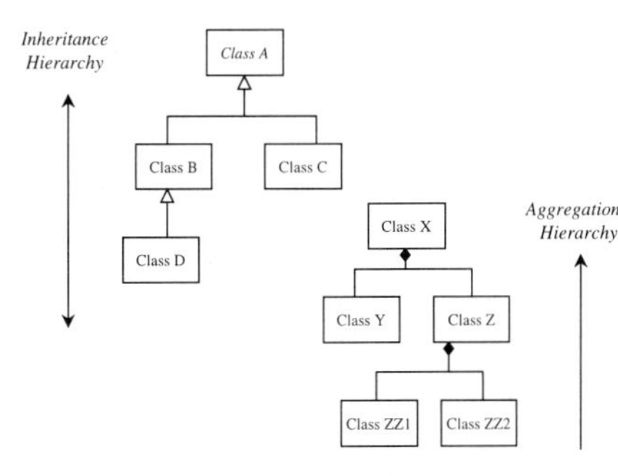

Figure 13-3. Testing Inheritance and Aggregation Hierarchies

(in which case recurse the process). Figure 13-3 summarizes the order for testing connections in an inheritance hierarchy.

Step 6: Testing Aggregation Hierarchies

When testing an aggregation hierarchy, test "from the bottom up". Use of the phrase "from the bottom up" means that, assuming a Class at the leaf level of a hierarchy has successfully been Class-tested, test the Class' connection to its immediate "whole" Class. Testing "from the bottom up" means to test the Class connections of an aggregation hierarchy in the reverse order of their aggregation. Figure 13-3 also summarizes the order for testing connections in an aggregation hierarchy.

For the SEM, this means that the connection between the `Window` and `Annunciator` Classes is tested before the connection between the `Panel` and `Annunciator` Classes.

Step 7: Testing Association Relationships (Dependencies)

There are many kinds of dependencies to be tested, including but not limited to:

- References
- Instantiates
- Calls.

For a *references* dependency, combinations of constructors and Attribute set and query Methods are required to test the connection. For *instantiates* dependencies, the connection of a Class to the specific Instance of the instantiation needs to be tested because the Parameterized Class *cannot* be tested. Finally, for *calls*, the connection needs to test that the results provided by the called entity are captured correctly by the Class in question.

Step 8: Determine under What Conditions, if Any, Test by Inspection Is Permitted

There are *no* conditions under which test by inspection is acceptable for testing connections between Classes, regardless of whether the connection is intra- or inter-Category.

Step 9: Agree upon Kinds of Inputs

There is a great deal of material written on testing already in the marketplace. As with GUI and database issues, a detailed discussion of valid inputs is outside the scope of this book. Each project must have an agreed-upon approach to the specification of the inputs to be used in testing the connections between Classes within a Category, or in testing the connections between Categories. As previously stated, there are many different kinds of Class connections: references, instantiates, and calls. It seems appropriate that sets of inputs can be categorized to accommodate these kinds of connections.

Step 10: Identify Class to Be Stubbed Out

For both intra-Category and inter-Category testing, agree upon the Class stubs that need to be used. Of course the Class stubs reside in the stub library. Table 13-3 suggests one such definition. Table 13-3 indicates that in intra-Category testing, all Hardware Interface Classes, foreign Category Classes (within the Domain), Software COTS/GFS/CFS Classes, and the actual database connection be stubbed out. For inter-Category testing, the actual Category Classes from foreign Categories within a Domain replace the Class stubs used during intra-Category testing. In inter-Category testing, Class stubs from a stub library are still used to represent the Hardware Interface Classes and COTS/GFS/CFS Classes. The actual hardware, database, and COTS/GFS/CFS software are integrated and tested during SWIT.

Step 11: Decide upon Basis for Intra- and Inter-Category Testing

The bases for *intra*-Category testing are the connections between Classes within the Category under test. When these connections are *not* Operator-driven, test drivers are appropriate. However, there may be cases within intra-Category testing, and most certainly within inter-Category testing, where the test case is Operator-driven. This is particularly true for *inter*-Category testing because the basis for that testing is the set of

Table 13-3. Class Stubs Usage in Intra- and Inter-Category Testing

Class Stub Utilization: Intra- and Inter-Category Testing		
	Intra-Category Testing	**Inter-Category Testing**
Hardware Interface Classes	Class Stub	Class Stub
Foreign Category Classes	Class Stub	Actual Class
COTS/GFS/CFS Interface Classes	Class Stub	Class Stub
Database	Simulate	Actual or Simulate

Use Cases allocated to the set of Categories that comprise the Domain under test. If testing tools that capture keyboard entries and mouse clicks, for example, preVue-X™ and Xrunner®, are *not* available to the Project Team, then a form, like that shown in Figure 13-4, needs to be developed for structuring and defining a test when the test is executed through Operator actions. The form can also be used to structure the tests, even if a tool is available. Note as currently designed the Use Case Test Design Worksheet does *not* currently support the specification of pre- and post-conditions. The form is easily modified to accomodate this information, either by adding a block comment preceding the specification of Operator Actions or as extra rows within the body of the worksheet.

This form captures:

- Which Use Case or supporting ID is being tested
- Which Category owns the Use Case under test
- The author of the test
- The tester and date tested
- The sequence of actions that are to be performed to test the Use Case
- Test case failures.

A simple form like this goes a long way to providing consistency and direction for a project.

Use Case Test Design Worksheet

Use Case #: ______________________ **Author:** ____________
Supporting ID: ______________________ **Tester:** ____________
Owning Category: ____________ **Date:** ____________

Sequence Number	**Operator Action**	**Input**	**Software Reaction**	**Pass**	**Fail**	**Comments**

Figure 13-4. Sample Use Case Test Design Worksheet Template

Step 12: What about Using a _View Class as a Driver?

A _View Class can be used as a driver as long as the inputs and outputs are captured. In this case, self-documenting tests are *not* appropriate at all. Again, if an appropriate test tool for capturing keyboard entries and mouse clicks is *not* available, consider modifying Figure 13-4 above by adding another column, "GUI Utilized," to document the particular GUI used. Figure 13-4 already supports the recording of the actual data entered.

Example

Here is a sample template for a Category test driver and a sample template for test cases within a Category test driver. Remember, modify these templates as required! Figure 13-5 shows a sample template for each individual Category test case, while Figure 13-6 shows a sample template for a Category test driver. Both Figures 13-5 and 13-6 represent samples for a C++ implementation.

Pragmatic Project Issues

Class Test CASE Tool

Most Class Test CASE tools that exist in the marketplace today can be utilized to perform Category testing as well. If a project has committed to using a specific tool, the template and contents of each Category test driver and each Category test case will be influenced by the CASE tool.

C++

```
//============================================================
// TEST CASE n
//
// INPUTS: << list required inputs by variable name >>
// EXPECTED RESULTS: << list expected results by variable name>>
// PURPOSE: << text to describe purpose of test case >>
// CONNECTION TESTED: << specify the connection(s) tested by
// Class>>
// USES: << list other resources required>>
{
    //BLOCK FOR TEST CASE n:
      << code for test case n >>
    //END BLOCK FOR TEST CASE n:
}
//============================================================
```

Figure 13-5. Sample C++ Category Test Case Template

```
/*==============================================================
//==============================================================
// Copyright P. P. Texel & C. B. Williams 1996
//
// FILENAME: << Name of Class Test Driver File>>
//
// AUTHOR: << Name of author>>
//
// CLASS UNDER TEST: <<Class Name followed by Class file names>>
//
// OWNING CATEGORY: <<Name of owning Category>>
//
// CATEGORY TEST: << Specify inter- or intra- Category Test >>
//
// DESCRIPTION: <<Words that describe the series of test cases
// within this Category Test Driver>>
//
// DATE CREATED: <<Date created >>
//
// TEST ENVIRONMENT: << Description of hardware and software
// environment used>>
// =============================================================
============================================================ */

// RESOURCES REQUIRED BY ALL TEST CASES
// #includes <<list all required Classes>>
void
main()
{

// global data
// establishing results file

      fstream filename; // C++ results file name is filename

      // open file as "filename.ctr"
      filename.open("filename.ctr", ios: : out);
      if (!filename)
      {
         cout << "Error opening filename.ctr << "\n";
      }

      //position filepointer at the beginning of the file
      filename.seekp (0L, ios: : beg);
```

Figure 13-6. Sample C++ Category Test Driver Template

```
        // write title to file
        filename << "========================================"
                 << "\n";
        filename << "INTRA-CATEGORY TEST: <Category Name>"
                 << "\n";
        filename << "Results for filename " << "\n" ;
        // write date of execution to file
        struct date theDate;
        getdate(& theDate); // fills theDate with current date
        filename << "lq_ctd_1.cpp executed on: " << "\n"
                 << "\n" ;
        filename << "month: " << (int)theDate.da_mon << "\n";
        filename << "day: " << (int)theDate.da_day << "\n";
        filename << "year: " << theDate.da_year << "\n"
                 << "\n" ;

        // write the time of execution to file
        struct time theTime;
        gettime(& theTime); // fills theTime with current time
        filename << "lq_ctd_1.cpp executed at: " << "\n"
                 << "\n" ;
        filename << "hour: " << (int)theTime.ti_hour << "\n";
        filename << "minutes: " << (int)theTime.ti_min
                 << "\n";
        filename << "seconds: " << (int)theTime.ti_sec
                 << "\n";
        filename << "========================================"
                 << "\n";
        filename << "\n";
//================================================================
// TEST CASE 1
//
// INPUTS: << list required inputs by variable name>>
// EXPECTED RESULTS: << list expected results by variable name>>
// PURPOSE: << text to describe purpose of test case >>
// CONNECTION TESTED: << specify the connection(s) tested by
// Class>>
// USES: << list other resources required>>
{
    //BLOCK FOR TEST CASE 1:
    << code for test case 1>>
    //END BLOCK FOR TEST CASE 1:
}
```

Figure 13-6. Sample C++ Category Test Driver Template (*continued*)

```
//=============================================================
// TEST CASE 2
//
// INPUTS: << list required inputs by variable name>>
// EXPECTED RESULTS: << list expected results by variable name>>
// PURPOSE: << text to describe purpose of test case >>
// CONNECTION TESTED: << specify the connection(s) tested by
// Class>>
// USES: << list other resources required>>
{
   //BLOCK FOR TEST CASE 2:
   << code for Test Case 2>>
   //END BLOCK FOR TEST CASE 2:
}
//=============================================================

// global clean up for all test cases
filename.close();                            // close the file
}
```

Figure 13-6. Sample C++ Category Test Driver Template (*continued*)

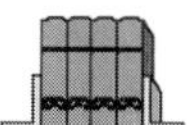

Product(s)

The products of this activity are as follows:

- A Category test strategy
- A template for a Category test driver
- A template for a Category test case.

13.2 DEVELOP CATEGORY TEST DRIVERS

Purpose

> The purpose of this Activity is to develop the Category test drivers for a Category for the current build following the agreed-upon Category test strategy.

Process

Coming into this Activity, we have the following: successfully tested Classes, Connection Matrices, and test templates for Category testing. All that remains is to develop the Category test drivers.

Step 1: Structure the Test Drivers for a Class

After examining the Class Connection Matrices that specify which connections must be tested, determine how many test drivers are required for a Class and what the test cases in each driver are to be. A sample structuring might be as follows:

- Intra-Category test drivers:
  - `lq_ctd_4.cpp` => test cases to test `Deviation()` Method's connection with the `Living_Quarter_CAT Hall` Class
  - `lq_ctd_5.cpp` => test cases to test `Deviation()` Method's connection with the `Living_Quarter_CAT Room` Class
- Inter-Category test drivers:
  - `lq_ctd_7.cpp` => test cases to test `Deviation()` Method's connection with EC Classes and DB Classes
  - `lq_ctd_7.cpp` => test cases to test `Deviation()` Method's connection with `Sensor` Classes
  - `lq_ctd_8.cpp` => test cases to test `Deviation()` Method's connection with all Classes

and so on. Note that there is a plan to slowly integrate with the Classes internal to `Living_Quarter_CAT`, as well as a plan for integrating Classes from external Categories. The connections are *not* all tested at once. This, of course, makes the debugging process easier. Providing some initial thought into the structuring of test drivers and test cases can reap benefits when actually developing the cases.

Step 2: Develop Category Test Drivers

Develop the actual test drivers, specifically produce the `.cpp` files (in C++), that are to be used to test a Class and its connections to other Classes, both internal and external to its owning Category.

Example

What follows is one Category test driver, coded in C++. As previously stated, providing the code for the other three languages does not add any significant benefit.

This Category test driver is *exactly the same* test driver that was developed during Phase 12, Class Test! All that changed was the way that some of the inputs were provided. In Category testing, the inputs are provided by the *actual* Class, rather than by a Class stub from the stub library. The `LivingQuarter` Class' `Deviation()` Method was tested during Class Test in isolation of other Classes and used Class stubs provided by the stub library. Also, the example in the previous Phase used a stub for the `FlatFileDatabase` Class. By changing the values returned in the `FlatFileDatabase` Class stub, different run-time situations were reproduced. Now, in this phase, Category Test, the Class stubs utilized in the previous phase are systematically replaced with the *actual* Classes. First, use the actual Classes within the

Category, and Class stubs for Classes in external Categories (intra-Category testing), and then replace the Class stubs for the Classes from external Categories with the *actual* Classes (inter-Category testing).

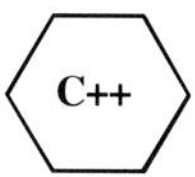

Figure 13-7(a) shows the Category test driver for the `Living_Quarter` Class, which tests the `Deviation()` Method for air pressure only. This Category test driver uses the actual `FlatFileDatabase` Class and a sample database. This driver, therefore, is an example of an inter-Category test driver.

```
/* ==========================================================
//==========================================================
// Copyright P. P. Texel & C. B. Williams 1996
//
// FILENAME: lq_ctd_4.cpp
//
// AUTHOR: Putnam Texel
//
// CLASS UNDER TEST: LivingQuarter (lq_lq.h & lq_lq.cpp)
//
// OWNING CATEGORY: Living_Quarter_CAT
//
// CATEGORY TEST: Inter-Category: DB_CAT
//
// CONNECTION TESTED: FlatFileDatabase connection
//
// DESCRIPTION: All test cases in this file test the Deviation()
// Method for the AirPressure only
//
// DATE CREATED: 1 October 1996
//
// TEST ENVIRONMENT: Borland C++ V4.5 and Micron P150
//==========================================================
========================================================== */
// RESOURCES REQUIRED BY ALL TEST CASES
// #includes
#include <iostream.h>
#include <fstream.h>
#include <dos.h>
#include <string.h>
// LIVING_QUARTER_CAT
```

Figure 13-7(a). Sample Category Test Driver

```
#include "lq_lq.h"
// ENVIRONMENTAL_CONDITION_CAT
#include "ec_environ.h"

void
main()
{

// global for all test cases

    fstream lq_ctd_4; // file for results

    // open file
    lq_ctd_4.open("lq_ctd_4.ctr", ios: : out);
    if (!lq_ctd_4)
    {
            cout << "Error opening lq_ctd_4.ctr" << "\n";
    }

    //position filepointer at the beginning of the file
    lq_ctd_4.seekp (0L, ios: : beg);
    // write title to file
    lq_ctd_4 << "=========================================="
             << "\n";
    lq_ctd_4 << "INTER-CATEGORY TEST: Living_Quarter_CAT"
       << "\n" ;
    lq_ctd_4 << "Results for lq_ctd_4.cpp test driver" <<
       "\n" ;

    // write date of execution to file
    struct date theDate;
    getdate(& theDate); // fills theDate with current date
    lq_ctd_4 << "lq_4_ctd.cpp executed on: " << "\n"
             << "\n" ;
    lq_ctd_4 << "month: " << (int)theDate.da_mon << "\n";
    lq_ctd_4 << "day: " << (int)theDate.da_day << "\n";
    lq_ctd_4 << "year: " << theDate.da_year << "\n" <<
       "\n" ;

    // write the time of execution to file
    struct time theTime;
    gettime(& theTime); // fills theDate with current date
    lq_ctd_4 << "lq_1_ctd.cpp executed at: " << "\n"
             << "\n" ;
    lq_ctd_4 << "hour: " << (int)theTime.ti_hour << "\n";
    lq_ctd_4 << "minutes: " << (int)theTime.ti_min
```

Figure 13-7(a). Sample Category Test Driver (*continued*)

```
            << "\n";
    lq_ctd_4 << "seconds: " << (int)theTime.ti_sec
            << "\n";
    lq_ctd_4 << "========================================"
            << "\n";
    lq_ctd_4 << "\n";

//==========================================================
// TEST CASE 1
//
// INPUTS:   HallId = A, RoomId = 2,
//        CurrentValue = 0.0
//        NomialValue = 20.0
// EXPECTED RESULTS: expect exception "Cannot Compute" to be
// thrown
// PURPOSE: to force Cannot Compute exception to be thrown
// CONNECTION TESTED: That the deviation returned is
//                    correct for the Hall, Room & EC
//                    Subclass specified.
// USES:
// EnvironmentalCondition Class
{
    //BLOCK FOR TEST CASE 1:

    LivingQuarter myLivingQuarter('A', 2);    // aLQ
    double theDeviation;                      // the result
    EnvironmentalCondition::Kind theKind = // AirPressure only
        EnvironmentalCondition::AirPressure;

    try
    {
    // get deviation
    theDeviation = myLivingQuarter.Deviation(theKind);
    lq_ctd_4 << "TEST CASE 1 FAILED" ; // want to get the
                                       // exception

    }
    catch (char * str)
    {
        cout << "Error: " << str << "\n";
        lq_ctd_4 << "TEST CASE 1 PASSED" ; // got the exception
    }
    //END BLOCK FOR TEST CASE 1:
}
```

Figure 13-7(a). Sample Category Test Driver (*continued*)

```
//==============================================================
// TEST CASE 2
{
      << and so on >>
}
//==========================================================
// TEST CASE 3
{
      << and so on >>
}
//==============================================================
//==============================================================
// global clean up for all test cases
    lq_ctd_4.close(); // close the file
}
```

Figure 13-7(a). Sample Category Test Driver (*continued*)

Figure 13-7(b) shows the `FlatFileDatabase` Class from the `DB_CAT` that was used to run the test, while Figure 13-7(c) shows the flat file implementation of the database with a value of 20.0 as the air pressure nominal value for living quarter (A,2). Each row in Figure 13-7(c) represents the three environmental conditions for one specific living quarter: the first entry after the hall and room identifiers represents the air pressure value, the second represents the oxygen value, and the third represents the temperature value. The final value in each row represents the occupational status of the living quarter: '1' represents occupied while '0' represents unoccupied.

```
/* ============================================================
// Copyright P. P. Texel & C. B. Williams 1996
//
// FILENAME: db_ffdatabase.h
//
// AUTHOR: P. Texel
//
// DESCRIPTION: Database Class for maintaining nominal
// values for the Living Quarters as well as
// their occupational status.
//
// DATE CREATED: 19 September 1996
//
==============================================================*/
```

Figure 13-7(b). FlatFileDatabase Class Implementation

```
#ifndef _FFDATABASE_H
#define _FFDATABASE_H

// SENSOR_CAT
#include "sr_address.h"
// DB_CAT
#include "db_database.h"

typedef int bool; // bool not supported in V4.5

class FlatFileDatabase: public Database
{
public:

   FlatFileDatabase(); // opens the file
   ~FlatFileDatabase(); // closes the file

   void Commit();
   void Rollback();
   void StartTransaction();

   // throws "DatabaseDown"
   double Read(Address anAddress)const;
   // throws "DatabaseDown"
   bool ReadLQStatus(Address anAddress)const;
   // both writes throw "DatabaseDown"
   void Write(Address anAddress, double aValue);
   void WriteLQStatus(Address anAddress, bool aValue);
};
#endif
/* ============================================================
// Copyright P. P. Texel & C. B. Williams 1996
//
// FILENAME db_ffdatabase.cpp
//
// AUTHOR: P. Texel
//
// DESCRIPTION: Current nominal values
// Implementation as Flat File - "semdata.dat"
//
// DATE CREATED: 19 September 1996
//
============================================================*/
#include <fstream.h>
#include <iostream.h>
```

Figure 13-7(b). FlatFileDatabase Class Implementation (*continued*)

```
#include "db_ff_database.h"

   // one instance of the database, retaining values
   // between calls
static fstream semdatabase;
   // set up block moves for the file pointer
const HallBlock = 176; // 8 rows of bytes for one Hall
const RoomBlock = 22; // 22 bytes per row inc. <lf> <cr>
// other local data

   // local function that uses the Hall Letter to determine
   // how many blocks of bytes to move to get to the right Hall
   // part of the file
int MapHallToMultiplier (char aCharacter)
{
   int Result; // value to be returned

   switch (aCharacter)
   {
         case 'A': {Result = 0; break; }
         case 'B': {Result = 1; break; }
         case 'C': {Result = 2; break; }
         case 'D': {Result = 3; break; }
         case 'E': {Result = 4; break; }
         case 'F': {Result = 5; break; }
         default: {Result = 0; break; }
   }
   return Result;
}

   // local function that uses the Sensor Number to determine
   // how many bytes to move in the row (from the beginning of
   // the row ) to get the right reading
int SensorOffset(int theSensorPart)
{
   const AirOffset = 4; // bytes from beginning of row
   const OxyOffset = 9; // bytes from beginning of row
   const TempOffset = 14; // bytes from the beginning of row
   int Result; // the value to be returned
   switch (theSensorPart)
   {
      case 1: {Result = AirOffset; break; }
      case 2: {Result = OxyOffset; break; }
```

Figure 13-7(b). FlatFileDatabase Class Implementation (*continued*)

```
        case 3: {Result = TempOffset; break; }
        default: {Result = 0; break; }
    }
    return Result;
}
int CalculateSensorFilePointerPosition (Address anAddress)
{
        // get the hall, room, and sensor id for the read
    char HallKey = anAddress.AddressHallPart();
    int RoomKey = anAddress.AddressRoomPart();
    int SensorKey = anAddress.AddressSensorPart();
        // calculate where to place file pointer
    int FilePointerPosition = 0;
        // implicit cast to int
    int HallMultiplier = MapHallToMultiplier(HallKey);
    int RoomMultiplier = RoomKey - 1; // already at room one at 0L
    int SensorOffsetInRow = SensorOffset(SensorKey);
    FilePointerPosition = // start of Hall values
        HallMultiplier * HallBlock + // start of Room values
        RoomMultiplier * RoomBlock + // find Sensor in row
        SensorOffsetInRow;
    return FilePointerPosition;
}
int CalculateLQStatusFilePointerPosition(Address anAddress)
{   // not shown to save space

}
FlatFileDatabase::FlatFileDatabase()
{
}
FlatFileDatabase::~FlatFileDatabase()
{
    // fstream automaticaly closes file when the
    // file goes out of scope
}
void FlatFileDatabase::Commit() // not shown to save space
{
}
void FlatFileDatabase::Rollback() // not shown to save space
{
}
```

Figure 13-7(b). FlatFileDatabase Class Implementation (*continued*)

```
void FlatFileDatabase::StartTransaction()
{
        // open file
        // throw DatabaseDown if can't open the file
    semdatabase.open("semdata.dat", ios::in | ios::out);
    if (!semdatabase)
    {
        throw "DatabaseDown";
    }
}
double FlatFileDatabase::Read(Address anAddress) const
{
    double Answer; // value to be returned
        // get the position in the file for the read
    int IndexIntoFile;
    IndexIntoFile =
    CalculateSensorFilePointerPosition(anAddress);
    semdatabase.seekg(IndexIntoFile, ios::beg); // move pointer
semdatabase >> Answer; // do the read
return Answer;
}
bool FlatFileDatabase::ReadLQStatus(Address anAddress)
// not shown to save space
{
}
void FlatFileDatabase::Write(Address anAddress, double aValue)
{
int IndexIntoFile;
IndexIntoFile =
    CalculateSensorFilePointerPosition (an Address);
semdatabase.seekp (IndexIntoFile, ios::beg);
semdatabase << avalue;
}
void FlatFileDatabase::WriteLQStatus
  (Address anAddress, bool aValue)
// not shown to save space
{
}
```

Figure 13-7(b). FlatFileDatabase Class Implementation (*continued*)

When a test is initiated by an Operator, rather than by the software itself, a different kind of test case needs to be developed. Figure 13-8 shows how the Use Case Design Worksheet can be used to design one or more test cases driven by Operator input.

A 1 15.7 22.9 55.9 1
A 2 20.0 22.9 55.6 0
A 3 35.7 26.9 55.8 1
A 4 45.7 22.9 55.6 1
A 5 55.7 22.9 55.6 1
A 6 65.7 22.9 55.6 0
A 7 75.7 22.9 55.6 1
A 8 85.7 22.9 55.6 1
B 1 11.1 22.2 33.3 1
. . .

Figure 13-7(c). Database as Flat File "semdata.dat"

Use Case Test Design Worksheet

Use Case #: 16 Operator_Updates_Nominal_Values_In_DB **Author:** P. P. Texel
Supporting ID: **Tester:** C. Williams
Owning Category: LQ **Date:** 11.7.96

Sequence Number	Operator Action	Input	Software Reaction	Pass	Fail	Comments
1	Operator selects Update All button on SEM_Desktop_View		Update_All_View displayed as active window			
2	Operator enters a Temperature value	150.0	150.0 is displayed			No constraint checking performed yet
3	Operator enters new Temperature value	72.5	Any Operator action is accepted			
4	Operator enters Air Pressure value	202.0	202.0 is displayed			
5	Operator enters Oxygen value	18.0	Any operation action is accepted			
6	Operator selects OK	—	Error message window displayed			Constraint checking throws out 202.0 air pressure value
7						
8						
. . .						

Figure 13-8. Use Case Design Worksheet: UC16_Operator_Updates_Nominal_Values_In_DB

Pragmatic Project Issues

Review Class Test Cases

Review the set of Category test cases in each Category test driver to ensure proper coverage. Alternatively, if a CASE tool has been provided for the project that can detect test coverage, utilize the tool.

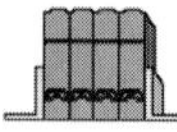

Product(s)

The products of this Activity are: 1) a set of Category test drivers, or `<<classname>>_ctd_#.cpp` files in C++, for each intra-Category Class connection in the Category under test, and 2) a set of Use Case Design Worksheets.

13.3 PERFORM INTRA-CATEGORY TESTS

Purpose

> The purpose of this Activity is to execute the intra-Category test drivers to test the Classes in question.

Process

Step 1: Execute the Tests

On a Class-by-Class, Category test driver-by-Category test driver basis, execute the test drivers for the intra-Category tests. For each test case that fails, resolve the issue.

Step 2: Correct Errors

To aid in the debugging process, rerun the PDL processor to obtain an updated Declared/Referenced PDL Report (Table 11-1). This information can help in the debugging process.

Example

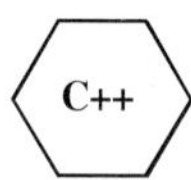

Figure 13-9 shows the contents of the `lq_ctd_4.ctr` file that was produced as a result of executing the Category test driver `lq_ctd_4.cpp`.

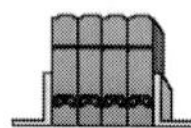

Products

The products of this Activity are a set of Category test results, or `.ctr` files, for each Category under test.

```
==================================================
INTRA_CATEGORY TEST: Living_Quarter_CAT
Results for lq_ctd_4.cpp test driver
lq_ctd_4.cpp executed on:

month: 10
day: 7
year: 1996

lq_ctd_4.cpp executed at:

hour: 12
minutes: 15
seconds: 33
==================================================
TEST CASE 1 PASSED
```

Figure 13-9. Sample Intra-Category Test Results File

13.4 PERFORM INTER-CATEGORY TESTS

Purpose

> The purpose of this Activity is to execute the inter-Category test drivers to test the Classes in question.

Process

Step 1: Execute the Tests

On a Class-by-Class, Category test driver-by-Category test driver basis, execute the test drivers for the inter-Category tests. For each test case that fails, resolve the issue.

Step 2: Correct Errors

To aid in the debugging process, rerun the PDL processor to obtain an updated Declared/Referenced PDL Report (Table 11-1).

Example

Figure 13-10 shows the contents of the `lq_ctd_8.ctr` file that was produced as a result of executing the test driver `lq_ctd_8.cpp`. Note the first line in the results file indicates that this represents results from an inter-Category test, specifically the connections with the `Sensor_CAT` and `Environmental_Condition_CAT`.

```
=================================================
INTER_CATEGORY TEST: Sensor_CAT & Environmental_Condition_CAT
Results for lq_ctd_8.cpp test driver
lq_ctd_8.cpp executed on:

month: 10
day: 7
year: 1996

lq_ctd_8.cpp executed at:

hour: 12
minutes: 15
seconds: 33
=================================================
TEST CASE 1 PASSED
```

Figure 13-10. Sample Inter-Category Test Results File

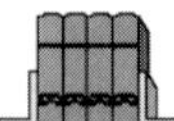

Products

The products of this activity are: 1) a set of Category test results, or `.ctr` files, for each Category under test, and 2) a set of Use Case Worksheets.

Phase Transition Criteria

Transition to the next Phase when the Class connections for the build have been tested, and the Class code and Category test results have been reviewed. The review criteria listed in Table 13-4 can help make this decision.

Review Criteria

Table 13-4. Category Test Review Criteria

#	Category Test Review Criteria	Class Test
1	Is there a Category test strategy that provides direction for each of the issues identified in Activity 13.1?	√
2	Does the strategy cover both intra- and inter-Category testing?	√
3	Has the directory structure been established on the system?	√
4	Is there a Category test driver template? Have the developers been notified?	√
5	Is there a Category test case template? Have the developers been notified?	√
6	Have the Classes required for Category Test been Class tested?	√
7	Have the Category test drivers/test cases/results been reviewed?	√
8	Has the Category test strategy been adhered to?	√

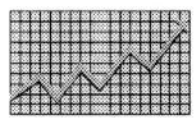

Tracking Progress

Table 13-5 shows the project management spreadsheet updated for this Phase. This Phase can be monitored at two distinct levels of abstraction. The first is the number of actual connections tested per Category (both inter- and intra-) can be monitored, as a percentage of the number requiring testing. Also, the Phase can be monitored at the Class level, monitoring the number of Classes whose connections have been tested as a percentage of the total number of Classes per Category that require testing. Again, these percentages need to be captured at the Category, Domain, and project levels.

Table 13-5. Project Management Worksheet: Phase 13

HCC Project Management Spreadsheet						
Number	**Phase Name**	**Activity**	**Charge Number**	**Product**	**Progress Metric**	**% Weight**
13	**Category Test**		**SW-CT-13**			
13.1		Develop Category Test Strategy	SW-CT-13.1	Category Test Strategy	1 Category test strategy completed	
13.2		Develop Category Test Drivers	SW-CT-13.2	<class>_ctd_#.*ext* Result source file	# Category test drivers and test cases (%)	0.50
13.3		Perform Intra-Category Test	SW-CT-13.3	Result files	# intra-tests run and % passed	0.25
13.4		Perform Inter-Category Test	SW-CT-13.4	Result files	# inter-tests run and % passed	0.25

PHASE 14

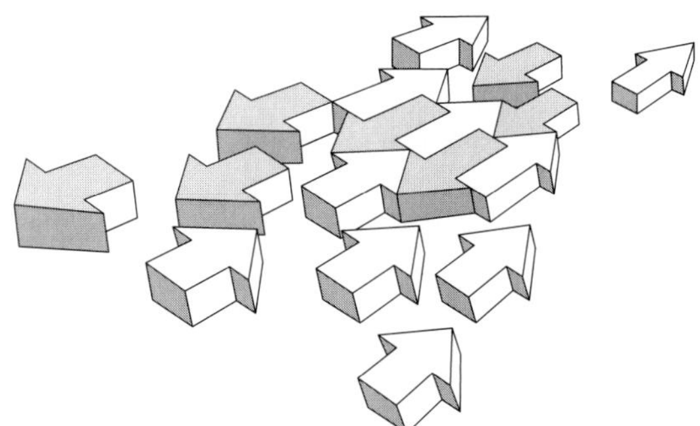

Software Integration and Test (SWIT)

PHASE OVERVIEW

Figure 14-1 represents the diagram for this Phase. There really is *not* a lot to say about SWIT. SWIT basically focuses on testing the functional capability of the software for a specific release, except now the functionality is represented by Use Cases. The following quote from Jacobson [JAC96] states this position very succinctly.

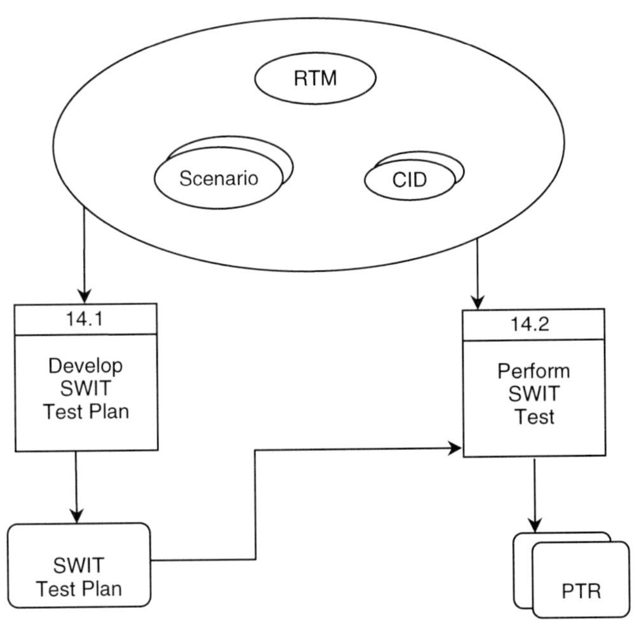

Figure 14-1. SWIT Phase Description Diagram

> "Test Cases are derived from Use Cases, either explicitly or implicitly. In actuality, those who have developed and tested a real system have identified its Use Cases, whether they formally labeled them as such or not. Hence the idea of testing on the basis of a use case is not new."

Up until now, all software testing was performed *on the development environment* by the *developers.* In Phase 12, Class Test, the testing effort focused on testing the required Classes for a build in isolation of other Classes. In Phase 13, Category Test, connections between Classes *within a Category* were tested first, followed by testing the connections *between* Categories *within the same Domain* for a specific build. Now SWIT, highlighted in Figure 14-2, focuses on integrating *all Domains on a standalone test bed* that duplicates, as much as possible, the final target platform. SWIT represents the *first* time that *all* the Domains are integrated and tested by an *independent* software testing organization.

The goal of SWIT is to ensure that the software system, viewed as a collection of *successfully tested* Classes, Categories, and Domains, satisfies the requirements as specified by Use Cases in the RTM for the current *release.*

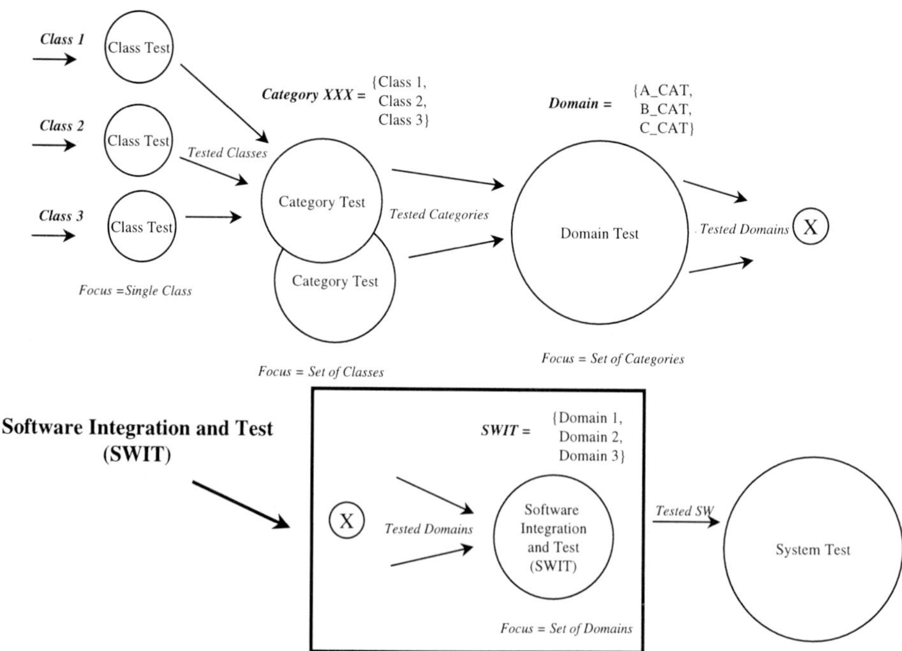

Figure 14-2. Overall Testing Philosophy: Focus on SWIT

14.1 DEVELOP SWIT TEST PLAN

Purpose

> The purpose of this Activity is to develop and agree upon the strategy for SWIT. The strategy must cover integrating all domain software (preferably on a duplicate of the target platform), recording test results, reporting bugs, and incorporating fixes.

Process

Step 1: Establish Order of Use Case Testing

Test the supplier Use Cases first. Test the Use Cases that are tightly coupled to multiple Use Cases and multiple Domains last. Establish a reasonable order for testing those Use Cases in between these two extremes, based on the dependency of the Use Cases and Domains. Basically, it does *not* make sense to spend time testing Use Cases that depend on other Use Cases if the Use Cases upon which they depend have *not* yet been tested.

The dependency of Use Cases is captured in the CIDs, therefore, examine the CIDs to establish the order of Use Case testing.

Step 2: Test Tool Capability

There are many test tools on the marketplace that can be used for this level of testing. Tools like Performance Awareness Corporation's preVue-X[1] and Mercury Interactive Corporation's Xrunner[2] capture keyboard entries and mouse clicks and record these actions in a file that can later be reused in regression testing. The January 1995 issue of UNIX Review provides a comparison of these two test tools, along with others. Additionally, the web site

http://www.yahoo.com/Computers_and_Internet/Software/Programming_Tools/Testing

yields a wealth of information with respect to software testing tools.

Step 3: Test Logically Related Use Cases

Within a release, look for Use Cases that represent similar functionality where the Subjects of the Use Cases represent Classes belonging to the same inheritance hierarchy. These Use Cases can be collected into one SWIT session. The same holds true for aggregation hierarchies. Collect Use Cases whose Subjects are parts of a composition hierarchy together for one SWIT session.

[1] Surf to http://www.PACorp.com for more information on the preVue tool set.

[2] Surf to http://www.merc-int.com for more information on Xrunner.

Table 14-1. Class Stubs Usage for Intra- and Inter-Category Testing: Phase 13

Class Stub Utilization: Intra- and Inter-Category Test		
	Intra-Category Testing	**Inter-Category Testing**
Hardware Interface Classes	Class Stub	Class Stub
Foreign Category Classes	Class Stub	Actual Class
COTS/GFS/CFS Interface Classes	Class Stub	Class Stub
Database	Simulate	Actual or Simulate

Step 4: Specify Software to Be Integrated

In both Class and Category testing, the distinction between and definition of the actual software to be tested and Class stubs was explicitly identified. Recall Table 13-1, repeated here as Table 14-1. For SWIT, a decision needs to be made with respect to Hardware Interface Classes and COTS/GFS/CFS Interface Classes that were represented by Class stubs in Class and Category tests. Is the actual software/hardware to be used in SWIT, or will Class stubs be used? At the very least, SWIT needs to integrate the actual GFS/CFS/COTS software and, if possible, the actual hardware. Table 14-2 updates Table 14-1 and now reflects the actual software and Class stub usage for all testing Phases up to and including SWIT.

Step 5: Develop SWIT Plan

Surfing the Internet provides a wealth of test plan outlines! Take your pick. Figure 14-3 shows a sample test plan outline.[3] When writing the SWIT Test Plan, simply ensure that the findings of the preceding steps are included.

Example

Table 14-3 summarizes information both with respect to Use Case dependency and with respect to Domains and Categories. Read the table as follows: the `Alarm_CAT` (AL) depends on the `IF_CAT` (IF). The `DB_CAT` does *not* depend on any other Category. Consequently, it is clear from Table 14-3 that Use Cases 18 and 21 should

Table 14-2. Class Stubs Usage for Intra- and Inter-Category Testing, and SWIT

Class Stub Utilization: Intra- and Inter-Category Tests and SWIT			
	Intra-Category Testing	**Inter-Category Testing**	**SWIT**
Hardware Interface Classes	Class Stub	Class Stub	Actual Hardware
Foreign Category Classes	Class Stub	Actual Class	Actual Class
COTS/GFS/CFS Interface Classes	Class Stub	Class Stub	Actual Software
Database	Simulate	Simulate/Actual	Actual

[3]This test plan outline is a blend of various test plans, but is primarily based on the NASA Midas Project.

1.0 INTRODUCTION
- 1.1 Document Objective
- 1.2 Document Scope
- 1.3 Applicable Documents
- 1.4 Facilities
- 1.5 Abbreviations
- 1.6 Definitions
- 1.7 Test Program Philosophy

2.0 TEST PLANS, PROCEDURES, AND REPORTS
- 2.1 Test Plans
- 2.2 Test Procedures
- 2.3 Test Reports
  - 2.3.1 Test Data Analysis

3.0 GENERAL TEST REQUIREMENTS
- 3.1 Safety
- 3.2 Product Assurance
- 3.3 Test Failures and Procedural Variations
  - 3.3.1 Test Failures
  - 3.3.2 Procedural Variation
- 3.4 Test Requirements
- 3.5 Environmental Control
- 3.6 Test Equipment Calibration
- 3.7 Documentation
  - 3.7.1 Test Equipment and Instrumentation
  - 3.7.2 Visual Inspection and Test Data
  - 3.7.3 Photographic/Video Documentation
- 3.8 Meetings, Briefings, and Reviews
  - 3.8.1 Test Coordination Meeting
  - 3.8.2 Test Readiness Review
  - 3.8.3 Set-Up and Post-Test Reviews
  - 3.8.4 Personnel Briefings
- 3.9 Test Condition Tolerances
- 3.10 Organization and Staffing
  - 3.10.1 Test Implementation and Control
  - 3.10.2 Role of the Engineering Test Manager
  - 3.10.3 Role of the Test Director
  - 3.10.4 Role of the Test Conductor
  - 3.10.5 Program Assurance Support

4.0 DEVELOPMENT TESTING - Prototype:

5.0 QUALIFICATION AND ACCEPTANCE TESTING

6.0 SUBSYSTEM INTEGRATION TESTING

7.0 TEST REQUIREMENTS CRITERIA:
- 7.1 Rationale for Establishing Test Environments

Figure 14-3. Sample SWIT Test Plan Outline

be tested first because the `Alarm_CAT` and its Use Cases do *not* depend upon any other Use Cases or domains.[4] Because Use Case 1 depends on the `Panel_CAT`, it makes sense to test the `Panel_CAT` Use Cases first.

[4]It does not matter at this point if the Use Cases were allocated to a Class Method or not. During SWIT, the Use Case must be "tested."

Table 14-3. SWIT Planning Data: Domain and Use Case Dependencies

	Domain Category Dependency								
	AL	**DB**	**DY**	**EC**	**IF**	**LQ**	**PL**	**SR**	**TR**
Error Notification Domain: UC #18, 21									
AL	—				√				
Monitoring Domain: UC # 1, 3, 16, 17, 25, 26 and UC # 6, 7, 8, 10, 12, 13									
DY[5]			—	√		√	√		
PL				√		√	—		
EC				—					
IF					—				
LQ	√	√		√		—	√	√	√
SR				√	√			—	
TR						√			—
Database Domain:									
DB		—							

14.2 PERFORM SWIT

Purpose

> The purpose of this Activity is to test the software for a specific release.

Definition(s)

Problem Trouble Report (PTR): A **PTR** is a record of a detected problem in either documentation or code. **PTR**s are known by various names, such as Trouble Report (TR), Bug Report (BR), Defect Report (DR), and so on.

Process

Step 1: Perform SWIT

This process is organization-specific. Each organization must fill in the specific Steps for this process.

Step 2: Generate PTRs

PTRs are generated and captured by Category and Domain Teams. Capturing PTRs by Category and Domain Teams enables the detection of a team in trouble and highlights where training and/or support is required.

[5]The acronym DY represents Display_CAT, the Category that owns the _View Classes.

Step 3: Incorporate Changes

Once the development staff addresses the PTRs and makes the code changes, SWIT must incorporate the updated code.

Step 4: Repeat Step 1

SWIT is a recursive process within itself. SWIT is *not* complete until all PTRs have been resolved. The resolution of a PTR means that the test case that caused the generation of the PTR now passes and any other Use Cases that depend on the Use Case (that originally failed) are retested and pass.

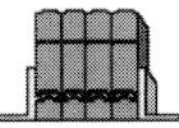

Product(s)

The products of this Activity are a set of PTRs for the build in question.

Phase Transition Criteria

Transition to the next Phase when all PTRs have been resolved. Resolving a PTR means that the test that originally caused the PTR now passes, and any other Use Cases affected by the code changes have been regression tested and *still* pass.

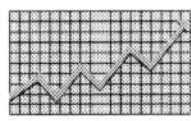

Tracking Progress

Table 14-4 shows the project management spreadsheet updated for this Phase. The number of Use Cases tested as a percentage of the total number of Use Cases requiring testing can be monitored, as well as the number of PTRs generated. Again, these data need to be captured by Category, Domain, and project.

Table 14-4. Project Management Spreadsheet: Phase 14

HCC Project Management Spreadsheet						
Number	**Phase Name**	**Activity**	**Charge Number**	**Product**	**Progress Metric**	**% Weight**
13	**Category Test**		**SW-CT-13**			
13.1		Develop Category Test Strategy	SW-CT-13.1	Category Test Strategy	1 Category test strategy completed	
13.2		Develop Category Test Drivers	SW-CT-13.2	<class>_ctd_#.*ext* Result source file	# Category test drivers and test cases	0.50
13.3		Perform Intra-Category Test	SW-CT-13.3	Result files	# intra-tests run and % passed	0.25
13.4		Perform Inter-Category Test	SW-CT-13.4	Result files	# inter-tests run and % passed	0.25
14	**SWIT**		**SW-UCT-14**			
14.1		Develop SWIT Test Plan	SW-UT-14.1	SWIT Test Plan	1 SWIT Plan completed	0.25
14.3		Perform SWIT Test Plan	SW-UT-14.2	PTR	# PTRs, #test cases #Use Cases tested (% passed)	0.75

PHASE 15

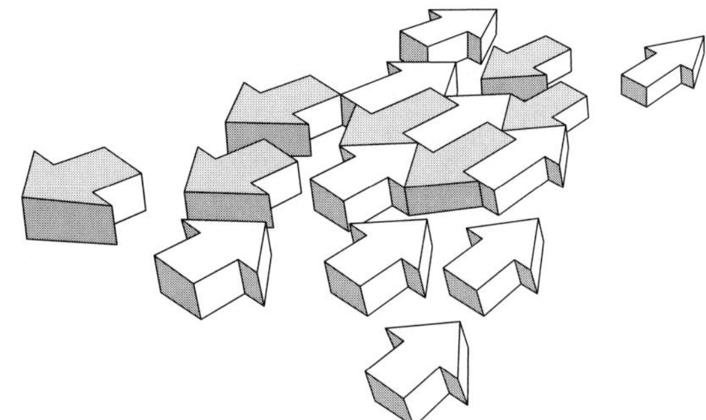

System Integration and Test (SIT)

PHASE OVERVIEW

Figure 15-1 is the diagram for this Phase. SIT basically focuses on testing the functional capability of the software for a specific release, as represented by the Use Cases for that release. The goal of SIT is to ensure that the software system satisfies the requirements as specified by Use Cases in the RTM for the *release* in question.

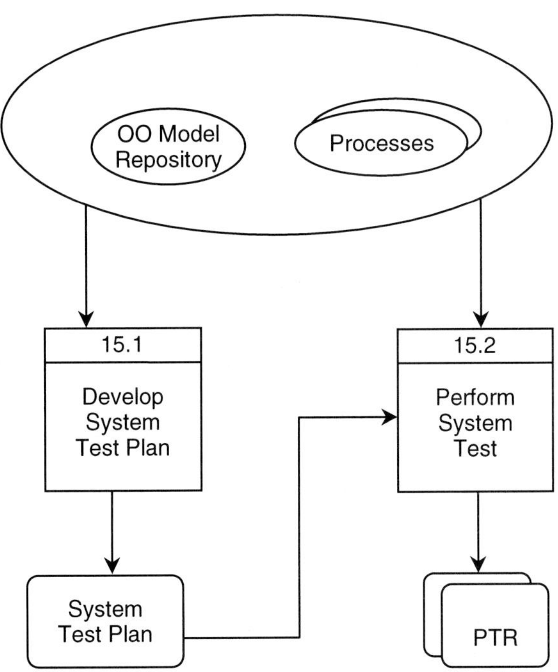

Figure 15-1. SIT Phase Description Diagram

SWIT (Phase 14) focused on integrating *all* Domains on a stand-alone test bed that duplicates, as much as possible, the final *target platform*. SWIT is the first time that *all* the Domains were integrated and tested by an independent software testing organization. Now, in SIT (also referred to as Acceptance Testing), the entire system is tested by the Customer. This testing is done either on a test bed, as in Phase 14, or on the actual environment platform on which the system will be executed. SIT is the last time where actual hardware and software elements *not* previously tested are integrated into the test environment.

15.1 DEVELOP SIT TEST PLAN

Purpose

> The purpose of this Activity is to develop and agree upon the strategy for SIT. The strategy must cover integrating of all domain software, recording test results, reporting bugs, and incorporating fixes. This plan also forms the basis for the acceptance of the system.

Process

Step 1: Establish Order of Use Case Testing

Since the system has already passed SWIT (a requirement for moving into this Phase), the order in which the Use Cases are tested is *not* important. The same order used in SWIT may also be used here, or the Use Cases may be tested in the order in which they appear in the RTM.

In addition to Use Case testing, SIT must include

- Performance testing, where applicable
- Client/Server performance testing.

Step 2: Test Tool Capability

The same test tools used in SWIT should be used in SIT, as any preparation required to use these tools (test drivers, scripts, etc.) has already been done and may possibly be reused.

Step 3: Specify Software to be Integrated

In SWIT, the definition of the actual software to be tested and the specification of Class stubs was explicitly identified. Recall Table 14-1, repeated here as Table 15-1. For SIT, any Class stubs *not* replaced in SWIT need to be replaced with the *actual* in-

Table 15-1. Class Usage for Intra- and Inter-Category Testing, and SWIT

Class Stub Utilization: Intra- and Inter-Category Test and SWIT			
	Intra-Category Testing	**Inter-Category Testing**	**SWIT**
Hardware Interface Classes	Class Stub	Class Stub	Actual Hardware
Foreign Category Classes	Class Stub	Actual Class	Actual Class
COTS/GFS/CFS Interface Classes	Class Stub	Class Stub	Actual Software
Database	Simulate	Actual/Simulated	Actual

terfaces. Note that since SWIT ideally incorporates all of the actual interfaces, there is the possibiliy that no additional interfaces will need to be added for SIT. However, in some organizations, the *live* database is *not* used until SIT.

Step 4: Develop SIT Test Plan

The sample test plan for SWIT (see Figure 14-3) can also be used as a guideline for a SIT Test Plan.

15.2 PERFORM SIT TEST

Purpose

The purpose of this Activity is to test the software for a specific release.

Process

Step 1: Perform SIT

This process is organization-specific. Each organization must fill in the specific Steps for this process.

Step 2: Generate PTRs

PTRs are generated and need to be captured by Domain. Capturing PTRs by Domain facilitates the detection of a team in trouble and highlights where training and/or support is required.

Product(s)

The products of this Activity are a set of PTRs for the release in question.

Phase Transition Criteria

Transition the software to the customer when all PTRs have been resolved. This Phase is iterated until all PTRs have been resolved. There are two issues to consider when resolving PTRs. First, a change in the code to fix a PTR will result in testing the new code from Class Test, Phase 12, through to SWIT, Phase 14, and regression testing the entire system (SIT). Second, with customer approval, a PTR can be resolved by noting that it will be addressed in the next release of the system. This action makes the PTR a new requirement for Phase 17, Maintenance.

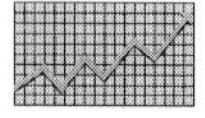

Tracking Progress

Table 15-2 shows the project management spreadsheet updated for this Phase. The number of Use Cases tested as a percentage of the total number of Use Cases requiring testing can be monitored, as well as the number of PTRs generated. Again, these data need to be captured by Domain.

Table 15-2. Project Management Spreadsheet: Phase 15

HCC Project Management Spreadsheet						
Number	**Phase Name**	**Activity**	**Charge Number**	**Product**	**Progress Metric**	**% Weight**
13	**Category Test**		**SW-CT-13**			
13.1		Develop Category Test Strategy	SW-CT-13.1	Category Test Strategy	1 Category test strategy completed	
13.2		Develop Category Test Drivers	SW-CT-13.2	<class>_ctd_#.*ext* Result source file	# Category test drivers and test cases	0.50
13.3		Perform Intra-Category Test	SW-CT-13.3	Result files	# intra-tests run and % passed	0.25
13.4		Perform Inter-Category Test	SW-CT-13.4	Result files	# Inter-tests run and % passed	0.25
14	**SWIT**		**SW-UCT-14**			
14.1		Develop SWIT Test Plan	SW-UT-14.1	SWIT Test Plan	1 SWIT Plan completed	0.25
14.3		Perform SWIT Test Plan	SW-UT-14.2	PTR	# PTRs, #test cases #Use Cases tested (% passed)	0.75
15	**System Test**		**SYS-TST-15**			
15.1		Develop System Test Plan	SYS-TST-15.1	System Test Plan	1 System Test Plan completed	0.25
15.2		Perform System Test	SYS-TST-15.2	PTRs	# PTRs, #test cases, #Use Cases tested (% passed)	0.75

PHASE 16

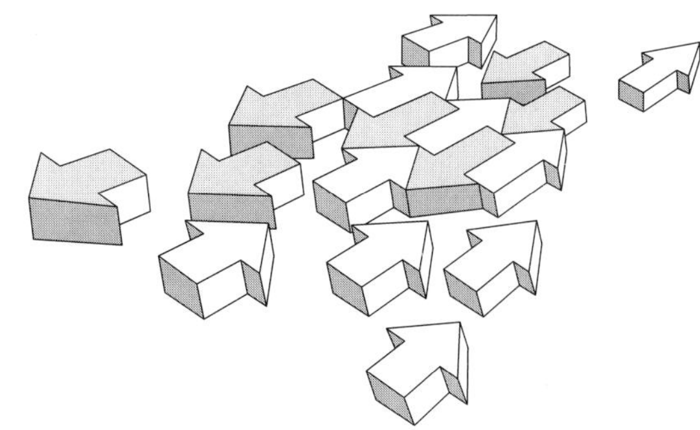

Requirements Trace

PHASE OVERVIEW

The system development process presented in this book began with Phase 1, Requirements Engineering, which established a set of requirements, both hardware and software, for a system development effort. These requirements, recorded as entries in an RTM, were next categorized (hardware, software, performance, and so on) and allocated to a specific build and release. The set of software functional requirements for a build were then migrated to Use Cases for development. Phases 1 through 15 defined the Activities and provided examples of the work products involved to produce the software to satisfy the requirements.

This Phase introduces a vehicle for tracing, or mapping, the original requirements to the implementation entities in the OO model. This Phase also identifies the source code files that are responsible for, or participate in, satisfying each requirement. Figure 16-1 depicts the Activities for this Phase. As the figure shows, there are two kinds of mappings:

- Forward Requirements Trace (FRT)
- Reverse Requirements Trace (RRT)

The FRT starts with an entry in the RTM (a Use Case) and maps it to the Categories that participate in the requirement, then to the specific Classes within the Categories that participate, then to the specific Methods in the Classes, and finally to the actual source code files. Thus, given a software requirement as an entry in the RTM, the FRT identifies the entities, both OO model and source code files, that are required to satisfy that requirement.

The RRT begins with a Method in a Class and traces the Method *back* to the set of requirements that utilize the Method. Thus, given a change in a Method, the RRT identifies the entities, both OO model and source code files, that are affected by that change.

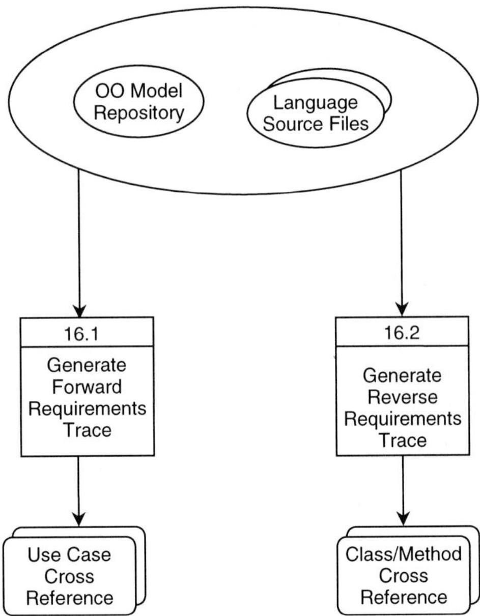

Figure 16-1. Requirements Trace Phase Description Diagram

The selected CASE tool should support this Phase, but in reality, none do at this point in time. Consequently, the FRT and RRT must be produced by developing scripts that extract the information from the project's repository.

Once the ability exists to extract this information from the repository, the information can be used during development, as well as during Phase 17, Maintenance. During development, the information is used to estimate the impact of new builds and releases, as well as the impact of new requirements requested by the customer. Once the system is delivered, this information is vital to the maintenance activities of fixing bugs and adding new capabilities.

To promote better understanding of this Phase, examples are embedded *within* the discussion of a Step in the Process section.

16.1 GENERATE FORWARD REQUIREMENTS TRACE (FRT)

Purpose

> The purpose of this Activity is to produce a list of entities, both OO model entities and source code entities, that participate in the satisfaction of a requirement.

The real benefit of this Activity is that given either an error in the implementation of a Use Case or a requested change in a Use Case, the FRT identifies all the entities that are involved in the satisfaction of the Use Case, which of course are the entities that are impacted by any change.

Process

Step 1: Decide Whether to Include Process and Controller Classes

This issue centers around whether or not to include the Process and Controller Classes in the FRT. Process Classes are the implementation of the executable code. The PAD, PCADs, and PID represent the static and dynamic process architecture. This information can be traced in the ID corresponding to the Use Case. Including the Process Classes in the FRT does *not* appear to yield any significant benefits. On the other hand, the Controller Classes provide information with respect to Class collaboration. This information is exactly what the FRT is attempting to capture. Consequently, the Controller Classes *are* included in the FRT in the following Steps. Of course, these decisions are project-specific.

Step 2: Identify the Categories that Participate in the Requirements

Initiate the FRT Matrix by capturing the software functional requirements entries from the RTM. Table 16-1 shows the primary step in creating an FRT Matrix. Note that for each Use Case, the Categories that participate in the satisfaction of the Use Case are indicated. This information is extracted from the IDs (UML Sequence Diagrams) that are stored in the repository. Recall that each software functional requirement is migrated to a Use Case, and that there is one Scenario per Use Case which is reflected in one primary ID (UML Sequence Diagram). To summarize, the ID reflects the Classes that participate in the Use Case. Finally, recall that each Class is owned by a Category. Consequently, it is easy to extract the Categories that participate in the ID (or requirement). The acronyms for each Category are used in the table to save space.

Another alternative is to list the information textually per Use Case, as is shown in Table 16-2.

Step 3: Identify the Classes within the Participating Categories

This Step can be accomplished with the same ease with which the previous Step was accomplished. Recall that the Classes on the ID are used to extract the Category information required for Step 1. In this Step, many matrices are produced (one matrix for each Category) that specify *which* Classes in a Category participate in the satisfaction of the requirement. Of course, only those requirements which the Category supports need to be included in these matrices. Table 16-3 shows a sample matrix for the `Sensor_CAT`. Looking back at Table 16-1, the `Sensor_CAT` is only involved in Use Cases 1, 3, and 25; consequently, only these rows of the original RTM need to be included in this part of the FRT.

Table 16-1. HCC FRT: Requirements to Category

		HCC FRT: Uses Cases to Category									
Entry #	**Use Case Name**	**AL_CAT**	**DB_CAT**	**DY_CAT**	**EC_CAT**	**IF_CAT**	**LQ_CAT**	**PN_CAT**	**SR_CAT**	**RU_CAT**	**TR_CAT**
1	UC1_SW_Monitors_Living_Quarters	√	√	√	√	√	√	√	√		√
2	n/a										
3	UC3_Timer_Triggers_Living_Quarter _Sensor				√	√	√		√		√
4	n/a										
5	n/a										
6	UC6_SW_Lights_Window			√				√			
7	UC7_SW_ Flashes_Window_2X			√				√			√
8	UC8_SW_ Flashes_Window_4X			√				√			√
9	n/a										
10	UC10_SW_Displays_Panel			√				√			
11	n/a										
12	UC12_SW_Displays_Annunciator			√				√			
13	UC13_SW_Displays_Window			√				√			
14	n/a										
15	Duplicate (UC16)										
16	UC16_Operator_Updates_Nominal_ Values_In_DB		√	√	√		√				
17	UC17_Operator_Updates_Living_ Quarter_Nominal_Value		√	√	√		√				
18	UC18_SW_Sounds_Alarm	√				√					
19	Duplicate (UCs 7 and 8)										
20	Duplicate (UCs 18 and 19)										
21	UC21_Operator_Turns_Off_Alarm	√		√		√					
22	UC22_Operator_Turns_Off_Window			√				√			
23											
24											
25	UC25_Operator_Resets_SEM	√	√	√	√	√	√	√	√	√	√
26	UC26_Operator_Sets_Living_ Quarter_State		√	√			√	√			

Table 16-2. FRT to Categories: Alternative Approach

Use Case 1: FRT to Categories			
√	Alarm_CAT	√	Living_Quarter_CAT
√	Database_CAT	√	Panel_CAT
√	View_CAT		Reusable_CAT
√	Environmental_Condition_CAT	√	Sensor_CAT
√	IF_CAT	√	Timer_CAT

Looking at Table 16-3, it is clear that every Class in the `Sensor_CAT` participates in each of the three requirements. This is *not* always the case. Examine Table 16-4, which shows a trace for the classes owned by the `Living_Quarter_CAT`. Table 16-4 indicates that the `Deviation` Class only participates in Uses Cases 1 and 25. The `Deviation` Class is *not* required for those Use Cases that just act on the `Living_Quarter` Class, yet have nothing to do with the actual calculation of the deviation.

An alternative is to add the Classes as columns to the initial FRT, Table 16-1. This approach requires only one matrix. On a real project, one FRT matrix gets quite large!

Table 16-3. FRT to Classes per Category: Sensor_CAT

FRT: Use Cases to Classes: Sensor_CAT					
Entry #	**Use Case Name**	**Air_Pressure_ Sensor**	**Oxygen_ Sensor**	**Sensor**	**Temperature_ Sensor**
1	UC1_SW_Monitors_Living_Quarters	√	√	√	√
3	UC3_Timer_Triggers_Living_Quarter _Sensor	√	√	√	√
25	UC25_Operator_Resets_SEM	√	√	√	√

Table 16-4. FRT to Classes per Category: Living_Quarter_CAT

FRT: Use Cases to Classes: Living_Quarter_CAT					
Entry #	**Use Case Name**	**Deviation**	**Hall**	**Living_Quarter**	**Room**
1	UC1_SW_Monitors_Living_Quarters	√	√	√	√
3	UC3_Timer_Triggers_Living_Quarter _Sensor		√	√	√
16	UC16_Operator_Updates_Nominal_ Values_In_DB		√	√	√
17	UC17_Operator_Updates_Living_ Quarter_Nominal_Value		√	√	√
25	UC25_Operator_Resets_SEM	√	√	√	√
26	UC26_Operator_Sets_Living_ Quarter_State		√	√	√

Step 4: Identify the Methods within the Participating Class

Once again, this Step is easily accomplished. The Methods are identified as Messages on the ID. Add the Method information to the same FRT Matrix by once again augmenting Table 16-1, or provide a separate matrix for *each* Class. The choice is up to each Project Team. For the SEM, the decision was made to provide one matrix for each Class. Table 16-5 shows the trace of the requirements to the Methods in the `Living_Quarter` Class in the `Living_Quarter_CAT`.

Step 5: Identify the Source Code Files that Participate

With an appropriate naming convention defined, source code files are easily extracted from the source code directory. For example, the `Living_Quarter` Class source code is found in the `code` subdirectory of the `/src` directory for the Category, specifically in `/src/lq/code`. The path names to the files are: `/src/lq/code/lq_lq.h` and `/src/lq/code/lq_lq.cpp`. This information can now be added to the appropriate matrices.

Pragmatic Project Issues

Need Repository Knowledge

To perform this Activity, knowledge of the structure of the repository is needed to enable the script writers to generate the necessary reports. Alternatively, the CASE tool vendor needs to provide appropriate browsing and report generation capability.

Staff Hours are Required

Staff hours are required to learn the repository structure and to generate and analyze the scripts. Project Teams are typically under-staffed, but it is hard to imagine a project succeeding without staff hours to generate the required scripts.

Table 16-5. FRT to Methods per Class: Living_Quarter Class

FRT: Use Cases to Methods: Living_Quarter Class: Living_Quarter_CAT						
Entry #	**Use Case Name**	**Change State**	**Create**	**Current State**	**Deviation**	**Update Value**
1	UC1_SW_Monitors_ Living_Quarters			√	√	
3	UC3_Timer_Triggers_ Living_Quarter_Sensor					
16	UC16_Operator_Updates_ Nominal_Values_In_DB					√
17	UC17_Operator_Updates_ Living_Quarter_Nominal_Value					√
25	UC25_Operator_Resets_SEM			√	√	
26	UC26_Operator_Sets_Living_ Quarter_State	√		√		

16.2 GENERATE REVERSE REQUIREMENTS TRACE (RRT)

Purpose

> The purpose of this Activity is to produce a trace so that if a Method changes in its implementation, the impact of that change can be identified.

If a Method should change within the OO model, or even within the source code, it is important to identify the entities affected by that change for the purpose of regression testing. The entities that are affected at the highest level of abstraction are the *initial requirements* that utilize the Method in question. Between the Method and the requirements there are the *Classes* that are affected (Classes that call the Method), the *Category* that owns the Classes that call the Method, and so on up the chain. This information is vital to understanding the effect of a change in a Method.

Process

Step 1: Initiate Category/Class RRT

The preferred approach is to produce one matrix per Class. For each Class, establish a matrix that contains the *public* Methods as columns of the matrix. The rows of the matrix are the Classes that utilize the services of the Class in question, organized by Category. Stated differently, view the Class in question as a Supplier Class, and the rows of the matrix as the clients of the Class, listed by Category. Table 16-6 depicts the start of an RRT for the `Living_Quarter` Class. The table clearly shows that *any* change in *any* Method impacts the `LivingQuarterController`, and therefore *all* Use Cases managed by that controller.

Step 2: Add Use Cases

Table 16-7, augmenting the previous RRT shown in Table 16-6, shows one way that the Use Cases are included in the trace. The Use Cases involved are simply added to the appropriate grid in the matrix. Table 16-8 shows an alternative mechanism, by which the clients for each Method of a Class are listed by Class. Then of course, these individual matrices can be collected and presented by Category.

Table 16-6. RRT: Living_Quarter Class: Methods to Classes

	RRT: LivingQuarter Class: Methods to Classes				
	Change State()	**Create()**	**Current State()**	**Deviation()**	**Update()**
Living_Quarter_CAT					
LivingQuarterController	√	√	√	√	√

Table 16-7. RRT: Living_Quarter Class Methods to Use Cases

	RRT: Living Quarter Class: Living_Quarter_CAT				
	ChangeState()	**Create()**	**CurrentState()**	**Deviation()**	**Update()**
Living_Quarter_CAT					
LivingQuarterController	**UC26**	**UC1**	**UC1, UC25, UC26**	**UC1, UC25**	

Pragmatic Project Issues

Format Not Crucial

The format in which the information is displayed is *not* crucial. The content *is* crucial to help define regression testing requirements. Please do *not* spend time discussing the format! Furthermore, it is wise to let the individuals who write the scripts provide input to the format so that their job is *not* unnecessarily complex. Again, what is important is the content!

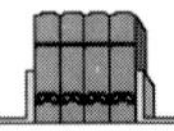

Product(s)

The products produced during this Phase are a set of matrices (or one) that trace a Use Case forward to the Categories, to the Classes within the Categories, to the Methods of the Classes within the Categories, and finally to the source code files that participate in

Table 16-8. RRT: Living_Quarter Class Methods to Use Cases: An Alternative Approach

- **LivingQuarter::ChangeState()**
  - *Class Clients:*
    - Living_Quarter_CAT:
      - LivingQuarterController
  - *Use Cases Served:*
    - UC26
- **LivingQuarter::Create()**
  - *Class Clients:*
    - Living_Quarter_CAT:
      - LivingQuarterController
  - *Use Cases Served:*
    - UC1
- **LivingQuarter::CurrentState()**
  - *Class Clients:*
    - Living_Quarter_CAT:
      - LivingQuarterController
  - *Use Cases Served:*
    - UC1, 25, and 26

. . .

the satisfaction of the Use Case (FRT). The products also include matrices that traces a Method of a Class to the clients of the Method, specifically to the Classes and Categories that utilize the services of that Method. Finally, this backward trace is completed by tracing back to the Use Cases that utilize the Method (RRT).

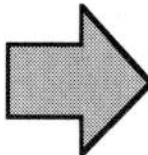

Phase Transition Criteria

This is a Phase that can start concurrently with Phase 1 and continue throughout the lifetime of a project. Consequently, a discussion of Phase Transition is inappropriate.

PART VIII

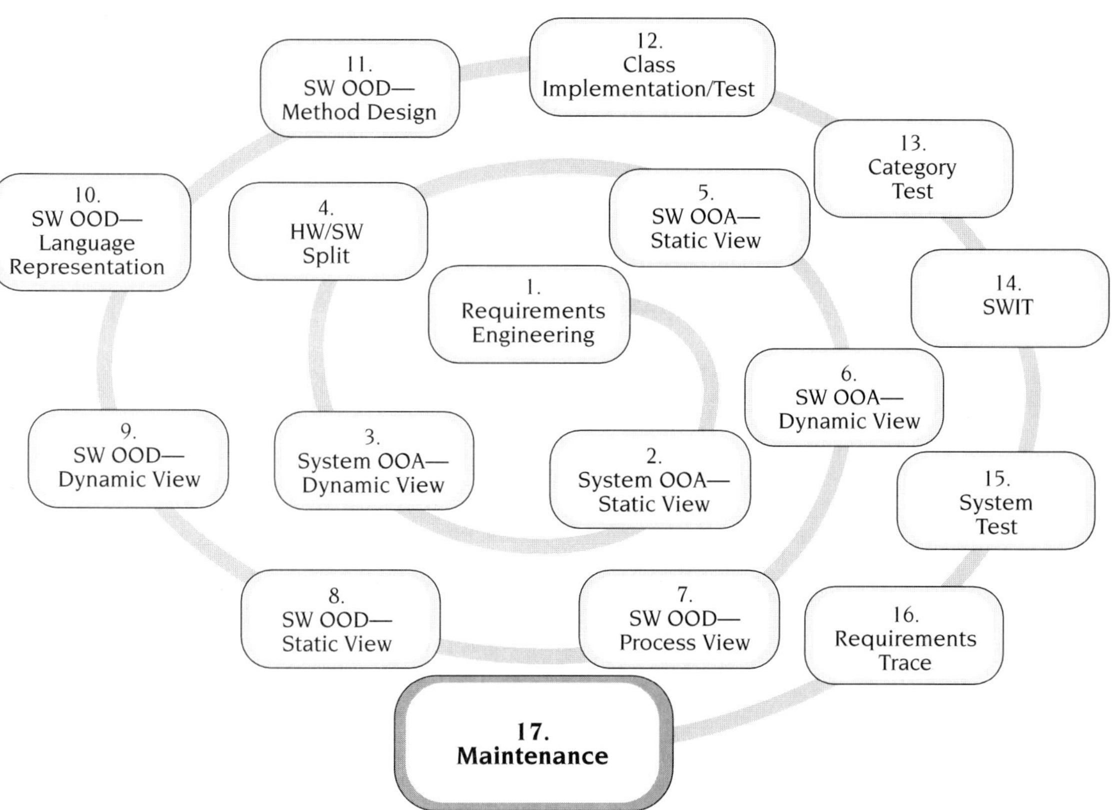

Post Delivery

PHASE 17

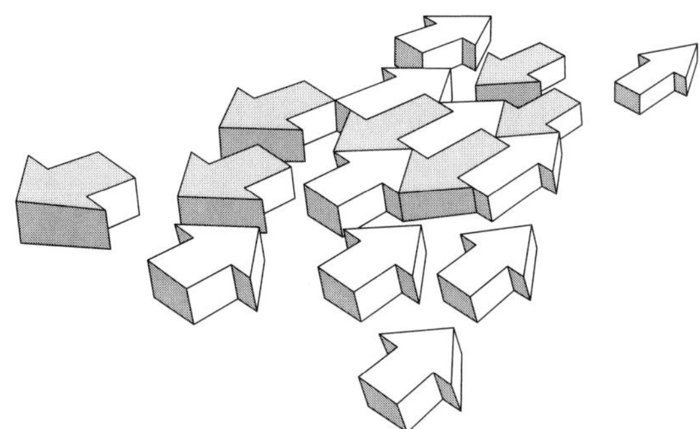

Maintenance

PHASE OVERVIEW

Here is where the benefits of all the previous work are reaped!

As shown by Figure 17-1, this phase is nothing more than iterating through the previous 16 development Phases. Table 17-1 summarizes the OO products produced and in what Phase they were initially created (C) and in what Phase they were *explicitly* updated (U). Here is how Table 17-1 can be used. If a new requirement is identi-

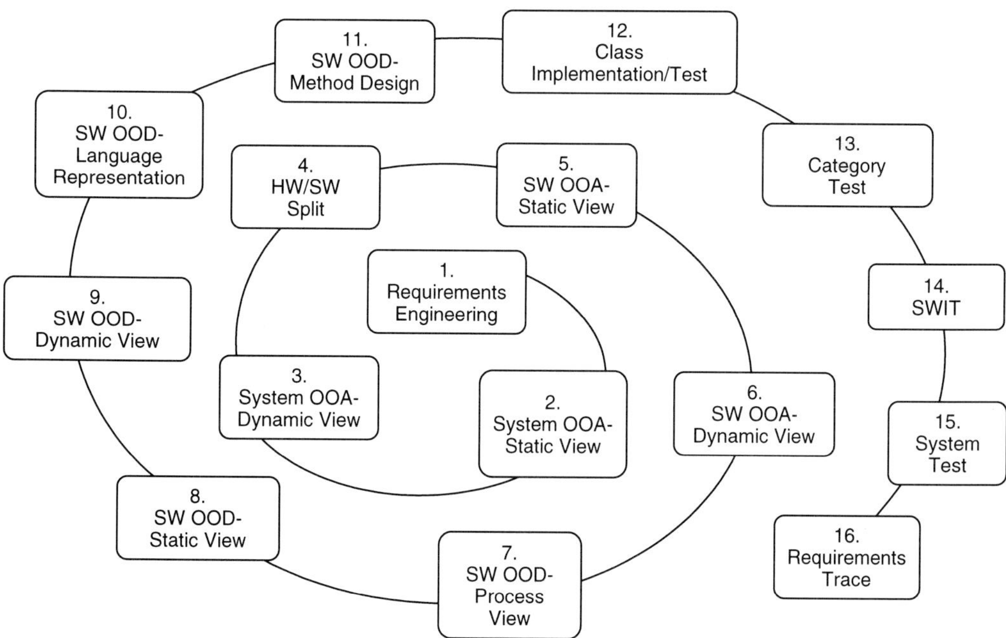

Figure 17-1. Maintenance Phase Description Diagram

Table 17-1. OO Product Summary

Phase	Phase Title	RTM	Category List	Scenario	SCD	CID	CCD	ID	PAD	PCAD	PID	Language Design Files	PDL	Source Files	Test Driver Files	Test Results Files	Use Case Design Worksheet	PTR
1	Requirements Engineering	C																
2	System OOA–Static	U	C	C	C													
3	System OOA–Dynamic					C												
4	HW/SW						C											
5	SW OOA–Static						C											
6	SW OOA–Dynamic							C										
7	Process								C	C	C							
8	SW OOD–Static						U											
9	SW OOD–Dynamic							U										
10	Language											C						
11	Method												C					
12	Implementation													C	C	C		
13	Category Test														C	C		
14	SWIT														C	C	C	C
15	SIT														C	C	C	C
16	Requirements Trace																	

Note: All products are continually updated. Only when the process calls out for explicit updates to a product is the letter U entered into this table.

fied, the RTM is the product that is affected (because it maintains the requirements); therefore, the maintenance process *must* begin at Phase 1 and iterate through all the remaining Phases. For example, if the requirement to log all Operator requests is added to the SEM, Phase 1 is where the maintenance process would begin. On the other hand, if a range of values for an Attribute is modified[1], the CCD and CS are impacted and the maintenance process begins at Phase 5. For a *specific* example, if the lower bound of the range of allowable temperatures for a living quarter was to change from 50.0 degrees to 65.0 degrees, both the Environmental_Condition_CAT_CCD and CS for the `Temperature_Environmental_Condition` Class would change. Phase 5 would then become the starting point for the maintenance process and all succeeding Phases would be analyzed for impact. To summarize, Table 17-1 provides a starting point for identification of the beginning of the maintenance process.

For this Phase a new requirement is to be implemented; specifically, the customer's request to log all Operator requests. All IDs in this Phase are in a generic format.

17.1 REQUIREMENTS ENGINEERING

Because there is a new requirement for the SEM, specifically to log all Operator requests, the maintenance process begins at Phase 1. This newly agreed-upon requirement must be added to the RTM. Table 17-2 shows the updated RTM with the new entry, Entry 27, with its type specified as software (SW), its allocation to Build 5, and its corresponding Use Case.

17.2 SYSTEM OOA

Upon analyzing the new requirement, it is clear that none of the existing Categories are appropriate for claiming its ownership. Consequently, a new Category is introduced, named `Log_CAT`. Table 17-3 shows the RTM updated once again, this time to reflect the allocation of the requirement to the `Log_CAT`, while Table 17-4 shows the updated Category List and the assignment of `Log_CAT` to a new domain, a logging domain.

Because `Log_CAT` is a new Category which is an application-specific Category, the SCD must also be updated. Figure 17-2 shows the updated SCD with the `Log_CAT` added. The `Log_CAT` has only one association, the association with the `Operator_CAT`. This was a very easy modification because the `Log_CAT` does *not currently* interface with any other Category. The original solution is very flexible and can easily accommodate a new requirement—one, for example, that might require any database activity to be logged as well. If this were the case, only one association would need to be added—from the `DB_CAT` to the `Log_CAT`.

Finally, Figure 17-3 shows the new Scenario created by the Systems organization to support the Use Case.

[1]This assumes that the range of allowable values did not appear in the RTM.

Table 17-2. Updated RTM: Requirement Added

Entry #	Para #	HCC Problem Statement	Type	Build #	Use Case Name	Class	Method	Category
25	-	Because the Operator can reset the nominal values in the DB, he/she needs to be able to reset the SEM to operate on those new values.	SW, DR	B4	UC25_Operator_ Resets_SEM			
26	-	The SEM does not need to monitor unoccupied living quarters, so the Operator can set living quarters to occupied/unoc- cupied to enable the SEM to operate more efficiently.	SW, DR,	B4	UC26_Operator_Sets_ Living_Quarter_State			Living- Quarter_CAT
27	Letter-Dated xx/xx/96	All Operator requests shall be captured in a message log, recording the date, time, and action requested.	SW	B5	UC27_Log_All_Operator_ Actions_In_Log			

Table 17-3. Updated RTM:Category Allocation

Entry #	Para #	HCC Problem Statement	Type	Build #	Use Case Name	Class	Method	Category
25	-	Because the Operator can reset the nominal values in the DB, he/she needs to be able to reset the SEM to operate on those new values.	SW, DR	B4	UC25_Operator_ Resets_SEM			
26	-	The SEM does not need to monitor unoc- cupied living quarters, so the Operator can set living quarters to occupied/unoccupied to enable the SEM to operate more efficiently.	SW, DR,	B4	UC26_Operator_Sets_ Living_Quarter_State			Living- Quarter_CAT
27	Letter-Dated xx/xx/96	All Operator requests shall be captured in a message log, recording the date, time, and action requested.	SW	B5	UC27_Log_All_Operator_ Actions_In_Log			LOG_CAT

Table 17-4. Updated Category List

HCC Category Name	Abbreviation	Domain	SME
Alarm_CAT	AL	Error Notification	Paul M.
DB_CAT	DB	Database	Peter H.
Display_CAT	DY	Monitor	Lucy J.
Environmental_Condition_CAT	EC	Monitor	Jack G.
IF_CAT	IF		
Interim_CAT	IM		
Living_Quarter_CAT	LQ	Monitor	Jack G.
Log_CAT	***LG***	***Log***	***Ivan F.***
Operator_CAT	OP	Monitor	Jack G.
Panel_CAT	PL	Monitor	Jack G.
Process_CAT	PS		
Sensor_CAT	SR	Monitor	Jack G.
Reusable_CAT	RU		
Timer_CAT	TR	Monitor	Jack G.
View_CAT	DY	Monitor	Jack G.

17.3 SYSTEM OOA–DYNAMIC VIEW

Only those CIDs that involve the `Operator_CAT` or `Operator` Class must be modified to reflect the logging of the Operator's actions and a new CID must be produced for the new Use Case. Here is where scripts that browse the repository can help enormously. As it turns out, the CIDs for Use Cases 16, 17, 22, 25, and 26 are the only CIDs affected. For the rest of this Phase, the examples focus only on Use Case 16, Operator_Updates_Nominal Values_In_Database.

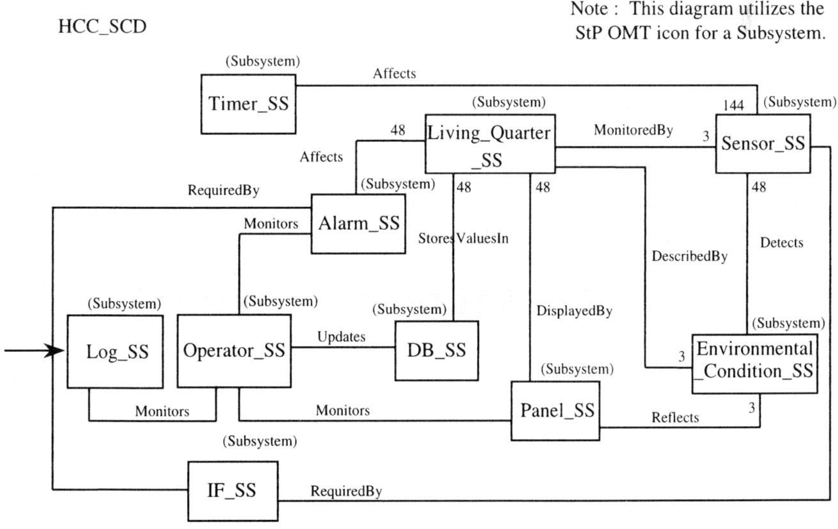

Figure 17-2. Updated SCD : Log_SS Added

Use Case 27: SW_Log_Operator_Actions

Overview:

This Use Case logs all operator requests to a flat file. The file is named "oplog.txt" and it is to be opened upon system boot, and closed only when the application fails or is exited. The log remains open while the application (SEM) is executing.

Preconditions:

1. The SEM is executing.
2. "oplog.txt" is open.

Scenario:

Action	Software Reaction
1. Create a message	1. Initiate a message with text representing one of the following: • Update_all selected • Reset selected • Window off selected • Update one lq selected • Alarm off selected
2. Date/Time-stamp the message	2. Message date/time-stamped
3. Add the message to "oplog.txt"	3. Message added to the file

Scenario Notes:

The log is to be maintained with the last message first in the file. Each message in the file should have a unique number assigned to it.

If the file is too full to accept a new message, delete the first 100 messages in the file.

Post Conditions:

1. The number of messages in the file is one more than before.

Required GUI:

None

Use Cases Utilized:

None

Exceptions:

None

Timing Constraints:

None

Figure 17-3. Scenario for Use Case 27

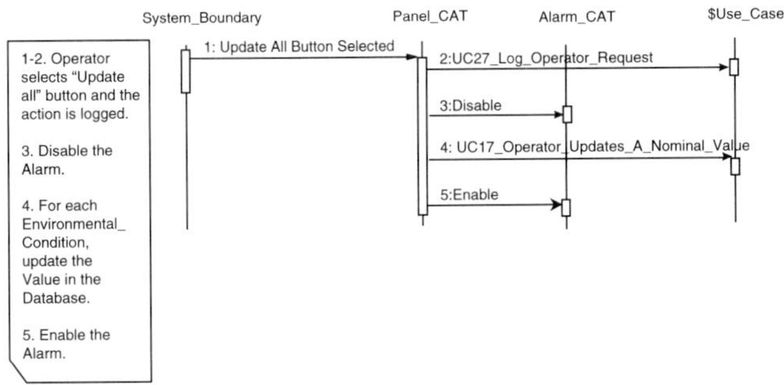

Figure 17-4. Updated CID : UC16

Figure 17-4 depicts the CID for Use Case 16, updated to reflect the new requirement, while Figure 17-5 shows the new CID for Use Case 27.

17.4 HARDWARE/SOFTWARE SPLIT

The decision as to the partitioning of the Category is also easy—the `Log_CAT` is *all* software. Consequently, Figure 17-6 shows the initiation of the Log_CAT_CCD, with a `Log` Class at the root, representing a placeholder for future types of logs.

17.5 SOFTWARE OOA–STATIC VIEW

During the analysis of the Scenario, it is clear that the `Log` Class requires the following Methods: `Open()`, `Close()`, `Add()`, `Delete()`, and `CurrentNumberOfMessages()`. It is also clear from the Scenario that there is a `Message` Class.

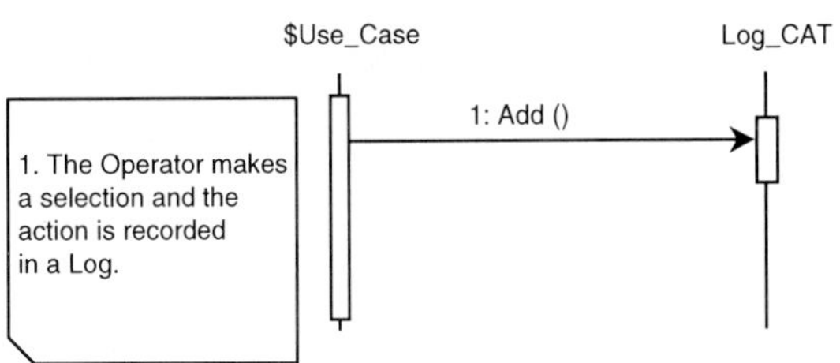

Figure 17-5. UC27_Log_Operator_Action CID

Log_CAT_CCD

Log

Figure 17-6. Initial Log_CAT_CCD

The question now becomes whether there needs to be a `Message_CAT` as well. One solution is to add a `Message_CAT`, anticipating that there may be other kinds of messages in the future, for example, error messages. Establishing the `Message_CAT` now will make life easier in the future and provide a common look for all Messages in the system. The other approach is to simply create one `Message` Class in the `Log_CAT` and hope that the Message requirements do *not* grow. This is the easy way out and will *not* be as flexible in its accommodation of new requirements. The approach taken by this book is to add a `Message_CAT`, establish an inheritance hierarchy—all to protect the design approach currently utilized.

Figure 17-7 represents the Category List updated once again, to reflect the addition of `Message_CAT`.

Upon analyzing the Scenario, the developer had several questions and documented the following answers to those questions as the annotations for the Use Case, as shown in Figure 17-8.

The annotations indicate the necessity for a `Renumber()` Method for the `Log` Class, as well a requirement to have one date time stamp. Figure 17-9 reflects the updated Log_CAT_CCD and Figure 17-10 reflects the new Message_CAT_CCD. Both

HCC Category Name	Abbreviation	Domain	SME
Alarm_CAT	AL	Error Notification	Paul M.
DB_CAT	DB	Database	Peter H.
Environmental_Condition_CAT	EC	Monitor	Jack G.
IF_CAT	IF		
Interim_CAT	IM		
Living_Quarter_CAT	LQ	Monitor	Jack G.
Log_CAT	LG	Log	Ivan F.
Message_CAT	***MS***	***Log***	***Ivan F.***
Operator_CAT	OP	Monitor	Jack G.
Panel_CAT	PL	Monitor	Jack G.
Process_CAT	PS		
Sensor_CAT	SR	Monitor	Jack G.
Reusable_CAT	RU		
Timer_CAT	TR	Monitor	Jack G.

Figure 17-7. Updated Category List

Q1. There is only one log for recording Operator actions?

A1. True.

Q2. Each message in the log will consist of the date and time of the message, as well as one of the indicated text strings listed in the scenario and that is all?

A2. No, each message must also have a unique number associated with it.

Q3. The reason each message has a unique number is because of purging the first 100 messages in the file if the log is full . . . which means that the messages will need to be renumbered if the delete occurs.

A3. True.

Q4. The log file would benefit from a date/time stamp for its creation.

A4. Good idea, let's do it.

Q5. Do the values for the environmental conditions entered by the Operator get recorded?

A5. No, just the fact that the Operator requested a specific GUI is what needs to be recorded.

Figure 17-8. Annotations to Use Case 27

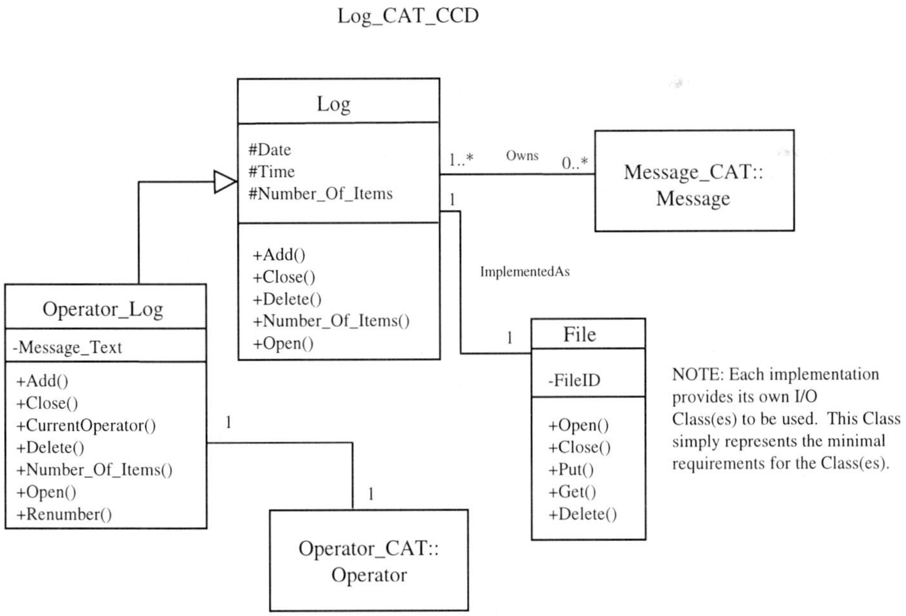

Figure 17-9. Log_CAT_CCD after OOA : UML Notation

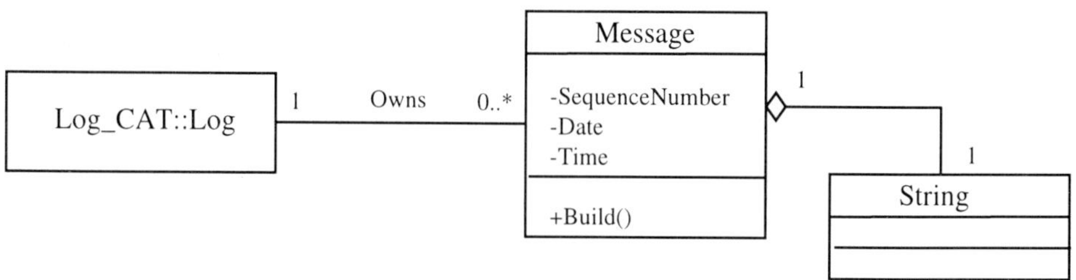

Figure 17-10. Message_CAT_CCD after OOA : UML Notation

figures are in UML notation. A decision was made *not* to initiate an inheritance hierarchy for the `Message` Class because the SEM is *not* a very complex system and it is envisioned that any messages would simply be text with a date/timestamp. On a more complex system however, a `Message` inheritance hierarchy is advised.

The View_CAT_CCD needs updating to reflect an association with the `Operator_Log` Class in the `Log_CAT` and the `Message` Class in the `Message_CAT`. Here is a case where the actual association identified in the SCD is lost when migrating to OOA. This is okay and indeed happens on occasion.

The CSs for the new Classes need to be completed. STDs are *not* deemed necessary for these new Classes. Finally, the SCD needs updating again to reflect the new Category, `Message_CAT`, and its association with the `Log_CAT`. Figure 17-11 reflects the updated SCD with the addition of the `Message_CAT`. If the `Message_CAT` is made a *child* Category of the `Log_CAT`, then it would appear in the Category List as a child Category of the `Log_CAT` in a separate column and would *not* be included on the SCD.

17.6 SOFTWARE OOA–DYNAMIC VIEW

The refinement of the ID for Use Case 16 during OOA is reflected in Figure 17-12. Implementing the refinement is relatively easy as all that needs to be done is to reference the new Use Case in the ID. The message sequence numbers change, if originally included[2], therefore the notes also change.

[2]This is an option on many CASE tools.

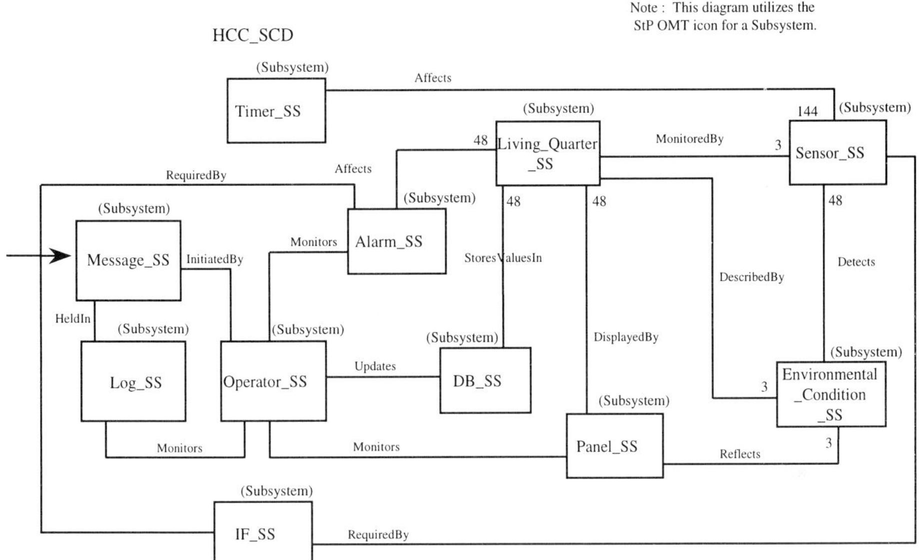

Figure 17.11. SCD Updated with Message_SS

The refinement of the CID, yielding the ID for Use Case 27, is shown in Figure 17-13. The figure is self-explanatory. Pay attention to the `Delete()` Method, which is conceived as being called internally by the Class when the file is full.

17.7 SOFTWARE OOD–PROCESS VIEW

The logging process can either be embedded in the `Display_Persistent_Process` (because selection of a _View Class initiates the logging) or it can exist as its own process. For this book, the idea of adding a *new* process is appealing to show how easy the updates are to the previously developed PAD, PCADs, and PID. The refined PAD (Figure 17-14) indicates that the message logging process is indeed a persistent process and will execute on the processor used for displaying the GUI. Having the log process and log file on the same processor (the Pentium processor) keeps interprocessor communication to a minimum.

The PCAD for the new process (Figure 17-15) shows that the new process requires all the new Classes in both the `Log_CAT` and `Message_CAT` to execute. None of the other PCADs need modification.

Finally, the updated PID (Figure 17-16) indicates that the `Log_Persistent_Process`, is under the control of the `Display_Persistent_Process`, which

UC16_Operator_Updates_Nominal_Values_In_DB_ID

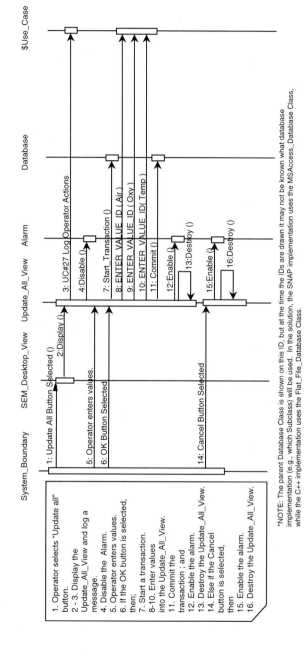

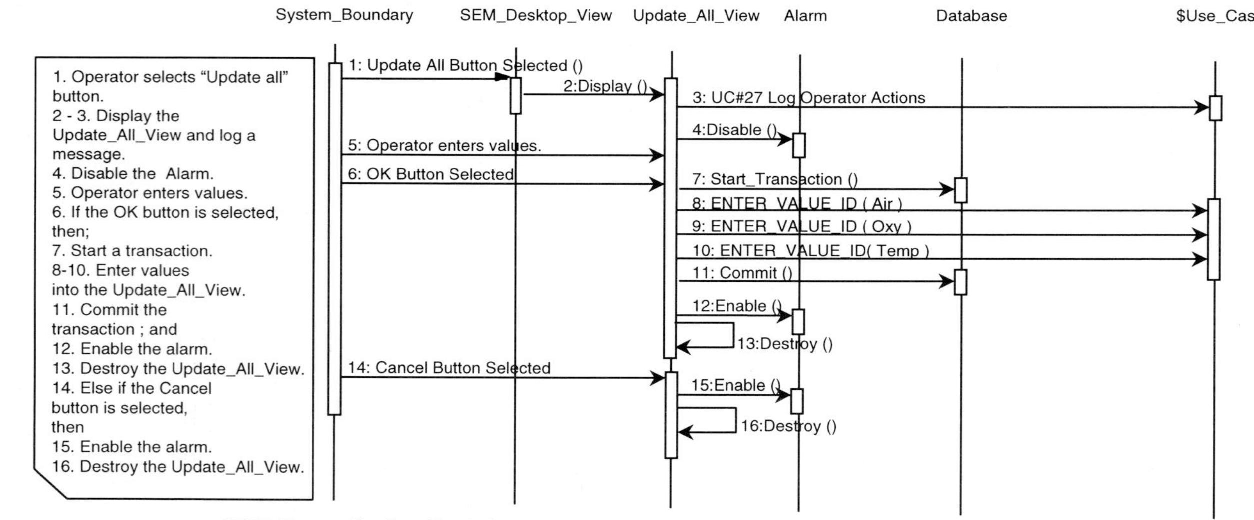
System_Boundary
SEM_Desktop_View
Update_All_View
Alarm
Database
$Use_Case
1. Operator selects "Update all" button.
2 - 3. Display the Update_All_View and log a message.
4. Disable the Alarm.
5. Operator enters values.
6. If the OK button is selected, then;
7. Start a transaction.
8-10. Enter values into the Update_All_View.
11. Commit the transaction ; and
12. Enable the alarm.
13. Destroy the Update_All_View.
14. Else if the Cancel button is selected, then
15. Enable the alarm.
16. Destroy the Update_All_View.
1: Update All Button Selected ()
2:Display ()
3: UC#27 Log Operator Actions
4:Disable ()
5: Operator enters values.
6: OK Button Selected
7: Start_Transaction ()
8: ENTER_VALUE_ID (Air)
9: ENTER_VALUE_ID (Oxy)
10: ENTER_VALUE_ID(Temp)
11: Commit ()
12:Enable ()
13:Destroy ()
14: Cancel Button Selected
15:Enable ()
16:Destroy ()

*NOTE: The parent Database Class is shown on this ID, but at the time the IDs are drawn it may not be known what database implementation (e.g., which Subclass) will be used. In the solution, the SNAP implementation uses the MSAccess_Database Class, while the C++ implementation uses the Flat_File_Database Class.

Figure 17-12. Updated UC16 ID after OOA

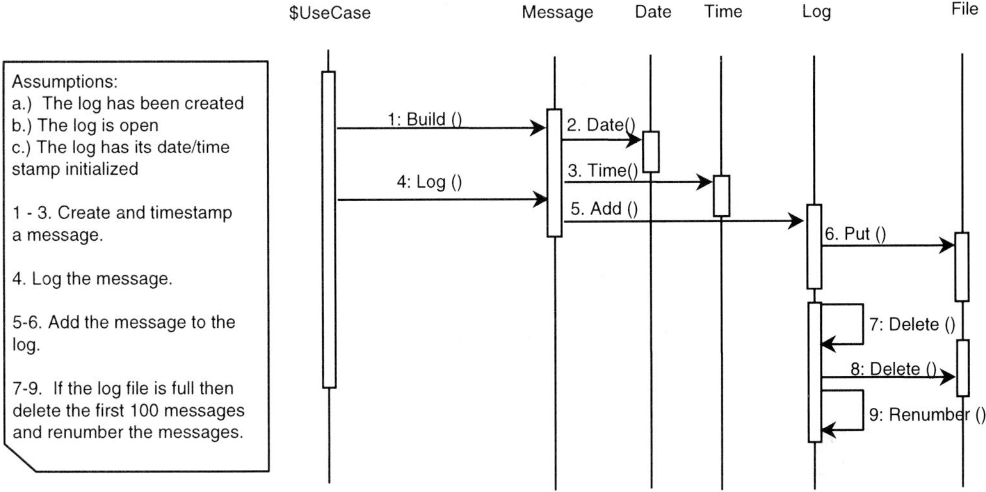

Figure 17-13. ID UC27 after OOA

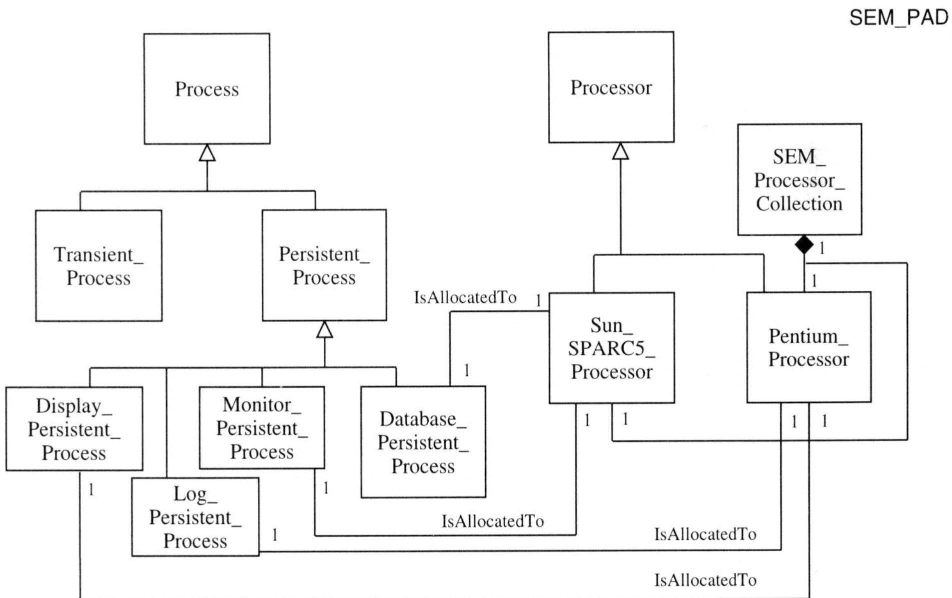

Figure 17-14. Updated PAD : UML Notation

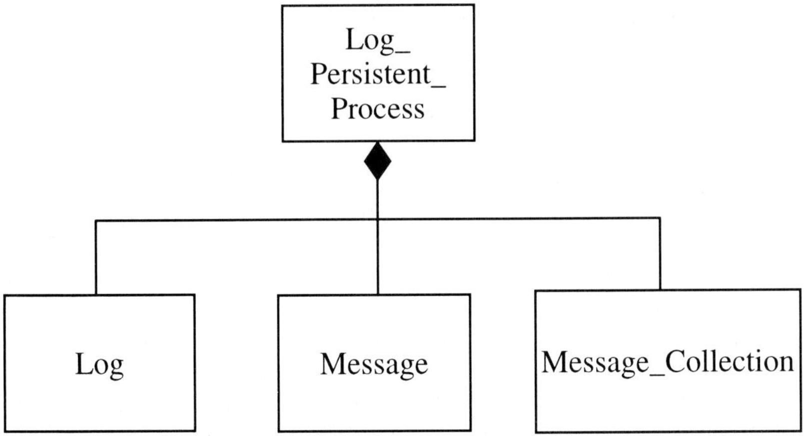

Figure 17-15. Log_Persistent_Process PCAD

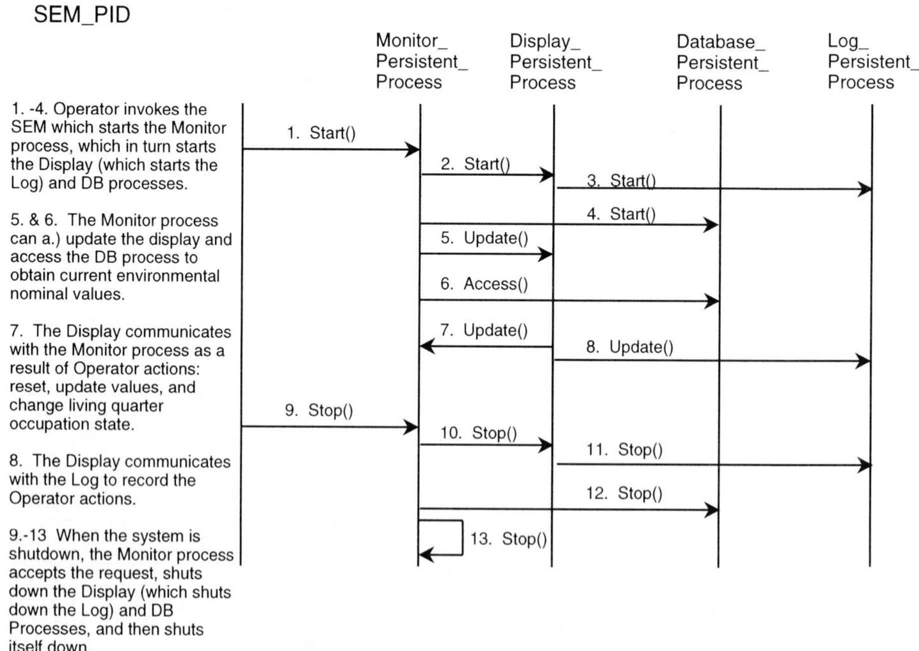

Figure 17-16. Updated PID

makes sense because it is the result of an Operator request for a GUI that causes the operator action to be recorded. This communication between the `Display_Persistent_Process` and `Log_Persistent_Process` will also be reflected in the updates to the IDs performed during OOD.

17.8 SOFTWARE OOD–STATIC VIEW

The Message_CAT_CCD and Log_CAT_CCD need to be refined according to the guidelines provided for Phase 8. The results are shown in Figures 17-17 and 17-18, respectively. In the Message_CAT_CCD (Figure 17-17) the `Message_Collection` Class has been introduced as well as its aggregation association to the `Message` Class. The `Message_Collection` Class can exist without any messages because the `Message_Collection` Class has its own Attributes (e.g., date/time stamp) and exists independently of the messages with which it is associated. In the Log_CAT_CCD (Figure 17-18) the association that existed between the `Operator_Log` and `Message` Classes is now replaced by an association to the `Message_Collection` Class. The fact that the `Log` Class is an Abstract Class has been indicated by italics and the associations have been migrated to Uses Relationships (UML Dependencies).

Finally, the CSs for these new Classes need to be completed.

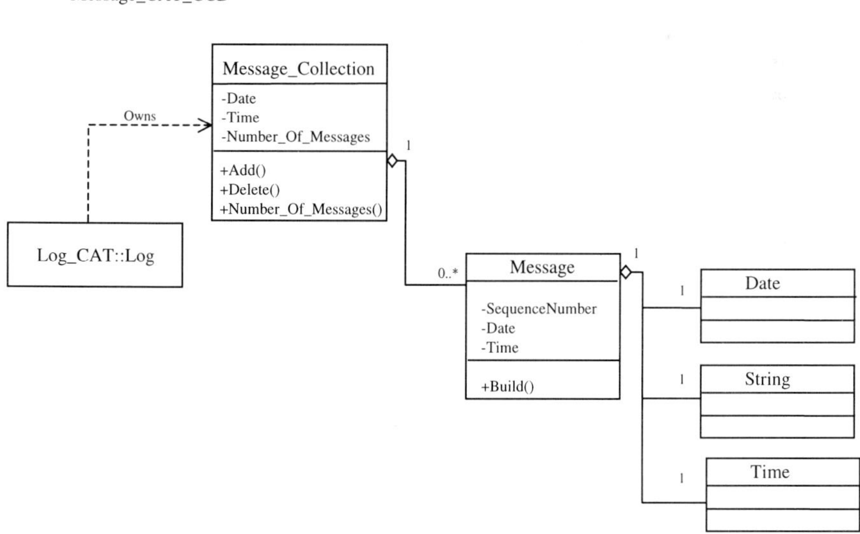

Figure 17-17. Message_CAT_CCD after OOD : UML Notation

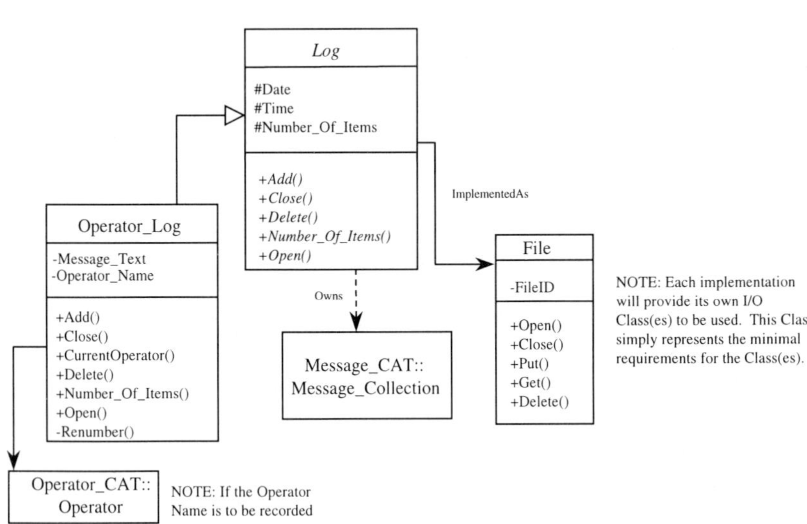

Figure 17-18. Log_CAT_CCD after OOD

17.9 SOFTWARE OOD–DYNAMIC VIEW

The update to the ID for Use Case 16 is reflected in Figure 17-19. Figure 17-20 reflects the update to the ID for Use Case 27. The ID representing Use Case 27 at the end of OOA, was reflected in Figure 17-12. Figure 17-20 also introduces a `Log_Controller` Class to handle the interaction between the `Log` and `Message` Classes.

17.10 LANGUAGE REPRESENTATION

The migration of the Classes to the target language is left as an exercise for the reader. One new Controller Class for the `Log_CAT` is required for the SEM.

17.11 METHOD DESIGN

The development of any required PDL is left as an exercise for the reader.

17.12 CLASS IMPLEMENTATION/CLASS TEST

Because new Classes have been added in support of the new requirements, these Classes must be completely implemented and tested. These modifications are also left as an exercise for the reader, as is the development of Class test drivers and executing

UC16_Operator_Updates_Nominal_Values_In_DB_ID

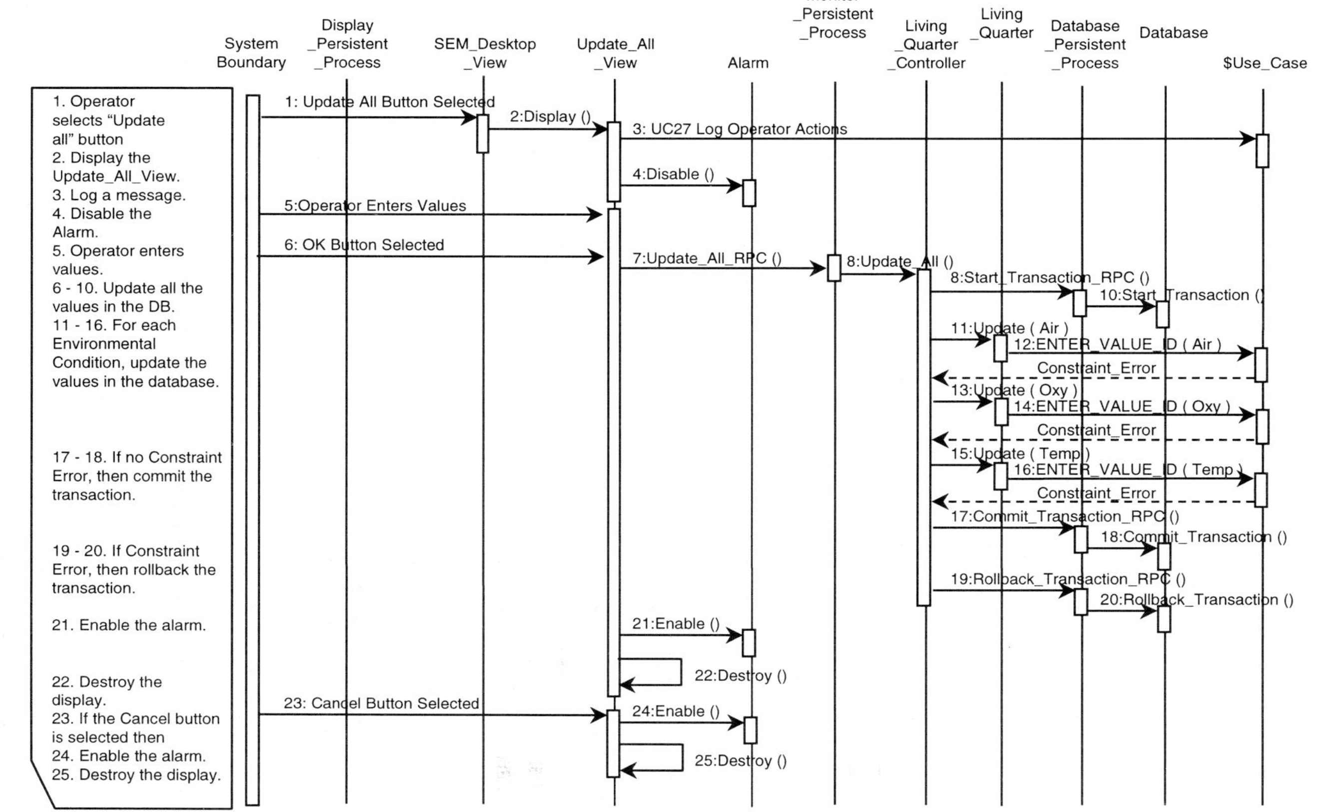

*NOTE: The parent Database Class is shown on this ID, but at the time the IDs are drawn it may not be known what database implementation (e.g., which Subclass) will be used. In the solution, the SNAP implementation uses the MSAccess_Database Class, while the C++ implementation uses the Flat_File_Database Class.

Figure 17-19. Updated ID UC16 after OOD

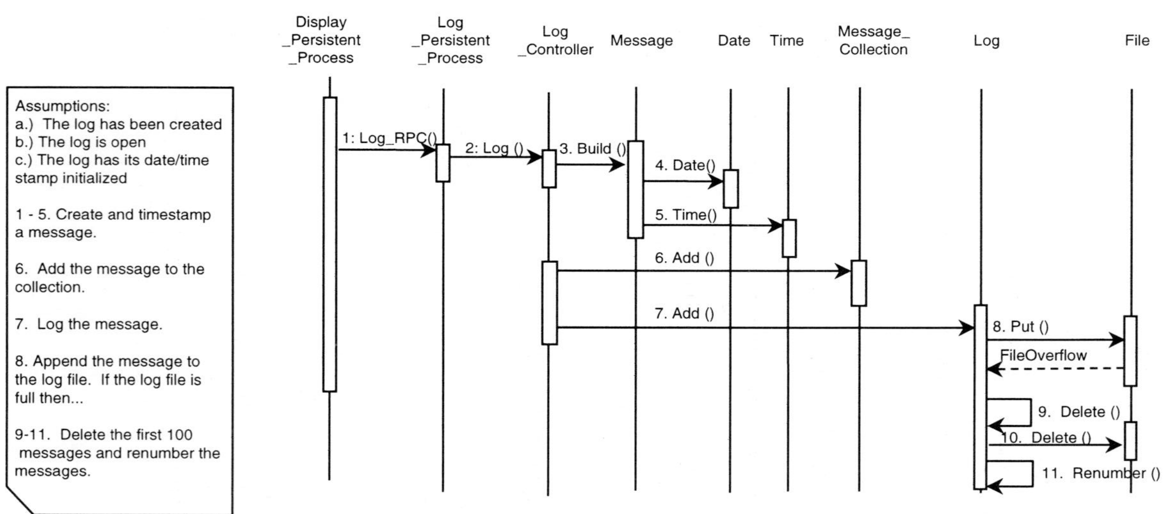

UC27_Log_Operator Actions_ID
Assumptions:
a.) The log has been created
b.) The log is open
c.) The log has its date/time stamp initialized
1 - 5. Create and timestamp a message.
6. Add the message to the collection.
7. Log the message.
8. Append the message to the log file. If the log file is full then...
9-11. Delete the first 100 messages and renumber the messages.
Display _Persistent _Process
Log _Persistent _Process
Log _Controller
Message
Date
Time
Message_ Collection
Log
File
1: Log_RPC()
2: Log ()
3. Build ()
4. Date()
5. Time()
6. Add ()
7. Add ()
8. Put ()
FileOverflow
9. Delete ()
10. Delete ()
11. Renumber ()

Figure 17-20. Updated ID UC27 after OOD

the tests as described in Phase 12. The changed Methods in the_`View` Classes should also be regression tested as per Phase 12.

17.13 CATEGORY TEST

Because two new Categories (`Log_CAT` and `Message_CAT`) have been added to the project, these Categories need to be completely tested as described in Phase 13. The development of intra- and inter Category test drivers and running the tests is left as an exercise for the reader.

The `View_CAT` needs to be regression tested as changes were made to callback functions in the Classes in this Category.

17.14 SOFTWARE INTEGRATION AND TEST (SWIT)

SWIT for the additional requirements specified for the SEM is nothing more than a complete regression test of all of the Use Cases containing an Operator action, specifically Use Cases 16, 17, 22, 25, and 26. Because the new Categories added for the new requirements are all software, there is no need to specify any additional Interface Classes, so there are no additional test Interface Class stubs required.

17.15 SYSTEM INTEGRATION TEST (SIT)

Just as for SWIT, the SIT for the additional requirements is nothing more than a complete regression test of all the Use Cases containing an Operator action, specifically Use Cases 16, 17, 22, 25, and 26.

17.16 REQUIREMENTS TRACE

Update the Forwards Requirements Trace (FRT) and Reverse Requirements Trace (RRT) to include the new requirements, new Categories, new Classes, and new Methods. This is trivial if the FRT and RRT are generated directly from the CASE tool repository and source code directory structure.

APPENDIX A

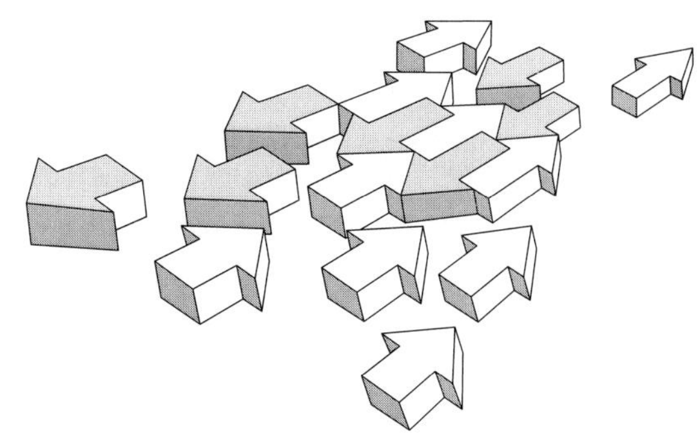

Acronym List

AD	Activity Diagram
CCCD	Class-Centric Class Diagram
CCD	Category Class Diagram
CD	Collaboration Diagram
CID	Category Interaction Diagram
CFS	Customer-Furnished Software
COTS	Commercial Off The Shelf Software
CS	Class Specification
CSD	Class Specification Document
ERD	Entity Relationship Diagram
FRT	Forward Requirements Trace
GFS	Government-Furnished Software
GUI	Graphical User Interface
HCC	Habitat Control Center
HCCD	Hardware Category Class Diagram
HW	Hardware
ID	Interaction Diagram
IF	Interface
IPC	Inter-Process Communication
OO	Object-Oriented
OOA	Object-Oriented Analysis
OOD	Object-Oriented Design
OOSE	Object-Oriented Software Engineering
OCD	Operational Concept Document
OMT	Object Modeling Technique

PAD	Process Architecture Diagram
PCAD	Process-to-Class Allocation Diagram
PDL	Program Design Language
PID	Process Interaction Diagram
RFP	Request For Proposal
RPC	Remote Procedure Call
RRT	Reverse Requirements Trace
RTM	Requirements Traceability Matrix
SCD	System Category Diagram
SD	Sequence Diagram
SEM	Sealed Environment Monitor
SIT	System Integration and Test
SOW	Statement Of Work
SQA	Software Quality Assurance
STD	State Transition Diagram
STT	State Transition Table
StP OMT	Software through Pictures (OMT CASE Tool)
SW	Software
SWIT	Software Integration and Test
UC	Use Case
UML	Unified Modeling Language

APPENDIX B

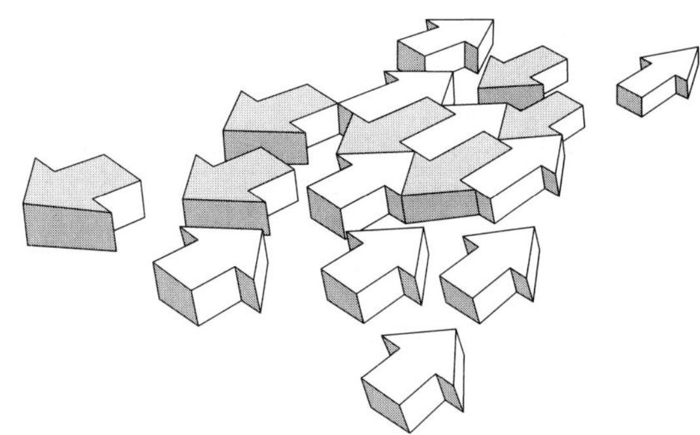

Glossary

Abstract Class: An **Abstract Class** is a Superclass in an inheritance hierarchy that does *not* have any Instances (Objects).

Ada95 Package: A **package** is an Ada95 construct that is utilized to represent a Class. A package has two parts: a package specification (specifies the contract, or interface, to clients) and a package body (provides the implementation of the Class).

Aggregation Hierarchy: An **aggregation hierarchy** is a set of Classes related through an aggregation relationship, with one root Class. All remaining Classes in the hierarchy are parts of, either directly or indirectly, and help comprise, the root Class.

Aggregation Relationship: An **aggregation relationship** is an Association between Classes that focuses on one Class being "made up of" another Class. An **aggregation relationship** is an Association that exists between "whole" Classes and "part" Classes. In UML there are two kinds of **aggregation relationships:** aggregation by value and aggregation by reference.

Annotation: An **annotation** is simply a set of notes, compiled by the developer, that records his/her understanding of the Scenario resulting from further research on the Scenario and/or discussions with domain experts/systems engineering. In other words, an **annotation** is a clarification of a Scenario.

Association: An **Association** is a semantic relationship that exists between two Categories or two Classes. There are three kinds of **Associations**:

- Aggregation relationship
- Inheritance relationship
- Association relationship.

Association Relationship: An **Association Relationship** is an Association that is based on a semantic relationship between two Categories (or Classes) and that is *not* inheritance and *not* aggregation. When graphically depicted, an **Association**

Relationship requires a label that describes the relationship, as well as the definition of its multiplicity (how many instances participate).

Attribute: An **Attribute** is a single characteristic of a Class that needs to be remembered by the software. An **Attribute** can either be transient or persistent. A **transient Attribute** is an Attribute of a Class whose value is *not* maintained after the application terminates. A **persistent Attribute** is an Attribute of a Class whose value *is* retained after the application terminates.

Black Box Testing: Black box testing is the process of testing the contract that the entity under test has made with its clients. A test, or set of tests, that focus on **black box testing,** are designed to ensure that the specification of the contract, given specific inputs, produces the required outputs without attention to the actual control paths in the code.

"Body": A "**body"** is the implementation of a Class contract. A "**body**" is represented as a compilable Ada95 package body or a `.cpp` file in C++. The concept of a "body" is not applicable to Java or SNAP.

"Body" Structure: A "**body" structure** is the overall structure of the implementation of the Methods of a Class, without the implementation of the Methods. A **"body" structure** does *not* contain the implementation of the algorithms. In Ada95, the "**body" structure** is developed using Ada95 stubs in the package body, while in C++ and Java, a "**body" structure** is developed by including the opening and closing curly braces ({ }) and a single return statement when required (when the function returns a value).

Build: A **build** is a specification of software functionality to be developed by a specific date. A **build** is part of a release, used for internal management purposes to track the development of a release to a customer. For inheritance hierarchies, the first **build** implements the root Class and one branch of an inheritance hierarchy down to a leaf Class. Subsequent **builds** add respective Subclass branches.

.cpp File: A **.cpp file** is a file that typically contains the C++ implementation of the Class Methods, with the exception of those functions coded in-line in the C++ header file. A **.cpp file** is *not* part of the interface, or contract, of a Class.

C++ Class: A **C++ Class** is a C++ language construct that is utilized to represent a Class. A **C++ Class** is represented by both a header file that provides the contract or interface to the clients and a `.cpp` file that provides the set of all function definitions appropriate to the Class.

C++ Header File: A **C++ header file** is a file that specifies the interface of a C++ Class to its clients. The contract that a Class makes with its clients is represented in the **C++ header file**.

Category Class Diagram (CCD): A **CCD** for *one* Category is a Class Diagram that depicts all Classes owned by the Category, all Classes required by the Classes in the

Category that are owned by other Categories (imported Classes), and all Associations between these Classes. There is one CCD per Category. Recall that a CCD is created as a Booch or UML Class Diagram or an OMT Object Diagram.

Category Interaction Diagram (CID): A **CID** is a graphical representation of the interactions between Categories required to satisfy, or implement, a Use Case using the notation of the CASE tool. OMT provides Event Traces while Booch provides Interaction Diagrams and Object Scenario Diagrams. In UML 1.0 terminology, an Interaction Diagram is any diagram that depicts interaction at the Instance level, and can be either a Sequence Diagram or a Collaboration Diagram.

Category Test Case: A **Category test case** is a description (minimally, in terms of 1) what is being tested, 2) required inputs, and 3) expected results) of a *single* test, along with the resulting code that executes the test.

Category Test Driver: A **Category test driver** is an executable piece of software that comprises one or more tests (called test cases) for the set of connections under test.

Category Test Results: **Category test results** record the results of executing a Category test driver.

Child Category: A **child Category** is a Category that is *owned* by another Category - the parent Category - and represents a logical collection of Classes of the parent Category, or equivalently, a subset of the parent Category.

Class: A **Class** is a static abstraction of a set of real world entities that have the same characteristics (Attributes) and exhibit the same behavior (Methods).

Class-Centric Class Diagram (CCCD): A **CCCD** for a Class within a Category is a kind of Class Diagram that represents, for *one* Class, all Classes and Associations in which the Class participates. These diagrams, of course, are optional. Remember that **CCCD**s are created as Booch/UML Class Diagrams or OMT Object Diagrams.

Class Contract: A **Class contract** is the interface of a Class to its clients. A **Class contract** represents the resources of a Class that are accessible by the clients of a Class.

Class Specification (CS): A **CS** is a description of a Class that includes, at a minimum, a textual description of the Class, the list of Class Attributes and Methods, a description of each Class Attribute and Method, and so on. The specific contents of a **CS** are project-specific. The specific implementation of a **CS** in a CASE tool is vendor-dependent. For example, StP OMT keeps some information in a Class table, while the rest is kept as annotations to a Class. Rose captures this information in a window, and produces a pre-formatted document including the information for each Class. To summarize, the contents of a **CS** are project-specific because of the dependency upon time available and the CASE tool being utilized. In the author's opinion, some CASE tools go overboard on the data to be entered to describe a Class.

Class Specification Document (CSD): A **CSD** is a project deliverable that contains CSs at a minimum, organized by Category. A **CSD** might also include CCDs and STDs.

Class Test: **Class Test** represents the process of testing a Class *in isolation of* other Classes in the software system.

Class Test Case: A **Class test case** describes, minimally, 1) what is being tested, 2) the required inputs, and 3) the expected results of a *single* test, along with the code that executes the single test.

Class Test Driver: A **Class test driver** is an executable piece of software that comprises one or more tests (called Class test cases) for an entity under test.

Class Test Results: **Class test results** record the results of executing a Class test driver.

Commercial Off-The-Shelf Software (COTS): **COTS** is software that is already written, or under development, that can be used to implement a portion of the required software functionality. The **COTS** copyright is typically owned by the organization that developed the software. Some examples of **COTS** products are Oracle, Microsoft Office, Netscape, and so on.

Concrete Class: A **Concrete Class** is a Class that has Instances.

Context Diagram: A **Context Diagram** is a diagram consisting of one circle (or ellipse), which represents the system, that is typically placed in the **center** of the diagram; rectangles are used to represent entities, both hardware and software, that are external, yet required interfaces, to the system to be developed; and finally, a pair of double lines represents any data store that is required/produced.

Controller Class: A **Controller Class** is a Class that is responsible for defining the necessary collaboration between Domain and View Classes to achieve a specific functionality. Basically, a **Controller Class** is an example of a Facade Design Pattern [GAM95].

Customer-Furnished Software (CFS): **CFS** is software that is supplied by a customer, and that is to be incorporated into the software under development. **CFS** is a term that is commonly used in the commercial arena. The copyright to **CFS** is typically owned by the customer.

Data Store: A **data store** is used to represent persistent data that are accessed by the system.

Derived Requirement: A **derived requirement** is a specification of system functionality that is conceived as knowledge of the semantics of the "shall" sentences accumulates. A **derived requirement** does *not* represent a sentence that includes the word "shall." A **derived requirement** is a requirement that is deduced from other system knowledge, yet is *not* explicitly stated in the System Specification (or any other document).

Domain Class: A **Domain Class** is a Class which defines a real world entity extracted from the problem space.

Exception: An **exception** is an error condition that occurs during run-time, and that without associated corrective processing, results in system failure.

Exception Handler: An **exception handler** is a piece of code, or processing, that executes and provides corrective action when an exception occurs.

External Interface: An **external interface** is an entity that is *not* currently part of the system being developed, yet provides resources that are required by or affected by the system currently under development.

Facade: A **Facade** design pattern is a mechanism that supplies an interface to a collection of interfaces. A **Facade** design pattern is a Class that filters requests for services from a collection of Classes, routing a request to the correct Class.

Government-Furnished Software (GFS): **GFS** is software that is already written, or under development, that can be used to implement a portion of the required software functionality. The **GFS** copyright is typically owned by the Government and therefore is public domain software.

Hardware Category Class Diagram (HCCD): An **HCCD** is a diagram for a Category that represents the hardware Classes owned by the Category and their Associations to other Classes in the Category as well as their Associations to Classes from foreign Categories. An **HCCD** is drawn as a Booch Class Diagram, an OMT Object Diagram, or a UML Class Diagram.

Inheritance Hierarchy: An **inheritance hierarchy** is set of Classes related through inheritance relationships, with one root Class. All remaining Classes in the hierarchy are descended, either directly or indirectly, from the root Class.

Inheritance Relationship: An **inheritance relationship** is an Association between Classes that focuses on similarities and dissimilarities between the Classes with respect to the Classes' Attributes and Methods. An **inheritance relationship** is an Association that exists between a Superclass and its Subclasses.

Instance: An **Instance** is a single, unique, real world entity that belongs to a Class. The term Object is used synonymously with **Instance** in this text.

Interaction Diagram (ID): An **ID** is a diagram, using the graphical notation previously introduced in Phase 3, System OOA, when the CIDs were produced, that represents the *refinement* of a CID or supporting CID. An **ID** portrays the functionality of a thread of control (Use Case) at the software level, in a manner that identifies which Classes, and which Methods of each Class, are required to satisfy a Use Case.

Inter-Category Test: **Inter-Category test** is the process of testing the connections between successfully tested Classes in *different* Categories.

Intra-Category Test: Intra-Category test is the process of testing the connections between successfully tested Classes within the *same* Category.

Java Package: A **Java package** is a Java construct that provides a mechanism to group-related Classes and interfaces.

Leaf Class: A **leaf Class** is a Class that is the lowest-level Class in an inheritance or aggregation hierarchy. Within an aggregation hierarchy, a **leaf Class** does *not* have any "part" Classes. Within an inheritance hierarchy, a **leaf Class** does *not* have any Subclasses.

Method: A **Method** is a single functional capability of a Class that can be performed on an Instance of the Class.

Multiplicity: Multiplicity defines the number of Instances that participate in either an association relationship or aggregation relationship. **Multiplicity** is synonymous with cardinality.

Package Body: A **package body** is an Ada95 construct that is utilized to represent the implementation of a Class. A **package body** is *not* part of the interface to the Class's clients.

Package Specification: A **package specification** is an Ada95 language construct that is utilized to represent the specification of a Class. A **package specification** represents the interface, or contract, that the Class makes with its potential clients.

Parameterized Class: A **Parameterized Class** is a Class that is used as the base Class description for a new Class. **Parameterized Classes** are implemented as templates in C++, or as generics in Ada95.

Parent Category: A **parent Category** represents a Category that, because of its size, is decomposed into a logical collection of child Categories.

Performance Requirement: A **performance requirement** is a statement that specifies either a timing or sizing restriction on either a hardware device or a functional subset of the software.

Persistent Data: **Persistent data** are data that remain after the termination of an application. There are various implementation mechanisms for **persistent data**, for example: a database, flat file, and so on.

Persistent Process: A **persistent process** is a process that is active for the lifetime of an application.

Private: A **private** access right *prohibits* access by external Classes to a Class' Attributes and/or Methods that are designated as **private**. A **private** access right permits access by Subclasses that inherit privately from the Class in question. The graphical symbol to represent private access is a minus sign (–).

Problem Trouble Report (PTR): A **PTR** is a record of a detected problem in either documentation or code. **PTR**s are known by various names, such as Trouble Report (TR), Bug Report (BR), Defect Report (DR), and so on.

Process: A **process** is an executable entity that comprises Classes (and their Methods). A process executes on a processor.

Process Architecture Diagram (PAD): A **PAD** is a Class Diagram that depicts the identified `Processor` and `Process` Classes in the software system, and the `Process` to `Processor` allocation.

Process Interaction Diagram (PID): A **PID** is a diagram that is drawn just like an ID (a Jacobson Interaction Diagram, Booch Object Scenario Diagram, OMT Event Trace Diagram, or UML Sequence Diagram), and which shows how the processes interact.

Processor: A **processor** is a physical hardware device that can execute processes.

Processor-to-Class Allocation Diagram (PCAD): A **PCAD** is a Booch/UML Class Diagram or OMT Object Diagram that for each identified process, depicts the set of Classes required by the process. One PCAD is produced for each process.

Program Design Language (PDL): **PDL** is a language used to represent design information. **PDL** is often called pseudo code because it resembles code and indicates, in its own syntax, the behavior of a specific functionality.

Propagation: **Propagation** is the re-raising of an exception to the next level, where "level" is defined by the programming language. The next "level" can be a block, calling routine, and so on.

Protected: A **protected** access right *permits* access by Subclasses to their Superclasses' Attributes and Methods that have been designated as **protected**. A **protected** access right *prohibits* access by *non*-Subclasses to a Class' Attributes and/or Methods. The graphical symbol to represent protected access is a pound sign (#).

Public: A **public** access right allows *all* Client Classes visibility to a Class' Attributes and/or Methods that are designated as **public**. The graphical symbol to represent public access is the plus sign (+).

Release: A **release** is a distribution of software functionality to the customer. A **release** is made up of one or more builds. A **release** has a specific version number associated with it to help identify the specific set of functionality included in the delivered software.

Repository: Each CASE tool maintains its information in a database, the format and content of which are typically vendor-specific. This book utilizes the word "**repository**" to represent a CASE tool database for one specific project. Thus, if a CASE tool supports two projects named A and B, respectively, there are two **repositories**—one for Project A and one for Project B.

Requirements Trace Matrix (RTM): An **RTM** is a matrix that initially contains the set of requirements for a system. The **RTM** is continually enhanced throughout Phases 1 and 2. The **RTM** is continually maintained throughout the lifetime of a project.

Rose: **Rose** is a software CASE tool developed by the Rational Corporation that supports the Booch and OMT methods.

Self-Documenting Test: A **self-documenting test** is a test case that is coded in such a way that when executed, can determine whether the test passed or failed, and outputs either a "PASS" or "FAIL" string to the results file. A **self-documenting test** therefore knows inputs and expected results, and compares actual results against expected results to determine whether a test passes or fails.

"shall" statement: A single **"shall" statement** is a sentence that includes the word **"shall"**. The **statement** is extracted from the System Specification (and any other agreed-to documentation). A **"shall" statement** indicates a contractual requirement for the system to be developed.

Shared Class: A **shared Class** is a Class that has Instances that are required by more than one process, regardless of whether the processes are on the same or different processors. When an Instance of a Class is required by more than one process, a strategy must be devised to keep the Instances of the Class synchronized. Shared memory is one approach, where the Instances are maintained in shared memory and all processes access the Instance through shared memory. If the processes require non-intersecting portions of the Class in question, the Class can perhaps be decomposed into two Classes, with each process utilizing the appropriate partition of the Class. For example, if only one of multiple processes needs to access the Instance information in the *database*, the Class can be broken into two Classes providing direct access to the database Methods in the process that requires those services, thus avoiding database activity being linked into all processes. Another alternative is message passing to keep the Instances synchronized. Each Project Team makes its own decision here.

SNAP Class Definition File: A **SNAP Class Definition File** (`.cd` file) is a file that typically contains the SNAP interface and implementation of a Class.

Software Constraint: A **software constraint** is a restriction potentially placed on the software implementation. For example, consider the fact that a living quarter has three sensors. The number three is a potential software ***constraint***, and can be implemented as an array upper bound, size of a bounded linked list, and so on. The same can be said for the number of halls, rooms, and therefore, the number of living quarters.

Software Through Pictures (StP) OMT: **OMT** is a CASE tool that supports the OMT methodology.

Stub Library: A **stub library** is a library of *Classes*, their *contracts* (interface specification) and "body" *structure*. The Classes in a **stub library** are those Classes that interface to any foreign Category, thus permitting developers to compile Classes within their Category that require access to Classes, without relying on other Categories' development schedules.

Subclass: A **Subclass** is a Class that is derived from another Class, its Superclass or base Class. A **Subclass** inherits all the Attributes and Methods of its parent Superclass.

Superclass: A **Superclass** is a Class from which other Classes, named Subclasses, are derived. A Superclass provides Attributes and Methods that are common to all its Subclasses.

Supporting Interaction Diagram: A **Supporting Interaction Diagram** is an Interaction Diagram that represents common processing, utilized by many Use Cases, that itself is *not* a Use Case. Again a Supporting Interaction Diagram is drawn using the notation provided by the CASE tool.

System Category Diagram (SCD): An **SCD** is a Category-level diagram. An **SCD** for a project is a Class Diagram (either a Booch Class Diagram or OMT Object Diagram) that depicts all known Categories and all Associations between the Categories. In UML, the **SCD** is drawn between UML packages, and the SCD portrays a UML *dependency*, rather than an Association.

Test By Inspection: **Test by inspection** is a testing technique that relies on visual examination of an entity under test according to predefined criteria.

Transient Process: A **transient process** is a process that is temporally active. In other words, a transient process is activated for a short period of time to perform a specific functionality, and then it is deactivated when its processing has completed.

UML Activity Diagram (AD): A **UML AD** is a diagram that depicts the execution steps to be performed by a Method. A **UML AD** depicts the steps that a Method executes to perform its intended processing. The diagram considers the steps that a Method executes through various states of the state machine represented by the Method. The notation for an **UML AD** provides for concurrency, branching, and multiple Instances.

UML Aggregation: **Aggregation** is an aggregation relationship where the "whole" Class does *not* have to create its "part" Classes, but rather, refers to the "part" Classes by reference or pointer. An Instance of a part Class has been potentially created by another Class and the "whole" Class requires access to the Instance to complete its aggregation. **Aggregation** permits parts to be easily replaced. **Aggregation** indicates a weaker coupling between the "whole" and its "part" Classes than is indicated with composition. The graphical representation of **aggregation** is an unfilled diamond (◊).

UML Collaboration Diagram: A **UML Collaboration Diagram** is the new UML name for the Booch Object Scenario Diagram.

UML Composition: **Composition** is an aggregation relationship where the "whole" Class is responsible for creating its "part" Classes directly. With composition the lifetime of an Instance of a "whole" Class is dependent on the lifetime of its "part" Class. If an Instance of a "part" Class "dies," so does the Instance of the "whole" Class (unless the multiplicity permitted '0' Instances to participate). **Composition** indicates a tighter coupling between the "whole" and "part" Classes than is indicated with aggregation. The graphical representation of a **composition** is a filled diamond (♦).

UML Dependency: A **UML dependency** between two entities, whether the two entities are Categories or Classes, indicates that one of the entities depends upon, or requires the resources of, the other entity. A **UML dependency** is depicted with a dashed line, with an arrow at one or both ends. The entity at the tail of the arrow depends upon the entity at the head of the arrow. A **UML dependency** between two entities means that the dependent entity requires visibility, or access, to the unit upon which it depends.

UML Interaction Diagram: A **UML Interaction Diagram** refers to both UML Sequence Diagrams and UML Collaboration Diagrams. Both kinds of diagrams represent general behavior, specifically interactions between Objects (Instances).

UML Package: A **UML package** is a collection of cohesive entities. There are different kinds of **UML packages**: a Category (a collection of Classes), a Subsystem (a collection of source code files), and so on. Each different kind of **UML package** is called a stereotype. A **UML package** has its own distinct symbol, a tabbed rectangle.

UML Sequence Diagram: A **UML Sequence Diagram** is the UML name for the Jacobson Interaction Diagram. Whereas a Jacobson Interaction Diagram portrayed collaboration between Classes, a **UML Sequence Diagram** shows the collaboration required between Objects (Instances). Additionally a UML sequence Diagram provides new notational enhancements for representing creation/destruction of Instances, conditional flow of control and so on.

UML Stereotype: A **UML stereotype** identifies a kind of element in UML. The **stereotype** Category package indicates that Category is a kind of package, while the **stereotype** Exception Class indicates that Exception is a kind of Class. A **UML stereotype** has its own distinct symbol, the name of the **stereotype** enclosed in double angled brackets, as in <<Class>>.

Uses Relationship: A Booch "uses" relationship is identical to a UML Dependency, indicating visibility from the source Class (requires resources) of the "uses" relationship to the target Class (supplies resources). The symbol utilized to represent a "uses" relationship is an unfilled circle attached to the source Class with a solid line to the target Class.

View Class: A **View Class** is a Class which defines how information in a Domain Class is displayed by the system. A **View Class** may provide controls to interact with the system.

White Box Testing: **White box testing** is the process of testing the internal workings, or structure, of an entity under test. A test, or set of tests, that focus on **white box testing**, are designed to ensure that all paths, or a critical set of paths, are exercised during the test.

APPENDIX C

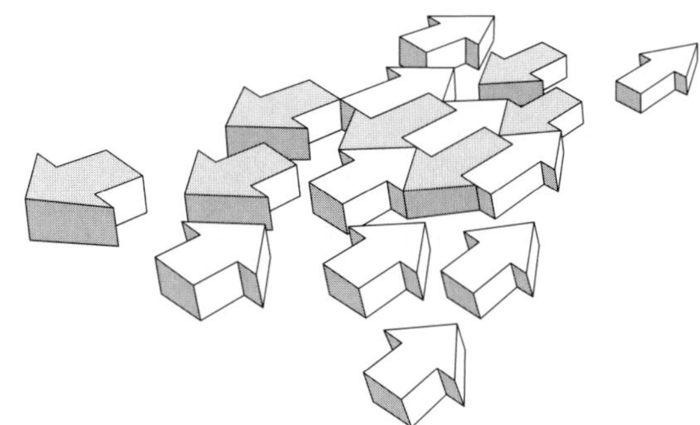

Bibliography

BIBLIOGRAPHY PART I

Object-Oriented/Software Engineering

[ATK91] Atkinson, Colin. Object-Oriented Reuse, Concurrency and Distribution. ACM Press. 1991.

[BOO91] Booch, Grady. Object-Oriented Design with Applications. Benjamin Cummings Publishing Company. 1991.

[BOO94] Booch, Grady. Object-Oriented Analysis and Design with Applications. Second Edition. Benjamin Cummings Publishing Company. 1994.

[BOO96] Booch, Grady. Object Solutions: Managing the Object-Oriented Project. Addison-Wesley Publishing Company. 1996.

[CAR94] Edited by Carmichael, Andy. Object Development Methods. SIGS Books, Inc. 1994.

[CAS89] Cashman, M. On O-O Domain Analysis. ACM Software Engineering Notes. Vol. 14 No. 6. October 1989.

[CMU95] Carnegie Mellon University Software Engineering Institute. The Capability Maturity Model: Guidelines for Improving the Software Process. Addison-Wesley Publishing Company. 1995.

[COA89] Coad, Peter and Yourdan, Ed. Object-Oriented Analysis. Prentice Hall. 1989.

[COA91A] Coad, Peter and Yourdan, Ed. Object-Oriented Analysis, Second Edition. Prentice Hall. 1991.

[COA91B] Coad, Peter and Yourdan, Ed. Object-Oriented Design. Prentice Hall. 1991.

[ENT95] Entsminger, Gary. The Tao of Objects: A Beginners Guide to Object-Oriented Programming, Second Edition. M&T Books. 1995.

[EVB88] EVB Software Engineering, Inc. "Object-Oriented Requirements Analysis" Proceedings of a Seminar for Washington, DC Chapter of the ACM. November 10, 1988.

[GAM94] Gamma, Eric, et al. Design Patterns: Elements of Reusable Object-Oriented Software. Addison-Wesley Publishing Company. 1994.

[GRA91] Graham, Ian. Object-Oriented Methods. Addison-Wesley Publishing Company. 1991.

[HUM89] Humphrey, Watts S. Managing the Software Process. Addison-Wesley Publishing Company. 1992.

[JAC92] Jacobson, Ivar, et al. Object-Oriented Software Engineering. Addison-Wesley Publishing Company. 1992.

[JAC96] Jacobson, Ivar, et al. Use Case Engineering: Unlocking The Power. Object Magazine. October 1996 6(8).

[KER89] Kerth, Norman L. Editor. Hotline of Object-Oriented Technology, Book Review of [COA89]. Vol. 1 No. 1 November 1989.

[KHO90] Khoshafian, S. and Abnous, R. Object-Orientation: Concepts, Languages, Databases, User Interfaces. John Wiley & Sons, Inc. 1990.

[LOR94] Lorenz, Mark and Kidd, Jeff. Object-Oriented Software Metrics. Prentice Hall. 1994.

[MAR92] Martin, James and Odell, James J. Object-Oriented Analysis & Design. Prentice Hall. 1992.

[MAR93] Martin, James. Principles of Object-Oriented Analysis & Design. Prentice Hall. 1993.

[McG92] McGregor, John and Sykes, David. Object-Oriented Software Development: Engineering Software for Reuse. Van Nostrand Reinhold. 1992.

[MEY88A] Meyer, Bertrand. Object-Oriented Design & Programming: A Software Engineering Perspective. Course Notes from Interactive Software Engineering, Inc,. Seminar. 1988.

[MEY88B] Meyer, Bertrand. Object-Oriented Software Construction. Prentice Hall. 1988.

[NEW88] Newton, M. and Watkins, J. "The Combination of Logic and Objects for Knowledge Representation." The Journal of Object-Oriented Programming. Vol. 1 No. 4. November/December 1988.

[RAT95] Unified Method For Object-Oriented Development. Document Set V0.8. Rational Software Corporation. 1995.

[RAT96] The Unified Modeling Language For Object-Oriented Development. Document Set V0.91 Addendum UML Update . Rational Software Corporation. 1996.

[RAT97] The Unified Modeling Language. Document Set V1.0. Rational Software Corporation. 1997.

[RUM91] Rumbaugh, James et al. Object-Oriented Modeling & Design. Prentice Hall. 1991.

[SAU89] Saunders, J.H. "A Survey of Object-Oriented Programming Languages." The Journal of Object-Oriented Programming Languages. Vol. 1 No. 6. March/April 1989.

[SHL88] Shlaer, S. and Mellor, S. J. Object-Oriented Systems Analysis: Modeling the World in Data. Yourdan Press. 1988.

[SHL89A] Shlaer, S. and Mellor, S. J. "Understanding Object-Oriented Analysis" Design Center Magazine, A Hewlett-Packard Publication. 1989.

[SHL89B] Shlaer, S. and Mellor, S. J. "An Object-Oriented Approach to Domain Analysis." Software Engineering Notes ACM Press. July 1989.

[SHL92] Shlaer, S. and Mellor, S. J. Object Life Cycles: Modeling the World in States. Prentice Hall. 1992.

[SHU92] Shumate, K. and Keller, M. Software Specification and Design: A Disciplined Approach for Real-Time Systems. John Wiley & Sons, Inc. 1992.

[SOM85] Somerville, I. Software Engineering, Second Edition. Addison-Wesley Publishing Company. 1985.

[TEX89] P. P. Texel & Company, Inc. Object-Oriented Requirements Specification for the Fire Support Planning Operational Category. 1989.

[TEX96] Texel, Putnam P. Use Cases & Categories: The Basis For Project Infra-Structure. Proceedings of the Tenth Annual ASEET Symposium. June 1996.

[VIC84] Vick, C. R., Ph.D. and Ramamoorthy, C. V. , Ph.D. Handbook of Software Engineering. Van Nostrand Reinhold. 1984.

[WIR90] Wirfs-Broch, Rebecca and Wilkerson, Brian. Designing Object-Oriented Software. Prentice Hall. 1990.

[YOU82] Yourdon, E. Writings of the Revolution, Selected Readings on Software Engineering. Yourdon Press. 1982.

[YOU94] Yourdon, E. Object-Oriented Systems Design: An Integrated Approach. Yourdon Press. 1994.

BIBLIOGRAPHY PART II

Ada

[AUS85] Ausnit, Christine, et al. Ada In Practice. Springer-Verlag. 1985.

[BAR94] Barnes, J. G. P. Programming in Ada, Fourth Edition. Addison-Wesley Publishing Company. 1994.

[BAR95] Barnes, J. G. P. Programming in Ada95. Addison-Wesley Publishing Company. 1995.

[BOO87A] Booch, Grady. Software Engineering with Ada, Second Edition. Benjamin Cummings Publishing Company. 1987.

[BOO87B] Booch, Grady. Software Components with Ada: Structures, Tools, and Subsystems. Benjamin Cummings Publishing Company. 1987.

[BUR85] Burns, Alan. Concurrent Programming in Ada. Cambridge University Press. 1985.

[CEC82] Using Selected Features of Ada: A Collection of Papers. U. S. Army-CECOM. 1982.

[COH96] Cohen, Norman. Ada As a Second Language (Based on Ada95, Second Edition). McGraw-Hill Companies, Inc. 1996.

[DOW82] Downes, V. A. and Goldsack, S. J. Programming Embedded Systems with Ada. Prentice Hall International. 1982.

[FEL85] Feldman, Michael B. Data Structures with Ada. Reston Publishing Company. 1985.

[GEH83] Gehani, Narain. Ada: An Advanced Introduction. Prentice Hall. 1983.

[GEH84] Gehani, Narain. Ada: Concurrent Programming. Prentice Hall. 1984.

[GIL86] Gilpin, Geoff. Ada: A Guided Tour & Tutorial. Prentice Hall. 1986.

[GON91] Gonzalez, Dean W. Ada Programmers Handbook. Benjamin Cummings Publishing Company. 1991.

[GOO87] Goos, G. and Hartmanis, J. A Review of Ada Tasking. Lecture Notes in Computer Science. No. 262. Springer-Verlag. 1987.

[HAB83] Haberman, A. Nico and Perry, Dewayne E. Ada for Experienced Programmers. Addison-Wesley Publishing Company. 1983.

[HIB83] Hibbard, Peter, et al. Studies in Ada Style. Springer-Verlag. 1983.

[ICH80] Ichbiah, Jean, et al. Notes from Course December 2, 1990. Honeywell/Alsys. 1980.

[INT95A] Ada95 Reference Manual. Intermetrics. 1995.

[INT95B] Ada95 Rationale. Intermetrics. 1995.

[KAT82] Katzan, Harry Jr. Invitation to Ada & Ada Reference Manual. Petrocelli Books, Inc. 1982.

[LED83] Ledgard, Henry. Ada: An Introduction, Second Edition. Springer-Verlag. 1983.

[LRM83] The Reference Manual for the Ada Programming Language. Department of Defense. 1983.

[McG82] McGettrick, A. D. Program Verification Using Ada. Cambridge University Press. 1982.

[NIE92] Nielson, Kjell. Object-Oriented Design with Ada. Bantam Books. 1992.

[OLS83] Olsen, Eric W. & Whitehill, Stephen B. Ada for Programmers. Reston Publishing Company. 1983.

[SAI85] Saib, Sabina. Ada: An Introduction. Holt, Reinhart and Winston. 1985.

[SAX83] Saxon, James A. and Fritz, Robert E. Beginning Programming with Ada. Prentice Hall. 1983.

[SPC89] Software Productivity Consortium. Ada: Quality and Style. Van Nostrand Reinhold. 1989.

[STA85] Stanley, James, et al. Ada: A Programmer's Guide with Microcomputer Examples. Addison-Wesley Publishing Company. 1985.

[TEX86] Texel, Putnam P. Introduction to Ada: Programming with Packages. Wadsworth Publishing Company. 1986.

[TEX91] Texel, Putnam P. Ada Supplement to Accompany Concepts in Data Structures and Software Development (Schneider & Burell). West Publishing Company. 1991.

[WEG80] Wegner, Peter. Programming with Ada: An Introduction by Means of Graduated Examples. Prentice Hall. 1980.

[WIE83] Wiener, Richard and Sincovec, Richard. Programming in Ada. John Wiley & Sons. 1983.

[YOU83] Young, S. J. An Introduction to Ada. Ellis Horwood Ltd. 1983.

BIBLIOGRAPHY PART III

C++

[ARN95] Arnush, Craig. Teach Yourself Turbo C++ 4.5 for Windows in 21 Days. Sams Publishing Company. 1995.

[ATK92] Atkinson, L. and Atkinson, M. Using Borland C++, Second Edition. QUE Corporation Programming Series. 1992.

[BOR91A] Borland International, Inc. Turbo C++ Users Guide, Second Edition. 1991.

[BOR91B] Borland International, Inc. The World of C++. 1991.

[CAR95] Carroll, Martin D. and Ellis, Margaret A. Designing and Coding Reusable C++. Addison-Wesley Publishing Company. 1995.

[COP92] Coplein, James O. Advanced C++ Programming Styles and Idioms. Addison-Wesley Publishing Company. 1992.

[DAV96A] Davis, Stephen R. C++ For Dummies. Second Edition. IDG Books. 1996.

[DAV96B] Davis, Stephen R. More C++ For Dummies. IDG Books. 1996.

[ECK93] Eckel, Bruce. C++ Inside & Out. Osborne McGraw Hill. 1993.

[ELL90] Ellis, Margaret A. and Stroustroup, B. The Annotated C++ Reference Manual. Addison-Wesley Publishing Company. 1990.

[KER88] Kernighan, Brian and Ritchie, Dennis. The C Programming Language. Second Edition. Prentice Hall. 1988.

[LIP90] Lippman, Stanley B. C++ Primer. Addison-Wesley Publishing Company. 1990.

[MIT92] Mitchell, Ed, et al. Secrets of the Borland C++ Masters. Sams Publishing Company. 1993.

[MUR93] Murray, Robert B. C++ Strategies and Tactics. Addison-Wesley Publishing Company. 1993.

[PER93] Perny, Greg. C++ Programming 101. Sams Publishing Company. 1993.

[SCH92] Schildt, Herbert. Teach Yourself C++. Osborne McGraw-Hill. 1992.

[STR86] Stroustroup, B. The C++ Programming Language. Addison-Wesley Publishing Company. 1986.

BIBLIOGRAPHY PART IV

JAVA

[FLA96] Flanagan, David. Java in a Nutshell: A Desktop Quick Reference for Java Programmers. O'Reilly & Associates, Inc. 1996.

[LEM96] Lemay, Laura and Perkins, Charles L. Teach Yourself Java in 21 Days. Sams.net Publishing. 1996.

[SAM96] Java Unleashed. Sams.net Publishing. 1996.

[VAN96] Vanhelsuwe, Laurence, et al. Mastering Java. Sybex, Inc. 1996.

BIBLIOGRAPHY PART V

SNAP[1]

SNAP Language Reference

SNAP Library Reference: Volume 1 Class Specifications
Volume 2 Module Specifications

Users Guide to the SNAP Development Process

Users Guide to the SNAP Development Environment

Users Guide to the SNAP Graphic User Interface Component

Users Guide to the SNAP Permanent Storage Component

Users Guide to the SNAP Communication Component

Users Guide to the SNAP External Application Software Component

[1]The publications cited for SNAP are supplied with SNAP, available from Template Software, Inc. 1-800-4TEMPLATE.

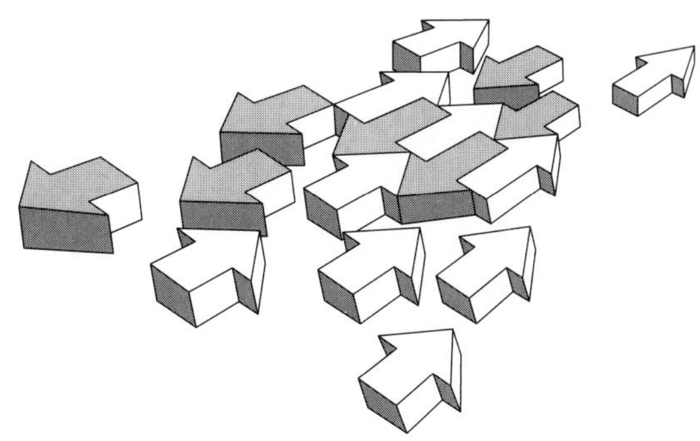

Index

Note : A bold page number represents the page where the definition of the term is provided.

D

E

LICENSE AGREEMENT AND LIMITED WARRANTY

READ THE FOLLOWING TERMS AND CONDITIONS CAREFULLY BEFORE OPENING THIS DISK PACKAGE. THIS LEGAL DOCUMENT IS AN AGREEMENT BETWEEN YOU AND PRENTICE-HALL, INC. (THE "COMPANY"). BY OPENING THIS SEALED DISK PACKAGE, YOU ARE AGREEING TO BE BOUND BY THESE TERMS AND CONDITIONS. IF YOU DO NOT AGREE WITH THESE TERMS AND CONDITIONS, DO NOT OPEN THE DISK PACKAGE. PROMPTLY RETURN THE UNOPENED DISK PACKAGE AND ALL ACCOMPANYING ITEMS TO THE PLACE YOU OBTAINED THEM FOR A FULL REFUND OF ANY SUMS YOU HAVE PAID.

1. **GRANT OF LICENSE:** In consideration of your payment of the license fee, which is part of the price you paid for this product, and your agreement to abide by the terms and conditions of this Agreement, the Company grants to you a nonexclusive right to use and display the copy of the enclosed software program (hereinafter the "SOFTWARE") on a single computer (i.e., with a single CPU) at a single location so long as you comply with the terms of this Agreement. The Company reserves all rights not expressly granted to you under this Agreement.

2. **OWNERSHIP OF SOFTWARE:** You own only the magnetic or physical media (the enclosed disks) on which the SOFTWARE is recorded or fixed, but the Company retains all the rights, title, and ownership to the SOFTWARE recorded on the original disk copy(ies) and all subsequent copies of the SOFTWARE, regardless of the form or media on which the original or other copies may exist. This license is not a sale of the original SOFTWARE or any copy to you.

3. **COPY RESTRICTIONS:** This SOFTWARE and the accompanying printed materials and user manual (the "Documentation") are the subject of copyright. You may not copy the Documentation or the SOFTWARE, except that you may make a single copy of the SOFTWARE for backup or archival purposes only. You may be held legally responsible for any copying or copyright infringement which is caused or encouraged by your failure to abide by the terms of this restriction.

4. **USE RESTRICTIONS:** You may not network the SOFTWARE or otherwise use it on more than one computer or computer terminal at the same time. You may physically transfer the SOFTWARE from one computer to another provided that the SOFTWARE is used on only one computer at a time. You may not distribute copies of the SOFTWARE or Documentation to others. You may not reverse engineer, disassemble, decompile, modify, adapt, translate, or create derivative works based on the SOFTWARE or the Documentation without the prior written consent of the Company.

5. **TRANSFER RESTRICTIONS:** The enclosed SOFTWARE is licensed only to you and may not be transferred to any one else without the prior written consent of the Company. Any unauthorized transfer of the SOFTWARE shall result in the immediate termination of this Agreement.

6. **TERMINATION:** This license is effective until terminated. This license will terminate automatically without notice from the Company and become null and void if you fail to comply with any provisions or limitations of this license. Upon termination, you shall destroy the Documentation and all copies of the SOFTWARE. All provisions of this Agreement as to warranties, limitation of liability, remedies or damages, and our ownership rights shall survive termination.

7. **MISCELLANEOUS:** This Agreement shall be construed in accordance with the laws of the United States of America and the State of New York and shall benefit the Company, its affiliates, and assignees.

8. **LIMITED WARRANTY AND DISCLAIMER OF WARRANTY:** The Company warrants that the SOFTWARE, when properly used in accordance with the Documentation, will operate in substantial conformity with the description of the SOFTWARE set forth in the Documentation. The Company does not warrant that the SOFTWARE will meet your requirements or that the operation of the SOFTWARE will be

uninterrupted or error-free. The Company warrants that the media on which the SOFTWARE is delivered shall be free from defects in materials and workmanship under normal use for a period of thirty (30) days from the date of your purchase. Your only remedy and the Company's only obligation under these limited warranties is, at the Company's option, return of the warranted item for a refund of any amounts paid by you or replacement of the item. Any replacement of SOFTWARE or media under the warranties shall not extend the original warranty period. The limited warranty set forth above shall not apply to any SOFTWARE which the Company determines in good faith has been subject to misuse, neglect, improper installation, repair, alteration, or damage by you. EXCEPT FOR THE EXPRESSED WARRANTIES SET FORTH ABOVE, THE COMPANY DISCLAIMS ALL WARRANTIES, EXPRESS OR IMPLIED, INCLUDING WITHOUT LIMITATION, THE IMPLIED WARRANTIES OF MERCHANTABILITY AND FITNESS FOR A PARTICULAR PURPOSE. EXCEPT FOR THE EXPRESS WARRANTY SET FORTH ABOVE, THE COMPANY DOES NOT WARRANT, GUARANTEE, OR MAKE ANY REPRESENTATION REGARDING THE USE OR THE RESULTS OF THE USE OF THE SOFTWARE IN TERMS OF ITS CORRECTNESS, ACCURACY, RELIABILITY, CURRENTNESS, OR OTHERWISE.

IN NO EVENT, SHALL THE COMPANY OR ITS EMPLOYEES, AGENTS, SUPPLIERS, OR CONTRACTORS BE LIABLE FOR ANY INCIDENTAL, INDIRECT, SPECIAL, OR CONSEQUENTIAL DAMAGES ARISING OUT OF OR IN CONNECTION WITH THE LICENSE GRANTED UNDER THIS AGREEMENT, OR FOR LOSS OF USE, LOSS OF DATA, LOSS OF INCOME OR PROFIT, OR OTHER LOSSES, SUSTAINED AS A RESULT OF INJURY TO ANY PERSON, OR LOSS OF OR DAMAGE TO PROPERTY, OR CLAIMS OF THIRD PARTIES, EVEN IF THE COMPANY OR AN AUTHORIZED REPRESENTATIVE OF THE COMPANY HAS BEEN ADVISED OF THE POSSIBILITY OF SUCH DAMAGES. IN NO EVENT SHALL LIABILITY OF THE COMPANY FOR DAMAGES WITH RESPECT TO THE SOFTWARE EXCEED THE AMOUNTS ACTUALLY PAID BY YOU, IF ANY, FOR THE SOFTWARE.

SOME JURISDICTIONS DO NOT ALLOW THE LIMITATION OF IMPLIED WARRANTIES OR LIABILITY FOR INCIDENTAL, INDIRECT, SPECIAL, OR CONSEQUENTIAL DAMAGES, SO THE ABOVE LIMITATIONS MAY NOT ALWAYS APPLY. THE WARRANTIES IN THIS AGREEMENT GIVE YOU SPECIFIC LEGAL RIGHTS AND YOU MAY ALSO HAVE OTHER RIGHTS WHICH VARY IN ACCORDANCE WITH LOCAL LAW.

ACKNOWLEDGMENT

YOU ACKNOWLEDGE THAT YOU HAVE READ THIS AGREEMENT, UNDERSTAND IT, AND AGREE TO BE BOUND BY ITS TERMS AND CONDITIONS. YOU ALSO AGREE THAT THIS AGREEMENT IS THE COMPLETE AND EXCLUSIVE STATEMENT OF THE AGREEMENT BETWEEN YOU AND THE COMPANY AND SUPERSEDES ALL PROPOSALS OR PRIOR AGREEMENTS, ORAL, OR WRITTEN, AND ANY OTHER COMMUNICATIONS BETWEEN YOU AND THE COMPANY OR ANY REPRESENTATIVE OF THE COMPANY RELATING TO THE SUBJECT MATTER OF THIS AGREEMENT.

Should you have any questions concerning this Agreement or if you wish to contact the Company for any reason, please contact in writing at the address below.

Robin Short
Prentice Hall PTR
One Lake Street
Upper Saddle River, New Jersey 07458